Global Financial Deregulation

Global Financial Deregulation

Commercial Banking at the Crossroads

Itzhak Swary and Barry Topf

BLACKWELL
Finance

Itzhak Swary and Barry Topf are hereby identified as authors of this work in accordance with Section 77 of the Copyright, Designs and Patents Act 1988.

First published 1992

Blackwell Publishers
3 Cambridge Center
Cambridge, Massachusetts 02142, USA

108 Cowley Road, Oxford, OX4 1JF, UK

Library of Congress Cataloging in Publication Data
Swary, Itzhak, 1946–
Global financial deregulation: commercial banking at the crossroads/ Itzhak Swary and Barry Topf.
p. cm.
Includes index.
ISBN 0-631-18188-1 (acid-free paper):
1. Banks and banking. International. 2. Financial services industry. 3. Banks and banking—Deregulation. I. Topf. Barry.
II. Title. III. Title: Commercial banking.
HG3881.S855 1991
332.1′2—dc20 91-13566
CIP

British Library Cataloguing in Publication Data
A CIP catalogue record for this book is available from the British Library.

Typeset in 11 on 13pt Ehrhardt by Butler and Tanner Ltd, Frome
Printed in Great Britain by TJ Press Ltd, Padstow, Cornwall.

This book is printed on acid-free paper.

Contents

Preface

Financial markets in general, and banking in particular, are confronted by continual rapid change. Often it seems that the only constant in the area of financial services is the steady acceleration in the pace of transformation. Hence any study of the subject must focus on the process of change itself; all static descriptions quickly become obsolete. In this book, we have tried to focus on two of the more important trends that have influenced banking worldwide: deregulation and globalization.

The regulation/deregulation dynamic is at work in almost all developed countries, and although progress has been uneven, its impact has been, and will continue to be, extensive. We have tried to describe the dynamic process in as broad a context as possible, as we feel that it will leave few aspects of banking untouched as the century draws to a close.

Banking has become in many ways a global industry, yet national banking systems are almost invariably analyzed separately. International banking on the other hand is studied in isolation, as though it was detached from the domestic systems which support it. To remedy this, we have provided an extensive national survey of banking in seven industrialized countries, in the belief that broad knowledge of developments in individual banking systems is essential to understanding their fusion at the level of global banking.

We have created many debts in the course of writing this book. The book itself grew out of a research project sponsored by the Israel International Institute for Applied Economic Policy Review in Tel Aviv, and is one part of the Institute's research program on promoting Israel's international financial relations, and the harmonization of banking and capital market regulation. Without the Institute's support and assistance, this book would never have been attempted, much less completed. Special thanks are due to Professor Zvi Sussman, the Institute's director of research, for suggesting the topic and for his valuable advice during all stages of the project, to the Institute's president Steve Marcus, and to the staff for their help, encouragement, and generous support.

Many professionals around the world reviewed sections of this book and provided data as well as valuable suggestions and comments. We would specifically like to acknowledge the contribution of Dr Amnon Goldsmidt, Israel's Supervisor of Banks, and Dr David Rutenberg, Director of research in the Bank Supervision Department at the Bank of Israel; Prof. Dr Christine Hersowitcz of the Swiss Banking School, Prof. Marshall Sarnat of the Hebrew University, Prof. Jean Dermine, INSEAD, France; G. Broker of the OECD; Mr M. Schmeider and Dr Neumann of the Federal Banking Supervisory Office, Berlin; Michael MacKenzie and J. Anne Lamont of the Superintendent of Financial Institutions, Canada; J. A. Hoskins of the Bank of England; Salomon Brothers, New York Bank Research Area, Shlomo Piotrokovsky of the First International Bank; Henny Sender of Institutional Investor, Japan; Mr Israel Hayon, Mr Shlomo Pergament, and Mr Topor, all of Bank Leumi. Pynchas Katz, Yoav Nardi, Uri Cohen, and Semadar Glick provided valuable assistance, and Mazie Cohen, Adele Zarmati, Ran Benor, and Helene Balouka who were indispensable in preparing the manuscript for publication. Finally, and most importantly, our largest debt is undoubtedly to our wives Edia and Carol, and to our children Etgar, Gili, and Jonathan Swary, and Chani, Rivka, Asher, and Naama Topf for their patience, understanding, and support.

1

Overview

Financial markets in developed countries have undergone profound structural changes in recent years, which have greatly increased competition in the provision of financial services. Prominent amongst these changes are:

- Securitization
- Internationalization
- Deregulation
- Reduced segmentation and increased competition amongst financial institutions.

1.1 Securitization

The flow of funds in any financial system can be either direct, or indirect using intermediaries. The former consists of the direct exchange of obligations between final borrower and lender, usually involving equity, debt, or other financial instruments. Indirect financing involves the services of various intermediaries mediating between ultimate borrowers and lenders.

The relative importance of each method within the financial system varies among countries and changes over time, because of factors such as regulatory rules and intervention, tax policy, level of development, and economic structure. For example, underdeveloped countries, lacking efficient capital markets, usually rely heavily on financial intermediaries, especially banks. Because of the primary role of banks and the absence of alternative financial markets, as well as the high-risk environment in which they operate, the level of regulation in these countries is usually very high.

In more developed countries, however, technological and economic conditions are more favorable to the development of capital markets, enabling direct financing to compete with intermediaries. Moreover, regulatory restrictions imposed on intermediaries, primarily commercial banks, including minimum capital ratios and liquidity requirements (and the monetary tax they imply), can inhibit the ability of intermediaries to compete with direct financing. As such restrictions on intermediaries become broader and more effective, their share in financial activities shrinks, and that of direct financing grows. Thus, during the last decade commercial banks in many countries lost their comparative advantage as providers of credit to large borrowers. Many large businesses replaced borrowing from the banking system with the issuance of securities such as bonds, commercial paper, or Euronotes. While retail markets have been less affected, the impact on wholesale markets of such securitization – the replacement of intermediated financial flows by direct obligations – has been marked. However, banks are also increasing their involvement in the capital markets, becoming participants in the direct flow of funds. The combination of decreased involvement in intermediation and increased involvement in capital markets constitutes a marked change in the role of commercial banks.

1.2 Internationalization

The market for capital and financing services is becoming increasingly globalized and national borders are playing an ever decreasing role. National banking systems have been exposed to competition from foreign banks, while being allowed (and sometimes forced by competitive pressures) to compete in foreign and international markets.

Banking deregulation has been both a cause and a result of the globalization of financial markets. Protective regulation has often been dismantled in order to stimulate competition in the provision of financial services or as part of a more general move towards freer competition; this has frequently necessitated fuller deregulation to allow banks to survive and compete in the more competitive markets that have emerged.

The development of global markets has increased the need for international coordination of regulatory policies and convergence in their content and implementation. Increasingly this has meant supervising and regulating the general risk level at which banks operate, while minimizing operative interference in banking activity. Moreover, current trends and developments in financial markets put the continued expansion of international banking in doubt.

It is our assertion that international banking activity will slow and even decline, accompanied by basic changes in its nature, paralleling the transformation of the banks' role in the financial system.

1.3 Deregulation

Banking systems around the world have been affected to varying degrees by the global trend of deregulation. In some cases this deregulation has taken the form of interest rate liberalization – including the removal of deposit rate restrictions – which resulted in a reduction in bank interest margin income (this in turn was the result of increased competition, including competition from foreign banks). In other cases, deregulation meant the reduction of reserve requirements, removal of restrictions on geographic expansion and non-bank activities, and reduced protection from foreign competitors.

The deregulation process has also provided banks with the opportunity to engage in activities related to investment banking, thus allowing them to generate substantial fees and trading income. However, regulatory authorities in various countries adopt different approaches to such participation; these differing paths have shaped the nature of the banking system and the scope of bank activities in the individual countries.

In the United Kingdom, Canada, France, and Japan, regulatory reforms have increased the ability of commercial banks to participate in the capital markets. In Switzerland and the Federal Republic of Germany, regulatory authorities have long allowed banks to participate in the capital markets. Therefore, the deregulation process in these countries has been reflected primarily both in the possibility of using new financial instruments and in the participation of foreign banks in the domestic capital markets. However, in the United States the 1933 Glass-Steagall Act prevents banks from underwriting securities such as corporate debt and equity, certain municipal revenue bonds, and securitized mortgages on private obligations. Nevertheless, US commercial banks have steadily increased their presence in other merchant banking activities, including government and municipal securities, foreign exchange trading, mergers and acquisitions, leveraged buyout financing, interest rate swaps, and Eurobond underwriting. Furthermore, the US banking system is currently engaged in an effort to update the Glass-Steagall Act so as to permit competitive activities on a par with other countries, and to put commercial banks on an equal footing with investment banks which can already provide commercial banking services without carrying the regulatory burden.

Participation of banks in capital markets is an important determinant of the banking structure. The development of non-banking competition in domestic markets, as well as competition from foreign banks, has forced banks to seek additional sources of income. This has naturally led to involvement in capital market activities. The involvement of banks in direct (capital market) financing, as a substitute for and supplement to conventional banking intermediation, has resulted in the stabilization of overall bank income. However, it has also given rise to significant disadvantages, particularly in terms of the high risk inherent in capital market activities. This high risk can undermine the stability of the banking system (one of the original motivations for the Glass-Steagall Act). Moreover, investment and commercial banking activities can entail potential conflicts of interests that may arise from bank operations as a multi-product financial firm which has some monopoly power in the credit market. However, since recently even US regulators seem to have reached the conclusion that the advantages incurred in capital market related activities far exceed the disadvantages, they have tended to approve the involvement of banks in such activities.

1.4 Reduced Segmentation

An important feature of increased competition is the "despecialization" of the financial services industry. This process applies in particular to savings institutions which, in most countries, traditionally attracted small savings which were then channelled into housing or government securities. However, savings institutions have gradually been allowed to become an integral part of the commercial banking system. Such a process occurred in the United Kingdom when the 1986 Building Societies Act was passed, by which building societies were given commercial banking powers. A similar, though less extensive, process has occurred in the United States (the Depository Institution Act of 1982), France, and Japan.

In addition to heightened competition among deposit taking institutions, decreased institutional segmentation has also brought increased competition from other financial and even non-financial firms. The removal of protective barriers means that a variety of firms can offer essentially the same services and products as commercial banks, with the latter by no means assured of any advantage in their production or marketing. This has led to the need for commercial banks to re-evaluate those areas and functions in which they remain competitive.

1.5 Organization of the Book

The book is divided into two parts. Part I presents a survey of the banking system in seven leading industrialized countries. Part II is devoted to the analysis of prominent issues in commercial banking worldwide.

The development and structure of banking systems in Switzerland, the Federal Republic of Germany, France, the United Kingdom, Japan, Canada, and the United States are considered in Part I. The analysis includes an overview of the environment in which these systems operate and an examination of regulatory provisions, taxation, accounting reportage, the role of the banking system in the economy, the various types of financial institutions, capital market efficiency, foreign bank competition, non-banking competition, and national involvement in international banking. The influence of these factors on the performance of banks is examined and measured in terms of interest margins, the composition of income, the growth of loan portfolios, expenses, and capital adequacy.

The response of each banking system to the challenges posed by the changing financial environment is considered within the framework of global trends and developments.

Part II describes and analyzes the major issues facing commercial banking, and their implications regarding the future role and development of commercial banks. The developments and trends analyzed include the following.

1.5.1 Securitization and Financial Innovation

The rapid pace of innovation has left few areas of financial activity unaffected. In its various forms, including general trends, new products, and structural changes, its impact on commercial banking has been especially profound. The previously unique role of banks in financial intermediation has been severely undermined, so that banks will need to develop new areas of competitive advantage to ensure their future profitability.

1.5.2 Non-banking Activities

In the shrinking banking market, the expansion of securitization as a substitute for commercial bank lending emphasizes the importance of the non-banking activities of commercial banks. In examining the non- banking activities to which banks can expand, the most significant, in terms of potential economies of scope, is the securities field. In other areas such as real estate and industrial or commercial activity (even where permitted under the system of universal banking) the volume of bank expansion has never been significant, probably because they lack synergy benefits. Banks, due to their established infrastructure and branch networks and their expertise in credit evaluation, may emerge as the prominent specialists in the sponsoring and originating of securities and their subsequent servicing as underwriters and trustees. The involvement of banks in securities activities is of special importance because it provides stability by allowing them to participate in all forms of credit channelling in the economy.

1.5.3 Capital Adequacy

Regulators from the "Group of Ten" countries (The United States, Canada, Japan, Britain, Germany, France, Italy, Belgium, Sweden, Switzerland, and the Netherlands) have jointly agreed to make uniform capital adequacy standards their primary tool in controlling bank risk. Minimum capital ratios, computed on a risk weighted basis, including the riskiness of new financial instruments and off-balance-sheet activities, and common definitions of capital, have been established and are in the process of being imposed. While the new standards suffer from some deficiencies, these are expected to be corrected over time. The new standards are having far reaching impacts on both individual bank decision-making, as well as the structure of entire banking systems in different countries. They affect the relative profitability of different assets, liabilities, and off-balance-sheet activities, the securitization process, bank mergers and acquisitions, loan sales, dividend policy, and risk taking by banks. From the regulatory viewpoint, they represent the trend toward prudential supervision with less operational intervention.

1.5.4 1992 and the Single European Market

The completion of the internal European market in financial services represents a milestone in the response of banks to a changing environment. However, rather than causing drastic changes, it will probably accelerate changes which were inevitable in any case. The removal of national borders as a factor in the provision of banking services, the expansion of markets, increased competition, and convergence of regulatory policy, will all have a direct impact on economies of scale and scope, operational and allocational efficiency, structure and concentration, and a host of other issues.

These and other developments surveyed in this book have significant implications for the banking industry and its regulation. The major issues addressed include the following.

The dynamics of bank regulation

The current level of bank regulation in industrialized countries represents a fragile balance between protection and intervention. The purpose of banks' market share protection is to complement and offset, to a degree, the inefficiencies caused by regulatory interference.

The well documented process of deregulation around the world has been accompanied by a reduction in supervisory protection and hence by increased competition, which has increased banks' risk exposure. A notable exception to the trend toward a less-regulated, less-protected banking industry is the safety net provided by regulators. An extreme example is the almost full coverage of deposit insurance provided in the United States. This type of insurance contradicts the trend to bank deregulation and constitutes a major challenge for regulators. The level of insurance coverage is expected to be reduced in the future.

The reshaping of banking systems

The newly deregulated, less-protected banks operating in an environment of increased competition and efficiency are more vulnerable to risk. The deregulation/deprotection trend in banking is expected to lead to the first stage of a major reshaping that will be accompanied by bank failures and bank mergers. Inefficient banks are likely to disappear and any potential economies of scale and/or scope are more likely to be exploited. The magnitude and significance of this process is more radical and painful in those countries which were heavily regulated in the past such as the United States and Japan. The Single European Market is also expected to have a similar effect, especially in those member countries which currently employ relatively high levels of bank regulation (intervention and protection).

The future of international banking

The convergence of the financial system globally will reduce the role of international banking. International banks will be just another type of intermediary which participates in the process of capital flows among countries with a minimum physical foreign presence. This conclusion is based on factors such as: the newly imposed capital adequacy requirements, deregulation, reduced tax rates, securitization in international markets, and advanced communication technology and innovation which allow for unbundling of different risks.

1.6 The Outlook for Commercial Banking

The cumulative result of recent developments has been the extensive erosion of the uniqueness of commercial banking. Bank products are becoming increasingly indistinguishable from the products of other financial and non-financial firms. Clearly, the future shape of banking systems will be the "universal" banking model prevailing in Europe rather than the highly segmented American/Japanese model.

Moreover, banks everywhere are likely to see a significant change in their basic economic function. They are likely to experience a marked decline in their role in direct intermediation, or asset transformation. Thus, their traditional role of accepting deposits and extending short-term credit will continue to diminish. In its stead, they will increase their involvement in indirect intermediation, specializing in and servicing capital markets, thus becoming essentially pure information processors. This evolution will pose significant challenges to individual banks and regulatory authorities, due to the change it will bring to the banking industry, payment mechanism, and monetary system.

PART I

COUNTRY SURVEY

2

Switzerland

2.1 Structure of the Financial System

2.1.1 Introduction

The financial system in Switzerland has long been characterized by two very Swiss qualities: safety and stability. No other banking system has enjoyed nearly the same degree of success in winning the confidence of the investment community, or in building on such confidence to develop a large and prosperous financial industry. However, in the face of future fierce global competition, and relentless innovation and change, it is unclear whether these Swiss qualities will be sufficient for continued success in the financial industry.

The well-deserved reputation of Swiss banks is rooted in the structure of the Swiss nation and the behavior of its people. The Swiss confederation's long history of a stable and unique political system, together with its jealously guarded neutrality, has made centrally located Switzerland a natural "safe haven" for capital fleeing strife torn countries, first in Europe and later around the world. The secrecy and confidentiality for which Swiss banks are well known has contributed to the growth of financial centers in Zurich, Basle, Geneva, and to a lesser extent Lugano and Berne. The violation of banking secrecy constitutes a criminal offense and such secrecy can be lifted only for what is considered a crime by Swiss law (tax evasion is not a crime in Switzerland). Switzerland's fiscal probity and the hard currency status of the Swiss Franc have provided the environment necessary for banking to become one of Switzerland's major industries.

Nevertheless, Swiss banking faces a number of challenges. Increasing financial deregulation around the world, and high internal costs (turnover taxes, withholding tax and salaries), have resulted in serious competition, both from offshore and semi-offshore centers. Given the limitations of the domestic Swiss market, and the indisputable fact that Zurich has become a second rank financial center (behind Tokyo, London, and New York), Swiss banks will have to look overseas and for new financial trends to achieve further growth and profitability.

Table 2.1 Switzerland – Major economic indicators and the banking system

	1980	*1984*	*1989*
Gross domestic product, US$ bil.	101.6	91.1	183.7
Current account, US$ bil.	−1.54	6.15	8.3
Rate of inflation, annual %	6.5	3.4	3.2
Exchange rate (SFr per US$) (year-end)	1.76	2.58	1.54
Average interest rate[a], %	2.29	3.34	6.5
Population (mil.)	6.3	6.4	6.7
Number of banks	557	581	631
Total branches	3,855	3,951	4,336
Number of ATMs	211	1,397	1,423
Population per branch	1,634	1,620	1,545
Population per ATM	29,858	4,581	4,708
Bank employees (thou.)	86.6	98.5	126.0
Bank employees as % of total population	1.4	1.5	1.9

[a] Money market rates.

Source: IMF, *International Financial Statistics Yearbook, 1990*, Banque Nationale Suisse, *Das Schweizerische Bankwesen*

2.1.2 *Financial Markets and Institutions*

Financial markets in Switzerland are predominantly indirect in nature, with large intermediaries playing the primary role. Markets for the direct exchange of capital are of secondary importance. Five major banks (or four since the recent Crédit Suisse-Bank Leu merger), or Grossbanken, dominate the banking industry and collectively account for 49.2 percent of the total assets of all Swiss banks (table 2.2). It should be noted that the "Big Three" – Union Bank of Switzerland (UBS), Swiss Bank Corporation (SBC), and Crédit Suisse – comprise 90 percent of the Grossbanken total assets, dwarfing the other two members – Swiss Volksbank and Bank Leu – which are included in the category more by tradition than because of their present size. The next largest group of Swiss banks, the 29 cantonal banks, account for 19 percent of the total assets. The Grossbanken have been increasing their dominance within Swiss banking since 1973. Their share of balance sheets has grown from 44 percent in that year to 49.2 percent in 1989, an increase of 240 percent. In contrast, the cantonal banks grew by 162 percent in the same period, reducing their share of total assets from 22 to 19 percent. The extensive domestic branch network of the Grossbanken has enabled them to increase market share within Switzerland, and to augment their dominance of foreign banking.

The Grossbanken are universal banks in the full sense of the term. They combine the functions of commercial and merchant banks, with broad fiduciary responsibilities. Apart from accepting deposits and making loans, the Grossbanken also underwrite and distribute securities, act as financial and corporate advisors, trade stocks and precious metals and, most notably, they serve as investment trust managers and portfolio managers.

Unlike US money centers or Japanese city-banks, the Grossbanken are highly liquid. Excess liquidity is concentrated in the interbank market, with over 90 percent in overseas accounts. As with other Swiss institutions, the Grossbanken maintain large hidden reserves, making any comparison of capital and profitability with foreign banks difficult. Fiduciary accounts, which are peculiar to Switzerland, are also not included in Grossbanken balance sheets. These are funds placed abroad by a Swiss bank in its name, but at the sole risk of the client who provides the funds. The bank is paid a pro rata fee for its services while the client is assured full anonymity. Such funds have grown rapidly in recent years, between 1973 and 1989 by 574 percent (148 percent between 1980 and 1989). Their current size, SFr 299 billion as of December 1989, is clearly one of the factors that have helped Swiss banks to achieve their major role in international banking.

The 29 cantonal banks are another uniquely Swiss institution. Established and owned by individual cantons (at least one such bank in each canton), their liabilities are, for the most part, guaranteed by the Canton. While their original purpose was to expand and strengthen banking services beyond those provided by private banks, they have over time increased the scope of their activities. Based upon the acceptance of small savings (they hold 36 percent of all Swiss bank accounts) their traditional focus has been the provision of credit to agriculture, small businesses and mortgage lenders in their home cantons, a location to which they are usually limited by law. More recently, cantonal banks have expanded into commercial credit, portfolio management, securities business, and even into financing of foreign trade. The distinctly regional nature of cantonal banks, and their inability to participate in international banking, has severely hampered their growth, with the result that their share of total banking industry assets, 22 percent in 1978, fell to 19 percent in 1989. Interestingly, while cantonal banks must be profitable, strict profit maximization is not

Table 2.2 The Swiss banking system

	Number of institutions			*Number of branches*[a]			*Total assets SFr billion*			*Percent of total*	*% change in assets*
	1980	*1984*	*1989*	*1980*	*1984*	*1989*	*1980*	*1984*	*1989*	*1989*	*1980–9*
Grossbanken	5	5	5	759	821	933	239.4	368.2	509.7	49.2	112.9
Cantonal banks	24	29	29	719	659	755	100.4	134.3	195.2	18.8	94.4
Regional and savings banks	220	217	210	609	616	664	45.6	59.9	88.6	8.6	94.3
Credit coops and loan associates[b]	2	2	2	1,214	1,232	1,229	13.2	18.9	31.2	3.0	136.4
Branches of foreign banks	16	15	17	27	27	32	9.2	14.1	27.4	2.7	197.8
Private banks	25	24	22	26	25	26	2.6	3.5	5.6	0.5	115.3
Finance companies	84	103	137	88	112	148	11.1	16.2	25.1	2.4	126.1
Other Swiss banks	93	82	91	241	249	301	21.7	33.9	55.9	5.4	157.6
Foreign-owned banks	83	104	118	172	210	248	45.0	73.8	97.8	9.4	117.3
Total	552	581	631	3,855	3,951	4,336	488.2	722.8	1,036.5	100.0	112.3

[a] Domestic and abroad.
[b] Composed of over 1,200 individual institutions.

Source: Banque Nationale Suisse

necessarily their primary goal; moreover, what profit they make (usually exempt from most taxes) is applied towards "public tasks".

The 210 regional and savings banks include various (mainly small) mortgage, savings, and localized commercial banks. What distinguishes them from the cantonal banks is their form of ownership: rather than being state-owned, these are joint stock companies or cooperatives. Consisting of small- to medium-sized institutions, the regional and savings banks have been unable to provide the range and scope of services offered by the Grossbanken, and their growth has been curtailed by the local and regional limits of their activities. While they have continued to grow in absolute size, their share of total Swiss banking assets fell from 12 percent in 1973 to 8.6 percent in 1989.

Over 1,200 small credit cooperatives and loan associations, widely distributed throughout the country, are organized into two large nationwide federations. These mutually-owned bodies use local surpluses to give loans and primary mortgages to their members. At the end of 1989 their collective balance sheet totalled SFr 31.2 billion, or 3.0 percent of total banking system assets.

Twenty-two private banks are distinguished by the fact that their owners bear unlimited personal liability. Their primary role is in security business and portfolio management. Thus, while private banks are Switzerland's oldest banks, dating from the 18th century, they represent at present a mere 0.5 percent of the total banking system assets. (However, a significant part of their operations are defined as off-balance-sheet items.)

Two types of finance companies exist: a very small number of deposit taking companies, which must conform to virtually all banking regulations; and others which do not take deposits, but are free to undertake almost all other banking activities. The latter have proved to be attractive to foreign interests and have consequently experienced considerable growth, reaching 2.4 percent of the total Swiss banking system in 1989.

Finally, other banks in Switzerland represent 14.8 percent of the banking system. These have grown from 65 banks in 1950 to 209 in 1989. 118 are foreign- owned or controlled and hold 64 percent of this category's total assets (or 9.4 percent of total Swiss banking assets). Their growth has been very rapid, especially in fiduciary operations, and they have become a popular vehicle for foreign banks to establish a banking presence in Switzerland. The 91 Swiss-controlled banks are divided into the following four sub-categories: commercial banks; stockbrokerage, securities trading and portfolio management institutions; personal loans and consumer finance banks; and other types.

Money markets

The Swiss Franc money market is extremely underdeveloped and of minimal importance. One of the reasons is the stamp duty leveled at a flat rate on all security transactions, regardless of maturity or of the nature of the transaction. The flat rate of the stamp duty (0.15 percent for residents, 0.30 percent for non-residents), on an annualized yield basis makes the issuance or trading of short-term instruments prohibitively expensive. Because both corporations and exporters rely on banks for short-term financing, viable markets in commercial paper and bankers acceptances have never developed. Since, historically, most banks have had excessive liquidity, they have been able to meet any credit demand without having to borrow, which has removed the incentive to develop short-term markets. In fact, the international interbank market has served the Swiss banking system as an outlet for surplus liquidity, with the regional, cantonal, and foreign-owned banks lending to the Grossbanken, which in turn place funds in the short-term Euromarket. The extensive use of foreign markets is illustrated by the fact that at the end of 1989, 37 percent of all assets and 30 percent of all liabilities of the Swiss banking system were with foreign banks and foreign clients.

Bond markets

In contrast to the money market, the Swiss Franc bond market is well developed and of some importance. Swiss banks maintain an overwhelmingly dominant role in all aspects of the bond market. The Grossbanken have succeeded in dominating most sectors of this market, a situation similar to that of the Federal Republic of Germany. Domestic primary issuance is controlled by a syndicate of the Grossbanken and private banks. Foreign concerns, after applying pressure, have recently been permitted to join the syndicate. Foreign bond issuance is also controlled by a syndicate, and while foreign banks have participated in the process since the early 1980s with their own syndicate, the dominant role has again shifted to the Grossbanken and private banks.

The Swiss bond market is characterized by the unusual relative size of various sectors: the domestic SFr bond market is of minimal importance; the foreign bond sector is very large; and the Eurobond market is nonexistent. This latter is a result of a strict prohibition on the issuance of SFr denominated bonds abroad, enforced by the Swiss National Bank in order to maintain firm control over monetary policy. Though this means that the SFr is the only major currency without an external bond market, it has not prevented the Swiss Franc from capturing a major share of fixed rate bond issues (19 percent of outstanding issues in 1989, third only to the US dollar and the Japanese yen), due to its large share of foreign bond issues (38 percent in 1989, as opposed to 19 percent in yen and 30 percent in US dollars). The issue profile of SFr bonds also differs sharply from other markets, with a breakdown of 61 percent foreign issues, 3.2 percent federal bonds, 4.5 percent cantons, 16.6 percent financial sector, and 14.6 percent industry.

Swiss banks also play a major role as investors in the bond market due to their considerable domestic and international placing power, and their important role in portfolio management and investment advisory services. While the SFr bond market is extremely illiquid compared with other major bank markets (since the major amount of paper purchased is held to maturity), all secondary market trading is dominated by the banks both on the exchanges and in the over-the-counter market.

While there is no SFr Eurobond market, Swiss banks have nevertheless secured an important role in the major Eurobond markets. However, because of a relatively unfavorable tax treatment, there is little Eurobond business in Switzerland (London has captured the bulk of this business). The withholding tax, applicable to all interest income other than that on foreign fiduciary accounts and foreign bond issues, and the stamp (or turnover) tax have discouraged the growth of bond trading in Zurich. And though the SFr bond market has been relatively open and, recently, partially deregulated (foreign participation in underwriting was permitted in 1982; elimination of ceilings on sizes was enacted in 1985, and elimination of note/bond segmentation in 1989), the key issues of virtual monopoly control of syndication, the absence of Euro SFr bonds, and the stamp tax, continue to inhibit the growth of the SFr bond market.

2.1.3 Banking Product and Bank Competition

Swiss banks are, in theory, fully universal. However, the historical development, and the federal structure of Switzerland have encouraged a degree of specialization in most Swiss banking institutions, except for the Grossbanken.

The Grossbanken, and primarily the big three, are in practice complete universal banks. Though engaging in virtually every type of financial business, their emphasis has long been on wholesale banking, corporate lending, and international activities. Recently, the Grossbanken have expanded into areas of domestic banking previously less emphasized, such as developing large branch networks to serve individual clients and engaging in mortgage and consumer lending. These activities have led to more direct competition with smaller regional banks. Given the intensity of the banking industry in Switzerland, the Grossbanken have probably outgrown the domestic banking market and will continue to look abroad for further growth opportunities. Efforts to expand the range of activities overseas include an involvement in investment banking, securities trading, and other fee income generating business, rather than the more traditional commercial banking activities. These efforts have taken different routes with each of the big three: Crédit Suisse through joint venture (Crédit Suisse First Boston London), UBS by acquisition (Phillips & Drew), and SBC by branch network (Swiss Bank International London.).

Strong representation abroad will be important if Swiss banks are to maintain a strong international position, since it is no longer clear if Switzerland will provide a sufficient base. This is because the advantages that made Switzerland an international financial center, based on specific features rather than volume or size, might not be as important in the future. For example, the removal of capital restrictions by many countries, and the spread of off-shore markets have reduced Switzerland's advantages in regulation. Further, Switzerland has lagged behind other financial centers in tax burden relief, with the result that it is at a comparative disadvantage today with regard to the taxation of financial services. Failure to remove the stamp duty (0.15 percent to 0.30 percent on all transactions in securities) has inhibited the growth of money markets. The withholding tax on interest and dividend income (at a rate of 35 percent) is one of the highest in the industrialized world, though it is waived on foreign bond issues and on fiduciary accounts.

The increasing use of off-balance-sheet instruments in other financial centers has not been matched in Switzerland; according to one report, Zurich has only a 1 percent share in the financial swaps market, possibly the most important new market developed in the 1980s. Moreover, while Swiss asset management has been based primarily on funds from private individuals, the rapidly progressing institutionalization of investment management (through pension funds, mutual funds, etc.) will probably limit future growth in this area. Nevertheless, the Grossbanken have a number of competitive advantages in the global banking market. Due to their long, and mostly successful experience in fully universal banking, a substantial portion of their earnings stem from fee income and investment banking activities rather than interest income. Foreign assets already amount to half their balance sheet totals, and international activities have long provided a disproportionate share of both growth and profits. Factors such as the Grossbanken's reputation for sound management and finances, including relatively high capital ratios; their solid domestic deposit base, and ability to attract funds from abroad; and their relatively low exposure to the debt crisis are a firm base for the future activities of the Grossbanken. These considerations undoubtedly influence their strategic plans.

The cantonal and regional banks, while mostly unregulated in terms of type of business, are severely curtailed in geographic terms. Due to their inability to engage in international banking, and most other activities outside their home cantons, they have never challenged the Grossbanken in the area of wholesale banking. Instead, cantonal banks have focused on the collection of savings (usually through acceptance of deposits), lending to agriculture and small business, and mortgage lending. While they have lost market share to the Grossbanken and foreign banks, cantonal banks have begun to compete more directly with the larger banks by expanding their commercial credit activities, offering portfolio management services, and entering the securities business. In 1972, all cantonal banks were admitted into the Cartel of Swiss Banks for foreign bond issues. Most recently, the cantonal banks that have specialized in savings and mortgage activities have generally fared better than those which emphasized commercial banking activities.

The numerous credit cooperatives, local savings and loan banks, and mutual credit agencies – virtually all single branch operations – have also seen their relative share of Swiss banking decline as a result of not having a role in more rapidly expanding sectors. Nevertheless, given their solid record and expertise in very localized markets, the cooperatives and credit agencies will probably continue to do business in much the same way as before. Foreign banks have been the most rapidly growing group in Switzerland, and are the greatest competition for the Grossbanken, especially in international finance. While it seems that their number will continue to increase, their ability to grow in the domestic market is probably limited.

Private banks have been declining in both number (from approximately 50 in the early 1960s to 22 in 1989) and market share, although their actual volume of business has expanded. Facing increasing competition, private banks are turning to the exploitation of "niches" in the banking market, such as private investment management, or customized banking for high net worth individuals.

A number of trends are thus apparent in Swiss banking. One is the increasing concentration of the market share in the hands of the large and foreign banks at the expense of the other banking groups. Another is that of greater competition between banking groups, with a resultant increase in the variety of services offered. Nevertheless, a number of laws limit competition in the domestic banking system. Cartels, although regulated, are legal in Switzerland. However, in 1989, the Cartel Commission, an independent government body, published an analysis of the numerous cartel agreements of the banks and recommended the loosening up or total abolishment of most cartels. If implemented, these recommendations are likely to enhance competition in the domestic Swiss banking industry. Further, given the limited scale of the domestic market, developments in international markets will play a greater role in determining the future of Swiss banking.

2.1.4 *International Involvement*

Switzerland is characterized by a small, open economy with a large banking and financial sector. Swiss banks have, historically, been active internationally, primarily serving as conduits for the capital exports that the Swiss economy generates. Swiss bankers have long maintained strong trading capabilities, especially in precious metals and foreign exchange. Early involvement in such activities has led to a strong international orientation, the maintenance of a network of overseas contacts, and a firm base for the development of non-interest income sources. Swiss bankers have always exploited the advantages of neutrality, stability, and secrecy to establish a "safe haven" reputation for international capital. As a result, the growth in fiduciary accounts has in the past two decades far outstripped the growth of balance sheets in general, reaching 28.9 percent of combined balance sheets by 1989. Indeed, the increased share of total Swiss banking assets, of both the Grossbanken and the foreign banks, is primarily accounted for by foreign asset growth. These two groups are virtually the only Swiss banks with international involvement. Since foreign activities have grown 25 percent faster than domestic activities in recent years, those Swiss banks with no significant international involvement have experienced a constantly diminishing share of activity. By 1989 Swiss banks had established 91 branches and 60 subsidiaries abroad, ensuring a presence in virtually every financial center in the world.

Concomitant with the overseas expansion of Swiss banks, there has been a growing foreign bank involvement in Switzerland. In addition to the advantages and prestige offered by a banking presence in Switzerland, foreign banks have been attracted by the possibility of tapping Swiss capital surpluses, providing fiduciary services to non-Swiss; and the ability to serve multinational clients. By the end of 1989, 17 branches of foreign banks were established, while 118 foreign-controlled banks accounted for the bulk of this sector. The number of employees of foreign banks has risen, to 16,826. The growth of foreign involvement in the Swiss banking system is summarized in table 2.3.

Table 2.3 International involvement of the banking system

		1980	1984	1989	Change 1980–9 (percent)
A. Foreign banks					
Subsidiaries and branches					
Number of branches		199	237	280	40.7
Total assets (SFr bil.)		54.2	87.9	125.2	130.9
Assets as a percent of total system assets		11.1	12.2	12.1	
			1984	1989	
B. Banks operating in foreign countries					
Number of branches			77	91	
Number of other offices			86	110[a]	
Total assets, (SFr. bil.)			118.9	147.2[a]	
Total assets (%)			16.4	15.2[a]	

		1980	1984	1988	1989
C. Assets and liabilities held against foreigners					
All banks					
Assets	Total	182.5	289	375.9	382.2
	Interbank	79.1	138.6	191.8	169.1[a]
	Securities	–	17.6	61.3	66.2
Liabilities	Total	141.9	230.3	289.1	309.1
	Interbank	–	78.9	134.2	145.1
	Securities	–	4.2	–	–
Swiss accounts only					
Assets	Total	–	171.3	231.4	226.5
Liabilities	Total	–	134.1	168.7	186.4
Fiduciary assets as a percent of total assets		24.7	32.1	23.4	28.9

[a] 1988 figures.

Source: Banque Nationale Suisse

2.2 The Regulatory Environment

2.2.1 The Regulatory Framework

Bank regulation in Switzerland is based on Article 31 quarter of the Swiss Federal Constitution, which gives the Federal Government the authority to enact legislation concerning the banking industry. The most prominent regulation is the Swiss National Bank Law, last amended in 1988. The Federal Banking Commission, which enjoys considerable independence, reports to the Federal Council and to the Swiss Parliament and is charged with implementing Swiss banking law. The commission has been accorded fairly wide supervisory powers, which include the actual licensing of banks and establishing and monitoring compliance with regulations concerning lending limits, liquidity, capital adequacy, foreign exchange and cross-country risk exposure. The commission operates through a network of licensed private auditing firms which directly audit the banks and report back to the commission, and also to the board of the respective bank.

There is no special regulatory requirement for establishing a banking entity overseas. Nevertheless, the Swiss parent bank must prepare financial statements on a consolidated basis (only for sums above SFr 5 million), and overseas branches and subsidiaries must generally comply with all regulations affecting domestic banks. Swiss banking law does not differentiate, for the most part, between domestic- and foreign-owned banks: the Federal Banking Commission regulates branches of foreign banks according to a special ordinance. There are additional requirements such as the need for reciprocal treatment of Swiss banks overseas.

The Swiss National Bank was established in 1906, with authority to issue banknotes and implement monetary policy. While it has no direct role in bank supervision, it is expected to take an interest in, and be consulted on bank affairs. Moreover, it can demand that banks provide it with data and information as deemed necessary. Although there is no formal obligation, it is generally assumed that the Swiss National Bank would fulfil the role of lender of last resort in a banking crisis.

The Swiss Bankers' Association plays a larger role in Switzerland than similar organizations in other countries. In addition to the general role of industry association, the Bankers' Association represents the banking industry before federal and cantonal authorities, and is expected to comment on legislation and regulation affecting banks.

Overall, the regulatory authority granted to the Federal Banking Commission and the Swiss National Bank is more limited than that of similar bodies in the United States or the Federal Republic of Germany. One exception is in the area of bank secrecy, where the customer's and the bank's right to secrecy are enshrined in both bank, and criminal law. The progress of deregulation in the banking industry in Switzerland is far less advanced than in other countries, due partly, perhaps, to the semi-advisory role played by the authorities.

2.2.2 *Major Bank Regulations*

Following are summations of the predominant features of Swiss banking regulations.

Scope of business – a universal bank

The legal framework of Swiss banks allows them to operate as universal banks. They engage in both short-term intermediation and long-term financing. Numerous institutions provide services in the fields of portfolio management, securities operations and other financial businesses. As in other countries with a system of universal or full-service banks, it is difficult to classify banks in Switzerland according to their economic functions.

Switzerland has always been regarded as a very liberal financial center. This reputation was strengthened in 1986, when restrictions regarding duration (central bank approval for long-term issuance) and the early repayment of public bonds on foreign debt were abolished. Furthermore, the Swiss have permitted local affiliates of foreign banks to lead (manage) Swiss franc bonds and dual currency issues featuring Swiss francs. However, the Grossbanken, with their massive placing power and retail banking franchises, continue to lead in this market.

The Swiss capital market consists of a rather unimportant domestic market (because of the small size of the country) and a much larger foreign sector. There is no Eurocapital market in Swiss francs, since the Swiss National Bank does not allow the issue of SFr foreign debts abroad. Together the three largest banks have approximately a 70 percent market share in the issue of foreign bonds and notes.

Foreign capital flowing into Switzerland is placed with banks and finance companies for long-term investment in portfolio management.

Fiduciary transactions are unique to Switzerland. They are investments and credits made by a bank in its name, but on account, and at the risk of the customer. The customer, who is the principal in the transaction, receives the full profits, and the bank earns a commission. Fiduciary transactions are off-balance-sheet items. They reached SFr 299 billion in 1989 (29 percent of total assets). The main reason for their existence is to avoid the Swiss withholding tax, which is 35 percent. Since intermediation in foreign funds (deposits and loans) in a third country are exempt from this tax, banks must present these transactions as off-balance-sheet items.

Because of their capital market involvement, the non-interest income generated by Swiss universal banks is far greater (almost twice) than their interest income. The bulk of Swiss non-interest income is derived from agency and stockbrokerage fees and custody revenues.

Insurance activity is subject to special statutory, licensing, and regulatory requirements; banks do not engage in the selling of insurance or underwriting. The direct involvement of banks in real estate activities is limited to investment in bank premises. There is no general limitation on the ability of a bank to invest in shares of industrial firms, although it is required to set aside capital covering 40 percent of any such investment.

Lending limitations

Loans to a single borrower cannot exceed 20 percent of a bank's capital for unsecured loans, 40 percent for secured loans, and 50 percent for loans to other banks. The Federal Banking Commission can demand that some loans be reduced if these limits are exceeded. Borrowers from a single group are considered an entity only if more than 50 percent of their assets are owned by the group.

Liquidity requirements

The Bank Law (the revised version of which came in force on January 1, 1988) requires that banks place their funds so that solvency is assured on a permanent basis. Accordingly, banks must maintain an adequate balance between liquid assets (primary liquidity), marketable assets (secondary liquidity) and short-term liabilities.

Liquid assets, marketable assets and short-term liabilities, are defined by law. The liquidity statement form (filled out periodically) is used to calculate primary and secondary liquidity, with secondary liquidity being the more important. The implementing ordinance requires that a bank maintain its liquid and the total of its easily marketable assets at given percentages of short-term liabilities.

Capital adequacy

Article 4 of the Swiss Banking Law dictates that banks maintain an adequate relationship between their equity and their assets. The minimum capital adequacy requirements are set in terms of percentages of risk commitments. The book value of each category of risk commitment is multiplied by the applicable percentage weighting, with the funds of the bank (as defined) being at least equal to the sum of the weighted risk commitments. The risk commitments include assets, contingent liabilities, and open positions in foreign currencies and precious metals. These equity requirements are not applicable to Swiss branches of foreign banks.

Article 21 of the Swiss Banking Law stipulates that unsecured obligations to a single borrower may not exceed 20 percent, and secured loans may not exceed 40 percent of a bank's capital.

Swiss banks have one of the most conservative capital adequacy standards in the world. They also have one of the highest equity-to-asset ratios (above 6 percent); this is understated as a result of non-taxed hidden reserves. The Swiss authorities included off-balance-sheet commitments in the risk asset capital ratio before their international counterparts included them (i.e., the Bank for International Settlement (BIS) Capital Adequacy Requirements).

Legal reserve

Swiss banks are compelled to establish a legal reserve and to restrict its use. Every year 5 percent of the net profit is allocated to a general reserve fund (legal reserve) until this fund amounts to one-fifth of the paid-in capital.

As long as the general reserve fund does not exceed 50 percent of capital, it can only be used to cover losses and to support the company through periods of depressed business.

Other regulations

Country risk

The Swiss Banking Law states that the issuance of foreign debt certificates and the granting of credit to foreign borrowers is subject to prior authorization if such transactions amount to SFr 10 million or more, and are for a period in excess of one year. The Federal Banking Commission does not impose specific methods for analyzing country risk, although it does require that an appropriate method be employed. As a complement to country risk analysis, each bank is expected to make appropriate provisions for loan losses. Since 1983 the Swiss Banking Commission has regularly increased recommended reserves of developing-country exposure (limited to certain countries), amounting to 50 percent in 1989. This reserve ratio has become mandatory since 1987.

Foreign banks operating in Switzerland

Foreign-controlled banks and Swiss branches of foreign banks comprise a significant part of the Swiss banking system. There are currently over 200 foreign banking institutions in Switzerland (including finance companies), making it one of the largest international financial centers. The Swiss Banking Law applies equally to all banks conducting business in Switzerland. Foreign banks must prove that reciprocity is granted to Swiss banks in their home country (which is a problem for Japanese banks and is discussed in chapter 12).

2.2.3 *Foreign Exchange Control*

The Swiss monetary authorities, acting through the National Bank, have had to deal with a currency which, in general terms, has appreciated substantially against the currencies of other countries. Therefore, in the context of restraining foreign demand for the Swiss franc, the National Bank has the power to impose negative interest rates, to forbid the payment of interest on foreign deposits in Swiss banks, and to restrict forward transactions with foreigners. The National Bank may also compel banks to balance their foreign exchange positions daily.

A bank may deal in commodities only if it is allowed to do so by its Articles of Association. The Banking Commission does not favor bank trading in commodities; however once a bank has obtained a trading license, the Commission may only control its conditions of dealing. These restrictions do not apply to precious metals trading, as there is no commodities exchange in Switzerland.

Since 1979 the Swiss National Bank has lifted nearly all restrictions on capital inflows. The most significant changes are, that there is no more limit on forward sale of Swiss Francs; that the ban on payment of interest and the levy of negative interest rates on increases in Swiss francs deposits of non-residents has been removed; and that there is no longer a license requirement for borrowing abroad by Swiss residents.

2.2.4 *Key Accounting Issues*

Under Swiss Federal Banking Law all banks, whatever their corporate form, must publish annual financial statements consisting of a balance sheet and a profit and loss account. Furthermore, banks with a balance sheet total over SFr 50 million must prepare semi-annual interim reports, and those with a total over SFr 200 million, a quarterly balance sheet.

The published reports of Swiss banks, particularly those of the larger banks, are of a high standard. They are coherent, consistent and presented in the format prescribed by law. However, these reports are understated, since hidden reserves are permitted and even encouraged by Swiss law.

The most significant accounting standards include the following:

Consolidation

There is no general requirement for consolidated financial statements. However, consolidated balance sheets must be submitted to the bank commission, principally for the purpose of determining consolidated equity (if total assets exceed SFr 5 million).

Moreover, a draft of the revised Banking Law shows a clear intention to require the publication of group accounts.

Loan loss reserves

Loan loss provisions as a form of hidden reserves are endemic to Swiss banking practice. There is a distinction between taxed reserves and inner reserves that are not taxable. In general, the tax authorities in Switzerland are generous in allowing provisions for loan losses: in 1989, they totalled SFr 5,587 million of which SFr 2,447 million were attributed to the five major banks. Provisions for inner reserves are not taxable, although there are timing differences between tax treatment and public reporting. There is no requirement, legal or otherwise, to identify the amounts of inner reserves or the accounts of prepaid or deferred tax in reported accounts. Furthermore, published figures do not indicate reserves, write-back of reserves, charge-offs of loans, or the provision to inner reserves. There is no clear distinction between the general and the specific provisions for loan losses.

Loan losses

As in many countries, taxation is a major consideration with regard to loan loss provisioning in Swiss banks. Because of the political structure of the Swiss Confederation, the tax system is complex. However, it is possible to state that generally Swiss tax authorities are especially generous in allowing deductions for provisions for loan losses.

The general rule for commercial enterprises in Switzerland is that they may make tax-allowable provisions, to build up a reserve of 5 percent of the book value of domestic accounts receivable and 10 percent of foreign accounts. In some cantons the percentages are 10 percent domestic and 15 percent foreign accounts receivable. For banks it is much more a matter of individual negotiation with the tax authorities. Normally, provisions against specific doubtful loans will be allowed and the authorities will, by international standards, be generous in regard to general provisions against loan losses. As for sovereign risks, in December 1982 the Federal Banking Commission requested a report from all banks exposed to such risks. The report detailed the bank's evaluation of the risk for each loan and the amount of loan loss provision for each risk. This study enabled the Commission to establish an industry norm for the amount of provisions required, and strongly encouraged banks with less than this norm to adjust their figures appropriately. Banks could either ear-mark hidden reserves or set aside new provisions out of income. In either case the amount, subject to negotiation, would normally be allowed as a deduction from taxable income.

Each bank's independent auditors must report to the Banking Commission on their evaluation of all likely risks, the consequent adjustments to asset values deemed necessary, and the provisions and inner reserves set up to cover them. Swiss banks do not write-off loans until all security is exhausted, and there is absolutely no chance of recovery; this usually occurs after the termination of legal proceedings.

Disclosure

Disclosure by Swiss banks of loan losses and hidden reserves is non-existent, the latter by definition (estimated as 20 percent of total industry net worth at the end of 1987). Swiss bankers regard their policy as perfectly normal and satisfactory, and consequently there is no significant movement for change toward greater disclosure. Since independent auditors must present recalculated balance sheets and income statements (including both inner reserves and hidden assets) in their annual reports to the Banking Commission, the regulatory authorities believe that there is no pressing need to fundamentally alter the information published, particularly in view of the impending revision of company and banking laws. To date, the Commission exercises considerable power over what should or should not be disclosed. For example, the Commission can require publication of the use of hidden reserves to keep a bank alive, despite structural weaknesses in the institution.

Another special feature of the published accounts of Swiss banks is that loans are stated as net of undisclosed specific loan loss reserves. Consequently, all other assets are likely to be undervalued and net of depreciation. The definition of sundry liabilities includes the balance of undisclosed reserves and general loan loss/risk reserves.

Hidden reserves

Essentially, Swiss banks maintain two distinct types of hidden reserves – inner, and hidden assets.

Inner reserves

The setting up of inner reserves, and the distribution of regular dividends, are done for the purpose of profit-smoothing. Provisions to inner reserves are derived from understating interest and other income items (e.g. by failing to accrue interest receivable). The tax treatment of these provisions is subject to negotiation. Under certain circumstances, hidden reserves may be considered as part of "own funds". Inner reserves may also be created by an upward revaluation of assets (previously written down) to original cost; in this case published balance-sheet totals rise by the amount of the revaluation.

Hidden assets

The banking law also implicitly permits "hidden" assets, which are created by deliberate undervaluation in the balance sheet. These "reserves" are used by banks to cover losses in times of crisis and are taken into account by the independent auditors' reports to the Banking Commission.

The banking industry believes that the stability and flexibility offered by hidden reserves far outweigh the disadvantages of the reported undervaluation of fixed assets in the balance sheet. However, a bank may not stay in business merely on the strength of its hidden reserves. In such a case, the Banking Commission would intervene and require that the situation be publicized.

Foreign exchange

The normal Swiss practice is not to recognize unrealized foreign exchange profits. However, balances in foreign currencies and forward exchange transactions should be translated at the year-end rate.

Fiduciary accounts

Fiduciary transactions are recorded as an off-balance-sheet item. The Grossbanken have reported the total of their fiduciary accounts in recent years. These represented 20.4 percent of their total balance sheet at the end of 1989 (table 2.4). For the entire Swiss banking system fiduciary transactions represented 28.9 percent of total assets in that year.

2.2.5 *Taxation*

The Swiss tax system is a reflection of the country's federal structure. While the federal tax law applies throughout Switzerland, each of the 26 sovereign cantons has its own tax law. Cantons in turn are subdivided into more than 3,000 municipalities that also charge taxes. Therefore, a Swiss bank pays taxes to at least three different public bodies. Tax rates and taxable income vary widely between the different systems. These differences include the base period, the deductibility of taxes paid and loss carry forward periods. The key elements of this system are as follows.

Corporate tax rates

Swiss corporate income tax rates are almost exclusively determined on the basis of profits. The rate of federal income is graduated from the basic tax rate of 3.63 to 9.8 percent. A surcharge of 4.84 percent applies to taxable income exceeding 4 percent of equity; an additional surcharge applies to taxable income exceeding 8 percent of equity. The maximum tax rate is 9.8 percent and applies if taxable income equals at least 23.15 percent of equity. Cantonal basic tax rates vary widely. The federal tax, cantonal and municipal taxes are generally graduated depending on the relationship of taxable income to capital. The maximum tax rates, taking into account the deductibility of taxes, for certain cantons are:

Basle – 20%
Berne – 23%
Geneva – 24%
Zurich – 25%

Swiss tax laws do not allow for consolidation.

Allowances for Doubtful Loans

The Zurich tax administration uses the following guidelines for banks:

- Accounts with other banks determined on a case-by-case basis
- Current and fixed loans: generally 5 percent (excluding mortgages), 7 percent on foreign receivables.

In 1989, the Swiss Banking Commission increased recommended reserves for developing-country exposure (which is tax deductible) to 50 percent. Leading Swiss banks have probably accumulated higher reserves.

Losses

Losses incurred in prior periods may be offset against current period profits. The federal tax law does not allow loss carrybacks, and loss carryforwards are limited to a maximum of three biannual computation periods.

Interest paid by banks

Interest paid to non-resident depositors is subject to a 35 percent withholding tax (unless a treaty affords relief). Since October 1986, all interbank (Swiss or foreign) deposits are exempt from the withholding tax (up to 1986, deposits for more than 12 months were subject to the tax). Since fiduciary deposits are not deposits with the accepting Swiss bank, interest payments are not subject to Swiss withholding. Interest paid by Swiss debtors to Swiss banks is also not subject to withholding.

Stamp duty

Transfer of securities

Federal stamp duty is levied on all transfers of securities to which a Swiss dealer (Swiss bank, broker or qualified holding company) is a party or in which it has acted as an intermediary, whether the transaction is between Swiss parties, foreign parties, or between both Swiss and foreign parties. The tax is also levied on original placements of securities by foreign debtors.

Taxable documents are:

- Bonds, certificates of deposit, debentures, shares, participating certificates, shares in investment funds, bills of exchange, and similar documents issued by domestic persons.
- Documents with a similar economic purpose issued by foreign persons (e.g., bankers acceptances, certificates of participation, commercial paper, notes, promissory notes, treasury bonds, and treasury bills).
- Documents evidencing a participation in such documents or in loans.

The rates of federal stamp duty are 0.15 percent for securities issued by a Swiss party and 0.30 percent for securities issued by a foreign party.

In the case of banks acting as intermediaries between two foreign parties, the tax is reduced by 50 percent if the transaction is concluded outside Switzerland, and one of the foreign parties is a bank.

The securities transfer duty provisions of the stamp tax law are to be revised during the current period of legislation (i.e., 1989–91). The most likely change will be a reduction of duty on the transfer of certain short-term securities and foreign transactions.

Issuance of stock

Federal stamp duty at 3 percent is levied on all amounts received by a Swiss corporation from its shareholders or related persons upon incorporation, in return for the issuance of rights of participation (mainly shares). It is also levied on all amounts constituting further capital contributions to such corporations. Reduced rates apply to capital issues resulting from mergers or reorganizations of Swiss corporations (1 percent), and on the transfer of a corporation's registered head office from another country to Switzerland (1.5 percent).

The rate of the stamp duty levied on the issuance of investment fund shares is 0.9 percent.

Table 2.4 Major assets of Swiss banks (SFr bil.)

	Total assets	%[a]	*Interbank deposits*	%	*Mortgage loans*	%	*Other loans*	%	*Securities*	%	*Fiduciary accounts*	*Fiduciary accounts as % of total assets*[b]
All banks[c]												
1980	488.2	100.0	111.5	100.0	109.6	100.0	166.1	100.0	33.0	100.0	120.7	24.7
1984	722.8	100.0	180.4	100.0	155.6	100.0	230.2	100.0	44.6	100.0	232.0	32.1
1988	967.5	100.0	251.8	100.0	229.3	100.0	324.2	100.0	68.2	100.0	226.5	23.4
1989	1,036.5	100.0	229.8	100.0	257.9	100.0	376.2	100.0	72.0	100.0	299.2	28.9
Big banks												
1980	239.4	49.0	63.8	57.2	30.1	27.5	93.6	56.4	13.2	40.0	47.4	19.8
1984	368.2	50.9	101.5	56.3	47.8	30.7	121.1	52.6	18.0	40.4	79.6	21.6
1988	483.5	50.0	142.7	56.7	78.0	34.0	177.8	54.8	25.9	38.0	78.6	16.3
1989	509.7	49.2	117.4	51.1	89.5	34.7	213.0	56.6	28.8	40.0	103.8	20.4
Cantonal banks												
1980	100.4	20.6	12.2	10.9	45.1	41.1	30.1	18.1	7.6	23.0	2.0	2.0
1984	134.3	18.6	18.6	10.3	58.9	37.9	39.8	17.3	8.9	20.0	2.8	2.1
1988	179.7	18.6	23.9	9.5	80.0	34.9	54.9	16.9	12.2	17.9	3.4	1.9
1989	195.2	18.8	20.9	9.1	89.7	34.8	62.8	16.7	12.7	17.6	5.9	3.0
Regional and savings banks												
1980	45.6	9.3	2.1	1.9	23.9	21.8	11.9	7.2	4.8	14.5	0.5	1.1
1984	59.9	8.3	3.5	1.9	31.8	20.4	15.4	6.7	5.4	12.1	0.7	1.2
1988	82.4	8.5	4.1	1.6	44.1	19.2	23.3	7.2	6.8	10.0	0.8	1.0
1989	88.6	8.5	4.4	1.9	47.9	18.6	25.4	6.8	6.5	9.0	1.7	1.9

Other Swiss banks												
1980	21.7	4.4	4.6	4.1	3.0	2.7	9.3	5.6	1.7	5.1	14.4	66.4
1984	33.9	4.7	7.9	4.4	4.6	3.0	13.7	6.0	2.3	5.2	23.3	68.7
1988	50.5	5.2	12.1	4.8	8.4	3.7	20.0	6.2	4.0	5.9	28.2	55.8
1989	55.9	5.4	12.7	5.5	9.3	3.6	22.9	6.1	4.5	6.2	37.9	67.8
Foreign-owned banks												
1980	45.0	9.2	17.4	15.6	0.3	0.3	17.7	10.7	3.6	10.9	34.6	76.9
1984	73.8	10.2	32.5	18.0	0.4	0.3	25.0	10.9	6.2	13.9	87.9	119.1
1988	91.5	9.5	39.2	15.6	0.7	0.3	30.6	9.4	12.2	17.9	78.7	86.0
1989	97.8	9.4	38.0	16.5	0.8	0.3	34.3	9.8	13.5	18.7	108.2	110.6
Branches of[d] foreign banks												
1984	14.1	2.0	6.7	3.7	–	–	5.1	2.2	1.1	2.5	23.6	167.4
1988	24.1	2.5	14.3	5.7	–	–	5.6	1.7	1.0	1.5	20.0	83.0
1989	27.4	2.6	17.6	7.7	–	–	5.7	1.5	0.9	1.2	21.4	78.1

[a] As a percentage of all banks.

[b] Fiduciary accounts are off-balance-sheet items.

[c] All banks also includes private banks, loan associations, agricultural credit cooperatives, and finance companies.

[d] Data for 1980 is not available.

Source: Banque Nationale Suisse, various issues

Table 2.4a Major domestic liabilities of Swiss banks

	Total assets	%[a]	*Interbank borrowing*	%	*Non-Bank deposits*	%	*Securities issued*	%	*Total equity*	%
All banks[b]										
1980	488.2	100.0	113.5	100.0	247.8	100.0	69.2	100.0	29.7	100.0
1984	722.8	100.0	143.5	100.0	389.2	100.0	104.9	100.0	43.2	100.0
1988	967.5	100.0	216.9	100.0	476.9	100.0	151.3	100.0	62.6	100.0
1989	1,036.5	100.0	233.3	100.0	531.0	100.0	164.4	100.0	67.9	100.0
Big banks										
1980	239.4	49.0	66.3	58.4	115.5	46.6	28.9	41.8	14.8	49.8
1984	368.2	50.9	77.8	54.2	209.5	53.8	38.2	36.4	19.8	45.8
1988	483.5	50.0	116.2	53.6	246.8	51.8	57.6	38.1	29.7	47.4
1989	509.7	49.2	121.9	52.3	261.7	49.3	58.7	35.7	33.1	48.7
Cantonal banks										
1980	100.4	20.6	6.1	5.4	63.2	25.5	23.1	33.4	4.3	14.5
1984	134.3	18.6	7.7	5.4	76.4	19.6	37.4	35.7	5.8	13.4
1988	179.7	18.6	10.5	4.8	100.6	21.1	51.5	34.0	7.6	12.1
1989	195.2	18.8	11.9	5.1	106.7	20.1	57.7	35.1	8.1	11.9
Regional and savings banks										
1980	45.6	9.3	1.5	1.3	29.4	11.9	10.6	15.3	2.6	8.8
1984	59.9	8.3	2.2	1.5	34.2	8.8	18.1	17.3	3.1	7.2
1988	82.4	8.5	4.8	2.2	44.6	9.4	25.8	17.1	4.0	6.4
1989	88.6	8.5	5.4	2.3	46.0	8.7	29.1	17.7	4.2	6.2

Other Swiss banks										
1980	21.7	4.4	4.3	3.8	10.9	4.4	2.5	3.6	2.5	8.4
1984	33.9	4.7	5.9	4.1	18.1	4.7	3.9	3.7	3.4	7.9
1988	50.5	5.2	10.2	4.7	24.9	5.2	6.3	4.2	5.4	8.6
1989	55.9	5.4	11.2	4.8	26.7	5.0	7.6	4.6	6.1	9.0
Foreign-owned banks										
1980	45.0	9.2	22.1	19.5	13.5	5.4	1.8	2.6	5.0	16.8
1984	73.8	10.2	29.8	20.8	29.3	7.5	2.8	2.7	7.3	16.9
1988	91.5	9.5	40.1	18.5	31.0	6.5	3.7	2.4	10.5	16.8
1989	97.8	9.4	42.9	18.4	32.9	6.2	3.7	2.3	11.0	16.2
Branches of[c] foreign banks										
1984	14.1	2.0	9.5	6.6	3.2	0.8	0.3	0.3	0.5	1.2
1988	24.1	2.5	20.2	9.3	2.2	0.5	–	–	0.4	0.6
1989	27.4	2.6	23.4	10.1	2.1	0.4	–	–	0.3	0.4

[a] As a percentage of all banks.

[b] All banks also includes private banks, loan associations, agricultural credit cooperatives, and finance companies.

[c] Data for 1980 is not available.

Source: Banque Nationale Suisse, various issues

2.3 Bank Performance

The performance of Swiss banks in the last four years is a direct result of the regulatory environment combined with the special characteristics of the Swiss banking system. The analysis in this section will examine the structure of the consolidated income statement of the Swiss banking system. The analysis is carried out separately for the five major banks involved in wholesale international banking, and also for a sample of primarily domestic retail banks.

2.3.1 Structure of Assets and Liabilities

Table 2.4 shows the general similarity of the structure of assets and liabilities for the different categories of Swiss banks. The various groups are involved in almost all the same activities, with differences in magnitude rather than scope of activity. This is a result of the universal nature of the Swiss banking system and its relative lack of product segmentation.

As shown in table 2.2, the market share of the five major banks at the end of 1989 was about 50 percent of the banking industry. A lower percentage of branches, characteristic of the major banks, is an indicator of the wholesale nature of their activities. Since the growth of this group paralleled the growth of the entire industry, the market share of the major banks remained stable during the period 1980-89. (However, it did grow during the period 1973–80.)

Table 2.4 shows that the major banks dominate the interbank market (51.1 percent) and the general loan market (56.6 percent). In the securities market an increasing foreign bank presence can be observed. The five big banks increased their share in the mortgage loan market from 27.5 percent in 1980 to 34.7 percent in 1989; while the market share of the cantonal banks and regional and savings banks declined in that period. During the period examined (1984–9) the big banks increased their share of retail domestic banking at the expense of cantonal banks and regional and savings banks, reflecting increased competition in this market. Another indication of this change is the increase of the share in non-bank deposits of the big banks, from 46.6 percent in 1980 to 49.3 percent in 1989. This increase was also at the expense of cantonal banks and regional and savings banks. The big banks have been investors (depositors) in the interbank market, although 1989 saw a major reversal in this, when a sharp decline in the Grossbanken's deposits with other banks turned them into net borrowers. However, when assets and liabilities held against foreigners are excluded, it is clear that the big banks are net borrowers in the *domestic* interbank market, whereas cantonal banks are net investors.

A more comprehensive analysis of the structure of assets and liabilities by groups of banks is presented in tables 2.5 and 2.6, whose data are based on detailed financial statements.

The structure of banking activities, as revealed in the combined balance sheet of the five major banks, is presented in table 2.5. The percentage of earning assets reached almost 90 percent of total assets; the percentage of loans and mortgages is 70 percent of earning assets when interbank loans and deposits with banks are netted out. Investment in securities are 18 percent and non-earning assets (primarily premises and reserve requirements) are 12 percent. The major sources of bank funds are deposits from the public, about 70 percent of the total. Long-term and other borrowing are 22 percent and equity capital is 8 percent. The structure of activities reveals a high degree of traditional intermediation (70 percent) and some involvement in capital market activities. It should be noted that the involvement of these banks in fiduciary intermediation comprises 34.3 percent of the loan portfolio, and 20.4 percent of total assets (table 2.4). The share of fiduciary accounts in this group was stable over time (19.8 percent in 1980).

Table 2.6 illustrates that the average size of the (sample) group of cantonal banks is much smaller than the larger multinational banks. In addition, the structure of assets and liabilities of the cantonal bank group differs with respect to the multinational bank group by:

- the composition of the loan portfolio. This includes a much greater proportion of mortgage loans reflecting the retail nature of cantonal banks
- the share of traditional intermediation. Loans and deposits are more than 80 percent of total assets when interbank activity is excluded
- the substantially lower equity capital-to-total assets ratio (about 4 percent) compared with the multinational group. This characteristic is not found in other countries examined here, in which large banks generally operate with a lower equity ratio than smaller banks.

Table 2.4 shows that the group of foreign banks (branches and subsidiaries) is less involved in traditional banking than the other two groups, and much more involved in capital market activity. The structure of assets and liabilities of foreign bank branch offices indicates a clear domination of foreign interbank business and fiduciary accounts, which usually considerably exceeds their total assets. The fiduciary accounts of foreign-owned banks represent an amount roughly equal to total assets in the years 1984 and 1989, much above the industry average. The branches of foreign

Table 2.5 Combined balance sheet (five major banks)

		31/12/88	*31/12/88*	*31/12/87*	*31/12/86*	*31/12/85*
		(US$ mil.)		*(SFr. mil.)*		
A	Loans					
	1 Customer loans	115511	173728	146670	134438	126449
	2 Mortgages	51856	77991	68993	60201	53302
	Total A	167367	251719	215663	194639	179751
B	Other earning assets					
	1 Deposits with banks	94905	142738	135700	132805	112359
	2 Short-term investments	11141	16756	25097	26777	27284
	3 Other investments	17233	25919	26786	26204	20727
	4 Equity investments	2910	4377	4065	3883	3285
	Total B	126189	189790	191648	189669	163655
C	Total earning assets (A + B)	293556	441509	407311	384308	343406
D	Fixed assets	4364	6564	5924	5607	5022
E	Non-earning assets					
	1 Cash and due from banks	3673	5524	14774	14587	13836
	2 Other	17120	25749	28453	29069	29731
F	Total assets	318713	479346	456462	433571	391995
G	Customer and short-term funding					
	1 Demand deposits	31435	47279	52982	48881	48014
	2 Savings deposits	46926	70576	65537	57767	53061
	3 Time deposits	85871	129150	113078	114291	109046
	4 Inter-bank	77242	116171	119212	113385	91653
	Total G	241474	363176	350809	334324	301774
H	Other funding					
	1 Long-term debt	33747	50755	48109	44411	40305
	2 Subordinated debt	4583	6893	4931	4564	3069
I	Other (non-int. bearing)	19175	28843	24510	23952	23503
J	Risk capital	19734	29679	28103	26320	23344
K	Total liabilities & risk capital	318713	479346	456462	433571	391995
	Exchange rate (US$1 = SFr)		1.504	1.28	1.62	2.08
	Ratios (%)					
	Deposits/loans		98.1	107.4	113.5	116.9
	Loans/total assets		52.5	47.2	44.9	45.9
	Fixed assets/risk capital		22.1	21.1	21.3	21.5
	Risk capital/total assets		6.2	6.2	6.1	6.0

Source: IBCA data base

Table 2.6 Combined balance sheet (five cantonal banks)[a]

		31/12/88 (US$ mil.)	31/12/88 (SFr. mil.)	31/12/87	31/12/86	31/12/85
A	Loans					
	1 Customer loans	17090	25703	23244	21696	21232
	2 Mortgages	19085	28704	26152	23705	21669
	Total A	36175	54407	49396	45401	42901
B	Other earning assets					
	1 Deposits with banks	6237	9381	10406	8935	7378
	2 Short-term investments	545	819	754	713	673
	3 Other investments	3031	4558	4037	3735	3524
	4 Equity investments	13	20	18	16	14
	Total B	9826	14778	15215	13399	11589
C	Total earning assets (A+B)	46001	69185	64611	58800	54490
D	Fixed assets	528	795	670	639	542
E	Non-earning assets					
	1 Cash and due from banks	575	864	1427	1281	1147
	2 Other	1096	1649	1639	1383	1250
F	Total assets	48200	72493	68347	62103	57429
G	Customer and short-term funding					
	1 Demand deposits	3421	5145	5199	4419	3969
	2 Savings deposits	17756	26705	25191	23334	22027
	3 Time deposits	4492	6756	6213	4953	4568
	4 Inter-bank	3808	5728	5424	5117	4842
	Total G	29477	44334	42027	37823	35406
H	Other funding					
	1 Long-term debt	14106	21216	19722	18305	16637
	2 Subordinated debt	43	65	65	65	65
I	Other (Non-int. bearing)	2527	3800	3624	3255	2904
J	Risk capital	2047	3078	2909	2655	2417
K	Total liabilities & risk capital	48200	72493	68347	62103	57429
Exchange rate (US$1 = SFr)			1.504	1.28	1.62	2.08
Ratios (%)						
Deposits/loans			71.0	74.1	72.0	71.2
Loans/total assets			75.1	72.3	73.1	74.7
Fixed assets/risk capital			25.8	23.0	24.1	22.4
Risk capital/total assets			4.2	4.3	4.3	4.2

[a] The relevant banks are the Bank Julius Baer, Banque Cantonale de Berne, Luzerner Kantonalbank, St Gallische Kantonalbank, Zurcher Kantonalbank.

Source: IBCA Data base

Table 2.7 Combined income statement of the Swiss banking system (SFr mil.)

	Net[a] *interest income*	%[b]	*Non-interest income*	%	*Personnel expenses*	%	*Other operating expenses*	%	*Provisions net*	*Taxes*	*Net income*	*Net*[c] *income to equity* (%)
All banks[d]												
1984	6,353	100.0	11,796	100.0	6,573	100.0	3,217	100.0	3,343	1,422	3,594	9.8
1985	7,220	100.0	13,770	100.0	7,308	100.0	3,670	100.0	4,032	1,700	4,280	9.9
1986	7,449	100.0	15,910	100.0	8,163	100.0	4,232	100.0	4,388	1,807	4,769	9.9
1987	7,449	100.0	17,435	100.0	9,002	100.0	4,705	100.0	4,724	1,803	4,650	8.6
1988	8,392	100.0	17,155	100.0	9,695	100.0	5,026	100.0	4,399	1,677	4,750	8.1
1989	8,974	100.0	20,755	100.0	10,713	100.0	5,653	100.0	5,587	1,788	5,988	9.6
Big banks												
1984	3,228	50.8	5,576	47.3	3,292	50.1	1,556	48.4	1,612	726	1,618	9.0
1985	3,716	51.5	6,427	46.7	3,610	49.4	1,757	47.9	1,972	854	1,950	9.8
1986	3,870	52.0	7,328	46.1	3,982	48.8	2,002	47.3	2,153	872	2,189	9.4
1987	3,879	52.1	7,739	44.4	4,340	48.2	2,169	46.1	2,128	849	2,132	8.1
1988	4,432	52.8	7,808	45.5	4,700	48.5	2,329	46.3	2,177	823	2,211	8.0
1989	4,592	51.2	9,088	43.8	5,242	48.9	2,607	46.1	2,447	827	2,557	8.6
Cantonal banks												
1984	1,046	16.5	945	8.0	846	12.9	336	10.4	357	42	410	7.5
1985	1,132	15.7	1,071	7.8	921	12.6	376	10.2	417	49	440	7.6
1986	1,194	16.0	1,209	7.6	993	12.2	428	10.1	458	52	472	7.7
1987	1,248	16.8	1,312	7.5	1,053	11.7	470	10.0	482	60	495	7.5
1988	1,379	16.4	1,316	7.7	1,124	11.6	512	10.2	468	60	531	7.1
1989	1,525	17.0	1,437	6.9	1,210	11.3	561	9.9	546	60	585	7.7
Regional and savings banks												
1984	449	7.1	511	4.3	370	5.6	178	5.5	138	82	192	6.6
1985	484	6.7	556	4.0	399	5.5	197	5.4	152	87	205	6.6
1986	524	7.0	603	3.8	435	5.3	227	5.4	163	87	215	7.0
1987	543	7.3	700	4.0	456	5.1	244	5.2	230	90	223	6.4
1988	625	7.4	660	3.8	489	5.0	265	5.3	201	90	240	6.3
1989	714	8.0	687	3.3	519	4.8	284	5.0	252	91	255	6.4

Other Swiss banks													
1984	531	8.4	1,247	10.6	638	9.7	359	11.2	317	158	306	10.2
1985	605	8.4	1,553	11.3	757	10.4	434	11.8	405	192	370	10.9
1986	656	8.8	1,938	12.2	889	10.9	513	12.1	474	252	466	11.9
1987	696	9.3	2,155	12.4	979	10.9	578	12.3	537	270	487	10.5
1988	750	8.9	2,020	11.8	1,000	10.3	588	11.7	467	249	466	9.0
1989	970	10.8	2,405	11.6	1,162	10.8	698	12.3	682	251	582	10.8
Foreign-owned banks												
1984	621	9.8	2,193	18.6	894	13.6	469	14.6	647	226	578	8.6
1985	723	10.0	2,489	18.1	971	13.3	514	14.0	748	277	702	9.6
1986	602	8.1	2,721	17.1	1,091	13.4	575	13.6	683	249	725	9.2
1987	535	7.2	3,137	18.0	1,260	14.0	641	13.6	818	246	707	8.2
1988	607	7.2	3,295	19.2	1,444	14.9	730	14.5	769	238	721	7.7
1989	584	6.5	4,653	22.4	1,569	14.6	851	15.1	1,112	290	1,415	13.5
Branches of foreign banks												
1984	129	2.0	311	2.6	152	2.3	101	3.1	61	32	94	24.9
1985	137	1.9	457	3.3	182	2.5	125	3.4	87	56	144	28.8
1986	143	1.9	497	3.1	209	2.6	143	3.4	91	50	147	32.4
1987	130	1.7	505	2.9	239	2.7	168	3.6	91	39	98	25.3
1988	142	1.7	460	2.7	242	2.5	163	3.2	62	31	104	26.8
1989	116	1.3	550	2.6	242	2.3	176	3.1	176	22	50	12.5

[a] Net interest income, including profit,from changes in market value of securities.
[b] Percentage of all banks included in this table.
[c] Net income to equity capital at the beginning of the year.
[d] All banks also includes private banks, loan associations, agriculture cooperatives, and finance companies.

Source: Banque Nationale Suisse, various issues

banks' share of the fiduciary banking market is also above industry average. However, after a peak in 1984, a major decline occurred in the period ending in December 1989 (from 167.4 percent of total assets in 1984 to 78.1 percent in 1989). Therefore, the total equity-to-total assets of the foreign-owned banks is clearly higher than the industry average (28.9 percent at the end of 1989).

International business involvement is concentrated in the five big banks and foreign banks. The largest Swiss banks have roughly 50 percent of the market, and the foreign-owned banks about 70 percent of their assets abroad.

2.3.2 Income Statement

The limited disclosure that characterizes the reported earnings of Swiss banks does not permit a comparative evaluation with banking systems in other countries. This is especially true since the provision for doubtful loans is constructed in a very conservative fashion, and does not disclose allowable hidden reserves.

Underlying earning fundamentals have strengthened recently, largely reflecting the 1984–6 global stock and bond market boom which propelled fee income, portfolio management fees, and trading profits. Stock market activity in Switzerland and abroad peaked in 1986 and decreased following the 1987 market crash. Nevertheless, these activities have continued to grow, due to Switzerland's ability to attract funds seeking conservative management. The banks have therefore sustained their dominance of the SFr bond market.

As seen in table 2.7, the interest income of the largest banks has increased during the period examined, by 42.2 percent, slightly above the industry average of 41.1 percent. As a result, the share of the industry net interest income gained by the largest banks reached 51.2 percent in 1989, compared with 50.8 percent in 1984. During the same period the share of foreign banks decreased. This structural change reflects the shift in composition of the loan portfolio of the largest banks toward domestic/mortgage loans. The non-interest income in the banking industry during the period examined increased by 75.9 percent. For foreign-controlled banks, non-interest income increased by 107.8 percent and for Swiss banks by 92.9 percent. This source of operating income increased in these groups above the industry average. At the same time, the large banks' (62.9 percent) and cantonal banks' (52.0 percent) non-interest income increased less than the industry average. The non-interest income of the Grossbanken is their major source of income (197.9 percent of interest income in 1989 compared with 266.0 percent for the rest of the banking system, although this is mostly due to the foreign bank sector).

Operating expenses, as a percentage of non-interest income (83.0 percent in 1984 compared with 78.8 percent in 1989), increased for the big banks, in particular. Personnel expenses increased during the period examined by 62.9 percent, mostly as a result of an increase in the number of employees (28.0 percent) and an increase in salaries. The most significant increase was that of the foreign banks (branches and subsidiaries). Other operating expenses increased by 75.7 percent in all groups of banks. Operating expenses increased, but were still lower than the industry average. Finally, the net income-to-equity ratio remained stable at 9.8 percent in 1984 and 9.6 percent in 1989. This stability is the consequence of an increase in non-interest income, which almost covered the increased cost necessary to develop retail banking and capital market activities. This development is common to all groups. A more detailed analysis of the sample groups of banks is presented in tables 2.9 and 2.10.

Net income to average equity for the big banks has been very steady due to smoothing for reporting purposes. Nevertheless, it declined from 9.0 percent in 1985 to 8.7 percent in 1988, and increased again in 1989.

The earnings of the largest banks have been subject to the universal trend of contracting margins on corporate business and increases in data processing expense (table 2.8). The ratio of net interest margins to other operating income has been stable at 62 percent from 1980 to 1988, indicating the importance of fee income compared with interest rate income. The continuous decline of interest rate margins in recent years ceased in 1988, when interest margins stabilized and even slightly increased. Additionally, personnel expenses were 50 percent of total operating expenses, a reflection of the relatively large expense of data processing. Finally, the tax provision was steady over the period, reaching 28 percent of pre-tax profit (almost the same as the statutory tax rate).

The stable reported earnings of 9 percent on average equity largely understates real profits. Nevertheless, 9 percent does reflect a high return on investment, especially given the relatively high equity (and low risk) of the banks.

The income statements of the cantonal banks (table 2.10) reflect the following structure of their operations:

- Less involvement in capital market operations and fiduciary transactions compared with the large multinational banks and foreign banks.
- Interest rate margins similar to that of the large multinational banks. This similarity reflects the universal nature of the multinational group.

Table 2.8 Combined income statement (five major banks)

	1988	1987	1986	1985
		(SFr. mil.)		
1 Interest received	23327	20675	19400	20453
2 Interest paid	18894	16796	15530	16737
3 Net interest revenue	4433	3879	3870	3716
4 Other operating income	7176	7188	6843	5996
5 Other income	632	551	486	431
6 Personnel expenses	4700	4340	3982	3611
7 Other non-interest expenses	4503	4294	4153	3726
8 Pre-tax profit	3038	2984	3064	2806
9 Taxes	823	849	872	854
10 Net income	2215	2135	2192	1952
Ratio analysis				
Average total assets	467904	445017	412783	391995
Average earning assets	424410	395809	363857	328849
Average risk capital	28891	27212	24832	21598
Inflation rate (%)	1.9	1.4	0.8	3.4
Ratios to average earning assets (%)				
Interest received	5.50	5.22	5.33	6.22
Interest paid	4.45	4.24	4.27	5.09
Net interest revenue	1.05	0.98	1.06	1.13
Interest on capital employed	0.30	0.29	0.30	0.35
Net spread	0.75	0.69	0.76	0.78
Other ratios (%)				
Personnel expenses/net interest	106	112	103	97
Other oper. expe./net interest	102	111	107	100
Net interest/non-interest income	57	50	53	58
Total oper. exp./non-interest income	118	112	111	114
Net income/total assets	0.46	0.47	0.51	0.50
Net income/risk capital	7.67	7.85	8.83	9.04

Source: IBCA Data Base

- Personnel expenses as a percentage of total operating expenses (67 percent in 1989) equal to the banking system average (table 2.7).

It can therefore be seen that the cantonal banking group is less profitable than the large multinational and foreign banks. Foreign banks are involved mostly in capital market activities and fiduciary accounts, which results in

Table 2.9 Selected financial data for the five major Swiss banks as at 31 December, 1988 (SFr. mil.)

	Union Bank of Switzerland	*Swiss Bank Corp.*	*Crédit Suisse*	*Swiss Volksbank*	*Bank Leu*	*Totals for the five major banks*
Total assets	158833	144553	106170	32195	14711	456462
Total loans	73562	69653	47139	20933	4376	215663
Total deposits	77330	76529	51549	20708	5480	231597
Risk capital	9746	8761	6613	1888	1095	28103
Personnel expenses	1653	1332	1154	438	123	4700
Net income	778	675	592	124	46	2215

Source: IBCA Data Base

their high return on equity. Net interest income has remained constant during the period examined, despite the increase in the loan portfolio.

2.3.3 Sources of Income

Interest margins constituted only 31 percent of 1989 gross operating income for the Swiss banking system, almost the same percentage as in 1984 (35 percent), (table 2.7). Nevertheless, significant differences exist among different groups. For the big banks interest income covered 34 percent of total income, for foreign banks only 11.6 percent, and for the retail-oriented cantonal and regional banks about 50 percent. These differences result from the involvement of the big banks in international lending (with even lower margins) and capital market activity. During the period examined, the loan portfolio of all banks increased by about 64.3 percent (with an increase in the share of mortgages from 40.3 to 40.7 percent). However, net interest income increased by only 41.2 percent (tables 2.4 and 2.7). Non-interest income increased by 75.9 percent.

Interest margins

Table 2.4 illustrates that the loan portfolio of the big banks increased by 79.1 percent, while the interest income increased by only 42.2 percent. This difference indicates a reduction in interest margins. Due to the similarity of margins across different types of loans, the composition of the loan portfolio plays a less important role in determining interest income.

The relatively modest 1 percent margin reported by the major and

Table 2.10 Combined income statement (five cantonal banks)[a]

	1988	1987	1986	1985
		(SFr. millions)		
1 Interest received	2912	2778	2655	2540
2 Interest paid	2319	2236	2138	2054
3 Net interest revenue	593	542	517	486
4 Other operating income	641	626	572	496
5 Other income	88	84	71	68
6 Personnel expenses	571	532	495	455
7 Other non-interest expenses	510	488	457	403
8 Pre-tax profit	241	232	208	192
9 Taxes	46	45	36	33
10 Net income	195	187	172	159
Ratio analysis				
Average earning assets	66898	61705	56645	52568
Average risk capital	2993	2782	2536	2360
Ratio to average earning assets (%)				
Interest received	4.35	4.50	4.69	4.83
Interest paid	3.46	3.62	3.78	3.91
Net interest revenue	0.89	0.88	0.91	0.92
Interest on capital employed	0.15	0.16	0.17	0.17
Net spread	0.74	0.71	0.75	0.75
Other ratios (%)				
Personnel expenses/net interest	96	98	96	94
Other oper. exp./net interest	86	90	88	83
Net interest/non-interest income	81	76	80	86
Total oper. exp./non-interest income	148	144	148	152
Net income/total assets	0.27	0.27	0.28	0.28
Net income/risk capital	6.52	6.72	6.78	6.74

[a] The relevant banks are the Bank Julius Baer, Banque Cantonale de Berne, Luzerner Kantonalbank, St Gallische Kantonalbank, Zurcher Kantonalbank.

Source: IBCA data base

cantonal banks in Switzerland reflects a highly competitive market. Furthermore, interest margins continued to decline during the period examined, reaching 1.04 percent in 1989. The effective interest rate margins are even lower since the major Swiss banks enjoy relatively large amounts of free capital (i.e., equity capital less investment in fixed assets). Free capital is considered (in accounting reporting) as costless funds. If the net interest revenue was reclassified to separate the income on free capital from the net interest margins on pure intermediation, the interest margins would be found to be as low as 0.75 percent in 1988.

Low liquidity requirements (see section 2.2.2) and the low monetary tax allow banks to operate with such low margins. It should also be noted that the reported average interest rate margins were composed of three major sources: wholesale intermediation, domestic retail banking (i.e., small to mid-sized corporations), and investments. The decline in overall interest rate margins was partially offset by a shift from wholesale corporate credits toward retail and small- middle-market businesses, which are less competitive and hence have higher margins. The relatively low interest rate margins on intermediation in Switzerland prevents, to a large extent, further disintermediation, and improves the position of Swiss banks in the globalization of banking.

The decline in interest margins was partially offset by the real increase in the size of the loan portfolio. Also, the interest margins reported were undoubtedly understated, due to the provisions for doubtful loans which are not reported.

For the cantonal bank sample the net spread is very similar to that of the big banks (table 2.10). Since the non-interest income of cantonal banks is lower, overall performance was worse than the big banks during the period examined. The loan portfolio and their interest income increased by 54.5 percent and 45.8 percent respectively (table 2.4). For foreign banks, the marginal increase in their loan portfolio was sufficient to offset the reduction in margin and net interest income at the same level.

Non-interest income

Non-interest income contributed 66.4 percent of the gross income of the big banks in 1989 (table 2.8). Recent growth in Swiss bank earnings has been generated by securities-related activities. The global stock and bond market booms of the mid-1980s have produced earnings in the form of brokerage fees, custody and investment advisory fees, and portfolio management. A major source of non-interest income is the income derived from fiduciary accounts, which is highly concentrated in the multinational and foreign bank group (table 2.4).

Additionally, the equity holdings of the major banks in Switzerland contribute further to their profits (which are understated because of unrealized profits). Operating non-interest income slowed down as a result of the October 1987 stock market crash. This development underscored the vulnerability of Swiss banks to the globalization of capital markets. Non-interest income is much less stable than traditional margins in intermediation, which is based on bank-customer relationships. Therefore, the competitive power of Swiss banks in market-related activities will certainly expose them to future operating risks.

For the cantonal, regional, and savings banks, non-interest income is less significant than for the largest banks, contributing 49 percent of total income in 1989 (table 2.7). The significance of non-interest income to this group continues to increase over time, reflecting the penetration of the group into capital markets. The increased importance of non-interest income to cantonal, regional, and savings banks represents the impact of deregulation on the Swiss banking system, as previously described.

For other Swiss and foreign banks non-interest income is a major source of income. Non-interest income to total income for other Swiss banks was 71.2 percent in 1989 (69.7 percent in 1984), and for foreign banks 88 percent in 1989 (77 percent in 1984).

2.3.4 Expenses

The three major sources of bank expenses are personnel, other overheads, and taxes. As can be seen in tables 2.7, 2.8 and 2.10, the relative magnitude of expenses is very similar in all bank categories. Personnel expenses are 66 percent of operating expenses (table 2.7). This is a relatively low percentage given the universal nature of Swiss banks. The big banks employ about 50 percent of all employees in the banking system, and account for 48.9 percent of personnel expenses. In terms of productivity the total revenue per SFr 1 of personnel expenses in the big banks declined from SFr 2.67 in 1984 to SFr 2.60 in 1989; the net interest income-to-personnel expense ratio declined from 0.98 in 1984 to 0.88 in 1989 (table 2.7). This trend reflects both increased expenses and the decline in interest income. Further examination of the net interest income to total operating expenses reveals a decline from 66 percent in 1984 to 58 percent in 1989. Within the banking industry net interest margins and total operating expenses are considered to be fixed for the short-run. Therefore, increased operating risk for the major banks is expected. The relative increase in personnel expenses in the big banks represents the additional costs required to increase retail banking and securities-related activities.

The non-personnel expenses represent mostly investment in electronic data processing (depreciation represents a small portion of other operating expenses reflecting low investment in fixed assets). Other operating expenses of the big banks have increased even more than personnel expense, especially investment in computer operations. Finally, the provisions for taxes represent 28 to 30 percent of gross profits (23 percent in 1989), very close to the statutory tax rate. This is due to the fact that almost the entire provision for doubtful loans is tax deductible.

From the sample of retail cantonal banks and regional and savings banks, the expenses are not significantly different from that of the large banks, a result of the universal nature of the big banks. The cantonal group employed 14.2 percent of all bank employees in 1989. However, the group share in personnel expenses was lower (11.3 percent), since employees in retail banking are lower paid (compared with those in securities-related activities and wholesale banking). During the period examined the increase in personnel expenses for this group (43.0 percent) was below the industry average (63.0 percent). For other operating expenses, the increase (67.0 percent) was also below the industry average growth rate (75.7 percent).

In 1989, other Swiss and foreign banks employed 9.2 percent and 14 percent, respectively, of all bank employees. Their share of personnel expenses in the entire banking system was 10.8 percent and 14.6 percent respectively (table 2.7), reflecting the high cost of employees required for capital market activities.

2.3.5 *Capital Adequacy*

The capital-to-asset ratio reached 6.5 percent at the end of 1989 (table 2.4), a figure undoubtedly below the true ratio. As discussed earlier, the current equity-to-asset ratio reflects the strict statutory risk-asset based guidelines enforced by the Swiss Bank Commission, which is calculated on a consolidated basis. Risk-asset coefficients are applied at 8 percent for an unsecured loan, 4 percent for bank deposits, and 20 percent for unquoted shares which also includes off-balance-sheet activities. Furthermore, capital is conservatively defined to include only equity. Consequently, Swiss banks not only have the most conservative capital adequacy guidelines, but also the highest visible equity-to-asset standard.

The reported capital-to-asset ratio should be adjusted for two major factors: exclusion of interbank deposits, which results in a rise of the capital asset ratio to 8.3 percent; and exclusion of taxed and non-taxed hidden reserves, which are estimated to increase the reported ratio of 6.0 percent by about 40 percent. The capital ratios in Switzerland, both on a capital/asset ratio basis and a weighted capital/risk asset basis, are among the highest in all the developed countries. It is unlikely that the Bank for International Settlement (BIS) globally-set minimum will encourage bank authorities in Switzerland to adjust their reporting requirements with respect to hidden reserves. The Banking Law of Switzerland provides for the creation of hidden reserves, which is beyond the practice of most other countries. As mentioned above, Swiss banks are obligated to make capital provisions for certain contingent liabilities and off-balance-sheet transactions, such as an open position in foreign currency (10 percent) and precious metals (20 percent), as well as for guarantees. No provisions, however, are required for portfolio management and underwriting obligations, which also entail risks.

References

Banque Nationale Suisse, *Das Schweizerische Bankwesen*, various issues.
IBCA, Banking Analysis Limited, London, *Data Base and Country Reports*.
IMF, *International Financial Statistics*, various issues.

3

The Federal Republic of Germany

3.1 Structure of the Financial System

3.1.1 Introduction

The West German (FRG) economy today is the proud product of the post-World War Two "economic miracle" – the rapid recovery and growth that enabled a defeated Germany to become the world's third largest economy. This economic miracle was the result of many factors, including a fairly intact industrial base; financial assistance in the form of the Marshall Plan; the traditional German discipline, organization, and work ethic; a highly skilled and motivated labor force; and successful economic policies. Thus, by the early 1970s West Germany was an integral part of the EC, the European Monetary System was virtually a Deutschmark bloc, inflation was dormant, unemployment low, and prosperity widespread. However, in the late 1970s and early 1980s this situation altered as a consequence of changing worldwide economic conditions. The FRG faced the unfamiliar problems of rising unemployment, from 3.3 percent in 1973 to 7.6 percent in 1988; an increase in inflation to 6.3 percent in 1981 (a frightening figure for a country still traumatized by past episodes of hyper-inflation); a slower growth rate; and a number of spectacular collapses of individual firms. While most industrial countries suffered similar difficulties during that period – and West Germany's economic performance since 1984 has been quite solid – considerable questions have nevertheless been raised concerning Germany's economic future. This is especially true regarding West Germany's ability to adapt to rapidly changing economic and industrial conditions and to compete in a world market characterized by the entry of newly industrialized countries.

More than any other Organisation for Economic Co-operation and Development (OECD) country, West Germany's economic strength has been based on traditional manufacturing products, especially automobiles, precision goods, chemicals, and optics. Indeed, manufacturing accounts for fully 31.8 percent of West Germany's GDP (compared with 30.5 percent in Japan, 25 percent in France, and 21 percent in the United States). However, in those areas expected to be industries of the future, such as consumer electronics, biotechnology, computers, semiconductors, and other high-technology products, West German industry has not kept pace with its competitors. This is also the case with the service sector, including financial services, with West Germany consistently lagging behind in areas such as deregulation and the development of new instruments and markets. Indeed, a 1984 OECD study found that difficulty in raising risk capital was one of three major problems facing the FRG, along with the low profitability of West German firms and the need to shift to higher technology products.

A number of cultural factors, such as negative population growth, distrust in materialism and technology represented by the "Greens" political movement, and a generalized and typically German "Angst", have all contributed to the uncertainty with which West Germans face their future. Thus, while the West German economy has considerable traditional strengths, its future course will depend on the development of both the flexibility and adaptability necessary in light of changing technological and economic conditions. Recent political events have, of course, considerably boosted the potential for growth and expansion of the West German economy. Massive immigration from Eastern Bloc countries has provided a new source of highly skilled labor. The possibility of vast new markets opening up in the former Comecon countries may result in an increased demand for FRG-produced capital and consumer goods, and investment. Moreover, despite economic distress in the short term, the reunification of the two Germanys may eventually create a European economic superpower which could easily dominate the entire continent.

German reunification

Political developments in Central Europe will certainly have a considerable impact on the German banking system, and on international banking in general. Under the terms of the German Economic and Monetary Union Agreement, which took effect in July 1990, and The German Unification Treaty (implemented October 3, 1990), the Federal Republic absorbed East Germany, adding to its former state 108,000 square kilometers (43 percent), 16.5 million people (27 percent), and 353 billion ostmark in GNP (approximately 10 percent).

The East German banking system was a one tier state-owned system which bore little resemblance to a Western style commercial banking system. It allocated income and credit on a centralized planning basis, in line with the command economy it served. Shortly before unification, the GDR's banking system had consolidated assets equivalent to DM 246 billion, representing a mere 7.5 percent of the consolidated balance sheet of the Federal Republic's banking system at that time. It comprised the State bank, ("Staatsbank"), which played the role of a central bank, some commercial and cooperative banks, and 196 savings banks.

Since unification, former East German territories have become part of The Federal Republic. All responsibility for monetary policy has been transferred to the Deutsche Bundesbank, the former GDR banking system has become subject to the Banking Act of the Federal Republic, and its institutions subject to supervision by the Federal Banking Supervisory Office. Banks licensed in the Federal Republic are now free to operate in the area of the GDR. There is no doubt that the former GDR area will be fully integrated into the FRG Banking System. The stated goal of the Deutsche Bundesbank is:

> the establishment in the GDR of an independent commercial banking system organized in line with free market principles. The current rudimentary banking system of the GDR must be developed in full into a financial sector structured along competitive lines...[1]

In fact, even before political union all the major West German universal banks began establishing themselves in the GDR. Some immediately began to assemble fully-fledged branch networks. While there are many questions regarding the economic consequences of German unification, German banks are sure to be the most involved. They will undoubtedly invest considerable resources in the banking infrastructure of East Germany, and its economic redevelopment. The impact of unification will obviously be the largest single factor affecting German banks' strategies and development in the immediate future, supplanting to some degree the importance of the Single European Market in 1992 and other developments, which, for now have been shifted aside.

3.1.2 Financial Markets and Institutions in the FRG

The West German economy is characterized by a remarkably high domestic savings rate, in which household saving is the most important sector. Domestic savings have consistently exceeded the high level of domestic investment, resulting in a structural surplus in West Germany's current account.

The FRG financial system is predominantly oriented toward financial intermediation rather than direct financial markets. Banks are by far the most important type of financial intermediary, dominating virtually every type of financial activity. They receive nearly 60 percent of all household savings, provide most of the debt finance of private business, and own 40 percent of all bonds. Other traits of the FRG financial system are directly related to the relative importance of West German banks, in financing both short- and long-term loans. These traits include a relatively small role for non-bank financial intermediaries; the relative unimportance of securities markets, especially for shares; and a high debt-to-equity ratio in business financing. Additionally, banks are the key to nearly all other sources, since they also handle most new issues of marketable securities and provide consultancy and brokerage services in securing foreign government and non-bank loans.

Table 3.1 West Germany – major economic indicators and the banking system

	1980	*1984*	*1989*
Gross domestic product US$ bil.	820	623	1,189
Current account, US$ bil.	−13.9	9.8	55.5
Rate of inflation (annual %)	6.3	2.4	2.8
Exchange rate (DM per US$) (year-end)	1.96	3.15	1.70
Interest rate[a] (%)	7.5	4.5	6.0
Population, (mil.)	61.6	61.2	61.6
Number of banks	4,355	4,701	4,202
Total branches	44,666	44,583	44,002
Number of ATMs	n.a.	n.a.	5,000
Population per branch	1,379	1,373	1,401
Population per ATM	n.a.	n.a.	12,320
Bank employees, (thou.)	532.3	571.8	624.6[b]
Bank employees as % of total population	0.86	0.93	1.02

n.a. not available.
[a] Discount rate, end of period.
[b] Data for 1988.

Source: IMF, International Financial Statistics, various issues; *Monthly Report of the Deutsche Bundesbank*, various issues

Banks

The dominant role of commercial banks in West Germany results from the fact that they are universal full service banks in the widest possible sense of the term. They maintain large branch networks, with the three largest banks operating throughout the FRG. Business is done on a national and, increasingly, international scale, even by regional banks. Services include deposit-taking of all types, sizes and terms; the extension of short-, medium- and long-term loans; payments and transfers; and the trading of foreign exchange, securities, and precious metals. Unlike many other countries, West German banks are intensely involved in all aspects of the securities business: underwriting, new issue management, secondary market trading and market making; safe-custody, the representation of share owners and execution of their rights, etc. Some FRG banks even maintain considerable equity interests in industrial conglomerates, an association which has had considerable influence on the development of the relationship between private industry and the banking sector.

As noted by Cable (1985), banks were represented on 61 of the top 100 companies, and supplied 20 board chairmen and six deputy chairmen. Cable concludes his study (p. 130)

> Empirical estimates show that, despite the banks' denial of exercising control over industry, there is a significant, positive relationship between the degree of bank involvement in leading industrial companies and their financial performance.... it is clear from the results that the relationship between industrial banking and firm performance has more to it than the provision of credit alone: it is bank control as well as bank lending which raises profitability.

Banks in West Germany can be categorized by their legal form, size, structure and business strategy. However, there is little structural division of functions. Bank groups differ primarily in the emphasis they place on different aspects of their business. Banks in West Germany can be divided into two main groups (table 3.2): 324 commercial banks, which are overwhelmingly universal full-service institutions and hold some 25 percent of total assets; and a large number of specialized institutions controlling the remaining 75 percent of total assets (savings banks and credit cooperatives).

Commercial banks

The largest banking institutions in West Germany are the three large branch bank – Deutsche, Dresdner and Commerzbank (known as Grossbanken). Each of these banks own an independent subsidiary in Berlin and maintain nationwide branch networks of more than 3,000 branches. These banks controlled 9.6 percent of total domestic banking assets by December 1989 (including mortgage and other subsidiaries). However, this figure is not a true indication of the importance of these banks to the banking system. For example, the Grossbanken handle 60 percent of West Germany's foreign trade payments, account for 50 percent

Table 3.2 The West German banking system[a]

Type of banks[b]	Number of institutions 1978	1984	1989	Number of domestic branches 1978	1984	1989	Total assets (DM billion) 1978	1984	1989	% of total assets 1989	% change in assets 1978–89
A Commercial banks											
Big banks	6[c]	6	6	3,074	3,125	3,116	210	242	410	9.6	95.2
Regional and other banks	110	103	170	2,555	2,604	2,990	218	306	506	11.8	132.1
Branches of foreign banks	53	62	60	96	112	94	38	72	81	1.9	113.2
Private banks	96	76	88	370	343	407	32	36	66	1.6	106.2
Total commercial banks	265	247	324	6,095	6,184	6,607	498	656	1,063	24.9	113.4
B Savings banks sector											
Regional giros	12	12	11	349	257	230	325	488	663	15.5	104.0
Savings banks	611	591	583	17,167	17,722	17,942	433	665	916	21.4	111.5
Total savings banks sector	623	603	594	17,516	17,979	18,172	758	1,153	1,579	36.9	108.3
C Credit cooperative sector											
Regional credit corp.	10	9	6	67	55	36	84	131	184	4.3	119.0
Credit cooperative	2,313	3,707	3,225	19,439	19,587	19,012	201	348	523	12.2	160.2
Total credit cooperative sector	2,323	3,716	3,231	19,506	19,642	19,048	285	479	707	16.5	148.1
D Specialized banks sector											
Mortgage banks	39	37	37	68	65	75	261	439	577	13.5	121.1
Sales financing	133	82	–	600	619	–	23	37	–	–	–
Special functions	17	16	16	47	94	100	124	201	290	6.8	133.8
Postal giro	–	–	–	–	–	–	39	49	61	1.4	56.4
Total specialized banks sector	189	135	53	715	778	175	447	726	928	21.7	107.6
Total banking system	3,400	4,701	4,202	43,832	44,583	44,002	1,988	3,014	4,277	100.0	115.1

[a] Based on domestic operations only.
[b] Excluding postal giro offices and buildings and loan associations.
[c] Including three Berlin subsidiaries of the big banks.

Source: Monthly Report of the Deutsche Bundesbank, various issues

of all bonds underwritten by banks, and hold 40 percent of all securities in safe custody with FRG banks. Moreover, they exert a great deal of influence on West German industrial conglomerates, often typified by their representation on boards of directors. This influence is due to two factors unique to West German commercial banking: the arrangement by which banks (with shareholder permission) exercise the voting rights of shares deposited with them for safe-keeping; and the direct investment of banks in private concerns. Deutsche Bank, for example, is a part owner of such leading firms as Volkswagen, Bosch, Bayer, and Siemens.

Regional banks

Regional banks include all banks organized in West Germany with limited liability under various forms (AG, GmbH, or KGaA). This is a very heterogenous group; while most of these banks maintain a distinct regional orientation, several operate nationwide and internationally, such as Bayerische Vereinsbank, Bayerische Hypobank, BfG and BHF. (Bayerische Vereinsbank and Nordeutsche Hypo enjoy special status as mixed banks and engage in large scale real estate lending, an activity not permitted other private commercial banks). The nationwide BfG, owned by the German Trade Union Confederation, and banks which specialize in foreign business, such as European Asian Bank AG and Ibero-American Bank AG, are also considered regional banks.

Private banks

The oldest group of West German banks, private banks are organized as sole proprietorships (an arrangement no longer permitted in the establishment of new banks) and represent 1.6 percent of bank assets. However, their influence is greater than indicated by size, since private banks generally (and increasingly) specialize in off-balance- sheet activities or services only partially represented on balance sheets. Private banks differ considerably in their business activities, some of which include foreign trade financing, securities issuance and syndication, portfolio management, trustee services, and corporate lending.

Foreign banks

Traditionally, foreign banks have been represented in West Germany by branches, but the recent trend is toward incorporation. There are 60 established branches of foreign banks with 94 offices in the FRG. These branches are considered domestic credit institutions and are free of any restrictions on competition with other domestic banks in all areas of banking. Foreign banks tend to specialize as bankers to subsidiaries of foreign concerns.

Savings banks (Sparkassen)

There were 583 savings banks in West Germany at year-end 1989, with assets of DM 916 billion. Savings banks are, with a few exceptions, owned by regional governments or town councils and operate within local areas. Originally employed only in the collection of savings from the public and in lending on real estate, savings banks now operate as full commercial banks, although their original emphasis remains. Eleven central savings institutes (Landesbanken) serve as regional money center banks for the Sparkassen. As the depository of the Sparkassen's liquidity reserves, they play a prominent role in the West German money market, and have been increasingly important in wholesale banking and international activities. Additionally, savings banks act as bankers for the federal states and their municipalities, and as mortgage banks through the refinancing of mortgages via bond issuance.

Cooperative banks

Cooperative banks were formed in the last century as part of a wider "self help" movement, and as such were intended to collect savings and extend credit to members. Today 3,225 local cooperatives, with about 20,000 branches and nine million shareholders, act as universal banks for their shareholders and other clients. These banks are served by six regional cooperative banks that act as money centers. Regional cooperative banks manage member banks liquidity and provide services such as financing and managerial consultancy. These regional banks are in turn served by the central commercial bank of the cooperative sector, Deutsche Genossenschafts-bank Frankfurt (DG-Bank) which, with DM 83.2 billion in assets, engages in all aspects of the banking business including international transactions.

Specialized banks

Specialized banks accounted for 21.7 percent of all banking activity in West Germany (at year-end 1989). The most important of these institutions are the 25 private, and 9 public, mortgage banks. Concentrating on long-term loans for residences and other projects secured by real estate liens, these banks also play a substantial role as lenders to public authorities. They obtain funds primarily through the floatation of mortgage and communal bonds in the public market. Other housing and loan societies finance owner-occupied dwellings by collecting funds via various savings schemes, some of which enjoy government incentives and tax advantages. Additional specialized banking institutions include:

- Installment credit institutions, which specialize mainly in consumer loans and to a lesser extent in medium-term industrial loans
- Collective Securities Depositories (Kassenverein), which engage in securities clearing and safekeeping on behalf of member banks
- Guarantee banks, which extend guarantees to small and medium-size businesses, allowing them to obtain loans at larger banks
- Investment Companies, which operate unit trusts and mutual funds specializing in foreign and domestic shares, bonds, and real estate
- Postal Giro and postal savings, which offer savings deposits and sight deposits for payment purposes
- Special Purpose banks, some of which are government owned, formed to further specific goals such as export finance, railroad financial operations, or agricultural development. Examples of special purpose banks include the Reconstruction Loan Corporation, the Equalization of Burdens Bank, the Industrial Bank of Berlin, and the German Transport Bank.

Financial markets

Although there are various institutions engaged in financial markets in West Germany, the role played by banks is so overwhelmingly dominant that they can virtually be considered interbank markets. This situation has influenced the capital markets and has resulted in the curtailed development of short-term money markets. The market for short-term balances is thus an interbank market, used for the transfer of liquidity among the 200 or so credit institutions that trade actively. Since both savings banks and cooperative banks operate internal markets, with their central institutions in turn trading on the general market, liquidity can be transferred efficiently throughout the system. Although non-bank entities are not prohibited from participating, their role in the financial markets is insignificant.

While the deposit market is used to transfer liquidity horizontally among banks, the short-term paper market serves as an instrument of monetary policy. This is because virtually all trading is done between the Bundesbank and the credit institutions. As a result, there is no market in direct short-term obligations, such as commercial paper, which have been so important in other countries.

The long-term securities markets in West Germany are large and fairly well developed, but play a much less important role than their size would indicate. The bond market, while the third largest in the world (after the United States and Japan), with outstanding public issues equivalent to $847 billion at the end of 1989, is also dominated by the banking system. Fully 53 percent of all German bonds at the end of 1988 were bank bonds;

of the rest, 33 percent were public sector debt, 14. percent international issues, and a minuscule 0.2 percent were non-bank corporate bonds. Moreover, while primary issuance is large, most issues are held to maturity or infrequently traded. As a result, secondary market trading is narrow and illiquid. The market itself is dominated by the banks, with new issues (including public debt) being bought through fixed syndicates of the major banks and in coordination with both the Bundesbank and the Central Capital Market Committee. The secondary market is predominantly over-the-counter in nature, with direct dealing far surpassing turnover on the exchanges.

The stock market in West Germany is much smaller than the bond market, with a year-end 1989 value of $334 billion, and relatively smaller than that of most other major industrial countries. Growth of the share market in recent years has been slow, with West German firms continuing to rely heavily on long-term debt (i.e., bank loans) for their financing. In contrast, the foreign exchange market has always been important in West Germany. This is due to the large role of the foreign sector in the economy and to the early (1958) deregulation of capital flows and convertibility of the DM. By far the largest market is that of Frankfurt which, like foreign exchange markets all over the world, is an interbank telephone and electronic market. Frankfurt is part of the second tier of world foreign exchange markets, following London, Tokyo and New York. It has recently lost some of its market share to other secondary centers such as Zurich, Paris, and Singapore. Other financial markets in West Germany are relatively unimportant; options trading is insignificant and the first financial futures and options exchange began operation only in 1990.

3.1.3 Banking Product and Bank Competition

Due to the universal nature of West German banking, virtually any financial product or service is provided by the banks. While specialized banks do exist, most types of financial products are offered by every bank. FRG banks therefore are differentiated not by type of service offered, but rather by a variety of factors such as legal form and regional or sector orientation. However, even these distinctions are becoming irrelevant as a result of the competition among banks to offer wider services. Thus, while the Grossbanken once concentrated on servicing the corporate sector, in recent years they have begun cultivating the urban retail customer. In so doing they have come into direct competition with the savings and cooperative banks. The cooperative banks, primarily through their central institutions (the Landesbanken and DG-bank), have in turn made important strides in wholesale banking both by winning corporate customers and by entering new fields such as international banking and the securities business. In rural areas where the Grossbanken have not been well represented, the main competition is between the savings and cooperative banks. It should be noted that there is relatively little intragroup competition, as both savings banks and cooperative banks maintain "unity and harmony, as a result of the regional organization which practically excludes competition within each group. On the other hand, commercial banks work together only on general economic issues and public relations."[2]

A number of trends have contributed to the current state of competition among West German banks. Firstly, there has been a tremendous degree of concentration in the banking sector. Since 1950, the number of independent units in the FRG banking system has declined by two-thirds, primarily as a result of mergers. This has eliminated weaker institutions, with those remaining being both larger and better able to compete domestically and internationally. Secondly, there has been a tremendous expansion of branch networks, enabling banks to compete in virtually every locale. Thirdly, the homogeneity of the bank product and lack of structural segmentation has encouraged banks to increase the scope of their activities and to offer services originally provided by specialized institutions. This has led, for example, to the entry of the Grossbanken into retail banking, an area previously dominated by regional and savings banks. At the same time regional and savings banks have challenged the Grossbanken in the area of wholesale banking.

Foreign banks have also provided considerable competition, focusing primarily on medium-size corporate customers, export industries and local subsidiaries of foreign firms. A more recent source of competition, especially in the securities market, has come from foreign investment banks.

Competition has further grown with the progressive liberalization of the Frankfurt market, which has led to the establishment of a local presence by foreign investment banks. Some foreign banks even joined various underwriting syndicates. Nevertheless, the vitality of the Frankfurt market has been undermined recently by the fact that a great deal of the bond and equity trading has moved to more dynamic and innovative markets overseas, especially London.

The banking system in West Germany is thus quite competitive and can possibly be described as "overbanked," having by far the largest ratio of banks to population in the world at one office per 1,400 inhabitants (compared with one to 4,100 in the United Kingdom, one to 4,200 in the United States and one to 2,700 in Japan). However this profusion of banks is misleading since there is very little non-bank competition in Germany.

The relative insignificance of the non-bank financial sector is the result of many factors, including the generous and far-reaching state pension system that has precluded the development of large institutional investors, pension funds, insurance companies, and other such institutions. Also, as a result of the close ties between banks and non-financial firms in West Germany, industrial and retail firms have in general shown no interest in expanding the financial aspects of their business.

The extent of FRG bank involvement and influence in non-financial firms has become a controversial issue. In contrast to banks in the United States, West German banks are permitted to own direct equity interests in non-financial firms, and they have done so to a considerable degree. Although recent data is lacking, in 1976 banks held 5.7 percent of all outstanding shares, and 22 percent of their holdings represented outright voting rights and controlling shares in firms (over 50 percent of the voting rights). Moreover, according to West German law, shares deposited with banks for safekeeping can be exercised by the banks, thus greatly increasing the banking sector's influence on corporate affairs. Cable (1985), noted that: "when proxies are added, the overall proportion of votes in the top 100 companies controlled by the banks rises to 36 percent . . .". Since West German banks also provide other services such as long-term financial advice and securities underwriting, the potential for conflicts of interest is readily apparent. A number of commissions have noted this potential for abuse and have issued various rules and recommendations. As a result of these recommendations and other factors, West German banks have begun to reduce their holdings of non-financial firms, especially in those cases in which holdings represent ownership of 25 percent or more of the firm.

3.1.4 International Involvement

The West German economy has long been an open one, with international trade playing an important role. However, the foreign sector in banking has a shorter history than in other countries such as the United Kingdom and Switzerland. This sector has recently been growing in importance, and current trends, such as a cautious process of liberalization of the financial markets, preparations for the united European market in 1992, and the opportunities presented by the reunification of Germany and the democratization of Eastern Europe, would appear to encourage this growth.

Foreign banks in West Germany

While there have been few restrictions placed on branches of foreign banks in the FRG, the scale of such operations has not been impressive. By the end of 1989, 60 foreign banks maintained only 94 branches in West Germany, with approximately a 2 percent share of banking business (table 3.3). In addition to full branches, there are some 300 representative offices and 30 subsidiaries of foreign banks. The motivation for foreign banks in establishing branches in West Germany is similar to that of any foreign operation: the provision of services to local subsidiaries of foreign firms with a prior banking relationship; trade financing; provision of international services such as foreign exchange and funds transfer; representation in an important financial center; and to some extent the exploitation of ethnic ties. For the most part, foreign banks have concentrated on wholesale banking, especially short- and medium-term lending to corporate customers; participation in the interbank, Euroloan, and foreign exchange markets; and international payments services.

Frankfurt's role as an international financial center has been hampered by regulation which has encouraged the migration of financial markets, primarily to London. With domestic monetary policy considerations foremost in mind, the West German authorities have prohibited the growth of new financial markets and instruments. Deutschmark denominated floating rate notes, certificates of deposits, and zero coupon bonds were only permitted in 1985 and 1986, years after they became established in other markets. Index linked and European currency unit (ECU) denominated accounts are still prohibited. Additionally, a stamp tax has inhibited secondary market trading in securities, with a badly managed proposal for withholding tax on coupon income causing a massive flow of capital out of West Germany in l988 and 1989.

It is generally perceived that the FRG financial industry, especially the securities industry, has lagged behind its major competitors in terms of innovation and customer service. This perception has contributed to the view of Frankfurt as a distinctly secondary market behind New York, London and Tokyo. Nevertheless, there are indications that Frankfurt is becoming a more serious competitor on the international scene. It has clearly achieved a dominant role in West Germany, concentrating financial activities that were once carried out in cities like Hamburg, Dusseldorf, and Munich. There have also been changes on the regulatory front, with new instruments being introduced (floating rate notes, currency swaps, zero coupon bonds in 1985, CDs in 1986), the opening up of new markets to foreigners (certain types of government bonds, Bundes Obligation in 1988) and the lowering of structural barriers (non-German firms have been

Table 3.3 International involvement of the West German banking system

	1980	*1984*	*1989*	*Change 1980–89*
A. Foreign banks				
Branches of foreign banks	56	62	60	7.1
Number of offices of foreign banks	106	112	94	–11.3
Total assets (DM bil.)	43.1	71.9	81.5	89.1
As a percent of banking system	1.9	2.4	1.9	
Foreign owned banks	n.a.	n.a.	102	
Numbers of offices	n.a.	n.a.	590	
Total assets (DM bil.)	n.a.	n.a.	197.3	
As a percent of banking system			4.3	
B. Banks operating in foreign countries				
Number of banks with foreign branches	16	22	25	56
Number of foreign branches	88	115	164	86.4
Volume of business	95	189	297	212.6
Foreign banking subsidiaries	51	63	87	70.6
Volume of business	n.a.	190	262	
Foreign subsidiaries, Luxembourg	28	26	29	3.6
Volume of business	47.5	157.6	184	287.4

C. Assets and liabilities held against foreigners (DM bil.)

Year	*Total assets*	*Lending to foreign banks*	*Lending to foreign banks*	*Foreign securities*	*Total liabilities*	*Liabilities to foreign banks*	*Deposits of foreign non-banks*
1978	133.5	72.1	56.2	5.2	105.9	78.7	27.2
1980	166.3	85.5	70.1	10.7	141.2	111.6	29.6
1984	236.2	134.4	92.3	9.6	179.6	128.3	51.3
1988	408.7	275.0	111.3	22.4	229.5	168.3	61.2
1989	517.6	362.0	109.0	28.1	271.5	196.6	70.9

n.a. not available.
Source: Monthly Report of the Deutsche Bundesbank, various issues

allowed to lead-manage DM and Euro-DM bonds since 1985). In response, major foreign financial firms have been establishing an investment and/or commercial banking presence in West Germany, including the three largest Swiss banks, the American firm Salomon Brothers and, most recently, major Japanese banks.

Foreign activity of West German banks

Although West German banks have long had branches abroad, the disruption caused by the Second World War resulted in FRG banks keeping a low profile overseas. Foreign branch networks first began to be reestablished only in the 1970s. Luxembourg was the first important "offshore" center for West German banks. Subsidiaries were set up in Luxembourg to avoid minimum reserve requirements on deposits and direct control by West German authorities. Although the latter advantage was eliminated by the introduction of consolidated reporting in the German Banking Law of 1985, Luxembourg remains a major center for FRG banks. While the Grossbanken were the first to establish branch networks abroad, and still account for approximately one-third of overseas branches, the regional banks and central banking institutions have also established a presence overseas, first in Western Europe and, more recently, in North and South America and the Far East. Although overseas activities will undoubtedly remain a very important area for West German banks, it is evident that recent under-performance of foreign branches will result in a reorganization in this area.

3.2 The Regulatory Environment

3.2.1 The Regulatory Framework

The regulatory framework in West Germany is a rule-based system, similar to that of the United States, and unlike the prudential regulatory system of the United Kingdom. Nevertheless, banking rules in the FRG have tended to be interpreted extremely narrowly, resulting in the exploitation of "loopholes" and circumvention of the intent of the rule. The supervisory bodies are endowed with considerable independence as well as broad and meaningful authority.

The Federal Banking Supervisory Office (FBSO)

Situated in Berlin and established by the 1961 Banking Law, the FBSO is an independent Federal Authority entrusted with maintaining the safety and integrity of all banking institutions in West Germany. While theoretically subservient to the Minister of Finance, it has in practice acted with considerable autonomy. The FBSO must obtain the agreement and cooperation of the Bundesbank for all its policies. The most important powers granted the FBSO for the exercise of prudential control of banking institutions in West Germany include:

1 the issuance and withdrawal of banking licenses
2 the promulgation of regulations concerning capital adequacy, liquidity, and lending limits
3 the determination of standards for auditing and the internal organization of banks
4 the right to request reports and information of any type and to conduct investigations as it sees fit
5 the approval of the selection of bank management
6 the extensive intervention in the affairs of a bank when deemed necessary.

The Deutsche Bundesbank

Authorized by the Central Bank Act of 1957, the Bundesbank enjoys authority and independence unparalleled in other major central banks. However, it does not have the responsibility for prudential supervision of banks. Nevertheless, due both to its other central bank functions (monetary policy, banker to the government, banker to the banks) and its mandated role of cooperation with the FBSO, the Bundesbank plays an important de facto role in the supervisory system. For example, most bank reports are submitted first to the Bundesbank, and are then passed on to the FBSO with its comments. Its role in monetary policy, including the setting of critical interest rates such as the Lombard and Discount rates and the setting of minimum reserve requirements, accord it further importance as a regulatory body for the banking system. While the Bundesbank is the provider of liquidity to the banking system, it has made clear that it will not automatically guarantee the solvency of a failing bank.

The Banking Associations

Each of the major banking groups (privatbanken, sparkassen, cooperative banks, etc.) maintain a banking association. These associations are expected to represent members' interests to the authorities and to provide mutual advice and assistance. They also play a role in the voluntary deposit protection schemes.

Deposit insurance

While there is no statutory deposit insurance, most banks belong to one of a variety of voluntary, mutual deposit protection plans, usually organized in the framework of the various banking associations. Funded through an annual levy on deposits, member banks contribute to a central fund, which then guarantees to non-bank depositors the repayment of a portion of their deposits. Additionally, the Landesbanken and Central Cooperative banks maintain guarantee funds intended to support their member banks in the case of illiquidity.

Foreign banks

There is no special regulatory treatment for branches of foreign banks. Instead, foreign banks are considered domestic banks for all supervisory purposes.

3.2.2 Major Bank Regulations

Scope of business

Banks are permitted to perform non-banking activities, and are required to report to the Bundesbank the commencement and termination of any such activity. In addition to banking, FRG banks engage in unlimited securities activities and insurance through affiliates, and are permitted to own shares in industrial and commercial companies. Mixed banks, which are involved in both mortgage and non-mortgage business, are required to present two separate returns for these activities. This broad range of activities allows banks to enjoy considerable non-interest sources of income. Banks have to report to the Federal banking supervisory board and to the Bundesbank on the acquisition and disposal of a participation in another enterprise, and changes in the participation should it exceed 5 percent of capital.

Lending limitations

The Banking Act contains detailed rules on legal lending limits and procedures for the approval of loans (Sections 13 to 20). Section 19 defines the term "loan" to include guarantees, repurchase agreements, and leasing. All companies constituting a group of related companies and their majority shareholders are regarded as a single borrower.

The legal lending limits are detailed in Section 13. Loans to a single borrower, whether domestic or foreign, exceeding 15 percent of equity capital ("liable funds") on a consolidated basis must be reported to the Bundesbank (e.g., large loans). This does not apply to loans amounting to less than DM 100,000, unless such loans exceed 50 percent of equity capital. Large loans must be reported again if they are increased by more than 20 percent of the prior reported amount. Banks are also required to report loans of DM 1 million or more on a three months basis. All such reports are transferred to the FBSO with comments from the Bundesbank.

In addition to reporting requirements, the Act imposes the following restrictions on lending: (1) no loan is allowed to exceed 50 percent of bank capital; (2) a bank's aggregate large loans must not exceed eight times its equity capital (liable funds); (3) large loans must be approved by all bank managers prior to or immediately after granting; (4) a bank that grants credit of more than DM 100,000 to a single borrower *must* obtain a disclosure of the creditor's business situation, i.e., an annual financial statement.

Sections 15 and 16 restrict loans made to managers, members of the supervisory board, officers and other borrowers connected to a bank. Such loans require prior approval by all bank managers (a unanimous decision) and the explicit approval of the supervisory board of the bank. Bank managers may be liable to compensate the bank for losses incurred if such loans are granted in violation of the rules.

Liquidity requirements

The German Banking Act's liquidity requirements – covering liquidity and interest rate risk, and serving monetary policy – is one of the most advanced banking regulatory frameworks in the world. Principles I and III require that banks must at all times maintain sufficient liquidity. Principle II attempts to keep long-term assets in reasonable proportion to long-term financial liabilities by controlling the interest rate risk exposure of commercial banks. The act defines the list of long-term assets as: unlisted securities, loans with original maturity of four years or more, real estate, and long-term funds. The latter include: equity capital, 60 percent of savings deposits, and bonds with an original maturity of four years. This principle states that a bank's long-term assets should not exceed its long-term funds.

Table 3.4 Required reserve ratios, February 1987

	Up to DM 10 Million %	*DM 10 to 100 Million %*	*Over DM 100 Million %*
Deposits of residents			
Demand	6.60	9.90	12.1
Time	4.95	4.95	4.95
Savings	4.15	4.15	4.15
Deposits of non-residents			
Demand	12.1	12.1	12.1
Time	4.95	4.95	4.95
Savings	4.15	4.15	4.15

As can be seen, demand deposits are subject to progressive rate classes based on the volume of deposits.

Principle III requires that medium-term assets are adequately funded.

Assets in this category include 20 percent of loans with original maturity between three months and four years, listed stocks and investment fund shares, and promissory notes. Sources of funds in this category are defined as 20 percent of savings deposits and 80 percent of the amount owed to other banks for advanced drawings. Principle III requires that the sum of assets in this category be not less than the sources of funds, thus reducing the possibility of mismatching throughout the portfolio.

Under Section 16 of the Federal Bank Act, banks are required to maintain interest free deposits with the Federal Bank. Exempted from this requirement are liabilities to West German banks and the Federal bank, liabilities with an original maturity of four years or more, and matched intermediation in foreign currency, (see table 3.4).

Capital adequacy

The Banking Act requires banks to maintain adequate equity capital at all times (Section 10 of the Banking Act defines liable funds). The rules were set by Principle I, which states that the loans and equity participation of a bank (less provisions for loan losses) must not exceed 18 times its equity capital. Since January 1985, Principle I has been applied on a consolidated basis. Equity participation applies to all banking participations, domestic and foreign, in which 40 percent or more of voting rights are controlled by banks. Recently the German Banking Act amendments tightened the implications of the 18 times rule by requiring FRG banks to include figures on their branches and subsidiaries in calculating this ratio.

In June 1986, a new rule was introduced that requires banks to cover themselves against off-balance-sheet risks. For example, 50 percent of NIFs (Note Issuance Facilities) should be counted as a loan for the purpose of calculating the capital-to-lending ratio. Further, Section 12 of the Banking Act limits the total permanent investments (real estate, furniture, ships, participation in banks and non-banks exceeding 10 percent of the equity of the enterprise) to the equity capital of the bank.

On October 1, 1990, the Federal Banking Supervisory Office amended Principles I and Ia. The new provisions are designed to take supervisory account of the dynamic trend in the off-balance-sheet transactions of West German banks. These transactions expanded during 1986–9, from 29 percent to approximately 56 percent of the banks' on-balance-sheet business (Monthly Report of the Deutsche Bundesbank, August 1990).

In such transactions, the exposure of the liable capital to the risk of the counterparty failure is covered under Principle I. In addition to book credits and participating interests, Principle I will in the future also require that the overall risk of counterparty failure arising from financial swaps, forwards, and options be limited to 18 times the bank's liable capital. The FRG law adopted the method provided by the EC Solvency Ratio Directive in calculating credit equivalent amounts. Accordingly, banks may use either the original exposure method or the marking-to-market-method. Under the original method the credit equivalent exposure is calculated by multiplying the relevant factor (listed in table 3.5) by the notional amount of the contract:

Table 3.5 Original method of calculating off-balance-sheet exposures

	Interest rate contracts %	*Currency contracts* %
Up to one year	0.5	2
More than one year but less than two years	1.0	5
For every additional year	1.0	3

Under the marking-to-market method, the credit equivalent exposure is the market value of the contract, according to the following table:

Table 3.5a Marking-to-market method for calculating off-balance-sheet exposures

	Interest-rate contracts	*Currency contracts*
1 Basis	contract replacement cost	contract replacement cost
2 Add on:		
Residual maturity		
Up to one year	0.0%	1%
More than one year	0.5%	5%

Deposit protection

Virtually all banks conducting deposit business belong to one of the deposit guarantee funds set up on a voluntary basis by the banking associations. The fund established by the commercial banks is aimed primarily at protecting depositors, while the schemes operated by savings bank and credit cooperative sectors are designed to avert member banks' insolvency. Foreign banks are permitted to raise funds from non-banks only if these funds are protected by a deposit protection scheme (for West German deposits). This means that foreign banks can only obtain deposit protection through participation in the deposit protection fund of the Federal Association of German Commercial Banks. Such participation requires some prerequisite evaluation including that of performance, level of equity, and the meeting of the standard for conducting banking business.

The deposit protection funds for commercial banks cover liabilities (domestic and in foreign branches) to each non-bank depositor up to an aggregate amount of 30 percent of the equity capital of the member bank. The annual insurance premium is 0.03 percent of liabilities to non-banks at financial year-end (the premium is subject to change according to fund needs). There is also a special entrance fee into the fund. For foreign bank subsidiaries, the deposit protection fund may request a guarantee from the parent company. In the case of savings banks, two schemes, the regional savings bank guarantee funds and the reserve funds of the local banks/regional giro institution, act as an extra safeguard for depositors.

In order to prevent a liquidity crisis in the wake of bank failure, the Deutsche Bundesbank and the FRG banking industry set up the Liquidity Consortium Bank in 1974, which grants liquidity assistance to banks of unquestioned soundness.

Foreign exchange exposure

Principle Ia provides that, at the close of each business day, a bank's net open position in foreign currency and precious metals must not exceed 30 percent of equity capital and reserves. The net position (assets minus liabilities) is determined separately for each currency and each precious metal irrespective of the maturity date of individual commitments.

Other requirements included in Principle Ia are:

- At the close of any business day, the maturing net position in any one calendar month must not exceed 40 percent of the bank's equity capital.
- At the close of any business day, the maturing net position in the first half of any calendar year must not exceed 40 percent of its equity capital.

The October 1990 amendment to Principle Ia aimed to limit price risks, in particular those arising from off-balance-sheet financial instruments, to 60 percent of a bank's liable capital. Off-balance-sheet transactions are thus classified in individual risk categories. The different risk categories are as follows (limits are given as a percentage of liable funds):

- *Foreign currency and precious metals price risk* – The assets and liabilities components previously used to determine the open foreign currency have been extended to include: financial swaps, options, delivery, and payment positions arising from spot and forward contracts. (30% limit.)
- *Interest rate risks* – Arising from interest rate forward contracts and interest rate options, to the extent that they increase the risk posed by other open

(especially on-balance-sheet) positions (the risk coefficients are calculated and computed for several scenarios). (20% limit.)

- *Other price risks* – Arising from forward contracts and options involving other price risk. (10% limit.)

3.2.3 Foreign Exchange Control

West Germany has already abolished all capital controls. In recent years this has resulted in a flow of capital to Luxembourg and Switzerland. A withholding tax of 10 percent on most savings and investments imposed on January 1, 1989, caused a further flow of funds out of the FRG until it was effectively rescinded.

West Germany currently imposes no capital controls on borrowing or lending abroad. However reports on cross-border investments are required for:

- Residents holding claims against or liabilities to non-residents, and payments by residents to non-residents.
- Both residents and non-residents on the sale and purchase of participations in companies and branches. Certain fixed interest securities by non-residents are subject to approval by the Federal Government. There are no restrictions on the repatriation of investments.

Foreign operations in the banking sector are subject to the same regulations as those facing FRG banks. However, the foreign banks have had difficulty breaking into this area, partly because of the large size of domestic banks' equity holdings in West German industrial companies.

3.2.4 Key Accounting Issues

Bank accounting principles in West Germany are regulated by a variety of laws, regulations and standards. Specific bank-related accounting principles are laid down by the Supervisory Agency. (The BIS capital adequacy proposals could lead to a change in public reporting.) The accounting treatment of key banking issues is described below.

Consolidation

The 1985 amendment of the Banking Act requires banking groups to maintain adequate equity on a consolidated basis. Since January 1, 1985, the limits laid down by the Banking Act for "large loans" must be applied on a consolidated basis. Consolidation has been further changed through the introduction of the seventh EC directive into West German Law (with a transition period through December 31, 1989), which includes:

- Consolidation of all subsidiaries, including subsidiaries abroad in which a majority holding exists
- Equity accounting for participations between 20–50 percent.

Valuation of securities and hidden reserves

FRG banks essentially maintain two distinct types of hidden reserves – section 26a reserves and undervalued assets. Section 26a of the Banking Act allows banks to set up reserves against the particular risks of the banks' line of business. Examples are excessive specific provisions in respect of bank debtors and the creation of a general provision for bad debts in excess of what is reasonably required. These provisions are not tax deductible.

The second source of hidden reserves is the adoption of conservative valuation, i.e., by valuating investment down to the lower of cost or market value. However, while general commercial law requires public and limited liability companies to write back any amount previously written off as soon as the reason for the initial write-off has disappeared, banks are allowed to maintain the write-off if debt or dealing investments are involved. The reasoning behind this specific provision is the fear that general accounting rules do not account sufficiently for the special risk inherent in banking.

Loan loss reserves

For tax and reporting purposes there are two basic types of reserves – specific and general. Specific bad debt allowances are set up on a case by case basis whereby individual loans are evaluated as to their future collectability. The allowance may vary from a low percentage, such as 5 percent of the face value, to a complete write-off if the loan is unsecured. The interest related to written-off amounts is no longer accrued if future collection is doubtful. Banks assume that any provision against a specific doubtful or bad loan is *tax deductible*. There are no clear criteria to define doubtful loans. Banks are required to classify risks according to certain categories: special notes, doubtful loans, and bad debt.

Bank management may decide to establish general allowances for a group of debts that cannot individually be evaluated. The basis for such an allowance is formed by each group of assets *after deduction of items covered by specific allowances*. The amount set off will be based on the bank's past performance, and will normally be deducted from the asset concerned.

Although the formation of a general provision is not compulsory, it is prescribed by the supervisory agency. The minimum general allowance percentage applicable to various loans is based on the type of loan and its maturity.

Banks may provide reserves using a higher percentage than that stipulated, but *these additional reserves are not allowed for tax purposes.*

General allowances, unlike specific allowances, are shown on the liabilities side (they are not offset against the corresponding asset balances). West German banks do not write-off loans until there is absolutely no chance of recovery. If no relevant specific provision has been previously made, such a write-off is deductible.

Foreign exchange

Assets and liabilities in foreign currencies are translated into Deutschmarks at the spot rate prevailing at year-end. The most comprehensive presentation of foreign exchange accounting is probably included in the pronouncement by the banking committee, which includes hedge transactions, swap deals, and open forward positions.

The net open forward and swap position is limited under Principle Ia. For the purpose of the pronouncement, closed or open positions are defined more narrowly when assets and liabilities for each currency fall due within the same business year. Net position in *each currency* must be accounted for individually. Unrealized profits must be identified separately by grouping balance sheet assets and liabilities to match forward positions that fall due within the same business year. Unrealized losses from uncompleted contracts can be balanced with unrealized profits (of the same maturity). Any excess loss has to be accrued and any excess profits cannot be taken into account.

The valuation of transactions is made on the following basis.

- *Swap deals* are matched in amount and due date by currency, they are valued by the exchange rate prevailing at the acquisition date, for the part of the transaction carried in the balance sheet, and the contracted rate for the forward part of the transaction. Premiums or discounts are accounted for on a pro rata basis if they arise from differences in interest rates.
- *Foreign currency* assets and liabilities, which are carried in the balance sheet, are valued at the average buy/sell rate of the closing day. Profits or losses arising from the valuation at the closing rate, compared with the original acquisition cost for each currency, are credited or charged to the profit and loss account except for unrealized profits. Unrealized profits in this context exist when a transaction is not yet completed. For example, this occurs when a foreign currency receivable would yield a higher Deutschmark amount at the closing date than the Deutschmark countervalue initially paid out to the debtor. Unrealized profits also exist when the repayment of a liability would result in a lower Deutschmark amount than the Deutschmark countervalue initially received from the creditor.
- *Potential future profit or loss*, inherent in forward sales and purchases of foreign

currencies, is determined by comparing the value at contracted rates with the value at the corresponding average forward rates prevailing at the closing date, separately for each future business year. The resulting profit or loss is corrected for the valuation of open positions (long or short). Profits which still exist, after adjusting for the valuation of open positions, may only be used to offset future losses calculated for the same currency in following years. Profits not set off are thereby disregarded for reporting purposes. Future losses not yet offset by future (unrealized) profits have to be accrued in a balance sheet. Open positions are valued, as described above, for the determination of unrealized profits included in balance sheet items.

Deferred taxes

A bank may record a deferred tax asset equal to the probable future tax reduction if the nature of the timing differences will eventually be reversed. There are limitations on profit distributions in the event that a tax asset is recorded. A profit distribution is only possible if, after the dividend distribution, the net retained earnings are at least equal to the tax asset that remains in the company.

3.2.5 Taxation

Generally, there are no differences between the taxation of banks and other industries in West Germany. However, most banking transactions are exempt from Value Added Tax (VAT) and therefore most input tax is not deductible. The major tax rules related to banks are of sufficient importance to be reviewed here.

Corporate tax rates

The standard tax rate of a corporation is 56 percent of retained profits and 36 percent of distributed profit (the tax rate on retained earnings was set to be reduced to 50 percent in 1990). Foreign banks operating in West Germany through a branch are considered non-resident taxpayers subject to taxes on their West German source income. Such branches pay a corporate tax at the flat rate of 50 percent on both retained and distributed income. No withholding tax is levied on profit distributed to the head office. In the case of income (e.g., dividend) subject to withholding, a rate of 25 percent is normally applied, which may be reduced by double taxation treaties. All capital gains are deemed to be ordinary income.

Losses

Losses of corporate subsidiaries and branches may be offset against other income of the bank arising in the same tax period. Losses may also be carried back for two years and forward for five years. A loss must first be carried back and offset against a prior year's income of up to DM 10 million.

Reserves and bad debt deduction

In general, the FRG tax authorities recognize the allowance for individual bad and doubtful loans required by commercial law as a deductible business expense. Loans that bear special risks are written down by deduction from the specific loan assets. All other debts not secured by banks or by state authorities, which bear only the usual risk, are subject to the statutory general reserve for loan losses determined by the supervisory authority. The rate of general reserve depends on the type of credit and bank setting up the reserve (in the range 0.1 to 1.8 percent). Generally, no interest is accrued on a bad loan.

Consolidation

A consolidated corporate tax return can be filed by the West German parent company for subsidiaries that form part of a fiscal unit. The details of the fiscal unit concept are quite complex, and define integration financially, economically, and in matters of organization.

Interest paid and received

Interest *charged* to a West German entity by a foreign related company or branch must be at market rates plus a reasonable margin. Interest paid by a West German resident debtor is not subject to any withholding tax. However, in the case of a "quasi" equity bond, a 25 percent withholding tax is applied. Interest from mortgages, deposits, and loans paid to a non-resident, if secured by West German land and buildings or West German ships, are subject to FRG income tax (no withholding tax). This interest income is taxed by assessment of net interest income (gross interest less interest and other related expenses). In 1989, a 10 percent withholding tax on almost all interest payments by West German debtors was introduced, although it was later effectively rescinded.

Other taxes

Trade tax

Municipal trade taxes are levied only on businesses. Trade tax is levied on income and capital based on the taxable profit and net worth as computed for corporate tax, after certain adjustments. Trade tax on income is 5 percent of the taxable income times the municipal multiple (e.g., 480 percent in Frankfurt, 450 percent in Munich, etc.). The basis of the trade tax on capital is 0.2 percent, *plus* a local multiplier of the same rate as for trade tax on income.

Value Added Tax (VAT)
Most bank related services are VAT-exempt. However, banks do not regularly receive a credit for VAT included in supplier invoices. Certain bank transactions are subject to a VAT rate of 14 percent. No VAT is levied on transactions between the bank branches and head offices.

Capital transaction taxes
These taxes are levied on two types of transactions:

- A 1 percent company tax on capital invested in a subsidiary or branch in West Germany. This tax is deductible in computing taxable income for corporate taxation
- A stock exchange transfer tax arising on transfer of title to securities. The tax rate is 0.25 percent on securities and is reduced to 0.1 percent on government and mortgage banks bonds, and 0.2 percent on certificate of investment fund. The above rates are cut in half if the purchase contract is concluded out of West Germany and only one of the parties is a resident of the FRG.

Stamp duty
A stamp tax of 0.15 percent becomes payable when a bill of exchange or draft of acceptance is first negotiated (checks are exempted). The tax is reduced to half when the transaction is carried out with a foreign resident.

Wealth tax
The annual tax on the total taxable net wealth is 0.4 percent for corporations and 0.5 percent for individuals. This tax is applied as well to branches or subsidiaries (subject to tax treaties) and is not deductible for income tax.

3.3 Bank Performance

The banks of all three banking groups (commercial banks, savings banks and credit cooperatives) are considered "universal banks" because they offer the full range of commercial and investment banking services. However, some specialization with respect to certain customers (regions) or business activities does exist. The Grossbanken are different with respect to two major activities: they hold shares and supervisory board mem-

Table 3.6 Major items in the balance sheet of domestic West German banks (DM bil.)

	Lending to non-banks	%	*Securities portfolio*	%	*Non-bank deposits*	%	*Bonds outstanding*	%	*Equity capital*	%
All categories of banks[a]										
1978	1,201	100.0	211	100.0	1,040	100.0	334	100.0	66	100.0
1980	1,482	100.0	228	100.0	1,185	100.0	414	100.0	77	100.0
1984	1,924	100.0	347	100.0	1,506	100.0	619	100.0	104	100.0
1988	2,304	100.0	502	100.0	1,983	100.0	705	100.0	145	100.0
1989	2,578	100.0	502	100.0	2,040	100.0	760	100.0	161	100.0
Big banks										
1978	115	9.6	15.3	7.3	131	12.6	8.3	2.5	9.2	13.9
1980	137	9.2	18.7	8.2	135	11.4	9.6	2.3	12.0	15.6
1984	151	7.8	25.9	7.5	153	10.2	11.4	1.8	13.2	12.7
1988	213	9.2	32.7	6.5	199	10.0	17.6	2.5	22.1	15.2
1989	267	10.4	37.5	7.5	223	10.9	23.0	3.0	26.9	16.7
Regional and other banks										
1978	129	10.7	17.5	8.3	103	9.9	28.3	8.5	9.3	14.1
1980	154	10.4	20.9	9.2	111	9.4	37.8	9.1	10.6	13.8
1984	197	10.2	33.4	9.6	133	8.8	60.0	9.7	13.2	12.7
1988	283	12.3	45.4	9.0	187	9.4	66.4	9.4	22.1	15.2
1989	341	13.2	51.4	10.2	200	9.8	77.7	10.2	24.7	15.4
Branches of foreign banks										
1978	10.0	0.8	3.3	1.6	3.3	0.3	–	–	2.5	3.8
1980	13.5	0.9	3.2	1.4	4.2	0.4	–	–	2.7	3.5
1984	22.7	1.2	6.4	1.8	7.1	0.5	–	–	3.6	3.5
1988	18.1	0.8	7.6	1.5	4.4	0.2	–	–	3.7	2.5
1989	23.8	0.9	7.2	1.4	5.7	0.3	–	–	4.0	2.5

Private bankers										
1978	15.8	1.3	4.3	2.0	16.0	1.5	–	–	1.7	2.6
1980	18.3	1.2	3.9	1.7	16.5	1.4	–	–	1.8	2.3
1984	20.6	1.1	5.9	1.7	19.9	1.3	–	–	2.0	1.9
1988	31.6	1.4	8.1	1.6	27.5	1.4	0.5	0.1	2.7	1.8
1989	38.7	1.5	7.6	1.5	30.0	1.5	0.6	0.1	3.8	2.4
Regional giro institutions										
1978	196	16.3	31.1	14.7	63	6.1	146	43.7	7.2	10.9
1980	239	16.1	35.7	15.7	70	5.9	179	43.2	8.5	11.0
1984	304	15.8	46.7	13.5	94	6.2	250	40.4	11.7	11.3
1988	332	14.4	51.6	10.3	138	7.0	266	37.7	14.6	10.1
1989	355	13.8	55.2	11.0	145	7.1	277	36.4	16.3	10.1
Savings banks										
1978	269	22.4	81	38.4	371	35.7	0.1	0.03	14.0	21.2
1980	345	23.3	84	36.8	428	36.1	0.6	0.1	17.2	22.3
1984	446	23.2	126	36.3	540	35.9	3.1	0.5	24.3	23.4
1988	528	22.9	201	40.0	660	33.3	18.2	2.6	32.6	22.5
1989	591	22.9	197	39.3	685	33.6	28.0	3.7	34.7	21.6
Regional credit cooperatives										
1978	16.9	1.4	12.2	5.8	10.4	1.0	4.1	1.2	2.6	3.9
1980	20.8	1.4	13.2	5.8	10.6	0.9	8.0	1.9	2.9	3.8
1984	27.7	1.4	25.8	7.4	13.0	0.9	11.7	1.9	4.6	4.4
1988	35.3	1.5	30.8	6.1	12.6	0.6	16.7	2.4	6.2	4.3
1989	54.5	2.1	34.2	6.8	12.6	0.6	18.5	2.4	6.7	4.2

Table 3.6 Major items in the balance sheet of domestic West Germany banks (dm bil.)—*contd.*

	Lending to non-banks	%	*Securities portfolio*	%	*Non-bank deposits*	%	*Bonds outstanding*	%	*Equity capital*	%
Credit cooperatives										
1978	126	10.5	27.6	13.1	167	16.1	–	–	7.6	11.5
1980	170	11.5	30.5	13.4	206	17.4	–	–	10.9	14.2
1984	229	11.9	50.9	14.7	281	18.7	2.4	0.4	13.1	12.6
1988	286	12.4	90.6	18.0	394	19.9	7.0	1.0	19.4	13.4
1989	324	12.6	92.0	18.3	416	20.4	9.5	1.2	20.4	12.7
Mortgage banks[b]										
1978	222	18.5	2.9	1.4	75	7.2	127	38.0	6.0	9.1
1980	270	18.2	2.2	1.0	91	7.7	156	37.7	7.1	9.2
1984	369	19.2	3.9	1.1	120	8.0	242	39.1	9.9	9.5
1988	421	18.3	7.6	1.5	198	10.0	255	36.2	13.4	9.2
1989	436	16.9	8.7	1.7	214	10.5	259	34.1	14.3	8.9
Banks with special functions										
1978	64	5.3	4.4	2.1	58	5.6	20.4	6.1	4.5	6.8
1980	75	5.1	4.0	1.8	64	5.4	22.0	5.3	4.9	6.4
1984	105	5.5	8.5	2.4	85	5.6	38.5	6.2	6.5	6.3
1988	131	5.7	11.1	2.2	104	5.2	57.5	8.2	8.5	5.9
1989	147	5.7	11.7	2.3	109	5.3	66.5	8.8	9.1	5.7

[a] Postal giro, postal savings bank and installment sale financing institutions are excluded.
[b] Mortgage banks include both private and public mortgage banks.
Source: Longer-term trends in the banking sector and market position of the individual categories of banks, *Monthly report of the Deutsche Bundesbank*, April 1989, 13–22 and 51–71

berships in non-bank companies and they transact a substantial part of their overall business through a European or global network of subsidiaries and affiliates. At the end of 1989 the total assets of subsidiaries and branches abroad reached about 13 percent of the total asset of domestic banks (about DM 559 billion).

The analysis in this section categorizes the *domestic* banking system according to structure and activities. A detailed analysis of the Grossbanken's *consolidated* financial statement and an examination of a sample of three major regional banks is also carried out here.[3]

3.3.1 Structure of Assets and Liabilities

During the decade 1978–89, West German banks enjoyed an annual rate of expansion of over 7 percent. A marked structural shift among the major categories of banks occurred. These developments included a massive influx of foreign banks, a sharp expansion of West German bank operations abroad, and a progressive introduction of computerized systems. Increased competition reduced the potential earnings from interest margins, a development that forced banks to broaden the range of their activities. New products included the linking of mortgage lending with real estate business, portfolio management, cash management services for corporate customers, and off-balance sheet activities (especially swap contracts).

There were also major changes in the structure of the traditional bank balance sheet during this period. Loan portfolios reached almost 80 percent of total assets when interbank activity was excluded. Investment in securities reached 15.6 percent (compared with 13.3 percent in 1978). Bonds outstanding increased by 127.5 percent from 1978 to 1989, whereas deposits grew by only 96.1 percent (table 3.6). This trend reflects the increased purchase of bank bonds and public bonds by banks. Within the banks' loan portfolios a major shift occurred in 1986 and 1987, from short- and medium-term maturities to long-term lending. This was due to the low interest rate during that period and to other, more fundamental causes. Partly as a reflection of this change banks have increased the "securitized" long-term sources of liabilities such as savings bonds and bank bonds, to reduce their interest rate exposure. This structural change has increased the cost of funds.

The sources of bank funds include deposits from the public at 64.2 percent of total liabilities at year-end 1989, excluding liabilities from banks (a decline from 69 percent in 1978). Bearer bonds outstanding increased from 22 percent in 1978 to 24 percent at year-end 1989. Equity capital increased from 4.4 percent in 1978 to 5.1 percent at year-end 1989 (3.76

Table 3.7 Combined income statement of West German domestic banks (DM Mil.)

Financial year	*Net interest*	*Net commission*	*% of net commission to net interest income*	*Securities & loan loss provision*	*Personnal expenses*	*% of personnel expenses to net interest income*	*Other operating expenses*	*Other (expenses) income*	*Provision for taxes*	*Net income*	*Net income to equity capital*[a]
All categories of banks											
1984	64,578	9,338	(14.5)	12,617	29,001	(44.9)	15,863	3,973	12,422	7,986	8.2
1985	67,741	10,965	(16.2)	13,884	31,675	(46.8)	17,849	5,627	12,833	8,092	7.8
1986	70,478	12,072	(17.1)	12,714	33,892	(48.1)	19,175	4,525	12,739	8,555	7.3
1987	72,468	11,828	(16.3)	11,707	35,803	(49.4)	19,993	4,657	11,550	9,900	6.2
1988	72,522	12,948	(17.9)	8,088	37,430	(51.6)	20,844	2,767	13,109	8,766	6.4
1989	73,143	15,024	(20.5)	16,740	38,680	(52.9)	22,108	8,500	10,497	8,642	6.0
Big banks											
1984	9,095	2,778	(30.5)	1,465	5,702	(62.7)	2,588	525	1,576	1,067	8.8
1985	9,416	3,343	(35.5)	933	6,104	(64.8)	2,959	756	2,017	1,502	11.3
1986	10,968	3,807	(34.7)	1,296	6,770	(61.7)	3,286	215	1,987	1,651	10.4
1987	9,999	3,671	(36.7)	1,329	7,012	(70.1)	3,430	519	1,201	1,217	6.5
1988	10,690	4,187	(39.2)	504	7,457	(69.8)	3,648	701	2,245	1,724	8.3
1989	11,398	4,812	(42.2)	1,035	7,702	(67.6)	3,869	943	2,493	2,054	9.3
Regional banks and others											
1984	6,966	1,561	(22.4)	1,722	3,541	(50.8)	1,893	367	914	824	7.3
1985	7,405	2,056	(27.8)	2,108	3,824	(51.6)	2,071	505	1,129	834	6.3
1986	9,186	2,341	(25.5)	2,740	4,901	(53.4)	2,897	1,433	1,391	1,031	7.0
1987	9,413	2,205	(23.4)	2,072	5,237	(55.6)	3,108	1,307	1,458	1,050	5.6
1988	9,516	2,343	(24.6)	1,631	5,508	(57.9)	3,306	1,262	1,509	1,167	5.6
1989	9,407	2,705	(28.8)	2,950	5,768	(61.3)	3,617	2,769	1,413	1,133	5.1

Branches of foreign banks											
1984	723	318	(44.0)	200	371	(51.3)	367	199	190	112	3.4
1985	784	370	(47.2)	179	387	(49.4)	383	125	225	105	2.9
1986	694	275	(39.6)	109	351	(50.6)	336	130	204	99	2.5
1987	596	182	(30.5)	106	342	(57.4)	333	271	207	61	1.6
1988	566	194	(34.3)	151	317	(56.0)	308	170	147	7	0.1
1989	465	184	(39.6)	310	326	(70.1)	334	266	96	(151)	(4.0)
Private banks											
1984	830	316	(38.1)	181	547	(65.9)	281	249	71	315	16.5
1985	756	393	(52.0)	142	537	(71.0)	304	304	88	382	19.1
1986	1,002	534	(53.3)	268	665	(66.4)	392	328	103	436	22.2
1987	1,071	473	(44.2)	296	736	(68.7)	453	359	78	340	12.9
1988	1,053	438	(41.6)	218	764	(72.6)	454	331	85	301	10.9
1989	1,066	569	(53.4)	329	789	(74.0)	500	364	88	293	10.8
Regional giro institutions											
1984	4,619	513	(11.1)	2,156	1,616	(35.0)	811	544	738	355	3.2
1985	4,784	572	(12.0)	2,740	1,738	(36.3)	838	1,177	796	421	3.6
1986	4,830	613	(12.7)	2,005	1,842	(38.1)	934	677	880	459	3.8
1987	4,715	556	(11.8)	1,787	1,942	(41.2)	977	679	747	497	3.7
1988	4,742	560	(11.8)	1,174	2,069	(43.6)	1,048	602	1,089	524	3.8
1989	4,703	648	(13.8)	1,090	2,171	(46.2)	1,137	793	1,016	730	5.0

Table 3.7 Combined income statement of West German domestic banks (DM Mil.)—*contd.*

Financial year	*Net interest*	*Net commission*	*% of net commission to net interest income*	*Securities & loan loss provision*	*Personnal expenses*	*% of personnel expenses to net interest income*	*Other operating expenses*	*Other (expenses) income*	*Provision for taxes*	*Net income*	*Net income to equity capital*[a]
Savings banks											
1984	22,276	2,132	(9.6)	3,038	9,152	(41.1)	4,902	274	5,256	2,334	10.5
1985	22,856	2,232	(9.8)	3,181	9,677	(42.3)	5,269	137	4,900	2,198	9.0
1986	23,354	2,356	(10.1)	3,142	10,283	(44.0)	5,598	214	4,762	2,139	8.1
1987	23,586	2,470	(10.5)	3,205	11,045	(46.8)	5,831	247	4,224	1,998	7.0
1988	24,443	2,619	(10.7)	2,420	11,542	(47.2)	6,138	(787)	4,095	2,080	6.8
1989	24,314	3,141	(12.9)	5,850	11,864	(48.8)	6,545	947	2,466	1,677	5.1
Regional credit cooperatives											
1984	1,704	259	(15.2)	241	471	(27.6)	325	78	537	467	11.4
1985	1,577	292	(18.5)	1,198	524	(33.2)	382	860	506	119	2.6
1986	1,707	353	(20.7)	283	536	(31.4)	496	218	529	434	8.0
1987	1,803	335	(18.6)	234	572	(31.7)	481	87	542	396	7.1
1988	1,732	371	(21.4)	34	554	(32.0)	475	(26)	585	429	7.0
1989	1,222	412	(33.7)	623	577	(47.2)	478	526	93	389	6.3
Credit cooperatives											
1984	11,503	1,222	(10.6)	1,904	5,790	(50.3)	3,611	1,492	1,968	944	7.9
1985	13,041	1,424	(10.9)	1,359	6,975	(53.5)	4,425	1,167	1,957	916	7.0
1986	13,301	1,556	(11.7)	1,408	7,331	(55.1)	4,599	1,344	1,943	920	5.7
1987	13,693	1,675	(12.2)	1,295	7,636	(55.8)	4,716	1,289	2,066	944	5.5
1988	14,045	1,957	(13.9)	755	7,876	(56.1)	4,759	812	2,357	1,067	5.8
1989	14,749	2,255	(15.3)	3,216	8,100	(54.9)	4,876	1,872	1,706	978	5.0

Mortgage banks[b]												
1984	3,642	–	–	766	616	(16.9)	335	(182)	750	993	10.1
1985	3,766	–	–	1,056	661	(17.6)	396	123	764	1,012	10.2
1986?	3,841	–	–	1,016	717	(18.7)	401	(132)	725	850	8.0
1987	3,962	–	–	900	769	(19.1)	409	(134)	793	957	8.2
1988	4,021	–	–	649	808	(20.1)	436	(421)	773	934	7.5
1989	4,062	–	–	716	821	(20.2)	461	(141)	894	1,029	7.7
Banks with special functions											
1984	1,323	235	(17.8)	371	418	(31.6)	176	30	233	390	6.4
1985	1,487	237	(15.9)	450	453	(30.5)	204	32	230	419	6.5
1986	1,595	237	(14.9)	447	496	(31.1)	236	98	215	536	7.6
1987	1,630	261	(16.0)	483	512	(31.4)	255	33	234	440	5.9
1988	1,714	279	(16.3)	552	535	(31.2)	272	123	224	533	6.7
1989	1,757	298	(17.0)	621	562	(32.0)	291	161	232	510	6.0

[a] Equity capital is measured at the beginning of the year.
[b] Mortgage banks include both private banks and public banks.

Source: The Profitability of German Banks in 1988, *Monthly Report of the Deutsche Bundesbank*, vol. 41, no. 8, August 1989

percent of total assets). However this increase in capital should be considered with caution, given the expansion in off-balance-sheet activities, which increased bank risk.

In considering the growth of the different categories of banks (table 3.2), it can be seen that the most rapid annual growth occurred in the credit cooperatives sector, followed by regional and special function banks.

By contrast, savings and commercial banks lost market share in West Germany. The commercial banks have offset this decline by expanding their international activity and off-balance-sheet activities.

Commercial banks group

Commercial banks involvement in interbank activities and investment in securities has declined. In lending to non-banks, commercial banks have increased their share (26.0 percent of total domestic bank lending to non-banks in 1989 compared with 23.4 percent in 1978). The Grossbanken share of medium- and long-term lending has been reduced, while their share of short-term lending increased. On the liabilities side, commercial bank market share in short-term deposits declined sharply, as a result of the transfer of funds to the Eurodollar market. The Grossbanken were the major losers in the field of both savings and bank savings bonds.

In summary, over time commercial banks, and especially the Grossbanken, have suffered from a decline in traditional banking activities, simultaneously increased their international activity, investment banking and off-balance-sheet activities. The situation is graphically illustrated by comparing the consolidated financial statement of the Grossbanken (table 3.8) with their domestic operations (table 3.7), which reveals that about 85 percent of all West German foreign banking activities are carried out by this group.

Savings bank sector

The lending share of the savings bank sector to non-banks decreased from 39 percent in 1978 to 37 percent in 1989 (table 3.6). However, this group has increased its share in securities investment. Savings banks have increased their reliance on borrowed funds at the expense of customer deposits and bond issues.

Credit cooperative sector

As a group, credit cooperatives have increased their market share in the savings deposit market at the expense of savings banks and commercial banks. The growth of credit cooperatives is mainly attributable to lending

Table 3.8 Combined income statement (the three big banks in West Germany)

	(DM millions) 1988	1987	1986	1985
1 Interest received	45467	41109	40885	41390
2 Interest paid	31959	28235	27233	29332
3 Net interest revenue	13508	12874	13652	12058
4 Net commission revenue	4915	4561	4195	3638
5 Other operating revenue	1705	1070	841	887
6 Personnel expenses	8784	8263	7701	6833
7 Other non-interest expenses	5839	5141	4459	4058
8 Operating profit (teilbetriebsergebnis)	5505	5101	6528	5692
9 Other – net (including loan loss reserves)	(360)	(1780)	(2084)	(1334)
10 Pre-tax profit	5145	3321	4444	4358
11 Taxes	2933	1762	2465	2466
12 Net income	2212	1559	1979	1892
Ratio analysis				
Average earning assets	652672	596275	541380	506776
Average risk capital	24636	22968	20471	17480
Ratios to average earning assets (%)				
Interest received	6.97	6.90	7.55	8.17
Interest paid	4.90	4.74	5.03	5.79
Net interest revenue	2.07	2.16	2.52	2.38
Interest on capital employed	0.20	0.20	0.23	0.23
Net spread	1.87	1.96	2.29	2.15
Other ratios (%)				
Personnel expenses/net interest	65	64	56	57
Other oper. exp./net interest	43	40	33	34
Personnel expenses/operating expense	60	62	63	63
Operating expenses/non-int. income	221	238	241	241
Net inte. income/non-int. income	204	229	271	266
Net income/total assets	0.34	0.23	0.35	0.37
Net income/risk capital	8.98	6.79	9.67	10.82

Source: IBCA data base

in the interbank market and to investments in securities, and less so to loan business.

3.3.2 Income Statement

The net income to equity capital (beginning of the year) for 1989 showed a figure of 6.0 percent for the entire FRG domestic banking system (compared with 8.2 percent for 1984). This figure reflected a continuing structural change in the component of the income statement, as well as major differences among categories of banking groups. As can be seen from table 3.7, the performance of the Grossbanken, private banks and mortgage banks was better than the industry average.

The improvement in net interest income and net commission was just sufficient to cover the rising cost of staff and other operating expenses. The major source of improvement in net 1988 income was the decline in the provision for doubtful loans (DM 11.7 billion in 1987, DM 8.1 billion in 1988). In 1989, the adverse impact of rising interest rates, and the valuation effects in the lending and securities business was very strong. Falling bond prices forced the banks to write off some DM 11 billion. This was particularly felt by savings banks and credit cooperatives.

Despite the greater significance of commission income from securitization trends and off-balance-sheet activities, interest margins remained by far the principal source of income, increasing by 2.9 percent during 1988 and 0.9 percent in 1989. Net commissions increased by 16 percent during 1989 (net commission reached 20.5 percent of net interest income). Administrative expenses increased by 6.1 percent. As a result, operating net income declined by 1.4 percent. There was an increase of loan and securities losses by DM 8.7 billion and, following a decline of 3.6 billion in 1989, an increase of other receipts of DM 5.8 billion, mostly in receipts from foreign exchange and security dealing. The major factor in the reduced loan and securities loss provision in 1988 was the approximately DM 4 billion allocated to general provisions in 1988. The creation of such provisions was approved for the first time in 1987. The sharp increase in loss provisions in 1989 was due to the general decline in securities prices.

The pre-tax return on capital grew from 14.4 percent (1987) to 15.5 percent (1988) and declined to 13.3 percent in 1989. The tax provision amounted to 55 to 60 percent of pre-tax profit, a very high tax rate close to the official rate.

The appreciable increase in pre-tax profit in 1987–8 was particularly marked in commercial banks and credit cooperatives. In 1989, the decline was significant for savings banks and credit cooperatives. Grossbanken registered the largest growth in net interest received. The banks in the credit cooperative sector did particularly well in non-interest business in 1989, reflecting the expansion of their various services. Their net commission income is now equivalent to about 42 percent of net interest income for this category of bank.

Saving banks and credit cooperatives pre-tax profit declined by 67 percent and 40 percent, respectively. Their net interest income declined accordingly.

During the five-year period examined the net income to capital ratio of the West German banks declined from 8.2 percent in 1984 to 6.0 percent in 1989, as a result of costs increasing much faster than operating income. Operating expenses increased during the period examined by 35.5 percent, whereas operating income increased by only 19.2 percent. The increase in other receipts somewhat offset this change. The decline in profitability in 1989 appeared mostly in savings banks, branches of foreign banks, credit cooperatives, and banks with special functions.

Finally, the results reported in tables 3.7 and 3.8 reflect the steep rise in the profits of West German bank subsidiaries abroad, especially in Luxembourg. The net income-to-equity capital on a consolidated basis for the Grossbanken reached 9 percent in 1988, compared with 8.3 percent for domestic operations.

3.3.3 Sources of Income

The three major sources of income for the West German banking system are net interest margin, net commission and other receipts. The other (extraordinary) receipts include income from securities dealings (from the bank's own account) and foreign exchange dealing.

Interest margins

Interest margins constitute the major source of income for the FRG banking system. In recent years a continuous process of decline in interest margins has occurred. This was caused by a shift of lending to the Euromarkets, as well as the public's preference for long-term borrowing. The drastic change in monetary policy in 1988 raised the cost of short-term funds which the banks needed to fund those borrowings. The net spread calculated for consolidated financial statements of the Grossbanken (table 3.8) shows a decline from 2.15 percent in 1985 to 1.87 percent in 1988. This decline represents both the effect of reductions in net spread and changes in the composition of the loan portfolio, with a decrease in foreign loans and an increase in the relative share of domestic loans (34 percent in 1985, which increased to 49.3 percent in 1988). Part of the increase in domestic loans might be the result of the decreased attractiveness of booking loans in Luxembourg, following the adoption of consolidated reporting in 1985. Because the loans provided by subsidiaries abroad are usually in wholesale banking, they are subject to a lower interest spread. It would therefore seem that the decline in the interest rate spread in domestic lending is even more significant. In summary, the net interest income increased during the period 1984–9 by 13.3 percent, while domestic lending increased by 34.0 percent. The results widely differ across categories of banks; for the big banks loan portfolio increased by 77.0 percent, although interest income increased by only 25.3 percent. For regional and other banks the loan portfolio increased by 73.0 percent and the interest income increased 35.0 percent. The decline in interest rate spread was the most drastic in 1989.

The rise in interest rates in 1989 had a marked impact on banks' profits when, as could be expected, a further squeeze in interest rate spread occurred, due to higher funding costs. Most FRG banks exposed themselves to interest rate risk by funding long-term lending with shorter-term liabilities.

Net commission income

Net commission income as a percentage of interest margin continued to increase in 1989 (table 3.7), reaching 20.5 percent for the domestic banking operation. This source of income is more significant for the big banks, branches of foreign banks, and private bankers. For these groups fee income exceeded 40 percent of net income. The improvement during 1989 was achieved in a broad range of services: the securities trading business, underwriting bonds, selling of investment funds units, and off-balance-sheet activities. Since domestic banks have always enjoyed full securities power, deregulation has played a minor role in West Germany.

The most significant developments have been the introduction of new instruments such as zero coupon bonds, and the opening up of the Federal Government underwriting syndicate to West German-based affiliates of foreign banks.

In contrast to the mixed trend of interest performance, the record increase in net commissions (16.0 percent) in 1989 was shared relatively equally by all banks, with the exception of the branches of foreign banks.

Other (extraordinary) receipts

In 1989 there was a fairly strong rise in receipts from foreign exchange and securities dealings. The gain registered in equity trading on the sale of shares in the 1989 bull market contributed to increased profits. This increase was used to offset other expenses and enlarge hidden reserves.

3.3.4 Expenses

The four major sources of expenses are personnel expenses, other overhead expenses, loan and securities loss reserves, and taxes. Personnel expenses cover about 53 percent of net interest income and above 64 percent of total operating expenses (table 3.7). The relative proportion of personnel expenses is common to all categories of banks, reflecting the universal nature of the FRG banking system. During the period examined (1984–9), personnel expenses increased 33.4 percent, caused by both an increase in the number of employees and real wage increases.

The increase in the number of employees represents the expansion of services provided by banks, including building societies, life insurance, and advisory services. Other operating expenses, despite relatively low investment in automation, increased during the period examined by 31.3 percent. Expenses also include loan loss reserves.

Like Swiss banks, the true profitability of West German banks is marked by generous allocations to reserves against loan and securities portfolios. The decline in loan losses during 1988 was the result of a regulatory change, which allowed for the transfer to special general reserves of about DM 4 billion. The provision represented 18 percent of net interest income and, in the big banks, 4.7 percent. It should be noted that no minimum loss reserves against developing-country exposure have been set. However, by the end of 1987, leading banks had almost 100 percent coverage. The credit quality of domestic loans suffered due to problems in the shipping, construction, shipbuilding, and residential real estate markets in 1984. By 1986, loan losses peaked, reaching almost 21 percent of net interest in all categories of banks. The apparently high tax rate is partially due to hidden reserves unrecognized for tax purposes. No doubt, West German banks adopt an extremely conservative approach with respect to loan and security loss provisions, resulting in considerable hidden reserves. Finally, the provisions for taxes represent 55 to 60 percent of pre-tax income, close to the statutory tax rate.

In 1989, general loan and securities provisions more than doubled, from DM 8.1 billion in 1988 to DM 16.7 billion. The major part of this increase was due to write-downs of bonds, some DM 11 billion against DM 3.4 billion in 1988. In accordance with current regulation some banks, to avoid write-downs, transferred part of the bond portfolio from current to fixed assets. This write-down was partially offset by a release from general loan loss provision (about DM 3.0 billion).

3.3.5 Capital Adequacy

Calculations by the Bundesbank reveal that the minimum BIS required solvency ratio for both core capital (4 percent) and total equity (8 percent) have on average already been met by the banks (with about 5 percent core and more than 9 percent total).[4] It should be noted, however, that the equity definition used by the German Banking Act is more restrictive than the one used by the Cooke Committee.[5] Under the Basle Agreement, applied in West Germany, a significant portion of the hidden reserves resulting from unrealized profits on property revaluation is considered part of the banks' equity capital.

Table 3.9 Average utilizations of Principles I, II, and III (all banks)

		Averages (annual)	
Year	*Principle I (limit: 18)*	*Principle II (limit: 100%)*	*Principle III (limit: 100%)*
1977	12,7	86,1	73,5
1978	13,0	87,4	73,4
1979	13,6	89,3	77,9
1980	14,0	91,7	82,9
1981	14,3	92,1	85,1
1982	14,1	91,0	83,4
1983	13,7	90,1	80,9
1984	13,6	89,9	80,4
1985	13,4	90,2	78,2
1986	12,7	87,9	71,3
1987	12,3	86,7	65,2

Table 3.10 Average utilizations of Principles I, II, and III in 1987 (banking groups)

		Averages (1987 basis)	
Banking groups	*Principle I (limit: 18)*	*Principle II (limit: 100%)*	*Principle III (limit: 100%)*
Commercial banks	12,7	84,18	83,2
Giro institutions	14,6	91,7	55,2
Regional institutions of the cooperative sector	6,7	83,2	47,6
Savings banks	12,0	87,7	52,1
Credit cooperatives	11,2	81,6	61,1
All banks	12,3	86,7	65,2

Source: Rudolph, Bernd (1990).

There is no doubt that capital adequacy requirements will continue to affect both West German bank operations and the in regulations. For example, in 1988 the Bundesbank, responding to pressure from other EC countries, allowed the general loan loss reserves to be included in the credit institution's own funds. The EC Commission intends to present a draft on solvency ratios that will closely follow the proposal of the Basle Committee. Therefore the Basle proposals will affect not only the relatively small number of international big banks, but all 4,200 West German banks. The adoption of the proposed community solvency directive and its implementation in national law is not expected to be completed before 1993. A prior adjustment of FRG capital adequacy (1990 amendment of Principle I), to incorporate off-balance-sheet activities among risk assets in calculating Principle I ratio, has been implemented. The current situation of the West German banking system, with respect to the previous capital adequacy requirement, is given in tables 3.9 and 3.10.

Table 3.11 Combined balance sheet[a] (the three big banks in West Germany)

	31/12/88 (US$ mil.)	*31/12/88*	*31/12/87*	*31/12/86*	*31/12/85*
			(DM, millions)		
A Loans					
1 Short-term loans	81354	144810	136285	123073	126658
2 Long-term loans					
(a) mortgages	55022	97939	93573	81008	70694
(b) public debt	47247	84099	81857	78557	74583
(c) other	56306	100225	93051	75886	68238
3 Assets leased	2649	4716	3959	2349	2024
Total A	242578	431789	408725	360873	342197
B Other earning assets					
1 Interbank					
(a) less than 4 years	83858	149267	137701	113661	100577
(b) more than 4 years	14320	25490	24719	22695	24760
2 Short-term investments	6257	11137	10926	12088	16044
3 Other investments	20839	37093	35036	34208	29024
4 Equity investments	9750	17355	16107	15812	10823
Total B	135024	240342	224489	198464	181228
C Total earning assets (A + B)	377602	672131	633214	559337	523425
D Fixed assets	3689	6567	6403	5593	4845
E Non-earning assets					
1 Cash and due from banks	9594	17077	18425	18779	18962
2 Other	3261	5805	5581	6827	4674
F Total assets	394146	701580	663623	590536	551906

Table 3.11 Combined balance sheet[a] (the three big banks in West Germany)

	31/12/88 (US$ mil.)	*31/12/88*	*31/12/87 (DM, millions)*	*31/12/86*	*31/12/85*
G Customer and short-term funding					
1 Demand	39654	70585	67474	58868	55140
2 Savings	38757	68987	69409	63364	53262
3 Time	84395	150223	136876	116138	105515
4 Inter-bank: less than 4 years	79216	141005	129968	120856	128288
5 Other	4331	7709	8044	9088	10824
Total G	246353	438509	411771	368314	353029
H Other funding					
1 Inter-bank: more than 4 years	13266	23613	22917	18305	16216
2 Long-term debt	107458	191274	183315	162356	145331
I Other (non-int. bearing)	12912	22984	21549	19695	18254
J Risk capital					
1 Equity	13918	24775	23646	21441	18651
2 Near equity	239	425	425	425	425
Total J	14157	25200	24071	21866	19076
K Total liabilities & risk capital	394146	701580	663623	590536	551906
Exchange rate (US$1 = DM)		1.780	1.583	1.940	2.461
Ratios (%)					
Deposits/loans		67.1	67.0	66.1	62.5
Loans/total assets		61.5	61.6	61.1	62.0
Fixed assets/risk capital		26.1	26.6	25.6	25.4
Risk capital/total assets		3.6	3.6	3.7	3.5

[a] Consolidated basis including operations abroad.
Source: IBCA data base

Table 3.12 Selected financial data as at December 31, 1988 (DM mil.)

	Deutsche	*Dresdner*	*Commerz.*	*Total*
Total assets	297548	226654	177378	701580
Total loans	190915	139348	101526	431789
Total deposits	111570	94369	83856	289795
Risk capital	11785	7712	5703	25200
Average number of employees[a]	52594	37580	26147	116321
Number of branches[a]	1498	1425	882	3805
Personnel expenses	4088	2179	1977	8784
Net income	1203	519	490	2212
Net income/risk capital (%)	10.2	6.7	8.6	8.8

[a] As of December 31, 1987.
Source: IBCA data base

Table 3.13: Combined balance sheet (three other banks in West Germany)[a]

	31/12/88 (US$ mil.)	*31/12/88*	*31/12/87*	*31/12/86*	*31/12/85*
		(DM, millions)			
A Loans					
1 Short-term loans	20448	36398	35172	36812	38312
2 Long-term loans					
(a) mortgages	34051	60611	57490	54885	50837
(b) public debt	39156	69698	67798	62073	60009
(c) other	14479	25772	24131	25542	26482
Total A	108134	192479	184591	179312	175640
B Other earning assets					
1. Interbank					
(a) less than 4 years	32469	57795	48772	45231	35465
(b) more than 4 years	14008	24935	21179	20570	18741
2. Short-term investments	1229	2187	2520	2610	6717
3. Other investments	11655	20746	20040	19224	16885
4. Equity investments	2130	3791	3434	3370	2931
Total B	61491	109454	95945	91005	80739
C Total earning assets (A+B)	169625	301933	280536	270317	256379
D Fixed assets	1875	3338	2916	2764	2563
E Non-earning assets					
1 Cash and due from banks	2460	4378	4193	4731	4147
2 Other	2714	4832	4793	3935	4013
F Total assets	176674	314481	292438	281747	267102
G Customer and short-term funding					
1 Demand	7683	13677	13678	13574	10527
2 Savings	12265	21831	20697	20633	20209
3 Time	24280	43218	38177	35887	34052
4 Interbank: less than 4 years	35327	62882	54320	56920	56855
5 Other	466	829	716	1003	1489
Total G	80021	142437	127588	128017	123132
H Other funding					
1 Inter-bank: more than 4 years	10418	18544	13874	11686	9678
2 Long-term debt	75007	133513	131947	124323	117627

Table 3.13: Combined balance sheet (three other banks in West Germany)[a]

	31/12/88 (US$ mil.)	31/12/88	31/12/87	31/12/86	31/12/85
		(DM, millions)			
I Other (non-int. bearing)	6267	11155	10472	9697	9402
J Risk capital	4961	8832	8557	8024	7263
K Total liabilities & risk capital	176674	314481	292438	281747	267102
Exchange rate (US$1 = DM)		1.780	1.583	1.940	2.461
Ratios (%)					
Deposits/loans		40.9	39.3	39.1	36.9
Loans/total assets		61.2	63.1	63.6	65.8
Fixed assets/risk capital		37.8	34.1	34.4	35.3
Risk capital/total assets		2.8	2.9	2.8	2.7

[a] Including Hypo Bank, Vereins – und Westbank & Westdeutsche Landesbank.
Source: IBCA data base.

Table 3.14 Combined income statement (three other banks in West Germany)[a]

	1988	1987	1986	1985
	(DM, millions)			
1 Interest received	20874	20217	19948	20600
2 Interest paid	16501	15854	15642	16429
3 Net interest revenue	4373	4363	4306	4171
4 Net commission revenue	825	800	808	710
5 Other operating revenue	417	391	360	243
6 Personnel expenses	2282	2128	2035	1843
7 Other non-interest expenses	1446	1319	1227	1040
8 Operating profit (teilbetriebsergebnis)	1887	2107	2212	2241
9 Other – net (including loan loss reserves)	(727)	(1094)	(1171)	(1428)
10 Pre-tax profit	1160	1013	1041	813
11 Taxes	695	603	612	505
12 Net income	465	410	429	308
Ratio analysis				
Average earning assets	291235	275427	263348	256379
Average risk capital	8695	8291	7644	7263
Ratios to average earning assets (%)				
Interest received	7.17	7.34	7.57	8.03
Interest paid	5.67	5.76	5.94	6.41
Net interest revenue	1.50	1.58	1.63	1.62

Table 3.14 Combined income statement (three other banks in West Germany)[a]

	(DM, millions)			
	1988	*1987*	*1986*	*1985*
Interest on capital employed	0.14	0.15	0.15	0.15
Net spread	1.36	1.43	1.48	1.47
Other ratios (%)				
Personnel expenses/net interest	52	49	47	44
Other oper. expe./net interest	33	30	28	25
Personnel expenses/operating expenses	61	62	62	64
Operating expenses/non-int. income	300	289	279	303
Net int. income/non-int. income	352	366	369	438
Net income/total assets	0.16	0.15	0.16	0.12
Net income/risk capital	5.35	4.95	5.61	4.24

[a] Including Hypo Bank, Vereins – und Westbank & Westdeutsche Landesbank.
Source: IBCA data base

Notes

1 *Monthly Report of the Deutsche Bundesbank* vol. 42, no. 7, July 1990, 16.
2 See Scheidl, K. West Germany, in Anne Hendrie (ed), Banking in the EEC, 1988 Structure and Sources of Finance, London 113 (*Financial Times Business Information*).
3 This section is based on data provided in the tables of this chapter and in Longer-term trends in the banking sector and the market position of the individual categories of banks, *Monthly Report of the Deutsche Bundesbank*, April 1989.
4 See Rudolph, B. Capital requirements of German banks and the EEC proposals on banking supervision, in Dermine, Jean (ed), European Banking in the 1990s.
5 For example, the BIS rules state that 45 percent of unrealized gains on "securities" holdings can be counted in Tier 2 capital. The application of this rule to holdings in industrial companies shares is not clear.

References

Cable, John (1985) Capital market information and industrial performance: The role of West German banks, *Economic Journal*, vol 95, 118–32.
Dermine, Jean (ed) (1990) European Banking in the 1990s, Basil Blackwell, Oxford.
Deutsche Bundesbank, *Monthly Report*, various issues.
Rudolph, Bernd (1990) Capital requirements of German Banks and European Economic Community proposal on banking supervision, in *European Banking in the 1990s*, Jean Dermine (ed), Basil Blackwell, Oxford, 357–68.
Scheidl, Karl (1988) West Germany in *Banking in the EEC, 1988 Structure and Sources of Finance*, Anne Hendrie (ed), London, 113 Financial Times Business Information.

4

France

4.1 Structure of the Financial System

4.1.1 Introduction

Since World War Two France has displayed an admirable economic record, becoming the Western world's fourth largest economy after the United States, Japan, and West Germany. While attracting less attention than other industrial countries, France actually has the fastest growth rate after Japan, and since the 1950s has grown considerably faster than other OECD countries, including West Germany. Compared with other industrialized nations, France's agricultural sector is large, with the percentage of workers employed at 6.7 percent in 1985, a rate much higher than most other OECD nations. While it is the world's fourth largest exporter, France is relatively less dependent on international trade than other EC members such as the United Kingdom, West Germany, or the Netherlands.

France does however face economic problems. Labor market imbalances are proving intractable; unemployment, while declining, is still higher than in most other countries. Moreover, the labor force is disproportionately balanced against new entrants, especially the young. Foreign trade imbalances have also proven persistent; France experienced a number of large trade deficits during the 1980s and has had to devalue the franc within the European monetary system a number of times. France's industrial development has often been criticized as being too specialized and narrow, and lacking in diversification and dynamism. While there have been some achievements in modern high growth areas, France has not enjoyed the success of Japan and the United States in moving into new technologies.

One of the notable structural features of the French economy, and very evident in its financial system, has been a high degree of central government involvement, direction, and even control of economic affairs. This is reflected by the role of government in both the nationalization of key industries and firms, and in planning and regulatory functions. The degree of state involvement, and its evolution, have been central influences in shaping the structure and function of the French financial system.

4.1.2 *Financial Markets and Institutions*

The French financial system has been characterized by the dominance of indirect flows, especially via deposit taking intermediaries such as banks, and the resultant relative unimportance of the capital markets. Another notable feature has been the high degree of government involvement in virtually every aspect of the financial markets. As a result, the financial system has been rather inefficient and unwieldy, with a high degree of concentration and lack of competition. Recently, however, a marked turning point in government policy has set in motion a number of developments whose impact has been at least a partial reversal of these characteristics. Thus, although until the mid-1980s, France had one of the most regulated financial systems of the industrialized world, this is no longer the case. In fact, at present it has one of Europe's most balanced bank regulatory environments.

Table 4.1 France – major economic indicators and the banking system

	1980	*1984*	*1988*
Gross domestic product (US$ bil.)	670	494	948
Current account (US$ bil.)	−4.2	−0.9	−3.5
Consumer inflation (pc pa)	13.4	5.7	2.6
Exchange rate (FFr per US$)	4.51	9.59	6.06
Interest rate (pc pa)	11.8	11.8	7.5
Population (mil.)	53.7	54.9	55.9
Total bank branches	23,659	25,477	25,780
Number of ATMs	1,000[a]	5,100[b]	12,000
Number of bank employees (thou.)	–	251	249
Population per branch	2,270	2,155	2,168
Population per ATM	53,700	10,764	4,658
Bank employees as % of total population	–	0.46	0.45

[a] 1978.
[b] 1983.

Source: Banque de France; IMF, *International Financial Statistics Yearbook*

The high degree of state involvement in the financial system was designed to achieve both regulatory and allocative goals. The need for rebuilding after World War Two, combined with France's tradition of state involvement and Paris-based central control and direction, resulted in government involvement in all areas and levels of the financial market. Many important financial institutions were nationalized outright in the post-war period, or had government appointed boards of directors. (However, while nationalized status certainly affected the economic decision-making of these concerns, many did act as essentially commercial entities in day-to-day operations.) Additionally, a vast array of government and government-owned financial agencies were established to promote specific goals, such as La Banque Française du Commerce Extérieur (foreign trade finance), Le Crédit National (long-term industrial finance), Le Crédit Foncier (real estate finance), and the Crédit d'Équipement des Petites et Moyennes Entreprises (CEPME), (small business finance).

In addition to its institutional presence, the government maintained an array of controls on interest rates and capital flows. Direct credit subsidization, quantitative controls, and discriminatory tax treatment were so extensively used that it can rightly be said that, "Prior to the current reform of the financial markets, market mechanisms played a fairly minor role in the way the financing of the French economy functioned" (OECD, France, June 1987).

The highly regulated and compartmentalized nature of the financial system was one reason for the distinctly secondary importance of the capital markets. Interestingly, conditions would seem to have favored the development of a large capital market. The household savings rate in France is relatively high compared with that of the United Kingdom or United States, while the corporate sector has maintained a low level of self-financing. Yet, for a variety of reasons, direct capital flows remained subsidiary to intermediation. Corporations shunned expensive equity capital, preferring debt which, in an inflationary environment, was often subsidized by the government. As a result of being "crowded out" of the long-term markets by the government, corporations became dependent on short-term debt, primarily bank credit, which provided for 70 percent of external financing of non-financial enterprises in the 1974–88 period.

Households, while maintaining a high savings rate, displayed a marked preference for maintaining savings either in real estate (partly due to generous government incentives), or short-term liquid instruments (which constituted the bulk of financial savings). Many of the short-term savings products enjoyed preferential tax treatment as well, to help meet financing needs, and to help finance housing. As a result, long-term financial savings of households has been relatively unimportant.

Institutional investors in France are of much less importance than in other countries. To a considerable extent this is due to the extensive nature of pension schemes operating on a "pay as you go" rather than a fully-funded basis. Thus, pension funds and other institutions such as insurance companies, have never developed the large investment role of these institutions in other countries. Nevertheless, they have been assuming greater importance since the mid-1980s.

Against this background, and considering the shocks and changes affecting financial markets throughout the world since the 1970s, financial reform in France became a high priority. Increased inflation and volatility in financial markets highlighted the need for flexible, efficient markets. The increasing public sector deficit in France emphasized the necessity of lowering debt costs and lengthening maturities. The public sector deficit also suggested the need for more competitive and efficient financial markets, not only to facilitate government debt policy but to contribute to the efficiency and competitiveness of French industry, and the maintenance and promotion of Paris' role as an international financial center. Thus, while reform and deregulation were seen as vital, the initiative was the result of the government's needs and perceptions of the direction the financial community should take.

Since 1985, both the magnitude and pace of reform have changed dramatically. Until then, the government had been mainly involved in decreasing the role of so-called "treasury financing channels" (official and semi-official intermediaries who received preferential treatment but were required to deposit funds with the treasury) in financing the government debt. These measures strengthened both the bank sector and, to a lesser extent, direct finance methods. As far back as 1967, banking reform reduced institutional segmentation and, theoretically, opened up competition between the banques de dépôts and the banques d'affaires (commercial and investment banks). However, the new banking law of January 1984 had much wider goals, essentially bringing the whole banking system under one unified framework, thereby reducing compartmentalization, eliminating privileges, and providing a more "level playing field." A wider range of asset and loan forms was offered to a larger group of participants. Foreign exchange controls were reduced and the money market, once highly restricted and essentially an interbank market, was opened up. New instruments, such as CDs, Commercial Paper, and treasury bills, provided the conditions for a true money market to develop.

The commercial paper (CP) market in France was launched in December 1985, giving borrowers a wider choice of financial instruments. Commercial paper may be issued only by non-bank French companies and subsidiaries of foreign companies. A rating agency has been set up. The law requires extensive disclosure and a guaranteed liquidity line (at least 95 percent of the CP outstanding). The maturity can range from between ten days to two years. Most issues have been in the 20 to 40 day range. By December 1986, outstanding CP had reached FFr 26 billion with well over 100 issuers, including subsidiaries of foreign companies. By 1989, FFr 85 billion of CP were outstanding, equivalent to 15 percent of short-term bank loans to business firms.

The most dramatic developments, however, have been in the capital markets, where the previously somnolent bond and stock markets have recently been among the most dynamic and fastest growing in the world. Primary and secondary market fees and taxes have been reduced and made negotiable, as have underwriting fees; new issue queues were eliminated, and the trading methods on the stock exchange streamlined and modernized. A mortgage agency modeled on the US Federal National Mortgage Association was established to reduce housing finance costs and rationalize the mortgage market. A second tier equity market was established, as well as a futures exchange (MATIF) which contributed significantly to the growth and liquidity of the bond markets. New institutions were allowed to participate in the markets, including open-end funds (SICAV), unit trusts (FCP), asset-backed securities funds (fonds commun de créance), securities houses (maison de titres), jobbers, and the "banques d'arbitrage."

The government itself contributed to this growth through its financing policy, creating a larger, more homogeneous, and liquid government securities market. Additionally, the privatization program that began in 1985 gave a considerable impetus to the share market and encouraged individual shareholding. The effects have been dramatic, with both the bond and share markets expanding significantly and attracting growing interest not only from domestic investors but from the international community as well. As a result, share market capitalization rose from 5.9 percent of GNP in 1982 to 16.0 percent in 1987 (still much lower than the 20 percent level in West Germany, 50 percent in the United States, 60 percent in Japan, and 65 percent in the United Kingdom). Moreover, the share of liquid assets in the growth of financial assets held by the non-financial sector fell from 67.9 percent in 1979 to 31.7 percent in 1985. While it is premature to judge the reform's impact on such macroeconomic variables as the savings rate and economic efficiency, the above statistics clearly have strong implications for the traditional role of financial intermediaries, such as banks.

4.1.3 *Banking Product and Bank Competition*

In France, indirect financing (borrowing from banks) was dominant until the end of the 1970s. Capital markets were under-developed, compared with the United States, the United Kingdom, Canada, and most other major industrialized countries. The role of the Paris stock exchange was marginal in the savings-investment process. From 1978 onwards, a rapid period of financial innovation ensued. In addition to computerization, new financial instruments were introduced such as the Commercial Paper Market (December 1985), Treasury bills, the Financial Futures Market (February 1986), the Options Market (September 1987), and Future Contracts on a Stock Index (September 1988). This process substantially increased the volume of direct financing through equity, debt, and other financial assets.

The breakdown of the banking system includes the following institutions.

Commercial banks

Universal banks

While banks in France are in theory universal, in practice they have tended to specialize in specific functions. The Banking Act of 1984 defined various types of credit institutions and brought them into a more or less uniform framework. The most important group is the universal banks, corresponding to commercial banks in the United States (table 4.2). Among universal banks, the three largest (Banque Nationale de Paris BNP, Crédit Lyonnais and Société Générale) dominate the financial market, with a combined 30 percent of total balance sheet of the credit system at year-end 1988. There are some 190 other universal banks with either a nationwide or provincial orientation, as well as some 145 foreign banks, operating mostly in Paris. The three largest banks were nationalized in 1945, and 36 other universal banks were nationalized in 1982. However, since many nationalized banks or industries held interests in other banks, government ownership influenced at least 124 banks altogether. Banks which were not nationalized were either too small (less than one billion francs in deposits) or foreign-controlled.

Starting in 1986, the government started to privatize the banking sector and several major institutions, including Paribas, Crédit Commercial de France and Société Générale, which were sold off. However, the October 1987 stock market crash, and the 1988 change of government in France put a halt to the privatization program. Nevertheless, ownership of the banking sector in France remains an important issue, giving rise to considerable debate and controversy.

Table 4.2 The French banking system

	Number of institutions		*Number of branches*		*Total assets (FFr. bil.)*			*Total assets (%)*	*Change in assets (%)*
	1986	*1988*	*1986*	*1987*	*1981*	*1984*	*1988*	*1988*	*1981–1988*
A Commercial banks									
Universal banks[a]	386	400	9,917	9,939	2,391	3,722	5,139	47.8	114.9
Cooperative and mutual banks[b]	192	178	11,125	11,175	818	1,215	1,845	17.2	125.5
Other banks[c]	22	22	48	58	179	254	251	2.3	40.2
Total commercial banks	600	600	21,090	21,172	3,388	5,191	7,235	67.3	113.5
B Other financial institutions									
Savings and provident banks	421	281	4,374	4,378	872	1,267	1,611	15.0	84.7
Finance companies and securities houses	1,049	1,069	n.a.	n.a.	258	415	863	8.0	234.5
Specialized banks	31	32	n.a.	n.a.	467	798	1,037	9.7	122.1
Total other financial institutions	1,501	1,382	n.a.	n.a.	1,597	2,480	3,511	32.7	119.8
Total credit establishments	2,101	1,982	n.a.	n.a.	4,985	7,671	10,746	100.0	115.6

[a] Includes the group of foreign banks.
[b] Includes among others, Peoples' Bank, Crédit Agricole, CNCA, Crédit Mutuel, and Crédit Maritime.
[c] Other banks include French Bank for Foreign Trading and Crédit Municipal.
n.a. not available

Source: Banque de France

Cooperative and mutual banks

Cooperative and mutual institutions include People's banks, Crédit Agricole, and Crédit Mutuel. The former, comprised of 40 regional People's banks (Banques Populaires), were originally founded to extend credit to small and medium companies and small retail customers. Crédit Agricole is a massive organization composed at the end of 1988 of 3,000 local cooperatives, 92 regional organizations and a central body the Caisse Nationale de Crédit Agricole (CNCA). The role and functions of the agricultural credit system have been modified, and the range of permissible activities has been widened. The system enjoyed the monopoly of distributing subsidized credits to the agricultural sector until 1989, and on the other hand suffered some limitations as regards lending to non-agricultural sectors. These institutions also compete in international financial markets. As a group, they hold 28 percent of deposits and savings of credit institutions, with Crédit Agricole holding about two-thirds, while the remainder is almost equally divided between Banques Populaires and Crédit Mutuel.

Other financial institutions

Savings and provident banks

The Savings and Provident bank sector (CEP) displays a similar three-tiered structure: 281 banks at the end of 1988 (with 4,600 outlets), grouped into 21 regional societies, and a central organization, the CENCEP. However, in this case the central organization is specifically not a bank but an "economic grouping." More than 75 percent of CENCEP activity is based on the collection of small savings deposits, while a large part of their assets are centrally managed by the Caisse des Dépôts et Consignations (CDC).

Finance companies and securities houses

Finance companies, although not defined as banks under the 1984 Banking Act, do carry out "bank-like activities," either under specific legislation (Group A finance companies) or under individual authorization (Group B).[1] The former include categories such as mutual guarantee companies, telecommunications finance companies, and real estate finance companies, while the latter include leasing, factoring, venture capital, and consumer finance companies.

Specialized banks

There are also a number of specialized financial institutions, mostly of an official or quasi-official status, and having varying structures. Their liabilities often carry government guarantees, and their primary function is the provision of long-term financing to both private and public sector entities. They include BFCE, Crédit National, CEPME, Crédit Foncier, and CCCE.

In addition to the Bank of France and the Treasury, other public bodies act as central banks to the savings sector. The CNE is a postal savings corporative, the CNT is the national telecommunications fund, and the CP serves as a postal cheque service. Other financial entities include the open end investment funds (SICAV), many of which are managed by banks, closed unit trusts (FCP), securities houses, financial holding companies, and banking intermediaries. Although credit institutions in France are diverse in nature and relatively large in number, there is actually little competition in financial markets.

It has often been noted that while there is a wide choice of banks in France, there is little choice of banking products. Intense government regulation, the use of banks as channels for financing the government budget deficit or as conduits for distributing credit subsidies, and an array of limitations and preferential rules have produced a highly compartmentalized banking system. However, the sweeping reforms undertaken in recent years have begun to dramatically affect the financial environment, so much so that the banking industry in France, now less protected and sheltered, is facing the same developments and challenges as those of other countries.

The development and growth of the capital markets has accelerated the process of disintermediation, dramatically reducing the reliance of the corporate sector on bank credit. The capital market's share of total financing rose from 22 percent in 1982 to 41 percent in 1985. The lowering of regulatory barriers and the reduction of government involvement and interference in banking has reduced the "compartmentalization" of the banking industry, increasing competitive pressures while simultaneously opening new opportunities. Also, developments affecting banking systems worldwide, such as increasingly stringent capital adequacy requirements, shrinking net interest margins, technological change and the need for heavy investment in electronic data processing, are all having an impact on the French banking system.

While legal distinctions between the types of banks were more or less eliminated by 1966, universal banks still retain an element of specialization. The three largest banks maintain truly universal banking services, which run the gamut from both retail and wholesale banking to securities portfolio management and corporate finance functions. The declining use of bank credit in corporate finance has hurt one of the traditional roles of universal banks. This loss is being offset by increased involvement in fields such as retail banking, especially consumer finance, the increased marketing of investment products and portfolio management services. Additionally, several lease banks have recently entered the insurance field through joint ventures. However, the lowering of barriers has exposed universal banks to increased competition in these fields from the mutual and cooperative banks, savings banks, and finance companies. The former banques d'affaires such as the Paribas group and Banque IndoSuez, have for the most part maintained their wholesale and investment banking orientation.

The lack of extensive branch networks among the banques d'affaires has discouraged their entry into retail banking, while experience in securities markets and corporate finance has proven advantageous when positioning themselves for current market conditions. The relatively large number of foreign banks in France have been handicapped by the lack of a natural deposit base, as well as their virtual exclusion from the considerable volume of government generated business. As in most countries, foreign banks have therefore found themselves concentrating on wholesale banking and other "niches," such as foreign exchange and the servicing of international trade.

The cooperative and mutual banks, which originally provided credit primarily for modest farmers and small commercial enterprises, have developed into virtually full service banks. Crédit Agricole, composed of over 3,000 local entities, dominates retail banking, and with its considerable resources is making strides into wholesale and international banking as well. While banking reform is allowing these firms to enter new areas, it is at the same time reducing or eliminating many of their privileged positions, such as the role of distributors of subsidized credit and government-backed incentives.

The savings bank sector is still overwhelmingly reliant on the collection of small retail savings deposits for its funding, which are then lent at both local and interbank levels (the latter usually through regional or nationwide central bodies). The savings banks still enjoy the privilege of issuing a passbook for tax-exempt savings that are subject to specific individual limits. These institutions are not yet authorized to offer all banking services. Nevertheless, savings banks are expanding the banking products they offer, and will probably face increasing competitive pressures as protective limitations are progressively reduced.

More than 1,000 finance companies operate in a quasi-bank fashion, and are active in a wide area of activities, from consumer and real estate financing, to company finance, including special purpose financing vehicles, leasing, factoring, and venture capital. A great number of finance companies are affiliated in some way with a bank, with the resulting complicated holding structures often being quite difficult to interpret.

The many specialized financial institutions, mostly public sector concerns, are primarily involved in the medium- and long-term finance functions that have been virtually appropriated by the government. This role, while still sizable, is shrinking due to expanding capital markets, the entry of private institutions, and diminishing government involvement. The future role of specialized financial institutions in the markets will be dependent on the progress of reform and the direction of government policy.

4.1.4 International Involvement

French banks maintain a sizable presence abroad, ranking third after Japan and the United States in international banking activity. Given the smaller size of the French banking system, the relative importance of their role is even more notable. French banks have a long history of international involvement, with names such as Rothschild and Lazard known around the world, and firms such as Paribas having had foreign branch networks since the last century. France's colonial past has obviously been one of the prime influences in this area, with French banks naturally establishing themselves throughout the world in French colonies and possessions. However, the last two decades have seen both qualitative and quantitative change in the foreign activities of French banks.

By 1986 French banks had 286 branches and 110 subsidiaries in over 100 countries (Metais, 1990a). This activity was highly concentrated, with the three largest banks accounting for some two-thirds of foreign activity, and the next four largest banks accounting for most of the rest. This high degree of foreign activity was the result of the considerable domestic growth and expansion of the 1970s, when it appeared that the domestic banking market was approaching saturation. At the same time, the regimentation of the banking industry by the government limited profitable opportunities, while the spread of the "banking habit" ensured that available funds were growing faster than profitable uses. The natural response was to seek profitable expansion opportunities abroad.

The first avenue of expansion abroad was the servicing of the needs of French multinational firms and exports. The volume of French exports increased by almost a factor of five from 1969 to 1983, and in relative importance from 12 percent of GDP in 1959 to 18 percent in 1984. French banks, therefore, at first went overseas to provide local services to their domestic clients, as well as to provide such trade related functions as funds transmission, foreign exchange, and documentary credit. Once established overseas, however, French banks soon began to serve local clients and to become involved in the financing of foreign entities and government. At the same time French banks became major players in the rapidly developing Eurocurrency and Eurobond markets. These activities were encouraged by the government, which appreciated the role the Euromarkets were playing both in the international financial system and in the financing of private and public sector entities in France.

Eventually, the focus of foreign activity became overseas business proper, rather than the extension of domestic activities. This in turn led to changes in the distribution of activity by center, with Africa, North America, and Asia growing in importance. While the current debt crises and generally less favorable conditions abroad have somewhat eroded the attraction of overseas business, in 1984 foreign activities accounted for 57 percent of the profits of internationally active French banks.[2] For universal banks, the foreign sector represented some 30 percent of the balance sheet at the end of 1988 (table 4.3).

The presence of foreign banks in France has also grown dramatically, and for largely similar reasons. In 1969, 51 banks were under foreign control, while by 1987 145 banks from 35 countries were operating in France, of which almost half were from other European countries, followed by the United States, Great Britain, and Japan. Many foreign banks, most notably West German, have entered France through consortia or other associations, although these have recently established direct presences. The consortium bank remains a favorite form of organization for the numerous Arab and Soviet bloc banks which have established a presence in France.

Most foreign banks entered France to service domestic clients' overseas needs, to finance foreign trade and to diversify out of saturated home markets. Additional factors, such as catering to the needs of ethnic communities, have influenced the location of Southern European and North African banks in France. Other attractions include Paris' role as a financial center, especially in the Eurocurrency and Eurobond markets, and its role as an important center of trade among various blocs such as the Arab countries, the Soviet bloc, and the former French colonies. France's close relationship with a number of Arab countries has meant an important role in the petrodollar recycling of the 1970s and early 1980s, which accounts for the large number of joint French-Arab banking concerns.

The factors which drew foreign banks to France have to a large degree

Table 4.3 Assets and liabilities held against foreigners (FFr. bil.)

	Total	Share of total balance sheet (%)	Claims against non-banks			Claims against banks			Other claims
			FFr.	*Other currency*	*Total*	*FFr.*	*Other currency*	*Total*	
A Assets									
Universal banks									
1981	819	34.3	95	152	247	15	510	525	47
1984	1,341	36.0	136	317	453	18	813	831	57
1988	1,562	30.4	128	283	411	75	997	1,072	79
Total credit establishments									
1981	909	18.2	132	163	295	16	546	562	52
1984	1,521	19.8	197	342	539	20	885	905	77
1988	1,824	17.0	218	315	533	83	1,103	1,186	105
B Liabilities to foreigners									
Universal banks									
1981	761	31.8	14	67	81	21	626	647	33
1984	1,340	36.0	19	129	148	42	1,020	1,062	130
1988	1,539	29.9	38	104	142	94	1,111	1,205	192
Total credit establishments									
1981	884	17.7	15	68	83	23	707	730	71
1984	1,672	21.8	21	133	154	48	1,191	1,239	279
1988	1,925	17.8	42	114	156	106	1,310	1,416	353

Source: Banque de France

shaped their overall characteristics. These include a relatively large area of activity either denominated in foreign currencies or conducted with foreigners; the concentration in wholesale and especially interbank transactions; very small branch networks; a focus on portfolio management, consultative, and trade service; and trading and capital markets activity. The wholesale orientation and high funding costs of foreign banks are illustrated by their 10.7 percent share of credits granted in 1987, as opposed to only 9.2 percent of deposits, and their 1.14 percent average spread margin, compared with 3.25 percent for the three largest domestic French banks.

4.2 The Regulatory Environment

4.2.1 The Regulatory Framework

The regulatory climate in France is based on extensive and comprehensive statutes and regulations, somewhat similar to that of the United States. Moreover, the various supervisory bodies display few of the advisory and consultative practices that typify the UK system. In sharp contrast to the approach adopted in countries such as the Federal Republic of Germany and Switzerland, the supervisory bodies in France maintain a somewhat adversarial role vis a vis the banking system, although they have made efforts to consult the banks during the preparation of regulations.

The nature of such supervision is changing, with the degree of day-to-day operative interference declining and the supervisory process assuming more of a strictly prudential nature. Notwithstanding the considerable reforms already in place, the role of government is still considerable and its future course will be decisive in shaping the French banking industry.

During the 1960s and 70s, the credit market in France was highly regulated regarding both quantities and interest rates. The first shock caused by deregulation came in 1966–7, and consisted of several important steps:

- the almost complete liberalization of banks' lending rates
- the liberalization of branch banking
- the relaxed distinction between commercial and investment banking.

The 1984 Banking Act formed a single complex regulatory structure for the credit system. The Ministry of Finance retains overall responsibility for the credit system, although its authority is mostly delegated to other bodies. The Banque of France, along with its role as the central bank, is also responsible for the supervision of the banking system, although its powers are exercised indirectly for the most part.

There are four operative bodies involved in bank regulation. The Committee on Bank Regulation (CRB) determines and issues the rules governing banking system safety on accounting standards, reporting formats and frequency, prudential ratios, and regulations regulating matters such as single borrower limitations.

The Banking Commission essentially monitors compliance with the various rules and regulations, and thus carries actual responsibility for the soundness of the banking system. Its mandate extends to overseas branches and subsidiaries of French banks. The Credit Establishment Committee is responsible for the licensing of banks, and the handling of technical matters at the individual bank level, while the National Credit Council is essentially a consultative group that advises the Ministry of Finance on issues pertaining to the credit system. The Association of French Banques, a representative group in which membership is obligatory for registered banks, has been made more or less a part of the supervisory group rather than an independent actor. All French banks, including mutuelles and cooperatives, are members of the Association of French Credit Establishments (AFEC).

Accountants and auditors play an important role in the system. The former prepare various reports on a consolidated basis according to strict standards and at various required intervals; they are obligated by law to report certain matters to the Ministry of Justice. Auditors, drawn from a special list, must verify and countersign bank reports.

As government interference in operative and allocative questions has declined, the context of regulatory measures has focused more on prudential safeguards, such as single borrower limitations and foreign exchange and foreign lending exposure. The question of capital adequacy has been especially irksome, due to the low (by international standards) equity ratios of French banks, and the distorting effects of years of government involvement. Liquidity requirements have been changed dramatically and have almost replaced quantitative credit controls as tools for implementing monetary policy.

Foreign-owned banks in France are essentially treated as domestic banks, with no official discriminatory policies or rules in existence. The overseas operations of French banks are seen as the full responsibility of their French-based head offices. This is clearly demonstrated in the requirements for full consolidation and their inclusion in all ratios computed by the parent bank.

4.2.2 *Major Bank Regulations*

The current structure of the banking system was implemented by the Banking Reform Act of January 24, 1984, which groups all financial institutions into the single category of "credit establishment." Under the new definition, a credit establishment is an institution which carries out any of the following:

- receives deposits from the public
- conducts credit operations
- provides customers with means of payment
- manages methods of payment (e.g., credit card, travellers cheques).

The Act constitutes an important step in the government's efforts to reform and modernize the financial system through deregulation and privatization. The 1984 Banking Law led to a unification of the regulatory status of various financial institutions and it applies equally to nationalized banks and to private sector banks (which have the same reserve requirements, solvency ratios, etc.). The broad definition of credit establishment (compared with other banking systems) brings under regulation all kinds of "non-bank" banks. All credit institutions must obtain an operating license from the Comité des Etablissements de Crédit. There are no specific restrictions on the entry of foreign banks.

Scope of business

Credit institutions are allowed to engage in activities related to their main functions, although various limitations are imposed. For example, under a rule adopted in November 1986, the net income derived from accessory activities may not be greater than 10 percent of the net product of a credit institution.

Until January 1988, there were rigid "Chinese walls" between banks and stockbrokers, who had a monopoly power over the stock market. The January 1988 Act (N-88–70 of January 22, 1988) induced stockbrokers who had become specialized brokerage firms to increase their capital. Acquiring an equity participation in a stockbroking firm is subject to approval by the French Stockbroking Association and the Ministry of Finance. Banks are expected to be able to increase their equity participation over a three-year period, as follows: 30 percent in 1988, 40 percent in 1989 and 100 percent in 1990. The recapitalization of brokerage firms implies close cooperation and capital equity investment of banks in brokerage firms (by December 1988 more than 50 percent of the brokerage firms had banks as stockholders). The encouragement of active Government Treasury

Bonds and futures markets and the permission to buy control of stockbrokers have enabled banks to generate substantial non-interest income.

Investment in non-banking activities may not exceed 5 percent of the bank's own funds. Furthermore, such investments cannot exceed a total of 50 percent of the capital employed. With the implementation of the EC Second Banking Directive, these norms will be adjusted to 15 percent and 60 percent, respectively. The total of the participations by which an investor receives unlimited responsibility or control should not be more than 15 percent of equity capital. Completion guarantees given for sales of buildings are included in the weighed risks which must not exceed 20 times the amount of the bank's equity capital. Additionally, banks are required to supply summaries of sales-type lease operations.

Under a rule adopted by the CRB in November 1986, the net income derived from accessory activities (insurance, business etc.) may not exceed 10 percent of the global net product of a credit institution. Banks may generally engage in unlimited insurance activities through subsidiaries. Investments which exceed 10 percent of the company's capital are subject to prior approval by the Ministry of Finance. Banks may engage directly or indirectly in brokerage, and real estate development and management.

Lending limitations

Lending limitations, set out in a CRB instruction of September 1984, are designed to identify the risk related to any one entity. Banks may not carry net risks (advances plus guarantees given, less guarantees received) of any one beneficiary (a group being deemed as one beneficiary), which exceed a total of 50 percent of the bank's capital employed. In addition, beneficiaries for whom total risks carried represent more than 25 percent of the bank's capital employed must be reported. As of December 31, 1988, any single guarantee granted could not exceed 40 percent of shareholder equity. The total of all guarantees, each exceeding 15 percent of equity capital, could not exceed eight times equity capital.

Interest rate control

Lending rates of banks were deregulated in 1967, while deposit rates were kept under tight control by monetary authorities. Interest payments on demand deposits have been prohibited since 1967. At the same time, commission fees were not charged for bank services, although since 1986 they have been completely deregulated. Recent financial innovations in cash management techniques have generated market interest rates on financial instruments leading to disintermediation. Since 1986, interest rates on time deposits with maturity over three months have been freely determined. Traditionally, a major part of the credit in the French economy has been channelled through a subsidized interest rate to sectors such as housing, agriculture, and export investments. Despite the decline over time the proportion was still 42 percent at the end of 1987 (Boissieu, 1990). Further, the magnitude of the subsidy has declined over time.

Liquidity

Regulation 88–01 (February, 1988) stipulates the calculation of a liquidity ratio which must be at all times equal to 100 percent or greater, and must be reported every quarter. The ratio consists of short-term assets divided by short-term liabilities. Banks must also provide "observation ratios," which are similar to the liquidity ratio but forecast for the six months to come.

Capital adequacy

The risk-asset ratio, set out in June 1985 (CRB No. 85.08), is determined by calculating the ratio of capital employed (after exclusion of intangible assets and investments in other banks, unless consolidated) to risk items. To weigh the risks relating to each individual category (varying from 100 percent of ordinary customer advances to 5 percent of guarantees given to financial institutions), the required minimum ratio was set at 5 percent.

Credit institutions must have paid up capital at least equal to a sum fixed by the Comité de la Réglementation Bancaire, depending on their balance sheet and the type of institution. The 8 percent European solvency ratio will be reached in stages, becoming compulsory on January 1, 1993.

Regulation 86–17 (November, 1986), the coefficient of own funds and long-term resources, stipulates funding for fixed and other non-liquid assets. The ratio of adjusted own funds to fixed assets, fixed investments, and non-liquid assets must be at least 60 percent, from 1992 onwards.

By international standards, French banks are less undercapitalized than is usually thought, particularly when interbank operations are not considered. For all credit institutions, interbank operations represented 32 percent in December 1987 (Boissieu, 1990).

Branch banking

Between 1945 and 1967, any new branch had to be authorized by an individual decision. The full liberalization of branch banking in 1967 was still in effect until 1982, with the period 1982–6 being characterized by reregulation. Since 1986, banks have not needed an authorization to open new branches. These regulations led to rapid growth in the number of branches during the 1970s. This phenomenon has had negative effects on bank productivity and on the cost of intermediation. Since 1986, commercial banks have been closing branches in "over-branched" areas.

Table 4.4 The growth of branch networks

	Ordinary banks (no. of branches)	*Total credit establishments (no. of branches)*
1966	4,483	–
1970	6,426	15,937
1980	9,964	23,659
1987	9,939	25,550

Source: Boissieu, 1990

Interest rate risk

As yet, there is no formal regulation on interest rate exposure, although one is being planned. This regulation will require all institutions taking market risks to define their internal limits, and adopt appropriate methods of measuring, monitoring, and managing the risks incurred.

Foreign exchange risk

A 1989 regulation requires all institutions which regularly engage in foreign exchange operations to have a permanent method of measuring, monitoring, and controlling positions, risks, and results, and to assure compliance with the system. Institutions which are subject to the regulation must observe:

- a maximum ratio of 15 percent between their net position in each foreign currency and their own net funds
- a maximum ratio of 40 percent between their aggregate currency positions and net funds.

Provisioning

Although there are specific rules for the classification of poor quality loans, there is no minimum level of provisions. The supervisory authorities may use an inspection visit to require appropriate classification and provisioning. Similarly, there are no specific country risk regulations, although the supervisory authority can and does establish minimum levels of provisioning.

4.2.3 Foreign Exchange Control

France relied for a long time on extensive capital controls, which made it one of the most regulated countries in Europe. Virtually all exchange controls were abolished in 1990.

4.2.4 *Key Accounting Issues*

Banks are currently required to prepare their financial statements in conformity with a standard chart of accounts developed by the Bank Supervisory Commission (CCB) in 1978 which is applicable to banks. The 1978 "Plan Comptable" (as amended) is strong on format but not on the choice of appropriate accounting and valuation policies; hence, it allows significant leeway by individual French banks. The CRB is obliged to complete by 1993 its compliance with the recent EC Bank Accounting Directive.

Consolidation

French legislation pertaining to consolidated financial statements was enacted in 1985, following EC Directive No. 7. More precisely, CRB instruction No. 85–12 (November, 1985) followed the enactment of legislation on consolidation for commercial and industrial companies. This instruction applies to all banking and financial establishments. Methods of consolidation depend on the extent and nature of the given controlling interest

- *Absolute and exclusive control* – Total integration is applied when a single company holds more than 50 percent of another entity's voting rights or control of its management board. In banking additional requirements exist; no other shareholder may hold more equity than the bank and no individual shareholder may hold more than 5 percent of the capital of the controlled company.
- *Joint control* – When a small number of companies collectively control another company, the proportional integration method is to be applied (i.e., over the consolidating company's share of the assets, liabilities, etc.).
- *Significant influence* – The equity accounting method of consolidation is in force in this instance.

Instruction 85–13, issued by the CRB in November 1985, requires banking establishments to publish their consolidated results by July 31 of the year following the date on which the financial year closes.

The notes to the financial statement must describe the basis of consolidation, significant accounting policies adopted by the group, segmented contributions, and the geographical sector of operation.

Hidden reserves and valuation of assets

Specific provisions are deducted from related assets if they are not excessive; such an excessive general provision can be in the nature of reserves, but these are to be included in liabilities and not hidden as undisclosed deductions from assets. Land and buildings are presented at cost and are frequently undervalued in relation to current market value. Securities held for trading purposes are valued at the lower of cost and market value.

Loan loss reserve

For accounting purposes, overdue loans are classified as either doubtful loans and advances, or as non-performing loans and advances (i.e., delays have been incurred in the repayment of capital or interest). Provisions would normally relate only to doubtful loans. Non-performing loans are held "in suspense."

Management should raise specific provisions against any bad item, or where doubt exists as to the ability of the debtor to meet the repayment terms. In the last few years the Banking Commission has encouraged banks to set up general provisions against unidentified losses, including certain country risks. To date, criteria have not been specified as to the size of this general provision; therefore, the amount to be provided remains a matter of judgment by management.

As to the presentation of provisions in financial statements, specific provisions are deducted from the appropriate assets in the balance sheet. General provisions are included in liabilities, and grouped with other provisions, accruals etc., under the headings of "accruals, provisions, and sundry items."

Interest receivable on non-performing or doubtful loans, which has not actually been received, continues to be taken to income, however an equal amount is suspended and specifically provided against such income.

Most French banks deduct specific reserves constituted in the same currency as the asset. Reserves in francs against foreign currency assets are generally recorded on the liabilities side (as general provision). However, major French banks have deducted their sovereign risk reserves from the related assets for 1986 and later consolidated accounts. By year-end 1989, French banks had accumulated sovereign risk reserves providing coverage of about 53 percent of their aggregate exposure.

French banks tend not to write off loans, even if they are 100 percent provided for, until the debtor is in the status of legal liquidation. Thus, French banks usually have higher loan loss reserves as a proportion of total loans than do, for example, UK or US banks. Similarly, French banks have lower rates of recovery on loans written off.

Foreign currency operations

Regulation 89–01 (June, 1989) stipulates that on every accounting date, asset, liability, or off-balance-sheet items are to be valued at the market price in rule at either the statement date or the preceding date. The market

price in rule at either the statement date or the preceding date. The market price applicable to asset and liability items, and to spot foreign exchange is to be the spot rate of the currency concerned. The market price applicable to forward foreign exchange commitments is to be the forward rate of exchange of the currency concerned for the outstanding term. The difference stemming from the translation of investments in subsidiaries and associated companies is to be recorded in adjustment accounts.

Deferred tax

In most cases deferred tax is not recognized, other than in the consolidated accounts of institutions having an international reporting obligation. With a few exceptions, published accounts form the basis of taxable income. The principal timing differences consist of non-deductible general bad debt and other provisions. To date no specific guidelines have been issued. Increasingly, however, major French banks do account for deferred tax in their consolidated accounts.

Asset disposal and securities transactions

The accounting treatment of asset disposal and securities transactions is stipulated by Regulation 89–07 (July, 1989):

- asset items subject to an outright disposal (no repurchase option) cease to appear in the balance sheet, and the institution's statement of income includes the profit or loss caused by the disposal of those assets
- disposed asset items carrying a guarantee against risk of debtor default continue to appear in the balance sheet of the disposer institution (as debt equal to disposal price)
- a disposal transaction with option to repurchase is included in the disposer institution's income statement as profit from the sale.

The regulation takes into account that there is a strong probability of repurchase, and sets up rules of accounting treatment of such cases.

In February 1990, a comprehensive new regulation (90–01) was issued regarding the accounting treatment of securities operations, including trading securities, securities held for sale, and investment securities.

4.2.5 Taxation

Basically, there are no special tax regulations applicable to banks as distinct from commercial or industrial enterprises, except the loan loss provisions.

Corporate tax rate

The normal rate of French corporate income tax is 42 percent of net taxable income (whether distributed or not) for accounting periods beginning January 1, 1988. From January 1986, the rate had been 45 percent.

The effective rate of corporate income tax may be reduced by preferential rates applicable to certain long-term capital gains (15 percent in general, 25 percent on land and buildings). Under the Finance Act of 1988, all capital gains realized on securities transactions are taxed at a flat rate of 16 percent. A recent recommendation (by the Lebegue Committee) is for a gradual abolition of discrimination between income and capital gains. Another recommendation is for the generalization of withholding taxes at rates chosen after coordination between the EC member countries. Such moves will reduce, or even eliminate, the tax gap between residents and non-residents.

Valuation

Assets are valued on the lower of historical cost and market value at year-end.

Securities are initially valued at their purchase price for accounting and tax purposes. At year-end, their initial value is compared to (lower of):

- securities held for participation (use value)
- securities held for portfolio businesses (market price)
- securities held for investment (market price defined as the average price of the last month before year-end)
- securities held for trading portfolio (market price at the closing day).

Any reduction from initial value must be recorded as a reserve. The tax reserve is considered as a long-term capital loss to be offset against long-term capital gain. When a security for which a reserve has been taken into account is disposed of, the reserve is recaptured as a long-term capital gain.

Loan loss reserves

The general tax rules relating to provisions for risk assets require that such provisions should meet the following conditions:

- the risk of non-recovery must be determined and quantified on a case-by-case basis
- the provisions must be supported by facts, such as the debtor's financial position and/or legal proceedings for recovery
- the provisions must be recorded in the income statement.

Such rules indicate that only specific provisions are allowed.

Alternatively, the French Code does offer a concession to banking establishments by accepting "statistically calculated" general provisions. Such provisions may relate only to long- and medium-term loans granted for a period exceeding two years. This general provision is a tax-incentive device. It cannot be accumulated with specific provision.

The allowable rate is the lower of:

- 5 percent of annual profits, before tax and depreciation, and subsequent to the absorption of any prior year losses brought forward.
- 0.5 percent of total long- and medium-term loans.

Finally, in March 1987 the Treasury Department allowed the banks to deduct, for tax purposes, reserves on doubtful accounts with country specific risk. The Banking Commission established an average provision of 30 percent of the receivable account covered by such risk as a "reference" rate. In practice the three big French banks had an average provision of 60 percent at the end of 1989.

Losses

A net loss may be carried forward for five fiscal years to offset future taxable income, and may be carried back three preceding years (after meeting certain requirements).

French corporate tax reform, effective January 1988, allows a company and its 95 percent-owned subsidiaries to report on a consolidated basis. The net taxable income or loss for the group is the sum of the profit and loss by each of the various companies comprising the group.

Interest paid and received

Under the general tax rules, income is recorded when the service is rendered. Some special rules applicable to certain kinds of services should be noted, since they apply to interest-bearing loans (interest is accumulated on an accrual basis). Interest payment from foreign countries may be subject to a withholding tax that can be credited against corporate tax if a treaty has been signed. However, since June 1987, interest paid to a non-French resident is no longer subject to withholding tax in France (no reciprocal agreement is required).

Value Added Tax (VAT)

Banks may opt to apply the VAT regime. Some activities, however, are exempt from VAT. These activities comprise the major areas of lending, the supply of guarantees, treasury operations, foreign exchange operations, customer deposits and checking account operations. The most common

VAT rate is 18.6 percent (the other rates are 5 percent, 7 percent, and 33.33 percent, although these are often decreased to 5 percent and 22 percent). Activities which are automatically subject to VAT consist mainly of general service activities such as portfolio management, financial advisory credit information, and debt recovery services and safekeeping. Currently, VAT applies to bank net income mainly through commissions and fees. Being exempted from VAT, the French banking sector is largely subject to specific taxes as on wages.

4.3 Bank Performance

The most important characteristics of the French banking system are as follows:

- A heterogenous banking sector, although recent despecialization has increased competition.
- A highly concentrated banking system. The three large universal banks (BNP, Société Génerale and Crédit Lyonnais) accounted for 28.8 percent of the entire credit system at the end of 1988. The largest mutual bank (Crédit Agricole) accounted for 9 percent of the credit system that year.
- The relatively late introduction of securitization, which developed rapidly.
- The January 1988 Act, allowing bank participation in stockbroking firms, led to cooperation between these institutions.
- The practice of not charging usage fees on checking accounts, which resulted in a high level of non-interest-bearing deposits (for example, 9.4 percent of all assets in the four largest banks at the end of 1988.
- A very large interbank market, both domestic and international, which accounts for 31.8 percent of total assets and 33.8 percent of total liabilities of the banking system (tables 4.5 and 4.5a).

The following analysis of the performance of the French banking system is based on statistics provided by the Banque de France (tables 4.2 and 4.6), data derived from the financial statements of the four largest banks (tables 4.7, 4.8 and 4.9), and a sample of three of the universal banks (tables 4.10 and 4.11).

4.3.1 Structure of Assets and Liabilities

Because of the heterogenous nature of the French banking system, the structure of assets and liabilities are analyzed separately here for each type of bank.

Table 4.5 Major assets of French banks (FFr. bil.)

	Total balance sheet	%[a]	*Loans to private sector*	%	*Interbank deposits*[b]	%	*Securities*	%
A Commercial banks								
1 Universal banks								
1981	2,391	48.0	732	32.4	1,100	66.9	52	19.5
1984	3,722	48.6	1,001	31.1	1,727	67.2	123	26.3
1988	5,139	47.8	1,512	32.6	2,289	66.9	283	33.7
2 Cooperative and mutual banks								
1981	818	16.4	442	19.5	217	13.2	43	16.3
1984	1,215	15.8	616	19.1	361	14.1	62	13.3
1988	1,845	17.2	952	20.5	519	15.2	91	10.8
3 Other banks[c]								
1981	179	3.6	17	0.8	122	7.5	–	–
1984	254	3.3	28	0.9	137	5.3	–	–
1988	251	2.3	35	0.8	89	2.6	3	0.4
B Other financial institutions								
4 Savings and provident banks								
1981	872	17.5	521	23.0	140	8.5	144	54.1
1984	1,267	16.5	706	21.9	201	7.8	238	50.7
1988	1,611	15.0	821	17.7	286	8.3	368	43.8
5 Finance companies and security houses								
1981	258	5.2	190	8.4	22	1.3	23	8.6
1984	415	5.4	268	8.4	71	2.8	41	8.7
1988	863	8.0	507	10.9	162	4.7	74	8.8
6 Specialized banks								
1981	467	9.3	359	15.9	44	2.6	4	1.5
1984	798	10.4	599	18.6	72	2.8	5	1.0
1988	1,037	9.7	815	17.5	78	2.3	21	2.5
Total credit establishments								
1981	4,985	100.0	2,261	100.0	1,645	100.0	266	100.0
1984	7,671	100.0	3,218	100.0	2,569	100.0	469	100.0
1988	10,746	100.0	4,642	100.0	3,423	100.0	840	100.0

[a] Percentage of all credit establishments.
[b] Interbank deposits in domestic markets and interbank deposits against foreign banks (see table 4.3).
[c] Includes the French Bank for Foreign Trade and the Crédit Municipal.

Source: Banque de France

Table 4.5a Major liabilities of French banks (FFr. bil.)

	Non-bank savings and deposits[a]	%	*Interbank deposits*	%	*Securities issued*	%	*Equity capital*	%
A Commercial banks								
1 Universal banks								
1981	684	35.3	1,292	69.1	49	15.8	68	35.1
1984	866	32.9	2,066	67.6	115	21.1	121	40.3
1988	1,391	36.9	2,458	68.3	264	23.7	239	41.0
2 Cooperative and mutual banks								
1981	510	26.3	90	4.8	71	22.8	38	19.6
1984	720	27.3	179	5.9	108	19.8	47	15.7
1988	1,068	28.3	279	7.7	175	15.7	78	13.4
3 Other banks[b]								
1981	8	0.4	137	7.3	8	2.6	2	1.0
1984	12	0.5	162	5.3	12	2.2	3	1.0
1988	26	0.7	101	2.8	47	4.3	5	0.9
B Other financial institutions								
4 Savings and provident banks								
1981	693	35.7	31	1.7	–	–	30	15.5
1984	949	36.0	56	1.8	1	0.2	50	16.6
1988	1,217	32.2	54	1.5	19	1.7	100	17.2
5 Finance companies and security houses								
1981	19	1.0	163	8.7	29	9.3	39	20.1
1984	47	1.8	236	7.7	64	11.7	53	17.7
1988	54	1.4	432	12.0	172	15.4	125	21.4
6 Specialized banks								
1981	25	1.3	157	8.4	154	49.5	17	8.7
1984	40	1.5	358	11.7	246	45.0	26	8.7
1988	19	0.5	276	7.7	436	39.2	36	6.1
Total credit establishments								
1981	1,939	100.0	1,870	100.0	311	100.0	194	100.0
1984	2,634	100.0	3,057	100.0	546	100.0	300	100.0
1988	3,775	100.0	3,600	100.0	1,113	100.0	583	100.0

[a] Includes certificates of deposits as of 1985.
[b] Includes the French Bank for Foreign Trade and the Credit Municipal.

Source: Banque de France

Table 4.5b Major assets and liabilities of People's Bank and Crédit Agricole (FFr. bil.)[a]

	Assets						Liabilities					
	Total balance sheet	%[b]	*Non-bank credit*	%	*Security*	*Interbank deposits*	%[c]	*Savings and deposits*	%	*Interbank deposits*	%	*Equity capital*
People's bank												
1981	128	2.6	66	2.9	5	36	2.2	84	4.3	15	0.8	4
1984	193	2.5	84	2.6	3	70	2.7	112	4.3	28	1.0	7
1988	341	3.2	146	3.1	14	104	3.1	183	4.8	56	1.0	15
Crédit Agricole												
1981	560	11.2	322	14.2	24	133	8.1	338	17.4	58	3.1	30
1984	829	10.8	450	14.0	36	226	8.8	472	17.8	131	4.3	34
1988	1,175	10.9	662	14.3	26	304	8.9	676	17.9	169	4.7	45

[a] These banks are included in the group of cooperative and mutual banks
[b] As % of total French credit system
[c] Interbank deposits include both domestic markets and those against foreign banks

Source: Banque de France

Table 4.6 The domestic banking system (FFr. bil.)

	Universal Banks[a]				
	1984	*1985*	*1986*	*1987*	*1988*
Interest income	436.1	417.4	381.7	391.5	458.4
Interest expenses	347.2	322.4	278.8	288.0	347.1
Net interest income	88.9	95.0	102.9	103.5	111.3
Non-interest income	33.5	40.1	49.5	55.4	60.8
Gross income	122.4	135.1	152.4	158.9	172.1
Operating expenses	(79.6)	(85.2)	(90.9)	(96.2)	(102.4)
Operating income	42.8	49.9	61.5	62.7	69.7
Provisions	(33.4)	(35.9)	(43.7)	(44.4)	(47.6)
Income tax	(4.4)	(5.6)	(6.4)	(5.7)	(6.8)
Net income	5.0	8.4	11.4	12.6	15.3
Net income/equity capital[b](%)	5.1	7.1	8.3	7.6	8.1
Equity capital[b]					

[a] Excluding subsidiaries in foreign countries.
[b] Equity capital at the beginning of the year.

Source: Banque de France

Universal banks

The French banking system is dominated by the universal banks, which represented 47.8 percent of all bank assets at year-end 1988 (table 4.2). The almost 400 universal banks operate about 18,000 domestic branches. The group is comprised of three sub-groups: the three big banks, other universal banks, and foreign banks. The universal banks offer wholesale and retail banking, capital market activities, non-bank financial services, and portfolio management. They dominate both sides of the interbank market (67 percent at year-end 1988), that is, both domestic markets and foreign banks. However, the universal banks were not borrowers in the interbank market throughout the period studied. For the three big banks, interbank deposits accounted for 26.7 percent of total assets at year-end 1988, with interbank liabilities at 48.9 percent of total balance sheets for the same period (tables 4.5a and 4.7). Traditional lending to the private sector accounts for 29.4 percent of total assets of this group, and non-bank deposits and savings account for 27 percent of total balance sheets at year-end 1988.

The striking conclusion, derived from analyzing the market share and composition of assets and liabilities of the different sub-groups of universal banks, is that they have maintained stability over time, despite regulatory changes and increased competition among financial institutions. The most impressive change has been the growth of the entire credit system. For example, the rise in total assets during the period 1981–8 was 115.5 percent (average annual growth: 11.6 percent), with non-bank deposits increasing 94.7 percent (average annual growth: 10.0 percent (table 4.5)).

The three big banks (BNP, Société Générale and Crédit Lyonnais) control about 5,600 branches and accounted for 28.8 percent of total assets of credit institutions at year-end 1988. They controled 26.8 percent of total credit, and 26.8 percent of total deposits and savings of the credit system at year-end 1988. These banks are very active in portfolio management, retail and corporate banking, and capital market activities.

The other universal banks provide a varying range of services. Some of the larger institutions offer full services, while other companies specialize in investment banking and retail corporate lending. This is reflected in their estimated average net interest spread of 7.3 percent in 1986 (Salomon Brothers, *The French Banking System*, December 1987). The foreign bank group share of the market was about 17 percent at year-end 1988 (Commission Bancaire, Annual Report, 1988). Group operations are concentrated on the international interbank market. The involvement of this group in traditional domestic banking (loans and deposits) is insignificant.

Table 4.7 Combined balance sheet (four major French banks)

	31/12/88 *(US$ mil.)*	31/12/88	31/12/87 *(FFr. bil.)*	31/12/86	31/12/85
A Loans					
1 Customer loans	164219	995	848	775	788
2 Loans to banks	3961	24	18	15	17
3 Long-term loans					
(a) leased assets	17495	106	78	55	47
(b) other	65027	394	310	250	233
4 Other	87308	529	468	407	398
Total A	338010	2048	1722	1502	1483
B Other earning assets					
1 Deposits with banks	185014	1121	983	970	966
2 Short-term investments	56280	341	321	326	333
3 Other investments	21951	133	134	93	68
4 Equity investments	4291	26	18	14	13
Total B	267536	1621	1456	1403	1380
C Total earning assets (A+B)	605546	3669	3178	2905	2863
D Fixed assets	4291	26	24	20	20
E Non-earning assets					
1 Cash and due from banks	14359	87	76	64	80
2 Other	80376	487	374	329	296
F Total assets	704572	4269	3652	3318	3259
G Customer and short-term funding					
1 Demand deposits	66183	401	368	358	334
2 Savings deposits	87803	532	487	436	387
3 Time deposits	124443	754	616	573	549
4 Interbank					
(a) demand	35649	216	192	171	207
(b) time	239974	1454	1246	1135	1154
Total G	554052	3357	2909	2673	2631
H Other funding					
1 Long-term borrowing	46377	281	249	226	221
2 Subordinated debt	5942	36	9	7	11
3 Participating notes	660	4	4	4	4
I Other (non-int. bearing)	78726	477	385	324	334
J Loan loss reserves (memo)	13864	84	76	67	65
K Risk capital					
1 Equity	16174	98	83	72	52
2 Near equity	2641	16	13	12	6
Total K	18815	114	96	84	58
L Total liabilities & risk capital	704572	4269	3652	3318	3259
Exchange rate (US$1 = FFr)		6.059	5.340	6.455	7.561
Ratios (%)					
Deposits/loans		82.3	85.4	91.0	85.7
Loans/total assets		48.0	47.1	45.3	45.5
Fixed assets/risk capital		22.9	24.9	23.9	34.5
Loan loss reserves/loans		4.1	4.4	4.5	4.4
Risk capital/total assets		2.7	2.6	2.5	1.8

Source: IBCA data base

The net spread of these operations is relatively low, and was estimated at 1.14 percent in 1986 (Salomon Brothers, ibid.).

Cooperative and mutual institutions

This group operates more than 11,000 branches and accounts for 17.2 percent of the credit system at year-end 1988. Two credit companies are the most prominent: The People's Bank (3.1 percent of the credit system's total assets as of December 1989) and Crédit Agricole (8.9 percent of the credit system's total assets at year-end 1988). In addition, Crédit Mutuel constituted 2.2 percent of the system.

The People's Bank, with about 1,500 branches, is a full service bank extending credit to small corporations and professionals. The group is active in the lending market (42.8 percent of total assets of the group at year-end 1988) and deposits and savings (53.7 percent of total balance sheets of the group at year-end 1988 (table 4.5b). The People's Bank is a net lender in the interbank market.

Crédit Agricole has a three level structure: 3,000 local cooperatives (branches), 92 regional organizations, and the Paris based CNCA. In aggregate, this vast organization accounts for 10.9 percent of the entire French credit system, and operates as a dominant factor in retail banking (providing 14.3 percent of total credit in the system and 17.2 percent of deposits and savings at year-end 1988 (table 4.5b). The group is marginally involved in the interbank market, mostly by investing its surplus from traditional banking (deposits and savings).

Savings banks

Savings banks have a three tiered system made up of 4,400 retail branches, 21 regional units and a central body. This group underwent major restructuring from December 1986 to December 1988, which reduced the number of institutions from 421 to 281.

The savings banks account for 15 percent of the French credit system. Of their funds, 75.5 percent derive from retail deposits; 51 percent of funds are used for lending. The group enjoys a surplus of funds, which is invested in both the interbank and securities markets. The growth of savings banks was below the industry average during the period 1984–8 as a result of slower growth in lending (23.0 percent of the banking system at year-end 1981 compared with 17.7 percent at year-end 1988); hence the group lost market share (17.5 percent in 1981, 15.0 percent in 1988).

Finance companies

Finance companies include 1,069 institutions engaged in leasing, equipment finance, home loans, and consumer credit. Most finance companies are owned by the universal banks, and operate as affiliates specializing in this type of lending. The market share of the group is about 8 percent, and has grown in the period examined (5.2 percent at year-end 1984) as a consequence of the increase in lending activities. Finance companies raise funds mostly by interbank borrowing (50 percent of the total balance sheet at year-end 1988 (table 4.5a), and by issuing securities (20 percent at year-end 1988).

Specialized institutions

In France, specialized institutions operate like finance companies. Their market share at year-end 1988 was 9.7 percent. The major use of funds by these institutions is for special lending (78.6 percent of total assets at year-end 1988). The major funding sources of specialized institutions are securities issued (42.0 percent) and interbank borrowing (26.6 percent (table 4.5).

4.3.2 Income Statement

The present analysis of French commercial bank performance during 1985–8 is based on consolidated figures. However, due to database limitations, only certain parts of the French banking system can be analyzed. Table 4.8 contains the combined income statement analysis for the four big banks. Table 4.11 presents the income statement of a sample of three other universal banks.

The net income to average equity of the four big banks for 1985–8 shows a figure of 10.72 percent, with very low variations. This figure is similar to returns earned in other developed countries. By comparison, the performance of the group of all banks presented was, on average, worse than the four banks group.[3] The sample of three retail universal banks substantially improved their performance during this period, attaining 13.3 percent in 1988.

Despite the reduction on lending margins for the big banks (table 4.8), which declined from 2.07 percent in 1985 to 1.97 percent in 1988, net interest income increased by 19.2 percent. This was due to the increase in the size of the loan portfolio of these banks. A similar trend can be observed for the sample of retail banks presented in table 4.10. Non-interest income substantially increased during the period for the four big banks (by 54 percent), and for the three retail banks as well (71 percent). Non-interest

Table 4.8 Combined income statement (four major French banks) (FFr. bil.)

		1988	*1987*	*1986*	*1985*
1	Interest received	345.8	295.8	276.8	301.6
2	Interest paid	270.3	226.4	211.5	238.3
3	Net interest revenue	75.5	69.4	65.3	63.3
4	Other operating income	26.8	20.6	21.8	17.4
5	Other income	2.9	2.4	2.4	2.3
6	Provision for loan losses	17.5	13.1	17.9	16.3
7	Personnel expenses	40.3	37.3	35.3	34.0
8	Other non-interest expenses	30.1	26.1	23.0	21.8
9	Operating profit before exceptional items	17.3	15.9	13.3	10.9
10	Exceptional items (net)	(0.6)	(1.9)	0.5	(0.5)
11	Pre-tax profit	16.7	14.0	13.8	10.4
12	Taxes	6.0	4.9	4.6	4.7
13	Net income	10.7	9.1	9.2	5.7
	Ratio analysis				
	Average earning assets	3424	3042	2884	2863
	Average risk capital	105	90	71	58
	Ratios to average earning assets (%)				
	Interest received	10.10	9.72	9.60	10.53
	Interest paid	7.90	7.44	7.34	8.32
	Net interest revenue	2.20	2.28	2.26	2.21
	Interest on capital employed	0.23	0.21	0.17	0.14
	Net spread	1.97	2.07	2.09	2.07
	Other ratios (%)				
	Personnel expenses/net interest	53	54	54	54
	Other oper. expe./net interest	40	38	35	34
	Total oper. exp./non-interest income	237	276	241	283
	Net interest/non-interest income	254	302	269	321
	Prov. for loan lo./total loans	0.85	0.76	1.19	1.10
	Net income/total assets	0.25	0.25	0.28	0.18
	Net income/risk capital	10.19	10.11	12.96	9.83

Sample includes BNP, CNCA, Société Générale and Crédit Lyonnais.

Source: IBCA data base

Table 4.9 Selected financial data (four major French banks) (FFr, bil.)

	Total assets	*Total loans*	*Risk capital*	*Net income*
Banque Nationale de Paris	1193.3	563.7	32	3.2
Caisse Nationale de Crédit Agricole	1051.4	588.9	25.2	1.6
Crédit Lyonnais	1083.8	482.7	28.7	2.2
Société Générale	942.1	413.1	28.8	3.6
Total	4270.6	2048.4	114.7	10.6

Source: IBCA data base

income for both groups represented 26.2 percent of total operating income in 1988.

The increase in operating income for the big banks during the period 1985–8 (26.8 percent) exceeded the increase in personnel costs (17.6 percent), and loan provision (7.4 percent, see table 4.8). The increase in net income during this period paralleled the increase in equity, such that the return to equity remained stable. The performance of the sample of three retail banks improved, mostly as a result of the increase in non-interest income, which exceeded the increase in expenses. Tax provisions amounted to about 35 percent of the pre-tax profit of the big banks.

The French banking system saw its profitability deteriorate in 1989, with a 1 percent rise in operating income, a negative real result compared with 1989's 3.6 percent inflation rate. Although overheads declined in real terms (a 3.2 percent nominal rise was recorded), and income from consumer operations increased by a healthy 8.6 percent, rising interest rates and intensified competition led to additional pressure on interest rate margins on domestic operations. This was the primary cause of the banks' disappointing results. Although off-balance-sheet items continued to grow steadily (12 percent), banks displayed considerable caution in their capital market activities, with both securities investment and trading portfolios either shrinking or growing slowly (2 percent and 6 percent, respectively).

4.3.3 Sources of Income

The two major sources of income for the French banking system are net interest margins and other non-interest income.

Table 4.10 Combined balance sheet (three other French banks)[a]

	31/12/88 (US$ mil.)	31/12/88	31/12/87	31/12/86	31/12/85
		(FFr. bil.)			
A Loans					
1 Customer loans	19508	118.2	95.7	85.8	92.7
2 Long-term loans					
(a) Leased assets	578	3.5	2.0	1.5	0.6
(b) Other	8170	49.5	42.2	33.7	13.3
3 Other	528	3.2	3.4	0.1	0.3
Total A	28784	174.4	143.3	121.1	106.9
B Other earning assets					
1 Deposits with banks	12725	77.1	81.8	67.4	112.1
2 Short-term investments	8714	52.8	39.5	45.6	26.6
3 Other investments	2030	12.3	10.6	5.5	10.6
4 Equity investments	710	4.3	2.4	2.0	1.8
Total B	24179	146.5	134.3	120.5	151.1
C Total earning assets (A + B)	52963	320.9	277.6	241.6	258.0
D Fixed assets	693	4.2	3.8	3.4	2.1
E Non-earning assets					
1 Cash and due from banks	1336	8.1	11.4	8.0	5.0
2 Other	11537	69.9	50.4	51.5	34.9
F Total assets	66529	403.1	343.2	304.5	300.0
G Customer and short-term funding					
1 Demand deposits	11867	71.9	66.8	63.5	33.3
2 Savings deposits	8665	52.5	47.5	42.8	16.9
3 Time deposits	12477	75.6	59.9	47.3	73.6
4 Interbank					
(a) Demand	875	5.3	6.6	5.7	4.5
(b) Time	14507	87.9	79.2	62.0	115.1
Total G	48391	293.2	260.0	221.3	243.4
H Other funding					
1 Long-term borrowing	4258	25.8	26.0	27.2	13.2
2 Subordinated debt	743	4.5	0.3	0.3	0.6
I Other (non-int. bearing)	11008	66.7	47.0	47.5	36.0
J Loan loss reserves (memo)	446	2.7	2.3	0.0	0.0
K Risk capital	2129	12.9	9.9	8.2	6.8
L Total liabilities & risk capital	66529	403.1	343.2	304.5	300.0
Exchange rate (US$1 = FFr.)		6.059	5.340	6.455	7.561
Ratios (%)					
Deposits/loans		114.6	121.6	126.8	115.8
Loans/total assets		43.3	41.8	39.8	35.6
Fixed assets/risk capital		32.6	38.4	41.5	30.9
Loan loss reserves/loans		1.5	1.6	0.0	0.0
Risk capital/total assets		3.2	2.9	2.7	2.3

[a] Including Banque Audi (France), Banque Worms & Groupe des Banques Populaires.

Source: IBCA Data Base

Table 4.11 Combined income statement (three other French banks) (FFr. bil.)[a]

		1988	1987	1986	1985
1	Interest received	35.6	31.6	29.7	30.1
2	Interest paid	24.5	20.8	19.2	20.2
3	Net interest revenue	11.1	10.8	10.5	9.9
4	Other operating income	4.1	3.5	3.1	2.4
5	Other income	0.8	0.6	0.5	0.4
6	Provision for loan losses	1.1	1.0	1.1	0.8
7	Personnel expenses	6.9	6.6	6.4	6.2
8	Other non-interest expenses	6.6	6.2	5.6	5.0
9	Operating profit before exceptional items	1.4	1.1	1.0	0.7
10	Exceptional items (net)	0.1	0.2	0.1	−0.0
11	Pre-tax profit	1.5	1.3	1.1	0.7
12	Taxes	0.1	0.0	0.0	0.0
13	Net income	1.4	1.3	1.1	0.7
	Ratio analysis				
	Average earning assets	299	260	250	258
	Average risk capital	11	9	7	7
	Ratios to average earning assets (%)				
	Interest received	11.90	12.15	11.88	11.65
	Interest paid	8.20	8.00	7.68	7.82
	Net interest revenue	3.70	4.15	4.20	3.83
	Interest on capital employed	0.28	0.24	0.20	0.21
	Net spread	3.42	3.91	4.00	3.62
	Other ratios (%)				
	Personnel expenses/net interest	62.1	61.1	61.0	62.6
	Other oper. exp./net interest	59.3	57.4	53.3	50.5
	Total oper. exp./non-interest income	276	312	333	400
	Net interest/non-interest income	226	263	292	354
	Prov. for loan lo./total loans	0.63	0.70	0.91	0.75
	Net income/total assets	0.35	0.38	0.36	0.20
	Net income/risk capital	12.73	14.44	15.71	10.00

[a] Including Banque Audi (France), Banque Worms & Groupe des Banques Populaires.

Source: IBCA data base

Interest margins

The interest margins calculated and reported in tables 4.8 and 4.11 should be analyzed with caution. The calculated margins and spread refer to all earning assets, which are not homogenous. Traditional lending is only 60 percent of total earning assets of the four big banks (table 4.7) and the retail banks. The margins in traditional intermediation are larger than those of other earnings assets, namely of interbank activities and securities markets. Therefore, the margin and spread is biased downward for lending activities. Given the relatively large proportion of interbank activity in the French banking system (about 32 percent), the actual spread in lending activities is 4.0 percent to 4.3 percent.[4]

Additionally, the current regulation suspending explicit payment of interest on demand deposits has led to implicit interest payment, by means of free banking services and extensive branching. This has resulted in cross-subsidization, in the form of not paying interest on demand deposits and not charging for banking services. The Salomon Brothers' estimates of the costs of the clearing system are equivalent to 8 percent interest on non-interest-bearing deposits. This cross-subsidization, in turn, caused an upward bias in the overall calculated net interest income of the four big banks by 6 percent, again based on the Salomon Brothers' estimate.[5]

Table 4.12 Interest Rule Margins in France

	Margin on APB banks Domestic operations (%)
1984	6.87
1985	6.88
1986	7.04
1987	6.25
1988	5.61
1989	4.90[a]

[a] Estimate.

Source: *Commission Bancaire*, Annual Report 1989

During the period examined the four big banks enjoyed a substantial growth of 38 percent in their private sector lending. A decline in interest margins of 5 percent allowed for an increase of 20 percent in net interest income. It should be noted, when comparing interest margins, that the above-mentioned biases can be ignored, since both the ratio of interbank activities and the level of interest remained stable.

The trend in interest rate margins has clearly been negative. As table 4.12 shows, the rising cost of deposits, and increased bank and non-bank competition especially from the capital markets, have put market pressure on interest rate margins in recent years (table 4.12).

The interest income for the other retail universal banks in the sample increased by 12.1 percent. This increase is the result of both a more significant decline of 11.4 percent in the net spread (table 4.11), and a significant increase of roughly 44.0 percent in the size of the group's loan portfolio. The net spread of this group (3.42 percent) is significantly higher than that of the big banks (1.97 percent). It is estimated that for retail lending the net spread is in the range of 5 to 6 percent.

Non-interest income

Non-interest income of French banks is derived primarily from capital market activities. The securitization process has developed very rapidly in recent years, resulting in a marked increase in the share of non-interest income. The average proportion of non-interest income to total income was 15.4 percent in the period 1980–4 (Boissieu, 1989). This ratio has increased for the big banks to 26.2 percent in 1988, (26.9 percent in 1988 for the sample of three retail universal banks). The growth in non-interest income was derived from underwriting, securities placement activities, and credit card activities.

Non-interest income is also an indication of increased off-balance-sheet activities. Off-balance-sheet commitments on behalf of customers increased by almost 30 percent in 1988 (Commission Bancaire, Annual Report, 1988). The volume of off-balance-sheet financial instruments increased to 64 percent of total assets, due mainly to accounting transfers.

4.3.4 Expenses

The major expenses of the French credit system include personnel, loan loss reserve, taxes, and other operating expenses. Personnel expenses accounted for 57.2 percent of total expenses for the four big banks in 1988 (table 4.8), and 51.1 percent for the sample of retail banks (table 4.11). Personnel expenses have increased during the period examined by only 18.5 percent (less than the rate of inflation). Non-interest income coverage of personnel expenses increased from 51.2 percent in 1985 to 66.5 percent in 1988 for the four big banks (table 4.8). Typical of universal banks, the largest French banks operate vast nationwide branch networks that are labor intensive. Recently these banks have reduced (marginally) staff and improved customer service by investing in new technology.

The largest French banks have had operating costs comparable with those of the largest German universal banks. French retail banks are widely acknowledged to be at the forefront of electronic banking technology, particularly home banking technology (videotext equipment). The share of other operating expenses in total operating expenses among the largest banks increased from 39.1 percent in 1985 to 42.8 percent in 1988, resulting mainly from an increase in the use of technology and a reduction in staff (table 4.8). The increase in other operating expenses during the period examined was 38.1 percent (table 4.8) and 32.0 percent in the sample of other banks (table 4.11). The increase in other operating expenses represents the most significant increase among the different items on the income statement.

The relatively low return to equity of French banks during the first half of the 1980s was the consequence of heavy loan loss provisions against domestic and LDC credits. The restructuring of selected segments of the French economy such as steel, textiles, and engineering, resulted in substantial charges.[6] French banks have reserved heavily against less developed country (LDC) debt. Annual loan loss provisions averaged 1.3 to 1.4 percent of total loans during the period 1982–8.

The provision for loan losses came to approximately FFr 30 billion (about 50 percent in the largest banks). This feature is characterized by a decrease in the provision for domestic loans and an increase in the provision for LDC debt. The gross exposure to LDC debt of the French banking system is estimated to be about FFr 322 billion at the end of 1988, and the accumulated loan reserve to be FFr 160 billion. The annual average provision for loan losses as a percentage of net interest income was 23.6 percent during the period 1985–8. This figure is high compared to the banking systems of other developed countries. It is expected that this cost will be reduced in the future. Of other universal banks sampled, loan loss reserves were less significant, covering about 10 percent of net interest income (table 4.11). The coverage ratio for sovereign debt rose 5.7 percent to 43.7 percent, while the overall coverage ratio was 49.4 percent due to the 58.2 percent coverage ratio of private risks.

4.3.5 Capital Adequacy

French banks in general, and the largest banks in particular, maintain a relatively low capital ratio. The four big banks operated at year-end 1988 with an equity capital-to-total-assets ratio of 2.7 percent (table 4.7). The ratio was 1.8 percent at year-end 1984. The entire French banking system operates with an equity capital-to-total-asset ratio of 5.4 percent (table 4.5). The ratio was 3.9 percent at year-end 1984. In both cases, equity capital increased much faster than the total assets of the respective group. For example, in all credit institutions, equity capital increased between

December 1984 and December 1988 by 94.3 percent, whereas total assets increased by only 40.1 percent (table 4.5). The most impressive growth occurred in the universal and savings banks. In analyzing and comparing the equity adequacy of French banks, several important aspects should be kept in mind:

- Historically, government ownership and implicit support of the major banks allowed them to remain relatively poorly capitalized.
- The balance sheets of French banks include a significant portion of interbank activity. Because of the low risk inherent in this activity, the measure of total equity to total asset is biased downward.
- General loan losses for both domestic lending and LDC debt further reduced the equities position of French banks.

An estimate of the necessary adjustment for these factors was carried out by Salomon Brothers, (December 1987), based on 1986 data. It was found that French banks are well situated when compared with banks of other developed countries. The increase in equity participation debt and subordinated debt since 1986 has further improved the ability of French banks to meet the BIS requirement. Boissieu (1988) found that the risk-based capital ratio of the large French banks already equalled 7.5 percent in 1987. The Cooke ratio of the 16 most important French banks was 8.6 percent at the end of 1988, and 8.7 percent at the end of 1989. However some banks, particularly those which are state-owned, will find it difficult to comply with the 4 percent pure equity ratio imposed by the EC directive on all banks.

Notes

1 A large number are in fact subsidiaries or affiliates of the large commercial banks.
2 Waywell T.G., Internationalization of the French Banking System, *Institute of European Finance, Research Paper 88/7*.
3 See *Bank Profitability*, statistical supplement, OECD Paris, 1988.
4 See discussion of this bias in Boissieu (1990), 26.
5 Salomon Brothers, The French Banking System, December 1987.
6 See Salomon Brothers (1987) The French Banking System.

References

Banque de France, *Statistiques Monétaires et Financières Annuelles*, various issues.

Boissieu, Christian de (1990) The French Banking Sector in Light of European Financial Integration, in European Banking in the 1990s Jean Dermine (ed), Basil Blackwell, Oxford.

—— (ed), *Banking in France*, Routledge, London, 1990.

Commission Bancaire, *Annual Report 1989*.

Metais, Joel (1990) International Strategies of French Banks, in *Banking in France*, Christian de Boissieu (ed), Routledge, London.

OECD, *Economic Survey*, France, February 1984, January 1987.

—— *Bank Profitability Statistical Supplements Financial Statements of Banks*, Paris, 1988.

Salomon Brothers (1987) *The French Banking System.*

Waywell, T.G. (1988) Internationalization of The French Banking System, *Institute of European Finance Research Papers in Banking and Finance* 88/7, University College of North Wales, Bangor.

5

The United Kingdom

5.1 Structure of the Financial System

5.1.1 Introduction

The British economy has undergone considerable change in the past decade, possibly setting the foundations for a long-lasting transformation. The so-called "British Disease" – sluggish growth, low productivity, labor market rigidities, excessive government intervention – had turned the major industrial power of the world into the "sick man of Europe" by the late 1970s. By that time, most measures of international trade, employment, and per capita GNP ranked the United Kingdom at, or near, the bottom of the major industrial countries. However, with the accession to power of the Conservative Party in 1979, and the policies pursued by Margaret Thatcher until recently, a considerable turn-around appeared to have been effected. Inflation was moderated, profits and productivity climbed considerably, and a growing proportion of the population enjoyed greater prosperity.

However, by approximately 1988 much of the bloom began to fade from the Thatcherite revolution. Growth again slowed to below the OECD average, while inflation once more soared to levels well beyond the EC average (table 5.1). A number of severe imbalances emerged in asset prices, the external balance, the private savings rate and private investment. Once again, the United Kingdom was displaying close to the worst economic performance in Western Europe, prompting many to suggest that the economic achievements of the early to mid-1980s were more a passing bubble than a change in trend.

While other factors have certainly played a part in influencing economic conditions in the United Kingdom (such as North Sea oil production), and it is obviously too early to fully assess Mrs Thatcher's achievements, it seems that there have been positive changes in the UK economy, which have brought improved prospects for future economic performance. While

Table 5.1 The United Kingdom – major economic indicators and the banking system

	1980	*1984*	*1989*
Gross national product (US$ bil.)	534	437	835
Current account, (US$ bil.)	7.5	2.6	−34.1
Rate of inflation, (pcp)	11.9	6.0	7.8
Exchange rate, (pound-US$) (year-end)	2.38	1.15	1.61
Interest rate (percent)	15.6	7.6	13.9
Population, (mil.)	55.9	55.6	57.2
Number of authorized institutions		598	551
of which foreign-owned		240	256
Number of deposit-taking institutions		858	720
Number of authorized institutions domestic branches		14,382	13,711[a]
Population per branch		3,866	4,157[a]
Number of ATMs	2,189[b]	5,653[c]	11,000[d]
Population per ATM	25,537[b]	9,835[c]	5,182[d]
Bank employees (thou.)	466.1	520.8	618[e]
Bank employees as a percentage of total population	0.83	0.94	1.08
Financial sector employees (thou.)	729[f]	2,309[g]	2,630[e]

[b] 1988 figures [b] 1978 figures [c] 1983 figures
[d] 1987 figures [e] March 1989 [f] September 1981
[g] September 1984

Source: IMF, *International Financial Statistics*, 1989 Yearbook; Bank of England, *Quarterly Bulletin*, various issues

the future course of British economic policy, after Mrs Thatcher's replacement by John Major in 1990, is unclear, more than one observer has claimed to see the United Kingdom leading the world into the post-industrial era, in much the same role as it ushered in the industrial revolution. According to this view, the prosperous south of England, and especially the Greater London area, represent a forerunner of the services-centered information age economy. If this is the case, then international financial services, long centered in London, will play a leading role.

The post-1987 downturn in the financial industry, apparent over-capacity in the securities industry, and the decline in the previously robust growth of the "City", still need to be assessed in terms of long-term impact on the future structure and performance of the financial system.

5.1.2 *Financial Markets and Institutions*

The financial markets of the United Kingdom developed gradually over a long period, characterized by slow evolution. Only recently have the markets experienced rapid change, and that primarily as a result of financial deregulation and reform promoted as a part of the broader "Thatcherite revolution." Thus, until the present, it was correct to note that "The British financial system is characterized as an institution whose present roles have evolved through historical tradition rather than design or regulation."[1]

Any overview of the British financial system must begin with a survey of the City of London, the financial district in the heart of Greater London that is home to the headquarters of most British financial institutions. It has also long served as one of the most important financial centers in the world. Located in one of the world's great trading centers, and at the heart of the British Empire, the City became the locale for an unparalleled concentration of financial services. While the decreasing relative importance of the British economy meant that London as a financial center had a smaller domestic base than other such centers, its international orientation and unregulated nature helped make it one of the three financial centers, along with Tokyo and New York, which have established a tripartite division of world financial activity spanning the globe.

The City houses a number of important markets, both organized exchanges and over-the-counter markets, including the London Stock Exchange, the insurance and Foreign Exchange, shipping, commodities, the Eurobond market, gilts, and money markets. It also contains the highest concentration of banks in the world: over 600 major banking institutions maintain a presence in the City, including 254 branches of foreign banks. Most major British banks, insurance companies and finance houses, all have their headquarters in the City.

The structure of the banking system

A concise description and classification of British financial institutions is complicated by the rather ambiguous and overlapping roles of many of the financial institutions. Recent legislation (the Trustee Savings Bank Acts of 1976, 1978, and 1988; the Building Society Act of 1986; the Financial Services Act of 1985; and the Banking Act of 1987) has, however, clarified the situation somewhat.

Commercial banks

- Retail banks
  - *Clearing banks* are dominated by the so-called Clearers, primarily the "big four" – Barclays, Midland, National Westminster and Lloyds. The

"clearing" appellation is today of historical importance only, reflecting the once dominant role of these banks in the British money transmission and payment networks. This group accounted for 33.6 percent of total Sterling deposits and 23.2 percent of total banking sector assets at year-end 1988.

The "big four" commercial banks have extensive nationwide branch networks and Automated Teller Machines (ATMs) networks. During the 1970s and 1980s this group expanded and diversified their activities into overseas operations, the home loan market, and investment banking, and hence became universal banks. However, unlike the West German banks, they do not hold major equity positions in industrial corporations.

- *The TSB* (Trustee Savings Banks) group was created in 1985 as a holding company for its constituent members, who originated in the last century as public service trusts. During the 1960s they diversified away from small personal savings banks toward retail banking, and then into commercial banks. It is now the eighth largest bank in the United Kingdom.
- *The Cooperative Bank*, recognized as a clearer in 1975, is owned by 100 retail cooperatives and acts in a more limited manner, primarily providing personal banking services and local authority financing. The cooperative bank has a relatively small but expanding branch network.
- *The National Girobank (NG) and National Savings Bank (NSB)*, modelled after the European giro systems, provide various money transmission banking services, mainly deposits and cash withdrawal facilities, through post office branches throughout the United Kingdom. In 1986 NG announced that it would be offering mortgages. The NSB also offers various savings bonds and certificates and invests mostly in government securities. The National Giro was sold in 1990 to Alliance and Leicester Building Society.

- *Merchant banks* These comprise firms involved in both wholesale banking and investment banking, including corporate finance. Recently, their deposit taking and credit extension has been of less importance than other activities, including international trade finance, mergers and acquisitions, financial advisory services, investment management, foreign exchange, and securities trading. The core members of this group include the 16 former "accepting houses," who long enjoyed a special relationship with the Bank of England.
- *Other British banks* This a catch-all Bank of England classification, to include miscellaneous UK registered institutions, institutions in the Channel Islands and Isle of Man, British overseas banks, and finance companies. Some of the Channel Islands and Isle of Man institutions are treated as UK banks for statistical purposes, yet are not authorized under the 1987 Bank Act.

Foreign banks

Foreign-owned banks operating in London numbered 362 by year-end 1989, from 78 countries, including 259 branches, 69 subsidiaries, and 18 consortiums. There are also 184 representative offices of foreign banks, 55 from the United States, 32 from Japan, and 92 from EC countries. While a few are active in retail banking, primarily exploiting ethnic affinities, the majority concentrate on the corporate and wholesale banking markets.

Table 5.2 The domestic banking system
A Total assets

Type of institution	*Number of institutions*		*Total assets Pounds sterling bil.*			*% of total assets*	*% change*
	1984	*1989*	*1980*	*1984*	*1989*	*1989*	*1980–9*
A Commercial banks							
Retail banks[a]	19	21	73.0	152.9	391.7	27.2	436.6
Merchant banks[b]	36	31	12.8	26.6	51.5	3.6	302.3
Other British banks	224	168	43.0	91.8	61.0	4.2	41.9
Total	279	220	128.8	271.3	504.2	35.0	291.5
B Foreign banks							
American banks	64	44	60.0	116.3	118.7	8.3	97.8
Japanese banks	25	29	40.8	167.6	281.9	19.6	590.9
Other overseas banks[c]	290	289	73.6	204.7	329.3	22.9	347.4
Total	379	362	174.4	488.6	729.9	50.8	318.5
C Other deposit-taking institutes							
Discount houses	10	8	5.2	8.1	15.3	1.1	194.2
Building societies[d]	190	130	53.8	102.7	188.6	13.1	250.5
Total	200	138	59.0	110.8	203.9	14.2	245.6
Total banking system	858	720	362.2	870.7	1,438.0	100.0	297.0

[a] Since 1985 this group includes the Trustee Savings bank.
[b] Until 1984, known as accepting houses.
[c] Including consortium banks.
[d] These institutions are not part of the monetary base.

Source: Bank of England, *Quarterly Bulletin*, various issues.

Foreign banks held nearly 50.8 percent of the UK banking system's total assets at year-end 1989, but only 20.3 percent of Sterling deposits. Foreign banks are especially prominent in the Euromarket and in the UK securities market. The attraction of the London market to Japanese and US banks lies in the opportunity to engage in security businesses from which they are prohibited at home. The overseas banks are competing actively in the corporate financial services market as well as in the securities market, although they are not expected to be involved in the retail market. A noticeable change in recent years has been the growth in importance of Japanese banks (mostly full branches), and the relative decline of US banks. Japanese banks have increased their share of the total assets of the banking system from 11.3 percent in 1980 to 19.6 percent in 1989. The comparable figures for US banks are 16.6 percent in 1980 and 8.3 percent in 1989, (tables 5.2, 5.2a).

London is, of course, the most important center for international Japanese bank business. As of June 1987, 28 percent of Japanese banks' international assets were booked in London.[2] The most important element of international Japanese bank activity in London is fund-raising from banks located outside the UK and from the UK interbank market. Recently, Japanese banks in London have built up their merchant bank subsidiaries; these merchant banks were established to help clients tap the Eurobond market. The importance of sovereign lending has declined since the debt crisis of the early 1980s, and as a result Japanese banks see the UK domestic market as an area for potential growth.

Other deposit takers

With the exception of the discount houses this group is not included in the UK monetary sector. Building societies, however, are included in the wide monetary aggregate M4.

Building societies

By 1989 there were some 130 of these institutions, which originated as mutually-owned mortgage societies, and which now operate a large network of branches. Traditionally, they obtain funds from depositors and finance home purchases. However, they are increasingly in competition with the clearers in both commercial banking services and mortgage lending. During the 1970s, the mortgage market was dominated by the building societies (80 percent of outstanding mortgage lending). In the 1980s, other financial institutions began to participate more extensively. During 1986–7, when wholesale money was cheaper than retail funds, and societies were constrained by the 20 percent wholesale funding limit, banks and specialized mortgage lenders increased their market share by over 50 percent. The building societies are not part of the UK monetary sector; however, they are major deposit taking institutions and offer a wide range of financial services, including savings schemes. The 1986 Building Societies Act extended their permissible activities and they now offer insurance, credit cards, money transaction accounts, personal banking, and non-financial products. Societies are allowed to expand the non-mortgage element of

Table 5.2a The domestic banking system
B Sterling deposits

Type of institution	*Pounds sterling bil.* 1980	1984	1989	*% of sterling deposits* 1989	*% change* 1980–9
A Commercial banks					
Retail banks	48.3	97.4	266.4	39.7	451.5
Merchant banks	5.3	9.8	28.9	4.3	445.3
Other British banks	16.6	29.0	38.5	5.7	131.9
Total	70.2	136.2	333.8	49.7	375.5
B Foreign banks					
American banks	9.0	10.9	17.3	2.6	92.2
Japanese banks	1.1	8.4	33.3	5.0	2,927.2
Other overseas banks	9.9	25.5	84.9	12.7	757.6
Total	20.0	44.8	135.5	20.3	577.5
C Other deposit-taking institutions					
Discount houses	5.1	7.4	14.5	2.2	184.3
Building societies	53.8	102.7	186.6	27.8	246.8
Total	58.9	110.1	201.1	30.0	241.4
Total banking system	149.1	291.1	670.4	100.0	349.6

Source: Bank of England, *Quarterly Bulletin*, various issues

their business by stages to a maximum of 25 percent of their total commercial business. Even though the 1986 Act allows them to compete with the services provided by banks, in 1989 Abbey National, the largest building society, chose to go public and obtained a banking license. During 1987–9, building societies significantly increased their mortgage lending (15.7 percent per year) as a result of the rise in house prices, in owner occupation, and in numbers of new households, therefore their expansion in non-mortgage activities was modest.

Discount houses

These eight firms play a unique role in the UK banking system, acting primarily as intermediaries between the Bank of England and the rest of the banking system. Most discount house funds are obtained through the short-term money market. These funds are used for investment in short-term assets.

Finance houses
These number 43 members organized through the Finance House Association (FHA), established in 1945. They control 80 percent of the installment credit business in the United Kingdom. Most of the finance houses are controlled by banks. The bulk of their funds come from their parent banks or other financial institutions. Most of their assets are loans to finance the purchase of automobiles and commercial vehicles.

Other financial institutions

The London Stock Exchange
This is the third largest stock exchange in the world, with a market value of £486 billion ($880 billion) at year-end 1989, and has long played a significant role in both the UK and in international equity finance. The so-called "Big Bang" (October, 1986) radically overhauled the standards and functions of this and other markets. Related equity markets include the USM (unlisted security market), the third tier market and the OTC (over-the-counter market).

The Bond market
With $302 billion in issues outstanding at year-end 1989, the Bond market consists overwhelmingly of central government debt (so-called gilt-edged stock), which comprised 65.0 percent of the Sterling bond market in 1989. Only 8.3 percent were corporate bonds, and virtually all of the rest (26.5 percent) consisted of Eurosterling or foreign issues.

Other markets and institutions
These include the sterling commercial paper market, which has been playing an increasingly important role since its inception in 1986; Lloyds of London, the world center for reinsurance and insurance brokerage; LIFFE, today the leading European market in futures and options; and the commodities exchanges.

The Euromarkets

London is, by many measures, the leading center for international finance, a role demonstrated by the numerous over-the-counter markets centered in the City. The London Foreign Exchange Market has long been the world's largest, although Tokyo has recently challenged that title. Nevertheless, the Eurobond, Euro-equity, Eurodeposit, and Syndicated Loan Market are clearly London-based. Because of London's role as an international center, it has even succeeded in creating meaningful markets in domestic securities of other countries. There is a large market in US treasury securities, and by some accounts more West German government bonds are traded daily out of London than in the Federal Republic of Germany.

5.1.3 Banking Product and Bank Competition

The worldwide trend of decreasing segmentation in the provision of financial services, and increasing competition among the providers of these services, is clearly evident in recent developments in the British banking system.

Retail banking

Due to their crucial role in the payments system, the clearing banks have dominated retail banking services. While the 1984 Child report deregulated the payment system and removed it from the monopoly of the clearing banks, their traditional role and extensive branch network (12,500 in 1987) have ensured continued dominance of the sector. Until recently, the clearers operated in a relatively straightforward manner: they extended short-term credit, primarily in the form of overdraft facilities and short-term unsecured lending, while funding was based on current accounts and the acceptance of deposits. However, deregulation (such as the TSB Acts of 1976 and 1978) has allowed new competition in these fields, resulting in greater pressure on the clearing banks' operating margins. The cooperative banks, National Savings bank, and National Giro bank have all made some (generally limited) inroads in the provision of personal banking services. The most serious competition has come from the building societies, which, with their large deposit base and 7,000 branches, are potentially formidable threats. Previously limited to making loans secured by real estate, the scope of their permitted activities has recently been enlarged, enabling the building societies to compete more directly for retail business. Also, the traditional self-imposed interest rate cartel, which restricted interest rate competition among the societies, was abandoned in 1983 in the face of growing competition from banks.

The clearers, for their part, have increased their range of services, and in so doing have come to resemble the universal banks common on the continent of Europe. Thus the clearers are operating credit card companies and unit trusts and are becoming active in trustee and insurance activities. One notable area of new activity is the provision of mortgages. Whereas building societies provided 90 percent of home mortgages in 1977, their share of mortgages ten years later had fallen to around 50 percent, largely as a result of competition from the clearers in the provision of home loans.

The building societies, in turn, have since 1986 been able to compete with the clearers in the provision of unsecured personal loans.

Wholesale banking

The clearing banks have vastly increased the range of services they provide to corporate customers. At one time, the clearers advanced short-term financing to provide working capital for their commercial customers, while medium- and long-term financing was the specialty of the merchant banks. Now, however, they are increasingly providing loans for periods of up to 20 years; through subsidiaries and venture capital companies the clearers are even providing equity capital to small start-up firms. As part of their transition into universal banks, the clearers have begun to enter a wide variety of allied businesses, including factoring, leasing, and payroll services.

While foreign banks have not penetrated the UK retail market to any great extent, they have enjoyed considerable success in the corporate market. By 1989 over 60 percent of loans to UK industry were extended by foreign banks, primarily to the large public companies. Another source of competition in both the corporate and retail banking sector is non-bank competition. Large non-financial corporations, such as the retail giant Marks & Spencer and British Petroleum, are beginning to offer bank-like services.

Further, the development and evolution of capital markets, especially the process of securitization, is threatening the traditional financial intermediary's activities. The growth of the sterling commercial paper market, and the introduction of mortgage backed securities in the United Kingdom, clearly threaten the long established domination of short-term business lending and home financing by banking institutions and building societies.

In March 1986 the issue of sterling commercial paper (with maturities between seven and 364 days) was allowed by the Bank, followed by similar steps a year later regarding the issue of short-term (one to five year) corporate bonds. Banks and building societies can issue short-term paper in the form of certificates of deposits. The large central government budget surplus (Public Sector Borrowing Requirement (PSBR)), and the resultant contraction in long-term government debt, suggest that the issuance of long-term corporate debt will assume meaningful proportions for the first time, further diminishing the role of traditional financial intermediaries.

Investment banking

The clearers have all taken major steps to enter the investment banking field. Primarily through a wave of acquisitions and expansion of subsidiaries prior to the big bang, all the clearers now have major international investment banking arms – Barclays de Zoete & Wedd, Lloyds Merchant Bank, Samuel Montagu (Midland), and County Bank (National Westminster). By expanding into such fields as securities underwriting and trading, funds management, and mergers and acquisitions, the UK clearers hope to both compensate for increased competition in their traditional field of commercial banking, and to obtain the depth and breadth needed to compete effectively against universal banks such as Deutsche Bank or Swiss Bank Corp. The large merchant banks have also acquired jobbers, stockbrokers, and discount houses. For example, Hambros acquired Strauss & Turnbull and S.G. Warburg acquired Akroyd & Smithers and Rowe & Pitman. The downturn in investment banking activity and the securities markets since 1987 has produced disappointing results in this area. Nowadays, there is a marked tendency for banks to restrict their activities or even to withdraw entirely from the field.

5.1.4 International Involvement

London has long been, and still remains today, the preeminent international banking center. Originating in medieval times, when London's role as a trading center attracted money lenders and merchant bankers, continuing through the colonial period when the British Empire's financial activities were concentrated in the city, until emergence as the home of the Euromarket in the 1970s, the level of international banking activity conducted in London has always been substantial. British banks, including the clearers, the merchant banks and British overseas banks (a descriptive category comprising banks, such as Standard Chartered and Grindlays, which, although headquartered in London, conducted most of their business overseas), began their international activities in the fields of international trade financing, documentary credits, export/import financing, and essential services such as foreign exchange and money transmission.

Colonies and Commonwealth countries alike provided a natural base for the establishment of branch networks abroad, a path followed most intensively by Barclays bank, while Lloyds bank concentrated on Europe and Latin America. Particularly rapid growth followed the oil price shocks of 1973 and 1978, in which commercial banks played a primary role in the international intermediation of funds – petrodollar recycling. London's already well developed financial center, the advantages of fairly lenient tax treatment, and the relative lack of regulation, ensured that it would become the site for the bulk of the vast growth in international financial activity which followed. This included the phenomenal growth in the Eurodeposit, and later the Eurosecurities, markets. The UK banks engaged in their share of the business, with Natwest and Midland joining Barclays and Lloyds in establishing overseas networks, most notably through acquisitions in the United States.

The slide in oil prices that began in the early 1980s, however, and the emergence of the debt crisis in 1982 took some of the bloom off international lending, and the Third World debt exposure of British banks became a matter of considerable concern. The decreasing profitability of overseas operations, including Midland's one billion sterling loss in its acquisition of Crocker National Bank in California, led to considerable rethinking of their strategic plans by UK banks, and a renewed emphasis on their domestic markets. The securitization of international finance, which saw traditional syndicated loans decrease in importance relative to securitized assets such as FRNs (floating rate notes), Eurobonds and NIFs (note issuance facilities), led British banks to place greater emphasis on trading and dealing activities centered in London, with less reliance on overseas branch networks engaged in more traditional banking activities.

While UK banks appear to be de-emphasizing their overseas activities, London appears to have lost little of its attraction to foreign banks. Despite some loss of market share, primarily to Japan's offshore market, London remains by far the world's foremost single center for international bankers. At year-end 1989, some 530 foreign banks were represented in London, 512 directly and 18 indirectly (primarily through consortium banks). All of the largest 100 banks in the world are present in London, with some 72,000 people employed by foreign banks. While most foreign banks have concentrated on wholesale banking and corporate finance, some have used ethnic ties to develop a retail presence. Citibank has made a determined effort to develop a broad-based retail network, although it is now apparently reconsidering this strategy. A number of foreign banks, primarily American, have made inroads into the mortgage market. The concentration and share of foreign bank activity in the wholesale market can be gleaned from comparing their 20.3 percent share of sterling deposits to their 50.8 percent share of total liabilities (table 5.4). It is estimated that, in 1989 foreign banks accounted for 80 percent of international claims booked in the United Kingdom, and about 43 percent of claims in the UK private sector.

As the importance of securities issuance, trading, and corporate finance (funds management, mergers and acquisition, and advisory work) grows

Table 5.3 International investment of the UK banking system

	1980	1984	1989	% change 1980–9
A Foreign banks				
Total assets, bil. pounds	174	488	730	319.5
Sterling deposits, bil. pounds	20	44.8	136	580.0

B Banks and other financial institutions: external liabilities and claim analysis by currency and sector

	Liabilities		Claims (assets)	
	1984	1989	1984	1989
	(US$ billions)			
Currencies				
Sterling	35.2	118.9	27.0	73.7
US dollars	406.9	533.5	366.8	500.5
Deutschmarks	36.6	133.3	39.6	118.5
Swiss francs	16.2	33.0	19.2	39.9
Japanese yen	12.6	90.3	13.9	106.5
Other currencies	24.0	118.9	22.8	84.8
Total	531.5	1,027.9	489.3	923.9
Sector				
Central monetary instit.	53.6	93.4	13.0	21.5
Other banks	331.5	657.3	331.5	682.2
Other non-residents	146.4	252.3	144.8	220.2
Securities	–	24.9	–	–
Total	531.5	1,027.9	489.3	923.9

Source: Bank of England, *Quarterly Bulletin*, various issues

and to some extent supplants traditional banking activities (deposit taking and lending), London offers other attractions. Banks that are not permitted to engage in certain activities at home, foremost among them the US and Japanese banks, can develop expertise and a base in the loosely regulated Eurobond, Euro-equity, and Euro-CP markets based in London. Moreover, even the universal banks of Switzerland, the Federal Republic of Germany, and France find it advantageous to be active in the efficient, relatively unregulated London-based markets, rather than remain in their comparatively undeveloped and somewhat dormant domestic markets. In this regard, the concentration of some 120 securities houses in London, and its emergence as one of the centers of the international securities markets, is of some note. The eventual effect of a single, unified European market for financial services in 1992 cannot yet be judged, but it obviously figures highly in the formulation of business strategy for UK banks in the years ahead.

5.2 The Regulatory Environment

5.2.1 The Regulatory Framework

Until quite recently there was relatively little statutory provision for banking supervision in the United Kingdom, with even the definition of a bank for regulatory purposes being very unclear. The Bank of England ("The Bank"), due to its centrality to the British banking system, maintained a rather informal supervisory system characterized by "moral suasion" – constant discussion with bank management, consultation on specific problems, and the use of "gentlemanly persuasion" should the need arise. The system was notable for its considerable reliance upon self regulation by the institutions concerned. There was very little in the way of formal regulation, mandatory rules, or prescribed codes. While this uniquely British approach worked very well for a long period of time, the accelerating pace of developments in financial markets in recent years made the adoption of a more formal and coherent regulatory structure highly desirable. More specific impetus was provided by the secondary banking crisis of 1973–5 and the collapse of Johnson Matthey Bankers (JMB) in 1984, which made further banking legislation virtually inevitable. While there were many developments in supervision in the past two decades, the form and context of bank regulation today is largely the result of two pieces of legislation intended to define and codify broad ranges of activities: the Banking Act of 1987, and the Financial Services Act of 1986.

The Banking Acts of 1974 and 1987 formalized the Bank of England's duties as regulator of the banking industry and mandated the establishment of the Board of Banking Supervision, an advisory panel authorized to oversee all areas of banking supervision. They also established independent reviews; reports by accountants who answered directly to the Bank of England; audits of statistics; and internal control systems. Additionally, they allowed a role for the Treasury in bank supervision.

In September 1987, the Bank published a guide to banking supervision, which summarized the relevant provisions and provided guidance on the manner in which supervision would be conducted. In the words of the Bank:

> The Bank's supervisory system is based on regular discussion with management of the financial information contained in prudential/statistical returns. These discussions assist the bank in its assessment of the quality of management and in satisfying itself that each authorized institution continues to conduct its business prudently and to meet other criteria.[3]

Through this act, the Bank established the quantity, content, and frequency of the returns and enforced penalties where relevant. In 1988–9, 551 authorized institutions submitted reports, and over 3,000 "interviews" (the regular discussions mentioned above) were held, including visits to branches of UK banks abroad and head offices of foreign banks that maintain offices in the United Kingdom. More thorough contacts include visits, reviews, and statutory investigations. In 1989–90, there were 116 review team visits to subsidiaries and branches of foreign banks. Further, the Bank is responsible for the authorization of new institutions (26 in 1988–89), for surrenders of authorization, and for revocations or restrictions.

The supervision of UK branches of foreign banks is in accordance with the Basle Concordat, which prescribes shared responsibility. Thus the Bank monitors the UK branch, while relying on the home supervisor to monitor the capital adequacy and management of the bank as a whole. Nevertheless, the Banking Act authorizes the Bank to take a wide range of positions, depending on its evaluation of the home supervisor, from total reliance to near total disregard.

The Financial Services Act of 1986 was intended to ensure the safety and protection of the investor. It set up a large and somewhat complex network of Self Regulatory Organizations (SROs), meant to authorize and supervise participation in various financial services (securities dealing, insurance, futures, and options, etc.). The various SROs in turn report to the Securities and Investment Board (SIB), which has the specific authority to ensure investor protection. While not specifically dealing with banks, the Act does affect many areas of banking business: wholesale market dealing (foreign exchange, precious metals); portfolio management; securities dealing; and advisory services.

The 1986 Building Societies Act, which came into effect in January 1987, provides for the creation of a Building Societies Commission responsible for supervising the societies. The Act allowed the societies to purchase in the wholesale financial markets up to 20 percent of borrowed funds, which was increased to 40 percent in 1988. The new Act also allows societies to extend

Table 5.4 Major items in the balance sheet of domestic banks (pounds sterling bil.)

		Sterling assets and liabilities							*Other currencies*				
Type of banks	*Total balance sheet*	*UK private sector deposits*	*%*	*Interbank deposits*	*CDs*	*Money market loans*	*UK private sector advances*	*%*	*Overseas deposits*	*%*	*UK private sector advances*	*Overseas loans*	*%*
A Commercial banks													
Retail banks													
1980	73.0	40.9	38.6	1.7	1.8	8.3	29.5	33.2	8.6	6.9	0.9	6.9	5.1
1984	152.9	72.0	37.4	10.1	5.7	19.7	64.2	35.3	21.6	6.4	3.9	17.4	4.7
1988	283.0	137.4	39.9	20.2	12.0	39.0	147.9	37.7	26.4	7.1	7.6	30.4	7.5
1989	391.7	197.8	48.7	25.2	15.6	47.4	207.6	43.8	40.3	8.8	12.2	46.7	9.8
Merchant banks													
1980	12.8	3.0	2.8	1.4	0.3	3.1	1.6	1.8	3.7	3.0	0.4	3.5	2.6
1984	26.6	6.1	3.2	1.7	0.8	6.3	2.8	1.5	7.4	2.2	1.0	7.4	2.0
1988	42.2	13.0	3.8	6.2	2.4	15.5	7.8	2.0	7.2	1.9	1.3	8.1	2.0
1989	51.5	14.1	3.5	10.2	2.2	16.2	11.5	2.4	8.3	1.8	2.0	10.2	2.2
Other British banks													
1980	43.0	6.9	6.5	5.6	1.0	8.5	7.4	8.3	13.6	11.0	1.9	15.3	11.4
1984	91.8	8.4	4.4	13.9	1.2	13.0	17.4	9.5	31.0	9.2	3.9	38.8	10.5
1988	74.6	15.3	4.4	13.7	4.0	18.2	26.7	6.8	11.1	3.0	2.2	15.6	3.9
1989	61.0	14.0	3.5	16.3	1.5	13.2	29.8	6.3	7.3	1.6	1.2	7.7	1.6
B Foreign banks													
American banks													
1980	60.0	2.2	2.1	3.3	1.8	3.1	4.4	5.0	31.6	25.5	2.4	37.6	28.0
1984	116.3	2.5	1.3	4.0	1.1	4.8	5.9	3.2	60.2	17.9	10.0	77.5	20.8
1988	96.7	4.9	1.4	3.6	1.4	4.9	9.7	2.5	47.7	12.8	15.6	51.9	12.8
[illegible]	[illegible]	[illegible]	[illegible]	[illegible]	[illegible]	7.6	[illegible]	2.1	50.2	12.9	22.0	60.6	12.8

1980	40.8	–		0.8	–	0.4	0.4	0.5	24.2	19.5	1.0	28.2	21.0
1984	167.6	0.7	0.4	4.7	0.8	4.5	1.0	0.5	96.4	28.6	5.3	111.3	30.0
1988	245.9	5.7	1.7	9.4	6.2	14.4	8.1	2.1	143.3	38.3	11.9	169.8	42.0
1989	281.9	7.6	1.9	11.3	8.2	15.2	13.4	2.8	169.3	36.9	17.5	189.8	40.1
Other foreign banks[a]													
1980	73.6	1.9	1.8	4.7	0.8	5.7	3.1	3.5	42.2	34.1	2.0	42.7	31.9
1984	204.7	5.3	2.7	8.7	1.5	13.8	9.4	5.1	120.1	35.7	9.6	118.8	32.0
1988	275.0	13.6	4.0	19.8	11.7	31.6	36.0	9.2	137.8	36.8	18.0	128.3	31.8
1989	329.3	18.6	4.6	22.7	14.0	33.7	46.0	9.7	172.9	37.6	23.0	158.6	33.5
C Other deposit taking institutes													
Discount houses													
1980	5.2	0.3	0.3	4.8	–	5.2	–	–	–	–			
1984	8.1	1.2	0.6	6.1	–	7.7	–	–	–	–			
1988	12.0	3.3	1.0	8.2	–	11.8	–	–	–	–			
1989	15.3	4.4	1.1	10.4		14.6	–	–	–	–			
Building societies													
1980	53.8	50.7	47.9	0.3	0.5	8.9	42.4[c]	47.7	–	–	–		
1984	102.7	96.5	50.0	0.4[d]	0.8	15.7	81.9	44.9	–	–	–		
1988	192.0	150.8[b]	43.8	8.9	4.4	20.5	156.4	39.7	0.4	0.1	–		
1989[e]	188.6	142.7	35.2	11.0	5.6	20.7	156.2	32.9	2.0	0.4			
Total banking system													
1980	362.2	105.9	100.0	22.6	6.2	43.2	88.8	100.0	123.9	100.0	8.6	134.2	100.0
1984	870.7	192.7	100.0	49.6	11.9	85.5	182.6	100.0	336.7	100.0	33.7	371.2	100.0
1988	1,221.4	344.0	100.0	90.0	42.1	155.9	392.6	100.0	373.9	100.0	56.6	404.1	100.0
1989	1,438.0	405.2	100.0	111.1	48.4	168.6	474.5	100.0	459.3	100.0	77.9	473.6	100.0

[a] Including consortium banks.
[b] Including shares and deposits.
[c] Mortgages.
[d] Estimated.
[e] In 1989, Abbey National Bank was reclassified from building society to retail bank.

Source: Bank of England *Quarterly Bulletin*, various issues

their traditional role of providing loans secured on a first mortgage of residential property, by making unsecured loans if they have commercial assets (total assets, less fixed assets) of more than 100 million pounds, up to 10 percent of a society's commercial assets. These rules open up new diversification possibilities for the societies.

The philosophy behind the regulatory approach in the United Kingdom is that during rapid changes in the marketplace, regulation by function rather than restriction on activities is the best way to oversee the financial services industry. This institutional expansion into other markets has increased actual and potential competition, and has increased stability, by not limiting exposure to risk to only one line of business. The influx of foreign financial institutions, has further increased the competition and strength of these markets.

At the end of 1987, the joint UK/US proposals for international convergence of capital measurement and standards were superseded by those drawn up by the Basle Supervisors Committee. The proposals dealt with a common definition of capital; a common system of risk weights for all balance sheet and off-balance-sheet items; and a standard minimum level of risk adjusted capital. This minimum was set to reach 8 percent by the end of 1992. As a member of the EC, UK banks are affected by the proposals included in the plans for the completion of the Community's internal market in 1992. As of 1988, the British criteria met EC minimum standards concerning such items as large exposures, deposit protection arrangements, and consolidation. By the end of 1989, the United Kingdom had also taken all the necessary measures to implement the EC's Own Funds and Solvency Ratio directives, which affect all banks in the member state, and not only international banks to which the Basle Agreement applies.

5.2.2 Major Bank Regulations

The traditional approach to bank supervision in the United Kingdom was based on cooperation and frequent consultation between the Bank and senior management of commercial banks. The supervisory system developed through a framework of prudential guidelines and extensive general reporting requirements, rather than specific rules. A fundamental precept of the Bank's approach to supervision has long been that the banking system should be able, subject to the satisfaction of basic prudential guidelines, to accommodate rather than to restrict different kinds of banking business. The application of this philosophy has been severely criticized in light of the banking crisis (1973–5) and the collapse of Johnson Matthey

Bankers in 1984. Since 1975, the Bank of England has issued formal prudential regulations for the UK banking system, and the Banking Acts of 1979 and 1987 provided for a number of new areas of supervision.

Scope of activities

Recently banking management has diversified into non-banking activities such as insurance, asset management, and estate management. By tradition and regulation, the UK clearing banks were not broadly active in key capital market activities. But with the Big Bang of deregulation in October 1986, banks have been able to raise their holdings in Stock Exchange member firms over the previous limit of 29.9 percent and, in most cases, have chosen to make 100 percent acquisition. The Clearing banks had a competitive advantage in this area because of their extensive branch distribution system.

The deregulation also helped banks to produce impressive improvements in the share of non-interest income of total income to 37 percent in 1988 (it was 26 percent in 1983).

The scope of permitted activities and investment

The United Kingdom's banking law generally imposes no restrictions on the activities in which banks may engage or the investments they may make. It should be noted that, although there are no formal general limits on investments, they are subject to case-by-case limits if they are significant in a bank's portfolio. Accordingly:

- Retail banks may engage in securities activities, most of which are carried out through subsidiaries. Merchant banks also traditionally have the power to accept deposits and engage in commercial banking.
- Banks may also make investments in companies, including those that are wholly-owned, which engage in insurance brokerage and underwriting activities. Banks have systematically expanded into this field.
- Banks are also permitted to engage in real estate activities, including investing in and developing real estate and acting as a real-estate broker. Bank expansion in this field has also typically been accomplished through subsidiaries.
- There are no statutory limitations on investment in industrial companies.

Lending limitations (large exposure)

The 1987 Banking Act introduced for the first time a legal requirement for approval of large exposures (after April 1, 1988), including notification of the following:

- a transaction (broadly interpreted) with a single borrower that exposes the bank to the risk of losing 10 percent of its equity capital;

- a prior notice of proposed transactions putting the bank at risk for 25 percent or more of its capital. The Bank policy is that the exposure should be very exceptional (e.g., overseas central banks).

Exposures are normally supervised on a group basis. The notification requirements apply to banks whose principal place of business is in the United Kingdom. The principle as far as possible, is to be applied to UK branches of overseas banks.

Liquidity

The Bank does not seek to impose a standard ratio of liquidity, but instead takes into account the particular circumstances of each institution and its place within the banking system. In the supervisory note of July 1982, the Bank emphasized its intention that banks should apply a prudent combination of liquidity measures, including holding liquid assets, making a future profile of cash flows, and maintaining an adequate deposit base. Liquidity measurement is based on a cash flow approach. Liabilities and assets are matched on a "maturity ladder," with their net mismatch positions used as a measure of the liquidity position.

The consultative papers issued in 1986 and 1988 differ from the earlier proposals by drawing a distinction between assets and liabilities in sterling and other currencies. The Bank proposes to set Tier 1 and Tier 2 liquid assets against a bank's gross liabilities at sight (up to eight days). Tier 1 assets are included without limit. Tier 2 is defined as liquid assets that are risky within a limit, and hence are accepted to a certain extent (a conversion factor of 20 percent). The Tier 2 liquid asset comprises only readily realizable assets with low credit risk, such as the Bank or other monetary authorities would be prepared to purchase.

As can be seen, liquidity requirements are informal. They intend by a broad margin to ensure liquidity and limit interest rate risk, without imposing a "monetary tax." Therefore, this factor cannot explain the relatively large interest margins in the UK banking system.

After issuance of the 1988 consultative paper, and in view of the possibility that any new requirement would have to be later adjusted to EC policy, the Bank decided not to introduce any new requirements. Rather, it chose to strengthen its assessment on the adequacy of bank liquidity on the basis of the 1982 Measurement of Liquidity notice.

Capital adequacy

The Bank of England regards the maintenance of adequate capital as the cornerstone of sound banking. In December 1987, the Committee on Banking Regulations and Supervisory Practices (the Cooke Committee) at the Bank for International Settlements (BIS) issued a consultative paper entitled "Proposals for international convergence of capital measurement and capital standards." These proposals will, in due course, ensure that the different types of risks carried on both balance sheet and off-balance-sheet activities will be included in the measuring of capital adequacy. The capital adequacy framework, which has emerged from the discussions in the BIS and the EC Second Banking Directive, were implemented by the Bank of England's "explanatory paper." The Bank emphasized that the 8 percent standard contained in the proposal is a minimum, and that in the great majority of cases the ratios agreed upon for individual banks are expected to exceed this percentage. The detailed timetable of the BIS proposals is for full implementation to be achieved by the end of 1992. In October 1988, the Bank set out how it would apply the framework to UK-incorporated banks. The Basle Convergence Agreement was implemented in the United Kingdom at the end of December 1989, on both a consolidated and an unconsolidated basis. The Bank did not take the option to adopt a transitional period until year-end 1992, except for implementation of general provisions in Tier 2 capital. The European Commission's parallel work on the Own Funds and Solvency Ratio Directives appear likely to result in a very similar framework.

The BIS proposals include three basic parts:

- *The constitution of capital* – Core (primary) capital must make up at least 50 percent of the total capital base. Supplementary capital consists of undisclosed reserves, revaluation reserves, general loan loss reserves up to 1.25 percent of risk assets, hybrid debt capital instruments, subordinated term debt up to 50 percent of core capital while deductions from the capital base, goodwill, and any investment in subsidiaries engaged in banking and financial activities.
- *The risk weights* – Five risk weights are to be used, namely 0 percent, 10 percent, 20 percent, 50 percent, and 100 percent. The weightings assigned to the on-balance-sheet assets are based primarily on credit risk. The proposed risk weights differ in a number of respects from those currently applied by the Bank, notably in the greater recognition given to the risk-reducing effect of collateral and guarantees and the lower weights proposed for residential mortgages and land premises. Risks of the full range of off-balance-sheet business are included for the first time.
- *A target standard ratio* – The minimum proposed ratio for all international banks is 8 percent, of which the core capital element must be at least 4 percent (transitional arrangements will, however, apply until year-end 1992). The Bank will require all UK banks to meet these minimum standards.

In aggregate, large British banks are likely to have the capacity to meet at the outset the minimum standards agreed upon under the Basle convergence proposals. The Building Societies Commission's approach to capital adequacy is essentially a form of risk assets formula. The required ratio is slightly higher, to reflect their exposure to interest rate risk and the fact that the societies are less diversified.

Foreign exchange exposure

The Bank of England supervisory notice on foreign currency exposure of April 1981, sets out the basis for measuring and monitoring bank exposure to movements in exchange rates. Although such exposure is only one of the many types of risks in banking, the Bank considers that, because of the short time scale in which significant losses can be incurred, special arrangements are justified for these exposures. The Bank therefore made a distinction between dealing positions arising from "normal" banking operations and those structural positions intended to be of a long-term nature, and arising from activities such as loan capital and investment in subsidiaries. The guidelines are expressed in terms of the relationship between the dealing position and individual bank capital. As a general rule, for banks experienced in foreign exchange the Bank will impose the following guidelines:

- The net open dealing position in any one currency is to be no more than 10 percent of the adjusted capital base, as defined in the paper "The Measurement of Capital."
- The net short open dealing positions of all currencies taken together are to be no more than 15 percent of the adjusted capital base.

Overseas branches of UK-incorporated banks are to be included in these arrangements, and the Bank intends in due course to include both domestic and overseas subsidiaries on a consolidated basis. For UK branches of foreign banks, the main responsibility for supervision rests with the home country supervisory authority.

Foreign currency exposure reports are to be made to the Bank on a monthly basis. The records are to include the net spot and forward long or short position in each currency at the close of business on the reporting day. The Bank recognizes that an anticipated flow of income and expense can give rise to exposure to interest rate risk in that currency. Such exposure, insofar as it is determinable, should in principle be measured. In calculating the dealing limits of a covered position, currency swaps and structural positions are excluded. An April 1984 explanatory note details the Bank's policy on foreign currency options, which should be included in the measurement of foreign currency exposure, within existing guidelines. The Bank has developed its own formula for measuring the extent of exposure on currency options.

As can be seen, regulators devote considerable effort to measure and monitor foreign currency exposure. This is due to the involvement of UK banks in international banking and to the fact that London serves as an important international center.

Country debt provisions – the Bank's matrix

The Bank has concentrated on ensuring that banks have adequate capital for the risks they run. Concomitantly the Bank has consistently shown itself unwilling to specify publicly how much banks should provide against their problem country exposure, leaving the question to the bank management and auditors. Acting alone, during 1987 the large British banks significantly increased their provisions from 25 percent to 35 percent of their exposure to problem countries. However, in August 1987, the Bank did circulate to UK banks a matrix it had devised to assist the banks in their calculation of appropriate reserve levels. The particular virtue of the matrix is that it provides common parameters by which an assessment can be made. The matrix identifies a range of factors that point to the likelihood of a partial or total failure to repay, based on a scoring system. A country is scored against a total of 15 different criteria, with different weightings divided into three categories:

"A" factors, evidencing a borrower's inability or unwillingness to meet its debt services obligations (e.g., two or more reschedulings);

"B" factors, evidencing a borrower's current debt service problems (e.g., arrears of interest on original and rescheduled loans from other external creditors);

"C" factors, covering a range of economic and other indicators of future performance (e.g., the debt service ratio).

The scores for each item are summed to provide an overall country score, which is then translated into an appropriate provisions range. The Bank updates the scores from time to time. By working within the matrix guidelines, the five largest British banks have significantly increased their provisions to an average level of around 30 percent of problem country exposure in 1987 and 60 percent in 1989. The matrix scores are periodically reviewed and provide a common reference point for banks when discussing provision levels with their auditors, the Inland Revenue, and the Bank itself. In 1989, a revised matrix was introduced, which retains the basic structure of the previous one, with a few technical and implemental changes.

In some cases the provision has created tax losses, and banks in turn have created a deferred tax asset to recognize the carry forward of losses. The Bank is now considering whether shareholder funds represented by deferred tax assets should be included in equity capital.

UK branches of overseas banks

The Banking Act of 1987 empowered the Bank to rely on the home supervisory authority in monitoring UK branches of overseas banks. Thus, the Bank may be satisfied that its requirements have been met if the supervisory authority in the home country covers these issues and the overall soundness of the bank. In accordance with the Basle Concordat,[4] the Bank monitors the activities of the UK branch while relying on the home supervisor to monitor capital adequacy and management as a whole.

Two regulations of note

Ownership and control of banks

Over the past few years, control of a number of UK banks has changed hands. The Bank's presumption is that there will remain a strong and continued British presence in the banking system of the United Kingdom. The 1987 Banking Act gives the Bank authority to object to the takeover of British banks by foreigners in the interest of depositors, in the same manner that they may block any control considered not fit or proper.

Loan transfer and securitization

British banks have shown growing interest in developing schemes for transferring risk, such as through the sale of individual loans and the packaging, securitizing and sale of residential mortgages. In December 1987, the Bank published a consultative paper entitled "Loan Transfer and Securitization." This paper described the most common forms of transfer, analyzed the legal position underlying such transactions, and looked at the general principles for determining the risk asset ratio treatment in each case. In February 1989, the Bank issued a policy notice including criteria for excluding a single loan or pool of loans sold from a bank's balance sheet. It also requires that a bank may not provide liquidity support to its vehicles, nor intentionally bear an interest rate risk arising from the scheme.

5.2.3 Foreign Exchange Control

There are currently no restrictions on capital flows out of the United Kingdom. All such controls were abolished in 1979, and there are now:

- no restrictions on borrowing from abroad
- no restrictions on direct investments. Proposed mergers may be subject to approval by the Monopolies and Merger Commission
- no restrictions on the repatriation of investments.

The United Kingdom has traditionally taken a liberal attitude toward issuing licenses for operations within the banking sector. Foreign branches and representative offices are viewed as an integral part of their parent institutions and are not required to maintain dedicated capital for their UK operations.

5.2.4 *Key Accounting Issues*

Consolidation

Standard accounting practice maintains that the group account should be prepared in the form of a single set of consolidated financial statements covering the holding company and its subsidiary abroad. Dissimilarity of business, lack of control, or temporary control justify the exclusion of a subsidiary.

The following matters are also worthy of consideration:

- Uniform accounting policies should be followed by the group;
- Common accounting dates should be used.

Foreign exchange

Accounting for foreign currency translation is dealt with in the Statement of Standard Accounting Practice (SSAP) 20. This standard attempts to compromise between the two underlying concepts invoked in the consolidation of a foreign subsidiary: the temporal basis (FAS 82 in the United States), and the closing rate basis (FAS 52 in the United States). Therefore, foreign assets and liabilities are translated at the closing rate revenue items, and are translated at the average rate for the year or closing rate. Any difference arising from the translation is transferred to reserves and must be disclosed. This standard does not deal with the method of calculating profits or losses arising from a bank's normal currency dealing operation.

The standard provides that monetary assets and liabilities maintained in foreign currencies are to be translated at exchange rates current at the balance sheet date, or at the rate at which the transaction is contracted. Any differences must be taken to the profit and loss account.

Loan losses and provisions for doubtful loans

As a matter of prudent financial policy, banks will make provisions against bad and doubtful debts. This is normally assessed on a case by-case basis. A *specific provision* is raised against each loan where it is anticipated that there will be a loss, after taking into account the value of any security held. The distinction between specific and general provisions is important for tax purposes. Normally, the Inland Revenue will allow specific loan loss provisions as a deduction.

The general provision revealed a fair amount of confusion in defining such concepts as "unidentified banking risks" and the extent to which this provision should be presented net of the tax relief, since it is not a short-term timing difference.

In the case of consumer credit, due to the large number of loans it is impractical to evaluate each loan separately. The provision required is instead to be calculated using a statistical formula based on past experience. Where interest on the loan is not likely to be collected, either a provision will be raised against the likely loss or the interest will not be credited to income. Banks differ considerably in the stage at which the charge-off loans are implemented. Finally, the assessment of the potential loss and the appropriate "general" and "specific" provisions are always to be a management decision.

Deferred tax

Accounting for deferred taxation is dealt with in the Statement of Standard Accounting Practice 15. This standard has had the most effect on the accounts of the major British banks. It determines that deferred taxation, using the liability method, be provided where the timing difference that gave rise to the deferral is likely to be reversed in the foreseeable future (short-term timing differences).

British banks have taken (through subsidiaries) substantial advantage of the tax "shelter" afforded by asset leasing. Until SSAP 15 was adopted, considerable deferred tax liabilities were built up. SSAP 15 allowed British banks to release a large part of these liabilities (long-term timing differences). However, a slowing down in asset-leasing can increase tax payment by banks.

5.2.5 *Taxation*

Corporate tax rates

The rate of corporation tax is set by each year's Finance Act. A company pays corporation tax at a single rate on all its profits, whether distributed or undistributed. For the year ended March 31, 1989, the corporation tax rate was 35 percent. There is a reduced rate of corporation tax (25 percent) for UK resident companies whose annual profits do not exceed 100,000 pounds sterling.

Losses

Losses incurred in trading may be relieved in the following ways:

- set against other income and capital gains arising in the same year
- used to offset profits in the preceding year set against profits of the same trade in future years, such carry forward being without time limit
- surrendered as "group relief," i.e., to be offset against the income or gains of other companies in the same group. It is required that the surrendering claimant companies are resident in the United Kingdom, and that not less than 75 percent of the share capital of each is directly or indirectly owned by the same UK corporate entity.

Loan loss reserves

Only a provision for loan loss allocated against specific bad or doubtful loans is deductible for tax purposes, whereas a general provision is not tax deductible. The Inland Revenue is entitled to check all relevant facts to examine the validity of the provision. Circumstances could arise whereby a specific provision would be allowable for tax purposes because, although the maturity date of the debt has not been reached, it is unlikely that the loan will ever be repaid.

The Inland Revenue has stated that specific provisions against foreign risk debt will be allowed, if they can be justified under normal criteria governing loan loss provisions. In 1987, the Bank issued a matrix formula that banks were required to follow, to determine levels of provision on a country by country basis. The Inland Revenue is accepting provisions based on the matrix for tax purposes.

Interest paid and received

Interest paid is tax exempt, if payable in the United Kingdom from another bank carrying on "arms length" banking business in the United Kingdom, or payable by a bank carrying on arms length banking business in the United Kingdom in the ordinary course of business. Interest would not be considered if it arose on a debt forming part of the capital structure, such as subordinated debt. In such cases income tax must be withheld at the basic rate, currently 25 percent. A bank is required to deduct income tax at a composite rate of 23.25 percent from interest paid to individuals ordinarily resident in the United Kingdom (with certain exceptions).

Annual interest paid by a UK resident company must normally be subjected to withholding tax at the basic rate of 25 percent. However, for interest paid in the United Kingdom on an advance from a bank there is no requirement to withhold income tax. Short-term interest (in a loan for less than a year) and interest paid by individuals are not subject to withholding tax.

Other taxes

Advance Corporation Tax (ACT)

The United Kingdom operates an imputation system, under which part of a UK resident company's corporation tax liabilities can be credited against a UK resident shareholders' liability to income tax on "qualifying distribution" paid by the company (e.g., a cash dividend). For example, when a UK resident company pays a dividend of 150 pounds and the basic tax rate is 25 percent, the ACT will be 50 pounds (25 percent of (150 + 50 pounds)). A UK resident individual shareholder is entitled to a tax credit of 50 pounds and is liable for an income tax of 200 pounds. There are circumstances under which ACT can report an additional tax liability, in particular when a UK resident company paying a dividend would not otherwise be liable to corporation tax.

Value Added Tax (VAT)

VAT is chargeable at two rates: the standard rate of 15 percent and the zero rate. Most bank transactions, such as loans and credit, dealing in money, financial guarantees, etc., are exempted.

5.3 Bank Performance

The UK financial system has experienced rapid structural change since the early 1980s. This change has been the result of both increased uncertainty caused by the volatility of interest and exchange rates, and the general economic recession of the early 1980s. UK banks have placed more emphasis on asset and liability management, and have had to obtain an increasing share of their funds from the wholesale money market. Substantial changes have also occurred in the provision of retail financial services, particularly regarding the increased competition between banks and building societies in the housing mortgage market.

5.3.1 *Structure of Assets and Liabilities*

Retail banks

The retail banking sector includes about 13,500 branches and the National Giro, a state-operated giro system that operates through 22,000 Post Offices. The basic functions of the retail (clearing) banks are money transmission, deposits, lending, international business, and financial services. Retail bank share of total assets of the banking system at year-end 1989 was 27.2 percent with 39.7 percent of total Sterling deposits. Competition from other institutions has led to higher rates in recent years (the retail group attracts 48.8 percent of all private sector deposits). The sector operates 10,800 ATMs for money transmission services.

The lending operations of the retail banking sector are concentrated on short-term loans. However, retail banks have recently moved into medium- and long-term lending. In the area of personal lending, changes have been especially significant, with the December 1989 balance of personal lending by retail banks amounting to 43 billion pounds, about 25 percent of the UK market.

The reliance of retail banks on the personal borrower for a substantial proportion of their income continues to bring them into competition with the building societies. Major structural changes have occurred in the composition of the loan portfolio, with a reduction in international lending and an increase in personal lending. Additionally, the provision of financial services has been the largest growth area for the retail banks. Such services include unit trusts, personal equity plans and portfolio management. All major banks also operate merchant bank subsidiaries.

Merchant banks (accepting houses)

Merchant banking covers a variety of activities, such as international banking and investment management (pension funds, insurance companies etc.) The widely held perception at the time of the Big Bang that successful British merchant banks would need to become integrated global houses has not yet proved to be the case. The intermediation of this group is mostly in wholesale markets.

Foreign banks

Most foreign banks concentrate on international banking, the wholesale markets, and capital markets. There has been a steady increase in foreign bank engagement in domestic business. Their UK private sector advances have increased from 13.3 billion pounds in 1980 to 131.9 billion pounds in 1989 (table 5.4). Foreign banks have been very active in the housing mortgage market. During the period examined, American banks grew at a much slower rate than Japanese and other foreign banks. Hence, the market share of Japanese banks has increased at the expense of American banks. Japanese foreign banks are characterized as net borrowers in the London market; the funds raised are used in subsidiaries around the world. Japanese banks operate mainly in the non-sterling money markets and in corporate lending.

The claims of Japanese banks on their own offices outside the UK stood at $63 billion at the end of September 1987,5 and the amount of funds from other Japanese banks outside the UK totalled $110.4 billion (net borrowing of $47 billion). Japanese banks as a group are also major players on both sides of the interbank market (claims $39 billion, liabilities $58.6 billion). Lending to UK non-bank residents is small (8.1 billion pounds sterling at year-end 1988), representing 5.6 percent of total lending by UK financial institutions (1 percent at year-end 1980). Japanese banks lend mainly to Japanese trading companies doing business in the UK, to building societies, and to securities dealers.

Building societies

The major source of funds for building societies is comprised of shares and deposits from the public (79 percent of total assets), (table 5.4). The building societies operate about 7,000 branches; their share of UK private sector deposits is 41 percent of this market. The retail market is increasingly innovative, with the building societies and other financial institutions offering a wide range of products. Building societies concentrate on long-term larger wholesale deposits which increase their funding costs. The competition between banks and building societies has intensified following deregulation and the Building Societies Act. This Act enables societies to expand their activities into unsecured lending, credit cards, and investment services. Also, since 1986 building societies have been allowed to borrow wholesale up to 20 percent of their overall funding (eventually increasing to 40 percent). Wholesale borrowing at year-end 1989 reached about 18.2 percent of total assets. As a result, the demarcation between retail bank and building society activity was progressively eroded in the 1980s.

The building societies finance mortgage lending by retail and wholesale borrowing. Their ability (particularly since 1983) to tap a variety of wholesale sources of funds has given the societies greater flexibility in funding and liquidity management. The wholesale borrowing of this group as a percentage of other liabilities has increased from 1.5 percent in 1980 to 18.2 percent at-year end 1989. The popular wholesale funding includes bond issue, floating rate notes, and CDs.

Discount houses

Discount houses serve mostly as intermediaries in both the wholesale market and international trade finance. The activity of discount houses is predominantly in the wholesale markets, where they are subject to interest rate risk.

5.3.2 Income Statements

The sharp deterioration in the property markets and the corporate sector in 1989, together with the worsening of the position of some problematic sovereign-debtors, led to a substantial regression of bank profitability. Large banks still saw some growth in trading profit, but small banks were not able to cope with increased competition.

The performance of large UK banks is presented in table 5.5 for 1985–9. There was steady growth in the return on equity and on total assets until the sharp downturn in 1989. Allowance for the provision of doubtful South American debts was made mostly in 1987 and 1989 and had a significant impact on these years' results. Net interest income increased during this period 43.3 percent; the increase in average earning assets was about the same. The decline in net spread occurred despite the change in the composition of the loan portfolio, which constituted a reduction in international loans and an increase in retail lending.

Non-interest income increased by 90.0 percent, mostly in fees and commissions. The steady growth in the importance of non-interest income is reflected in its share of total income in this group (31.4 percent in 1985 compared with 37.7 percent in 1989) (table 5.6). Operating expenses rose during the period examined by 59.0 percent. Bank costs have been rising as a result of technological change, marketing costs, and other expenditures. The competitive pressure on margins and the increasing difficulty of generating more fee income continues to cause banks to reexamine their operating costs.

The provision for loan losses reached 17 to 18 percent of net interest income during the entire period examined. The provision against problem country debt, based on the matrix score, reached 60.3 percent of the debts

Table 5.5 Large British banks: indicators of income, costs and earnings

(*Pounds sterling, billions*)	*1985*	*1986*	*1987*	*1988*	*1989*
Income					
Net interest	9.71	10.40	11.06	12.32	13.92
Other	4.44	5.23	6.02	7.02	8.44
Total	14.15	15.63	17.08	19.34	22.36
Total operating costs	9.43	10.35	11.35	12.86	14.99
Pre-tax profit	3.29	3.84	0.73	5.67	0.86
Post-tax profit	1.80	2.48	0.09	3.68	0.50
Provision/gross exposure to problem-country debt			30.5	32.3	60.3
Return on equity	13.4	15.7	0.5	17.8	2.2

Source: Bank of England, Banking Act Report for 1989/90, tables II to VI

by year-end 1989. The annual average return on equity for the four largest British banks was therefore 9.92 percent, including the exceptional years 1987 and 1989.

A net profit of 120 million pounds for 1989 was reported by the four big banks (4.4 billion pounds in 1988), after they provided a staggering 4.5 billion pounds for LDC lending. In recent years, these four generated over 80 percent of their profits from the UK domestic market. However, the 1989 recession slowed growth in the volume of domestic business and led to a surge in the UK domestic debt provision (407 million pounds in 1988, compared with 787 million pounds in 1989).

The performance of a sample of three foreign banks is presented in table 5.7. Foreign banks took advantage of the demand for property-related finance to expand their sterling portfolio. Major banks also developed the medium-sized corporate market and leasing activity. Japanese banks continued to occupy a key position in the wholesale market: CDs, syndicated credits, and money market dealing. The strength of both the domestic and international economy in 1988 enabled many overseas banks to improve their performance. However, as in other countries, overseas operations are less profitable than domestic because of the difficulty in penetrating local markets.

Table 5.6 Combined income statement (four British clearing banks)[a]

	(Pounds sterling, millions) 1988	1987	1986	1985
1 Interest received	29293	25459	25711	26385
2 Interest paid	19450	16682	17372	18563
3 Net interest revenue	9843	8777	8339	7822
4 Other operating income	5351	4717	4095	3583
5 Other income	549	391	388	316
6 Provisions for loan losses				
(a) exceptional for sov. risks		3405		
(b) other loan losses	940	945	1361	1442
7 Personnel expenses	6165	5490	5103	4675
8 Other non-interest expenses	4195	3725	3293	3048
9 Pre-tax profit	4443	320	3065	2556
10 Taxes	1568	346	1078	1192
11 Net income	2875	(26)	1987	1364
Average earning assets	261522	239755	228288	221301
Ratios to earning assets (%)				
Interest received	11.20	10.62	11.26	11.92
Interest paid	7.44	6.96	7.61	8.39
Net interest revenue	3.76	3.66	3.65	3.53
Interest on capital employed	0.60	0.51	0.60	0.49
Net spread	3.16	3.15	3.05	3.04
Other ratios (%)				
Personnel expenses/net interest	63	63	61	60
Other oper. exp./net interest	43	42	39	39
Operating expenses/non-interest income	176	180	187	198
Interest income/non-interest income	167	172	186	201
Prov. for loan lo./total loans	0.47	2.70	0.86	0.95
Net income/total assets	0.99	-0.01	0.79	0.56
Net income/risk capital	14.50	-0.15	12.58	11.62

[a] Including Barclays, Natwest, Lloyds, and Midland

Source: IBCA data base

Table 5.7 Combined income statement (three foreign banks in the UK)[a]

	(*Pound sterling, millions*) 1988	1987	1986	1985
1 Pre-tax profit	30.1	9.8	47.0	37.9
2 Taxes	11.0	6.3	14.5	15.1
3 Net income	19.1	3.5	32.5	22.8
Net income/total assets	0.32%	0.06%	5.52%	0.37%
Net income/risk capital	6.85%	1.29%	12.70%	10.05%

[a] Including: Industrial Bank of Japan, Banque Nationale de Paris & Scandinavian Bank Group.

Source: IBCA data base

5.3.3 *Sources of Income*

The large UK banks enjoyed a substantial rise in both net interest income and fee income during the period 1985–9. Net interest income grew more quickly than total assets, despite the slight decline in net spread from 3.6 percent in 1985 to 3.4 percent in 1989, due to the change in composition of the loan portfolio which resulted from a move toward higher margin domestic business.

The interest margins of the large British banks are shown in table 5.8.

Table 5.8 Large British banks' interest margins

	1981	1984	1985	1986	1987	1988	1989
				(%)			
Domestic	6.9	5.62	5.67	5.59	5.50	5.0	4.7
International	2.1	2.18	2.16	2.03	1.81	1.4	1.8
Net interest revenue	4.1	3.42	3.62	3.64	3.64	3.6	3.4
Net interest income of building societies		1.69	1.89	1.90	1.96	2.03	2.0

Source: Bank of England Annual Report under the Banking Act for 1989/90, table III, and for building societies The development of the building societies sector in the 1980s, Bank of England Quarterly Bulletin, November 1990, p. 561

Spreads on lending to large corporate borrowers remained tight, reflecting competition with capital markets and other financial institutions. Bank lending rose 28 percent in 1988, and 22 percent in 1989/90; the growth was mostly in the corporate sector (34 percent in 1988 and 27 percent in 1989/90) and in property companies (56 percent in 1988, and 43 percent in 1989/90) following the 1988 property boom. In 1989, banks increasingly took funding of property investment away from building societies. Bank's losses have been relatively small although, recently, several large property development companies have gone into bankruptcy. The interest margins of banks and building societies are significantly different due to differing funding and lending structures. A very high percentage of bank lending is carried out on an unsecured basis, which generates higher risk.

Non-interest income has grown steadily, a function of the deliberate policy that banks have pursued to increase fee income through diversification into such activities as insurance, asset management, and estate agency.

The sources of non-interest income of the four largest banks are shown in table 5.9.

Table 5.9 Large banks' non-interest income

	1984	*1985*	*1986*	*1987*	*1988*
	(*billions of pounds Sterling*)				
Foreign exchange	0.26	0.28	0.41	0.36	0.38
Fees and commission	2.98	2.99	3.30	3.80	4.19
Others	0.52	0.47	0.56	0.75	0.99
Total	3.76	3.74	4.27	4.91	5.56

Source: Bank of England Annual Report under the Banking Act for 1988/1989, Table VI.

Activities closely related to the stock market were severely affected in 1988 by the market's difficulties (low turnover) following the sharp adjustment of October 1987. Other activities grew in 1988, including trustcard, credit card, insurance and investment services, leasing, and personal service.

5.3.4 *Expenses*

The major expenses of the UK banking industry include personnel expenses, other operating expenses, loan loss reserves and taxes. Personnel expenses account for about 60 percent of total operating expenses for the four largest banks.

The non-interest income coverage of personnel expenses increased from 78.7 percent in 1985 to 99.0 percent in 1989 (table 5.5). The increase in personnel expenses throughout this period (52 percent) was slightly lower than the increase in total income, 58 percent. The increase in personnel expenses stemmed mostly from an increase of about 20 percent in the number of bank employees, and from salary increases (Table 5.1). The four largest banks, more than the rest of the industry, face the problem of controlling overhead while investing in expansion into new fields. The cost breakdown of the largest British banks (major retail banks) is presented in table 5.10.

Table 5.10 Large British banks' expenses

	1984	*1985*	*1986*	*1987*	*1988*	*1989*
	(*billions of pounds sterling*)					
Staff	5.60	5.64	6.18	6.64	7.56	8.50
Premises and equipment	1.75	1.77	1.91	2.02	2.21	2.56
Other expenses	2.03	2.02	2.26	2.68	3.09	3.93
Total	9.38	9.43	10.35	11.34	12.86	14.99

Source: Bank of England Annual Report under the Banking Act for 1989/90, table III.

The increase in costs for premises (plant) and equipment is a result of the need to invest in branch modernization and technology to provide more cost-efficient services. The rapid growth in other expenses partly reflects the marketing costs present in penetrating into new fields. Recently, the four big banks (especially the Midland) have moved away from diversification and growth for their own sake.

Commercial bad debt experience in 1988 was better than in 1987, when the largest banks increased the overall provision against problem-country debt from 10 to 30 percent. In 1988, the provision against such debt was increased from 30 to 32 percent. However, 1989 saw another major increase in provision for problem-country debt, which brought overall provisions against such debt to over 60 percent of gross exposure. The total exposure of the four big banks to such debt is approximately 14 billion pounds, representing about 50 percent of these bank's equity capital. For Barclays Bank and National Westminster, the net exposure exceeded equity capital. The sum of provision against this debt as of December 1988 was about 4.5 billion pounds.

The provision of the four largest UK banks against LDC debt (32 percent in December 1988) was considered relatively low by American and European standards, where provisions were above 50 percent. During 1989, however, the four more than doubled their loan loss provision against LDC debt by adding 4.5 billion pounds. Individual banks increased their coverage against this debt as follows: Lloyds 75 percent; Natwest 72 percent; Barclays 70 percent; and Midland 50 percent.

Table 5.11 Combined balance sheet (four British clearing banks)

	31/12/88 (US$, mil.)	*31/12/88 (pound, millions)*	*31/12/87*	*31/12/86*	*31/12/85*
A Loans					
1 Customer loans	343353	189874	158366	151307	143323
2 Consumer loans	11085	6130	4823	4249	4049
3 Lease receivables	21817	12065	10034	9486	9048
4 (Unearned income)	5754	3182	2821	2758	2617
5 (Loan loss reserves)	12344	6826	6841	4218	3916
Total A	358157	198061	163561	158066	149887
B Other earning assets					
1 Bank deposits and placings	109394	60495	59539	59365	53562
2 Short-term investments	16649	9207	6821	4943	4725
3 UK Listed gov. securities	5790	3202	4183	5487	3745
4 Other investments	12114	6699	6304	7700	6561
5 Securities – long positions	2418	1337	883	706	0
6 Equity investments	3143	1738	1013	939	889
Total B	149508	82678	78743	79140	69482
C Total earning assets (A + B)	507665	280739	242304	237206	219369
D Fixed assets	14177	7840	6155	5537	4877
E Non-earning assets					
1 Cash and due from banks	14894	8236	8693	8390	8238
2 Other	25380	14035	11090	12142	7109
F Total assets	562116	310850	268242	263275	239593
G Customer and short-term funding					
1 Demand deposits	121591	67240	51326	46484	47956
2 Savings deposits	60481	33446	40225	36639	31698
3 Time deposits	281595	155722	132997	135373	126340
4 Other	8687	4804	3501	3416	2765
Total G	472354	261212	228049	221912	208759
H Other funding					
1 Long term	2307	1276	1087	1311	1118
2 Other	1052	581	770	548	0
3 Subordinated, non-primary	10541	5829	4513	4610	5030
I Other (non-int. bearing)					
1 Securities – short positions	1186	656	4 34	471	0
2 Other	34969	19338	15699	16766	10759
J Risk capital					
1 Equity	33049	18276	14335	13394	10707
2 Near equity	6658	3682	3355	4263	3220
Total J	39707	21958	17690	17657	13927
K Total liabilities & risk capital	562116	310850	268242	263275	239593
Exchange rate (US$1 = GBP)		0.553	0.538	0.678	0.692
Ratios (%)					
Deposits/loans		132	139	140	139
Loans/total assets		64	61	60	63
Fixed assets/risk capital		36	35	31	35
Loan loss reserves/loans		3.45	4.18	2.67	2.61
Risk capital/total assets		7.06	6.59	6.71	5.81

Source: IBCA data base

In the domestic market, difficulties worsened, particularly in the property and personnel sectors, and in international operations (other than problem-country debt). The 1989 charge was lower than those in the early 1980s; however, current economic conditions are likely to cause it to increase significantly in 1990.

Finally, the provision for taxes in 1986 and 1988 accounted for 35 percent of pre-tax income, representing the statutory tax rate.

5.3.5 *Capital Adequacy*

The equity capital to total assets ratio of the four largest banks is relatively high and has increased in recent years from 5.81 percent in 1985 to 7.06 percent in 1988 (table 5.11). The capital ratio of these banks meets the minimum standard agreed upon under the Basle convergence proposals. The strength of retained earnings and the raising of new equity has improved Tier 1 capital. Tier 2 capital includes perpetual debt, general reserves, hidden reserves, and property revaluation reserves. A number of banks have capitalized part of their revaluation reserves by issuing shares against them. The Bank agreed that the share capital so created was indistinguishable from other equity, and should therefore be treated as Tier 1 capital. Most UK banks already meet the minimum standard capital ratio set within the framework. The major sources of capital growth of large British banks are given in table 5.12.

Table 5.12 Sources of capital growth

	1984	*1985*	*1986*	*1987*	*1988*	*1989*
	(*billions of pounds sterling*)					
Retained earnings	0.78	1.39	1.91	(0.64)	2.74	(0.57)
Perpetual debt	1.20	3.82	1.25	0.09	0.01	0.93
Term subordinated debt	1.29	0.05	(0.29)	0.44	1.56	0.11
Share issues	0.28	0.70	1.42	1.96	1.33	0.33
	3.55	5.96	4.29	1.85	5.64	0.80
Total capital	20.92	25.72	29.97	29.50	36.64	38.77
Risk-asset ratio		9.7	10.5	9.7	10.0	9.2

Source: Bank of England Annual Report under the Banking Act for 1989/90, Tables VI and VIII.

The current BIS ratio for the four largest banks is around 10 percent.

The decision of large UK banks to add substantial provisions against problem-country debt in 1989 had a sharp impact on the risk-asset ratio. Little share capital was issued for cash, although, as in 1988, some banks capitalized part of their property revaluation reserves. The growth of lending, together with a relatively small increase in capital, resulted in a decline in the risk-asset ratio.

Table 5.13 Combined balance sheet and income statement (three foreign banks in the UK)

	31/12/88 (*US$, mil.*)	31/12/88 (*pound, millions*)	31/12/87	31/12/86	31/12/85
A Loans					
1 Loans & advances	4255	2353	2633	2596	2541
2 Local auth./bank loans	109	60	81	110	111
3 Lease receivable	76	42	51	66	67
4 Loans > 1 year	1184	655	774	995	1083
Total A	5624	3110	3539	3767	3802
B Other earning assets					
1 Bank deposits and placings	4770	2638	2272	2365	2049
2 Short-term investments	7	4	4	4	4
3 UK listed gov. securities	62	34	55	222	81
4 Equity investments	7	4	8	5	5
Total B	4846	2680	2339	2596	2139
C Total earning assets (A + B)	10470	5790	5878	6363	5941
D Fixed assets	109	60	41	37	34
E Non-earning assets					
1 Cash and due from banks	7	4	7	16	10
2 Other	309	171	148	111	97
F Total assets	10895	6025	6074	6527	6082
G Customer and short-term funding					
1 Demand deposits					
2 Savings deposits					
3 Time deposits	8646	4781	5253	5832	5248
4 Other	678	375	224	123	257
Total G	9324	5156	5477	5955	5505
H Other funding					
1 Long term	165	91	69	13	10
2 Subordinated, non-primary	141	78	63	69	69
I Other (non-int. bearing)	761	421	193	234	270
J Risk capital	504	279	272	256	227
K Total liabilities & risk capital	10895	6025	6074	6527	6081
Exchange rate (US$1 = GBP)		0.553	0.538	0.678	0.692
Ratios (%)					
Deposits/loans		166	155	158	145
Loans/total assets		52	58	58	63
Fixed assets/risk capital		22	15	14	15
Risk capital/total assets		4.63	4.47	3.92	3.73

Source: IBCA data base

Table 5.14 Selected financial data (four British clearing banks)

Dec. 31, 1988	*Barclays*	*Natwest*	*Midland*	*Lloyds*	*Total*
	(Pounds sterling, millions)				
Total assets	104645	98642	55729	51834	310850
Total loans	65585	61214	34041	37221	198061
Total deposits	86136	84981	46176	43919	261212
Risk capital	6574	7052	4068	4264	21958
Net income	893	944	420	618	2875

Source: IBCA data base

Notes

1 *Merrill Lynch International Bank Guide*, Merrill Lynch, New York, 1986.
2 See Japanese Banks in London, *Bank of England Quarterly Bulletin*, 1987, vol 27, 516–24.
3 *Bank of England Annual Report under the Banking Act for 1988/9*, 46.
4 Principles for the supervision on banks' foreign establishment, May 1983
5 See Japanese Banks in London, *Bank of England Quarterly Bulletin*, 1987, vol 27, 518–24.

References

Bank of England, *Annual Report* and *Quarterly Bulletin*, various issues.
Banque de France, *Statistiques Monétaires et Financières Annuelles*, various issues.
Merrill Lynch, *Merrill Lynch International Bank Guide*, New York, 1986.

6

Japan

6.1 Structure of the Financial System

6.1.1 Introduction

As might be expected, Japan's financial system reflects to a great degree the characteristics of the Japanese economy and society. Compared with other major industrialized economies, Japan's financial markets display considerable segmentation and specialization, supported by an extensive structure of regulation and constraints, both formal and informal. Financial markets in Japan, moreover, have never been seen as independent mechanisms for the allocation of resources; rather, they have been a means of allocating resources as determined by policy makers. The well-known Japanese emphasis on collective and group achievement applies to the financial sector as well. Thus, outright conflict and confrontational tactics are avoided – although competition, where permissible, can be fierce. This cooperative spirit is facilitated by the widespread movement of individuals between the public and private sectors. Government officials frequently expect to begin a second career working for the very firms they previously regulated.

The Japanese emphasis on loyalty and tradition also influences the structure of Japan's financial system. Given the clearly perceived hierarchical ranking of banks in Japan, the prestige associated with a business deal can be an important factor influencing decisions. These characteristic features of loyalty, tradition, and hierarchy have resulted, until recently, in a slower pace of change and adaptation in Japan than in any of the other major economies. Stability is often seen as a goal in and of itself, and has been achieved to a great degree. Thus, while the United States has experienced an ever increasing number of bank failures – 200 in 1988 alone – Japan has had only one bank failure since World War Two. Recently, the well-protected banking industry – which had benefited from clientele and profit margins virtually guaranteed by the Ministry of Finance (MOF) – has been exposed to increased risk and declining profit because of continuous deregulation. The regulatory response to new risks and potential bank failures is still unknown.

Table 6.1 Japan – major economic indicators and the banking system

	1980	*1984*	*1989*
Gross domestic product, (US$ bil.)	1,062	1,256	2,830
Current account, (US$ bil.)	−10.8	+35.0	+56.8
Consumer inflation (percent)	4.9	2.1	2.3
Exchange rate, (yen-US$) (year-end)	203	251	138
Interest rate[a] per annum (percent)	2.25	5.0	4.3
Population (mil.)	116.8	120.02	123.1
Number of depository institutions	7,456	7,263	6,744
Number of offices	40,697	42,527	45,314
Population per office	2,870	2,822	2,717
Number of ATMs	n/a	58,000	68,200
Population per ATM	n/a	2,069	1,805

n/a not available
[a] Central bank discount rate.

6.1.2 Financial Markets and Institutions

Financial markets

Until recently, Japan's financial markets were characterized by a fairly rigid structure, with a large number of highly specialized institutions in well-defined (and usually well-protected) roles. The resultant structural barriers, combined with the considerable power and influence of official policy makers, have produced a financial market that lags behind other major nations in terms of innovation, completeness, and efficiency. This is clearly the result of two critical periods in Japan's recent history: the rapid industrialization of the country following the Meji restoration of 1866, and the reconstruction and rebuilding of the Japanese economy following the Second World War. The period of industrialization was characterized by the concentration of power and control in interlocking corporate groupings (called Zaibatsu prior to the Second World War, and Keiretsu in their somewhat weakened post-war form). This form of corporate structure encouraged a strong tradition of binding loyalty in business relationships, including financial activities. The post-war period saw the coordination and concentration of resources on behalf of national goals, an effort achieved through the almost total identification of official and private institutions and the general population with such goals.

Direct finance

Indirect finance remains the main vehicle of financial market flows, especially in smaller business. As a result, financial intermediaries rather than markets have played the crucial role. During the period 1980–4, 89 percent of all financial market activity was indirect finance, with only 11 percent representing direct financial flows (Suzuki, 1987, 13). Thus, for example, the securities markets have been until recently rather unimportant as a source of financing. Instead, Japanese companies have relied heavily on debt (usually loans provided by banks) in their balance sheets, reaching a debt to equity ratio as high as 4:1 (compared with an average 1:1 in the United States; Viner 1987, p.49).

Moreover, approximately 65 percent of equity in companies listed on the Tokyo Stock Exchange is held in an interlocking fashion by firms in the same Keiretsu, or with a similar close relationship (Viner, p. 46). One of the characteristics of Japanese indirect finance is the "main bank" system, whereby a special single bank represents a banking syndicate.

The stock exchanges had been relegated to a marginal role by frequent speculative cycles and suggestions of unsound practices (such as insider trading and manipulation). However, in the past decade the volume and extent of trading have grown tremendously, undoubtedly marking a turning point in the role of the exchanges both as a source of funding for companies and as a venue for investment by the public. Indeed, the Tokyo Stock Exchange is presently the world's largest, with a total capitalization in September 1989 of $4,250 billion (41 percent of global equity markets), far surpassing the $3,548 billion of the New York Stock Exchange. Only ten years earlier the market value of the Tokyo Stock Exchange (TSE) companies was only $250 billion. Even in yen terms the period 1978–9 saw an increase of TSE market value of over 1,000 percent, while average daily trading volume rose by nearly 650 percent. The phenomenal growth of the TSE, along with its tremendous volatility (including large declines in 1990) make it a somewhat special case, and thus difficult to compare to other markets.

The privatization of government firms through flotations on the exchange has contributed to this rapid growth. In fact, the market value of one such firm, Nippon Telephone and Telegraph (in 1988, the largest firm in the world by market value), was greater than that of *all* listed West German industrials combined. Clearly, the TSE has become a major factor in Japanese financial markets, both as a venue for raising capital and as an investment alternative for individuals and institutional fund managers. It now presents increased competition for Japan's banks.

The bond market in Japan, including the huge government bond market, while enormous in size, ($1,980 billion at year-end 1989, 19 percent of the global bond market) is overwhelmingly dominated by public sector debt, 64 percent of the total. Bonds issued by private non-financial corporations constitute a marginal part of the bond market (7.7 percent).

Direct financing by Japanese banks has been virtually prohibited by Article 65 of the Securities and Exchange Law (sometimes called the "Japanese Glass-Steagall"), which rigidly defines the roles of financial institutions. Since banks are banned from the securities markets, security companies have filled this vacuum. There are 224 such firms in Japan, with an overwhelming concentration of influence and market share in the so called "big four" – Nomura, Daiwa, Nikko and Yamaichi. While dominating the securities industry in Japan, these firms have also acquired considerable worldwide influence. And as the barriers among financial institutions in Japan are reduced, they will undoubtedly come into more direct competition with the banking industry. For example, in January 1980, security companies began selling small denomination certificates of participation in bond trusts. The trusts, known as Chukoku funds since they invest primarily in medium term government bonds, are essentially similar to Money Market Mutual Funds in the United States. The ability of security firms to offer a close substitute to a bank deposit represented a significant blurring of the line between the security business and banking. In fact, the volume of such funds grew rapidly until 1987, when the deregulation of deposit interest rates slowed and eventually reversed their growth.

The short-term money market in Japan is extremely underdeveloped compared with those of other major industrialized countries. Whereas the volume of outstanding short-term debt in the United States in 1985 was equivalent to 40 percent of GNP, in Japan the figure was only 8 percent. Moreover, the market continues to be highly regulated and controlled, and most reforms enacted in recent years have been largely the result of foreign pressure.

Until 1980, the short-term market consisted of just two instruments: call money (available in maturities of up to seven days and used for settling bank reserve positions); and the bill discount market (in maturities from one to four months and used for transferring liquidity among financial institutions). Access to both instruments is extremely curtailed by the Bank of Japan (BOJ), which also controls the interest rates according to its monetary objectives. The first "free" short-term market, in which interest rates were able to respond to supply and demand, was the Gensaki or collateralized loan market (security repurchase agreement) established in 1970. In addition to having market-sensitive rates, the Gensaki is open to a wider range of participants. Individuals, however, cannot enter the market, and city bank activities are subject to various restrictions. Since 1984, three short-term market instruments have been created: short-term government bonds with a maturity of six months were introduced in February 1986; bonds with a three-month maturity began to be issued in September 1989; and yen-denominated bankers' acceptances were brought forth in June 1985.

Moreover, the combination of domestic demand and foreign pressure has resulted in a number of financial innovations in recent years, including yen CDs in 1984, and the introduction of foreign commercial paper in 1987. Nevertheless, the market is still encumbered by a wide range of restrictions due to both pressure from special interest groups and characteristic Japanese conservatism and caution in introducing change. The BOJ influences the money market by its leverage over the brokers, known as Tanshi, through whom many money market transactions must be channelled. These brokers are traditionally ex-BOJ officials, and as a matter of course consult the BOJ as to the calibration of crucial money market interest rates. Nevertheless, present trends clearly indicate that a freer, more integrated market is evolving.

The banking industry

The rigid structure of Japanese financial markets is apparent in the banking sector, composed of a number of distinct types of institutions with clear functional divisions. Financial institutions have had their roles clearly defined by the triple segmentation of financial activity: the separation of direct and indirect finance (Article 65); the separation of banking and trust business; and the separation between short- and long-term finance. In Japan, both wholesale and retail banking operations are performed together as an integrated unit.

Commercial banks

The most important commercial banks are the so-called city banks, roughly equivalent to American money center banks. These 13 institutions (12 following the merger of Mitsui and Taiyo Kobe banks) some direct descendants of Zaibatsu banks, function on a nationwide level and have traditionally been the primary suppliers of funds to Japanese corporations. They have often enjoyed close, nearly exclusive relations with large concerns and other firms. The city banks, usually cash poor, depend heavily on the interbank market for funds and have extremely limited access to long-term funding. At the same time, the growing access of Japanese firms to less expensive direct funding (e.g., commercial paper) has led these banks to search for new areas of activity to maintain growth and profitability. BIS capital rules, and the 1990 declines in the TSE, further encouraged city banks to reduce their size. Moreover, most city banks have huge exposure to US LBOs, construction developers, and real estate lending.

The 64 regional banks, whose activities are usually limited to a specific locality, are major institutions. Indeed, most regional banks are ranked within the largest 500 banks in the world. However, unlike the city banks, regional banks have an abundant base of funds supplied by their retail depositors, and they are large net suppliers of funds in the interbank market. Local firms and borrowers, rather than the large nationwide concerns, are their principal customers for credit.

Foreign banks in Japan play a relatively limited role. With no natural customer base, restricted access to yen funding, and handicapped by cultural differences, the bulk of their business is in foreign exchange and other related areas. While the number of foreign banks has grown from 16 in 1968 to 82 in 1989, their collective share of the market has actually declined in recent years, and a few foreign firms have withdrawn from banking activity in Japan.

Specialized financial institutions

Alongside the commercial banks there exists a variety of special purpose institutions, created and nurtured to fulfil specific functions. Specialization and segmentation imply that access to designated areas is prohibited or restricted, so that only special institutions are allowed to enter. However, as the highly regulated environment in which special purpose banks function gradually becomes more competitive, they will be forced to adapt to a less protected environment.

Three banks were assigned the exclusive role of providing long-term credit to industry following the destruction caused by World War Two. In a sense, these banks formed a surrogate long-term capital market. To enable them to perform this function, the long-term credit banks were given the nearly exclusive ability to raise long-term yen funding (primarily by issuing debentures), sheltering them from direct competition with commercial banks. However, the recent and rapid trend toward longer lendings by ordinary banks, and shorter lendings by long-term credit banks, is increasing the resemblance between the two kinds of institutions.

In Japan, only 18 banks are allowed to conduct trust business. They are presently comprised of seven trust banks, two ordinary banks, and nine trust banks affiliated with foreign banks. These banks operate under special legislation and have two specialized functions: long-term financing and financial management. They maintain extensive commercial banking activities while specializing in trust management, primarily pension funds. Several hundred other institutions specialize in serving small business. They include Sogo (mutual savings and loan banks), Shinkin (credit associations including 454 local establishments), credit cooperatives, and credit associations, and operate in a highly localized fashion serving relatively small customers. The main legal distinction between Sogo and ordinary banks is that Sogo banks are authorized to engage in the mutual instalment loan business, whereas this is denied ordinary banks. The Sogo banks were one-line savings banks. Over the past two years, 66 out of 68 have given up their mutual status to become secondary regional banks (table 6.2). Interestingly, each category has a central bank of its own, which has become a major institution in its own right by combining the resources of its individual members. For example, the Zenshinren bank serves some 470 credit associations and is ranked 70th among the world's largest banks. Finally, while small businesses continue to be the main customer of Sogo bank financing, in recent years ordinary banks have rapidly increased their provision for this type of lending as well.

The agricultural sector in Japan (long a source of considerable economic and political power) is served by several thousand rural credit cooperatives located in virtually every town and village. The surplus funds of these cooperatives are deposited in the Norinchukin bank, the Central Cooperative Bank for Agriculture and Forestry. The enormous scope of the Norinchukin Bank's resources has allowed it to become a major player in the money markets; indeed, it has the largest domestic deposits of any bank in Japan.

Government financial institutions play a significant role in the financial system. A number of institutions, including the Export Import Bank of Japan, The Overseas Economic Cooperation Fund, and ten finance companies, such as the Small Business Finance Corporation and the Housing Loan Corporation, play an allocative role channelling credit according to government policy. The Trust Fund Bureau and the Japan Development Bank manage and invest the funds gathered by the postal savings system.

The postal savings system was designed to encourage small personal savings, and to accomplish this, accounts were granted a tax exemption up to a limit of JPY 3 million per individual. As a result, postal savings assumed a major share of personal savings, and grew from 16 percent of individual deposits in 1965 to 32 percent in 1985. However, the tax exemption feature and other aspects of the system have generated considerable criticism regarding distortions of the financial system and the role of the government. In April 1988, postal deposits were subjected to the same 20 percent withholding tax as other deposits, and since then they have started to decline as a share of total deposits (to 31.7 percent in September 1989).

6.1.3 Banking Product and Bank Competition

Until recently, there was a strict correspondence between the type of banking institution and its product and range of activities, usually mandated by statute. Because of this strictly segmented financial system, competition within each grouping was intense, while competition between the groups was almost nonexistent. Thus, commercial banks, banned from both the securities business and long-term credit markets, collected deposits and extended short-term credit. Within the commercial bank group, the city banks focused on wholesale banking by maintaining a close relationship with the larger blue chip companies and serving their needs both domestically and abroad. By contrast, the regional banks served small and regional firms, obtained funding through a large natural deposit base, and often lent those funds through the interbank market to the liquidity-starved city banks. Foreign banks, with little access to domestic business, were relegated to the margins of the system and concentrated on foreign exchange and on serving subsidiaries of foreign firms.

The specialized banks had even more distinctly defined products and roles. The long-term credit banks, given their monopoly in obtaining long-term funding, dominated long-term lending. The trust banks, while providing some commercial banking products, concentrated on managing funds they were entrusted with. The various mutual savings and loans banks, credit cooperatives, and credit associations had clearly defined customer bases and roles. The cohesive nature of each of these groupings is highlighted by the role played by the various central banking institutions serving each category.

Under this system, not only were banks limited in their activities, they were also protected from non-bank competition by Article 65 and other regulations and statutes. These administrative guidelines were based on the separation between financial intermediation and direct financing, long- and short-term lending, deposit based and trust based activities, and the maintenance of specialized institutions for specific purposes.

As a result of both basic changes in the Japanese economy and the worldwide movement toward deregulation and liberalization, the rigid structure of the Japanese banking system has begun to change, but at a

Table 6.2 The Japanese banking system

Type of banks	Number of institutions			Number of business offices[c]		Total assets (yen trillions)			% of total	% change
	1980[a]	1984	1989	1984	1989	1980	1984	1989	1989	1980–89
A Ordinary (commercial) banks										
City banks	13	13	13	2,987	3,387	122.8	170.2	328.3	34.2	167.3
Regional banks	63	64	64	6,657	7,350	68.8	99.0	164.5	17.2	139.1
Secondary regional banks[b]	–	–	68	–	4,547	–	–	62.6	6.5	–
Foreign banks	64	76	82	114	121	6.6	11.9	13.7	1.4	107.6
Total	140	153	227	9,758	15,405	198.2	281.1	569.1	59.3	187.1
B Financial institutions for Long-term credit										
Long-term credit banks	3	3	3	61	67	26.8	34.1	69.8	7.3	160.4
Trust banks[d]	7	7	7	356	372	12.4	24.0	51.1	5.3	312.1
Total	10	10	10	417	439	39.2	58.1	120.9	12.6	208.4
C Financial institutions for small businesses										
Sogo (mutual) banks	71	69	–	4,033	–	33.0	41.3	–	–	–
The Shinkin banks	461	456	454	6,368	7,455	40.9	55.4	87.4	9.1	113.7
The Zenshinren banks (federation)	1	1	1	17	17	3.2	5.6	10.8	1.2	237.5
Credit cooperatives	476	461	414	2,337	2,529	9.4	13.0	20.2	2.1	114.9

National federation of credit cooperatives	1	1	1	12	12	0.8	1.6	3.0	0.3	275.0
Labor credit association	35	64	186	527	598	3.1	4.7	6.8	0.7	119.3
The national federation of labor credit associations	1	1	1	1	1	0.7	1.2	2.2	0.2	214.3
The Shoko Chukin bank	1	1	1	94	95	5.7	8.5	12.1	1.3	112.3
Total	1,047	1,054	1,058	13,389	10,707	96.8	131.3	142.5	14.9	47.2
D Financial Institutions for Agriculture, Forestry and Fishing										
The Norinchukin Bank	1	1	1	37	37	12.2	18.5	26.2	2.7	114.7
Agriculture Cooperative	4,490	4,272	3,723	16,437	16,364	30.4	40.4	54.2	5.7	78.3
Credit Federations of Agriculture Coop.	47	47	47	240	244	17.7	27.5	40.4	4.2	128.2
Fishery cooperatives	1,686	1,691	1,673	2,125	2,115	2.2	2.7	3.6	0.4	63.6
Credit Federations of Fishery Coop.	35	35	35	124	124	1.2	1.6	2.0	0.2	66.7
Total	6,259	6,046	5,479	18,963	18,884	63.7	90.7	126.4	13.2	98.4
Total Depository Institutions	7,456	7,263	6,774	42,527	45,435	397.9	561.2	958.9	100.0	141.0

[a] Data in this table are based on figures at end December of the relevant year.
[b] Since the end of 1989, ordinary banks include member banks of the Second Association of Regional Banks, including the Sogo banks.
[c] Figures for financial institutions, agriculture, forestry, and fishing are based on 1988 data.
[d] Domestic pure trust banks only.

Source: *Economics Statistics Annual, 1989,* March 1990, The Bank of Japan.

very measured pace. These changes are designed to force institutions enjoying a protected existence to adapt to competition in both their original markets and in new areas. One of the basic characteristics of the Japanese economy after World War Two was a tremendous shortage of capital. This meant that bankers enjoyed a lender's market for many years. In fact, the power of Japanese bankers had been so great that Japan was long known as "the banker's kingdom."

Today, however, Japanese firms and the nation as a whole generate tremendous capital surpluses. Thus, Japan has now become a borrower's market, and as Japanese firms have become cash rich and less dependent on their bankers, the importance of long-term relationships and corporate loyalty has diminished. In its place a more transaction and performance focused orientation has developed, similar to that in other industrial nations. Greater use of direct finance, seen in both equity (the booming stock exchange) and debt (spreading securitization), has further reduced the dominance of the banks. The regulatory authorities, both to develop more efficient markets and in response to increasing foreign pressure, have slowly and steadily reduced their involvement in the financial markets. For example, in recent years new financial instruments have been permitted, tax distortions reduced, interest rate and deposit regulations removed, and foreign exchange controls relaxed. Euro-yen CDs were introduced in December 1984, a Euro-yen commercial paper market was launched in November 1987, and Euro-yen lending has been deregulated. The ongoing reform of the financial process and the resultant increased competition (together with the BIS capital requirements and a poorly performing capital market) have increased banking risk. The MOF policy, so far, is to encourage strong institutions to assist weaker ones (Sender, 1990).

In response, Japanese banks have widened the scope of their activities. Commercial banks, faced with decreased loan demand and reduced interest margins, are increasingly seeking fee generating activities such as foreign exchange and securities trading, the issuing of mortgage loans,credit card companies, international operations, and even investment banking activities (security underwriting, mergers and acquisition business). Legislative weakening of Article 65 will eventually enable commercial banks to compete with securities houses. As a result, competition from the "big four" security houses in areas close to commercial banking activities, such as money market mutual funds and foreign exchange, is expected to be fierce.

The long-term credit banks, facing declining demand for long-term bank loans, are transforming themselves into investment banks while maintaining their emphasis on long-term financing. They have been very aggressive in courting international business and have become important players in the Euromarkets. The regional banks, notwithstanding their appellation, have increasingly entered national and even international markets. They have established a nationwide automatic teller machine (ATM) network and have established ties with the large, blue chip concerns that were once the exclusive preserve of the city banks.

Reform of the institutional structure of the Japanese financial system was examined in an official 1989 report entitled "On a New Japanese Financial System." The report dealt with the highly segmented nature of the system, including the issues of the separation between securities and banking, and the fragmented nature of the banking system itself, including commercial, trust, and long-term banking. Five avenues of reform were examined, including:

- The piecemeal approach, maintaining the present system while allowing gradual blurring of lines;
- Separate subsidiaries, allowing financial firms to establish single purpose subsidiaries in different areas of finance;
- Multi-functional subsidiaries, allowing firms to set up a subsidiary which would engage in a variety of activities;
- Holding companies, to allow banks and securities firms to establish holding companies which would in turn own various financial subsidiaries;
- A universal banking system, which would introduce a European style fully universal banking system permitting all activities in a single entity.

While no final conclusions were drawn, the report indicated that the most likely course would be either the separated subsidiary or multi-functional subsidiary approach, or a combination of the two, in addition to other supplementary measures to expand the areas of activity permitted financial firms.

While its pace may be uncertain and irregular, it seems clear that the trend toward less regulated and more liberalized financial markets in Japan will continue. There is no doubt that this will result in increased risks, due to the reduction of protective segmentation and the intensified competition. The Shinkin group, for example, has misinterpreted the process and has increased yields paid on deposits without assuring themselves of higher asset returns. The resulting erosion of interest rate margins, along with increased competition from the larger banks, has caused difficulties. The Sogo regional banks, lacking a deposit base and with a record of poor investments, are in an even worse situation. Indeed, it seems that the small institutions lack the basic tools to manage the interest, market, and even credit risks that they must now face. The MOF is expecting regional and city banks to help troubled banks (e.g., by merger) and thus prevent bank runs. So far, it has not met with the desired response, and it is entirely possible that some actual bank closures must be expected.

6.1.4 International Involvement

The growing economic importance of Japan is clearly demonstrated by dramatic changes in its financial sector over the last decade. Through the accumulation of enormous trade and current account surpluses (95 and 79 billion US$ respectively in 1988, 77 and 57 billion in 1989), Japan has become the world's largest creditor nation and an unprecedented exporter of capital (131 billion US$ in 1988). Japanese financial institutions have mirrored their nation's growing preeminence on the world scene. The Tokyo Stock Exchange is now the world's largest, capitalized at 50 percent more than the New York exchange. Japan's big four securities firms are among the top ten lead managers of international bonds. Japanese banks have achieved incredible dominance in the global banking industry; the ten largest banks in the world by market capitalization are all Japanese. When ranked by deposits, seven Japanese banks are in the top ten and 46 Japanese banks are in the top 200 banks in the world. Moreover, four of the ten fastest growing banks in terms of total assets in 1987 were Japanese (*Institutional Investor*, June 1988). Their role in international banking is even more predominant. In 1987, Japan surpassed the United States to become the second largest center for international banking, after the United Kingdom. Japanese banks are by far the largest participants in international banking, accounting for fully half of the total growth in international assets in 1987, and an incredible 89 percent in 1988. By the end of that year their share in international bank assets was 38 percent of the total, compared with just 15 percent for all US banks, the next largest group. Finally, Japanese banks account for about 42 percent of foreign bank activity in the US and about 27 percent of total assets and liabilities in UK financial markets. However, some major Japanese banks will have a hard time meeting the BIS capital adequacy requirements, and their weak performance will slow down Japanese expansion abroad.

Expansion of the Euro-yen Market

The internationalization of the yen has included several important steps:

1 Euro-yen CDs were introduced in December 1984. Eligible issuers are non-resident banks, as well as branches and affiliate institutions of Japanese banks.
2 The Euro-yen commercial paper (CP) market was launched in November 1987, limited to non-resident issuers.

3 In June 1984, the MOF lifted the ban on yen lending by banks outside Japan to Japanese residents.
4 Long-term Euro-yen lending to residents was permitted in May 1989.
5 As to Euro-yen bond issues by non-residents, the only eligibility requirement since 1986 has been the acceptable credit rating of the issuer. This approval led to yen-denominated bonds being issued in Japan by non-residents. The size of the Euro-yen bonds market by December 1989 was 10,118 billion yen (750 billion in 1984); yen bonds issued in Japan by non-residents totalled 5,000 billion yen (4,171 in 1984).
6 Euro-yen issues by Japanese residents were permitted in April 1984, and the withholding tax on non-residents was abolished in 1985.

Foreign banks in Japan

The growing importance of Japan as a financial center is illustrated by the increased presence of foreign banks. Only eight banks were represented in Japan before World War Two; by 1968 the number had only grown to sixteen. In that year international pressure on Japan to liberalize the licensing of foreign banks began to bear fruit, resulting in the number of foreign banks with branches in Japan increasing to 50 by 1978, and 82 by 1989 (table 6.3).

An additional 124 banks maintained representative offices in Japan by 1987. In July 1985, permission was granted to foreign banks to open trust banks and by 1986 eight such autonomous trust banks were established. Foreign interest extended also to the capital markets; by late 1988, 47 securities firms from ten foreign countries had branches and/or subsidiaries operating in Tokyo.

Foreign banks in Japan lack a natural yen deposit base, because foreign institutions lack branch networks. As foreign banks engage to a certain degree in wholesale banking, they tend to depend on corporate bonds and short-term financial markets. However, foreign banks are prevented from issuing bank bonds, and therefore have been dependent on the money market and yen swap market for yen funds, and on borrowed funds (primarily from their head offices and the Euromarkets) for foreign currency denominated funds. During periods of capital shortage in Japan, foreign banks do have access to imported capital, and their ability to lend this capital to Japanese corporations has generated sizable profits in the past. However, such activity has become much less profitable in recent years, due to the declining demand for loans by the corporate customers, increased access to foreign funds on the part of Japanese banks, and easier access to foreign capital markets as a result of the integration and internationalization of financial markets. In June 1985 foreign banks were allowed to set up

Table 6.3 International involvement of the banking system

	1980	*1984*	*1989*	*% change 1980–1989*
A Foreign banks				
Number of foreign banks in Japan	64	76	82	28.1
Number of branches	85	107	121	42.3
Assets (trillion yen)	7.5	12.3	13.7	82.7
Percent of banking system asset	1.9	2.2	1.4	
B Banks operating in foreign countries				
Number of Japanese banks with offices abroad	23	24	41	78.2
Number of branches	142	177	272	91.5
Assets (trillion yen)	38.4	105.8	175.6	357.3
Assets as a percent of banking system	9.7	18.9	18.3	
C Assets and liabilities held against foreigners				
Total external assets of banks (trillion yen)	13.3	31.8	116.0[a]	
As a percentage of banking system, total assets	3.3	5.7	12.1	

[a] Including Japanese offshore market.

Source: *Economic Statistics Annual, 1989*, March 1990. The Bank of Japan

trust banking subsidiaries in Japan. In November 1984, they were allowed to deal in government bonds.

Foreign banks in Japan have always been very active in the Tokyo foreign exchange market, in trade financing, and letters of credit. To offset declining corporate lending, foreign banks are seeking to increase their investment in areas such as consumer and housing finance, factoring, and leasing. They emphasize their ability to provide Japanese firms with consultation and data on international markets and operations; information vital to the Japanese effort to maintain growth in overseas trade. These services have probably been the main reason that many Japanese corporations have maintained a relationship with foreign banks.

The entry of foreign banks into the trust banking business is seen as potentially very profitable. With the development of a freer market in asset management, many foreign banks believe that their experience in overseas funds management will enable them to capture a significant market share. Given the vast pool of assets in Japan, such potential fees would be very attractive. So far, the foreign bank presence in Japan has been marginal, representing about 1.4 percent of total assets of the banking system.

Access of foreign financial institutions to the securities markets has also improved, after the issue was raised by a number of foreign governments, including the UK and US. Foreign banks were allowed into the government bond underwriting syndicate in April 1984, and in October 1988 the share per foreign institution was raised from 0.07 percent to 1 percent, with the aggregate foreign share in the syndicate rising from 2.5 percent to 8 percent. Access to the market was further eased in April 1989 when four foreign security firms were appointed lead managers of the syndicate, and the auctioned share of the ten year government bond was increased from 20 percent to 40 percent. As of 1989, 18 foreign banks and 48 foreign security firms were permitted to deal in public bonds, and 25 foreign security firms were regular members of the Tokyo Stock Exchange. The number of foreign security firms in Japan grew from 12 in 1984 to 48 at the end of 1989.

The Japanese offshore market (JOM)

Seeking to remain competitive with the large banking centers of London, New York (IBF), Singapore, and Hong Kong, Japan established its offshore market in late 1986. (Concerns of the BOJ regarding its ability to control monetary policy, and of the Ministry of Finance regarding tax revenue, delayed the opening by years.) Japan's offshore center remains more regulated than other such centers, since local taxes and stamp duties are required and there are limitations on participation by domestic and non-bank entities. Transactions are exempted from interest rate regulation, reserve requirements, deposit insurance, and withholding tax on non-residents. However, despite these limitations, Japan's offshore market has displayed healthy growth and has furthered the internationalization of Japanese finance, especially among institutions without developed foreign networks (such as regional and Sogo banks). Total assets booked on the JOM reached $496 billion by the end of 1989.

Japanese banks abroad

The role of Japanese banks abroad has not only grown enormously in scope, but has changed in nature. The city banks, once primarily domestic-oriented, have since the 1980s increased their overseas involvement and become the largest international lenders. Japanese banks are major participants in syndicated loans, sovereign lending, interbank lending, and related markets such as the Euro floating-rate note market. This development is the result of the enormous increase of liquidity in Japan and the relative decline in domestic demand for funds. Another factor is the low capital-to-assets ratio maintained by Japanese banks (2.6 percent in 1989 versus 5 to 6 percent for US banks), which has enabled them to compete more effectively for international business. The adoption of new capital adequacy guidelines will certainly be of some importance in this regard, although it is not clear just how great their impact will be.

Japanese banks abroad have also profited from strategies similar to those used by other Japanese industries in penetrating foreign markets: they have concentrated on market share rather than profit margins, and have focused on long-term plans rather than short-term results. Japanese financial institutions also enjoy the added advantage of open markets abroad and protected markets at home. Foreign firms have had considerable difficulty establishing themselves in Japan. This difficulty is due not only to the inaccessibility of Japan's protected markets, but also to such objective difficulties as language, cultural differences and the general force of tradition.

By the end of 1989, 41 Japanese banks had established 272 branches abroad, as well as 194 subsidiaries (by 1988), and 396 representative offices – a massive overseas presence. While located throughout the world, the largest share (about 70 percent) was in the United States, with an especially strong presence in California. In fact, five of the eleven largest banks in California are Japanese-owned. In addition to domestic business, they serve more than 1,000 subsidiaries of Japanese firms and the sizable Japanese population located in California. By year-end 1988, commercial and industrial loans to US residents reached $60 billion. Also, US offices of Japanese banks are large net borrowers in the domestic interbank market. In most UK branches of Japanese banks, assets and liabilities are denominated in currencies other than Sterling. Branches of Japanese banks in the UK, unlike their US offices, deal mainly in foreign currency with non-UK residents. UK branches of Japanese banks are large net borrowers in the interbank Eurocurrency market and are the largest issuer of Euro-CDs. These funds are used to finance related offices in other countries, including head offices in Japan (table 6.3a).

Japanese banks have also been aggressive in pursuing every form of business in the Euromarkets. All the city banks have London branches, and an increasing number are opening operations in the Federal Republic of Germany, Switzerland, and other continental centers. By so doing, they

Table 6.3a The UK and US activities of Japanese banks (US$. bil.)

	Total assets and liabilities	*%*[a]	*Securities*	*Loan*	*[Net] liabilities to banks*	*Deposits*
US branches and agencies						
1980	60.8	31.2	1.4	36.5	11.7	10.1
1984	130.8	31.1	6.4	57.8	30.7	9.0
1988	306.7	27.4	23.2	131.6	85.4	27.6

	Total assets	*%*[a]	*Overseas residents: Related office*	*Overseas residents: Others*	*UK residents*
UK branches and agencies					
1980	97.6	46.8	32.7	37.7	24.9
1984	194.1	46.1	51.3	85.7	40.7
1988	444.6	39.7	143.2	164.0	59.0
Liabilities					
1980			16.5	41.3	36.3
1984			25.8	92.4	70.1
1988			91.4	167.9	123.4

[a] Percentage of total foreign branches of Japanese banks.
Source: Terrell, Dohner, and Lowrey (1990) The Activities of Japanese Banks in the United Kingdom and in the United States, 1980–1988, *Federal Reserve Bulletin*

have acquired experience in securities dealing, experience that will be invaluable once Article 65 is relaxed. Such involvement was most dramatically illustrated by the Sumitomo bank investment of US$ 500m to obtain a limited interest in Goldman Sachs, the US investment banking partnership. As a condition for approval of the deal, Sumitomo bank received no voting rights in return for its investment.

6.2. The Regulatory Environment

6.2.1 *The Regulatory Framework*

The regulation and supervision of banks in Japan is probably the most extensive and comprehensive of any developed nation. While the overt manifestations of such regulation can sometimes be subtle and indirect, the regulatory influence is in fact pervasive and decisive, affecting bank policy and activity in virtually every area and at almost every level.

Formally, the Bank of Japan, the nation's central bank, presides over the banking system in Japan in a manner somewhat analogous to that of the Bank of England in the United Kingdom. To a great extent, the Bank of Japan's relationship with other banks is contractual rather than statutory; in fact, BOJ decisions do not necessarily carry the weight of law, which has led to some lack of clarity concerning the Bank of Japan's role in bank supervision. This lack of clarity has been overcome by the Japanese inclination to seek accommodation and cooperation, enabling the Bank of Japan to, in fact, have extensive control. Where the central bank does have statutory authority – in the issuing of currency and the control of the credit system – it has not hesitated to closely dictate the behavior of banks in such matters as the level of interest rates and the volume of credit. Additionally, the Bank of Japan is accorded the role of provider of liquidity to the banking system (lender of last resort), is widely perceived to be the guarantor of solvency for the Japanese banking system, and conducts monetary policy.

Japanese banking law gives actual supervisory authority over banks to the seemingly all-powerful Ministry of Finance. The MOF, in addition to being able to regulate interest rates on bank liabilities, can require banks to divulge virtually any information it deems necessary. It can enforce policy using either non-binding voluntary directives (so-called administrative guidance), or through the issuance of binding rules based on its authority under the banking law. The MOF is responsible for approving the business operations and merger of banks, as well as the opening of new branches.

The regulatory structure of banks in Japan is currently in a state of considerable flux. At present, regulations concerning capital adequacy, liquidity, and loans to single borrowers are formulated and enforced by the Ministry of Finance. The ministry has also devised a set of guidelines concerning international lending by Japanese banks, including a set of "administrative guidelines" for country-risk evaluation systems. The supervision of overseas branches and subsidiaries is done on a fully consolidated basis, and has been considerably tightened in recent years.

Formally, foreign banks operating in Japan operate under the same laws and guidelines as domestic banks. In practice, however, the treatment of foreign banks is determined by the treatment accorded Japan's banks in the country of origin.

6.2.2 *Major Bank Regulations*

This section summarizes major bank regulations in terms of their potential impact on bank performance.

Scope of business – capital market activities

The banking industry is regulated by Article 65 of the Security and Exchange Law, a Glass-Steagall type barrier between banking and the securities (investment banking) business. According to this article, banks are permitted to invest and participate in the underwriting of Japanese National, Municipal and Government guaranteed bonds. In Japan, commercial paper is not considered a security but a bill discounted. As a result of compromise, both banks and securities firms are allowed to handle commercial paper. Overseas affiliates of Japanese banks are permitted to underwrite Eurobond issues by non-Japanese firms. Significantly, most city banks place a high priority on overseas expansion by focusing on securities-related activities. It is expected that progressive liberalization will gradually take place over the next few years. In terms of bank performance, the contribution of non-interest income is currently relatively modest.

These are a number of principal securities powers available to Japanese banks and their subsidiaries:

- Japanese banks may underwrite and deal in government bonds (as of the beginning of the 1980s)
- they may underwrite and deal in commercial paper
- they may serve as the private placement agent of corporate and other debt securities
- they may render investment advice; under the 1986 investment advisory business law, bank subsidiaries may provide investment advisory services
- Japanese banks may buy and sell securities for their own portfolio investment account
- the banks may engage in futures activities both for their own account and for customers.

However, Japanese banks may not engage in insurance activities or in real estate.

Another important regulation that has segmented the banking industry is the provision that only long-term credit banks can issue long-term obligations in the underdeveloped capital market. Consequently, these banks have become an important supplier of long-term funds (especially for foreign borrowing).

Lending limitations

Ordinary commercial banks are prohibited from extending loans to a single borrower (and its affiliates) in excess of 20 percent of the bank's capital stock and reserve. In the case of long-term credit banks, the restriction is set at 30 percent and for specialized foreign exchange banks at 40 percent. There are two additional complementary constraints, to wit:

- total loans and indirect credit extension (e.g. guarantees, acceptances, commercial letters of credit) to a single borrower by an ordinary commercial bank must not exceed 30 percent of the bank's capital stock and reserves
- total loans and indirect credit extension to a borrower and its subsidiaries must not exceed 40 percent of the bank's capital stock and reserves.

These restrictions impose a certain level of diversification, by reducing the possibility that a single borrower's default could lead to a bank failure. These restrictions also contribute to a clear distinction between wholesale banking and retail banking, in accordance with the size of the bank's equity base.

The Temporary Interest Rate Control Law

Lending and deposit rates in Japan have traditionally been set by the regulatory authorities. Under the Temporary Interest Rates Control Law, the MOF has the authority to establish maximum limits on interest rates of private financial institutions.

As of Sept. 1, 1986 the maximum limits on rates were as in table 6.4.

Table 6.4 Maximum interest rates

	Rate per annum percent
Deposits:	
Time deposit	4.38
Demand deposit	0
Other	0.63
Short-term loans	15.00

Exempt from the above regulation are:

1 large denomination time deposits (over $0.7 million since 1987)
2 certificates of deposit and money market instruments
3 yen accounts of foreign governments and international organizations
4 foreign currency deposits and loans
5 long-term loans.

Rates of interest on short-term yen loans are established within a range between the bank's prime rate of interest and the maximum limit set by law. The prime rate of interest is 50 basis points higher than the Bank of Japan official discount rate. However, on large denomination deposits, the rate deregulation that occurred in 1985 has led to an increase in rates and a margin squeeze. The rapid deregulation (by April 1990 about 70 percent of deposits were deregulated) had a greater impact on smaller institutions which were unable to diversify or manage risk.

Long-term lending rates are not regulated. In practice, prime rates of interest on long-term loans of trust banks and long-term credit banks are pegged at about 90 basis points higher than their five year funding cost.

It is not clear to what extent the low margin on financial intermediation is the result of regulatory intervention. It is evident, however, that these interest rate margins are among the lowest in the world.

Liquidity – reserve deposit system

Banks are required to maintain non-interest-bearing demand deposits with the Bank of Japan. The current reserve ratios for banks, which were implemented on July 1, 1986, depend upon their balance of deposits at the end of the previous year. These are shown in table 6.5.

Table 6.5 Reserve requirements

Balance of deposits	*Time deposits and negotiable CDs*
Less than yen 800 billion	0.125
Yen 800 billion to 2,500 billion	0.625
More than yen 2,500 billion	1.625

These reserve requirements are very low compared with other countries. Such low reserve requirements enable banks to operate with low interest margins. Furthermore, the schedule of reserve requirements subsidizes small banks at the expense of large banks.

The MOF also encourages banks to keep the following operating ratios:

1 the average balance of current assets to total deposits should exceed 30 percent
2 at least 45 percent of term lending for one year or more should be funded by term deposits or other debts of over one year's maturity
3 the average ratio of loans to deposits should be below 80 percent.

Capital adequacy

For purposes of capital adequacy, capital is defined as equity capital plus reserves. Until recently, the MOF has provided banks with administrative guidance that includes the following ratios:

1 a bank's own capital must be greater than 10 percent of total deposits
2 fixed assets and equipment must not exceed 40 percent of equity capital
3 dividends are generally limited to 15 percent of equity capital and 40 percent of after tax net income.

In May 1986 the MOF introduced new guidelines for all domestic banks, requiring that the capital-to-asset ratio reach approximately 4 percent by the end of 1990 (currently the ratio is 2.6 percent). The new guidelines also call upon Japanese banks with overseas branches to achieve a capital adequacy ratio of 6 percent. Also, the Japanese regulators have introduced the concept of a risk asset ratio that applies only to a bank's foreign assets. This ratio establishes a limit of 3.5 times net worth, which includes 70 percent of unrealized profit on securities. The MOF intends to reduce this limit to 2.5 times net worth.

Following the agreement of the Basle Committee, the MOF amended its capital requirements in December 1988. A new standard based on the Cooke Committee agreement was introduced for banks with international operations. At the same time, the MOF maintained its own existing standard for banks with purely domestic operations.

The new system of measuring capital adequacy for banks with international operations was introduced retroactively commencing March 31, 1988. However, the target ratio came into force on March 31, 1991, when it reached 7.25 percent. From March 1993, the target ratio will be 8.0 percent, of which half must be core capital (Tier 1). Due to deregulation of interest rates, Japanese banks found the asset growth strategy emphasized in the past to be neither interesting nor profitable. The BIS requirement encourages capital formation, and improving return on assets.

The domestic standard

The standard of capital adequacy that will be applied to banks without international operations is the following pre-existing capital ratio:

$$\text{Capital ratio} = \frac{\begin{array}{l}\text{shareholders equity plus various reserves}\\ \text{plus other specialized items}\end{array}}{\begin{array}{l}\text{average total assets (excluding acceptances,}\\ \text{but including guarantees) less}\\ \text{specific loan loss reserve}\end{array}} \times 100$$

The target was 4 percent, and commenced at the end of March 1991.

Deposit insurance

The Deposit Insurance Law was enacted and implemented in 1971. Insured deposits include principal guaranteed money trusts, but exclude deposits in offshore branches, certificates of deposit, and foreign currency deposits. The premium charged is constant at 0.012 percent per annum of the total insured deposits balance outstanding at the end of the preceding year. Deposits are insured up to yen 10 million per depositor. The practices of the Deposit Insurance Corporation are very similar to its US counterpart, including the provision of assistance to banks acquiring a troubled financial institution. But while the Deposit Insurance System in Japan acts in ways similar to its US counterpart, in practice it is of far less importance due to the negligible number of bank failures in Japan.

Foreign exchange exposure

The foreign currency operations of banks authorized to engage in foreign exchange transactions are monitored. The MOF sets limits on a daily basis for each bank's net spot position and for spot plus forward positions. There are further guidelines with respect to the degree of allowed maturity mismatching. Banks generally keep their foreign exchange exposure below 10 percent of their equity.

Other regulations

1 Legal earned reserve. A domestic bank paying cash dividends to its stockholders is required to contribute an amount equivalent to 20 percent or more of cash dividends to legally earned reserves, until such reserves equal the amount of its capital stock.
2 The dividend payout ratio (total dividend/net income) should not exceed 40 percent in any one year, unless the dividends do not exceed 10 percent of the par value of the share.
3 Foreign banks operating in Japan. Until recently there were no subsidiaries of foreign banks in Japan. For a foreign bank to operate a subsidiary, approval was required from several government authorities under different laws; obtaining such approval was virtually impossible. Foreign banks have had no access to the low cost funds of private individuals, resulting in 90 percent of their funds being obtained on the short-term money markets. Eighty-two branches of foreign banks operated in Japan in 1989. In the summer of 1985 nine foreign banks were allowed to open trust banks in Japan.

In summary, regulatory intervention in Japan, in terms of market segmentation, is substantial (long-term vs. short-term intermediation, commercial vs. investment banking, domestic vs. foreign banks). By contrast, regulatory intervention in banking operations has been relatively flexible, allowing banks to pursue efficient banking practices.

6.2.3 Foreign Exchange Control

The Foreign Exchange and Foreign Trade Control Law of 1949 was completely amended in December 1979. The method of control was changed to one of general permission, with restrictions only on specific classes of transactions. Foreign exchange is conducted by MOF authorized foreign exchange banks. There were 252 authorized foreign exchange banks as of December 1988, including the Bank of Tokyo, city banks, regional banks, long-term credit banks and mutual (Sogo) banks.

The Act provides various controls over authorized foreign exchange banks, regarding transactions with customers and other banks and net foreign exchange positions. Authorized foreign exchange banks are limited to a maximum net foreign exchange position (spot plus forward) at the daily close of business of an amount specified by the MOF.[1] The purpose of this regulation is to prevent speculation and ensure control over the temporary inflow of foreign capital. Under the Foreign Exchange Law, authorized foreign exchange banks are required to submit a number of reports for control and statistical purposes, including reports on foreign exchange positions and on loans and deposits.

Until March 1984, forward exchange trading in Japan had been confined to transactions related to actual trade flows (for example, hedging transactions associated with export contracts). The removal of the rule in April 1984 resulted in a considerable widening of scope for active foreign exchange management by the non-bank sector. In 1986, the MOF gradually removed the regulations that restrict Japanese institutional investors from purchasing foreign securities.

6.2.4 Key Accounting Issues

Banks must provide shareholders with annual and semi-annual reports. These reports are not detailed, lacking both consolidated figures and specific information on the types and maturities of loans and deposits.

The BIS capital adequacy proposals may lead to changes in the kind of information banks make public, by requiring more consolidated financial statements and disclosure of hidden reserves.

Specifically, Japanese accounting standards include the following details.

Consolidation

Banks are not obliged to publish consolidated financial statements, except for those banks which have listed securities (subject to materiality). The approach employed for consolidation is the "total integration" method, which is also used in the United States (APB 18). It should be noted that, since December 1987, the Anti-Monopoly Law prohibits banks from owning 5 percent or more of other companies unless they have specific permission.

Valuation of securities – hidden reserves

Banks must report two categories of securities holdings: those for investment and those for trading. Investment and trading securities include listed bonds and other securities, which are valued at the lower of cost or market value (in the case of government securities, the MOF allows the cost basis). Unlisted securities are valued at cost, adjusted for permanent decline. In the case of most equities, cost is far below market value, giving rise to hidden reserves.

Additionally, banks are required to establish two reserves:

1 National bonds price fluctuation reserve of 2 percent of the increase during the year of the carrying value of the Japanese National Bond.
2 Reserve for losses on trading account securities of 10 percent of net profit on the sale of trading accounts securities (up to 20 percent of equity capital).

Loan loss reserves

In terms of disclosure, loan loss reserves appear separately on the liabilities side of the balance sheet. There are three components of the loan loss reserves although they are reported as one figure.

General loan loss reserves

The MOF requires that a bank's general loan loss reserve should be the maximum amount provided for by the tax law. However, while this maximum amount (currently 0.3 percent) has been reduced, loan totals have been rising. The general loan loss reserves include two elements provided out of taxed and untaxed income.

Reserves for problem country loans

The MOF has specified particular countries for which bank exposure is at special risk. The requirement to provide against such exposure was first introduced for the fiscal year ending March 1983. The maximum reserve is currently 10 percent (until March 1988 it was 5 percent) of unconsolidated credit, of which only 1 percent is tax deductible. The reserve against exposure to a particular country may be as high as 100 percent, but the average reserve against total unconsolidated exposure to qualifying countries must not exceed 10 percent.

Specific loan loss reserve

A bank may set up specific loan loss reserves under the Banking Bureau's rules only if the MOF is satisfied that such a need exists. It must be shown that the debtor has insufficient assets or income stream to meet its liabilities, and/or has failed to comply with the loan conditions. The Taxation Bureau is more stringent, since it requires a court judgment impugning the debtor's solvency before it will allow a specific provision against tax. Even then, the Bureau may allow only 50 percent of any provision made, depending on its view of the risk of loss. In all cases of dishonored cheques and debts arising under the Corporate Reorganization Law (equivalent to Chapter 11 of the Bankruptcy Act in the United States or a Vergleich in the Federal Republic of Germany), a maximum tax-deductible provision of 50 percent is mandated by the Bureau.

Japan therefore differs from most other countries, in that the MOF (in the guise of the Banking Bureau) has final approval on specific or general provisions in excess of the taxable limit. In other countries this decision resides with bank management.

Public reporting

As already noted, only one figure is published in bank balance sheets, a figure that combines three types of loan loss reserves. Likewise, only one combined figure of transfer from income to the three types of reserves is disclosed. Charge-offs against income are separately reported in the published income statement, as are any recoveries of amounts previously written-off.

One of the explanatory schedules given in bank securities reports shows movements during the reporting period in loan loss reserves; however, it analyzes only the one combined figure of loan loss reserve. This schedule shows the opening and composite balance, foreign exchange adjustment, the total transfer out of the reserve back to income, the total transfer in from income, any charge-offs against reserves, and the closing balance. Sometimes an addendum to this schedule provides enough information for an educated guess of the level of a bank's general loan loss reserve.

Foreign currency translation

In consolidated accounts the foreign currency assets, liabilities and net income of foreign subsidiaries are converted according to Financial Accounting Standard (FAS) No. 52. This essentially involves conversion at year-end rates.

Foreign exchange

Japanese bank accounting standards allow two accounting methods for foreign exchange: (1) the total net position method, including forward contracts; and (2) the separate position method. Once adopted, the method chosen must be consistently applied, but it can be changed if there is reasonable cause.

(1) The total net position method (spot and forward)

Yen equivalent of total net currencies (including forward contracts)	– XXX
The amount equivalent to unearned interest on export bills in foreign currency, bought in yen	– XXX
Less: Total net position of assets in Yen (historical rates) book value	–(XXX)
Valuation gain or Loss	– XXX

(2) The separate position method

Yen equivalent of total assets in foreign currencies (excluding forward exchange contracts) spot rate	– XXX
Less: Spot position at historical rate	–(XXX)
Subtotal (A)	XXX
Yen equivalent of forward contracts	XXX
Less: Forward contracts (at historical spot rate at the day of contract)	(XXX)
Subtotal (B)	XXX
Spot position at current spot rate	XXX
Less: Spot position at average historical spot rate for past six months	(XXX)
Subtotal (C)	XXX

In case $|B| < |C|$ total gain $A + B$

In case $|B| > |C|$ total gain $A - B$

If there is a translation gain on the net forward position, the loss should be deducted from the evaluation loss on the net spot position, to the extent of translation gains on the net spot position.

New reporting requirements

In September 1989, Japanese banks began reporting profitability in accordance with new standards. The major change involved the replacement of operating profits with a new concept: business profit. The business profit does not include profits from the sale of equity holdings, enterprise taxes, or additions to loan reserves. Thus, business profits represent a closer measure of profits from current operation. Restating profits generally will result in business profit levels in line with old operating profits.

6.2.5 Taxation

Corporate tax rates

Since 1987 the effective tax rate on corporate income has been 56 percent, including corporation tax, business tax, and inhabitant tax (Prefectural and Municipal taxes). There is a special tax rate for small corporations (paid up capital of less than 100 million yen) of 31 percent on undistributed profit of up to 8 million yen.

The corporation tax (National tax) rates on undistributed taxable income, for accounting periods ending on or after April 1, 1987 were:

1987 – 42 percent
1988 – 40 percent
1989 – 37.5 percent

The business tax (Prefectural tax) rates are:

Taxable income	Tax rate[a]	Increased tax rate
0 – 3.0 million yen	6%	6.6%
3.5 – 7.0 million yen	9%	9.9%
over 7.0 million yen	12%	13.2%

[a] A deduction is allowed for business tax paid.

Increased rates apply according to government discretion (e.g., the Tokyo Metropolitan Government increased the rates to large corporations). The Inhabitant tax is based on the corporate tax. The standard tax rate is 17.3 percent on corporate tax, and the rate may be increased to 20.7 percent.

An assessment for per capita taxes, which range from 50,000 to 4.35 million yen per annum, is included in the Inhabitant tax. The per capita tax is based on capitalization and number of employees.

Valuation

Net taxable income is based on the corporation's accounting books and records kept in accordance with regulations, under which national and other bonds, other securities, and gold assets are valued at lower of cost or market value. Shares in subsidiaries and securities not listed should be valued at cost.

Reserves

A corporation may establish a tax deductible reserve for unsecured bad debt. The amount of reserve is based on either the statutory percentage or the corporation's average bad debt experience during the preceding three years. The statutory rate for banks is 0.3 percent. In specific cases an additional special reserve of up to 50 percent of certain debt may be recorded.

Under the Uniform Accounting Principles for banks, the following reserves are required:

1. All provisions and reserves permitted by the tax law (including bad debt, employee severance);
2. A provision for national bond price fluctuations equal to 1 percent of the bank value of national bonds at the end of each accounting period;
3. A provision for losses on trade of marketable securities.

Losses

Losses can be carried back for one year and carried forward for five years. However, the carryback provision has been suspended for losses reported in 1986 and 1987. Furthermore, for accounting periods ending between April 1, 1986 and March 31, 1988, a tax loss reported for the preceding one-year period cannot be carried forward and deducted during this period.

Interest paid and received

Intrabank interest costs

Intrabank interest costs are allowed if the cost is reasonable and does not exceed the amount computed, based on the Eurodollar market rate. Any excess portion will be disallowed unless the bank can substantiate the actual rate. Where intrabank interest charges to the Japanese branch are below market rate, the difference reduces the disallowed portion of interbank interest charges on funds taken from the same market (e.g., no offset can be made with respect to funds taken from different markets). Finally, the interest cost allowable for Japanese tax purposes is limited to funds used *directly* for income producing activities (for example, lease deposits on banking office premises, or the book value of fixed assets, cannot be used).

Interest payment by banks

Interest paid in Japan to a resident individual or company is subject to a 20 percent withholding income tax. Interest paid to a non-resident individual or non-resident company is subject to either a 20 percent withholding income tax or a lower rate if a tax treaty is applicable. Interest received by banks in the course of banking activities is exempted from withholding tax. Foreign banks are specifically required to apply for the withholding tax exemption for the purpose of reporting interest income.

6.3 Bank Performance

The performance of Japanese banks in the past five years is a direct result of both the regulatory environment and the economic conditions in Japan. The following evaluation of Japanese banks primarily examines the large wholesale city banks, a sample of regional banks, and a sample of foreign banks.

6.3.1 Structure of Assets and Liabilities

Bank regulation in Japan makes a clear distinction between different types of institutions.

City banks

The 13 city banks have a market share of about 34 percent (table 6.2). City banks are both wholesale and retail banks that function in the nationwide and international markets.

The combined balance sheet of the 13 city banks for four years ending March 31, 1989 is presented in table 6.6. The percentage of earning assets in March 1989 was about 95 percent of total assets. The majority of loans (almost 78 percent), when deposits with other banks are excluded, were made to large corporations. Especially noteworthy is the 49 percent growth rate of the city bank portfolio of loans between March 1985 and March 1989. This very impressive growth rate is the result of both increased

Table 6.6 Combined balance sheet (13 city banks)

	31/3/89 (US$, mil.)	*31/3/89*	*31/3/88 (Yen, bil.)*	*31/3/87*	*31/3/86*
A Loans					
1 Bills of exchange	618449	81759	83861	84500	81969
2 Overdrafts	211626	27977	23259	16771	10938
3 Loans on deeds	831157	109879	89495	69550	56720
Total A	1661232	219615	196615	170821	149627
B Other earning assets					
1 Deposits with banks	634213	83843	67105	60908	49720
2 Trading securities	5091	673	1049	1689	1616
3 Japanese govt bonds	92216	12191	10617	8829	7762
4 Other investments	144395	19089	17629	16100	12666
5 Equity investments	98056	12963	9767	7285	6555
Total B	973971	128759	106167	94811	78319
C Total earning assets (A+B)	2635203	348374	302782	265632	227946
D Fixed assets	11694	1546	1436	1323	1238
E Non-earning assets					
1 Cash and due from banks	245696	32481	28453	23383	20535
2 Other	36762	4860	3892	3203	2938
F Total assets	2929355	387261	336563	293541	252657
G Customer & short-term funding					
1 Demand	309538	40921	37545	34442	30464
2 Savings	231135	30556	26756	28185	24435
3 Time	1581952	209134	181929	151615	131043
4 Domestic interbank	333964	44150	37687	35834	29356
5 Other	180461	23857	19667	17007	13692
Total G	2637050	348618	303584	267083	228990
H Other funding					
1 Convertible bonds	9886	1307	441	104	157
I Other (non-int. bearing)	191436	25308	23067	19042	17026
J Loan loss reserves	12693	1678	1506	1354	1119
K Risk capital	78290	10350	7965	5958	5365
L Total liabilities & risk capital	2929355	387261	336563	293541	252657
Exchange rate (US$1 = JPY)		132.2	125.4	145.8	179.6
Ratios (%)					
Deposits/loans		127.8	125.2	125.4	124.3
Total loans/total assets		56.7	58.4	58.2	59.2
Fixed assets/risk capital		14.9	18.0	22.2	23.1
Risk capital/total assets		2.7	2.4	2.0	2.1

Source: IBCA data base

Table 6.7 Principal assets and liabilities (yen, billions)

	Lending to non-banks	%[a]	*Securities portfolio*	%	*Non-bank deposits*	%	*Bonds outstanding*	%	*Equity capital*	%
All banks										
1980	179,590	100.0	49,696	100.0	215,869	100.0	20,685	100.0	10,758	100.0
1984	266,053	100.0	66,459	100.0	293,603	100.0	29,643	100.0	11,323	100.0
1988	419,993	100.0	108,075	100.0	423,813	100.0	43,304	100.0	18,426	100.0
1989	466,667	100.0	125,097	100.0	481,943	100.0	45,875	100.0	25,467	100.0
City banks										
1980	66,631	37.1	16,827	33.9	85,418	39.5	1,395	6.7	4,463	41.5
1984	96,439	36.2	20,135	30.3	114,815	39.1	2,286	7.7	4,809	42.5
1988	177,183	42.2	37,102	34.3	172,817	40.8	4,148	9.6	8,930	48.5
1989	195,523	41.9	44,287	35.4	195,456	40.7	4,233	9.2	11,995	47.1
Regional banks										
1980	43,640	24.3	13,937	28.0	58,788	27.2	–	–	4,114	38.2
1984	65,431	24.6	18,315	27.6	83,731	28.5	–	–	4,226	37.3
1988	94,368	22.5	26,694	24.7	120,522	28.4	467	1.1	4,735	25.7
1989	106,759	22.9	30,291	24.2	135,969	28.2	355	0.8	5,975	23.5
Second association of regional banks[b]										
1989	39,222	8.4	9,831	7.9	52,554	10.9	38	0.1	1,867	7.3
Foreign banks										
1980	4,672	2.6	165	0.3	1,249	0.6	1,077	5.2	–	–
1984	6,849	2.6	391	0.6	1,712	0.6	263	0.9	–	–
1988	6,475	1.5	1,140	1.1	1,463	0.3	976	2.2	–	–
1989	6,966	1.5	1,366	1.1	2,163	0.4	328	0.7	–	–

Long-term credit banks										
1980	16,524	9.2	5,252	10.6	3,434	1.6	18,213	88.1	1,002	9.3
1984	24,087	9.1	7,638	11.5	4,888	1.7	27,094	91.4	1,058	9.3
1988	38,265	9.1	12,421	11.5	6,782	1.6	37,303	86.1	2,000	10.8
1989	41,980	9.0	14,226	11.4	7,923	1.6	40,391	88.0	2,437	9.6
Trust banks (banking activities)										
1980	4,844	2.7	4,078	8.2	5,338[c]	2.5	–	–	782	7.3
1984	12,113	4.6	6,470	9.7	7,596[c]	2.6	–	–	794	7.0
1988	22,702	5.4	11,796	10.9	10,485[c]	2.5	410	1.0	2,148	11.7
1989	23,509	5.0	13,949	11.1	13,599[c]	2.8	530	1.2	2,879	11.3
Sogo banks										
1980	16,932	9.4	3,766	7.6	27,167	12.6	–	–	167	1.5
1984	24,592	9.2	5,396	8.1	34,045	11.6	–	–	177	1.6
1988	35,097	8.4	8,729	8.1	46,170	10.9	–	–	310	1.7
The Shinkin banks										
1980	26,347	14.7	5,671	11.4	34,475	16.0	–	–	230	2.2
1984	36,542	13.7	8,114	12.2	46,816	15.9	–	–	259	2.3
1988	45,903	10.9	10,193	9.4	65,574	15.5	–	–	303	1.6
1989	52,708	11.3	11,147	8.9	74,279	15.4	–	–	314	1.2

[a] Percent of total banks in this table.
[b] Including Sogo banks.
[c] Amount due to trust accounts: 1980 – 3,523 yen billion
1984 – 9,089 yen billion
1988 – 15,080 yen billion
1989 – 14,642 yen billion

Source: Economic Statistics Annual, 1989, March 1990, The Bank of Japan

involvement in international markets and growth in the Japanese economy. In recent years, city banks have succeeded in penetrating the market for small business and individual loans. Additionally, city banks have also increased their share of longer lending for loans over a year (from 33.5 percent in 1981 to 41.9 percent in 1989).

Investment in securities reached only 12 percent of total assets, representing the relatively low involvement of banks in securities markets and the fact that the valuation of securities is below their market value. Investment in premises represents only 0.5 percent of total assets and 18 percent of equity capital and reserves. During 1989, rising interest rates (the central bank discount rate rose from 2.5 percent in 1988 to 4.5 percent in 1989) caused major losses in city banks' bond portfolios. Changes in accounting methods, and the use of futures and options, led to a growing degree of unrealized losses in the bond portfolios of banks.

The funds of city banks are based on deposits from the public (73 percent), borrowed money (24 percent), and equity capital (3 percent). About 60 percent of total deposits are large scale corporate deposits. The funding position of city banks has been one of net deficit throughout (table 6.7). This deficit has been financed through borrowing from the Bank of Japan and short-term financial markets. City banks have almost no access to long-term funding. The structure of assets and liabilities reveals a high degree of involvement in traditional intermediation (e.g., deposits taken from the public, extending loans etc.).

Regional banks

Regional banks are generally of medium and small size, although several equal city banks in size. The loan portfolio of regional banks, based on a sample of five (see table 6.8), represents 64 percent of total assets. This amount grew significantly (34 percent) during the period 1984–9. The main borrowers are local small- and medium-sized firms. Regional banks are much less involved than city banks in interbank money market transactions. Most funds (about 60 percent) are deposits of individuals, with 72 percent of these being deposits of one year or more. Regional banks have no access to long-term funds. As a result of their broad funds base, regional banks have a large ratio of security holdings and are major participants in financial markets. The retail nature of these banks is reflected in the structure of their assets and liabilities, being based mainly on traditional intermediation among a large number of depositors and borrowers.

Foreign banks

Foreign banks are an important part of the Tokyo dollar-call market and the Tokyo foreign exchange market. The main source of funds is Euromoney borrowing (interoffice). The lending operation involves short- term yen-denominated (60 percent of the loan portfolio) lending in foreign currency.

Long-term credit banks

The scope of activities of these banks involves long-term credit financed mostly by bank debentures. It should be noted that ordinary banks are not legally prohibited from offering long-term loans. The major distinction is that ordinary banks take short-term deposits and long-term credit banks issue long-term debentures. Therefore, ordinary banks are exposed to interest rate risks in their long-term lending. The total value of bank debentures issued by long-term credit banks was 40.4 trillion yen at year-end 1989. There are restrictions on the type of deposit these banks can accept, hence the outstanding amount of such deposits is small. Additionally, these banks are involved in securities-related operations, foreign exchange business, foreign trade financing, and international securities operations.

Trust banks

Trust banks jointly manage trust operations (accounts) and banking operations (accounts). The types managed include money trusts, securities trusts, movable property in trust, and real estate in trust. The banking accounts represent between 20 and 30 percent of total assets.

Sogo banks

The business activity of all Sogo banks is identical to those of ordinary banks, except that they are permitted mutual instalment operations. Article 2, paragraph 1, of the Sogo Banking Law defines mutual instalment payments over a period of time as the promise of payment of a fixed amount of money, either during or at the end of a determined period. In recent years, mutual instalment payments have declined sharply in importance and, hence, the volume of business for Sogo banks has grown at a slower pace than other areas of the Japanese banking system. Over the past two years, 66 of the 68 Sogo savings banks have given up their mutual status to become secondary regional banks. Deregulation and increased competition has led to poor performance and potential failure in this group.

Table 6.8 Combined balance sheet (five regional banks)

	31/3/89 (US$, mil.)	31/3/89	31/3/88 (Yen, bil.)	31/3/87	31/3/86
A Loans					
1 Bills of exchange	48948	6471	6818	6426	6418
2 Overdrafts	21127	2793	1608	1218	702
3 Loans on deeds	50666	6698	5554	4528	3823
Total A	120741	15962	13980	12172	10943
B Other earning assets					
1 Deposits with banks	26082	3448	2353	1360	1402
2 Trading securities	499	66	49	122	69
3 Japanese govt bonds	12549	1659	1384	1254	1158
4 Other investments	17360	2295	1667	1480	1171
5 Equity investments	4266	564	420	342	315
Total B	60756	8032	5873	4558	4115
C Total earning assets (A+B)	181497	23994	19853	16730	15058
D Fixed assets	1543	204	171	155	155
E Non-earning assets					
1 Cash and due from banks	12080	1597	1416	1262	1175
2 Other	1605	212	166	124	112
F Total assets	196725	26007	21606	18271	16500
G Customer & short-term funding					
1 Demand	30794	4071	3740	3374	2964
2 Savings	9115	1205	1136	1042	986
3 Time	125825	16634	13124	11219	10107
4 Domestic interbank	11112	1469	1437	683	591
5 Other	2050	271	115	134	159
Total G	178896	23650	19552	16452	14807
H Other funding					
1 Convertible bonds	893	118	24	5	0
I Other (non-int. bearing)	10378	1372	1297	1179	1113
K Loan loss reserves	598	79	73	70	68
L Risk capital	5960	788	660	565	512
M Total liabilities & risk capital	196725	26007	21606	18271	16500
Exchange rate (US$1 = JPY)		132.2	125.4	145.8	179.6
Ratios (%)					
Total loans/total assets		61.4	64.7	66.6	66.3
Reserves/total loans		0.5	0.5	0.6	0.6
Inter liab./earning assets		98.6	98.6	98.4	98.3
Risk capital/total assets		3.0	3.1	3.1	3.1
Fixed assets/risk capital		25.9	25.9	27.4	30.3

Source: IBCA data base

Including: Bank of Hiroshima, Bank of Kyoto, Chiba Bank, Hokuriko Bank & Iyo Bank.

The Shinkin banks

The operations of Shinkin banks are not particularly different from that of ordinary banks. These banks are organized, however, on a membership basis. Deposits at Shinkin banks (mostly by members), are mostly time deposits (more than 90 percent), and exceed the amount lent. Lending to non-members is not allowed to exceed 20 percent of total lending. Surplus funds are invested in a securities portfolio. Deregulation of interest rates and increased risk affect the soundness and performance of this group.

6.3.2 Income Statement

Net interest margins are significantly higher for domestic retail banks than for either city or other retail banks throughout the period examined (table 6.9). Moreover, there has been a continuous trend toward declining interest margins for all banking groups. The most drastic reduction in net interest during the period 1980–8 occurred in the city bank group (about 40 percent), while for the more retail-oriented groups of Sogo and Shinkin banks the reduction was lower (about 10 to 15 percent). The reduction in net interest income is somewhat offset by the significant reduction in the personnel and other operating expenses ratio. This reduction resulted from an increase in the volume of lending beyond the increase in personnel and other expenses.

Japanese banks have been severely affected by the progressive deregulation of deposit rates, which even before the deregulation of the interest rate margin were among the lowest in the world. Banks increased their reliance on funding through instruments with deregulated interest rates (from 17.8 percent of total deposits in 1985 to 50.3 percent in 1989). For city banks the average net interest margin was 0.99 percent in 1988–9 (table 6.10), and for regional banks it was 1.50 percent in 1988–9 (table 6.11). At present, rate limitations on large denomination time deposits have been removed, and retail deposits are likely to be deregulated in coming years. From 1985 onward, deposits with deregulated interest rates accounted for 40 to 70 percent of the total increase in financial assets, whereas the share of old-fashioned time deposits declined sharply.

The net result of deregulating rate limitations in 1985 was a reduction in margins. Further, in November 1987 the MOF authorized dealing in commercial paper, which can be underwritten and distributed by both banks and securities houses. As a result, corporate and individual liquidity has increasingly moved into the securities markets. The purchase of foreign securities by corporations expanded from 9.3 percent (1975–9) to 24.8 percent during 1980–9. Thus, Japanese borrowers are not only increasingly

Table 6.9 Income statement major indicators

Type of banks	*Yield on lending*	*Interest rates on deposits and debentures*	*Net interest margin*	*Personnel expense ratio*[a]	*Other operating expense ratio*[a]
City banks					
1980 (L.H)[b]	9.13	7.69	1.44	0.98	0.62
1985	6.72	5.80	0.92	0.66	0.45
1986	5.62	4.66	0.96	0.59	0.42
1987	5.19	4.37	0.82	0.50	0.40
1988	5.47	4.71	0.76	0.44	0.38
Regional banks					
1980 (LH)[b]	8.45	5.80	2.65	1.50	0.71
1985	6.58	4.61	1.97	1.27	0.62
1986	5.82	3.89	1.93	1.19	0.61
1987	5.16	3.43	1.73	1.09	0.58
1988	5.16	3.32	1.84	0.99	0.58
Sogo banks					
1980 (LH)[b]	8.69	5.96	2.73	1.64	0.83
1985	7.08	4.70	2.38	1.38	0.68
1986	6.55	4.04	2.51	1.34	0.67
1987	5.97	3.57	2.40	1.22	0.63
1988	5.89	3.42	2.47	1.16	0.63
Shinkin banks					
1980 (LH)[b]	8.84	5.63	3.21	1.89	0.62
1985	7.39	4.62	2.77	1.66	0.77
1986	6.89	4.05	2.84	1.59	0.75
1987	6.20	3.44	2.76	1.49	0.70
1988	5.93	3.11	2.82	1.41	0.67

[a] The ratio is calculated as personnel and other operating expenses per dollar of earning assets.
[b] FH and LH represent the first half (April–September) and the last half (September–March) of the reporting year.

Source: *Economic Statistics Annual 1989*, March 1990.The Bank of Japan

using the securities markets, but are also moving abroad to Euro-yen and other international markets. Foreign bonds accounted for 8 percent of total corporate financing in the 1985–8 period (Osugi, 1990). The fall in interest rate margins was more than compensated for by the 75 percent growth (between end-of-year balances for 1984 and 1989; (table 6.7)) of the loan portfolio, resulting in an increase in the net interest income during this period of 41 percent (table 6.12).

Other operating income increased by 191 percent between 1984–9 (table 6.12). This increase resulted from the increase in underwriting activities of government securities and bond trading. The ratio of other operating income to net interest income increased from 22.9 percent in 1984 to 47.4 percent in 1989 (table 6.12), indicating both the growing importance of fee income and the declining importance of interest rate margins. For the city banks, the significant decline in interest margins was more than compensated for by the growth of the loan portfolio during the period 1984–9 102.7 percent (table 6.7) resulting in an increase in the net interest income of 40.2 percent. Non-interest income, which was 20.9 percent of interest income in 1984, grew to 51.1 percent in 1989.

Personnel expenses for city banks comprised only about 45 percent of total operating expenses (in 1989). This low percentage represents both the wholesale nature of Japanese city banks, and their relatively large expenses on data processing. Japan actually leads the world in the ratio of ATMs to population.

The provision for loan losses averaged 2.4 percent of interest income, with the balance of loan loss reserve reaching 0.8 percent of the total loan portfolio as of March 31, 1989 (tables 6.7 and 6.12). These relatively low bad debt losses resulted from favorable economic conditions in Japan and the tendency of Japanese banks to restructure bad debt and avoid charges. The rate of tax provision was steady over the period examined, reaching about 50 percent of the pre-tax profit. This rate is almost equal to the statutory tax rate.

Thus, the overall performance of Japanese city banks resulted in stable earnings of 12 to 13 percent on risk capital, which increased during the period 1984–9 from 10.3 percent to 13.4 percent (table 6.10).

The structure of income statements for regional banks stems from the retail nature of their activities (as opposed to the wholesale nature of city banks). For this group of banks as well, the decline in interest margins was compensated for by the 63.1 percent growth in the loan portfolio. The net result was an 29.1 percent increase in interest income (table 6.12). Other operating income increased by 65 percent during the period 1984–9. The ratio of fee income to interest income increased from 7.8 percent in 1984

Table 6.10 Combined income statement (13 city banks)

	1988/89	*1987/88*	*1986/87*	*1985/86*
		(*Yen, billions*)		
Interest received	20261.0	16279.9	14379.2	14912.3
Interest paid	16548.4	12945.0	11347.5	12369.4
Net interest revenue	3712.6	3334.9	3031.7	2542.9
Other operating income	898.4	950.2	773.6	632.7
Provision for loan losses	218.3	102.8	76.1	34.2
Personnel expenses	1308.9	1277.7	1257.2	1235.5
Other overheads	1660.0	1449.5	1172.5	1021.1
Operating profit	1423.8	1455.1	1299.5	884.8
Securities items – net	1242.0	669.5	266.7	226.6
Special items – net	(48.3)	(31.9)	(88.2)	(15.4)
Pre-tax profit	2617.5	2092.7	1478.0	1096.0
Taxes	1388.1	1189.8	782.8	540.9
Net income	1229.4	902.9	695.2	555.1
Ratio analysis				
Average total assets	361912	315052	273099	246559
Average earning assets	325578	284207	246789	233460
Average risk capital	9157	6961	5661	5492
Average fixed assets	1491	1380	1281	1218
Ratios to average earning assets (%)				
Interest received	6.22	5.73	5.83	6.39
Interest paid	5.08	4.56	4.60	5.30
Net interest revenue	1.14	1.17	1.23	1.09
Interest on capital employed	0.15	0.11	0.10	0.12
Net spread	0.99	1.06	1.13	0.97
Other ratios (%)				
Personnel expenses/net interest	35	38	41	49
Other oper. expe./net interest	45	43	39	40
Interest income/non-interest income	413	351	392	402
Total oper. expe./non-interest income	330	287	314	357
Net income/total assets	0.34	0.29	0.25	0.23
Net income/risk capital	13.43	12.97	12.28	10.11

Source: IBCA data base

to 9.9 percent in 1989, a rate much lower than the 51.1 percent rate of city banks.

Personnel expenses for regional banks represent 57 percent of total operating expenses. The net result is that regional banks experienced lower returns on total equity capital (7 to 9 percent) than city banks (12 to 13 percent).

During the period 1988–9, regional banks and long-term credit banks outperformed the city and trust banks in operating profits. This is the result of a reduction in new loan making by city banks, an increase in loan loss reserve to developing countries and lower bond trading profits. At year-end 1988, the BOJ and MOF began a new policy of rewarding and punishing individual banks on the basis of their performance, by allowing differential growth rates on new bank loans.

6.3.3 Sources of Income

Interest income constituted about 67 percent of operating income for all commercial banks in 1989 (as opposed to 81.4 percent in 1984). Interest rate margins constituted 66.2 percent of the gross operating income of city banks in 1989 (83 percent in 1984). The impact of deregulation of deposit rates and increased securitization is expected to lead to a further significant reduction in margins. This tendency is only partially reflected in the figures presented here, since the period examined can be characterized as transitional (e.g., commercial paper was introduced in November 1987). In the future it is expected that interest margins and interest income will be reduced, as they have been in other countries with well-developed capital markets.

Japanese banks have traditionally used a "prime rate system" as a way of setting loan rates in the domestic market (announced by the leading bank). As a result, the fluctuations of loan rates have been much more moderate ("sticky") than those of other market rates. However, with the increased role of instruments with deregulated and flexible rates, major city banks decided in 1989 to adopt a new prime rate system, in which the prime rate is determined by adding a certain spread to a base rate. Thus, loan rates are expected to become more flexible.

The decrease in interest margins has been paralleled by the increased involvement of city banks in capital markets. Previously, banks were restricted from the underwriting and distribution of all domestic securities. However, since 1985 banks have been permitted to distribute and underwrite government securities. Furthermore, Japanese banks abroad are permitted to underwrite most Eurobond issues (except by Japanese firms) and are especially active in US corporate issues. The fee income from capital market activities and the income from bond trading is expected to compensate city banks for the decline in interest rate income. Moreover,

Table 6.11 Combined income statement (five regional banks) (Yen, billions)

	1988/89	*1987/88*	*1986/87*	*1985/86*
1 Interest received	1051	914	863	880
2 Interest paid	698	603	566	613
3 Net interest revenue	353	311	297	267
4 Other operating income	43	48	40	37
5 Provision for loan losses	11	7	9	1
6 Personnel expenses	141	140	140	138
7 Other non-interest expense	135	123	105	98
8 Operating profit before securities & special items	109	89	83	67
9 Securities items – net	19	15	16	15
10 Special items – net	(4)	(2)	(3)	(3)
11 Pre-tax profit	124	102	96	79
12 Taxes	67	51	53	43
13 Net income	57	51	43	36
Ratio analysis				
Average earning assets	21923	18292	15894	15056
Average risk capital	724	612	538	512
Ratios to earning assets (%)				
Interest received	4.79	5.00	5.43	5.84
Interest paid	3.18	3.30	3.56	4.07
Net interest revenue	1.61	1.70	1.87	1.77
Interest on capital employed	0.11	0.12	0.13	0.14
Net spread	1.50	1.58	1.74	1.63
Other ratios (%)				
Personnel expenses/net interest	40.0	45.0	47.2	51.7
Other oper. exp./net interest	38.2	39.5	35.3	36.7
Interest income/non-interest income	821	648	743	722
Total oper. exp./non-interest income	642	548	613	638
Prov. for loan lo./total loans	0.07	0.05	0.07	0.01
Net income/total assets	0.22	0.24	0.24	0.22
Net income/risk capital	7.87	8.50	8.00	7.07

Including: Bank of Hiroshima, Bank of Kyoto, Chiba Bank, Hokuriko Bank & Iyo Bank.

Source: IBCA data base

it is expected that the restrictions on placing power in the capital markets of commercial banks will be gradually eliminated.

The involvement of Japanese banks in capital market activities as both a substitute for and a supplement to conventional banking intermediation is likely to result in a stabilization of overall bank income. For example, during periods when high demand for capital market intermediation causes a decrease in bank intermediation, the banking system will be able to compensate by participating in the capital market. For regional banks the impact of deregulation is much less relevant, since the reduction in interest margins is smaller and the involvement of these banks in capital markets is marginal.

6.3.4 Expenses

The major sources of expenses analyzed are personnel expenses, other overheads, taxes, and loan loss reserves. For all banks, personnel expenses covered 47.9 percent of total operating expenses in 1989 (58 percent in 1984 (table 6.12)). The total revenue per one yen of personnel expenses rose from 2.54 yen in 1984 to 3.76 yen in 1989 (table 6.12). The net interest margin per one yen of personnel expenses rose from 2.07 yen in 1984 to 2.55 yen in 1989. The growth of loans and deposits was not paralleled by similar increases in personnel expenses. These economies of scale were the major impetus that enabled Japanese banks to retain their profitability, despite the decline in interest margins. The impact of these economies was particularly beneficial to city and trust banks, who have enjoyed the fastest growth in the banking industry.

The ratio of total net interest income to operating expenses remained stable (119.5 percent in 1984 compared with 122.1 percent in 1989). This is mainly due to the rise in other overheads (including investment in electronic data processing), and a relative decline in both personnel expenses and net interest income. The introduction of on-line real time systems in city banks has been completed, both within branches of the same bank and among financial institutions. The system is now expanding to include relations between banks and other enterprises and individuals. In the area of automated teller machines, Japan is well ahead of most industrial countries. As a result of these investments, other operating costs in the financial sector are being reduced, mainly through personnel cuts.

The tax provision represents 53 to 55 percent of gross income, very close to the statutory tax rate. This rate is typical, since accounting reserves are limited to the tax deductible percentage.

The loan loss reserve is relatively small as a proportion of net interest

Table 6.12 The banking system income statement (Yen, billions)

	Net interest income	%	*Non-interest income*	%[a]	*Personnel expenses*	%	*Other operating expenses*	*Other income (expenses)*	*Loan loss provision*	*Provision for taxes*	*Net income*	*Net income to equity capital*[b]
All banks (87)												
1983/4	5,094	100	1,171	100	2,461	100	1,803	150	175	1,081	895	10.5
1984/5	5,153	100	1,479	100	2,559	100	1,965	153	183	1,149	929	9.9
1985/6	5,119	100	1,896	100	2,635	100	2,095	81	93	1,219	1,054	10.4
1986/7	6,037	100	2,234	100	2,718	100	2,340	14	195	1,669	1,363	12.2
1987/8	6,544	100	2,847	100	2,757	100	2,740	173	234	2,126	1,707	13.6
1988/9	7,189	100	3,408	100	2,819	100	3,067	291	387	2,429	2,186	13.9
City banks (13)												
1983/4	2,623	51.5	548	46.8	1,163	47.3	931	90	101	572	494	12.6
1984/5	2,633	51.1	705	47.6	1,190	46.5	1,007	72	92	618	503	11.6
1985/6	2,524	49.3	861	45.4	1,207	45.8	1,048	47	31	587	559	11.8
1986/7	3,010	49.9	976	43.6	1,251	46.0	1,156	(14)	76	784	705	13.2
1987/8	3,318	50.7	1,502	52.7	1,250	45.4	1,412	76	108	1,207	919	15.1
1988/9	3,678	51.2	1,880	55.2	1,277	45.3	1,579	163	222	1,394	1,249	15.8
Regional banks (64)												
1983/4	2,031	39.9	158	13.5	995	40.4	591	22	34	338	253	8.4
1984/5	2,077	40.3	205	13.9	1,052	41.1	645	31	38	319	259	7.9
1985/6	2,093	40.9	291	15.3	1,096	41.6	684	25	34	334	261	7.4
1986/7	2,286	37.8	276	12.4	1,109	40.8	735	40	63	393	302	8.1
1987/8	2,345	35.8	281	9.9	1,128	40.9	773	36	50	356	355	8.7
1988/9	2,622	36.5	261	7.7	1,143	40.5	859	37	58	448	412	9.8

Trust banks (7)												
1983/4	108	2.1	426	36.4	224	9.1	176	14	15	71	62	8.6
1984/5	124	2.4	509	34.4	232	9.1	201	31	32	121	78	9.6
1985/6	166	3.2	654	34.5	241	9.1	239	4	14	194	136	15.4
1986/7	277	4.6	918	41.1	264	9.7	312	6	29	360	236	23.7
1987/8	340	5.2	998	35.1	282	10.2	384	37	53	380	276	21.8
1988/9	276	3.8	1,194	35.0	295	10.5	447	44	49	400	323	18.8
Long-term credit (3)												
1983/4	332	6.5	39	3.3	79	3.2	105	24	25	100	86	9.9
1984/5	319	6.2	60	4.1	85	3.3	112	19	21	91	89	9.6
1985/6	336	6.6	90	4.8	91	3.5	124	5	14	104	98	9.9
1986/7	464	7.7	64	2.9	94	3.5	137	(18)	27	132	120	11.3
1987/8	541	8.3	66	2.3	97	3.5	171	24	23	183	157	13.7
1988/9	613	8.5	73	2.1	104	3.7	182	47	58	187	202	12.7

[a] Percentage of all banks in this table.
[b] Net income divided by equity capital at the end of March of the previous year.

Source: Analysis of financial statements of all member banks, Federation of Bankers Association of Japan

income (about 3 to 4 percent throughout the period examined). For city banks the ratio is very similar to other banks (table 6.12). Japanese city banks increased their loan loss reserve against outstanding loans to LDC debt problem by only 1 percent during 1988. There was a total LDC debt of 3,365 billion yen at year-end 1988, and a 734 billion yen debt for long-term credit banks. However, the proportion of developing country loans that have been covered by reserves comprised only 15 percent of their debt. This relatively low coverage is due to current tax and accounting practices in Japan.

6.3.5 Capital Adequacy

The equity capital and reserves to asset ratio of city banks reached 3.6 percent in March 1989. It has long been alleged that Japanese commercial banks possess an artificial competitive advantage in international lending markets, as a result of home country regulations permitting exceedingly low capitalization. In 1986, US government pressure for greater coordination of prudential controls (and competitive fairness) resulted in the adoption of a risk-based capital requirement within the context of the Bank for International Settlement (BIS).

This requirement was resisted by Japanese banks, who argued that part of their undisclosed holdings of securities should be counted as equity capital (the MOF modifies banks capital by 70 percent of their average unrealized capital gains over the previous five years). The final specific set of risk-based capital requirements was signed in mid-December 1987, and the final figure for unrealized capital gain was 45 percent (included in Tier 2 capital). Currently, the individual net worth of all Japanese city banks is still below the 4 percent standard established in the BIS proposal. There are two methods of raising the capital ratio, increasing the numerator (capital) or decreasing the denominator (assets). Several city banks have already achieved the 8 percent risk-adjusted ratio, with the average ratio for March 1989 of the Japanese city banks being 8.2 percent. In 1988, Japanese banks issued more than 2.2 trillion yen of equity, and their total unrealized profits increased to 45.2 trillion yen.

However, in September 1990, stock prices fell by 22 percent. The revaluation reserves in the Tier 2 capital of Japanese banks collapsed (45 percent of unrealized profit). It is estimated that for every 1,000 point fall of the Nikkei (stock price) index, city banks' capital ratios fall by 0.1 to 0.2 percent.[2] Since the end of March 1990, the market has fallen by 7,000 to 8,000 points. Moreover, Japanese banks have relied on subordinated debt to improve their Tier 2 capital. The cost of raising this type of capital has now become prohibitively high since Japan now faces interest rates similar to those of the rest of the world. At present most city banks, and many other banks, fall short of their 8 percent risk-weighted capital targets. Furthermore, rising bond yields are expected to cause unrealized losses in bond portfolios. Thus, instead of raising capital, Japanese banks may need to shrink their balance sheet by shifting the composition of assets, slowing their growth, and downsizing their activities to improve their capital ratio. Activities abroad present considerable potential for change. It seems that lending abroad will be affected (cut back) before lending at home, and Japanese banks may have to curtail their international expansion (mostly in the Single European market). Finally, the BIS requirements will increase the pressure to develop securitization of bank assets in Japan. Since March 1990, Japanese banks have been allowed to sell their domestic loans, and a secondary loan market is now taking form.

In addition, the MOF lowered the foreign assets to total net worth ratio (including 70 percent of unrealized gains) to 2.5 times, down from the 3.5 times mandated in September 1986. For example, assuming an 8 percent equity capital, foreign business cannot exceed 20 percent of total bank assets. However, even the new requirement is not currently binding.

The capital adequacy of the sample of regional banks is higher than the

Table 6.13 Selected financial data – city banks (Yen, billions)

March 31, 1989	*Total loans*	*Total assets*	*Total deposits*	*Risk capital*	*Net income*
Dai-Ichi Kangyo Bank	28744	50734	46097	1321	180
Sumitomo Bank	26189	48779	44313	1284	198
Fuji Bank	25557	46802	42574	1378	172
Mitsubishi Bank	24535	45764	42836	1284	167
Sanwa Bank	25308	44736	41196	1159	156
Tokai Bank	16630	29465	26972	742	60
Mitsui Bank	16673	27108	24418	720	79
Taiyo Kobe Bank	15284	23131	20950	578	54
Bank of Tokyo	11737	23119	17146	605	59
Kyowa Bank	8717	13881	12432	361	36
Saitama Bank	7504	12804	11727	345	29
Bank of Yokohama	6721	10892	9886	340	20
Hokkaido Takushoku	6016	10046	9072	232	19
Total city banks	219615	387261	349619	10349	1229

Source: IBCA data base

city banks, reaching 3.5 percent. However, since their unrealized capital gain is below that of city banks, most do not meet the Tier 1 requirement.

Notes

1 The "Swap Limit Rule" on banks' open spot position in foreign currencies was abolished in June 1984.
2 Salomon Brothers, Japanese banks – BIS targets now compel changes, New York, August 27, 1990.

References

Bank of Japan, *Economic Statistics Monthly*, and *Annual*, various issues. *Institutional Investor*, Ranking the world's largest banks, June 1988, 143–54.

Osugi, K. (1990) Japan's experience of financial deregulation since 1984 in an international perspective, *BIS Economic Papers* no. 26, BIS, Basle.

Salomon Brothers, *A Review of Bank Performance*, April 1990 edition.

— *Japanese banks – BIS Targets now Compel Changes*, Salomon Brothers, New York, August 27, 1990.

Sender, Henny (1990) Japan's not-so-mighty banks, *Institutional Investor*, November, 74–85.

Suzuki, Yoshio (ed) (1987) *The Japanese Financial System*, Clarendon Press, Oxford.

Terrell, Henry S., Robert S. Dohner and Barbara R. Lowrey (1989) The US and UK activities of Japanese banks 1980–1988, *Federal Reserve Bulletin*, 39–50.

Viner, Aron (1987) *Inside Japan's Financial Markets*, The Economist Pub., London.

7

Canada

7.1 Structure of the Financial System

7.1.1 Introduction

Canada and its economy are often assessed in light of the United States. While such a comparison is certainly legitimate and helpful, it does not provide a full picture of the many ways in which Canada differs from other major industrialized countries. For example, Canada's relatively recent colonial past (independence was achieved in 1867) still influences present day concerns, and its mixed heritage combines elements of both British and French cultural and political influences. Furthermore, natural resources and agriculture remain important aspects of Canada's economy. Canada is also relatively underpopulated in comparison with its major competitors and trading partners. Finally, there is the considerable impact of the much larger US economy on Canada's development, although this fact is sometimes overemphasized.

Along with these unique features, the Canadian economy can be characterized as primarily a market economy. As in other English-speaking countries, it displays a relatively low level of state interventionism, regulation, direction, and centralization. Its abundant natural resources, open frontiers, and immigration-based population growth have produced rapid economic development. The influence and example of the nearby larger and older US economy have extensively affected Canada's economy, including its relative openness and the importance of foreign trade.

7.1.2 Financial Markets and Institutions

The Canadian financial system has been, and continues to be, well-developed and efficient. It is unencumbered by the controls, regulations, and distortions that have characterized the financial markets of many other

Table 7.1 Canada – major economic indicators and the banking system

	1980	*1984*	*1989*
Gross domestic product, (US$ bil.)	258	327	532
Current account, (US$ bil.)	-0.96	2.6	-14.1
Consumer inflation (pc pa)	12.4	4.0	5.0
Exchange rate, (C$ per US$) (year-end)	1.19	1.32	1.16
Interest rate pc per annum	13.3	10.9	12.0
Population (mil.)	24.2	25.1	26.3
Number of bank employees in Canada[a] (thou.)	150	146	177
Number of branches[a]	7,426	7,055	7,307
Number of ATMs[a]	–	1,813	6,894
Population per branch	3,258	3,558	3,599
Population per ATM	–	13,844	3,815
Bank employees as percentage of population[a]	0.6	0.6	0.7

[a] Figures for chartered banks only.

Source: IMF, *International Financial Statistics Yearbook*, 1990
Bank of Canada Review, various issues

advanced economies. In a study of the Canadian financial system, the Organization for Economic Co-operation and Development wrote that

> The Canadian financial markets ... have displayed flexibility and a capacity to adapt to the changing needs of the suppliers and users of loanable funds, as well as a willingness to innovate. All aspects of intermediation have been present and active, and direct access to the capital markets by enterprises and households have been unfettered. Traditionally, the authorities have not interfered with the quantity or pricing of credit, and only minimal restrictions have been placed on investment in foreign securities.[1]

Nevertheless, Canada has also been affected by the worldwide trend of financial market reform. In fact, reform in Canada has been prompted by the same factors as in other countries: adapting the regulatory framework to structural and functional changes in financial markets, responding to the increased globalization and integration of financial services, and ensuring the safety of financial institutions in times of increased stress and pressure. The latter goal has assumed special significance due to increased problems afflicting Canadian banks since the early 1980s.

The financial sector in Canada is relatively large and is typical of an advanced financial system. Total financial assets as a ratio of GDP are approximately 4.4 to 1, similar to that of the United States, but considerably higher than that of the Federal Republic of Germany or Italy (3.6 and 3.9

respectively). Intermediated assets constitute 41 percent of total financial assets, slightly higher than in the United States (38 percent), but much lower than in the Federal Republic of Germany (47 percent),[2] where the dominant role played by German universal banks has pushed this ratio up. The direct capital markets have long been well-developed, with the share of securities in total credit flows (49.4 percent in 1984/85) not only greater than in the Federal Republic of Germany or France (36.4 percent and 42.5 percent, respectively) but also greater than in the United States (46.7 percent).

The household savings ratio in Canada declined during the 1980s, reaching some 11 percent in 1989; while the corporate sector, traditionally a net borrower, has been decreasing its deficit. The public sector also increased its net borrowing during the 1980s. As a result of these developments, Canada, which had been a net exporter of capital in the early 1980s, saw this trend reversed in the late 1980s. Interestingly, the conversion of the public sector into a large structural borrower, and the resulting increase in direct obligations issued by the government, did not cause any disintermediation. Rather, the maturity of the Canadian system was demonstrated by government obligations replacing other direct obligations in private portfolios, with the public long having adjusted its portfolio to the desired mix of direct/indirect claims. If anything, there appears to have been a slight increase in the weight of intermediated claims, as the public's preference increased for short-term financial assets (due to rapid inflation and low real interest rates) and pension and retirement funds (due to preferential tax treatment).

The traditional structure of the Canadian financial system is widely known as the Four Pillar Framework: chartered banks, near-banks (other deposit-taking institutions), investment dealers, and insurance companies. Clearly, this constitutes a system of structural separation of financial intermediation by function and product, similar to that of the United Kingdom and the United States and unlike the European model of the universal bank. While functional separation is distinct, there is no element of geographic restriction as in the United States; in fact, most financial intermediaries operate in Canada on a nationwide basis.

Chartered banks, comparable to commercial banks, numbered 66 as of July 1989. They hold some 72 percent of banking sector assets (table 7.2). These banks are categorized as either Schedule A (widely held domestic banks, numbering seven), or Schedule B (closely held domestic and foreign-owned banks, numbering 59) according to the Bank Act of 1980. In 1988, these categories were renamed Schedule I and Schedule II, respectively.[3]

The Schedule II banks have the same powers as Schedule I banks except for some restrictions on branching and size.

Table 7.2 The Canadian banking system

	Number of institutions			*Number of branches*[a]		*Total assets*[b] *(C$, bil).*			*Share of total assets*	*Change 1980–9*
	1980	*1984*	*1989*	*1984*	*1989*	*1980*	*1984*	*1989*	*1989*	*%*
A Chartered banks										
Foreign-owned banks	–	55	59	200	7,307	10.3	22.1	56.8	7.3	451.0
Canadian-owned banks[c]	11	14	7	6,855		270.9	383.5	497.6	64.3	83.7
Total	7,307	69	66	7,055	7,307	281.2	405.6	554.4	71.7	97.2
B Other financial institutions										
Trust and mortgage loan companies[d]						64.7	67.4	127.8	16.5	97.5
Credit unions						30.5	40.6	67.1	8.8	120.0
Sales finance and other consumer loan companies						14.1	14.2	24.0	3.1	70.2
Total						109.3	122.2	218.9	28.4	100.3
Total banking system						390.5	527.8	773.3	100.0	98.0

[a] Branches in Canada.
[b] Total assets on consolidated basis, as of October 31 of the relevant year.
[c] Mostly represent the big five banks.
[d] Excluding mortgage loan companies associated with chartered banks.

Source: *Bank of Canada Review*, various issues

The most important of the Schedule I banks are the big five nationwide banks, which with some 6,700 branches and 90 percent of chartered bank assets, dominate the banking sector. The big five are all among the 100 largest banks in the world. The other Schedule I banks are two regional banks. The banking system as it has evolved in Canada includes large branch networks to bring the capital of city institutions to remote towns and villages.

The 58 subsidiaries of foreign banks (there is only one closely held domestic bank), which are incorporated as Schedule II chartered banks, all operate under the 1980 Bank Act. Additionally, there are special rules and regulations that apply specifically to foreign banks.

The second pillar of the financial structure, trust companies and mortgage loan companies, can be termed near-banks. Although the two groups are of distinct origin, they have over the years developed into very similar institutions. To a considerable extent they have come to resemble commercial banks. The banking functions of trust companies include funding through savings and term deposits; the issuance of guaranteed investment certificates; and investments in mortgages, high grade securities, and collateralized loans. As opposed to chartered banks, trust companies need not maintain non-interest-bearing reserves with the central bank. However, their commercial lending is limited to 7 percent of total assets. Trust companies are unique in that they may undertake fiduciary activities. This allows them, for example, to administer estates and trusts and to provide portfolio and real estate management services.

Mortgage loan companies are funded primarily by accepting term deposits and issuing debentures. Most are subsidiaries of either trust companies or chartered banks. Since loan companies are not subject to Bank of Canada reserve requirements, they are used to channel mortgage lending more profitably.

A number of smaller institutions have specialized roles. These include cooperatively-owned credit unions (in Quebec called Caisses Populaires), savings and loan institutions, sales financing companies, and consumer loan companies.

The non-bank pillars traditionally include investment dealers and insurance companies. Investment dealers, similar to US investment banks and UK merchant banks, assist corporate clients in their financing and capital needs. This is done almost exclusively through securities transactions such as underwriting, distribution, and market making. Regulated by the provinces, the future role of investment dealers in the financial structure seems likely to increase given the growing securitization of financial markets. Unlike the investment dealers, the role of insurance companies is clearly in decline with their share of intermediated assets decreasing from 18 percent in 1965 to 14 percent in 1988. The annuities and savings schemes offered by the insurance companies have not been attractive in the face of both increased competition from other sources and a general preference for short-term liquid assets.

Outside the traditional four pillar structure, a number of relatively new, specialized financial institutions have begun to play a significant role as financial intermediaries. These include pension funds, mutual funds, leasing companies, and venture capital firms. Pension funds in particular have attracted an increasing share of household assets, playing a concomitantly important role in corporate financing. The many regulatory reforms and changes which have been either enacted or proposed in recent years, in tandem with market developments, seem likely to herald continued change in the institutional structure of Canadian financial markets.

The money and capital markets of Canada are well-developed and share many of the characteristics of the US and UK markets. The resemblance of Canadian markets to those of the United States is based not only on common background, but also on the relatively high degree of capital mobility between the two economies. As a result of the well-developed capital markets, securities account for a relatively high percentage of investments and have been incorporated into household portfolios for many years. The fact that portfolio preferences for direct claims have long been satisfied by a highly evolved market has helped Canada avoid sudden disintermediation when government deficit financing grew in importance in the early 1980s.

The securities market is regulated on a provincial basis, with the primary role played by Ontario. A dual structure is maintained that includes a retail segment, involving some 100 highly regulated firms, to ensure investor protection, and an exempt segment of wholesale and professional institutions, which is basically unregulated, there being no need to protect sophisticated investors.

The money market in Canada is estimated to be the third largest in the world, after the United States and the United Kingdom It is much more developed than that of far larger countries such as Japan, the Federal Republic of Germany, or France. Federal government treasury bills comprise the largest and most liquid part of the market, while the provinces also issue substantial amounts of paper. The bank sector includes a very active call money market, as well as term deposits, CDs, swap deposits, and Euro C$ deposits. The corporate sector includes finance paper (secured short-term promissory notes), commercial paper (unsecured promissory notes), and bankers acceptances (table 7.3). Finance company paper and other commercial papers are generally issued for terms of 30 to 365 days. Finance company paper is generally placed directly and held to maturity. The automobile finance companies, which account for a large proportion of the finance company paper issued, include a guarantee from their US parent. Canadian companies make more use of bankers' acceptances than commercial paper (table 7.3).

The Canadian bond market is the seventh largest in the world, with some C$326 billion (US$258 billion) in outstanding issues at year-end 1989. Federal government debt has been growing as a share of this market in the past decade, reaching 38 percent by 1989. Provincial and municipal bonds accounted for 31 percent: corporate paper 15 percent, and international issues 16 percent. All bonds are traded on an over-the-counter basis. Liquidity is quite high in the secondary market for government paper and, to a lesser extent, provincial bonds; the secondary market liquidity of corporate bonds is much lower.

Table 7.3 The Canadian dollar money market outstanding volume (C$ millions)

Year	*Federal treasury bills*	*Provincial & municipal bills*	*Finance paper*	*Commercial paper*	*Bankers acceptances*
1975	6,200	668	2,676	2,913	1,047
1980	20,735	1,177	3,077	8,554	5,365
1985	59,400	7,418	3,836	8,363	17,007
1989	120,100	11,805	9,898	19,569	43,666

Source: *Bank of Canada Review*, various issues

Five stock exchanges operate in Canada, although Toronto (with 75 percent) and Montreal (with 20 percent) account for virtually all the turnover on a value basis. The Canadian equity market is the world's fifth largest, with a market capitalization at the end of 1989 of C$401 billion (US$347 billion), and for some 1,207 companies listed on the Toronto and Montreal exchanges in 1989, turnover was 8.1 billion shares, with a market value of C$103 billion.

7.1.3 Banking Product and Bank Competition

While the institutional structure of Canadian banking has historically displayed considerable segmentation, functional competition in banking products has been considerable. This is because the market for various banking services is fairly open to competition by institutions from different sectors. Additionally, regulatory segmentation has been reduced and is likely to be reduced even further in the future. Thus, the Canadian banking industry is moving, albeit at an uneven pace, to a "level playing field" with less regulatory or structural differentiation among the various intermediaries.

The Schedule I chartered banks, and especially the big five that dominate the sector, constitute a fairly homogeneous sample of classic commercial banking. They are large, nationwide operations with well-developed branch networks providing a stable funding base of low cost deposits. Given the openness of the Canadian economy, their high degree of international involvement is well understood. In 1989, 31 percent of chartered bank assets were foreign currency denominated, although for the big five banks it ranged up to 50 percent. Approximately 16 percent of chartered bank assets were booked overseas. Important as their foreign involvement still is, however, it is clearly diminishing. Foreign currency assets were 39 percent of the total in 1980, climbing to 45 percent in 1984, before they began declining to 33 percent in 1988 and 31 percent in 1989. Foreign-booked assets, 16 percent in 1989, were 18.6 percent in 1980 and 24 percent in 1984. The tradition of sole banking relationships with large customers of Schedule I chartered banks has led to a notable degree of concentration in lending. However the near disastrous involvement of a number of them in the Dome Petroleum affair of 1982 has led to greater geographic and economic diversification. Their activities include the full range of both wholesale and retail banking services, including real estate lending via subsidiaries; all trust activities are forbidden. This emphasis on traditional banking activity is indicated by the fact that 75 to 80 percent of total revenue stems from net interest spread, with relatively minor non-interest income. The regional banks are active in the same product areas, with restricted geographical operations.

The Schedule II banks are essentially foreign-owned and can theoretically compete in the same range of services as domestic banks. However, due to their limited branching possibilities, they have generally refrained from competing for retail business. Instead, Schedule II chartered banks have concentrated on medium to large size corporate clients and on business with an international character.

The other near-bank intermediaries active in Canada are becoming increasingly like chartered banks in terms of activities. Trust companies, while retaining the unique ability to undertake fiduciary activities, also accept deposits and invest in a variety of loans (mainly real estate secured) as well as high quality securities (tables 7.5 and 7.5a). The restriction of direct competition between trust companies and chartered banks has been achieved by limiting their commercial lending to 7 percent of assets. Mortgage loan companies retain their emphasis on investing in secured mortgages, while competing with chartered banks in the collection of retail deposits. Credit unions have expanded the range of services they provide beyond their original goal of providing low cost credit to members. Today they provide a full range of personal banking services including checking accounts, credit cards, and personal loans. Cost considerations, economies of scale, and competitive pressure have resulted in a trend toward a smaller number of larger institutions, accomplished through a combination of merger, consolidation, and branching.

Sales, finance, and consumer loan companies, although not allowed to accept deposits, do compete with chartered banks by providing automobile and large appliance financing, personal loans, and commercial leasing. These firms have been losing market share to chartered banks and trust companies, due to the larger branch networks and increasing range of

Table 7.4 International involvement of the Canadian chartered banks

Major foreign currency assets and liabilities[a]

Year	*Foreign branches*	*Foreign currency assets*	*Per-centage of total assets*	*Loans*	*Securities*	*Deposits with banks*	*Total*[b] *liabilities*	*Deposits of banks*	*Other deposit*	*Other liabilities*
				(Canadian dollars, billions)						
1980	289	109.9	39.1	55.9	5.8	45.4	112.9	65.3	45.8	1.8
1984	269	182.8	45.1	116.6	10.1	47.7	187.3	86.7	90.0	10.6
1988	234	168.9	33.2	111.3	13.6	33.6	180.2	59.8	101.7	18.7
1989	235	171.8	31.0	112.9	13.8	33.4	179.7	57.1	101.4	21.2

[a] Includes total foreign assets and liabilities in Canada and abroad of chartered banks.
[b] The difference between the total assets and liabilities represent net foreign position.

Source: *Bank of Canada Review*, various issues

Table 7.4a International involvement of the Canadian chartered banks

Foreign currency assets and liabilities of chartered banks booked in Canada								*Of which, booked in US dollars*	
		Non-residents			*Canadian residents*				*Percentage of foreign currency assets booked in Canada*
Year	*Total*	*Banks*	*Others*	*Total*	*Banks*	*Others*	*Total*	*C$ billions*	
Assets									
1980	57.4	33.0	8.6	41.6	1.7	14.1	15.8	53.3	92.9
1984	85.3	44.4	7.8	52.2	4.2	28.9	33.1	79.5	93.2
1988	81.2	40.3	12.6	52.9	2.6	25.7	28.3	74.6	91.9
1989	82.7	41.7	11.4	53.1	2.6	27.0	29.6	76.0	92.0
Liabilities									
1980	61.0	28.6	19.8	48.4	1.8	10.8	12.6	58.0	94.9
1984	89.8	44.7	33.3	78.0	4.1	7.7	11.8	85.3	95.0
1988	87.8	43.9	32.9	76.8	2.6	8.4	11.0	80.1	91.2
1989	86.6	42.0	32.3	74.3	2.4	9.9	12.3	77.3	89.3

Source: *Bank of Canada Review*, various issues

services these institutions can provide. Legislation restricting the leasing of cars and personal property by banks has provided some protection for sales finance and consumer loan companies.

While there is a high degree of concentration in the banking industry in Canada, especially among the chartered banks, competition has not been reduced to any great extent. This is primarily due to the ability of various types of institutions to compete for essentially the same banking business, with the result that there are relatively few banking activities that can be considered protected. For example, personal banking services are provided

Table 7.5 Major items in total assets of Canadian banks (C$ billions)

	Total assets	%[a]	*Securities*	%	*General loans*	%	*Mortgages*	%	*Foreign currency*	%
All banks										
1980	390.5	100.0	25.6	100.0	113.9	100.0	66.0	100.0	103.0	100.0
1984	527.8	100.0	40.3	100.0	154.0	100.0	97.0	100.0	182.8	100.0
1988	702.6	100.0	50.0	100.0	204.4	100.0	175.4	100.0	168.9	100.0
1989	773.3	100.0	53.1	100.0	227.5	100.0	203.7	100.0	171.8	100.0
Chartered										
1980	281.2	72.0	18.1	70.7	93.1	81.7	18.5	28.0	103.0	100.0
1984	405.6	76.8	27.8	69.0	123.1	80.1	38.0	39.2	182.8	100.0
1988	508.6	72.4	36.0	72.0	155.4	76.0	75.7	43.2	168.9	100.0
1989	554.4	71.7	37.2	70.1	173.2	76.1	89.6	44.0	171.8	100.0
Trust and mortgage companies[b]										
1980	64.7	16.6	6.5	25.3	1.6	1.4	32.2	48.8	–	
1984	67.4	12.8	11.4	28.3	7.7	5.0	38.8	40.0	–	
1988	110.3	15.7	13.1	26.2	10.6	5.2	69.1	39.4	–	
1989	127.8	16.5	15.1	28.4	13.1	5.8	81.4	40.0		
Credit unions and caisses populaires										
1980	30.5	7.8	0.8	3.2	7.5	6.6	15.3	23.2	–	
1984	40.6	7.7	0.7	1.7	10.1	6.5	20.2	20.8	–	
1988	61.1	8.7	0.8	1.6	17.2	8.4	30.6	17.4	–	
1989	67.1	8.7	0.8	1.5	18.6	8.2	32.7	16.0		
Sales finance and consumer loans corporations										
1980	14.1	3.6	0.2	0.8	11.7	10.3	–		–	
1984	14.2	2.7	0.4	1.0	13.1	8.5	–		–	
1988	22.6	3.2	0.1	0.2	21.2	10.3	–			
1989	24.0	3.1	0.0	0.0	22.6	9.9				

by chartered banks, trust companies, mortgage loan companies and, to some extent, by sales, finance, and consumer loan companies as well. Even commercial lending is provided not only by the Schedule II chartered banks, but also by the foreign-owned banks and, to a limited extent, by trust companies.

Table 7.5a Major items in total liabilities of Canadian banks (C$ bil.)

	Personal savings deposits	%[a]	*Non-personal deposits*	%	*Foreign currency liabilities*	%	*Bank debentures*	%	*Shareholders equity*	%
All banks										
1980	139.9	100.0	59.1	100.0	114.1	100.0	9.8	100.0	15.8	100.0
1984	202.5	100.0	46.6	100.0	188.0	100.0	13.7	100.0	24.9	100.0
1988	311.4	100.0	79.6	100.0	181.7	100.0	19.9	100.0	37.4	100.0
1989	358.4	100.0	85.0	100.0	181.4	100.0	21.1	100.0	40.7	100.0
Chartered										
1980	74.9	53.5	59.1	100.0	112.9	99.0	2.2	22.4	6.7	42.4
1984	109.5	54.1	46.6	100.0	187.3	99.6	2.6	19.0	16.8	67.5
1988	161.9	52.0	79.6	100.0	180.2	99.2	2.4	12.1	25.7	68.7
1989	189.5	52.9	85.0	100.0	179.7	99.1	2.6	12.3	27.8	68.3
Trust and mortgage companies[b]										
1980	40.0	28.6					0.5	5.1	3.0	19.0
1984	57.9	28.6					1.7	12.4	3.6	14.4
1988	97.4	31.3					1.7	8.5	5.6	15.0
1989	111.1	31.0					1.7	8.0	6.3	15.5
Credit unions and caisses populaires										
1980	25.0	17.9							4.1	26.0
1984	35.1	17.3							2.8	11.3
1988	52.1	16.7							3.9	10.4
1989	57.8	16.1							4.2	10.3
Sales finance and consumer loans corporations										
1980	–		–		1.2	1.0	7.1	72.5	2.0	12.6
1984	–		–		0.7	0.4	9.4	68.6	1.7	6.8
1988	–		–		1.5	0.8	15.8	79.4	2.2	5.9
1989	–		–		1.7	0.9	16.8	79.7	2.4	5.9

[a] Percentage of total banking system.
[b] Excluding mortgage loan companies associated with chartered banks.

Source: *Bank of Canada Review*, various issues

Some areas do enjoy a relatively high degree of protection, especially by OECD standards. Foreign banking competition is perhaps the most prominent example, being subject to special legislation, restrictions on individual as well as aggregate size, restricted organization and with branches subject to regulatory approval. The securities industry is another example, with investment dealers enjoying considerable protection. Both personal and commercial lending are at least partially restricted from free competition. These exceptions aside, the overall picture of Canadian banking is one of fairly unrestricted competition, with a clear trend toward even less segmentation and restriction in the future.

A major step in reducing institutional segmentation in the market structure was the "Blue Paper" (policy paper) issued by the federal government in 1986. Although it dealt with a variety of issues, the theme of integration of the financial services industry was prominent.

The overall restructuring proposed by the Blue Paper involves removal of regulatory barriers and the implementation of common ownership of firms in the four pillars. Financial institutions would be permitted to establish wholly-owned subsidiaries to engage in the business of the other pillars.

Some reforms have already begun, including the removal of restrictions on the affiliations of banks and security firms. Other reforms are still in the planning stage such as the enhanced affiliations of banks and trust companies. In any event, Canada has decided that increased competition and removal of unnecessary impediments to free market forces will benefit the economy.

7.1.4 International Involvement

Canadian banks have a major stake in international business, a reflection of the openness of the Canadian economy and the sizable role of foreign trade within that economy. Canadian banks operate more than 300 branches and representative offices in over 55 countries. As mentioned above, 32 to 51 percent of the assets of the big five banks can be considered international assets.

The first overseas ventures, undertaken in the last century, were the establishment of banking presences in the major money centers abroad (mainly in New York and London). Access to international capital and the provision of foreign exchange services were the primary goals. Later, Canadian banks established branch networks in areas important to Canadian foreign trade, primarily in the western hemisphere (mainly in the Caribbean). Although the United States is by far the major area for

Canadian banks, Latin America has also attracted Canadian bank activity. This has resulted in large exposure to LDC debt, although such exposure has been reduced over the past few years. In the period since the Second World War, Canadian banks have been established in the financial centers of a large number of countries, regardless of their particular importance to the Canadian economy. In these countries banks have based their activity on wholesale banking with local clients, mainly due to a lack of retail branch networks and the absence of any connection with their domestic Canadian clients.

In fact, the nature of Canadian overseas bank operations has differed from that of many other nations in that they did not develop by following domestic customers abroad. Many Canadian companies are foreign owned, but relatively few Canadian firms operate on a multinational basis. Thus, Canadian banks initially operated overseas to raise funds for both the Canadian government and the private sector. Only later did they develop business generated by local or non-Canadian multinational firms. Canadian banks, therefore, have been at a relative disadvantage in some of their overseas operations due to the lack of a "natural" customer base and to relatively low "name recognition." Of continuing importance has been their involvement in trading and capital market activities, including foreign exchange, precious metals, and securities. With the lowering of national barriers and the increased integration of money and capital markets, these functions are likely to increase in importance. Until now, however, fee income has been of less significance to Canadian banks than to other national groupings in the international market.

Foreign banking activity in Canada has been relatively restricted, although there has been a recent trend toward loosening regulations. Until the Bank Act of 1980, foreign ownership of banks was limited to a 10 percent share. Therefore, the 40 foreign banks that did establish "affiliates", and those financial corporations which competed with chartered banks, could not call themselves banks or accept deposits. While foreign banks cannot branch into Canada they can establish subsidiaries as Schedule II chartered banks. To do so they must meet a number of requirements such as capital adequacy, the maintenance of local assets, and reciprocal treatment of Canadian banks in the foreign bank's home country. Foreign banks are severely restricted in their ability to open branches, with their licensing being at the discretion of the Canadian Minister of Finance. Entry approval allows a bank to open a head office and one branch; additional branches require specific further approval.

Perhaps the most profound restriction is the limiting of the aggregate domestic assets of foreign banks to a given share of Canadian banks' domestic assets. The limit, originally 8 percent, was raised to 16 percent in 1984. In 1989, when the free trade agreement with the United States took effect, US banks were removed from the restriction, which was then set at 12 percent for all other foreign banks. Additionally, aggregate non-resident ownership of a bank's shares may not exceed 25 percent of the shares of any class of Schedule I bank. Overall, it is probably correct to say that Canada's policy in this regard is the most restrictive of any of the major industrialized countries. Despite these restrictions, however, 58 Schedule II chartered banks from 17 countries, and some 30 representative offices, have been established in Canada. Their motives are typical for foreign expansion in any country: they have followed domestic customers and multinationals, sought trade financing, and serviced ethnic communities. A not inconsiderable goal has been to establish a presence in a politically stable, resource rich country with high growth potential. Given the fact that Canada has not been an international financial center, foreign banks have relied on acquiring local wholesale business, especially with medium to large firms. The high degree of foreign ownership of Canadian firms has helped many foreign banks to establish relationships in the corporate sector. They have also been effective in providing merchant bank and advisory services not supplied by the domestic banks.

7.2 The Regulatory Environment

7.2.1 The Regulatory Framework

The legislative basis of the Canadian banking system is the Bank Act which, according to the Canadian constitution, must be revised at least once every ten years. The aim of this mandatory review process is to keep banking statutes relevant to changing economic conditions. The last such full revision produced the Bank Act of 1980, which explicitly stated as its goal the stimulation of competition in the financial industry. The restructuring of banks into Schedule I and II chartered banks was a step in this direction.

The Act does not define banks, but simply states that "banks may engage in and carry on such business as generally pertaining to the business of banking." It does, however, specifically forbid certain activities, such as fiduciary and portfolio management, trade in goods, and equity investment of over 10 percent in Canadian firms (with some exceptions). The Act contains regulations affecting many other areas, including foreign banks, capital adequacy, securities trading, and leasing. Other important modern legislation includes the Canada Deposit Insurance Act of 1967, the Canadian Payments Association Act of 1980, and the Bank of Canada Act of 1980.

A number of factors, however, raised the issue of regulatory reform well before the next revision of the Bank Act was due. In 1984 the government announced its intention to undertake regulatory reform. In 1985 it issued The Regulation of Canadian Financial Institutions: Proposals for Discussion (the so-called Green Paper), and in 1986 a position paper entitled New Directions for the Financial Sector (the Blue Paper) which also presented proposals. Many, although not all, of the proposals have been finalized, some of which have already been adopted. The process of regulatory reform, however, is still very much in progress.

Responding to the same forces affecting financial systems everywhere, as well as specifically Canadian concerns (including perceived weaknesses in the supervisory system), the Blue Paper proposed reform based on four elements:

1 Integration of the financial services industry through the common ownership of institutions and extension of powers.
2 Pragmatic ownership policy which checks commercial-financial links, while maintaining balanced competition in the financial services sector.
3 A stronger framework for prudential regulation.
4 A modern and effective supervisory system.[4]

The basic approach of the reforms was to allow common ownership of firms within the four pillars, and removing unnecessary regulatory barriers between them, while maintaining separate institutional identities for supervisory purposes. Thus, financial firms are able to provide a full range of services, although often through affiliates rather than directly. For example, once banks were permitted to own securities subsidiaries, they expanded rapidly into the field and are estimated to indirectly control over 75 percent of the industry today. The extension of powers proposed included granting full commercial and consumer lending powers to trust, loan and insurance companies, and fiduciary and portfolio management services to banks. To protect against undue concentration in the industry, approval of the Ministry of Finance is required for acquisitions of financial services companies.

The issue of foreign participation in the Canadian market was also addressed, with consideration being given both to increased globalization and the ongoing discussions concerning international activity at both the bilateral and multilateral level (including the US-Canada Free Trade Agreement and the completion of the Internal European Market in 1992).

The Blue Paper's goals were:

1 To maintain a strong Canadian Presence in domestic markets;
2 To foster competition that will benefit Canadian consumers through foreign entry;

3 To protect the ability of Canadian financial institutions to be world class participants, by assuring that non residents' access to Canadian domestic markets reflects Canadian firms' access to markets abroad.[5]

Its conclusions were that there were no major changes needed in existing laws, pending international negotiations on the subject. Thus,

> ... non resident firms will be able to enter Canada...and will, as a general rule, enjoy the same extensions of powers as will domestic firms. Foreign owned firms wishing to expand will be required to do so by creating new firms rather than acquiring existing ones ... foreign owned firms in Canada will not be given preferential treatment over Canada's own institutions within Canada's borders.[6]

The Bank of Canada, as the central bank, influences the banking industry in an important, although primarily indirect, way. It controls the day to day management of monetary policy, thereby managing primary and secondary reserve requirements, and open market operations, and acts as lender of last resort for the chartered banks. The Central Bank has not hesitated to employ moral suasion when it has felt the need to do so.

Actual supervisory authority is entrusted to the Office of the Superintendent of Financial Institutions (OSFI) which replaced, in 1987, both the Office of the Inspector General of Banks and the Department of Insurance, which had regulated trust, loan, and insurance companies, investment companies and cooperatives. The new office was intended to strengthen the supervisory system through integration and concentration of supervisory powers.

The Superintendent is appointed by the government and reports to the Minister of Finance. The duties of the inspector include "responsibility to supervise the chartered banks and administer the Bank Act on behalf of the Minister of Finance." In practice this has meant overseeing the annual examination of banks to ascertain the sound financial condition and safety of depositors, creditors, and shareholders; certification of the correctness of the annual reports of banks; special examinations of banks; the imposition of capital adequacy requirements; and examination of the Canadian Payments Association. The supervisor is also authorized to monitor the activities of banks in areas not subject to legislation, and can issue "guidelines" concerning bank behavior in matters such as single customer exposure, lending to interested parties, and foreign exposure. Although these guidelines have no statutory standing, banks are expected to comply with them.

The Blue Paper also proposed a number of steps to strengthen prudential regulation of financial institutions, and protect their depositors. The existing framework was to be largely unchanged although updated, with additional regulations provided to control self dealing and limit conflicts of interest. Trust, loan, and insurance companies were to be provided with rules ensuring a "prudent portfolio" concept, involving diversification, matching the nature of assets and liabilities, and observing investment limits.

Banks must submit a wide range of periodic (ranging from weekly to annual) reports, as required by the Bank of Canada, the Bank Act, the OSFI or the Canadian Deposit Insurance Corporation (CDIC). Banks also issue quarterly reports to their shareholders. All banks must have two auditors who meet the requirements set forth in the Bank Act, although neither auditor may serve more than two consecutive years. Most banks therefore employ a panel of auditors on a rotating basis.

All deposit-taking institutions outside Quebec (chartered banks, trust companies, and loan companies) must belong to the CDIC. The province of Quebec operates its own deposit insurance scheme for institutions incorporated there. Although the Corporation's stated function is the protection of small depositors, non-binding statements have included the objective of "maintaining confidence and stability in the financial system." Recent public statements indicate, however, that it should not be assumed that the CDIC will commit itself in the future to any undertaking beyond that required by the letter of the law. The CDIC collects annual premiums from its members based on the level of insured deposits, which are then deposited with the Bank of Canada. Insurance is limited to domestic deposits of up to C$60,000 held by the private sector. The CDIC is empowered to inspect its members annually for financial standing and business practices, and any breach of regulations or fraud is reported to the authorities, who in turn can press for corrective steps.

The Canadian Payments Association, which operates the nationwide check-clearing system, imposes certain financial requirements (as well as CDIC membership) upon its members. The Canadian Banking Association is the banking industry's representative body, and undertakes lobbying, public relations, and educational activities.

7.2.2 Major Bank Regulations

Scope of business

1 The 1980 Bank Act provides that a bank may engage in activities that are considered to be bank business. Such activities include:

(a) opening branches
(b) lending with or without security

(c) guaranteeing the payment of money
(d) acting through a subsidiary in financial leasing
(e) issuing credit and charge cards
(f) acting as advisor to or administrator of real estate investment trust.

2 In general, banks are prohibited from making significant equity investments (defined as more than 10 percent of voting rights), except for the following entities:

(a) a bank service (such as leasing) corporation
(b) any Canadian company whose only activity is to promote the financing of exports from Canada
(c) a mortgage loan corporation
(d) a venture capital corporation
(e) a factoring or leasing corporation. No limit is placed on the voting rights of Schedule I bank-owned foreign corporations. However, Schedule II banks are subject to the 10 percent limit
(f) banks can hold a temporary investment (up to two years) of up to 50 percent, subject to ministerial approval.

3 The Bank Act permits banks to acquire and hold real property for their own use and occupation. Banks must have a controlling interest (more than 50 percent of the voting rights) in such property.

4 A bank may act either as a principal (for its investment portfolio), or as an agent for real property mortgages, bonds, and debentures. It may act only as a principal in buying and selling equity securities. Banks may not act as underwriters except in respect of bonds and debentures. Banks and their officers, employees, and control corporations are restricted from managing mutual funds.

5 The Bank Act prohibits all banks from engaging in certain specific activities, including:

(a) dealing in goods or merchandise or in any business other than banking
(b) engaging in fiduciary activities
(c) engaging portfolio management or investment counselling
(d) engaging in data processing services, other than banking-related data processing
(e) acquiring, dealing in, or lending more than C$50,000 in securities or shares or debentures of any other bank
(f) engaging in insurance activities
(g) investing or developing real estate, or acting as a real estate broker.

There is currently a substantial expansion in the scope of activities that banks are allowed to carry out, either directly or through subsidiaries. Similarly, other financial intermediaries have been permitted to expand into banking activities. On June 30, 1987, Canadian banks, foreign banks, trust companies, and insurance companies were allowed to enter the securities business which opened the door to increased foreign participation in the Canadian financial market. In June 1988 all ownership restrictions were lifted. The Blue Paper retained the basic policy aim of preventing banks from undertaking "commercial" activity; however, banks have generally only been permitted to establish subsidiary corporations to provide activities undertaken by the other institutions within the four pillars, e.g., trust companies, securities firms, and insurance companies.

Lending limitations

Schedule I banks must limit exposure to a single borrower or group of borrowers to less than 25 percent of common equity. Foreign bank subsidiaries must observe a limit of 50 percent of equity on single exposures, with aggregate large exposures limited to 400 percent of equity (exceptions can be granted with approval).

Bank management must have written guidelines in place regarding determination of connected borrowers. These limits are scheduled for revision in 1990. The proportion of a loan that may be secured by real estate is limited to 75 percent of the value of the property, unless the loan is guaranteed under the National Housing Act or it is insured. The total value of residential mortgages may not exceed 10 percent of a bank's Canadian dollar deposit and debenture liabilities. This latter limitation does not apply to a mortgage arranged by subsidiaries.

Reserve requirements

All chartered banks are subject to reserve requirements. Primary reserves must be held either in the form of non-interest bearing Canadian dollar deposits placed with the Bank of Canada, coins, or Bank of Canada notes. The required reserves include:

- 10 percent of Canadian currency demand deposits
- 2 percent of Canadian currency notice deposits up to C$500 million, 1 percent over C$500 million
- 3 percent of foreign currency deposits placed with the bank in Canada, or its subsidiary in Canada by Canadian residents.

Deposit liabilities do not include Canadian currency or foreign currency deposits of non-residents.

All banks are required to maintain secondary reserves to the extent deemed appropriate by the Bank of Canada. The secondary reserves must be held in the form of primary reserves or treasury bills of Canada, or day loans to authorized investment dealers. Since 1981, the secondary reserves must be 4 percent of the aggregate of both a bank's Canadian dollar deposits and foreign currency deposits by Canadian residents.

Capital adequacy

Canada implemented the BIS capital adequacy framework in 1988. Before that, the Inspector General, in a March 1983 letter to Canadian banks, set out capital adequacy guidelines that included definitions of capital. Total capital, referred to as "adjusted total capital," was divided into primary capital and secondary capital. Secondary capital includes preferred shares and subordinated debentures. Minority interests are included in primary capital. The following ratios were calculated:

$$\text{Primary capital leverage} = \frac{\text{Consolidated total assets plus off-balance-sheet claims, less investment in associated corporations}}{\text{Primary capital less investment in associated corporations}}$$

Total capital leverage = As above, with the caveat that instead of primary capital, total capital is used

Adjustments made with respect to investment in associated companies recognize a bank's potential commitment to an associated corporation in financial difficulties, and avoid the possibility of counting capital twice (i.e., double leverage). Within the overall guidelines set by the OSFI, the assessment of each bank's capital adequacy is based on that bank's risk exposure as reflected in its size, diversification, liquidity, and profitability.

The issue of capital adequacy assumed much greater importance during the first banking crisis in Canada in 65 years, which peaked in 1985 when a rescue package was put together for the Canadian Commercial Bank (CCB), Canada's tenth largest bank, and also for the Northland Bank.

Foreign exchange exposure

The Inspector General requires that at least 50 percent of the total Canadian dollar assets of foreign bank subsidiaries be funded by Canadian dollar liabilities.

Deposit insurance

The Canada Deposit Insurance Corporation (CDIC) was established in 1967. All deposit-taking institutions are required to be members of the CDIC, with the previously mentioned exception of Quebec incorporated entities. The CDIC has authorized capital of C$10 million. Each member institution pays an annual premium based on the level of its insurable deposits. Following the failure of several trust companies in 1984 and 1985, the constant insurance premiums to the CDIC were increased. Member institutions are examined at least once a year by the OSFI or provincial regulators. If the examination reveals that the institution is following unsound business practices, a report is submitted to the Board of Directors.

Since 1983 deposits covered by the CDIC have been limited to private sector domestic Canadian dollar deposits of up to C$60,000. There is no limit on the number of single eligible deposits that can be made by depositors (in different institutions).

In 1983, when CDIC legislation was amended, the Minister of State for Finance noted that an important objective of deposit insurance in Canada is "to assist in maintaining the confidence and stability in the financial system." The Canadian Bankers Association, among others, has recommended the introduction of a risk-related deposit insurance premium to help achieve the objective.

7.2.3 Foreign Exchange Control

There are at present no exchange controls in Canada.

7.2.4 Key Accounting Issues

The format of the financial statements of chartered banks in Canada is prescribed by the 1980 Bank Act and by the Minister of Finance. The standards of disclosures by Canadian banks are generally high. Following are the major accounting practices.

Consolidation

The 1980 Bank Act requires a bank to prepare its financial statements on a consolidated basis in respect of all corporations controlled by the bank (e.g., more than 50 percent of voting rights) and on an equity basis in respect to other investments in which the bank owns more than 20 percent.

Valuation of assets

Investments in securities held for trading purposes are revalued to their market value at each reporting date, with the resulting gain or loss reflected in income. Investments in other securities are carried at the lower of cost or market value. Revaluation of assets may be considered applicable primarily to fixed assets, otherwise, land is carried at cost and buildings at depreciated cost.

Foreign exchange

Assets and liabilities recorded in foreign currencies, and not covered by a forward contract, are translated using the closing rate provided by the Bank of Canada. Translation of the income statement is effected by using the average rate for the period. For those assets and liabilities covered by a forward exchange contract, translation is made using the amortized forward rate.

Loan loss reserves

On a periodic basis the loan portfolio is reviewed for specific bad accounts that must be written off, and for accounts considered to be doubtful. The total "actual loan loss" experience is deducted from the balance sheet value of the asset and charged to the appropriation for contingencies account. The appropriations for contingencies represent amounts set aside to meet both future loan losses arising from "normal" credit risk, and any major or exceptional loss that might arise from any of the bank's activities.

Until 1988, loan loss provisioning by Canadian banks allowed for the smoothing of the impact on income statements for any particular year. This was achieved by deducting from the income statement, as loan loss, an amount based on the five-year weighted average loan loss history, as opposed to the actual loss experience for that year. Thus, a differential between actual loss experience and that charged on a five-year average accumulates in the appropriation for contingencies account. This account is shown as a separate item in the balance sheet and movements are disclosed in a separate statement. Canadian banks are permitted, by the OSFI, to set up general reserves only for sovereign risks. Sovereign risks are also deducted from the related assets in the balance sheet. Canadian banks are required by the Inspector General to maintain a certain level of reserves against bad loan exposure on loans to specified problem countries. In 1988, new methodology for provisioning was introduced based on actual experience during the period, instead of historical averages.

Hidden reserves

Loan loss reserves account for the majority of the reserves maintained on the books of Canadian banks. The Bank Act provides for specific and general loan loss reserves. The specific loan loss reserve was described above; general reserves are charged against income essentially by applying the bank's five-year loss average to eligible loans outstanding. Further transfers can be made directly from retained earnings to appropriation for contingencies with certain limits. More concern has been expressed of late about the inadequacy of bank loan loss reserves than about the use of hidden reserves.

7.2.5 *Taxation*

A bank is considered for taxation purposes to be a corporation resident in Canada, and is subject to taxation on the same basis as other Canadian corporations.

Corporate tax rate

Under the Canadian corporate tax structure, the federal government imposes a flat tax rate of 35 percent. This rate is reduced by 10 percent of income earned in Canada. Corporations are also subject to a varying provincial tax. In 1988, federal corporate income tax rates were lowered.

The combined federal and provincial tax rates for several provinces are:

Alberta	– 43.84 percent	British Columbia	– 42.84 percent
Ontario	– 44.34 percent	Nova Scotia	– 43.84 percent
Quebec	– 34.74 percent		

Losses

Losses may be carried back three years and forward seven years in arriving at taxable income in those years. Losses, for this purpose, include one-half of capital losses (in excess of capital gains) on arm's length dispositions of shares, debt of small business corporations, losses arising when qualifying debt becomes bad debt, or losses when qualifying debt or qualifying shares become worthless due to bankruptcy. Losses cannot be carried forward if there occurs either a change of control or a cessation of the business in which the losses were incurred.

Reserves and loan losses

The Superintendent of Financial Institutions, under the authority of the Minister of Finance, issues annual rules for the determination of allowable provisions. Under these Prescribed Aggregate Reserve (PAR) rules, the provisions for loan losses are charged to income, while contingency reserves (for future loan losses) are charged to retained earnings. For example, the 1987 PAR was defined as 1.5 percent of the aggregate book value of eligible loans (total loans net of all specific and general reserves) up to a value of C$2 billion, plus 1 percent of the remainder, at year-end. Any excess loan loss provision must be transferred to retained earnings. This provision may be transferred back to tax allowable appropriations in a subsequent year, if the balance of the tax allowable provision, after making the PAR transfer for that year, is less than the PAR. The deduction for unclaimed loan losses carried forward is unrestricted; however, the deduction for unclaimed PAR transfers of prior years is limited to the excess of one-third PAR at year-end over the PAR transfer for the year. Once recorded for accounting purposes, the loan loss and PAR transfers are deductible for tax purposes.

In June 1987, the Minister of Finance announced proposals for tax reform, under which tax relief is to be calculated on the basis of actual loss experience (e.g., specific reserves for identified doubtful loans) based on a loan-by-loan examination or on a pooled basis. In August 1987, the Superintendent of Financial Institutions required Canadian banks to significantly raise the level of their sovereign risk reserves. The additional required provision is tax deductible. Further, banks will no longer be permitted to deduct actual losses from income for tax purposes on the basis of the five-year formula prescribed for financial reporting purposes. Banks were permitted to deduct write-offs and specific reserves effective for 1988 and subsequent tax years. In 1988, the PAR rules were phased out, replaced by new rules based on actual experience.

Foreign exchange fluctuations

Foreign exchange gains or losses arising from the repayment of loans and deposits or on the realization of trade debtor and creditor balances (e.g., of income nature), are considered to be tax deductible or allowable depending on the nature of the originating transaction. Foreign exchange gains and losses are normally recognized when realized. However, gains and losses of an income nature may be recognized on an accrual basis in accordance with normal business practice. Gains or losses on capital accounts are treated as capital gains or losses and are not recognized for tax purposes until actually realized.

Interest paid and received

Interest payment by banks

Generally, a deduction is allowed for reasonable amounts of interest paid to acquire business or income producing property. No deduction is allowed for interest on money borrowed either to earn exempt income or not used to earn income. However, the practice is to allow banks to deduct their full interest expense. Also, Canada imposes a 25 percent withholding tax on amounts of interest paid or credited to non-residents. The 25 percent rate is generally reduced to 15 percent under Canada's tax treaties.

However, the following interest payments are exempt from withholding tax:

- interest paid or credited to a non-resident on a foreign currency deposit with a Canadian bank;
- interest on bonds, debentures, and similar obligations issued after April 1966 and before 1989 by the federal government, a province, or a municipality.

Interest payments to banks
Interest income is taxable on an accrual basis. However, interest on income bonds, income debentures, small business bonds, and small business development bonds is reported as received. "Income bonds" and "income debentures" are very narrowly defined, usually only when the issuer is having specific financial difficulties.

Other taxes

Financial institutions are not subject to federal sales tax on their sales of financial services. However, purchases by financial institutions of items such as stationery, furniture, or buildings are subject to federal sales tax. The federal government proposed a Goods and Services Tax (GST) which took effect on January 1, 1991. This replaces the Federal Sales Tax. Financial transactions are exempt from the new tax.

7.3 Bank Performance

The financial system in Canada is divided into four categories: banking, insurance, trust companies, and securities dealers. By law, banks are not allowed to engage in underwriting, selling securities, or trust banking. Trust banks are allowed to lend only for real estate transactions. As mentioned before, the Green Paper intended to permit much greater integration through financial holding company vehicles. By establishing and operating fully-owned subsidiaries, banks would be allowed to engage in securities, trust business, and where provincial regulations allow, brokerage firms. Following these proposals, the existing legislation was amended in June 1987 to enable the ownership of shares in securities houses by banks and other financial institutions. Trust business has not as yet been permitted.

7.3.1 Structure of Assets and Liabilities

The five largest banks in Canada account for about 75 percent of the entire banking system. These banks operate a wide network of 6,600 branches for retail, wholesale, and international banking. In the late 1970s the government, ostensibly to increase competition, chartered regional banks and foreign banks. The regional banks have not been successful and have disappeared; foreign banks altogether make up only the equivalent of the seventh largest major bank. The big banks dominate the foreign currency market (almost 100 percent) and the commercial loan market (about 76 percent), and are quite active in the mortgage market (44.0 percent at year-end 1989) (table 7.5). Chartered bank loans for personal use make up a significant portion of their loan portfolio. By year-end 1989, the total of such loans amounted to about C$62.3 billion, or 23.1 percent of their loan portfolio. Retail loans (personal and residential mortgage loans) accounted for the impressive growth in the loan portfolio during the period 1984–9. The mortgage loan portfolio increased by 156 percent, and personal loans by 78.2 percent in that time, compared with total asset growth of 37 percent.

Chartered bank investment in government and municipal securities was about $23.6 billion (4.3 percent of total assets) by year-end 1989. This investment served as both a source of liquidity and a part of the securities-related activities of chartered banks. Chartered banks operate with a solid base of deposits that financc 74 percent of their Canadian dollar operations. A high proportion of all deposits, about 69 percent, are personal savings. This source of funds is considered relatively "cheap" and less sensitive to interest rate changes. Other financial institutions, such as trust and mortgage loan companies and credit unions, are active in the mortgage loan market (40 percent and 16 percent of the market, respectively). For the most part, these are specialized institutions in terms of activities and clients (or members).

Foreign currency assets were about 31 percent of total assets at year-end 1989, and have been declining for a number of years (39 percent of assets in 1980). Foreign currency operations are mainly concentrated within the big five chartered banks. The domestic foreign currency operation, mostly in US dollars, represented 15 percent of the Canadian banking system in 1988. The overseas activities of the Canadian chartered banks were 16 percent of total Canadian banking system assets in 1989.

The banking system as a whole has been characterized by marginal real growth (beyond inflation). However, a gradual change in the composition of the banking system can be observed. Chartered banks have increased their presence in the mortgage loan market (from 37.1 percent in 1980 to 44 percent in 1989). This increase has been at the expense of trust and mortgage loan companies. In turn, these institutions have increased their market share in commercial lending.

7.3.2 *Income Statement*

An income statement analysis of Canadian banks is presented in table 7.6. The data reflects separately the status of Canadian-owned and foreign-owned chartered banks. As can be seen, the increase in net interest income represents both an increase in activity, as well as an increase in net spread (margins). The provision for loan losses represented 19 to 25 percent of net interest income, with a significant increase for South American debt in 1986. Other income, mostly from securities activities, more than doubled during the period and represented 41.5 percent of net interest income in 1989 (28.9 percent in 1984). Operating expenses were about 83 percent of net interest income. All components of operating expenses (i.e., salaries, premises, and equipment) grew by about 60 to 80 percent, a real annual growth of approximately 4 to 5 percent. The provision for tax payment represented 20 to 38 percent of income before taxes. Finally, the net income-to equity capital of this group averaged 10.1 percent, a relatively high and stable return. The only exception was a 1987 loss, the result of the special provision for loan losses. The results for 1989 showed a decrease in net income of this group; the rate of return to equity declined to 9.0 percent. The decrease in net income was primarily the result of additional provisions for loan losses on less-developed countries' debts.

Foreign-owned chartered banks enjoyed a real increase in their loan portfolio and net interest income during this period. The difference in composition of the loan portfolio of the chartered and foreign-owned banks was revealed by the ratio of net interest margins to gross interest income. For example, in 1989 the net interest margins to gross interest income for the chartered banks were 29 percent (23.4 percent in 1984), whereas for the foreign-owned banks they were 18.6 percent (15.7 percent in 1984). This difference reflects the larger proportion of domestic retail loans in the chartered banks' loan portfolio. Nevertheless, the volume of activities of foreign-owned banks (which is constrained by regulations) compared with operating expenses (86 percent of net interest income and 66 percent of total income) and their relatively large equity investment (7.2 percent of total assets), did not allow sufficient profitability in this group. As a result, during this period foreign-owned chartered banks were characterized by an average annual net income-to-equity capital of 5.1 percent, much lower than that of Canadian chartered banks which enjoyed a 10.1 percent annual rate of return.

Table 7.6 Combined income statement (C$ billions)

	Canadian-owned chartered banks[a]						*Foreign-owned chartered banks*					
	1984	*1985*	*1986*	*1987*	*1988*[b]	*1989*	*1984*	*1985*	*1986*	*1987*	*1988*	*1989*
Interest income	38.4	38.8	37.7	35.9	40.2	49.7	2.42	2.41	2.39	2.96	3.38	4.58
Interest expense	(29.4)	(28.7)	(26.7)	(24.4)	(27.0)	(35.5)	(2.04)	(1.98)	(1.93)	(2.33)	(2.66)	(3.73)
Net interest income	9.0	10.1	11.0	11.5	13.2	14.2	0.38	0.43	0.46	0.63	0.72	0.85
Provision for loan losses[c]	(2.5)	(2.6)	(3.6)	(1.9)	(2.5)	(5.1)	(0.04)	(0.05)	(0.15)	(0.22)	(0.09)	(0.16)
Other income	2.6	3.1	3.6	4.5	5.2	5.9	0.11	0.16	0.22	0.29	0.33	0.41
Total income	9.1	10.6	11.0	14.1	15.9	15.0	0.45	0.54	0.53	0.70	0.96	1.10
Salaries	(4.3)	(4.7)	(5.0)	(5.3)	(6.0)	(6.8)	(0.14)	(0.16)	(0.18)	(0.30)	(0.32)	(0.36)
Premises and equipment	(1.3)	(1.5)	(1.6)	(1.7)	(2.0)	(2.2)	(0.06)	(0.07)	(0.08)	(0.13)	(0.14)	(0.15)
Other operating expenses	(1.5)	(1.7)	(2.0)	(2.2)	(2.4)	(2.8)	(0.10)	(0.11)	(0.14)	(0.19)	(0.20)	(0.22)
Total operating expenses	(7.1)	(7.9)	(8.6)	(9.2)	(10.4)	(11.8)	(0.30)	(0.34)	(0.40)	(0.62)	(0.66)	(0.73)
Income before taxes	2.0	2.7	2.4	4.9	5.5	3.2	0.15	0.20	0.13	0.08	0.30	0.37
Provision for taxes	(0.4)	(0.7)	(0.5)	(1.9)	(2.2)	(1.1)	(0.07)	(0.09)	(0.06)	(0.08)	(0.14)	(0.17)
Other income (exp.)	–	–	(0.1)		(0.1)		–	–	–	0.03	0.02	(0.03)
Special provision for losses in transborder claims	–	–	–	(3.5)	–	–	–	–	–	(0.01)	–	–
Net income (loss)	1.6	2.0	1.8	(0.5)	3.2	2.1	0.08	0.11	0.07	0.02	0.18	0.17
Net income[d] to Equity capital (%)	11.6	12.2	10.8	(0.3)	17.5	4.0	6.0	7.0	4.1	1.0	6.5	5.7

[a] Consolidated worldwide.
[b] Income statement for the year ended October 31.
[c] Restated to reflect the requirement that loan losses be deducted directly from earnings rather than averaged over a five-year period.
[d] Net income for the year divided by equity capital beginning of the year.

Source: *Bank of Canada Review*, various issues

7.3.3 *Sources of Income*

The major sources of income for Canadian chartered banks are net interest income and non-interest operating income. During the period 1984–9, the total income of Canadian chartered banks increased by about 65 percent. Interest income (after deducting provisions for doubtful loans) increased by about 40 percent; non-interest income increased by 127 percent. The share of non-interest to interest income increased from 28.5 percent in 1984 to 34.3 percent in 1989.

Net interest income grew substantially during the period examined, despite deregulation and the growing share of interest rate sensitive liabilities. Real growth in the size of the loan portfolio (43 percent, equivalent to 14 percent in real terms) contributed to this increase. Also, the net spread (table 7.7) increased from 2.59 percent in 1985 to 3.08 percent in 1988. The impressive growth in the interest rate margin reflected the change in the composition of bank loan portfolios: a major increase in residential mortgage loans (high interest spread) and a decline in international lending (especially by the Royal Bank of Canada and Scotia Bank). The share of mortgage loans and personal loans in the chartered banks' loan portfolio increased from 43.4 percent in 1984 to 57 percent in 1989. Business loans declined from 52.9 to 39 percent, while their share of this change in composition contributed to the improved position of Canadian chartered banks.

Non-interest income also dramatically increased during the period examined, as a result of the following factors:

- the significant investment by Canada's banks in technology during the period 1975–85;
- involvement in capital market activities (advisory services, private placement, and insurance);
- the growth in investment banking, and underwriting and selling of federal, provincial, and municipal bonds;
- the development of merchant banking.

The increased involvement of large Canadian banks in capital market activities contributed to the increased profitability of this group. It should be noted, however, that according to the Green Paper, Canadian banks are subject to competition in many areas from other financial institutions. For example, in the instalment business, the banks must contend with increased competition from sales, finance, and consumer loan organizations.

The foreign-owned chartered banks experienced even more impressive growth in their net interest income (about 124 percent). The source of this growth was the increase in the size of their loan portfolio and a significant

Table 7.7 Combined income statement (the five major Canadian banks)

	(C$, millions) 1988	1987	1986	1985
1 Interest received	37498	33261	34966	35791
2 Interest paid	24802	22130	24246	25901
3 Net interest revenue	12696	11131	10720	9890
4 Other income	4781	4105	3312	2878
5 Provisions				
-Special for transborder claims	0	5613	0	0
-Other loan losses	2292	1804	3159	2138
6 Personnel expenses	5547	4854	4536	4286
7 Other non-interest expense	4039	3671	3319	2879
8 Pre-tax profit	5599	(706)	3018	3465
9 Taxes	2548	(131)	1264	1553
10 Net income	3051	(575)	1754	1912
Ratio analysis				
Average total assets	380203	368035	354004	347581
Average earning assets	356776	346007	333408	327781
Average risk capital	21011	20022	18404	16761
Inflation rate	4.0%	4.4%	4.2%	4.0%
Ratios to average earning assets (%)				
Interest received	10.51	9.61	10.49	10.92
Interest paid	6.95	6.40	7.27	7.90
Net interest revenue	3.56	3.21	3.22	3.02
Interest on capital employed	0.48	0.43	0.45	0.43
Net spread	3.08	2.78	2.66	2.59
Other ratios (%)				
Personnel expenses/net interest	44	44	42	43
Other oper. exp./net interest	32	33	31	29
Net interest/non-interest income	266	271	324	344
Total oper. exp./non-interest income	200	208	237	249
Net income/total assets	0.8	-0.2	0.5	0.5
Net income/risk capital	14.5	-2.9	9.5	11.4

Source: IBCA data base

improvement in the net spread (from 0.80 percent in 1984 to 1.63 percent in 1988) (table 7.8). The net spread of foreign-owned chartered banks was much lower than that of Canadian banks. This difference represented the limited involvement of foreign banks in domestic operations due to their restricted branching power. The non-interest income of the foreign-owned

Canadian banks improved even more significantly. The non-interest income of this group represented 37 percent of total income in 1989 compared to 24.4 percent in 1984, and a growth of about 272 percent during the six-year period examined. This increase was based on the involvement of foreign-owned Canadian banks in capital market activities and foreign trade.

Table 7.8 Combined income statement (four foreign Canadian banks)

	(*C$, millions*)			
	1988	*1987*	*1986*	*1985*
1 Interest received	964	869	555	512
2 Interest paid	738	666	433	406
3 Net interest revenue	226	203	122	106
4 Other income	116	117	65	50
5 Provisions for loan loses	44	69	30	10
6 Personnel expenses	102	88	43	33
7 Other non-interest expense	104	96	50	38
8 Pre-tax profit	92	67	64	75
9 Taxes	49	34	12	37
10 Net income	43	33	52	38
Ratio analysis				
Average total assets	10427	8377	5682	5566
Average earning assets	9801	7913	5431	5372
Average risk capital	748	584	375	316
Inflation rate	4.0%	4.4%	4.2%	4.0%
Ratios to average earning assets (%)				
Interest received	9.84	10.98	10.21	9.53
Interest paid	7.53	8.42	7.97	7.55
Net interest revenue	2.31	2.56	2.24	1.98
Interest on capital employed	0.68	0.88	0.76	0.51
Net spread	1.63	1.68	1.48	1.47
Other ratios (%)				
Personnel expenses/net interest	45	43	35	31
Other oper. exp./net interest	46	47	41	36
Net interest/non-interest income	195	174	188	212
Total oper. exp./non-interest income	178	157	143	142
Net income/total assets	0.4	0.4	0.9	0.7
Net income/risk capital	5.7	5.7	13.8	12.0

Including: Bank of Tokyo Canada, CitiBank Canada, Crédit Lyonnais Canada & Lloyds Bank Canada
Source: IBCA data base

7.3.4 *Expenses*

The expenses of Canadian banks consist of four types: provision for loan loss, salaries, operating expenses, and income tax.

The provision for loan losses covered 28 percent of net interest income in 1984, increasing to 36.1 percent in 1989. During this period as a whole, the significance of this item increased, especially in 1987 (including the special provisions). During the period 1980–4 the amount of non-performing assets increased from 0.50 percent to 2.40 percent of total assets. This increase represents the substantial exposure to South American debt, especially for the Royal Bank and the Canadian Imperial Bank of Commerce. Since 1984, with the significant increase in loan loss reserves and the decline in South American debt, the non-performing loans have declined. Loan loss provisions for loans to 34 countries designated by the Superintendent of Financial Institutions rose to 45 percent of the exposure to those countries. In 1989, the provision for loan losses on less-developed countries (LDC) debt increased by another C$2,268 million.

Personnel expenses for Canadian banks increased by 58.1 percent, a real increase of about 27 percent. This is slightly greater than the increase in the number of employees during that period, 21 percent. The number of employees grew as a result of the increase in domestic/retail operations, such as mortgage lending and capital market activities. Other non-interest expenses have increased at an annual rate of about 11 percent (7 percent real rate), representing continued investment in facilities and equipment, and an increase in deposit insurance premiums during 1987. Total operating expenses have increased at an annual rate of 8.8 percent (in real terms about 5 percent), resulting from growth in retail banking and the investment in advanced technology of Canadian banks.

The provision of taxes on income increased from 20 percent in the period 1984–6 to about 34 percent in 1989.

The structure of expenses in foreign-owned banks is very similar to that of Canadian-owned banks. An increase in loan loss reserve occurred, from 10.5 percent of net interest in 1984 to 18.8 percent in 1989. A substantial increase in salaries (157 percent between 1984 and 1988), and an impressive growth in other operating expenses (120 percent), were characteristic of this period. This structure of expenses reflects the attempt of foreign-owned banks to penetrate the domestic Canadian market. Finally, the provision for taxes of this group is very close to the official rate throughout the period (about 45 percent).

7.3.5 *Capital Adequacy*

The average equity capital to total assets of Canadian banks at year-end 1988 reached 5 percent (Tier 1 capital ratio), based on the Canadian interpretation of the BIS risk-weighted capital standard. Tier 2 capital ratio of Canadian banks is short of the 8 percent total capital requirement standard. Canadian authorities have not permitted either the inclusion of part of loan loss reserves or the excess of the estimated market valuation (over book value) of real estate holdings. Canadian banks are expected to meet the BIS requirements by 1992. The Toronto Dominion Bank is by far the most capitalized institution in Canada, with a ratio of equity-to-total-assets of 6.3 percent at year-end 1988.

Foreign-owned banks operate with a much higher equity-to-total-asset-ratio. The ratio at year-end 1988 reached 6.5 percent (7.7 percent in our sample of four foreign banks (table 7.9)). This ratio is in effect, even higher, given the low percentage of investment in fixed assets (12 percent in the sample of four foreign banks, compared with 24 percent in Canadian banks).

Table 7.9 Combined balance sheet (four foreign Canadian banks)

	31/10/88 (US$, Mil.)	*31/10/88*	*31/10/87*	*31/10/86 (C$, millions)*	*31/10/85*
A Loans					
1 Day loans to invst dealers	5	6	16	13	50
2 Customer loans	5189	6330	6786	3212	3547
3 Loans to banks	49	60	51	62	99
4 Long-term loans					
(a) mortgages	677	826	736	492	454
(b) leased assets	337	412	380	708	175
5 Other	11	13	15	26	13
Total A	6268	7647	7984	4513	4338
B Other earning assets					
1 Deposits with banks	341	416	746	318	417
2 Short-term investments	261	318	267	17	2
3 Other investments	595	726	1152	608	585
4 Equity investments	130	159	185	36	31
Total B	1327	1619	2350	979	1035
C Total earning assets (A + B)	7595	9266	10334	5492	5373
D Fixed assets	74	90	96	33	29
E Non-earning assets					
1 Cash and due from banks	280	341	260	72	29
2 Other	164	200	265	203	137
F Total assets	8113	9897	10955	5800	5568
G Customer & short-term funding					
1 Demand deposits	215	262	245	43	100
2 Savings deposits	755	921	858	102	28
3 Time deposits	4750	5795	6421	4088	4461
4 Interbank deposits	890	1086	1494	672	158
Total G	6610	8064	9018	4905	4747
H Other funding					
1 Subordinated debentures	49	60	33	17	17
2 Other borrowings	98	120	142	30	38
I Other (non-int. bearing)	730	890	1029	413	450
J Loan loss reserves (memo)	176	215	206	8	0
K Risk capital	626	763	733	435	316
L Total liabilities & risk capital	8113	9897	10955	5800	5568
Exchange rate (US$1 = CAD)		1.22	1.316	1.39	1.367
Ratios (%)					
Deposits/loans		91.2	94.2	93.8	105.8
Loans/total assets		77.3	72.9	77.8	77.9
Fixed assets/risk capital		11.8	13.1	7.6	9.2
Risk capital/total assets		7.7	6.7	7.5	5.7

Source: IBCA data base

Table 7.10 Combined balance sheet (the five major Canadian banks)

	31/10/88 (US$, mil.)	31/10/88 (C$, millions)	31/10/87 (C$, millions)	31/10/86 (C$, millions)	31/10/85 (C$, millions)
A Loans					
1 Day loans to invst Dealers	2019	2464	2700	3204	2500
2 Customer loans	169242	206475	198332	192509	192830
3 Loans to banks	5611	6845	8969	11391	11113
4 Long-term Loans					
(a) Mortgages	59217	72244	60712	48759	39646
(b) Leased assets	1953	2383	2140	1848	1676
5 Other	822	1003	978	1141	1407
Total A	238864	291414	273831	258852	249172
B Other earning assets					
1 Deposits with banks	22484	27430	38923	41314	39774
2 Short-term Investments	10786	13159	16248	14359	15256
3 Other investments	18064	22039	20275	21693	21130
4 Equity investments	5354	6532	3701	2818	2449
Total B	56688	69160	79147	80184	78609
C Total earning assets (A + B)	295552	360574	352978	339036	327781
D Fixed assets	3904	4763	4409	4051	3814
E Non-earning assets					
1 Cash and due from banks	7706	9402	9389	10145	9866
2 Other	8217	10024	8868	7195	6121
F Total assets	315379	384763	375644	360427	347582
G Customer & short-term funding					
1 Demand deposits	23980	29256	28253	24695	26834
2 Savings deposits	89937	109723	103316	91344	81030
3 Time deposits	116126	141674	134166	138750	133597
4 Interbank deposits	42564	51929	69946	67900	74752
Total G	272607	332582	335681	322689	316213
H Other funding					
1 Subordinated debentures	2726	3325	2640	3072	2888
2 Other borrowings	5015	6118	2381	3283	3176
I Other (non-int. bearing)	16977	20712	14945	11336	8544
J Loan loss reserves (memo)	7461	9103	10797		
K Risk capital					
1 Equity	16899	20616	18484	18448	16351
2 Near Equity	1155	1410	1513	1599	410
Total K	18054	22026	19997	20047	16761
L Total liabilities & risk capital	315379	384763	375644	360427	347582
Exchange rate (US$1 = CAD)		1.22	1.316	1.39	1.367
Ratios (%)					
Deposits/loans		96.3	97.0	98.5	96.9
Loans/total assets		75.7	72.9	71.8	71.7
Fixed assets/risk capital		21.6	22.0	20.2	22.8
Risk capital/total assets		5.7	5.3	5.6	4.8

Source: IBCA data base

Table 7.11 Selected financial data (the five major Canadian banks) (C$, millions)

Oct. 31, 1988	*Total assets*	*Total loans*	*Total deposits*	*Risk capital*	*Net income*	*Net income/risk capital*
The Royal Bank of Canada	100515	77781	75414	5554	721	13.0%
Canadian Imperial Bank of Commonwealth	87208	67286	63706	5334	591	11.1%
Bank of Montreal	75324	51986	54443	3824	560	14.6%
The Bank of Nova Scotia	69022	50815	45713	3557	512	14.4%
Toronto Dominion Bank	52692	43546	41376	3756	668	17.8%
Total five major banks	384761	291414	280652	22025	3052	13.9%

Source: IBCA data base

Notes

1 *OECD Economic Surveys*, Canada, 1986/7, 15, 59.
2 Ibid., p. 41.
3 The main difference between the two types of banks is their ownership. The shares of Schedule I banks are widely held with no one interest holding more than 10 percent. The shares are held by the public and are listed on all the Canadian exchanges.
4 Hockin, T. New Directions for the Financial Sector, Executive Summary, 1986, p. 2.
5 Ibid., p. 7.
6 Ibid.

References

Bank of Canada *Review*, various issues.
Hockin, Thomas, New directions for the financial sector, Minister of State for Finance, Canada, December 1986.
IBCA, Banking Analysis Limited, London – *Data Base and Country Reports*.
OECD, *Economic Surveys*, Canada 1986–7, 1987–8.

8

The United States

8.1 Structure of the Financial System

8.1.1 Introduction

The United States economy is the largest and most diversified in the world. In fact, the US economy can be considered to be in a class of its own. The United States emerged as the world's foremost economic power following the First World War, and its dominance of the global economy peaked in the aftermath of the Second World War. Recently, the rehabilitation of the European industrial countries and the emergence of new economic powers in the Far East have reduced this US domination.

Following the "stagflation" of the 1970s and the recession of 1981–2 (the worst since the 1930s), the United States entered into a new period of expansion. New job creation was nothing short of remarkable, especially when compared with Western European countries. Unemployment declined to levels that were probably consistent with a long-term natural level. Output grew faster than in most other large OECD countries, and productivity growth rebounded considerably from the depressed levels of the 1970s. Inflation did not escalate to the degree expected at that stage of expansion. In the beginning of the 1990s, growth of the economy slowed considerably, turning negative by the end of 1990.

The US economy has recently been plagued by two major problems, referred to as the "twin deficits" – the unprecedented large peacetime government deficit and the huge trade deficit. By 1988 this had turned the United States into the world's largest debtor nation. By the end of the decade, however, both the trade and budget deficits began to decline, both in nominal terms and especially relative to GNP. The years of expansion did not suffice to improve living standards on a broad basis. According to several measures, the distribution of gains and patterns of growth led to a marked decline in income equality.

In many ways, the most disturbing aspect of recent US economic performance has been the deterioration of the savings-investment balance, the accounting identity counterpart of the twin deficit phenomena. Though recent data indicate some recovery, the overall performance of the savings-investment balance, especially for a period of expansion, was very poor.

Structural change has also been dramatic in the United States. It accelerated markedly in the 1980s with the ascendance of Ronald Reagan, with his distinct ideological program, to the presidency in 1980. Tax reform, deregulation, the attempted reduction of the role of government in economic life, as well as more general features of the Reagan presidency, have all had their impact on US economic performance. The financial sector in particular has seen dramatic change in the last decade.

Table 8.1 The United States – major economic indicators and the banking system

	1980	*1984*	*1988*	*1989*
Gross national product ($ bil.)	2,732	3,774	4,880	5,234
Current account ($ bil.)	1.8	−107.0	−126.0	−105.9
Consumer inflation[a]	10.4	3.5	3.5	4.8
Exchange rate, dollar per SDR	1.30	1.02	1.34	1.28
Interest rate[a,b]	13.4	10.2	7.6	9.2
Population (mil.)	227.7	236.6	246.3	249.4
Banks	15,296	15,489	13,791	
Branches	41,477	43,979	49,519	
Bank Employees (thousands)	n/a	n/a	1,530	
Number of ATMS	4,750	48,118	58,500	
Population per ATM	47,937	4,917	4,210	
Population per bank office	4,010	3,979	3,890	

n/a: not available.
[a] Percent per annum.
[b] Federal funds rates.

Source: IMF, International Financial Statistics, *Federal Reserve Bulletin*

8.1.2 Financial Markets and Institutions

The financial system of the United States is the most advanced and developed in the world. It comes closer than any other to meeting the criteria of being an efficient, complete, and perfect market. American markets are unparalleled in terms of the breadth and range of financial assets available, the liquidity and efficiency of markets (both primary and secondary), and the lack of restrictions facing the investor.

The sheer size of the US financial market is one factor that has contributed to its advanced structure. The outstanding stock of tradeable debt instruments surpasses $10 trillion, with the amount of treasury debt over $2 trillion, constituting the largest single debt market in the world. In relative terms as well, the financial market is huge. The ratio of non-financial sector debt to GNP has climbed rapidly in recent years, reaching a level of 1.86 in 1987.

The flow of funds in the American market is similar to that of most developed countries. The household sector is the largest net supplier of funds, with the foreign sector having assumed a greater role in the 1980s. The corporate and government sectors remain large deficit sectors. Most of the government deficit is attributable to the federal government, with local government remaining much closer to balance.

One of the outstanding features of the US financial system is the even development of its various areas, capital markets, and financial institutions. The household sector's financial assets, for example, include approximately 40 percent in direct holdings of equity and fixed income securities and 34 percent in deposits, with the remainder being investments in non-depository financial intermediaries (primarily pension funds and insurance companies).

The existence of well-developed direct financial markets and non-bank intermediaries, the prohibition of universal banking, and the greater progress of securitization have all led to a relatively smaller role for the US banking sector than in other countries. Only about 35 percent of all intermediation is done by banks in the United States as compared with 90 percent in the Federal Republic of Germany, 50 percent in the United Kingdom, and 50 percent in Canada. Moreover, the financial system in general, and banking in particular, is characterized by a high degree of dispersion with a very large number of relatively small participants, each with a limited market share. The traditional American dislike of concentrated financial power, as well as the regional fear of being dominated by large banks located elsewhere, have resulted in a state-based banking system.

The financial crisis of the 1930s had a decisive impact on the structure of financial markets over the past half century. The Securities and Exchange Commission (SEC), endowed in 1935 with substantive regulatory and enforcement powers, oversees and promotes fair practices in equity and bond markets. Other bodies regulate the commodity and other markets. Banking in particular received considerable attention, with legislation attempting to ensure bank stability through both structural restriction, limiting the areas of bank operations, and operative interference, most notably in the setting of interest rate ceilings.

The recent worldwide upsurge in both financial innovation and regulatory reform can be traced to the United States. As in other countries, these changes came in response to rising inflation and financial market volatility, high nominal and real interest rates, and the increased importance of international trade and capital flows. In the United States, however, these trends became significant earlier than in other countries. Moreover, there was early recognition that the regulatory structure was outmoded and that rather than solving problems, it aggravated them. Furthermore, the United States had the technological conditions needed to implement change – an advanced telecommunications network and data processing capability. Perhaps most important, the United States was fertile ground for financial market reform because, from the late 1970s, there has been a marked propensity to seek solutions to economic (and social) problems via the mechanisms of the free market. This called for a reduced role for government, deregulation, and curtailed intervention in financial markets.

Financial intermediaries

Financial intermediaries in the United States can be conveniently categorized into three major groups: depository institutions, contractual institutions, and all others.

Commercial banks remain the largest single category of depository institution, with 29.7 percent of intermediated assets. However, they play a much smaller role than their counterparts in other developed nations. This is due to the relatively smaller role of intermediation in the United States, as opposed to direct finance, and to limitations on areas of operations imposed upon commercial banks by both federal and state regulations. Moreover, this market is shared by a large number (almost 13,000) of individual banks. The commercial banking sector has been characterized by slower growth than other financial sectors, and this disparity has increased with time (see table 8.2).

Other depository institutions include savings and loan associations (S & Ls), mutual savings banks, and credit unions. S & Ls and mutual savings banks, often grouped together as "thrifts," differ only in their form of ownership. S & Ls are organized as conventional stock companies, while in mutual savings banks the owners are the depositors themselves. Both S & Ls and mutual savings banks receive savings and time deposits, often in passbook form, from individual households. Their assets are overwhelmingly composed of conventional mortgage loans or other real estate

Table 8.2 The banking system

	Number of institutions				*Total assets*[a] *(US$ bil.)*			
	1984	*1986*	*1988*	*1989*	*1984*	*1986*	*1988*	*1989*[d]
All banks[b]	13952	13733	12691	12323	2402	2754	2959	3112
Less than $300 million[c]	13218	12871	11796	11393	638	664	647	656
$300 million – $5 billion	668	779	800	831	640	738	804	842
Money center banks	9	9	9	9	590	645	641	643
Other large banks	57	74	86	90	534	707	867	971
Other financial institutions								
Mutual savings banks	267	359	n/a	n/a	204	237	261	257
Savings and loan associations	n/a	3136	3220	n/a	977	1164	1350	1251
Credit unions	n/a	n/a	n/a	n/a	96	148	175	183
Total financial institutions	–	–	–	–	3679	4303	4745	4803

n/a: not available.
[a] Average assets during the year.
[b] Insured commercial banks.
[c] End of period total assets.
[d] Figure for June 1989.

Source: Wolfson and Mclaughlin (1990) Recent Developments in the profitability and practices of commercial bonds, *Federal Reserve Bulletin*

related loans, with a small amount of consumer or other loans and liquid assets. The savings and loan sector has been in a crisis since the beginning of the 1980s. A number of factors, ranging from the macroeconomic (continuously rising interest rates at the end of the 1970s which resulted in S & L funding of long-term assets at substantial losses), to poor management (and apparently corruption) with grossly inadequate supervision have led to an unprecedented number of failures. This in turn has prompted the largest financial rescue scheme ever, entailing considerable restructuring of the S & L industry.

Credit unions in the United States are small but numerous, and cater to the savings and borrowing needs of their members. These are primarily middle-class, salaried employees sharing some common association – usually place of employment, but frequently church membership, union affiliation, or neighborhood. They are limited to serving the needs of their members, although the range of services they provide is becoming increasingly comprehensive, so that credit unions have become competitors of banks. Credit union funds come almost entirely from members' savings. These funds are used primarily to finance loans for members (mainly automobile and large appliance purchases), although almost one-third are held in low-risk liquid assets such as government securities and bank deposits. At present there are some 20,000 credit unions nationwide. However, there is a distinct trend toward a smaller number of larger institutions, providing a greater variety of services more efficiently.

Contractual institutions are becoming increasingly important. (This has resulted in the supplanting of the individual investor in the financial markets by the so-called institutional investor.) The most important and fastest growing of these are the pension funds. They hold over half the assets held by this category and account for over half the growth in assets. Funding is provided primarily by employer contributions and, to a much smaller extent, by employee contributions. Investment income has also grown in recent years as a source of funds. Due to the very long-term nature of their obligations, pension fund assets are similarly long term. Such assets include corporate equities and bonds, and government and agency obligations. A relatively small amount is held in short-term assets.

Life insurance companies play a large, although declining, role in financial intermediation. Since their liabilities – life insurance benefits, savings benefits and annuities – are long term, insurance companies have traditionally invested in similarly long-term assets – corporate bonds, equity, mortgages, and government securities. However, changing investor preferences, primarily an increased desire for more liquid and flexible assets, has adversely affected the predictability and level of premium payments. This has forced life insurance companies to be more innovative in liability and asset management.

Other insurance companies, property and casualty insurers, have long faced more highly variable liabilities, as reflected in their asset portfolios. Almost 50 percent consist of highly liquid bonds (mostly government), with the rest invested in corporate equity. Less liquid assets, such as mortgages and other loans, form a negligible portion of their portfolios.

One interesting development affecting pension funds, life insurance, and casualty insurers, is their increasing tendency to bypass both other intermediaries and financial markets, to become direct investors in final assets. The economies of scale achieved by many of these institutions have allowed them to buy securities directly from the issuers or to make direct investments in corporations, real estate developments and new ventures.

The third group of financial institutions includes mutual funds. These institutions are pure intermediaries. Despite the variety of forms, all are based on providing the individual investor with the benefits of risk, maturity, and denomination transformation. While the "professional management" benefit of mutual funds has been challenged, the opportunity of attaining wide diversification with controlled transaction costs certainly serves some risk-reduction function, while the benefits of maturity (liquidity) and denomination transformation appear to be indisputable.

Although the classic mutual fund was created to manage equity investments, recent growth has been mostly in a wide variety of specialized funds. These provide the investor with relatively low risk access to markets as diverse as bonds, foreign equity, venture capital and start ups, precious metals, foreign exchange, and a variety of industry groupings. While conceptually a sub-grouping of mutual funds, money market mutual funds have assumed an importance of their own. In fact, they far outweigh, by asset size, all other types of mutual funds combined. In addition to the benefits provided by other types of mutual funds, the money market funds enjoyed the special advantage of being exempt from the interest rate ceilings forced upon depository savings institutions by the Federal Reserve's Regulation Q. This regulation kept the interest rates of such institutions below rising market interest rates during the 1970s and early 1980s. This period was one of phenomenal growth for money market mutual funds, which were able to attract vast sums at the expense of depository institutions through a combination of higher yield and relative convenience, including some check writing facilities. Thus, money market funds played a major role in the process of financial disintermediation. They have also greatly complicated the implementation of monetary policy, by rendering obsolete traditional money quantity measures.

Finance companies have played a growing and changing role in the past decade. Traditionally divided into three categories by type of lending – consumer, sales finance, and commercial – trends toward consolidation and diversification have resulted in a smaller number of larger firms, often engaged in all three types of business. Some of the larger firms, such as General Motors Acceptance Corporation (GMAC), are among the largest financial firms in the United States today. Most credit extended by finance companies is for business loans, with consumer loans having a declining share. Sources of funds have been stable over time, with bank loans less than 10 percent of the total, short-term debt (mostly commercial paper) approximately 35 percent, long-term debt 30 percent, and own capital approximately 15 percent.

The investment bank or securities firm is one type of intermediary whose importance to the financial system is far greater than balance sheet measures indicate. One vital role they play is in the issuance and trading of securities of all types. Due to both the rapid growth of debt markets and their increased securitization, securities firms have become increasingly important to the financial system and to the economy as a whole. In the primary market they serve as the designers and initiators of new issues, and as underwriters and distributors. In the secondary market they serve the all-important role of market-maker by holding inventories and by buying and selling to customers (the dealer or risk assumption role).

The role of securities firms in corporate finance has led to the virtual financial restructuring of corporate America. Mergers, acquisitions, and leveraged buyouts have changed the ownership of American business. Securities firms have been among the most dynamic and innovative of financial firms, responsible for developments as diverse as the junk bond market, mortgage backed securities, quantitative portfolio management techniques (such as program trading, portfolio insurance and immunized portfolios), and many other innovations. They are also the source for a large proportion of US economic, financial, and corporate research, the generation and distribution of which play a major role in keeping US financial markets so efficient. While the securities industry has shown some signs of faltering, especially since the October 1987 market crash, their adaptable and considerable human resources will undoubtedly assure them a considerable role in the foreseeable future. One of the most recent moves of the securities firms has been the move into so-called "merchant banking," or the taking of a direct equity interest in other firms.

Other private sector financial intermediaries, of much less importance than those mentioned above , include mortgage bankers (primarily originating and servicing mortgages for other investors), leasing companies (often bank affiliates), and Real Estate Investment Trusts (REITs) which are essentially mutual funds investing in commercial real estate.

Although the US federal government's direct role in financial intermediation is not as large as in other countries, it is still considerable. There are three types of intermediaries: federally sponsored agencies, federally owned agencies, and government guarantee programs.

Federally-sponsored agencies conduct "off the budget" financing, operating in the private financial markets to raise funds for specific sectors. While not explicitly government guaranteed, their close association to and implicit moral support from the Treasury allow them to raise funds at below market rates – usually close to that which the Treasury pays for funds. Such agencies mainly finance either the housing or the agricultural sector. The former, much larger, sector includes the Federal National Mortgage Association, the Federal Home Loan banks, and the Federal Home Loan Mortgage Association. The latter sector includes the Farm Credit Banks, Federal Land Banks and Federal Intermediate Credit Banks.

All of these agencies raise funds by issuing securities; they receive no Treasury funds.

Federally-owned agencies, on the other hand, receive direct appropriations from the Treasury, both as financing and to cover the direct subsidy inherent in their lending operations. While in the past federally-owned agencies have borrowed directly in the markets, today such borrowing is channelled through the Federal Financing banks, so that all their borrowing directly increases the federal debt. The major government owned agencies are the Export-Import Bank, the Tennessee Valley Authority, and the Government National Mortgage Association. At the end of 1989, there was $412 billion of federal and federally sponsored debt outstanding.

Many of these institutions affect the financial markets by the issuance of guarantees, usually in amounts much larger than actual borrowings. While these do not appear directly in the flow of funds accounts, they undoubtedly have a major indirect effect on the size, direction and allocation of such flows.

By far the largest such guarantee program is that affecting mortgage pools. This program involves the packaging of large numbers of mortgages, interests in which are then sold (with agency guarantee) to investors. The growth in these pools has been extremely rapid, and has virtually revolutionized housing finance in the United States. The agencies involved in mortgage guarantee programs include the Government National Mortgage Association, the Federal Home Loan Mortgage Association, and the Farmers Home Administration.

Financial markets

The money markets

The short-term credit markets in the United States are absolutely unparalleled in terms of depth and coverage, with virtually every possible combination of credit quality, maturity, and denomination available. Liquidity is in most instances virtually unlimited and transaction size is huge. The federal government maintains a steady auction schedule of 91 day, 182 day, and 364 day treasury bills, and the dealer community maintains a large and liquid secondary market. This secondary market is made up of short-term default free securities with a continuous maturity of up to one year, providing a benchmark for all other short-term rates, and a convenient proxy for risk-free interest rates. At the end of 1989, $431 billion in bills were outstanding. In addition, various federal agencies are occasional issuers of short-term obligations.

Commercial paper is a short-term promissory note issued by a corporation either directly or through a dealer underwriter. Commercial paper is usually issued by large reputable firms to raise funds at low cost by accessing investors directly. It can therefore be used as a substitute for short-term bank loans.

Bankers acceptances are also short-term drafts or bills of exchange issued by a corporation; however, in addition they are guaranteed by a bank and can therefore be traded as an obligation of the bank. At year-end 1989, there was $529 billion of commercial paper and $63 billion of bankers acceptances outstanding.

Repurchase and Reverse Repurchase agreements (Repo and Reverse Repo) are the simultaneous purchase and sale of a (usually) low-risk security for different dates, thus constituting what is basically a collateralized loan with a huge and varied market (US government securities dealers reported $219 billion in repurchase agreements at the end of 1989). In addition to their own importance, Repo and Reverse Repo agreements have contributed significantly to the liquidity and efficiency of the markets for the underlying instruments they employ.

The banking system has also generated a huge money market, partly restricted to banks themselves, but to a great extent open to a variety of participants, individuals as well as institutions. The fed funds market is the interbank market for the lending of excess reserve balances held at the Federal Reserve. This market is usually very short-term (overnight) in nature. It is probably the most liquid market, and due to its role in monetary policy and credit availability, the fed funds rate is a closely watched financial indicator. The Eurodollar market, involving the placement or acceptance of dollar denominated deposits outside the United States, is important for US banks both as a source for (via overseas branches) and as a use of short-term funds. Certificates of deposit (domestic or Euro), with either fixed or floating rates of interest, are negotiable instruments with the creditworthiness of a deposit. Developed in the early 1960s, they are important tools for bank liability management and provide investors with a liquid short-term instrument that pays money market rates. Money Market Mutual Funds and Money Market Deposit Accounts have grown enormously in the past decade, and now represent one of the more important uses of short-term funds.

Capital markets

A variety of equity and quasi-equity instruments (preferred stock, convertible bonds, and warrants) are widely and actively traded in the United States. The New York Stock Exchange (NYSE) is the largest in the United

States and the second largest in the world, after the Tokyo Stock Exchange. The US equity market, capitalized at $3.6 trillion, constituted 34 percent of the global equity market at the end of 1989. The NYSE, the New York based American Stock Exchange, as well as ten smaller regional exchanges, provide an institutional framework for trading. Most recently, off-the-exchange trading of listed securities has grown in importance. There is also a very large and active over-the-counter market, with a large portion of the securities being listed on an automated, computerized trading system, the so-called NASDAQ (National Association of Security Dealers Automated Quotation System List).

While the outstanding market value of corporate equity has actually been shrinking in recent years (due to the restructuring of corporate ownership), and the market has become increasingly institutionally dominated, equity holdings are still a more important factor in individual portfolios than in most other countries.

The US public bond market totalled $5 trillion at the end of 1989, almost 48 percent of the world bond market.

Almost all fixed income securities are issued and traded on the dealer based over-the-counter market. The most important market is that for US government securities ($1,5 billion at the end of 1989), organized around some 40 primary dealers (large security houses that can deal directly with the Federal Reserve). A continuous stream of new issues of default-free, large, homogeneous issues covering a maturity spectrum up to 30 years, makes this by far the most liquid debt market in the world. Average daily dealer transactions in US government securities (bills, notes, and bonds) was more than $112 billion in 1989. In the same year, daily dealer transactions in agency securities amounted to an additional $19 billion.

State and local government obligations (municipal bonds) are held mostly by individual investors (increasingly via mutual funds), attracted by their exemption from federal income tax. Corporate bonds are widely issued and held, forming the second largest group of debt instruments in the United States after treasury issues – almost $800 billion at the end of 1989, 16 percent of the total. The availability and low cost of corporate access to the direct credit markets help explain the corporate sector's relatively low reliance on bank financing. Of special note has been the rapid expansion of the so-called junk bond market. Junk bonds are lower than investment grade securities issued by companies that in the past would not have enjoyed access to the debt market.

Mortgage pool securities represent the largest area of securitization, with over 35 percent of all residential mortgage debt now held in the form of securities (compared with approximately 5 percent in 1970). A great deal of growth in this area has been due to the explicit or implicit government guarantee that much mortgage debt carries. This growth has significantly increased the volume of credit that bypasses the banking system. Other asset backed securities, representing pooled claims on car loans, credit card receivables, and other obligations, are far less developed. These markets may enjoy significant growth in the future, further reducing the share of credit provided by the banking system.

Less than 2 percent of outstanding debt securities are foreign bonds. Such bonds are issued in the United States primarily by foreign government entities and supranational organizations, such as the World Bank.

Other financial markets

In addition, a large number of other related markets play an important role in the US financial system. In fact, it would be proper to include a third separate category, that of derivative financial markets, in the description. The development and growth of these markets since the late 1970s has been nothing short of phenomenal. Financial futures are standardized exchange traded agreements to buy or sell an underlying asset at a predetermined date. They exist for a wide variety of instruments – debt, equity, currencies, and even indices. These instruments play a major role in hedging and portfolio management. Introduced in 1975, the daily trading in treasury bond futures surpassed, in 1980, the volume of the cash markets. The bond futures market out-traded the bond market itself by approximately three to one in 1987.

Exchange-traded and over-the-counter options on equity, debt, currencies, indices, and related products (caps, floors, and collars) have found myriad uses and increased acceptance among financial market participants. The swap market for both interest rates and currencies has shown the fastest growth of any of the new instruments. It has had considerable impact on other markets, including the bond and syndicated loan markets. The various derivative products have been major influences in changing the financial system, and it is difficult to compartmentalize their impact. They have revolutionized risk management, hedging and portfolio management, encouraged efficiency, and altered market institutions – for example, by vastly increasing the importance of off-balance-sheet assets as opposed to traditional assets.

A large number of commodities exchanges, trading both products and derivative instruments (options, futures, indices), on a vast array of products (precious metals, energy, agricultural produce, raw materials), complement the financial markets.

The rapid pace of internationalization affecting US financial markets has had the cumulative effect of expanding the financial system from the point of view of the domestic American participant. Due to its own huge size, completeness, and the small relative role of international trade to the US economy there was, until fairly recently, a high degree of insularity with US participants tending to ignore foreign markets. However, increased awareness, technological changes, and free access to foreign financial opportunities for both American and foreign participants, have vastly increased the amount of flow in both directions.

8.1.3 Banking Product and Bank Competition

Due to the extent and complexity of the supervisory framework in the United States, it is extremely difficult to describe the nature and structure of the banking product and competition without constant reference to the supervisory process. The form of virtually every banking service, and the nature and extent of competition, is in large measure determined by legislative or supervisory constraints. The development and evolution of banking has similarly been inseparable from changes in regulatory policy and its execution. As a result the role of lawyers and lobbyists in shaping today's banking industry has been at least as great as that of business executives and financial innovators. Nevertheless, for the sake of clarity, the banking product and the nature of banking competition will be described here without reference to the regulatory environment, which will be considered separately.

Commercial banks remain the most comprehensive provider of financial services in the United States, even though their activities are not as widespread as universal banks in other countries. US commercial banks are virtually the only financial intermediaries that both lend to, and borrow from, all four of the major financial sectors – government, business, household, and overseas. The trend toward lowering structural barriers, regulatory reform, and the economics of technological and financial services are all likely to contribute to an expansion of banking services so that the commercial bank will more closely resemble a true financial supermarket.

Commercial banking activities can be usefully categorized into three primary groups: traditional (on-balance sheet) activities, off-balance-sheet (fee generating) activities, and related services. An analysis of the aggregate commercial bank balance sheet (tables 8.3 and 8.3a) shows the acceptance of deposits and the extension of credit accounts for over two-thirds of the balance sheet. (Obviously, there are great variations among both individual banks and different categories of banks.) Only 20 percent of funds come from low-cost transaction accounts, with time deposits being the largest single source of funds. Interestingly, real estate lending is the largest single use of funds, being slightly more important than commercial lending.

Off-balance-sheet activities are, by definition, much more difficult to quantify. However, there is little doubt that such activities have assumed a much greater relative share of commercial banking business in recent years. Some such as loan syndication, sales, and swaps result from balance sheet considerations. Other off-balance-sheet activities represent risk assumption and/or hedging activities such as the creation and trading of derivative products (options, forward sale agreements, and other forward agreements). The underwriting and trading of debt securities (with restrictions) is assuming greater importance, as is foreign exchange and precious metal trading. Correspondent banking services, payment transmissions in various forms, custody and safekeeping services, and foreign trade services are all important areas for many banks.

A number of other activities and related services are either engaged in by banks themselves or frequently by affiliates and bank holding companies. These include inter alia, trust services, the provision of financial and investment advice, leasing, certain (limited) insurance activities, arranging for equity real estate financing, data processing services, and discount brokerage.

The thrift banks have evolved from highly restricted institutions specializing in residential real estate financing into institutions closely resembling commercial banks in terms of both asset and liability management. With regard to deposit taking, thrifts no longer have either restrictions or advantages vis a vis commercial banks. Therefore, their operations are very similar to those of commercial banks in both type of account and interest rate paid. Overall, this has had the effect of substantially raising the cost of funds for these institutions. Although their ability to borrow funds has also been considerably broadened, thrifts typically remain less reliant on borrowed funds than commercial banks. On the asset side they have moved from almost total concentration on financing residential real estate into more diversified activities. Current regulations allow thrifts to invest up to 40 percent of assets in non-residential real estate, up to 30 percent in consumer loans, and up to 10 percent in unsecured commercial loans. Some thrifts have adopted a transactional approach to mortgage lending, by originating and servicing loans and selling them to other lenders. Others have adopted a consumer-oriented strategy, providing a variety of financial services for individual households in one location.

Credit unions are also being exposed to both the risks and opportunities presented by a less regulated environment. Although they remain almost

Table 8.3 Major items in total assets; combined balance sheet (US$ bil.)

	Loans							*Securities*		
	Commercial and industrial	%[b]	*Real estate*	%	*Consumer*	%	*Total*	*US government*	*Total*	*Money market*
All insured banks[a]										
1984	573	41.4	355	25.7	239	17.3	1383	239	396	253
1985	565	36.8	402	26.2	277	18.0	1537	243	397	255
1986	577	35.2	460	28.1	305	18.6	1637	256	444	272
1987	577	33.5	539	31.3	320	18.6	1723	290	482	280
1988	577	32.2	609	34.0	335	18.7	1792	308	499	272
1989	595	31.2	691	36.2	357	18.7	1907	336	521	267
Banks with less than $300 million in assets										
1984	93	27.8	125	37.4	80	24.0	334	123	183	53
1985	98	27.8	135	38.2	83	23.5	353	120	177	55
1986	93	26.3	144	40.8	81	22.9	353	118	178	67
1987	88	24.8	158	44.5	77	21.7	355	125	183	65
1988	82	23.4	166	47.3	73	20.8	351	127	182	54
1989	82	22.7	177	49.0	74	20.5	361	132	182	53
Banks with $300 million to $5 billion in assets										
1984	153	43.2	106	29.9	81	22.9	354	74	126	70
1985	128	30.9	123	29.7	96	23.2	414	76	125	63
1986	138	30.9	145	32.5	103	23.1	446	77	135	64
1987	150	29.9	178	35.5	115	23.0	501	89	146	64
1988	146	28.7	195	38.4	118	23.2	508	90	146	57
1989	147	27.2	218	40.3	128	23.7	541	99	152	53

Table 8.3 Major items in total assets; combined balance sheet (US$ bil.)

	Loans							*Securities*		
	Commercial and industrial	%[b]	*Real estate*	%	*Consumer*	%	*Total*	*US government*	*Total*	*Money market*
Nine money center banks										
1984	188	50.3	58	15.5	31	8.3	374	14	34	64
1985	182	46.8	65	16.7	36	9.3	389	14	36	71
1986	171	43.4	74	18.8	40	10.2	394	15	46	74
1987	157	40.8	81	21.0	39	10.1	385	14	53	84
1988	146	38.9	88	23.5	37	9.9	375	20	55	85
1989	140	36.7	104	27.3	38	10.0	381	21	57	78
Large banks other than money center banks										
1984	139	43.3	66	20.6	47	14.6	321	28	53	66
1985	157	41.2	79	20.7	62	16.3	381	33	59	66
1986	175	39.4	97	21.8	81	18.2	444	46	85	67
1987	182	37.8	122	25.3	89	18.5	482	62	100	67
1988	203	36.4	160	28.7	107	19.2	558	71	116	76
1989	226	36.2	192	30.8	117	18.8	624	84	130	83
Other financial institutions										
Savings and loans										
1984	12		641		34		687		242	13
1985	17		691		46		754		259	14
1986	24		697		52		773		323	18
1987	23		722		58		803		371	22
1988	34		765		62		861		401	26
1989	34		743		59		836		337	25

Mutual savings banks						
1984		103		128	60	5
1985		110		141	56	6
1986		118		153	63	6
1987		138		172	67	7
1988		148		179	61	7
1989 (may)		145		179	58	6
Credit unions						
1984				62		
1985				73		
1986				86		
1987				97		
1988				113		
1989				123		
Total other institutions						
1984	12	744	34	877	302	18
1985	17	801	46	968	315	20
1986	24	815	52	1012	386	24
1987	23	860	58	1072	438	29
1988	34	913	62	1153	462	33
1989	34	888	59	1138	395	31

[a] Average balances.
[b] Percent of total credit.
[c] Includes mortgage backed securities.

Source: Wolfson and Mclaughlin (1989); Duca and Mclaughlin (1990)

Table 8.3a Major items in total liabilities; combined balance sheet (US$ bil.)

	Total balance sheet	Deposit liabilities						Borrowed funds	Equity capital
				Domestic offices					
		Foreign offices	%	Large time	%	Other	Total deposits		
All banks									
1984	2402	311	16.6	294	15.7	1267	1872	248	144
1985	2560	323	16.3	294	14.8	1363	1980	285	158
1986	2754	320	15.1	297	14.0	1497	2114	337	171
1987	2883	326	14.8	305	13.8	1573	2205	360	175
1988	2959	318	14.1	328	14.5	1610	2257	373	180
1989	3112	311	13.2	358	15.2	1693	2361	398	196
Banks with less than $300 million in assets									
1984	638	0.4	–	70	12.5	488	559	15	51
1985	652	1	–	76	13.3	496	573	13	52
1986	664	0.4	–	76	13.0	509	586	12	53
1987	666	0.2	–	73	12.4	514	588	12	54
1988	647	0.3	–	70	12.3	498	569	12	53
1989	656	0.5	–	73	12.7	502	575	12	55
Banks with $300 million to $5 billion in assets									
1984	640	19	3.7	90	17.7	398	507	73	39
1985	685	18	3.3	93	17.0	435	546	75	44
1986	738	18	3.1	93	15.8	479	590	80	48
1987	808	20	3.2	101	15.9	513	634	99	53
1988	804	19	3.0	101	15.9	514	634	96	53
1989	842	17	2.6	107	16.3	534	658	99	57
Nine money center banks									
1984	590	208	48.8	63	14.8	155	426	75	27
1985	618	222	50.7	51	11.6	165	438	88	29
1986	645	223	49.6	47	10.4	180	450	104	31
1987	650	228	50.0	44	9.6	184	456	101	28
1988	641	218	48.9	46	10.3	182	446	100	28
1989	643	210	47.3	51	11.5	183	444	103	30
Large banks other than money center banks									
1984	534	84	22.0	71	18.6	226	381	85	27
1985	605	82	19.4	74	17.5	267	423	109	33
1986	707	78	16.0	81	16.6	329	488	141	39
1987	759	78	14.8	87	16.5	362	527	148	40
1988	867	81	13.3	111	18.3	416	608	165	46
1989	971	83	12.1	127	18.6	474	684	184	54

Source: Wolfson and Mclaughlin (1989); Duca and Mclaughlin (1990)

Table 8.3b Major items in total liabilities; combined balance sheet (US$ bil.)

	Total balance sheet	*Deposits and savings*	*Borrowed funds*	*Bonds*	*Equity capital*
Other financial institutions					
Savings and loan association					
1984	978	784	143	4	37
1985	1070	844	158	5	47
1986	1164	891	197	9	52
1987	1251	904	250	12	46
1988	1351	972	300	–	55
1989	1252	946	252	–	34
Mutual savings banks					
1984	204	187	12		12
1985	217	186	17		13
1986	237	192	25		18
1987	259	201	36		21
1988	261	202	36		20
1989(may)	257	200	33		20
Credit unions					
1984	93	84			
1985	118	106			
1986	148	134			
1987	169[a]	156			
1988	175	159			
1989	183	167			
Total other financial inst.					
1984	1275	1055	155	4	49
1985	1405	1136	175	5	60
1986	1549	1217	222	9	70
1987	1679	1261	286	12	67
1988	1787	1333	336	–	75
1989	1692	1313	285	–	54

[a] Data for 3/88.

Source: Wolfson and Mclaughlin (1989); Duca and Mclaughlin (1990)

totally dependent on member deposits for funds (some 90 percent of the total), credit unions are now permitted to offer various transaction-type accounts and to participate in various funds transmission mechanisms. On the asset side, while some 90 percent of all lending is to members, the composition of loans is changing. The share of automobile and appliance secured lending is declining, while unsecured consumer loans, real estate, and home improvement lending is increasing. Interestingly, some 30 percent of credit union assets are held in liquid assets, almost triple the amount held by commercial banks. In addition to their original function – providing savings accounts and loans to members – credit unions have begun to offer a far wider range of services including electronic funds transfer and payment services, money orders, financial planning, and even travel advisory services. In this manner, credit unions are participating in the homogenization, de-segmentation, and competition of the banking industry.

The competition facing US commercial banks is both extensive and intensive. This is, historically, the result of an explicit political policy to disperse financial power among many relatively small banks. The ban on interstate banking has resulted in the largest number of commercial banks of any country, at close to 14,000, compared with 87 in Japan, 316 in the Federal Republic of Germany, and 400 in France. The five largest US banks control only approximately 13 percent of total assets, while roughly comparable figures elsewhere are 38 percent in the Federal Republic of Germany, 47 percent in France, 45 percent in the United Kingdom, and 51 percent in Canada.

Due to the high degree of operative regulation prevailing until fairly recently, banks often competed against one another in a primarily non-price fashion. Because various interest rate ceilings were effective for long periods of time, competition took the form of convenience (number, size, and location of branches, opening hours, drive-in tellers), service (form and frequency of statements, Christmas clubs), or occasionally outright circumvention of interest rate ceilings (gifts for opening new accounts, manipulation of compounding frequency). But with the elimination of most such restrictions, competition has for the most part resumed more conventional forms. However, the mechanism of federal deposit insurance has, due to the introduction of moral hazard, somewhat distorted the nature of competition among banks.

Federally chartered thrift institutions were permitted a considerable expansion of their asset activities by the Garn-St Germain Act (1982), which included the following main points:

- Thrifts are allowed to hold up to 10 percent of their assets in commercial and industrial loans (this limit was passed in 1984);
- Consumer lending constraints were increased from 20 percent to 30 percent of assets;
- Thrifts are authorized to invest up to 10 percent of assets in personal property leases;
- Interest rate ceilings on all time deposits were removed;
- Constraints on investing in state and local government securities were removed.

Due to the large number and varied nature of US commercial banks, certain other categorizations of competition might be instructive. To a certain extent the New York money center banks compete with other money center banks, particularly those of California and Chicago. All the money center banks compete with the super regional and regional banks for customers in their areas. And, to a degree, all are competing with local banks for at least some local customers. Competition between commercial banks and other depository institutions (thrifts and credit unions) is direct and virtually unlimited, to the extent that most customers are unaware of differences between these institutions.

Other institutions offer services similar to those of commercial banks including limited check writing, electronic payment mechanisms, and automated payroll crediting. Many of these institutions are increasingly moving into competition with commercial banks by providing commercial credit and business loans. Commercial banks, freed from discriminatory interest rate ceilings previously in force, are competing with thrifts and credit unions for individual savings accounts, and are increasingly offering mortgage financing and personal loans.

Foreign banks provide another source of formidable competition for US commercial banks. Although the foreign share of US domestic assets (9.6 percent in 1988) is relatively low, it has been increasing rapidly. This increase is the result of a nearly total lack of restrictions on foreign bank activities in the United States. While the main area of competition by foreign banks remains the wholesale banking market, considerable effort has recently been made by foreign banks to establish themselves in the retail market, often on an ethnic affinity basis. This trend is illustrated by the attempt of Japanese banks to win a share of the important and growing California market. Most recently, foreign penetration has tended to be in the form of acquisition and joint venture, with direct expansion becoming relatively less popular.

Non-depository financial institutions have also provided intense competition for US commercial banks. An example of such competition was the rapid growth of money market mutual funds run by investment corporations. These grew from $11 billion in 1978 to $207 billion in 1982. Although uninsured, money market mutual funds are perceived as close substitutes for passbook accounts at banks. The fact that they paid market rates of interest while banks were still bound by interest ceiling regulations, fuelled their phenomenal growth during periods of rising interest rates. While the recent elimination of most interest rate ceilings on bank rates has slowed, and even reversed the growth of mutual funds, the variety and mix of financial services offered by non-bank financial institutions – deposit-like accounts, insurance, securities, and investment management – have proved to be a competitive advantage in winning business away from banks.

On the asset side, many non-bank entities are entering the field of commercial credit by extending loans to corporate customers. Finance companies have captured a growing share of business loans. Pension funds and insurance companies have also been directly extending loans to corporate customers, thereby eliminating the commercial bank intermediary. Investment banks, moving into the area of "merchant banking," have extended bridge and even term loans to corporate clients, and have been moving into such previously bank dominated areas as foreign exchange trading.

One of the more unexpected sources of competition has been that presented by non-financial corporations, which have been generating enormous numbers of financial transactions. Firms such as Sears Roebuck and General Motors have become major financial market factors due to economics of scale, a synthesis between commercial and financial business, and a vast nationwide presence. Other firms, such as British Petroleum and Kodak, have set up sophisticated internal trading operations as independent profit centers, essentially joining the interbank market for foreign exchange and credit as equal members.

To a certain extent, the success of non-bank competitors in winning a share of the banking market has been due to the discriminatory regulatory burden placed upon commercial banks. Limitations on branching, liquidity requirements, deposit insurance premiums, and restrictions on permissible activities put commercial banks at a disadvantage vis a vis their competitors. However, some of the forces at work are clearly long-term developments, independent of the particular institutional framework. Such forces include advances in data processing technology and improved telecommunications, combined with the scale of financial flows attained by many market participants. These have reduced the value of the specialist and intermediary functions played by commercial banks.

The rapid securitization of financial markets is also part of this trend. As more and more borrowers and lenders achieve the technical means and professional sophistication to meet in the direct capital markets, the role of the various intermediaries will continue to shrink. Thus, for example, commercial paper issuance has replaced short-term bank lending, while "junk bonds" have replaced longer-term bank financing, and asset-backed securities move mortgages, car loans, and even credit card receivables off bank balance sheets. In the long-term, basic economic and financial trends, rather than any specific set of institutions, might well prove the most serious source of competition for commercial banks.

8.1.4 International Involvement

The US economy has been, on a relative basis, less internationally-oriented than most advanced economies. Nevertheless, the absolute size of the US economy and its lack of capital controls and restrictive regulations, have made it a major force in international banking. Other factors have helped to make US banks major participants in foreign banking, as well as attracting considerable involvement in US banking markets from abroad. These include the dominant role of the dollar as the international reserve currency since the Second World War, New York's preeminence as a financial center for most of that period, the depth and dynamism of US capital markets, the leading role of US corporations in developing multinational business and, of course, the political and social stability of the United States.

Foreign banks have long had an interest in the vast US markets. Before the First World War, foreign banks (primarily headquartered in New York, but with a large presence in California) played a large role in meeting the United States' need for foreign capital. They were also significant in financing the construction of both the transcontinental railroad network and much of American industry.

By the onset of the First World War, 21 foreign banks were operating in New York City. In the aftermath of that war, with the US dollar replacing the Pound Sterling as the linchpin of international finance, and with the US role in international trade growing, New York became an even more attractive center. However, the slowdown in international trade during the Depression, and the disruption of the Second World War, delayed any rapid growth in foreign participation in US markets until the 1970s, when rapid growth was again initiated. In 1975, 79 banks from 24 countries had 147 offices in the United States. By 1989, 246 banks from 32 countries maintained 514 offices in the United States. The growth rate of foreign banks has slowed in the 1980s due to a number of factors, including a reevaluation of the profitability and risk of expansion into the

US domestic market, a refocusing of strategy on home and regional markets, and probably some degree of saturation of the market; by the late 1970s most of the large international banks already had a US presence. This is corroborated by the fact that most recent growth is accounted for by relatively small banks, not included among the top 500 banks in the world. The geographic distribution of these newest foreign banks has also become more diverse, with significant numbers of offices opening for the first time outside the traditional New York/Chicago/California centers (i.e., Atlanta, Miami, Seattle, etc.).

The geographic distribution of foreign banks by country of origin has also shifted, possibly mirroring the US shift from an Atlantic to a Pacific orientation. Banks headquartered in Asia had 207 of 514 foreign offices in 1987, and almost 60 percent of foreign bank gross assets in that year, compared with 46 percent of total assets in 1980. Almost all of that proportion was accounted for by 32 Japanese banks with 82 offices, which held some 55 percent of total foreign bank assets. Western European banks' share declined from 36 percent of total assets in 1980 to 30 percent, with the share of UK and German banks halving during that period to less than 3 percent each. Italian banks became the largest European group, rising from 6 percent of total foreign bank assets to almost 9 percent in 1987. The role of the largest US trading partner, Canada, fell from almost 10 percent to 7 percent in that period. Latin American banks suffered the largest loss; while their numbers increased from 37 to 58 from 1980 to 1987, their share of foreign bank gross assets actually decreased from 7.5 percent to just 2.2 percent.

Another means of expansion into the US market has been through the acquisition of subsidiaries. The popularity of this method has fluctuated along with changes in the dollar's exchange rate, the valuation of US bank shares, and the experiences of previous acquisitions, a number of which did not prove to be great successes.

Foreign banks have, with some exceptions, concentrated on wholesale banking in the United States. Some 72 percent of their liabilities are interbank, compared with an average of just 17 percent for US domestic banks; only 20.5 percent are non-bank deposits, compared with 62.6 percent for US banks. Their penetration of domestic US business is hard to determine, as a great deal of their activity is evidently conducted with US affiliates of overseas entities. This is especially true of Japanese banks. In December 1988, approximately one-third of their assets were direct claims on Japanese residents; however, if they are assessed on a basis of ultimate claim (i.e., on the parent), the share almost doubles to approximately two-thirds of total claims. While there are many anecdotal indications of increasingly aggressive foreign, and especially Japanese, penetration of commercial lending and other domestic banking activities, total foreign bank loans to US commercial borrowers increased 196 percent from 1980–8, slower than the 212 percent increase in total foreign bank assets during that period. Off-balance-sheet activities have been very important to foreign banks, especially the issuance of standby letters of credit and derivative financial products such as swaps and options. Another important function has been servicing the needs of home country corporations in their US activities, including foreign trade finance, foreign exchange, and advisory services. Foreign banks have also made inroads into the securities business, drawing on their overseas experience and large capital bases, with a number of UK and Japanese banks acquiring primary dealerships in US treasuries. This type of activity has recently slowed markedly, with a number of reverses by 1989.

A number of foreign banks have penetrated US retail markets. These include Japanese banks via statewide branching in California, and UK banks through acquisitions, not always successful, such as Midland's ill-fated purchase of Crocker National Bank and Standard Charter's purchase of the National Bank of North America. Ethnic affiliation has also been used to achieve a retail presence, especially by South American, Southern European, and Israeli banks.

American bank activities overseas, with the exception of a few institutions, have become important only in the past 25 years. Until the First World War, American banks were relatively small and inexperienced, and played a very small role overseas. In fact, it was only with the passage of the Federal Reserve Act in 1913 and subsequent amendments that nationally chartered banks obtained the legal basis for foreign branching. Nevertheless, very few banks entered foreign markets, with most activity concentrated in the hands of a few money center banks (especially Citibank, Bank of America, and Chase Manhattan Bank and, to a lesser extent, the First National Bank of Boston). On the eve of the Depression, US banks maintained 181 offices abroad; by 1955, they had only 115; by 1960, that number had again increased to 131 offices, accounted for by only eight banks. As late as 1966, only 13 banks had branches abroad, although the number of branches had grown to 244. The next two decades saw rapid growth: in 1975, 126 banks had 762 branches outside the United States, with a peak of 163 banks and 917 offices in 1984, declining to 153 and 902, respectively in 1987 (table 8.4). Activity remained highly concentrated, however, with the three largest banks alone accounting for approximately one-third of all overseas branches; the top nine banks held nearly 60 percent of the cross-border claims of US banks in 1987.

Table 8.4 International involvement of the banking system

	1980	*1984*	*1987*	*Change 1980–1987 (%)*
Number of foreign banks, with branches or agencies	153	233	246	60.8
Number of offices	328	469	514	56.7
Assets ($, billion)	148.0	273.2	579.5[a]	291.2
As a percent of banking system	5.8	7.9	12.0	
Number of US banks, with offices abroad	159	163	153	−3.8
Number of offices	787	917	902	14.6
Assets ($ billion)	400.5	458.2	545.0[a]	36.0[a]
As a percent of banking system	15.5	13.2	11.3	
External assets of banking system	176.9	409.6	599.3[a]	238.8[a]
(of which IBF)		188.6	342.9[a]	
As a percent of total system	6.9	11.8	12.5[a]	
(of which IBF)		5.4	7.1[a]	

[a] Figures for 1989.

Source: Houpt (1988) and *Federal Reserve Bulletin*, various issues

In organizing international activities, US banks choose among a variety of forms – branches, subsidiaries, Edge Act and Agreement corporations, joint ventures, and IBFs. While US banks had 899 foreign branches in 1986 with $331 billion in assets, they also had 860 subsidiaries with $132 billion, and 131 Edge Act corporations with $22 billion that same year. Nearly 500 international banking facilities have been established. The choice of form is a function of tax considerations, host country regulations (Mexico, Canada, and Australia, for example, do not allow foreign bank branches), and to some extent US regulatory practices.

In most cases, US banks have followed their customers abroad, especially in the post Second World War era. The rise of the American multinational corporation, and its penetration of foreign markets, created a demand for banking services that US banks could meet only by expanding overseas. As the balance of payments went into deficit and the US dollar weakened, US banks had additional reasons for establishing foreign presences. The Interest Equalization Tax of 1963, and the subsequent growth of the Eurodollar market, prompted US bank interest in offshore centers, especially in the Caribbean. The petrodollar recycling of the 1970s, and the phenomenal growth of international financial markets since then, have provided additional incentives for an international presence by American banks.

For the most part, the international business of US banks is wholesale in nature, involving interbank activity and corporate lending. In 1987, US banks accounted for 31 percent and 41 percent of international assets and liabilities, respectively. Although barred from most aspects of the domestic securities business, US banks abroad have been actively gaining experience in the field. This accounted for 7 percent of assets in 1987, a rapid increase over previous years.

8.2 The Regulatory Environment

8.2.1 The Regulatory Framework and Process

Development and form

The regulatory framework within which American banks (and other financial institutions) operate is exceedingly complex, with no overall structure or rational division of responsibility. The system as it stands today developed over a long period of time without benefit of a master plan or overall guiding principles. Regulations, instead, have been the haphazard result of attempts to satisfy a variety of contradictory goals and to react to specific events and developments. As Arthur F. Burns, then Chairman of the Federal Reserve Board, said in 1974

> I have no doubt that if we were setting out today to create a system of bank regulation when none existed before, we would arrive at something other than the present structure. Much of our present regulatory framework can be understood only by reference to historical developments in our country.[1]

Among the major factors that shaped the regulatory framework were the desire to avoid a concentration of financial power, the need to ensure a wide distribution of banks, and the maintenance of control over them. Finding expression in the framework of states' rights versus federal power, these motivations gave rise to the dual system of federal and state chartered banks. The piecemeal development of the system, and the desire to separate powers even at the federal level, resulted in supervisory authority distributed among a number of bodies. Thus virtually every bank in the United States is subject to the direct supervision of at least three bodies at both federal and state levels. While there has been a distinct trend toward the growth of federal regulatory power at the expense of state authorities, the latter have taken many initiatives in the area of reform and regulation.

The other significant influence on the structure of bank supervision in the United States has been the occurrence of periodic financial crises, characterized by bank failures. This is especially true of the traumatic events of the 1930s. The bank failures and profound financial crisis of those years provided the immediate impetus for the bulk of legislation and supervisory regulations which have determined the shape of American banking for the past half century. Moreover, the haphazard response to each perceived threat to the banking system of specific legislative or supervisory remedy has resulted in an ever increasing tangle of laws, restrictions, and regulations. Sometimes the resulting structure has actually undermined rather than strengthened the stability of the banking system.

It is far from certain whether current events could conceivably provide a similar stimulus for change in the supervisory structure. While less traumatic, the accelerated pace of change in the financial system has revealed profound stresses and weaknesses in the American banking system. The most obvious symptom is the current rate of bank failures, a rate unseen since the 1930s. This has, in turn, spurred a number of legislative and supervisory steps, in addition to proposals for more far-reaching and comprehensive actions. However, the supervisory system remains a complex and confusing tangle of overlapping authority and jurisdiction, with no overall rational structure. This awkward and somewhat ponderous regulatory structure has, in many ways, become the dominant factor influencing bank behaviour. To that extent, banking in the United States has been called a battlefield controlled by lawyers, courts, and regulators.

Legislative basis

Banks in the United States can be either nationally or state chartered. This is because the "entry and exit function of supervision" – the ability to grant and revoke charters to banks – is shared between the Office of the Comptroller of the Currency (OCC) at the federal level, and the various banking departments at state level. While practical differences between national and state chartered banks are rapidly diminishing, they are historically quite distinct. Regardless of charter, however, all banks are subject to both federal and state legislation. Although federal authority has, in general, been growing at the expense of state authority, in many areas state authority remains very important. Moreover, the federal government does cede authority to the states in certain areas, such as in the control of branching and the rights of geographic expansion.

A brief survey of landmark federal banking legislation is necessary to understand the development and structure of the US banking system. Beyond the major pieces of legislation mentioned here, there are many other federal statutes affecting banks directly or indirectly. There are also the separate bodies of law enacted by each of the 50 states that, in conjunction with federal law, determine the environment in which banks operate.

- *The National Currency Act* (1863), and the *National Bank Act* (1864), established the OCC and its power to charter national banks. This created the dual banking system, since individual states were already chartering banks. In addition, the NBA (1864), authorized the "business of banking" as deposit taking and the extension of credit, providing the definition of banking still in use today.
- *The Federal Reserve Act* (1913), established the central bank in its current form, granting it authority in the setting of monetary policy and a major role in the banking system and bank supervision.
- *The Edge Act* (1919), authorized banks to establish special purpose corporations to engage in international banking activities.
- *The McFadden Act* (1927), established the dominance of state banking laws in determining interstate banking structures, essentially prohibiting interstate branching.
- *The Banking Acts* of 1933 and 1935, were the major legislative responses to the banking crisis of the 1930s. Their most important provisions included:
    - The separation of commercial banking from the investment banking and securities businesses (Glass-Steagall).
    - The prohibition of the payment of interest on demand deposits and the establishment of ceilings on other creditory interest rates (Regulation Q).
    - The establishment of the Federal Deposit Insurance Corporation (FDIC), granting it regulatory powers.
    - The establishment of the Federal Open Market Committee (FOMC) to implement monetary policy and increase the Fed's supervisory authority.
    - The broadening of the OCC Supervisory powers.
    - The restriction of a variety of bank activities, including interlocking directorships, bank branching, and lending to insiders.
- *The Federal Home Loan Bank Act* (1932), *The Home Owners Loan Act* (1933), and *The National Housing Act* (1934), established a regulatory framework (including deposit insurance) for savings and loans parallel to that for commercial banks.
- *The Federal Credit Union Act* (1934), established federal chartering for credit unions.
- *The Bank Holding Company Act* (1956), and *Amendments* (1970), established the framework for federal regulation of bank holding companies and granted the Federal Reserve Board virtually exclusive authority in regulating them

- *The Bank Merger Act* (1960), required that applications for mergers and acquisitions by banks be processed through bank regulators, for either approval or denial. The Antitrust Department of the Department of Justice has only advisory responsibility. Bank merger activities were exempted from the Sherman Act and the Clayton Act.
- *The Savings and Loan Holding Company Act* (1967), established the framework for supervising Savings and Loan Holding Companies.
- *The Consumer Credit Protection Act* (1968), and subsequent legislation established the federal interest in consumer protection in banking matters.
- *The Financial Institutions Regulatory and Interest Rate Control Act* (FIRIRCA) (1978), established the Federal Financial Institutions Examination Council (FFIEC), increased various powers of federal supervisory agencies, and addressed various problems concerning electronic funds transfer systems.
- *The International Banking Act* (1978), provided the regulatory framework for foreign banks operating in the United States.
- *The Depository Institutions Deregulation and Monetary Control Act* (DIDMCA) (1980), was the first major piece of bank legislation since the 1930s. It attempted to reform the structure of the banking system, not altogether successfully. Its major provisions included:
  - The phasing out of deposit interest rate ceilings (Regulation Q).
  - The authorizing of nationwide NOW (negotiable order of withdrawal) accounts.
  - The expansion of the power of the FRB to establish required reserves for *all* depository institutions (rather than only member banks).
  - The expansion of the permissible activities of S & Ls.
- *The International Banking Facility (IBF)* (1981). In December 1981 the Federal Reserve amended its Regulation D (reserve requirements) and Regulation Q (interest on deposits) to permit the operation of IBFs. The purpose of the IBF is to enable US banks to compete more effectively with foreign banks without using an offshore operation.
- *The Garn–St Germain Depository Institutions Act* (1982), authorized Money Market Deposit Accounts, and included a number of measures aimed at strengthening the savings and loan industry.
- *The International Lending Supervision Act* (1983), established mandatory reporting and exposure standards for foreign loans.
- *The Competitive Equality Banking Act* (1987), attempted to promote increased and fairer competition in financial services by providing a "level playing field." Its most specific measure prohibited the establishment of new non-bank banks.
- *The Financial Institutions Reform, Recovery and Enforcement Act* (1989), included the following major points:
  - It authorized increased funding for closure and disposal of thrifts.
  - It changed the regulatory structure for the thrift industry, specifically it
    - Abolished the FSLIC, placing the thrift insurance fund (SAIF) under control of the FDIC.

- Created the Office of Thrift Supervision (OTS), a subdepartment of the Treasury Department, which replaced the FHLBB as the primary supervisor of thrifts.
- Created the Resolution Trust Corp. (RTC) to dispose of failed thrifts and the Resolution Finance Corp. (RFC), to manage the sale of failed thrift's assets.
- It restricted thrift's asset powers. The main restrictions included:
  - Thrifts must hold 70 percent of assets in "qualified assets," primarily residential mortgages and mortgage-backed securities.
  - Commercial real estate lending is limited to four times capital.
  - Investment in less than investment grade securities (junk bonds) is prohibited.

Administrative regulations

There is a large body of "administrative law," composed of various regulations drafted by regulatory bodies under authority delegated to them by the legislature. From a practical point of view, administrative regulations are as important as banking statutes themselves, since they provide the means by which the regulators implement legislative goals in practice.

State laws

Each of the 50 states is entitled to, and does in fact, charter and regulate state banks as part of the dual banking system. While the trend has been for federal authorities to encroach upon state regulations, state law remains an integral part of the regulatory system and an important determinant of many facets of the banking industry. The relationship between state and federal regulations is unclear, as are many aspects of bank supervision in the United States. In a formal sense, when a federal regulation is in conflict with a state regulation, the federal statute will usually be considered the prevailing authority. Nevertheless, various considerations generally restrain federal regulators from directly challenging state authority unless specifically backed by federal legislation.

The institutional framework

Regulatory and supervisory authority over banks is shared by a number of bodies at both federal and state levels. While the system has become less fragmented in recent years, and standardization and coordination among the agencies is increasing, banks are still subject to the rules and regulations of at least three regulatory bodies. These bodies can be grouped into federal agencies (OCC, FRB, FDIC, and FFIEC), other federal bodies (SEC, Department of Justice, Federal Trade Commission, etc.), and state authorities.

- The oldest federal body is the OCC, established in 1863. It is concerned solely with the supervision of the over 4,800 national banks, comprising 60 percent of total bank assets. Although it is a part of the Treasury Department, the OCC enjoys semi-autonomous standing in the government. Its powers originally stem from the OCC ability to grant and deny bank charters and branching applications. Subsequent legislation has expanded its role to include the more general functions of bank examination and supervision.
- The Federal Reserve System consists of the Federal Reserve Board in Washington and 12 Regional Federal Reserve banks. The FRS is an independent government agency, although political and other considerations ensure that its independence is far from absolute. Although its direct supervisory franchise over banks is relatively narrow compared with the OCC or FDIC, its influence is pervasive due to its central role in the financial system and control of monetary policy. Moreover, the supervisory functions of the FRS have been steadily expanding. It shares supervisory and examination responsibility with state banking authorities for some 1,000 state chartered FRS member banks, comprising 15 percent of total bank assets. Its more important regulatory role, however, is as the sole regulator and controller of both single and multi-bank holding companies, one of the few unshared areas of supervisory authority in the entire regulatory framework. As of 1984, the FRS supervised more than 6,000 such BHLS, comprising almost 90 percent of all bank assets. In addition to its general impact on the banking system through its control of monetary policy, since the passage of the DIDMCA (1980) the FRB has been authorized to establish required reserves for all depository institutions. Through its discount window, the Fed has often acted as the supplier of liquidity of last resort to the banking system, although this role is not formalized.
- The FDIC. The protection of depositors through a system of deposit insurance is the main goal of the FDIC. The achievement of this goal has meant that the FDIC has assumed a major role in bank supervision in general, and in dealing with problem and failed banks in particular. Since carrying FDIC coverage has become a competitive necessity for virtually all banks, the FDIC oversees, in some form, 98 percent of all US banks. However, since the OCC supervises national chartered banks and the FRS supervises state member banks, the FDIC concentrates on supervising some 8,500 state chartered, insured non-member banks with approximately 25 percent of commercial bank assets, a responsibility shared with state banking authorities.
- The Federal Financial Institutions Examination Council (FFIEC) is a coordinating body with a small staff and no direct supervisory or enforcement powers. However, its mandate is an important one. It develops a uniform reporting system for all depository institutions and coordinates examination and supervisory procedures among the various other agencies.

A number of other federal agencies play important, although largely indirect, roles in bank regulation. Among the more important:

- The Securities and Exchange Commission (SEC) regulations affect banks when they issue securities (through the same disclosure and registration requirements that apply to all issuers of securities), or when they perform other security related activities such as broker, dealer, or trust activities. The SEC has, however, generally been content to let the banking agencies play the primary role in supervising securities-related activities other than securities issues.
- The Department of Justice has responsibility for the anti-trust implications of BHC activities, bank mergers, and acquisitions.
- The Department of Labor has responsibility for certain areas of bank activities regarding fair labor practices. The Federal Trade Commission enforces some consumer protection regulations. Other groups have become involved in various bank activities that have been considered to have implications regarding civil rights legislation.

Each of the states has a bank supervisory body involved in the granting of charters, the controlling of branching, the drafting and enforcing of regulations, and the conducting of examinations. There are some 9,000 state chartered banks which state banking departments oversee, in the vast majority of cases in conjunction with either the FRB or the FDIC. These banks comprise about two-thirds of all commercial banks, although they control just over one-third of bank assets.

The Conference of State Bank Supervisors is a coordinating and representative body that attempts to promote efficiency and professionalism among state regulatory authorities. The FFIEC maintains a State Liaison Committee with representatives of a number of state banking authorities. The Committee's mandate is to promote coordination and cooperation between state banking authorities and federal agencies.

There are a number of banking industry associations that play various educational, public relations, and lobbying roles for the banking industry. Although they do not have any formal regulatory role, as advocates of commercial banking interests, these associations can attempt to shape the regulatory structure. The largest such body is the American Bankers Association, which has 13,000 members. The Association of Bank Holding Companies represents most of the larger BHLs, while the Independent Bankers Association of America represents the small "community" banks and their interests.

The regulatory process

The goals of the regulatory process in the United States can be categorized into four main areas of concern: bank safety, banking system structure, consumer protection, and international banking activities. While all four areas are interrelated to a great degree, this sort of categorization can provide a sense of order in the complex and confusing proliferation of authorities and regulations.

Bank safety is concerned with assuring the solvency and stability of individual banks, thereby ensuring the safety of deposits. The tools of regulatory authorities include operative interference in bank operations, monitoring and surveillance of bank performance, and establishment of general standards and guidelines.

Concern with the overall structure of the banking industry, aside from seeking to ensure bank safety at the system-wide level, also stems from concerns with the role of banks in the wider economy and in the body politic. The prime goals have been the prevention of overconcentration of financial power and the encouragement of a fair, but not destabilizing, degree of competition among banks. To attain these goals, the authorities have attempted to regulate the size and number of banks by both geographic and product area. This has been done through the use of exit and entry powers (chartering and branching), the control of bank holding companies, and bank ownership.

Consumer protection as a distinct goal is a relatively recent development, and can be seen as part of the general trend of growing concern for consumer and individual rights in a broad range of other areas. Both legislation and administrative decree, enforced by either existing supervisory authorities or special purpose government agencies, are used to achieve the goal of consumer protection. Primary responsibility for consumer protection lies with the FRB.

The control of international banking activities is an extremely complex area of banking regulation. It is for this reason that it can be considered a distinct part of the regulatory process.

Deposit insurance

Formal deposit insurance plays an important role in the American banking system, providing not only protection for depositors, but also an additional regulatory body and a framework for handling failed banks. It has been successful in maintaining the confidence of depositors, and in preventing runs and panics that threaten bank stability. However, certain aspects of the FDIC's operation can have negative economic implications, being in fact a destabilizing influence on the banking system. This is primarily due to the element of moral hazard introduced into banking operations. While, formally, FDIC coverage has been limited to a ceiling for depositors (currently $100,000), historically it has attempted to prevent any loss to depositors. This desire has generally been reflected in its method of choice for handling failing banks: straight pay off of insured deposits, facilitating merger of the failing bank with a stronger institution, or providing direct assistance to the bank in question to enable it to meet its obligations.

Bank safety

Supervision of bank safety is based upon the idea of monitoring safe and sound banking practices. In pursuing this goal bank regulators have relied upon operative interference in bank activities, the setting of minimum standards in various areas, and the monitoring of compliance and general bank performance. Operative restrictions include the prohibition of banks engaging in commerce or other restricted activities, the severe limitations placed upon bank involvement in the securities business (Glass-Steagall), regulation of the type and amount of securities held for investment purposes, and the relationship with and activities of affiliate companies. Lending activity, in addition to being subject to quality appraisals by various authorities, is also subject to statutory limitations by borrower, such as regarding loans granted to single borrowers, insiders, and/or affiliates, or by purpose of loan, such as real estate or securities lending. The regulation of interest rates paid on deposits, once one of the most important tools used by regulators to ensure bank safety, has now virtually ceased to exist.

Minimum standards are used to ensure liquidity and capital adequacy. While levels of liquidity are not specified, they are examined in the monitoring process. Minimum reserve requirements, extended to all depository institutions by the DIDMCA (1980), are primarily used by the Federal Reserve as a tool of monetary policy; however, they still play some role in maintaining standards of liquidity. Capital adequacy has increasingly become the focus of regulators looking to ensure bank safety. Minimum standards were adopted by the OCC, FDIC, and FRB in 1985, the first time capital adequacy has been the subject of specific regulations. Although state guidelines can sometimes differ, coordination among federal agencies ensures that uniform minimal standards now apply to virtually every bank in the country. The treatment of capital adequacy is still evolving, with major developments likely to focus on issues such as differential risk weighting for computing capital ratios, the treatment of off-balance-sheet and contingent liabilities, the definition of capital, and the meeting of international standards.

The monitoring of bank compliance and performance is accomplished by setting minimum accounting standards, mandatory reporting and disclosure requirements, carrying out special examinations and, when and if required, the taking of enforcement action. Given the number of agencies involved, their overlap and jurisdictional tangles, the setting of standards and coordination of activities have sometimes been difficult to achieve. Nevertheless, widely accepted reporting standards, formats, common surveillance, and evaluation systems have been established. The FFIEC has been instrumental in coordinating these efforts. As routine reporting needs have been more efficiently dealt with, the regulatory bodies have devoted increasing efforts to the specific problems facing banks in recent years. These include off-balance-sheet risks and specific loan problems (international exposure, real estate, agriculture, or energy); the new emphasis has caused a shift from reliance on routine reports and random sampling to a greater use of targeted examinations for specific problem areas and institutions.

The statistical reporting process begins with the report of condition and income that all banks must submit on a quarterly basis. Data culled from this report and from other sources is used to prepare the Uniform Bank Performance Report (UBPR). The UBPR is used by all federal agencies, and by state authorities, for routine monitoring of banks.

In addition to routine monitoring of reports on a more or less continual basis, periodic examinations of banking institutions are conducted by all federal agencies. These examinations are of a frequency ranging from annual (OCC), to once every two (FRB), or three (FDIC) years. The bank examination schedule is coordinated with state agencies to produce either joint or alternate examinations, as the situation requires. Needless to say, special examinations can and are conducted whenever needed. A common rating system, the Uniform Financial Institutions Rating System, has been adopted by the relevant agencies. The system, commonly known by its acronym CAMEL, examines five areas: Capital adequacy, Asset quality, Management quality, Earnings quality, and Liquidity. Bank Holding Companies are rated by the Federal Reserve on another scale, the BOPEC, representing five areas of concern: Bank subsidiary, Other subsidiaries, Parent company, Earnings consolidated, and Capital adequacy-consolidated. An "early warning system" to identify troubled banks has been developed by the OCC, known as the National Bank Surveillance System. The NBSS employs four mechanisms: a bank performance report, an anomaly severity rating system, a "human element" analysis, and an action control system.

Banking structure

The banking system structure is regulated primarily by entry and exit limitations (chartering and branching). While specifics differ from state to state, most emulate the OCC in its evaluation of chartering requests. This evaluation examines earnings prospects, capital adequacy, character and quality of management, and community needs. Many states also require FDIC membership, thus bringing the FDIC into the chartering process. Control of branching is based on the McFadden Act (1927), which essentially forbade interstate branching and allowed national banks to branch within their home state only to the extent allowed by state regulations. The overall effect was to effectively grant states the final say in determining the nature of the bank structure unit and limited branching to intrastate activity. State legislation has recently been quite active in using bank laws to permit various structures of regional branching. State power is not absolute in this regard, however, as both the FDIC and FRB are required to approve branching of member banks. The whole question of branching is currently under considerable scrutiny, due to structural pressures and to the implications of technological developments, such as automatic teller machines, electronic banking, and electronic point of sale funds transfer.

The ownership structure of banks has become an area of increasing concern to regulatory authorities. Proposed mergers and acquisitions need the approval of both federal and state agencies involved in the supervision of such banks. Moreover, the approval of the Department of Justice is needed to satisfy anti-trust considerations.

Bank holding companies are supervised only by the Federal Reserve, whose influence both directly and indirectly can extend virtually system wide. Based on the BHCA (1956), the minimum and maximum areas of bank and BHC activity are controlled by the Fed. Furthermore, the Fed can restrict geographic expansion, product areas, and ownership.

International banking activities

While international banking activities involving the United States began in the last century, specific supervisory attention has been increasing rapidly in recent years. This is due both to the vast expansion of international activity since the Second World War, and the considerable problems that have accompanied such growth.

The basic approach of the regulatory authorities concerning the international activities of American banks has been to encourage the adoption of a competitive position abroad, while attempting to limit any negative repercussions of such activities *vis-a-vis* the domestic goals of bank supervision. The attempt to ensure the competitiveness of American banks has resulted in their engaging in a much wider range of activities than permitted domestically, such as securities underwriting and ventures into commerce. The organizational form of foreign activity can include branching, forming

Edge Act or Agreement corporations, expansion via subsidiaries and affiliates, and the formation of International Banking Facilities (IBFs).

The delineation of supervisory responsibility for all forms of international banking activity is unclear. Since the regulatory policy of all jurisdictions is generally relevant, most banks are subject to the regulation of a number of national authorities. Therefore, in addition to regular supervision by regulators in the locale of operation, any special provisions enacted by regulators in the home country will also be relevant. The OCC and Federal Reserve cover international activities in regular examinations of domestic offices, and also make on-site inspections of foreign operations. The International Lending Supervision Act (ILSA, 1983), considerably strengthened the ability of the federal regulatory agencies to deal with some of the problems raised by the vast expansion of international activities. It mandated greater disclosure of country exposure, the establishment of specific reserves against loans to problem countries, specified the accounting treatment of overseas loan income, and granted the federal agencies authority to raise minimum capital ratios for large international banks.

The treatment of foreign banks in the United States was formulated in the International Banking Act (IBA, 1978), which adopted the principle of "national treatment," equalizing the requirements of foreign and domestic banks. Foreign banks can establish subsidiaries, making them subject to the BHCA and to the supervision of the Federal Reserve. Branches and agencies can be either state or federally chartered, and are subject to the provisions of the McFadden Act concerning interstate activities and home state branching. Also, in line with the approach of national treatment, Federal Reserve minimum reserve requirements and access to the discount window were extended to foreign banks. Foreign banks are also treated the same as domestic banks with regard to permitted activities and products. In 1985, the FFIEC enacted new standards for the collection and reporting of data from foreign banks, making those requirements essentially the same as for domestic banks. Branches and agencies of foreign banks are required to maintain capital equivalency accounts at a Federal Reserve member bank, while state laws often require certain standards of pledged assets.

Regulation of other financial institutions

Thrift institutions (savings and loans, savings banks, and credit unions) are regulated in a manner similar to that of commercial banks, regarding both dual federal-state regulation and the institutional framework of supervision. The Federal Home Loan Bank Board (FHLBB) was by far the most important body, as it combined functions of chartering, supervision and insurance, and even certain aspects of monetary control. Approximately

80 percent of all S & Ls and savings banks were supervised in some form by the FHLBB, while the FDIC oversees another 12 percent. The remaining state supervised institutions are predominantly small in size. There are approximately 4,000 Thrift institutions, with overall assets of around $1.5 trillion, somewhat less than half the assets of commercial banks. The Federal Reserve Bank plays a role, through its required reserve ratios and its responsibility for the enforcement of most consumer protection regulations.

The FHLBB, an independent agency with a structure similar to that of the Federal Reserve Board, operated primarily through the Federal Home Loan Bank system. Deposit insurance was handled by an independent subsidiary, the Federal Savings and Loan Corporation, which operated in a manner similar to that of the FDIC. Supervisory and examination functions were conducted for the FHLBB by the Office of Examinations and Supervision (OES), often in tandem with state authorities.

The Financial Institutions Reform, Recovery, and Enforcement Act of 1989 (FIRREA) reorganized the supervision of thrift institutions. The FHLBB was replaced as the primary supervisor of thrifts by a new Treasury subdepartment, the Office of Thrift Supervision (OTS), the FSLIC was replaced by the thrift insurance fund (SAIF) under the control of the FDIC, while the Resolution Trust Corp (RTC) was created to dispose of failed institutions and the Resolution Finance Corp (RFC) was formed to manage their assets.

The approximately 9,000 credit unions with $180 billion in assets, are federally supervised through the National Credit Union Administration. The NCUA charters, regulates, and examines credit unions; provides insurance through the National Credit Union Share Insurance Fund; and provides liquidity, when needed, through the Central Liquidity Facility. State authorities supervise non-federally insured credit unions.

8.2.2 Major Bank Regulations

US commercial banks are subject to extremely comprehensive and complex regulations, both compared with other regulated industries in the country, and with banks abroad. The major bank regulations include the following.

Scope of business

The Glass-Steagall Act

Among the most important restrictions on bank activities are those imposed through four sections of the Banking Act of 1933 (Sections 16, 20, 21, and 32, commonly called the Glass-Steagall Act). These restrictions are designed to differentiate commercial banks from investment banks (e.g., regarding the underwriting of securities, with some exceptions; the issuance of securities or stock; and the selling and distributing of securities). Since 1935, only minor changes have been made in the Glass-Steagall Act. However, market forces and legal interpretations of the Act have made it a considerably less impressive barrier than it once was. Of the countries in our sample, only Japan maintains a similar restriction.

In 1987 the Federal Reserve decided to allow commercial bank holding companies to establish separately capitalized affiliates to underwrite commercial paper, mutual funds, and mortgage-backed securities, so called "section 20 companies," as long as the revenues derived from such bank-ineligible securities do not exceed 10 percent of the affiliate's total revenues. In 1989 the list of permitted activities was expanded by the Federal Reserve to include the underwriting of corporate bonds. Thus, without congressional action, the Fed, through bank holding companies, have effectively reduced the Glass-Steagall Act's effectiveness.

Investment portfolio restrictions
Member banks cannot hold securities of any one issue (except issues of the US Treasury and States) amounting to more than 10 percent of their equity capital. Investment securities should exclude securities of a speculative nature, as determined by the criteria of various rating agencies.

Restrictions on non-banking activities
Under the Bank Holding Company Act of 1956 companies that owned banks were allowed only to conduct banking activities, or activities closely related to banking as approved by the FRB (such as leasing, mortgage lending, discount brokerage, and certain other services).

Lending limitations

Loans to a single borrower
Banks are prohibited from making unsecured loans to a single borrower in excess of 15 percent of unimpaired capital and surplus. Additional loans of 10 percent of equity capital can be made if such loans are fully secured by readily marketable securities. Loans to insiders (executive officers, directors, and principal shareholders) must be on more or less the same terms as those prevailing at the time for comparable transactions. Loans to affiliates are generally limited by statute to 10 percent of the equity capital to one affiliate and 20 percent to all affiliates. There are also limits on securities loans; a margin requirement of 50 percent has been in effect since 1974.

Liquidity requirements

Historically, only members of the FRS were required to maintain reserves against deposits. The DIDMCA (1980), however, required all categories of banks and non-bank depository institutions offering transaction accounts to maintain non-interest bearing reserves with the Federal Reserve.

By the end of 1990, reserve requirements were reduced to zero on all time deposits and Eurocurrency liabilities. On net transaction accounts required reserves were 3 percent of the amount, up to $41.1 million, and 12 percent of the amount exceeding $41.1 million.

Reserve requirements have been applied since 1983 to transaction accounts contemporaneously, instead of according to the lagged system previously in effect. Currently there is a lag of two days between the computation period and the maintenance period for transaction accounts, and a 17 day lag for non-personal time deposits and Eurocurrency liabilities.

Capital adequacy

Federal supervisory agencies have set minimal capital adequacy standards for eligible institutions. Since 1981, they have been based on two definitions of capital: primary, including equity and reserves, and total capital which includes, in addition, various types of subordinated and long-term debt. The standards were defined as minimum capital-to-total assets ratios. Different, although very similar, ratios are imposed on small (community), large (regional) and multinational banks, and on bank holding companies.

In January 1989, a new risk-based capital adequacy requirement was implemented by US regulators. It was based on the framework adopted on July 11, 1988, by the Basle Committee on Banking Regulations and Supervisory practices, which included supervisory authorities from 12 major industrial countries.

It is not yet clear whether the risk-based capital asset requirement will replace the previous minimum capital ratios, or be an addition to them. While the prior system makes no allowance for different risk weightings, it does provide a ceiling on total leverage, which risk-based requirements alone do not. The staff of the Federal Reserve Board have in fact recommended maintaining the existing capital-to-asset ratios along with the new risk-weighted requirements, at least initially (although not necessarily at the 5.5 percent and 6.0 percent level). However, the definitions of capital used must clearly be made compatible to facilitate a dual system.

The guidelines established a systematic framework that makes regulatory capital requirements more sensitive to differences in risk profiles among banking organizations, takes off-balance-sheet exposures into explicit account in assessing capital adequacy, and minimizes disincentives to holding liquid, low-risk assets. The guidelines provide for phasing in risk-based capital standards by the end of 1992, at which time the standards become fully effective. At that time, banking organizations will be required to have capital equivalent to 8 percent of assets, weighted by risk.

Banking organizations must have at least 4 percent Tier 1 capital, which consists of core capital elements, including common stockholder equity, retained earnings, and perpetual preferred stock, to weighted risk assets. The other half of required capital (Tier 2) can include, among other supplementary capital elements, limited-life preferred stock and subordinated debt, and loan loss reserves up to certain limits.

Initially, the risk-based capital guidelines did not establish a minimum level of capital. However, by year-end 1990, banking organizations were expected to meet a minimum interim target ratio for qualifying total capital to weighted risk assets of 7.25 percent, at least one-half of which should be in the form of Tier 1 capital.

Highlights of the guidelines include:

- Application of the two-tier requirement to bank holding companies. Bank holding companies may include cumulative perpetual preferred stock, as well as non-cumulative preferred stock, in Tier 1 capital. However, cumulative and non-cumulative perpetual preferred stock cannot exceed 25 percent of total Tier 1 capital.
- Bank holding companies are temporarily allowed to count goodwill, acquired before March 12, 1988, as capital in Tier 1, but they may not include in capital goodwill acquired subsequent to that date. After year-end 1992, however, all goodwill is to be deducted from bank holding companies' Tier 1 capital. In any case, banks must deduct all goodwill from capital immediately.
- Loans secured by first mortgages on residential properties of one to four units, either owner-occupied or rented, are assigned a 50 percent risk weight, rather than the 100 percent risk weight initially proposed, provided the loans are of a high quality and covered by an adequate margin of conservatively valued collateral.

The risk weights assigned to assets and for equivalent amounts of off-balance-sheet items are based primarily on credit risk. Other types of exposure such as interest rate, liquidity, funding risks, and asset quality problems, are not factored into the risk-based ratio. Such risks, however, will be taken into account in determining a final assessment of an organization's capital adequacy.

Deposit interest rate limits

Deposit interest rate limits were imposed in 1933 (Regulation Q) to prevent excessive competition among banks for funds. By 1980, the DIDMCA scheduled a six-year phase-out of depository institution rate ceilings. Since 1988, the only prohibition remaining is against the payment of interest on demand deposits of corporations, which cannot have NOW accounts. Thus, the majority of corporate deposits are turned over in the money market.

Deposit insurance

FDIC insurance protects each depositor up to the ceiling established by statute. This ceiling has been raised from $5,000 in 1934 to the present $100,000, which became effective in 1980. Premiums, collected as a flat rate, were 0.0833 percent from 1935 until 1989. They have since been raised rapidly, to 0.12 percent in 1989, 0.195 in January 1991 and to 0.23 percent in June 1991. Retail deposits of savings and loans associations are also covered by insurance through a similar organization, the SAIF.

The ceiling applies to individual depositors held "in the same capacity and the same right." This definition allows a depositor to increase insurance coverage by maintaining multiple accounts in different banks. The FDIC has estimated that 95 percent of all domestic deposit accounts, which cover 77 percent of all bank deposits, are covered by deposit insurance. The FDIC has three main methods to deal with failed banks: liquidation and "deposit pay off"; facilitation of purchase or merger of the weak bank with a sound bank; and provision of assistance to troubled banks (as was the case with Continental Illinois Corp. in 1984). It should be noted that only the latter two strategies ensure that all deposits are fully covered; they have been the method of choice in almost all cases of FDIC intervention.

Since it was established in 1933, the FDIC's major function has been to help ensure the stability of the banking system. The FDIC was successful in its efforts and kept the average bank failure rate to seven failed banks per year. However, since the 1980 deregulation of banks, the number of bank failures has grown, reaching 206 in 1989. It therefore seems impossible to maintain the traditional system of deposit protection in a climate of deregulation, because insurance coverage contributes to instability by encouraging excessive risk-taking. The FDIC and other agencies have made a variety of proposals for reforming the insurance system. At present no direct reform has been implemented, although the new capital adequacy requirement may be considered a means to control excessive risk taking.

By 1991 reform of deposit insurance was a major issue for two reasons: firstly, the experience of the thrift crisis and the insolvency of FSLIC, and the decline in the size of the Bank Insurance Fund, promoted serious doubts about the future cost and stability of the FDIC. Secondly, deposit insurance was itself identified as a contributing factor in the banking crisis, due to the flat rate premium system which effectively subsidized poorly run riskier institutions while penalizing stronger banks. Proposals to encourage greater stockholder discipline and depositor discipline included restricted coverage of insurance, risk based premiums, and explicit reconsideration of the "too big to fail" doctrine associated with FDIC policy since 1984. (See Berlin, Saunders and Udell, 1991).

Bank examination

The most basic tool used in bank supervision remains the report of condition and income, the "call report." From the call report and other data, bank regulatory authorities use a number of ratios that measure bank performance. These ratios are presented in the Uniform Bank Performance Report (UBPR), available to anyone upon request.

In the examination process, bank regulators use a uniform system for rating the conditions of banks. This system is called CAMEL – the Uniform Interagency Bank Rating System. It rates: Capital adequacy, Asset quality, Management, Earnings, Liquidity. Each of those attributes is rated on a 1 to 5 scale. The bank under examination is given a composite rating of 1 to 5 based on overall evaluation of each area.

The composite ratings are defined approximately as follows:

1 Banks in this group are considered sound.
2 Banks in this group are fundamentally sound, with slight correctable weaknesses.
3 Banks in this group show enough weaknesses as to be vulnerable to adverse business conditions.
4 The potential for failure is present but not pronounced.
5 Banks in this group have a high probability of failure.

The CAMEL rating for individual banks is considered confidential and is not available to the public.

Recent proposals

In February 1991, the Bush Administration presented its plan for the most sweeping overhaul of the US banking system since the Depression, entitled "Modernizing the financial system – Recommendations for safer more competitive banks". The report addressed four interrelated causes of the current banking crisis:

- *reduced bank competitiveness and financial strength* caused by legal restrictions that have prevented banking organizations from stemming the loss of traditional customers to competitors. The result has been underpriced loans, narrowed spreads, eroded underwriting standards, and hence diminished profitability, which undercut the safety and soundness of the banking system;
- *overextension of deposit insurance* coverage has extended well beyond its original

purpose of protecting small unsophisticated depositors, to include wealthier individuals and large institutions. Depositors, with no risk of loss, have been more than willing to supply funds to weaker banks. Undercapitalized banks have had a perverse incentive to take excessive risk – the "moral hazard" problem – exposing the taxpayer to even greater losses;

- *fragmented regulatory system* that has created an inefficient system lacking a single regulator with either the full information or the clear authority and responsibility necessary to take the decisive and timely action essential to deal with troubled banks;
- *an undercapitalized deposit insurance fund* which might not be sufficient to meet demands made upon it in the present high risk environment.

The major features of the administration's plans were:

- to permit industrial companies to own banks, although in such cases insured deposits would be held in a separate affiliate;
- to emphasize the role of capital adequacy in determining supervision, insurance premiums, and the activities allowed banks;
- to permit banks to open branches in other states without restrictions;
- to permit well-capitalized banks to have financial affiliates including mutual funds and corporate securities underwriters;
- to allow banks to sell insurance if that is allowed in the states where they operate. (Sixteen states now permit banks to sell insurance.)
- the regulation of banks and savings and loans would be consolidated;
- deposit insurance would be limited to $100,000 per institution for individual accounts and $100,000 per institution in retirement accounts. The long term goal is to limit coverage per depositor across all depository institutions, rather than limiting coverage per account.

The main focus of the plan was greater emphasis on safety and increased capital. The plan rewards financially strong banks by allowing them more freedom and establishes the amount of equity capital and the riskiness of its assets as the criteria for measuring bank strength.

8.2.3 Foreign Exchange Control and Foreign Bank Licensing

There is no foreign exchange control in the United States. Foreign banks operating in the United States are required to have specific regulatory approval either from the Comptroller of the Currency or the State Bank regulatory agency.

Entry requirements consider factors such as the adequacy of capital resources, the financial condition of the applicant, the general character of the proposed management, and the convenience and needs of the community to be served.

There are no limitations on the extent of ownership control in US banks. Any change of control in a US bank must be reported to the federal banking agencies and approved by them.

8.2.4 Key Accounting Issues

The specific accounting policies as practised in the United States are based primarily on the Financial Accounting Standard Board (FASB) statements, or the opinions of the Accounting Principle Board (APB).

Consolidation

Consolidated accounts are required by both bank authorities and the SEC. Consolidated statements present the position of the group as a single economic entity and are required by the SEC and bank regulatory authorities. Control is generally defined as ownership of over 50 percent of the outstanding voting shares. Majority-owned subsidiaries are included in consolidated financial statements, unless control is temporary or when control does not rest with the majority owners. Intercompany profits, transactions, and balances are eliminated in consolidated statements. The equity method is used for affiliates owned 20 to 50 percent, unconsolidated subsidiaries and corporate joint ventures. This involves bringing into the consolidated financial statements the attributable share profits, losses, assets, and liabilities.

Loan loss reserve

The allowance for loan losses is a valuation reserve disclosed on the balance sheet as a reduction of the total loan portfolio. The allowance is maintained at an amount determined by management to be adequate to cover all reasonably expectable losses inherent in the existing loan portfolio. This would also normally cover projected losses of any related interest receivable. Known and identified losses are to be promptly charged-off against the allowance along with interest accrued in prior periods. Current period interest accruals are reversed against current period income. The allowance is established by periodic provisions that are charged against income, and subsequent recoveries of previously charged off loans are credited to the allowance. The provision is reported on the income statement as a reduction of net interest income. FAS No. 5 on contingencies provides the basis for accruing losses, when it is probable that an asset and the amount of the loss can be reasonably estimated.

To implement the requirements of the International Lending and Supervision Act of 1983, bank regulatory authorities established new classification

categories for foreign loans. Mandatory reserve percentages are required for countries whose loans are deemed to be in the category of "value impaired." These reserves, called Allocated Transfer Risk Reserves, are not considered part of the regulator's definition of bank capital.

With the exception of Allocated Transfer Risk Reserves, minimum reserves are no longer mandated by supervisory authorities, unless it is determined that management has not estimated reserves based on a realistic assessment of the risks in the loan portfolio. Such an assessment typically includes the consideration of delinquencies, the level of "non-performing loans," loans classified or criticized by the bank examiners, the results of the bank's own credit review procedures, general economic factors, and a review of historical trends.

Additional disclosures of the risk elements of a loan portfolio are required by the SEC in its Guide 3, "Statistical Disclosures by Bank Holding Companies." These disclosures include the following:

1 Non-accrual, past due, and restructured loans from the past five years;
2 Potential problem loans as of the end of the current year;
3 Outstanding loans to foreign countries, individually over 1 percent of bank assets, and aggregate outstanding to foreign countries between 0.75 and 1 percent of bank assets;
4 Loan concentrations of over 10 percent of the current loan portfolio.

Also, the SEC has recently proposed amendments to Guide 3, which would require registrants to disclose further information regarding loans to borrowers in troubled foreign countries. Among other things, the amended guidance would call for an analysis of changes in outstanding balances and information regarding pre- and post-restructuring terms, if applicable.

Foreign exchange transactions and foreign currency translations

The key to US accounting policy for foreign exchange is the determination of an entity's functional currency, or the currency of the environment in which the entity primarily generates and expends cash. Transactions denominated in currencies other than the US dollar result in gains or losses during periods when the exchange rate changes. These gains or losses are recognized in net income during the period of rate changes, unless the transaction hedges a foreign currency commitment or a net investment in a foreign entity.

If the bank owns a foreign subsidiary or other entity whose functional currency is also the US dollar, but maintains its books in another currency, the accounts must be remeasured into the functional currency. The measurement produces the same results as if the records had been maintained in the functional currency. Remeasurement is accomplished by using current exchange rates for monetary items and historical costs for items carried at cost, such as securities, property and equipment, and deferred charges and credits. Exchange gains and losses from remeasurement are *included in net income*. Since the functional currency is also the reporting currency, there is no need for translation.

If the bank owns a foreign subsidiary or other foreign entity whose functional currency is other than the US dollar, the transactions of the entity should be measured in its functional currency. These statements are then translated to the reporting currency (US dollars) using current rates of exchange for the balance sheet and average rates of exchange for the income statement. Translation adjustments are not included in determining net income but are reported and accumulated as a separate component of stockholders' equity, until such time as the foreign entity is sold or liquidated.

Gains or losses on forward exchange contracts still open at the balance sheet date, and those that are not hedges of net investments in a foreign entity or a foreign currency commitment, are included in determining net income. Gains or losses on speculative contracts are computed using the difference between the contracted forward rate and the market rate available for the remainder of the contract. Gains and losses on other contracts, whether or not deferred, are computed by the difference in spot rates, with separate recognition given to the discount or premium.

The current authoritative source for foreign exchange accounting policies is FAS No. 52.

Valuation of assets

Generally accepted accounting principles in the United States are based on the historical cost accounting theory; revaluations of assets are normally prohibited. Accounting policies in selected areas, however, require the use of market values and subsequent changes in market values for recording assets. The following are among the most common examples:

1 Trading account securities are carried at lower of cost or market value under bank regulatory requirements;
2 Marketable equity securities included in investment securities portfolios are required to be written down to market value for both temporary and permanent declines in accord with FAS No. 15;
3 Other real estate owned is required to be carried at the lower of cost and market value;
4 Buildings under capital leases are valued at the lesser of fair market value and the present value of the lease payments;

5 Interest rate futures contracts and option contracts are carried at market value;
6 Foreign exchange futures contracts are carried at market value;
7 Goodwill is initially calculated by revaluing the assets acquired in a purchase transaction.

Supplementary disclosure of the effects of changing prices (inflation) is required of certain large, publicly held companies by FAS No. 33 and subsequent pronouncements. However, the FASB has tentatively agreed to withdraw the inflation accounting requirements of FAS No.33, and replace them with guidelines for suggested voluntary disclosures.

Finally, hidden reserves are not permitted in financial statements of banks or bank holding companies, prepared in accordance with generally accepted accounting principles or regulatory accounting principles.

Deferred tax

Accounting for income tax is based on comprehensive interperiod tax allocation, whereby the tax effects of current timing differences are deferred and allocated to tax expense in future periods. This is called the deferred method, by which the current amount of the tax effect is calculated by the difference between taxable income and pre-tax accounting income, without regard to new taxes or changes in future tax rates. When multiple timing differences exist, with items originating and reversing in a given period, the change in deferred taxes can be determined by either the gross change method or the net change method. These methods are used for loan loss provision, depreciation, discount accretion in securities and lease financing. The basic authoritative sources for policies on accounting for deferred taxes are APB No. 11 and APB No. 23. The latter statement presumes that undistributed earnings of subsidiaries will be distributed in the future and interperiod tax allocation is required (i.e., tax expense is to be accrued). However, when sufficient evidence exists that the subsidiary will reinvest its earnings, interperiod tax allocation is not required.

In December 1987, the FASB issued FAS No. 96, "Accounting for Income Taxes." The statement replaced APB No. 11, "Accounting for Income Taxes," and many other related AICPA and FASB interpretations and amendments. The FAS implemented a number of accounting changes, including a toughening of rules for recording deferred tax debits; eliminating the indefinite reversal exceptions to deferred tax accounting; adopting the liability method (replacing the currently required deferred method) for calculating deferred taxes on timing differences; and recording deferred taxes, for the tax effects of differences between assigned values and the tax basis of assets acquired and liabilities assumed in a tax-free purchase transaction.

As issued, statement No. 96 was effective for financial statements during fiscal years beginning after December 15, 1988. Recently, the Board has announced its intention to delay the initial adoption to the first interim period, which began after September 15, 1990 (FASB Action 89–29, July 19, 1989).

8.2.5 *Taxation*

There are certain special rules for determining taxable income that apply to banks; they are set out in Sections 581 to 585 of the Internal Revenue Code. Section 582 provides special rules for losses and gains with respect to securities held by financial institutions. Section 585 provides special rules for losses on bad debts.

Corporate tax rates

Prior to the Tax Reform Act of 1986, corporate taxable income was subject to tax under a five-bracket, graduated rate structure, with a top rate of 41 percent on taxable income over $100,000. An additional 5 percent tax was imposed on a corporation's taxable income over $1,000,000, such that corporations with taxable income of $1,405,000 or more, in effect paid a flat tax of 46 percent. The 1986 Act reduced the top corporate tax rate to 34 percent on taxable income of over $75,000, and provided a three-bracket, graduated rate structure for tax years beginning on or after 1 July, 1987. For years beginning on or after this date, taxable income not in excess of $50,000 is taxed at a 15 percent rate; income over $50,000 but not over $75,000 is taxed at a 25 percent rate.

The Act also limited the benefit of the lower rates to smaller corporations, by beginning the phase-out of the graduated rate structure at $100,000 of taxable income. Thus, an additional 5 percent tax is imposed on a corporation's taxable income over $100,000. Corporations with taxable income of $335,000 or more, in effect, pay a flat tax rate of 34 percent.

Allowances for doubtful loans

Specific statutory provisions govern the deductibility of amounts that represent bad debts owed to a taxpayer. For this purpose, the IRS authorizes bad debt deductions under either the specific charge-off, or the reserve method.

The Tax Reform Act of 1969 added Section 585 to the IRC, compelling commercial banks that use the reserve method to determine a reasonable addition to the reserve for loan losses, which does not exceed the amount determined under one of two methods prescribed by Section 585.

Banks that elect not to use the reserve method, or large banks precluded from its use, may take a deduction for a bad loan in the year in which the loan becomes partially or completely worthless. To take a deduction for partial worthlessness, the regulations require that the taxpayer actually charge-off on its books and records the worthless portion of the loan. The regulations also provide that, if a bank charges-off a loan pursuant to a regulatory order, the debt will be presumed to have become worthless to the extent it was charged-off during the taxable year. In the absence of a charge-off directed by regulation, controversies often arise between banks and the IRS as to the timing of bad debt deductions under the specific charge-off method.

A bank may also elect to use the reserve method, provided it is adopted in accordance with regulations. In contrast to the specific charge-off method, the reserve method minimizes controversy as to: (1) the exact year in which a loan may have become worthless, either in whole or in part; (2) the amount of partial worthlessness at the end of any taxable year; and (3) the necessity for charge-off of such partial worthlessness. For these and other reasons, most commercial banks have adopted the reserve method.

Section 585 of the IRC provides transitional rules with respect to the computation of additions to a reserve for loan losses by a commercial bank. During this transitional period, a bank may claim an addition to its reserve for the greater of the amounts computed under the "percentage method" or the "experience method." For taxable years beginning after 1987, only the experience method will be permitted.

Under the experience method, a bank is allowed to maintain a reserve for loan losses based on its actual loan loss experience in the current, and five preceding, taxable years. Accordingly, a bank's permissible reserve will equal the amount bearing the same ratio to loans outstanding at the close of the taxable year as the total net bad debts sustained to loans outstanding during the last six years.

Initiated in 1987, the Tax Reform Act of 1986 eliminated use of the reserve method for "large banks" and allowed only the specific charge-off methods. A bank is a large bank if, for the taxable year, the average adjusted basis of all assets of the bank exceeded $500 million. Additionally, a large bank must recapture its existing loan loss reserve into income over a four-year period, beginning with the year in which it becomes a large bank. Finally, if a large bank is "financially troubled" during any of the four recapture years, the recapture is suspended for that year (or years). A financially troubled institution is one whose non-performing loans exceed 75 percent of the bank's equity capital.

Losses

Net operating losses may generally be offset against other income or gains of the bank, including securities transactions, that occur in the same accounting period. Prior to the 1986 Act, a bank that incurred a net operating loss was allowed to carry that loss back ten years (and recover paid taxes). To the extent that a net operating loss was not absorbed by the 10–year carryback, any remaining loss could then be carried forward to each of the five succeeding taxable years. Any losses unrecovered at the end of the five-year carryforward period expired.

For taxable years beginning after 1986, banks are subject to the same general net operating loss carryback and carryover rules of other corporate taxpayers. That is, a net operating loss may be carried back three years and forward 15 years. A special exception exists for the portion of a pre-1994 net operating loss of a large bank (one that cannot use the reserve method for bad debts) attributable to loan losses. That portion of a net operating loss that is attributable to loan losses retains the 10-year carryback and five-year carryforward features of the prior law.

Interest paid and received

As a general rule, banks are not required to withhold US income tax on interest paid on deposit accounts. However, an exception exists when the depositor has failed to furnish the bank with its taxpayer identification number, or the IRS has notified the bank that it should begin withholding taxes on interest payments to the depositor. In these instances, the bank is required to withhold tax at a 20 percent rate. If the bank fails to withhold the tax it will be subject to penalties and interest.

As a general rule, interest payments to a resident bank or the US branch of a foreign bank are not subject to federal income tax withholding.

Foreign exchange fluctuations

Prior to the 1986 Tax Reform Act, US tax treatment of foreign exchange gains and losses was governed by a collection of revenue rulings and court cases that did not create a consistent set of rules regarding several significant issues. The principal issues were: when exchange gain or loss should be recognized; how to determine whether exchange gain or loss was ordinary or capital in nature; and how to determine the geographic source (whether domestic or foreign) of the exchange gain or loss. The 1986 Act added a series of IRS sections, which set forth a comprehensive and complex set of rules governing the tax treatment of foreign currency transactions involving US taxpayers.

The 1986 Act eliminated pre-existing uncertainties through the mechanism of the "functional currency" concept. Under this concept taxpayers are required to make all federal income tax determinations in their functional currency. In addition, the functional currency concept serves as the basis for measuring a taxpayer's exchange gain or loss. As a general rule, the term "functional currency" means the US dollar.

The law requires that foreign currency gain or loss attributable to specified transactions be computed separately and treated as ordinary income or loss. Recognition of foreign currency gain or loss, however, requires a closed and completed transaction, such as the payment of a liability.

In connection with transactions involving non-functional currency, foreign currency gain or loss will be recognized only to the extent of the total gain or loss from the transaction. Any gain or loss from such transactions, however, must first be attributed to foreign currency gain or loss. Thus, any gain realized by a debtor upon repayment of a loan in a non-functional currency will first be attributed to foreign currency gain. The amount of such gain equals the difference between the dollar value of the face amount of the obligation when issued and when discharged. Any remaining gain may be treated as income from the discharge of indebtedness or otherwise. As a general rule, foreign currency gains and losses of a bank will be treated as ordinary income or loss.

The 1986 Act authorizes the issuance of regulations that govern the treatment of foreign exchange transactions that are part of a hedge. Generally, these regulations provide that if any foreign exchange transaction is part of a hedge, all the hedging transactions must be integrated and treated as a single transaction, or must otherwise be treated consistently.

Valuation

Usually, a bank may acquire securities in one of two capacities, as a dealer or as an investor. When securities are acquired for resale at a profit to customers in the ordinary course of a bank's business, the bank is considered to be acting as a securities dealer. These securities are generally held in a trading account and are treated as inventory for federal income tax purposes. When securities are acquired as an investment, their value for tax purposes is the cost of the securities to the taxpayer.

A bank may determine the appropriate inventory accounting method and inventory valuation method for securities that are to be resold, by electing to use specifically defined methods in its initial year as a dealer. The most commonly used accounting methods to determine the basis of inventory at year-end are the first-in, first-out (FIFO) method, the last-in, first-out (LIFO) method, and the specific identification method. The specific identification method requires that each security be identified individually so that its time and point of sale may later be determined.

Treasury regulations allow valuation of a security dealer's closing inventory by one of three methods: original cost, the lower of cost, or market value. Closing inventory valued at cost reflects the original cost of the security. Any appreciation or depreciation in market value at year-end will not be reflected in the bank's income. The lower of cost, or market value method, results in recognition of unrealized losses in the inventory at year-end to market declines; unrealized gains due to appreciation in market value are not recognized. Finally, under the market value method, all unrealized gains and losses in closing inventory are recognized for taxes.

Capital gains tax

Prior to 1986, an alternative tax rate of 28 percent was applied to a corporation's net gain (excess of net long-term capital gain over net short-term capital loss) on the sale or exchange of capital assets. This rate applied when it was lower than the corporation's top regular tax rate.

The 1986 Tax Reform Act increases the alternative tax rate for a corporation's net capital gain to 34 percent, effective for tax years beginning after 1986. However, the alternative tax does not apply unless the top regular corporate tax rate for the taxable year is higher than 34 percent (determined without regard to the phase-out of the lower graduated rates).

Corporate capital losses are deductible only against corporate capital gains. The losses may not be used to reduce the corporation's ordinary income. If a corporation's capital losses exceed its capital gains, the losses may generally be carried back three years and forward five years, to offset net capital gains in those carryback and carryforward years. The 1986 Act does not change these capital loss rules. Thus, it is still necessary to distinguish ordinary income, capital gains, and capital losses, even though the corporation's net capital gain is no longer subject to a preferential tax rate for tax years beginning on or after July 1, 1987.

As a general rule, a bond, debenture, or other evidence of indebtedness constitutes a capital asset in the hands of a corporate taxpayer. Accordingly, any gain or loss on the sale or other disposition of these assets are subject to the rules outlined above. In the case of a corporation that meets the statutory definition of a bank, the sale or exchange of these types of securities, and other evidence of indebtedness, are not considered a sale or exchange of a capital asset. Consequently, gains and losses from the sale or exchange of securities held in the bank's investment portfolio are taxed as ordinary income or loss, as the case may be.

8.3 Bank Performance[2]

In recent years fluctuations in loss provisioning have caused considerable variation in profits, particularly those of large banks (see table 8.5). However, excluding loan-loss provisions, the return to equity has been quite stable. Other major developments that have affected bank performance include the following.

- *Capital adequacy requirements* – In January 1989, the Federal Reserve Board imposed risk-based capital adequacy requirements. These requirements should substantially affect bank management by altering the composition of assets and encouraging loan sales and securitization. Despite strong domestic demand for loans, overall asset growth has remained moderate.
- *Bank failures* – Since the beginning of the 1980s there has been a sharp and steady increase in bank failures, from ten closures in 1981, to 200 closures and 21 assistance transactions in 1988, and a record of 206 closures in 1989. The majority of bank failures were located in the southwest (167 out of 206 in 1989), reflecting economic conditions there.
- *Real estate loans* – Real estate lending has become a major component of bank loan portfolios. This is partly a result of the crisis in the thrift industry. In areas (such as the northeast region), which in previous years experienced significant property price increases, non-performing loans have increased from $2.6 billion at year-end 1987 to $9.1 billion at year-end 1989, or 4.6 percent of total loans (BIS, Annual Report, 1990, p. 108).
- *The thrift industry crisis* – In August 1989, the US Congress passed the Financial Institution Reform, Recovery and Enforcement Act, establishing a new government agency, the Resolution Trust Corporation. The law reduces the advantages of being classified as a thrift institution, thereby contributing to a major contraction of the industry. The long-standing problems of thrifts have improved the competitive position of commercial banks, especially with respect to real estate loans and retail deposits.
- *Geographic expansion* – The relaxation of both interstate and intrastate restrictions on geographic expansion has encouraged greater merger activity. As of mid-1989, 45 states have sanctioned some type of interstate expansion. Eleven states (Alaska, Arizona, Idaho, Maine, New Mexico, Nevada, Oklahoma, Oregon, Texas, Utah, and Wyoming) have enacted legislation permitting unrestricted interstate banking. This process will reshape the structure of the banking industry by giving rise to increased competition and potential economies of scale (super regional banks).
- *Securitization* – The growth of securitization, loan sales, and other off-balance-sheet activities (such as loan commitments and interest rate swaps) has been reflected in the growth of non-interest income, representing 44.3 percent of net interest income in 1989, compared to 32.8 percent in 1984.

Table 8.5 Combined income statement; profit and loss (US$ bil.)

	Gross interest income	*Gross interest expense*	*Net interest margin*	*Non-interest income*	%[a]	*Loan provision*	%[a]	*Other non-interest expense*	*Taxes*	*Net income*[b]	*Return to equity*	*Tax liabil. of pre-tax income*
All Banks												
1984	248.1	167.8	80.3	26.3	32.8	13.8	17.2	72.8	4.7	15.3	10.6	23.4
1985	245.2	155.5	89.7	30.6	34.1	17.5	19.5	80.8	5.4	17.2	11.2	23.3
1986	234.1	140.8	93.3	35.2	37.7	21.6	23.2	88.3	5.2	17.3	10.0	23.1
1987	240.6	142.6	98.0	40.7	41.5	36.6	37.3	94.9	5.3	3.1	1.8	63.1
1988	264.9	160.3	104.6	43.7	41.8	16.0	15.3	97.6	9.9	24.8	13.8	28.5
1989	308.7	199.4	109.3	48.4	44.3	28.7	26.3	103.9	9.5	15.6	7.9	37.8
Banks with less than $300 million in assets												
1984	68.6	42.7	25.9	5.0	19.3	3.7	14.3	20.7	1.3	5.2	10.4	19.7
1985	66.3	39.1	27.2	5.3	19.5	5.2	19.1	21.7	1.2	4.4	9.2	20.0
1986	61.0	34.6	26.4	5.4	20.5	5.8	22.0	22.1	1.0	2.9	7.4	20.4
1987	57.5	31.1	26.4	5.5	20.8	4.3	16.3	22.0	1.6	4.2	7.8	27.6
1988	57.6	31.6	26.0	5.5	21.2	3.3	12.7	21.5	1.9	4.8	8.9	28.4
1989	63.0	35.9	27.1	5.9	21.8	3.0	11.1	22.0	2.4	5.6	10.2	30.0
Banks with $300 million to $5 billion in assets												
1984	63.7	40.8	22.9	8.1	35.4	2.9	12.7	21.9	1.0	5.2	13.3	16.1
1985	64.6	38.8	25.8	9.0	34.9	3.8	14.7	24.2	1.2	5.7	12.8	17.4
1986	63.0	35.9	27.1	9.4	34.7	5.1	18.8	25.3	1.3	5.6	11.7	18.8
1987	66.6	36.9	29.7	10.7	36.0	6.3	21.2	27.6	2.1	4.7	8.8	30.9
1988	70.2	40.0	30.2	10.7	35.4	4.9	16.2	27.3	2.5	6.1	11.4	29.1
1989	81.0	48.7	32.3	11.4	35.3	6.1	18.9	28.8	2.6	6.2	10.9	29.5

Nine money center banks												
1984	62.0	46.3	15.7	6.8	43.3	3.0	19.1	14.9	1.5	3.1	11.4	32.6
1985	58.7	41.7	17.0	8.3	48.8	4.6	27.1	16.7	1.6	2.8	9.6	36.4
1986	53.3	36.0	17.3	10.4	60.1	5.1	29.5	19.1	1.4	3.0	9.7	31.8
1987	54.7	38.0	16.7	12.9	77.2	14.0	83.8	20.6	1.0	−5.6	−19.5	–
1988	61.2	42.5	18.7	13.5	72.2	2.4	12.8	20.4	2.6	6.8	24.3	27.7
1989	70.2	53.0	17.2	14.3	83.1	9.6	55.8	21.5	2.2	−1.8	−6.2	–
Large banks other than money center banks												
1984	53.8	38.0	15.8	6.4	40.5	4.2	26.6	15.3	0.9	1.8	6.6	33.3
1985	55.6	35.9	19.7	8.0	40.6	3.9	19.8	18.2	1.4	4.5	13.6	23.7
1986	56.8	34.3	22.5	10.0	44.4	5.6	24.9	21.8	1.5	4.8	12.2	23.8
1987	61.8	36.6	25.2	11.6	46.0	12.0	47.6	24.7	0.6	−0.2	−0.5	–
1988	75.9	46.2	29.7	14.0	47.1	5.4	18.2	28.4	2.9	7.1	15.4	29.0
1989	94.5	61.8	32.7	16.8	51.4	10.0	30.6	31.6	2.3	5.6	10.3	29.1

[a] As a percentage of net interest margins.

[b] Extraordinary items end securities gains or losses items are not presented.

Source: Wolfson and Mclaughlin (1989); Duca and Mclaughlin (1990)

8.3.1 Structure of Assets and Liabilities

Interest-earning assets of US commercial banks represented about 87 percent of total assets during the period 1984–9. Earning assets included the loan portfolio (60 percent of total assets), securities (17 percent of total assets), and money market lending (10 percent of total assets). The annual growth of total assets of US commercial banks during the period 1984–9 was 4.9 percent, and for the loan portfolio 6.3 percent.

Loans

The composition of the US bank credit portfolio has shifted from commercial and industrial loans toward residential mortgages. The fastest growing component of bank credit was real estate (15.8 percent annual growth), whereas commercial and industrial loans experienced only moderate growth (0.6 percent). By 1989, real estate loans had become the largest type of loan held by banks (36.2 percent of the loan portfolio). This expansion in real estate loans occurred across banks of all sizes by almost the same magnitude (table 8.3). The growth in real estate loans reflects the declining role of thrifts in the residential mortgage markets, the increase in property prices in certain regions, and the more favorable treatment of residential mortgages under the pending risk-based capital standard. Home equity loans have expanded rapidly since the passage of the Tax Reform Act of 1986, which phased out the deductibility of most non-mortgage debt.

The commercial and industrial loan share of US bank credit portfolio declined from 41.4 percent in 1984, to 31.2 percent in 1989. Most of this decline represents a change in composition in all categories of banks (table 8.3). This change was caused by a decline in business borrowing from banks due to the reliance of corporations on commercial paper and other forms of securitization, to a decrease in merger-related loans (such as LBOs), and to a decrease in demand emanating from the deterioration in the general economic outlook and problems specific to various industries (in 1988 and 1989).

The increased use of loan sales without recourse (e.g., originating loans and generating fee income without increasing required capital) has also contributed to the decline in importance of commercial and industrial loans.

The volume of such transactions is estimated at $70 billion for 1989. Consumer loans to individuals have remained stable despite the use of home equity loans to replace bank credit, and also because of increased securitization of consumer receivables (mostly credit card debt). Loans to foreign governments and business loans to foreign residents also contracted during the period examined. Banks sold some of these loans in the secondary markets to reduce their exposure to developing country debt.

Securities

Securities holdings by commercial banks were slightly up in 1989 for all categories of banks, especially for large banks, following a decline in previous years. The securities portfolio of commercial banks includes government bonds (44 percent in 1989), government-backed securities (20 percent in 1989), and tax-exempt state and local government bonds (20 percent in 1989, 40 percent in 1984). Tax-exempt securities issued by state and local governments declined as a result of two main causes. The first was the Tax Reform Act of 1986, which disallowed the deduction from taxable income of 80 percent of the cost of funding. However, the grandfathered provision contained in the Act encouraged banks to acquire a considerable volume before the enactment. The second cause for the decline in securities issued by state and local governments was the less favorable tax treatment of municipal securities, compared with that of US treasury securities and mortgage-backed securities. Bank holdings of mortgage-backed securities surged because of the supply by the troubled thrift institutions and because risk-based capital adequacy standards require less capital to be maintained for them than for most other balance sheet items.

Off-balance-sheet activities

The off-balance-sheet activities of US banks have expanded significantly and include loan sales, securitization, loan commitments, interest rate swaps, and revolving lines of credit.

Liabilities

Deposit liabilities as a share of total liabilities declined somewhat during the period 1984–9 (reaching 76.0 percent of total liabilities in 1989, compared with 77.9 percent in 1984). This decline was the result of a decrease in foreign deposits (from 12.9 percent of all liabilities in 1984, to 10.0 percent in 1989) and an increase in the share of domestic deposits. Several factors contributed to the change in the composition of bank liabilities. The share of demand deposits of total deposits declined sharply (see Duca and Mclaughlin, 1990), reflecting deregulation and rising interest rates (during 1988 and 1989). Retail deposits became a larger source of funds at the expense of the troubled thrift industry.

The US banking industry enjoys a core deposit base that is significantly larger than its credit portfolio. This base reduces the reliance on borrowed funds, especially for small and medium-sized banks.

Equity capital represented about 6.3 percent of total assets in 1989, (6.0 percent in 1984). The strongest capital base was in small banks (8.4 percent); the weakest was in the money center banks (4.7 percent). All banking groups improved their capital position during the period examined, except the money center banks, mostly because of huge provisions for developing country debt.

8.3.2 Income Statement

In recent years sizable additions to loan-loss provisions, especially by large banks, have accounted for large variations in profits (table 8.5). Loan-loss provisioning caused many large banks to report losses in 1987 and 1989. In contrast, small and medium-sized banks reported stable return to equity in the range of 8 to 12 percent per year. In 1987, almost all loan-loss provisions were made against loans to developing countries. In 1989, a substantial part of loss provisions reflected a deterioration in the quality of real estate loans.

Net interest income increased during the period examined by 36.1 percent (at an annual rate of growth of 6.4 percent). This increase was slightly below the annual rate of growth of the loan portfolio (6.8 percent), indicating a slight decrease in margins. This decline in margins occurred despite the structural change in the composition of the loan portfolio, i.e., the increased proportion of residential mortgages (with relatively high margins), the decline in the share of commercial and industrial loans, and loans to foreign countries (with low margins).

Non-interest income expanded at a much higher annual rate – 12.9 percent. Non-interest income represented 44.3 percent of net interest income at year-end 1989. This expansion is particularly evident in the money center and large banks. Non-interest expenses grew at an annual rate of 7.3 percent, representing 95.1 percent of net interest margins in 1989 (90.7 percent in 1984), and 225.8 percent of non-interest income (276.8 percent in 1984).

Finally, the effective tax rate was about 23.4 percent in 1984 and 1985 (before the tax reform), and increased to 63.1 percent in 1987, 28.5 percent in 1988, and 37.8 percent in 1989. This increase was mainly caused by the Tax Reform Act of 1986, which disallows the reserve method and allows deductions of actual net charge-offs in determining taxable income. As can be seen in table 8.5, money center banks had tax liabilities despite suffering losses in 1987 and 1989. The provision in the Tax Reform Act which disallowed 80 percent of the cost of funding of tax-exempt securities also contributed to the increase in the effective tax rate on banks.

During the six-year period examined, the average net income to equity capital of US banks was 9.2 percent, with variations between year, category of bank, and region. The major cause of these variations was the level of loan-loss provision.

Results in 1989 indicate that commercial bank performance followed to a large degree the pattern of overall economic conditions: recovery in the west (with problems remaining in the southwest), in contrast to deteriorating performance in the east.

8.3.3 Sources of Income

The two major sources of income for US banks are net interest income (69.4 percent of total income in 1989), and non-interest income (30.6 percent of total income). During the six-year period examined, net interest income increased by 36.1 percent (the average annual growth being 6.4 percent). The average annual growth of the sum of the loan portfolio and securities was also 6.4 percent. These figures indicate a stable interest rate spread for the entire portfolio and group of banks. However, this stability resulted from a decline in margins that was compensated for by a change in the composition of the loan and (declined) securities portfolio.[3] In other words, this stability was the result of a decrease in the share of foreign loans, commercial and industrial loans, and securities (assets with relatively low spread), and an increase in consumer and real estate loans (with relatively large margins). The magnitude of these changes differs across groups of banks (tables 8.3 and 8.5).

When considering the changes in interest rate margins among groups of banks, it can be seen that the greatest change occurred in the group of small and large banks (excepting money center banks). The change in composition of the loan portfolio for the small bank group was relatively modest, hence the increase in net interest margin between 1984 and 1989 was 4.6 percent (table 8.5). This increase was well below the growth of the loan portfolio (8.1 percent, table 8.3), reflecting the decline in net interest income. In contrast, the most drastic change in the composition of the loan portfolio occurred in the group of large banks. This was the result of greater involvement in residential mortgages, causing an increase in net interest income between 1984 and 1989 (106.9 percent), and exceeding the growth of the loan portfolio (94.4 percent). The changes in the composition of loans during the period examined brought banks of different sizes closer to each other, with large banks increasing their involvement in consumer lending.

Non-interest income for US banks has grown faster than any other item in the income statement during the period examined (the average annual growth being 12.9 percent). An important part of this increase is attributable to increased fees from merger-related activities, fee income, gains from trading accounts, and securitization. There is some evidence that the increase in non-interest income imposed an increase in non-interest expenses. For example, among large banks the cost of managing growing off-balance-sheet activity imposed additional non-interest expenses.

The growth of non-interest income varied across groups of banks. The expansion was much more significant for large banks (the average annual growth being 7.1 percent) than for small banks (3.4 percent). Table 8.5 illustrates how dramatic this expansion has been for money center banks, with the 83.1 percent ratio of non-interest income to interest income (compared with 51.4 percent, 35.3 percent and 21.8 percent for large, medium-sized and small banks, respectively). This figure represents both the growth of fee-income activities and the decline in net interest margins, and is part of a general trend in banking characterized by the decline in traditional intermediation and the growth of fee-generating activities such as loan sales, securitization, and off-balance-sheet activities.

Based on this development, the earnings outlook is favorable for money center institutions, since the impact of their loan-loss provisioning is fairly low, while the growth of non-interest income continues. In this respect it seems that economies of scale that were not found in previous studies do exist, and will be exploited in the future. Large banks, which do not enjoy economies of scale in traditional banking, may well enjoy economies of scale and scope in providing fee-income types of services.

8.3.4 Expenses

The three major sources of expenses are non-interest expenses (personnel and overhead), loan-loss reserves, and taxes. During the period examined, non-interest expenses grew by 42.7 percent (the average annual growth being 7.4 percent). The most significant growth occurred in the group of large banks (106.5 percent for the period), with a parallel growth in non-interest income (162.5 percent for the period). To further analyze the breakdown of this growth by component, in a sample of 35 banks (12 large banks and 23 regional banks)[4] it was found that the number of employees grew by 12.8 percent, with the personnel expenses per employee increasing for the large banks by 62.4 percent (the average annual growth being 10.5

percent), and for regional banks by 29.4 percent (the average annual growth being 5.3 percent during this period). The difference in personnel expenses between the groups (both in terms of level and growth) reflects the demand for high-quality employees to operate the expanded fee-income services of the large banks.

Variations in loss provisioning have accounted for changes over the years and among groups of banks. Presently, foreign loans are the most troubled loan category. Consumer loans (especially credit cards) suffer the second highest net loss, while loan losses on real estate were below the national average. In 1989, domestic loan losses became significant. Nevertheless, the percentage of loss provisions attributable to international business reached 88 percent in that year. At year-end 1989, with some of the most troubled loans charged-off, the reported quality of commercial bank credit improved and loan-loss allowances to non-current (past due) loans reached 85.96 percent (FDIC, Quarterly Banking Profile, Fourth Quarter, 1989).

Finally, as can be seen in table 8.5, the tax rate for the United States increased following the 1986 Tax Reform. The two major provisions of this Act are:

1 Loss provision is not allowed for deductions, except when the debt is actually charged off.
2 Eighty percent of the cost of funding of tax-exempt securities is disallowed.

These revisions have a greater impact on large banks, especially in years of large loan-loss provision.

8.3.5 Capital Adequacy

In 1989, new risk-based capital adequacy requirements were adopted by US regulators. Currently, many banks already meet the interim criterion for 1990 and final 1992 capital standards. Banks, especially those that are less well capitalized, continued to raise equity ratios in 1989 by securitizing loans and paring down low-earning assets. The risk-weighted capital adequacy standards adopted by bank regulators have had a significant impact on bank behavior. Treasury securities and federally guaranteed debt (such as GNMA) carry a zero weight, Federal Agency debt a 20 percent weight and conventional mortgages of one to four family dwellings a 50 percent weight. Similarly, total capital is defined as Tier 1 or Tier 2 Capital (including subordinated debt, convertible debt and loan-loss reserves). The current situation is illustrated in table 8.6, where it can be seen that Tier 2 equity capital represents a greater proportion of total equity of large banks. The capital ratios given are for the end of 1989.

Table 8.6 US Bank capital ratios

Bank	*Total assets (billions of dollars)*	*Tier 1 capital ratio %*	*Total capital ratio %*
Citicorp.	227.1	4.4	8.6
Chase Manhattan	107.4	5.8	10.6
Security Pacific	83.9	5.0	7.2
J.P. Morgan and Co.	82.2	6.8	12.1
Chemical Banking Corp.	71.5	6.9	12.2
Manufacturers Hanover	60.5	8.7	15.7
Bankers Trust of N.Y.	55.6	5.7	11.3
Bank of New York	48.9	6.0	8.3
First Chicago	47.9	6.8	10.3
Mellon Bank Corp.	31.5	7.0	10.1
Continental Bank Corp.	29.5	6.8	9.7
Republic N.Y. Corp.	25.5	8.8	14.8
Signet Banking Group	12.5	11.1	12.2
Valley National	10.5	7.2	10.8
Bancrop Hawaii Inc.	8.3	10.9	10.9

Source: Salomon Brothers (1990) A Review of Bank Performance

US banks can adjust their capital ratios both by securitization (removing assets from the balance sheet), and by shifting from higher risk weight assets into lower risk weight assets. An example would be swapping part of the portfolio from industrial revenue bonds for government-backed mortgages. For all banking groups, the investment in government-backed mortgages increased between year-end 1987 and year-end 1989 by 70 percent (from about $60 to $102 billion). At the same time, bank investment in state and local government securities decreased by 46 percent (from $180 billion to $98 billion). Since 1987, banks have securitized all kinds of mortgage and consumer loans at an accelerating pace. Securitization reduces lending costs, while enabling banks to continue to earn fee income from originating and servicing the loans backing securities.

Bank behavior in 1989 was not unexpected with respect to two issues: dividend policy and merger activity. Despite the decline in profitability, dividends paid increased as a percentage of total assets. In the Salomon Brothers sample of 35 banks, the amount of dividends declared increased from $3.7 billion to $4.4 billion. Thus, banks were not using dividend policy (cutting dividends) to improve their capital position.

Merger activity was expected to decline, since it worsens the capital position of merged banks. Nevertheless, in 1988 and 1989 the number of bank mergers reached 600 and 500 as compared with an average of 230 in the period 1980–6. By early 1991, more favorable market conditions encouraged many banks to raise fresh equity capital; in the first three months of 1991, banks raised $2.8 billion in new equity, more than they had raised in all of 1990.

Table 8.7 Balance sheet analysis (15 multinational banks) (US$ mil.)

	31/12/88	*31/12/87*	*31/12/86*	*31/12/85*
A Loans				
1 Loans	674252	668130	665155	625514
2 (Loan loss reserves)	25651	28021	12392	9595
Total A	648601	640109	652763	615919
B Other earning assets				
1 Deposits with banks	63495	73883	64554	57677
2 Short-term investments	71554	63418	63722	56031
3 Investment securities	93168	91289	76635	62699
Total B	228217	228590	204911	176407
C Total earning assets (A + B)	876818	868699	857674	792326
D Fixed assets	14887	14861	13219	11472
E Non-earning assets				
1 Cash and due from banks	57044	53045	61518	55460
2 Other	77811	77083	67602	68334
F Total assets	1026560	1013688	1000013	927592
G Customer & short-term funding				
1 Non-interest bearing	136689	134536	149213	128674
2 Interest bearing	531341	532712	494644	474748
Total G	668030	667248	643857	603422
H Other funding				
1 Short-term	168643	163508	180551	156863
2 Long-term	71326	70074	60907	55266
I Other (non-int. bearing)	66049	68674	64144	66861
J Loan loss reserves (see loans)				
K Risk capital	52512	44184	50554	45180
L Total liabilities & risk capital	1026560	1013688	1000013	927592
Ratios (%)				
Total loans/total assets	63.2	63.1	65.3	66.4
Reserves/total loans	3.8	4.2	1.9	1.5
Interest liabi./earning assets	88.0	88.2	85.8	86.7
Total equity/total assets	5.1	4.4	5.1	4.9

Source: IBCA data base

Table 8.8 Income statement analysis (15 multinational banks) (US$ mil.)

		1988	*1987*	*1986*	*1985*
1	Interest received	100328	88402	83577	88285
2	Interest paid	66999	58674	54603	61042
3	Net interest revenue	33329	29728	28974	27243
4	Other operating income	22693	21779	18778	14410
5	Provision for loan losses	6125	22035	8874	7425
6	Personnel expenses	18563	17918	16172	13410
7	Other overheads	18262	18096	15225	13794
8	Pre-tax profit	13072	(6542)	7481	7024
9	Taxes	4159	1259	2268	2228
10	Other adjustments	611	66	17	
11	Net income	9524	(7735)	5230	4796
Average earning assets		872758	863186	825000	792326
Ratios to average earning assets (%)					
Interest received		11.50	10.24	10.13	11.14
Interest paid		7.68	6.80	6.62	7.70
Net interest revenue		3.82	3.44	3.51	3.44
Interest on capital employed		0.50	0.35	0.46	0.47
Net spread		3.32	3.09	3.05	2.97
Other ratios (%)					
Provi. for lo. los./net int. inc		18.4	74.1	30.6	27.3
Non-int. income/non int. expense		61.6	60.5	59.8	53.0
Provi. for lo. los./total loans		0.9	3.4	1.4	1.2
Net income/total assets		0.9	−0.8	0.5	0.5
Net income/average equity		19.7	−16.3	10.9	11.9

Source: IBCA data base

Table 8.9 Major indicators (15 multinational banks) (US$ mil.)

	Loans	*Total assets*	*Risk capital*	*Net income*
CitiCorp	144992	207665	9864	1856
Chase Manhattan	66860	97455	4902	1059
Bank of America	65420	94647	4149	726
J.P. Morgan	26842	83923	5778	1002
Security Pacific	54329	77870	3843	639
Chemical	39550	67349	3967	754
Manufacturers Hanover	46678	66710	3251	952
First Interstate	36603	58194	2240	129
Bankers Trust	22801	57942	3499	648
Wells Fargo	36918	46617	2579	512
First Chicago	26558	44432	2369	513
Bank of Boston	25768	36061	2085	322
Melon Bank	18075	31153	1202	−65
Continental Illinois	15585	30578	1605	316
Marine Midland Bank	21622	25964	1179	161
Total 15 MNB	648601	1026560	52512	9524

Source: IBCA data base

Table 8.10 Balance sheet analysis (four other banks) (US$ mil.)

		31/12/88	31/12/87	31/12/86	31/12/85
A	Loans				
	1 Loans	20671	17836	16517	14784
	2 (Loan loss reserves)	302	297	247	220
	Total A	20369	17539	16270	14564
B	Other earning assets				
	1 Deposits with banks	1353	1344	922	973
	2 Short-term investments	689	668	547	956
	3 Investment securities	6235	5028	4794	4322
	Total B	8277	7040	6263	6251
C	Total earning assets (A+B)	28646	24579	22533	20815
D	Fixed assets	429	399	387	366
E	Non-earning assets				
	1 Cash and due from banks	2292	2107	2151	2022
	2 Other	919	737	659	717
F	Total assets	32286	27822	25730	23920
G	Customer & short-term funding				
	1 Non-interest bearing	5413	5222	5653	4910
	2 Interest bearing	20381	16371	15435	14766
	Total G	25794	21593	21088	19676
H	Other funding				
	1 Short-term	3478	3542	2193	1886
	2 Long-term	387	292	324	359
I	Other (non-int. bearing)	640	567	508	578
J	Loan loss reserves (see loans)				
K	Risk capital	1987	1828	1617	1421
L	Total liabilities & risk capital	32286	27822	25730	23920
Ratios (%)					
Total loans/total assets		63.1	63.0	63.2	60.9
Reserves/total loans		1.5	1.7	1.5	1.5
Interest liabilities/earning assets		84.6	82.2	79.7	81.7
Total equity/total assets		6.2	6.6	6.3	5.9

Source: IBCA data base

Table 8.11 Income statement analysis (four other banks) (US$ mil.)

		1988	*1987*	*1986*	*1985*
1	Interest received	2580	2220	2112	2038
2	Interest paid	1421	1174	1188	1203
3	Net interest revenue	1159	1046	924	835
4	Other operating income	423	393	358	285
5	Provision for loan losses	159	169	145	95
6	Personnel expenses	525	486	477	285
7	Other overheads	512	482	460	552
8	Pre-tax profit	386	302	200	188
9	Taxes	97	79	17	26
10	Other adjustments				
11	Net income	289	223	183	162
Average earning assets		26613	23556	21674	20814
Ratios to average earning assets (%)					
Interest received		9.69	9.42	9.74	9.79
Interest paid		5.34	4.98	5.48	5.78
Net interest revenue		4.35	4.44	4.26	4.01
Interest on capital employed		0.57	0.57	0.55	0.50
Net spread		3.78	3.87	3.71	3.51
Other ratios (%)					
Provi. for lo. los./net int. income		13.7	16.2	15.7	11.4
Non int. income/non int. expense		40.8	40.6	38.2	34.1
Provi. for lo. los./total loans		0.8	1.0	0.9	0.7
Net income/total assets		0.9	0.8	0.7	0.7
Net income/average equity		15.2	12.9	12.0	13.0

Source: IBCA data base

Notes

1 Arthur F. Burns, *Address to the American Banking Association Convention*, Honolulu, Hawaii, October 21, 1974.
2 This section draws heavily upon Duca and McLaughlin (1990), and Wolfson and McLaughlin (1989).
3 In analyzing the changes in net interest income over time, it should also be noted that under an agreement reached in 1988 banks issued new credits permitting Brazil to resume interest payments in 1988 of about $3 billion, thereby stopping the continued process of declining interest margins in the money center banks.
4 *A Review of Bank Performance*, 1990 Edition, Salomon Brothers, April 1990.

References

Berlin, Mitchell, Anthony Saunders and Gregory F. Udell (1991) Deposit insurance: What are the issues and what needs to be fixed? New York University Salomon Center *Working Paper Series* S-91-18.

Burns, Arthur F., "Maintaining the Soundness of our Banking System," addressed at the 1974 American Bankers Association, Honolulu, Hawaii, October, 21, 1974.

Duca, John V. and Mary M. Mclaughlin (1990) Developments affecting the profitability of commercial banks, *Federal Reserve Bulletin* of the Board of Governors of The Federal Reserve System. Vol 76, 477–95.

FDIC, *Quarterly Banking Profile*, various issues.

Federal Reserve Bulletin, Board of Governors of the Federal Reserve System, various issues.

Houpt, James V., International trends for US banks and banking markets, Board of Governors of the Federal Reserve System, *Staff Study* no. 156, Washington D.C., May 1988.

IBCA, Banking Analysis Limited, London – *Data Base and Country Reports.*

Salomon Brothers, *A Review of Bank Performance*, 1990 edition, April 1990.

Wolfson, Martin H. and Mary Mclaughlin (1989) Recent developments in the profitability and lending practices of commercial banks, *Federal Reserve Bulletin*, vol 75, 461–84.

PART II
COMPARATIVE ANALYSIS OF TRENDS AND DEVELOPMENTS

PART II
COMPARATIVE ANALYSIS OF TRENDS AND DEVELOPMENTS

9

Securitization and Financial Innovation

9.1 Financial Innovation

Financial innovation, however defined or measured, has recently been accelerating in pace and scope. In addition to fundamentally altering the financial environment, the resultant changes have raised serious concern regarding macroeconomic efficiency, the safety and soundness of the financial system, and the stability of individual financial institutions and whole classes of financial firms. Financial intermediaries, primarily depository institutions, are among those which have been most affected by the pace of financial innovation. A brief taxonomy of financial innovation, and a survey of some of its major causes and possible impacts, is a precondition to understanding the specific implications of such innovation for the banking system.

9.1.1 Forms of Financial Innovation

The process of financial innovation has produced general trends, new products, and structural changes. Needless to say, many specific developments fall into more than one category, but a general classification is still useful for analytical purposes.

General trends resulting from the process of financial innovation include securitization, integration, globalization, and the move to market mechanisms in pricing and distribution. Securitization, one of the most dramatic recent developments in financial markets, is examined separately in the following section. Integration of financial markets has continuously reduced the importance of geographical, institutional and regulatory factors in the determination of their function. In turn, it has played a crucial role in the growing globalization of the financial markets, in the creation of what is essentially a single, unified, worldwide market for financial services. This worldwide market involves both offshore markets, in which location of transaction is largely irrelevant, and domestic markets where distinctions of national origin of participants have lost any meaning. This process is far from complete, of course, and matters of protectionism and barriers to free trade in financial services are still an issue in Japan and in the single European market of 1992. Nevertheless, several large and important markets have already achieved a largely homogeneous worldwide, 24-hour character, including the foreign exchange, precious metals, and major government debt markets. Other markets, such as a number of futures and options exchanges and the corporate debt and equity markets, are making major strides in the same direction. Banks in particular have been increasingly attaining a global character, both in terms of geographic presence and market activity. As a result, globalization has been an increasingly important force affecting banking systems.

The move to freer market mechanisms is intimately connected with the move to deregulation and less government interference in financial markets. Indeed, it is sometimes difficult to distinguish the direction of causality in the dynamics of deregulation, financial innovation, and regulatory response. What is clear, however, is the growing role of free-market determination of price and quantity in financial markets, and the diminishing role for government regulatory interference in the determination of debitory and creditory interest rates and the allocation of credit.

The new financial products and services offered by the financial industry are truly many and varied. The market for derivative financial products, which developed only in the 1970s, has seen phenomenal growth since then. Exchange traded financial futures, especially interest rate futures, have expanded to rival, and even in some cases supplant, the market for the underlying assets. Exchange traded options on foreign exchange, equity, and other assets have assumed a major role. For example, the International Monetary Fund (IMF) listed 100 major financial futures and options contracts traded on 19 exchanges in 11 countries by 1988. The average daily trading volume of future contracts on the ten-year Japanese Government bond of 7–8 trillion yen vastly outweighs the one trillion yen average daily trading in the actual bonds; the average volume in the United States bond future has also outstripped turnover in the cash market. Over-the-counter markets have also developed, including forward rate agreements (generally on short-term interest rates) and options on both interest rates and foreign exchange, and have included many variations such as caps, collars, floors, and range options.

Innovative products in the fixed income area have included a bewildering number of combinations and permutations. Zero coupon and floating rate bonds, securities with various forms of linkages and option features, equity warrants, and partly paid securities have all developed into major markets. Floating rate notes constituted 35 percent of new international bond issues in 1985, declining to 10 percent in 1988; equity-related issues grew from 7 to 32 percent in the same period. Money markets have seen the development of new types of securities such as note issuance facilities, Eurocommercial paper, floating rate notes, and CDs. Not only the products but the markets themselves have changed. Primary and secondary market practices, syndication, auction, computerized market-making, intermarket linkages, and new clearing and safekeeping systems such as SWIFT, CHIPs, and Euroclear have all contributed to a vastly changed financial marketplace.

Off-balance-sheet financing has assumed increasing importance, especially in banking markets. Interest rate and foreign currency swaps, standby letters of credit, loan commitments, sales, and transfers and guarantees have become major activities for many banks. Interest rate swaps, first introduced in 1981, grew to outstandings of 81 billion US dollars in 1984, and over 1,000 billion US dollars by 1988. This in turn has had commensurate impact on strategy, profitability, and risk, all areas of considerable importance to regulators.

Structural change in financial markets has taken numerous forms. As already noted, national boundaries and geographic location have diminished as factors in the determination of financial function. Delineation of roles by institutional identity is declining as structural barriers in the provision of financial services are dismantled. Financial firms, no longer assured of a market by protective regulation, are reorganizing as either "financial supermarkets" or "boutiques" in order to exploit a niche in the marketplace. Banks have been expanding into non-traditional areas of activity, while other financial firms have been providing banking type services and forming "non-bank banks." A dramatic development has been the entry of non-financial firms into financial and even banking markets. The institutionalization of financial markets has also proceeded rapidly, leading to increased professionalism and sophistication on the part of all participants. Both investors and borrowers increasingly act in the market as institutions, with all the advantages that this entails. This trend has important implications for financial markets.

9.1.2 Causes of Financial Innovation

Technological progress has been both a facilitator and an impetus for financial innovation. Improved and inexpensive information processing capabilities, combined with the increased speed, availability and sophistication of telecommunications, has influenced the acceleration of financial innovation.

The macroeconomic environment has contributed to increased demand for a greater variety of financial services. The vast expansion of international trade and wealth caused a disproportionate growth in the financial sector of most developed economies. Imbalances in the distribution of income and wealth, including the petrodollar recycling of the 1970s, the great Japanese savings and capital surpluses of the 1980s, the large budget and trade imbalances among the industrialized countries, and the economic crisis of the developing countries, have resulted in new and greater uses of international capital markets.

Against the background of higher inflation, macroeconomic disturbances, and policy changes, interest rate and exchange rate volatility soared to a post-war high. While these developments led investors and borrowers to seek ways to minimize or transfer market (price) risk, methods for increasing liquidity and redistributing credit risk were spurred by regulatory changes and waves of instability in creditworthiness. At the same time, the microeconomics of financial markets made possible a number of important developments. Achievements in financial theory provided a direct impetus in a number of fields, including options pricing, indexation, and portfolio theory. The greater availability of information and financial data, the lower cost of obtaining and distributing it, and the vastly increased data processing capabilities made whole new classes of financial instruments and techniques feasible, from securitized debt to program trading.

9.1.3 Banks and Financial Innovation

As already noted, banks have been at the center of the process of financial innovation. While the impact of financial innovation on banks has been varied and complex, a consensus seems to have emerged that the general impact has been to reduce the traditional function of extending short-term credit funded by the collection of deposits. As prime borrowers obtained sufficient size and sophistication, investors' savings were increasingly funneled through institutional channels. At the same time, securitization provided attractive techniques and instruments, so that an increasing share of credit needs are now being met in direct capital markets, disintermediating banks and other depository institutions. Protective barriers insulating banks from competition, either geographically or by institutional definition, are being removed, while restrictions on bank entry into other fields remain largely intact. For the most part, the costs and burdens of monetary policy (reserve requirements) and prudential regulation (deposit insurance and especially capital adequacy requirements) fall disproportionably and almost exclusively on banks, possibly constituting a considerable competitive disadvantage. In addition, the move to market-determined creditory interest rates has greatly altered the structure and stability of bank liabilities, undoubtedly raising their overall funding costs. Similarly, changes in cash management techniques and the reduced uniqueness of bank-provided liquidity and payment mechanisms have further reduced the special status of banks in the monetary system.

Since banks, like all financial intermediaries, essentially owe their existence to a variety of market imperfections, the erosion of these imperfections has eliminated some of the economic justification for the banking firm. Due to technological, regulatory, and structural changes, and new products resulting from financial innovation, many non-financial firms and individuals can essentially duplicate the functions once provided by commercial banks (maturity, denomination and liquidity transformation, credit evaluation, and diversification) at lower costs.

Banks have reacted in a variety of ways to these changes and pressures, with individual banks often taking sharply different approaches. Changes in the funding structure of commercial banks have elicited a number of responses, including the policy known as liability management; the development of alternate funding sources such as CDs, Eurodollars and repurchase agreements; innovative deposit arrangements such as NOW and MMDAs; and the unbundling and explicit pricing of various services such as payments, collections, and checking accounts. Where banks have been hampered by product restrictions, as in the United States, Japan, and to some extent the United Kingdom, they have sought to either outflank them (by operating in restricted products overseas or through special purpose subsidiaries and holding companies) or directly challenge them.

Due to the pressure of increasingly uniform and stringent capital adequacy requirements, banks everywhere are placing greater emphasis on off-balance-sheet activities by providing loan guarantees, standby letters of credit, foreign exchange and other trading activities, and becoming involved in corporate restructuring. Banks are especially interested in promoting fee generating income such as mergers and acquisitions, securities underwriting, and funds management, long considered investment bank prerogatives. In addition many banks are engaging in strategic restructuring. For example, Bankers Trust Co. is abandoning retail and traditional commercial banking to concentrate on wholesale and merchant banking activities; Citibank, Deutsche, and Barclays are pursuing a global presence in a wide variety of areas. Many banks are also investing in non-banking activities through subsidiaries, leasing, insurance, and real estate activities being the most popular. However, except in the Federal Republic of Germany, strict separation between banking and commercial or industrial activities remains the norm.

Since the process of financial innovation seems to have attained a degree of permanence, it seems likely that banks and the banking system will continue to change and respond to new developments. If the pace of change and innovation continues at its recent rate, it seems likely that the impact on banks in the coming years will be both extensive and dramatic.

9.1.4 The Impact of Financial Innovation on Financial Reporting

One area in which the response to the torrid pace of innovation has been deficient is that of financial reporting. The goal of reports is to provide the managers, owners, and other interested parties with timely and accurate information reflecting a firm's status. However, rapid changes in financial markets and instruments have outstripped the accounting techniques used to measure profitability and risk. In the case of banks, the problems are especially severe. Off-balance-sheet activity, by its very nature, is difficult to capture accurately in traditional financial statements. This is because of difficulties in distinguishing trading activities from balance sheet activities, of accurately ascribing costs and risks to area of activity, of dealing with swaps, loan transfers and securitization, and derivative products such as futures and options. These problems greatly complicate the task of financial reporting, impacting on the reliability of regulatory reports necessary for prudential supervision.

9.1.5 Other Implications

Regulation, deregulation, and supervision of banks has been prominently and intimately connected to the process of financial innovation, in both causative and reactive roles. The removal of direct interest rate controls, the elimination of product, structure and geographic barriers, and other deregulatory moves have promoted innovation on the part of banks and at the same time are responses to developments in the marketplace. In many areas a dynamic situation was created in which it is increasingly difficult to differentiate cause from effect. For example, it has been suggested that the very existence of regulations in free, open economies promotes the flow of activity away from heavily regulated banks to unregulated competitors, thus undercutting the original goals of regulation. But extensive deregulation has certainly not proven to be a panacea for the banking industry, and there are claims that the process of deregulation and innovation on the part of banks has had a negative overall impact on bank stability.

What is clear is that those entrusted with ensuring the stability of the financial system will be forced to devote considerable resources to grappling with the implications of financial innovation on all levels – general, product, and structural. The Bank of England has formulated the goal of instituting a formal structure of regulation encompassing all institutions based on functional rather than institutional identity. Banking supervision will have to deal with increased and new forms of risk, including greater volatility in financial market activity, implications of changing technology, and possible excessive competition stemming from pressure on interest rate margins, non-bank competition, and bank entry into new areas of business.

The Governor of the Federal Reserve System has enunciated the goals of avoiding failure of the financial system, promoting competition and efficiency in the system, and protecting impartiality in the granting of credit. Among the means to be used to achieve these goals are "shock absorbers" at the system and the institutional level of adequate capital and liquidity, providing market or market-like incentives in management, ensuring symmetry of risk and reward, and repealing the Glass-Steagall Act.

Not only regulators, but also those in charge of monetary policy must be concerned with the impact of financial innovation. Definitions of money and credit, the nature of payments systems, and important behavioral characteristics of the financial system are all being changed by the various aspects of financial innovation, often in extremely fundamental ways. Even rather mundane tasks, such as the collection of basic statistical data, have become greatly complicated because of the effects of financial innovation.

9.2 Securitization: Definition and Development

The securitization of financial markets has been an outstanding recent development. In its most narrow sense, securitization requires the consolidation and transformation of illiquid, usually contractual claims (such as loans and deposits) into marketable claims, i.e., securities. In a broader sense, securitization involves financial intermediation through the sale and purchase of primary claims, rather than their transformation into secondary claims. In general, this results in the actual elimination of intermediation by the direct matching of suppliers and users of loanable funds.

Clearly, depository financial intermediaries, including commercial banks, are in the forefront of institutions involved in and affected by the securitization process. This process is most developed in the United States; however, the trend toward securitization is also clearly present in most OECD countries. The ratio of corporate debt securities to total bank lending appears to be increasing in all our sample countries (table 9.1). Moreover, international capital markets appear to be increasingly securities-based, with interbank borrowing and the syndicated loan market's share of total funds raised consistently declining.

Securitization is a phenomenon which affects the composition of banking assets and liabilities as follows:

- *The shift away from bank credit to the securities markets* – mostly through the use of the bond market, commercial paper, mortgage-backed securities, bankers' acceptances, and loan sales.
- *Banks as borrowers in the long-term securities markets* – primarily through the issuance of bonds (where allowed) and negotiable certificates of deposit.
- *Banks as participants in domestic (interbank) money markets* – through investments and borrowing in domestic short-term money market securities.
- *Banks as participants in the international (interbank) securities markets* – over the first half of the 1980s the composition of international lending shifted from mainly syndicated bank loans to predominantly securitized assets. Banks have become borrowers in the international bond market.

These changes have increased the liquidity and marketability of bank assets and liabilities. This chapter deals mostly with the first phenomenon, e.g., the shift away from bank credit to the alternative securities market. The narrow "asset sale" type of securitization is best exemplified by the pooling of homogeneous assets held by a bank and their subsequent sale as a security, thereby removing the assets from the bank's balance sheet altogether. By far the most important example of this trend is in the field of mortgage financing, which has been virtually transformed by the development of mortgage-backed securities (table 9.2). Since the first issue of Government National Mortgage Association (GNMA) certificates in 1970, the securitization of mortgages has undergone explosive growth, reaching 34.2 percent of outstanding residential mortgages in the United States in 1988, and 42 percent of new funds raised. (The latter figure peaked at 76 percent in 1986, apparently reflecting declining opportunities for securitizing the outstanding stock of mortgage claims.) Mortgage securities

Table 9.1 Outstanding securities and bank lending activities

	Non-bank corporate bond	*Commercial paper bankers acceptances*	*Other debt*	*Total corporate debt*	*Corporate debt securities as a percentage of bank lending*	*Total debt securities*[d] *domestic*	*Total debt securities*[d] *international*	*Total debt securities as a percentage of bank lending*
The US								
1984	421.9	310.2	287.1[a]	1,091.2	44.8	2,637	246	127.0
1988	715.8	526.6	749.8	1,992.2	70.2	4,495	472	175.5
The UK								
1984	9.2	23.3	–	32.5	14.8[b]	165.6	9.7	94.1
1988	23.2	39.2	–	62.4	15.8	309.9	73.6	80.1
Japan								
1984	12.5	–	–	12.5	1.6	217.3	19.6	121.9
1988	109.9	29.7	–	139.6	5.6	2,420.1	108.6	101.3
Canada								
1984	24.1	19.2	2.3[c]	45.6	24.0	152.7	5.4	83.0
1988	37.0	38.4	6.0	81.4	25.4	256.2	33.6	90.3
FRG								
1984	0.7	–	–	0.7	0.1	425.3	30.6	74.5
1988	1.3	–	–	1.3	0.1	646.8	106.3	58.4
Switzerland								
1984	11.2	–	–	11.2	7.5	33.8	48.7	55.6
1988	29.6	–	–	29.6	8.1	79.4	129.5	55.3
France								
1984	20.2	–	–	20.2	7.5	108.8	1.7	41.4
1988	62.7	10.5	–	73.2	13.0	330.9	12.0	61.1

[a] Mortgage-backed securities.
[b] Total corporate securities divided by domestic loans.
[c] Finance company paper.
[d] Includes government debt.

Source: 1 Benavides, Rosario (1989) How Big is the World Bond Market? – 1989 update,' Salomon Brothers, *International Bond Market Analysis*.
2 See notes to tables on the structure of assets and liabilities in the chapters on the different countries.
3 Edward P.M. Gardener, 1992 and the Future of Securitization in Western Europe, *Institute of European Finance, Research Paper in Banking and Finance*, 89/23.
4 G. Broker (1989) *Competition in Banking*, OECD, Paris.

comprise the vast bulk of asset backed securities, with other types being much more recently developed. These have included automobile loan backed securities developed in 1985, and credit card backed securities developed in 1986. Additionally, a broader use of securitization, in which securities or primary claims rather than secondary claims (such as bank loans and deposits) are exchanged, has been developing over a long period.

Table 9.2 The US credit market (US$, bil. outstanding)

			Share of total	
Securities	*1984*	*1988*	*1984*	*1988*
US government securities	1,101	1,749	21.4	22.4
State and local government	517	760	10.0	9.8
Corporate and foreign	668	1,188	12.9	15.2
Money market paper[a]	310	521	6.0	6.7
Mortgage-backed securities	287	749	5.6	9.6
Total	2,883	4,967	55.9	63.7
			Share of total	
Bank lending	*1984*	*1988*	*1984*	*1988*
Commercial and industrial	558	612	10.8	7.8
Mortgages and real estate	1,146	1,511	22.2	19.4
Consumer credit	284	397	5.5	5.1
Other loans	290	310	5.6	4.0
Total lending	2,278	2,830	44.1	36.3
Total	5,161	7,797	100.0	100.0

[a] Mostly commercial paper and bankers acceptances.

Sources: 1 Wolfson and Mclaughlin (1989), Duca and Mclaughlin (1990).
2 *Federal Reserve Bulletin*, various issues.
3 Benavides Rosario (1990).

In universal banking countries such as the Federal Republic of Germany and Switzerland, long-term external funds were historically and, to a great extent still are, provided by the banking system. This was not possible in non-universal banking systems such as in Japan, the United States, and Canada. In Japan, an institutional framework was developed to meet the need for long-term external funds – the framework included long-term credit banks and specialized financial institutions. In the English-speaking countries, capital markets developed to meet this need – bond markets developed and accounted for the bulk of long-term debt financing. In recent years, securities have accounted for a growing percentage of all forms of credit raised in the United States, and not simply for long-term credit. The best example of this phenomenon has been the growth of the commercial paper market.

Commercial paper is a short-term obligation issued (up to 270 days in the United States) on either an underwritten or non-underwritten basis, and placed with an investor. To a great extent, commercial paper is a direct substitute for short-term bank loans. The use of this form of lending has grown in the United States from approximately one-tenth of commercial and industrial loans to almost three-quarters in 1988. The impact however is much greater: since only the most creditworthy borrowers can issue in their own name and thereby realize the savings of borrowing directly rather than through a bank intermediary, the loan portfolios of commercial banks have been steadily deteriorating in terms of credit quality. Moreover, even when customers remain with banks, the existence of the commercial paper market has undoubtedly affected interest rate margins and loan conditions.

The Eurocurrency interbank market encompasses over 1,100 banks from 50 different countries. As of December 1989, cross-border interbank claims stood at $3,486.0, or approximately 69 percent of the international market (BIS). Apart from transactions in US dollars, which usually account for more than 55 percent of BIS reporting banks, there are flourishing interbank markets in German mark, Swiss franc, Japanese yen, British sterling, and French franc.

The international interbank market has also seen its share of the short-term debt market reduced. For a variety of reasons, Eurocommercial paper (ECP), Note Issuance Facilities (NIF), Multi-Option Facilities (MOFs), and Floating Rate Notes (FRNs) have accounted for a growing share of international funds raised, at the expense of traditional bank-based intermediation involving Euro-deposits and syndicated loans. The function of the Eurocurrency interbank market is to facilitate the international distribution of capital. Securitization has been fostered by the increasing efficiency of the Euro-bond markets, which have become broad and homogeneous. The international debt crisis has increased the desirability of highly liquid assets. It has therefore become common practice to issue bonds through multinational syndicates of large banks at short notice.

The amount of new international syndicated loans (gross) decreased from over $100 billion in 1981, to only $11 billion in 1988. In contrast to the declining credit intermediation in international bank lending, there was a rapid growth of issues in the international bond market.

Tentative steps have already been taken in the direction of the total

Table 9.3 Estimated net lending in international markets (US$, bil.)

Year	*Net bank lending*	*Net[a] bonds*	*Euro-notes*	*Total*	*Bank lending as % of total*
Excluding exchange rate effects					
1984	90.0	81.0	5.0	176.0	51.1
1986	195.0	160.3	13.0	368.3	53.0
1988	225.0	137.9	19.5	382.4	58.8
1989	330.0	171.6	6.9	508.5	64.9
Outstanding (end of period)					
1984	1,330.0	401.0	5.0	1,736.0	76.6
1986	1,630.0	680.7	28.0	2,338.7	69.7
1988	2,390.0	1,085.4	72.0	3,547.4	67.4
1989	2,640.0	1,252.3	79.0	3,971.3	66.5
Percent change 1984–89	98.5%	212.3%	1,480%		

[a] Fixed rates, floating rates, and convertible bonds.

Sources: 1 BIS, 59th Annual Report, Basle, 12 June, 1990.
2 International Banking and Financial Market Development, May 1990.

elimination of financial intermediation through the direct matching of final borrowers and lenders. A number of the largest and most creditworthy borrowers have begun placing debt directly with large institutional investors, while some lenders have begun to search for, and make investments directly with, borrowers. This development allows borrowers to dispense not only with the function of depository intermediaries, but even with the basic underwriting broker/dealer function of non-depository intermediaries. The growing share of securities in US financial markets is shown in table 9.2.

The varied forces responsible for the rapid growth of securitization can best be considered against the background of the basic role of the depository intermediaries. These financial firms have provided a better match for the needs of borrowers and lenders, through a series of "transformations" of credit, maturity, liquidity, denomination, and market risk. The mechanism used has been the issuance of claims against the intermediary itself, while obtaining claims against consumers, firms, and other borrowers. In other words, the growth of securitization is the result of the securities markets providing the same service more efficiently, due to a wide range of economic, behavioral, and regulatory changes.

Lending can be either direct or channelled through financial intermediaries. One way to consider the economic rationale for the existence of commercial banks is to compare their function in channelling funds from savers to investors to the alternative of direct lending (e.g., corporate bonds, CP). Within this framework it is clear that in an economy with capital markets in which all agents are price-takers, and in which there are neither frictions nor private or costly information, intermediaries need not exist since they can not improve on capital markets. However intermediaries do exist, apparently as a response to costly market imperfections. The existence of financial intermediaries is explained by two theories that differ in their conclusions regarding the ultimate allocation of resources. The first theory, associated with Leland and Pyle (1977), Campbell and Kracaw (1980), Chan (1983), and Boyd and Prescott (1986), concludes that indirect and direct lending lead to differing allocations of funds. Intermediaries are viewed as producers of information to overcome problems arising from asymmetrically informed lenders and borrowers. Financial intermediaries thereby resolve the public good and moral hazard problems of unreliable information.

The second theory emphasizes the comparative advantages and cost savings of intermediation compared to capital markets, assuming the same allocation of resources in the economy. Benston and Smith (1976) point to a reduction of transaction costs as a rationale for intermediation. Diamond (1984) regards financial intermediation as having a net monitoring cost advantage relative to direct lending. Finally, Deshmukh, Greenbaum and Kanatas (1983) distinguish between two main functions of financial intermediaries: that of brokers holding perfectly hedged positions, and that of asset transformers affecting the attributes of the financial claim purchased (e.g., maturity, divisibility, liquidity) and thereby assuming risk.

The emergence of the institutional investor on the one hand, and of large and sophisticated borrowers on the other, has greatly reduced the role of commercial banks in providing transformation services. Primary borrowers and lenders have reached a size where they have now attained genuine economies of scale, and the concomitant advantages of specialization which hitherto were the reserve of financial intermediaries alone. Technological changes, especially in telecommunications and data processing, have provided the infrastructure for the technically complex job of pooling securities, and furnished the vast amounts of information that the securities markets require. Regulatory requirements, including those of capital adequacy and reserves, have raised the cost of traditional intermediation and provided an impetus to move assets off the balance sheet; while other changes, such as SEC Rule 415 (allowing "shelf registration" of securities), have made the issuance of securities easier.

In addition, increased market risk reduced the profitability of traditional banking relationships. At the same time the development of derivative instruments to control financial risk made the trading of claims feasible.

It should be noted that securitization, while clearly related to disintermediation, is not identical to it: while the former involves a change in the form in which a financial asset is held, the latter involves only a change in the identity of the holder. Similarly, other forms of "asset sales," usually involving bank loans, are typically more limited in impact than securitization-based events. Sometimes, as in the sale of loan participations, securitization is essentially a form of funding. Other methods, such as assignment of loans (transfer of lenders' rights) or novation (the cancelling of a loan and its replacement with a new loan), while accomplishing some aspects of securitization, retain an intermediary depository role and a private contractual agreement between borrower and lender. A number of interesting "grey" areas of financing have been in existence for many years (such as certain types of private placements of securities or transferable loan agreements which display features of a true security).

9.3 An Example: The Commercial Paper Market

Securities which serve as a substitute for bank credit intermediation include several instruments: bonds (fixed rate, floating rate, convertible debt) as a substitute for long-term debt, and bankers acceptances and commercial paper as a substitute for short-term credit. In this section commercial paper, which is the most rapid growing security in most developed countries, is analyzed in detail. Commercial paper (CP) is a short-term (seven to 270 days), unsecured promissory note, with a fixed maturity. It is issued usually on a discount basis, mostly to institutional investors (pension funds, insurance companies). Borrowers include industrial and commercial companies, bank holding companies, subsidiaries of foreign-owned companies, and sovereign or sovereign backed borrowers. Commercial paper can be issued directly by the issuer or by a securities dealer.[1] New trends include backing of CP with a guarantee from insurance companies through surety bonds, and the collateralized issue of CP. Collateralized issues involve the pledge of an asset, such as accounts receivable or title to machinery, as backing to improve the papers' ranking.

The CP market is a long-established instrument in the United States and Canada. Recently, CP markets have emerged in France (1985), the United Kingdom (1986), and Japan (1987). The emergence of new CP markets owes much to the change in the regulatory environment toward reduction of structural rigidities and barriers to competition in corporate borrowing. Additionally, capital adequacy requirements further encourage the development of such markets as generators of fee income. The economic background of the CP market is based on lower borrowing costs, so that simple and flexible (tailored maturities) markets provide an opportunity to diversify sources of borrowing. Investors have increasingly preferred marketable assets rather than illiquid bank deposits, and CP has offered a higher return than bank deposits and most money market instruments. Another factor is the fact that many potential borrowers achieved higher credit ratings than the banks, due to a general decline in bank asset quality and the LDC debt crisis specifically. The attraction of CP clearly depends on the availability of other short-term borrowing and its cost (e.g., the cost imposed on commercial banking). The aggregate size of domestic CP markets at the end of 1988 was estimated as $510 billion (80 percent in the US markets).

In addition to the domestic commercial paper markets, international commercial paper (Euronotes and Eurocommercial paper) has evolved for borrowers located outside the country of issue. This market has complemented the longer-term international bond market. The US market is the model for the Euronote and Eurocommercial paper markets. There has been great variation in the manner of arrangements under which commercial paper has been issued. Until 1985, the most common arrangement was the note issuance facility (NIF), or revolving underwriting facility (RUF), under which banks guarantee the availability of funds to the borrower by purchasing any unsold notes (or standby credits). Recently non-underwritten facilities have become popular, with dealer distribution. Outstanding Euronote and Eurocommercial paper was estimated for the end of 1988 at $72 billion (BIS). These markets are almost entirely centered in London. The US and Euromarkets have been linked by a growing number of issuers who have set up programs for issuing simultaneously domestic commercial and Eurocommercial paper whereby borrowers can switch between markets according to cost and other considerations.

Finally, the expansion of international markets has coincided with the opening of domestic CP markets in several countries. Most notable is Japan where issues were first allowed in 1987, with CP accounting for 12 percent of total corporate borrowings in 1988 (BIS). The growth of domestic CP markets has also been significant during recent years in Canada, France, and the United Kingdom.

These trends illustrate that the emergence of the commercial paper markets has been an important factor leading to disintermediation and the decline of traditional banking, and the resultant decline in interest margins.

9.4 The Role of Depository Institutions

One of the effects of securitization has been the multiplicity of roles created to replace the lender, even in simple loan relationships. These may include the originator of the asset, the sponsor of securitization, the servicer of the security, a credit enhancer, a trustee, an underwriter and, of course, an investor. To a greater or lesser extent banks have fulfilled all of these roles. Due to their established infrastructure and branch networks, and their expertise in credit evaluation, banks have an advantage in the area of both sponsor/originator and servicer of a loan. Indeed, some observers believe that, as the process accelerates, banks will emerge as the prominent specialists in the area of originating and servicing loans.

Securitization of loans can also be used to manage the timing of income, by both accelerating the recognition of previously deferred fees and by creating non-fee income due to securitization itself.

After origination of a loan, the higher cost of bank funding (due to capital adequacy needs, reserve requirements and deposit insurance) means that the assets created will be shifted to other, lower cost funders (such as pension funds or insurance companies). Nevertheless, banks are also holders of securitized assets. Securitized assets have a number of advantages to banks as investors, including the speed with which they can be acquired, their liquidity, and the opportunity to diversify asset and loan portfolios beyond what is possible through loan origination.

The servicer, credit enhancer, and trustee roles are often attractive to banks as sources of fee income. However the introduction of risk-based capital requirements, which "capture" the risk inherent in credit enhancement, will probably reduce the role of banks in this function. The role of commercial banks in underwriting asset-based securities has been problematic in the United States due to the Glass-Steagall Act. While the matter has not been fully resolved, the general pattern has been to erode the institutional segmentation of financial markets. Banks have already been permitted the initial placement of asset-based securities they originate, and recent rulings appear to increase their freedom in this area, albeit with some restrictions.

The effects of increased securitization on the banking system are likely to be many and varied. As noted above, there is a possibility that banks will increasingly specialize in certain areas, such as the origination of a specific type of loan or the receiving of a certain category of deposit, rather than playing all the roles involved in financing. Moreover, banks appear to be less likely to be long-term holders of such obligations themselves, except insofar as they hold a working inventory of assets being processed into securities. While costs can be lowered and certain types of risks reduced, other risks may increase (such as those associated with credit or lack of information). Residual or moral recourse risks, inherent in securitization, may also grow. Additionally, market risk, financial exposure, and liquidity risk are not automatically eliminated in securitization, and they could theoretically increase as well. The "hollowing out" of banking that might result is not inherently negative, although there is a consensus that the exigencies of the securitization process tend to remove only the superior credits from a bank's balance sheet, thus shifting overall credit portfolio quality significantly downward. These and other considerations have heightened the concern of regulatory authorities about the securitization process.

9.5 The Regulatory Response

The process of securitization has raised a number of issues to be addressed by regulatory authorities. As is the case with many other financial innovations, practices are developing much faster than regulatory responses. In many cases, that response is being formulated only now.

The various risks inherent in securitization are essentially similar to those in standard depository intermediation. However, while in classic bank lending all risks are usually borne by a single institution (generally experienced in handling the various facets of risk created by the entire lending/funding process), securitization distributes the risk among a variety of institutions. As a result, the risk entailed in a transaction might not be as transparent as with a loan. Moreover, the "factionalization" of the risk holders can reduce overall risk monitoring and adjustment. Finally, various accounting and regulatory practices, appropriate for dealing with commercial credit situations, may prove to be insufficient in the case of securitized transactions. For example, credit risk is borne by a commercial bank in its role as investor in securitized assets, or insofar as it plays a credit enhancement role. For limited periods of time, moreover, banks acting as sponsors, originators, or underwriters will also bear some credit risk. Due to the dynamic process of securitization, and the apparent "transferability" of the risk, recognition of the risks involved might not always be full and comprehensive. Also, certain types of securitization do not fully transfer risk, but rather leave behind an underlying residual risk. Sometimes this residue is formal, as in sales of assets with recourse, insurance, or guarantees. However, it can often also be informal – "moral recourse" or the expectation that a commercial bank will compensate an investor who has purchased securitized assets, even when there is no contractual obligation to do so.

Obviously, these types of risk are difficult to capture or quantify. Additionally, the securitization process itself can, in theory, lead to a deterioration of the asset quality of a bank's portfolio. On the one hand, a "skinning-off" effect might develop whereby a bank securitizes its higher quality, more easily marketable assets, leaving the poorer credits on its books. On the other hand, banks could be tempted to acquire assets of lower quality, in the belief that they can be securitized later. Such assets can either fail to be transferred, or even if eventually transferred, can remain on the bank's books for a period of time. If this becomes a continuous process, average credit quality will be lowered. The division of creditor roles among many small securities holders rather than one bank will, in general, lead to less information and oversight of the debtor, as well as lower likelihood that a creditor will assist a troubled debtor to regain financial stability. Thus, the fragmentation of intermediation and the diminished role of relationships in financial transactions, may lead to diminished overall credit quality.

As with credit quality, other types of risk are not eliminated by securitization, but are instead transformed and redistributed. Liquidity, interest rate, and funding risks can be "managed" by banks trading marketable assets rather than holding non-marketable loans. However, risks (such as those inherent in maturity mismatching) can be as easily enhanced as reduced through poor management; advantages might be more apparent than real, as when liquidity disappears totally in unfavorable market conditions exactly when it is most needed.

The accounting treatment of securitization is crucial to both the feasibility of the process and to the formulation of supervisory procedures for banking institutions. The basic question involves the nature of the transaction – is it a sale of assets or a form of collateralized borrowing? If it is the former, then the assets involved are removed from the balance sheet of the originator, with a consequent increased return on both equity and assets due to decreased leverage. If the transaction is a form of collateralized borrowing, then the asset side of the balance sheet remains largely unaffected.

For depository institutions the impact is even greater, due to the "regulatory taxes" levied on balance sheet (and off-balance-sheet) obligations, including reserve requirements, capital adequacy, and deposit insurance premiums. The advantages of avoiding or alleviating the regulatory tax burden are obviously a major force promoting securitization, although not the sole factor given that non bank firms (such as the financing subsidiaries of manufacturing and retail companies) have also participated in the securitization of assets. In any event, the treatment allowed a transaction is pivotal in determining its economic feasibility.

In the United States there are two frameworks for determining the accounting treatment of commercial bank securitization: Generally Accepted Accounting Principles, (GAAP), and Regulatory Financing Reports (RAP). The former is used for the publication of financial statements, the latter by supervisory agencies for the preparation of financial reports used for regulatory purposes. In general, the two approaches prescribe largely identical guidelines, although in the case of securitization they can and do differ. For example, it is more difficult for a transaction to receive sales treatment under RAP then GAAP. Thus, a securitization transaction will sometimes be treated as a sale for the purpose of published financial statements, but as collateralized borrowing by regulators. A securitization transaction treated as collateralized borrowing necessitates capital requirements against the assets, as well as reserve requirements, and even deposit insurance premiums against the funding, which is viewed as a deposit.

In general, the test for sales treatment under GAAP is transfer of benefits, while RAP examines the transfer of risk. Only when there is absolutely no retention of risk, will regulatory authorities allow a transaction to be reported as a sale, and subsequently remove it from the balance sheet for all purposes. Under GAAP, sales treatment can be allowed under certain circumstances even when some risk (if it is quantifiable) is retained by the originator. For a depository institution RAP will ensure that, when there is any retention of risk, assets will remain on the balance sheet of the seller for regulatory purposes. That risk can stem from agreements involving any type of recourse granted the purchaser: a put option sold the purchaser, or a guarantee, letter of credit, or insurance agreement accompanying the transaction. It should be noted that even RAP treats certain mortgage-based transactions more leniently, usually when a federal program (GNMA, FNMA, FHLMC) is involved.

The response of regulatory authorities to the risks present in bank involvement in securitization has focused on ensuring competent management on the part of the bank, accurate monitoring and reporting of risks, and the provision of adequate supervision for those risks. A Bank of England policy paper states that the supervising authority should ensure that:

- banks can successfully execute the securitization transaction;
- all parties should fully understand all risks involved;
- risk should be captured by supervisors, especially with regard to capital adequacy.

The US Federal Reserve Board has noted that there is a need to:

- maintain the accuracy and usefulness of regulatory reports in reporting the risks associated with securitization;
- coordinate interagency regulatory policy;
- impose risk-based capital requirements;
- develop guidelines for examination procedures so that bank examiners can determine whether banks are following prudential policies with regard to securitization.

Among the points to be assessed concerning securitization are:

- the degree of its integration into the bank's strategy and organization;
- the degree of understanding of credit risk and other risks;
- the level of recognition of market risks;
- the ongoing avoidance of over-concentration or over-reliance;
- avoidance of conflicts of interests;
- determination that monitoring and management policies have been established to deal with the process.[2]

Regulators appear to be relying on risk-based capital adequacy requirements to provide the primary provisions for securitization oversight. Banks holding securitized assets will have to make explicit capital provisions for different classes of assets, based on each asset's perceived riskiness. These capital requirements are being broadly coordinated internationally in line with the BIS Cooke Committee's recommendations. Equally important, explicit capital provisions will need to be made for any off-balance-sheet risk stemming from letters of credit, guarantees, or other credit enhancements, as well as from sales or the transferring of asset with recourse by a bank or bank holding company.

In the United States, the role of commercial banks in underwriting and market-making of asset-backed securities has become a controversial issue. On the one hand, as commercial banks become prominent in the origination of such securities and hold a large portion of assets suitable for securitization, they are likely candidates for a role in the underwriting and subsequent secondary trading of such securities. On the other hand, most underwriting activities have long been denied commercial banks in conformance with the Glass-Steagall amendment. In the case of asset-based securities (although for different reasons) both the Federal Reserve Board and the comptroller of the currency have essentially approved such underwriting in a variety of cases. However, they have also imposed a number of limitations and restrictions on such activity, by banks and their affiliates, to prevent possible conflicts of interest, unsound credit practices or other deviations from safe banking policy.

9.6 Comparative Analysis

A comparative analysis of securitization in the countries in our sample is provided in tables 9.1 and 9.4. Table 9.1 includes data on the relative size of securities (bond) issued by domestic corporations (direct lending) and bank lending (indirect lending). The data provided allows for cross- country and over-time analysis. As can be seen in table 9.1, for all countries in our sample the importance of securities compared to bank lending has increased during the period 1984–8. The most significant growth of securities markets has occurred in the United States, Japan, and France, with the market being the most advanced in the United States. During the period examined (table 9.2), securities direct lending increased by 72.3, percent whereas bank lending grew by only 24.2 percent. Most notable is the dramatic increase in mortgage-backed securities (161.0 percent). In Japan and France securitization is a new phenomenon permitted by regulators only in recent years.

For all countries in our sample the bond market is dominated by governmental issues and international bond issues as described in table 9.5.

In recent years, exchange rate fluctuations and the expansion of previously less-developed bond markets (primarily the non-dollar markets) have changed the relatives shares of national markets in the worldwide total. The share of the US dollar has been declining, although in 1989 it rose to 47.7 percent after an all time low of 44.1 percent in 1987. In addition to variations in the strength of various currencies in the international bond market, the composition of many currency markets changed. Although one of the outstanding developments in world bond markets in the 1980s was the tremendous growth in government debt, budget surpluses in the United Kingdom and Switzerland led to declines in government debt in both these countries. The size of the overall securities (bond) market to bank lending

Table 9.4 Marketable securities in banks assets and liabilities

	Investment in securities as a percentage of total assets			*Securities outstanding as a percentage of total liabilities*		
	1980	*1984*	*1988*	*1980*	*1984*	*1988*
FRG	11.5	11.5	12.8	20.8	20.6	18.1
France	6.2	7.1	10.4	5.3	6.1	7.8
Switzerland	6.7	6.2	7.0	14.2	14.5	15.6
Japan	11.6	10.8	11.5	6.7	6.6	6.4
Canada	2.4	2.3	2.6	6.6	7.6	7.4
UK	11.1	9.9	12.7			
US	n.a.	18.4	18.5	n.a.	10.8	7.8

n.a. – not available.

Source: See tables in the corresponding chapters in this book

provides information on the depth of the bond market and its potential for growth.

A cross-country comparison of the level of direct lending (short-term and long-term) reveals that the process of securitization is much more developed in the United States. The magnitude of direct securities lending reached 70.2 percent of total bank lending at year-end 1988. However, in the universal banking countries (Switzerland and the Federal Republic of Germany) long- and short-term lending are provided by the banking system. In Canada and the United Kingdom the securities market is developed and represents a significant part (about 20 percent) of bank lending.

Finally, in Japan and France direct lending is relatively marginal, nevertheless given the process of securitization it is expected to expand. The BIS capital adequacy standard will foster this process since banks in both Japan and France will be at a disadvantage when these requirements are imposed.

Table 9.4 provides data on the share of marketable securities in the assets and liabilities of banks in our sample. In the Federal Republic of Germany and Switzerland securities issues represent the involvement of banks in domestic and international bond markets. In the United States the significant investment in securities represents both liquidity management and banks involvement in the securitization process.

Table 9.5 Global bond markets

Country and 1989 share of total 13 largest bond markets	*Size in local currency (billions)*	*Composition (%)*				
		Central gov't debt	*Government guaranteed and agency debt*	*Total corporate*	*Bank bonds*	*Int'l bonds*
The US (47.7)						
1970	553.7	28.9	21.8	33.5	n.a.	n.a.
1980	1,627.3	25.0	16.8	28.6	n.a.	3.9[a]
1989	5,483.0	28.0	22.5	24.3	n.a.	9.9
Japan (19.1)						
1970	20,511	17.5	29.3	14.5	30.1	0.0
1980	147,669	45.6	17.2	6.6	17.6	1.3
1989	326,418	48.4	15.3	7.7	18.0	4.6
FRG[b] (8.2)						
1970	176.4	6.9	7.0	4.4	66.8	11.0
1980	627.9	15.0	3.8	0.7	65.8	12.6
1989	1,438.0	26.0	4.0	0.2	52.9	14.4
The UK (2.9)						
1970	26.9	78.0	–	20.4	n.a.	n.a.
1980	88.8	92.0	–	6.0	n.a.	0.9
1989	188.5	65.1	–	8.3	n.a.	26.5
France[c] (4.4)						
1975	228.7	6.2	61.7	26.1	n.a.	2.2[a]
1980	497.6	15.6	56.8	21.7	n.a.	2.5
1989	2,636.7	40.9	38.6	16.0	n.a.	3.9
Canada (2.7)						
1970	30.2	45.7	3.3	34.4	n.a.	0.0
1980	118.0	32.3	0.4	24.2	n.a.	3.1
1989	326.0	37.6	0.0	42.6	n.a.	44.0
Switzerland (1.6)						
1970	34.2	10.3	–	29.8	28.7	17.0
1980	95.2	11.9	–	25.1	23.0	27.3
1989	251.7	3.9	–	22.2	21.8	46.8

n.a. – not available.

[a] Includes only Euro-issues.

[b] Excluding Schuldscheine (certificates of indebtedness).

[c] Data for 1970 not available.

Source: Benavides Rosario, How Big is the World Bond Market, 1990 update

Notes

1 There are several differences between commercial paper and bankers' acceptances (another short-term money market instrument). The primary difference is that bankers' acceptances are related in most cases to a specific transaction and are obligations of both the drawer and the accepting bank.

2 Boemio and Edwards, Asset Securitization: A Supervisory Perspective, *Federal Reserve Bulletin*, October 1989.

References

Bank for International Settlements *Annual Reports*, various issues.

Benavides, Rosario (1990) *How big is the World Bond Market? 1990 update*, Salomon Brothers, New York.

Benston, George J. and Clifford W. Smith, Jr. (1976) A transaction cost approach to the theory of financial intermediation, *Journal of Finance*, vol 31, 215–23.

Boemio, Thomas R. and Gerald A. Edwards (1989) Asset securitization: A supervisory perspective, *Federal Reserve Bulletin*, vol 75, 659–69.

Broker, Gunther, *Competition in Banking*, OECD, Paris, 1989.

Boyd, John H. and Edward Prescott (1986) Financial intermediary coalitions, *Journal of Economic Theory*, vol 38, 211–32.

Campbell, Tim S. and William A. Kracaw (1980) Information production, market signalling and the theory of financial intermediation, *Journal of Finance*, vol 35, 863–82.

Chan Yuk-Chee (1983) On the positive role of financial intermediation in allocation of venture capital in a market with imperfect information, *Journal of Finance*, vol 38, 1543–68.

Deshmukh, Sudhakar D., Stuart I. Greenbaum and George Kanatas (1983) Interest rate, uncertainty and the financial intermediation choice of exposure, *Journal of Finance*, vol 38, 141–47.

Diamond, Douglas W. (1984) Financial intermediaries and delegated monitoring, *Review of Economic Studies*, vol 51, 393–414.

Duca, John V. and Mary M. Mclaughlin (1990) Developments affecting the profitability of commercial banks, *Federal Reserve Bulletin* of the Board of Governors of The Federal Reserve System, vol 76, 477–95.

Federal Reserve Bulletin, Board of Governors of the Federal Reserve System, various issues.

Gardener, Edward P.M. (1989) 1992 and the future of securitization in Western Europe, *Institute of European Finance Research Papers in Banking and Finance* 89/23, University College of North Wales, Bangor.

Leland, Hayne E. and David H. Pyle, (1977) Information asymmetries, financial structure and financial intermediation, *Journal of Finance*, vol 32, 371–87.

Salomon Brothers, *A Review of Bank Performance*, April 1990 edition.

Wolfson, Martin H. and Mary McLaughlin (1989) Recent developments in the profitability and lending practices of commercial banks, *Federal Reserve Bulletin*, vol 75, 461–84.

10

Non-banking Activities of Banking Organizations

10.1 Background

Classically, commercial banks act as mediators by borrowing from depositors in order to lend to investors. Lending through a bank rather than directly is desirable if a bank has a comparative advantage over individuals and other organizations in, for example, the acquisition and analysis of information.

Over the course of time, however, banks in different countries have been attempting to expand into non-banking activities.[1] The volume of this expansion has accelerated in recent years as a result of the decline in traditional banking activity; banks that lost their unique advantage in banking began to seek other markets to improve their performance. Expansion into non-banking activities calls for a regulatory response in the form of a social cost-benefit analysis of such expansion, to determine the permissible activities for banks and bank holding companies (BHCs), and the appropriate form of organization to perform such activities (for example, a bank subsidiary or a BHC subsidiary). Some countries take a liberal approach to regulation by adopting universal banking. In its extreme form, universal banking allows a bank to engage "in house" in any activity associated with banking, insurance, securities, and commerce that can be undertaken in a department of the bank itself. A second approach could be to permit certain activities to be undertaken only by a bank subsidiary, as opposed to the bank itself. Countries with a universal structure for their financial services include the Federal Republic of Germany, Switzerland, and the United Kingdom. In the Federal Republic of Germany, while banking and securities activities are usually undertaken within the bank itself, insurance activities are often organized by a bank subsidiary. In the United Kingdom, securities activities are usually undertaken by a subsidiary of a bank. In the United States, regulators prefer the BHC form of organization for undertaking non-banking activities.

Expansion into non-banking activities is currently considered to be a major issue in bank regulation. On the one hand, banks have lost part of their traditional market, and expansion into new areas can compensate them in part for the diminished opportunities in their traditional business. On the other hand, this expansion confronts regulators with the problems arising from the increased freedom and subsequent risk to the banks, and also other potential adverse effects. These factors require regulators to weigh the social cost-benefit balance of such expansion. One of the main issues is the degree to which commercial banks provide a unique socially valuable service to the economy and the extent to which this uniqueness could be endangered by affiliation with non-bank firms.[2] The extent to which banks are special, in terms of the social costs of bank failure resulting from the contagion effect, is clearly controversial; it is the failure-uniqueness structure that leads regulators (Corrigan, 1982, Volcker, 1986) to advocate the continued separation of banking from commerce.

10.2 Rationale of Non-bank Expansion

The potential benefits to banks from expansion into non-banking activities depend upon several factors: (1) economies of scope; (2) economies of scale; (3) provision of a solution to the problem of asymmetric information; (4) diversification.

10.2.1 *Economies of Scope*

Gilligan and Smirlock (1984) have already shown that with a limited product set, there may be quite large economies of scope within a banking firm, especially in joint production of information services. The expansion of banks into non-banking activities is expected to provide them with a comparative advantage in producing closely related financial services (such as credit card systems, mortgage banking, and trust companies). In these services, as well as in banking activities, information serves as a major factor of production. Therefore, a bank's advantage in acquiring and analyzing information about the financial status of its customers provides it with an advantage in producing these complementary services. This is particularly true for those bank customers who have already been purchasing banking services and about whom information is readily available. For example, it is argued that expected production efficiency is the reason that the 1970 Amendment to the BHC Act required activities of non-bank subsidiaries of BHCs to be functionally related to banking, the term "functionally" implying that joint production increases the returns from information and/or reduces the market price of financial services. A related rationale for the non-bank expansion of banks is the convenience to customers of purchasing financial services from a single institution; this leads to production and consumption efficiency. However, the potential extent of such economies remains to be investigated.

10.2.2 Economies of Scale

Banking organizations attain economies of scale by issuing financial claims to carry out the financing function of the entire group, and providing operating funds to their existing affiliates that affect their leverage position. The evidence cited by Talley (1975), and Heggestad-Mingo (1975), indicates that the equity capital to total assets ratio for large BHCs is significantly lower than that of independent banks. Furthermore, the capital-to-asset ratios of banks acquired by BHCs tend to decline subsequent to their affiliation. Moreover, the group may enjoy the advantage of shifting resources among subsidiaries according to their investment opportunities, at transaction costs lower than those borne when issuing external claims; the flow of funds within the group, however, is limited by law. The subsidiary bank may lend up to 10 percent of its capital to any one affiliate and up to 20 percent of its capital to all affiliates. It can also transfer funds through dividends to the parent firm or management fees to other affiliates. However, the extent to which these movements can be made is limited, and transaction costs may be involved (such as taxes on dividends).

10.2.3 Asymmetric Information

In a world of asymmetric information, banks, as information processors and capital suppliers, will enjoy a comparative advantage if they become insiders of a non-bank firm. That is, by becoming equity owners rather than creditors, they will have access to inside information. Moreover, as insiders, banks continue to monitor the real and financial decision of the non-bank firm and will be motivated to resolve any agency problem that can be resolved (for example, by membership on the board of directors).

Cable (1985), for example, argues that a major factor underlying the remarkable performance of the German industrial sector since the Second World War has been its universal banking system. Under this universal banking system, the participation of banks in the decision-making of industrial firms has resulted in access to information and resolved the problem of asymmetric information between banks and borrowers.

10.2.4 Diversification

The expansion of banks into non-banking activities reduces the expected costs of bankruptcy by permitting greater product and geographic diversification. Several researchers have sought to analyze correlations among the returns on banking activities and returns on non-banking activities, using either accounting data or stock market data.

Brewer et al. (1988), summarize the findings of a number of studies on the risk of the bank-non-bank combination. Even though these studies differ in methodology, data, and sample period selected (table 10.1, reproduced from Brewer et. al., 1988), they generally conclude that there is some, though often limited, potential for risk reduction through diversification into non-bank activities.

These potential benefits support the deregulation of the segmentation of banking and commerce.

10.3 Types of Non-banking Activities

In traditional bank lending the bank's interest in the borrower's activities is limited to the risk of non-repayment with respect to the amounts and schedule originally agreed upon. It is for this reason that the borrower is required to provide "good" collateral or a guarantee that is not related to his or her business. BHC expansion into non-banking activities can be regarded as financing a given investment by purchasing equity instead of providing loans. The bank, as a stockholder, is entitled to share (uncertain) profits from the investment, but bears a residual risk with no capital or collateral protection.

Regarding the type of non-banking activity in which the investment is made, the question that needs to be asked is whether the rationales mentioned in the previous section imply that some areas of activity are more attractive to banks than others.

10.3.1 The Economies of Scope Rationale

Imply that investment by means of participation in equity will be desirable if the merger is a *synergistic* one and the bank cannot otherwise realize the potential efficiency to be gained. This efficiency is based on information

Table 10.1 Review of selected studies on the risk of non-bank activities[a]

Study	*Time period*	*Methodology*[b]	*Do non-bank activities reduce BHC risk?*
Accounting industry data			
Heggestad (1975)	1953–1967	COV	Yes. Impermissible activities, insurance agents and brokers and real estate agents, brokers, managers, holdings and investment companies and lessors of R.R., oil and mining properties. Banking is among the riskiest activities based on the coefficient variation in profits. (Studied activities of one-BHCs prior to 1970 BHC Act amendments.)
Johnson and Meinster (1974)	1954–1969 (annual data)	COV and portfolio analysis	Yes. Impermissible activities, insurance agents and brokers, holding and investment companies, real estate agents, brokers and managers. Studies 13 activities. Portfolio analysis based on earnings and cash flow conclude there are diversification benefits into non-bank activities but that the benefits are sensitive to the percentage of assets in each activity.
Wall and Eisenbeis (1984)	1970–1980	COV	Yes. Impermissible activities. S & Ls, security brokers and dealers, life insurance, general merchandise stores lessor of R.R. property. Permissible activities personal and business credit agency. Banking neither highest nor lowest risk based on coefficient of variation. Results are sensitive to time period.

Table 10.1 Review of selected studies on the risk of non-bank activities[a]—*contd.*

Study	*Time period*	*Methodology*[b]	*Do non-bank activities reduce BHC risk?*
Firm data			
Jessee and Seelig (1977)		COV	No. Risk reduction is not related to share of non-bank investment.
Meinster and Johnson (1979)	1973–1977	ROF	Yes. BHCs effectively diversified but slightly increased probability of capital impairment with debt financing (Sample of only 2 BHCs in 7 permissible activities of leasing, consumer finance, mortgage banking, bank management consulting, financial services, and foreign bank services.)
Litan (1987)	1978–1983	COV	As likely to reduce volatility of BHC income as to increase it. (Sample of 31 large BHCs.)
Wall (1986)	1976–1984	ROF	Non-bank activity either decreases BHC risk slightly or has no impact. The positive relationship between non-bank risk and BHC risk, BHC leverage, and bank risk is consistent with the possibility that management preferences influence the riskiness of the BHC's subsidiaries and determine the use of leverage to influence overall risk.
Boyd and Graham (1986)	1971–1983 (1971–1977 and 1978–1983)	ROF	Entire period: no significant relationship between non-bank activity and any risk or return measures. Less stringent policy period (1971–1977): no, non-bank activity is positively related to risk. More stringent policy period (1978–83): weak negative relationship between non-bank activity and risk.

Boyd and Graham (1988)	1971–1984 (annual date)	COV/ROF/MS	Study covers six impermissible activities. Yes for life insurance. The standard deviation and bankruptcy risk measures indicate risk is likely to increase for real estate development, securities firms, and property/casualty insurance activities, and increase slightly for other real estate and insurance agency and brokerage activities. BHC is lowest risk activity.
Brewer et. al. (1988)	1979–1985	COV	Yes. One standard deviation increase in investment in non-bank subsidiaries leads to 6 basispoint drop in BHC risk (approximately 7%.)
Industry and firm data			
Stover (1982)	1959–1968	Wealth maximization, debt capacity	Yes. Impermissible activities: S & Ls, investment banking, land development, fire and casualty insurance. Measures equity returns and diversification benefits of 14 permissible and impermissible activities in wealth maximization model.

Table 10.1 Review of selected studies on the risk of non-bank activities[a]—*contd.*

Study	*Time period*	*Methodology*[b]	*Do non-bank activities reduce BHC risk?*
Boyd, Hanweck and Pithyachariyakul	1971–1977	COV/ROF	Yes, but limited. Permissible activities, mortgage banking, factoring, consumer finance, credit card loan servicing, investment advisors, leasing (except auto community) welfare, data processing, credit life, accident and health insurance agents and underwriters, and Management consulting. No. (Any investment increases probability of bankruptcy). Permissible activities, commercial and sales finance industrial banks, trust services, auto leasing.
Market data			
Industry data			
Eisemann (1976)	1961–1968 (monthly data)	Industry (portfolio) selection model (COV)	Yes. Banking is minimum risk activity. Lowest risk BHC includes permissible activity of sales finance and impermissible activities of insurance, investment banking. Highest risk BHC includes permissible activity of data processing Studies 20 activities.
Firm data			
Wall (1984)	Select dates	Bond returns	No significant effect.
Wall and Eisenbeis (1984)	Select dates (monthly data)	Bond returns	No. (Study only covered permissible activity of discount brokerage)

Boyd and Graham (1988)	1971–1984 (annual data)	COV/ROF/MS	Studies six impermissible activities. Yes for life insurance, insurance agency and brokerage, and property/casualty insurance. Risk likely to increase for real estate development and securities firms, and increase slightly for other real estate. Based on standard deviation, bankruptcy and beta risk measures BHC is not lowest risk activity. Insurance agency and brokerage, and property and casualty insurance are lowest risk activities.
Brewer (1988)	1979–1985 (daily data)	COV	Yes. One standard deviation increase in investment in non-bank subsidiaries leads to an 8–11% basis point drop in BHC risk. Results are sensitive to the time period studied.
Brewer, Fortier and Pavel (1988)	1980–1982 and 1986 and 1979–83	COV/MS	Yes. Impermissible activities of insurance agents and brokers, property and casualty and life insurance underwriting. Investment of 5% or less for any of the tested activities would not increase the variance of the BHC significantly,but investment of 25% or more for all but the above listed activities would increase the riskiness of the BHC significantly. Examination of the impact of total investment in non-bank activities regardless of the specific activities finds increases non-bank activity tends to lower BHC risk significantly.

[a] Permissible activities refer to those non-bank activities currently permisible (May 1988), whether or not they were permissible at the time of the study. Impermissible activities also include activities not yet ruled upon by the Board at the time of the study.

[b] COV-analysis of coefficient of variation of rates of return of banking and non-banking activities. ROF-risk of failure (bankruptcy) analysis: MS-simulated merger analysis.

Source: Brewer, Elijah III, Diana Fortier and Christine Pavel (1988) Bank risk from non-bank activities, table 2, *Economic Perspectives*, Federal Reserve Bank of Chicago, vol. 12

about customers, and the role of such information in the production and consumption of banking services and closely related banking activities. To obtain the inherent synergistic gains the non-banking activities should be closely related to banking, such as other financial services and dealings in securities.

10.3.2 The Economies of Scale Rationale

Imply that any growth of the banking organization is advantageous regardless of the inherent desirability of the given field.

10.3.3 The Asymmetric Information Rationale

Implies that banks might hold shares of firms with which they do business. Such affiliations between banks and borrowing firms may result in lower information costs (monitoring). Accordingly, the fields of non-bank expansion should parallel the composition of the bank's loan portfolio.

10.3.4 The Diversification Rationale

Implies that the direction of non-bank expansion should be determined by the effect of the investment on the bank's risk. Such considerations should naturally lead to expansion into fields other than financial services. The latter are, after all, highly correlated with traditional banking services (table 10.1), and will therefore not effectively reduce the bank's operating risk.

The most detailed existing data on the composition of non-banking activities relates to the United States. According to Liang and Savage (1990, p. 285) "... A large percentage of non-bank assets is invested in traditional banking activities that can be conducted within the bank. Principally in commercial finance, mortgage banking, consumer finance and leasing account ... The remainder of non-bank assets is accounted for primarily by securities brokerage ...". However, it should be noted that the current choice of non-banking activities has been influenced by existing federal reserve regulations concerning permitted activities, and therefore does not necessarily indicate the *ex-ante* choice of banks in the absence of regulatory interference.

10.4 Regulatory Considerations

The potentially adverse effects of expansion by commercial banks into non-banking areas have led regulators in most countries to separate banking from commerce. Such effects include:

1. Increased risk of insolvency (investment risk);
2. Increased coverage of regulatory protection (either formal deposit insurance, or an informal safety net) to non-banking activity;
3. Conflicts of interest;
4. Excessive conglomeration.

10.4.1 Insolvency Risk

The bank's insolvency risk is the risk of ruin (closure or reorganization), which can be analyzed within a mean-variance framework considering its operations and equity capital. Therefore, the insolvency risk is determined by the return, risk, and equity. These factors are examined separately in the relevant literature. Several studies have sought to analyze the important question of whether the return performance of holding company banks is superior to that of their non-bank affiliates. Karna (1979), found lower returns. However, Desai and Stover (1985), using equity returns, found that acquisitions of non-bank affiliates resulted in positive abnormal returns while Swary (1981), and Saunders and Smirlock (1987), analyzing the acquisition of mortgage banks and discount house subsidiaries respectively, could find no significant return effects.

The most controversial element in the insolvency issue is the effect of non-bank expansion on bank risk. As noted earlier, a number of researchers have sought to analyze correlations among the returns on banking activities and returns on non-bank activities using either accounting data or stock market return data. In general, the results from a large number of studies provide no strong evidence that banks affiliated with non-banks in a holding company are any more risky than independent banks.

In this recent study of the non-bank activities of US bank holding companies, Liang and Savage (1990) found

> To date, the new data provided by the FR-Y11Q and FR-Y11AS on non-bank activities of bank holding companies are only available for three years. Nevertheless, the available data indicate that some of the nation's largest banking organizations have large holdings of non-bank assets. Furthermore, the overall share of holding company assets devoted to non-bank activities has increased significantly since data collection began in 1986.... Available evidence on non-bank activities of bank holding companies suggests that

> non-bank subsidiaries are more profitable than bank subsidiaries, but non-bank profits have moved in parallel with bank profits over the 1986–88 period. Furthermore, non-bank subsidiaries appear to be better capitalized than bank subsidiaries, although this may reflect double leveraging. However, various measures of risk involving loans or insolvency appear to indicate that non-bank subsidiaries are riskier than bank subsidiaries and therefore may be more than a device to circumvent restrictions on geographic expansion. Thus, the growth in the relative share of non-bank activities could have important implications for the safety and soundness of banking organizations (1990, p. 292).

In sum, the empirical evidence (see Benston, 1990, for a review) indicates that combining commercial and investment banking could result in higher returns. The findings also indicate a higher standard deviation of returns from investment banking than from commercial banking: the total mean-variance risk does not increase significantly.

10.4.2 Increased Coverage of Regulatory Protection

For several reasons, the regulatory protection provided to banks (formally or informally) can be extended to other fields, as follows.

Contagion effect

Non-bank subsidiaries are often closely associated with their bank affiliate even if no credit links or direct investment exist. Therefore, losses in non-bank affiliates may cause a loss of confidence in the bank which could in turn lead to a run on the bank. Such a run may occur because depositors doubt the effectiveness of the regulatory protection, or because they regard troubles in the non-bank affiliates as an indication of possible dishonesty and mismanagement of the bank affiliate (e.g., the Beverly Hills Bancrop failure, 1974).

Corporate separateness

The BHC might use its control over the bank to cover losses in the non-bank subsidiary. Black, Miller, and Posner (1978), suggest three alternatives to counter this potential effect: (1) Regulators may attempt to remove any impression on the part of creditors of the non-bank subsidiary that they are dealing with the bank, or that the bank is guaranteeing the debts of the non-bank affiliate (for example, by using different names and locations, as suggested by Black, et. al,. 1978). However, such an operational separation is clearly very costly and contradicts the basic concept of joint production of financial services. Obviously, it is in the interest of the bank to notify its customers of the production dependency among its bank and non-bank subsidiaries. As long as the dependency in production among subsidiaries exists it is expected that the creditors and the market will view management's problem in managing a non-bank subsidiary as information about the competence of the bank's management. (2) Regulators may consider excluding activities that are risky, relative to banking, from the list of permitted non-banking activities, or regulating the extent of investments in non-banking activities. The expected social benefit of such restrictions should be compared with the resulting losses of efficiency in producing the respective non-banking services. (3) Finally, regulators can choose to supervise the non-bank subsidiaries of banks. At the present time, non-banking activities represent a very small share of bank assets (see Liang and Savage, 1990, table 1), and the potential added risks are not likely to constitute a major threat to the banking industry as a whole. However, non-bank investment may affect, and actually has affected, the probability of an individual bank failure. Therefore, capital adequacy considerations are based on the evaluation of the entire organization.

Deposit insurance

The potential extension of deposit insurance subsidies to non-bank firms via holding company affiliations involves a potentially important moral hazard problem, that gives banks the incentive to increase their risk and hence their market value by expropriating the FDIC's claim (or the regulator's informal protection). Non-banking activities expand the bank's investment opportunity set, thereby increasing bank stockholders' investment incentives. Also, there is the risk that an affiliated non-bank firm might indirectly borrow subsidized deposits by obtaining loans from an affiliated bank (such loans, which are controlled by regulators in almost all countries, are in the United States limited to 10 percent of the bank's capital). In recent large bank failures in the United States, such as the First National Bank of Oklahoma City and Banc Texas, regulators forced creditors of the relevant holding company to bear some of the losses, and made deposit insurance applicable only to depositors of the bank affiliates.

Discount window loans

The Federal Reserve, or central banks in other countries, make secured loans to banks. These loans are usually given at less than the market rate, and are thus part of a safety net that benefits the banks.

10.4.3 Conflict of Interest

The potential conflicts of interest that may arise from banks operating as multi-product financial firms have proved to be of major concern to bank regulators. Indeed, conflict of interest was the prime reason for the passage of the Glass-Steagall Act of 1933 (Benston, 1990).[3] Saunders (1985), identifies the four major areas of potential concern:

1 Restriction of the amount of bank credit to competitors.
2 Use of a bank's monopoly power over its products to tie customers to other products of the bank that they might not necessarily want.
3 The making of loans to commercial firm affiliates.
4 The dissemination of inside information to such commercial affiliates regarding their competitors.

These are only some of the possible areas of conflict of interest. A common feature is the monopoly power that the bank has over the credit market, allowing it to ration credit, tie in customers to products, extend credit to affiliates, etc. While this might have been a realistic concern at the time of the Glass-Steagall Act, the banking and securities markets have since undergone a remarkable transformation. A dramatic decline has taken place in the relative importance of bank loans to the debt market, and access to the capital market by small and medium-sized firms has become easier. Especially relevant have been the growth of the commercial paper market, the long-term debt market, and the international securities market. This suggests that any monopoly power that banks had over corporate borrowers through loan contracts has been significantly reduced.

10.4.4 Excessive Conglomeration

One of the overriding reasons for the continued separation of banking and commerce has been the fear of industrial-banking conglomerations. The argument is that banking, as a protected and monopolistic industry, might use its monopoly rents to drive competition out of the industrial sector through discriminatory and unfair pricing, resulting in concentration of economic resources in the hands of a few large conglomerates.

These potential adverse effects have persuaded regulators in most countries to limit the expansion of banks into non-banking activity.

10.5 The Bank Holding Company Form of Organization

The BHC form of organization dominates the banking system in many countries. In most cases they were created in response to regulation, especially concerning non-bank activities.

The term BHC refers to a corporation which controls a banking institution. Most holding companies also control entities that engage in non-banking activities. The classic structure of the holding company organization is presented in the following diagram:

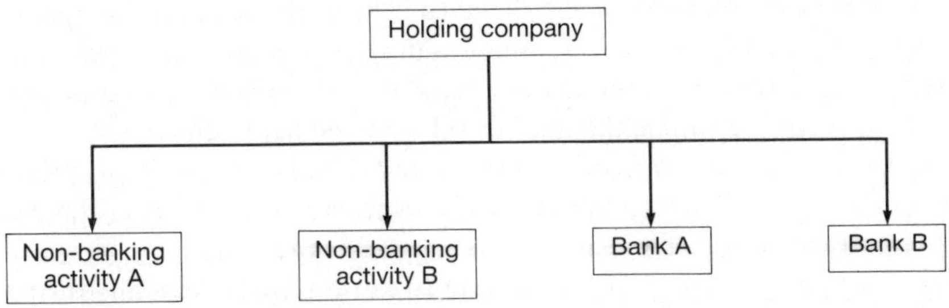

Figure 10.1

Alternatively, expansion into non-banking activities can be carried out directly by the banking institution in the following form.

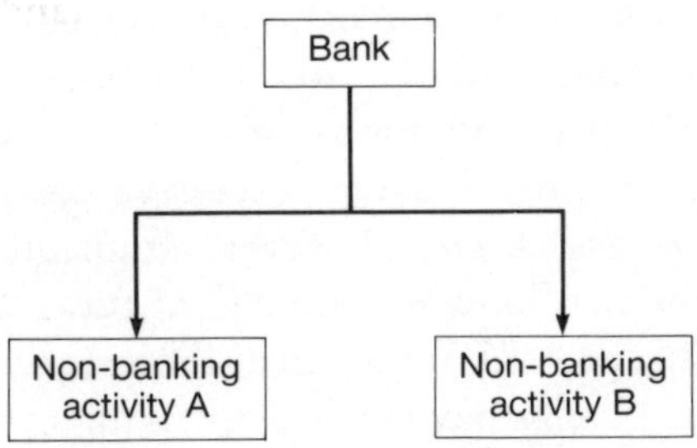

Figure 10.2

These two forms of organization serve the same purpose of allowing banks to expand into non-banking activities, the economic and legal differences between them notwithstanding. BHCs can represent vertical and/or horizontal mergers, that is the horizontal consolidation of several banking institutions (multi-bank holding company) or the vertical merger of banking and non-banking activities. This section deals with vertical expansion through a BHC.

The regulatory approach to BHCs is ambivalent; on the one hand, the BHC form of organization requires separation between banking and non-banking activities (the "Chinese Wall"). As a subsidiary of a BHC, the bank is maintained as a legally separate corporate entity that is isolated from any financial difficulties arising in other subsidiaries. Legally, a subsidiary of a holding company is not liable for debts of any other subsidiary. The only consequence of a failure of a non-bank subsidiary that leads to failure of the BHC would be a transfer of bank ownership. On the other hand, the public equates the BHCs' problems with those of their non-bank affiliates, even in cases where the holding company is reasonably sound. Moreover, the holding company management, in attempting to maximize the market value of the entire organization, need not necessarily maximize the market value of the bank affiliates.

In support of this contention, Orgler and Wolkowitz (1976, p. 78), cite the Beverly Hills Bancrop Failure, and Silverberg (1975, p. 204), describes the Southern California bank experience. Mayne (1978, p. 731), cites several additional cases where bank failure was related to losses by the non-bank affiliates of the respective holding companies.

The implications of the foregoing discussion for regulatory policy may vary from considering the entire organization as a single unit for regulatory purposes, to the other extreme of attempting to isolate the bank from the rest of the organization, via regulation.

The relevant literature has also dealt with several other issues related to bank affiliation with a holding company. One such issue is the concern that a proportion of bank returns will be "upstreamed" to strengthen the parent holding company (Mayne, 1980, for example). The methods identified for such dissipation of earnings include: excessive fee payments, dividend payments, transfer of assets, etc. However, empirical findings (Rose and Talley, 1984) indicate net "downstreaming" of funds from the parent and non-bank affiliates to the bank rather than the reverse. The evidence also suggests that affiliated banks have higher operating expenses and dividend payments than non-affiliated banks, though this has a logical explanation in the servicing of acquisition debt.

Another issue is corporate separateness. The area for concern is the ability of unsatisfied creditors of a failing non-bank affiliate to sue the affiliated bank. The risk is that creditors may be able to make a justifiable claim if they can show that the bank affiliate or BHC misled them into believing they were actually dealing with the bank (Eisenbeis, 1983, Black, Miller and Posner, 1978).

10.6 Comparative Analysis

In analyzing regulatory approaches toward non-banking activity of commercial banks, several activities should be considered:

1 Those closely related to banking;
2 Securities;
3 Insurance;
4 Real estate;
5 Industrial and commercial investment.

All the countries in our sample allow activities closely related to banking activities (such as leasing, credit card operations, etc.). These activities are, therefore, excluded from our analysis.[4]

10.6.1 Switzerland

Switzerland has a universal banking system which allows Swiss banks a full range of activities, as follows.

Securities

Unlimited securities activities are allowed, including underwriting corporate debt and equity, secondary market trading, and management services (membership of the stock exchange). Mutual funds are subject to a separate regulatory scheme.

Insurance

Banks generally do not engage in insurance marketing or underwriting activities.

Real estate

This area is limited mainly to investment in bank premises.

Industrial investment

Though there is no general limitation, the bank is required to set aside capital to cover 40 percent of the investment in permanent participations.

10.6.2 The Federal Republic of Germany

German banks have engaged in securities activities directly, in insurance and real estate activities through affiliates, and are permitted to own shares in industrial and commercial companies as well. The universal banking system in the Federal Republic of Germany has operated with a high level of efficiency, and has been credited with making a substantial contribution to the stability and success of the economy.

Securities

German banks engage directly in unlimited securities activities, including underwriting, dealing in corporate debt and equity securities, and sponsoring mutual funds.

Insurance

German banks may indirectly engage in unlimited insurance agency and underwriting activities through affiliates (though they usually do not have a controlling interest).

Real estate

Unlimited real estate activity is permitted. Real estate brokerage activities, development, and management are conducted through subsidiaries.

Industrial investment

There is no general limit, although such investments are treated as loans for lending limit purposes (loans to a single borrower), and are also considered in determining compliance with equity-based limits on aggregate investments.

It is important to note that the industrial holdings of the ten largest German banks in non-banking companies amounted to 0.7 percent of the aggregate assets of these banks in 1986 (this ratio has been declining over time). Most of their non-bank holdings result from reorganization during the depression.[5]

10.6.3 France

Recent legislative changes have removed the remaining restrictions and France now has a truly universal banking system. Banks are allowed to engage in securities, real estate, and insurance activities without restrictions, as well as make investments in industrial firms.

Securities activities

Banks are allowed to engage in underwriting, dealing, and full service investment banking. Banks may also create investment companies (Société d'Investissement à Capital Variable – SICAV) and manage mutual funds. It is estimated that more than 75 percent of all securities orders are transmitted through banks. Banks are also allowed to acquire control of stockbrokering firms.

Insurance

Banks may generally engage in unlimited insurance activities through subsidiaries (with the prior approval of the Ministry of Finance).

Real estate

Banks may engage, directly or indirectly, in brokerage, and developing and managing real estate.

Industrial investment

Banks may invest in industrial companies, although prior approval is required if the investment is more than 10 percent of the acquired company's capital.

10.6.4 United Kingdom

As a consequence of the significant changes that have been made in the United Kingdom, it has now effectively moved towards a universal banking system similar to that practised in other European countries.

Securities activities

Banks may engage in unlimited securities activities such as underwriting and dealing in corporate debt and equity securities; advising on investment and finance; advising on mergers and acquisitions; sponsoring, managing, advising, and underwriting open-end and closed-end investment companies. Most of these activities are carried out through merchant bank subsidiaries, which are primary dealers in UK government securities.

Insurance

Banks may make unlimited investments through subsidiaries in companies that engage in insurance brokerage and underwriting activities.

Real estate

Banks are permitted to engage in unlimited real estate activities, including developing and brokerage.

Industrial investment

There are no statutory limitations on investment in industrial companies.

10.6.5 Japan

The restructuring of Japan's financial markets has been accelerating since 1984, when the United States and Japan concluded agreements regarding the need for reform of the Japanese financial system. In December 1987, the Financial System Research Council issued a report concerning changes in the Japanese financial markets. Its major recommendation was that, in view of the global trend toward securitization, the legal separation of banking and securities activities should be reexamined.

Securities activities

Article 65 of the securities and exchange law prohibits banks from underwriting, selling, dealing, and brokering stocks or corporate banks. However, the following activities are allowed:

- Dealing in Japanese Government bonds.
- Underwriting and dealing in commercial paper.
- Providing investment advisory services (bank subsidiaries have been allowed to engage in these activities since 1986).
- Buying and selling securities for their own portfolio investment accounts.
- Futures activities, both for their own accounts and for customers (since 1988).

Insurance and real estate activities

Banks are not permitted to engage in these activities, either directly or indirectly.

Industrial investment

The Anti-monopoly Law prohibits banks from holding more than 5 percent of the shares of another firm unless permitted by the Fair Trade Commission (mostly investment in activities closely related to banking). It should be noted, however, that many Japanese banks have close interlocking relationships with non-banking firms in the framework of the Keiretsu conglomerates.

10.6.6 Canada

In order to increase competition, in recent years financial institutions have been allowed to offer a broader range of services to the general public, mainly through affiliates.

Securities activities

Under Canada's Bank Act, until 1987 banks could not underwrite or deal in corporate securities, engage in investment management services, act as a broker, or hold more than 10 percent of the voting shares of a firm engaged in such businesses. In June 1987, the restrictions on ownership of securities firms and securities dealers by banks were removed. Banks are now also allowed to distribute corporate equity and debt securities, trade in corporate equity securities, and provide portfolio management and investment advice.

Insurance

Banks cannot now engage directly, or through affiliates, in the insurance business. However, the federal government has announced in its Blue Paper proposals that it will expand the insurance powers available to banks in the near future.

Real estate

Banks may generally not invest in or develop real estate or act as real estate brokers.

Industrial investment

With certain limited exceptions, a bank may not own more than 10 percent of the voting shares of a Canadian corporation. The exceptions are related financial activities (e.g., mortgage loan corporations, securities firms, and data processing firms).

10.6.7 The United States

In the United States there is a distinct separation between commercial banking and investment banking. This is based on the Glass-Steagall Act (1933), and the 1956 BHC Act (and its 1970 Amendment).

Securities activities

With the following exceptions, banks are not allowed to issue, underwrite, sell, or distribute securities:

- US government obligations
- General obligation bonds of states and municipalities
- Buying or selling of securities without recourse, solely on the order and for the account of customers
- Investment in government bonds and high-grade bonds, on their own account.

Insurance

US banks are not permitted to deal in insurance.

Real estate

Banks are allowed to invest in real estate investment trusts (REIT).

Industrial investment

Under Section 4(c)(8) of the Bank Act banks are allowed to invest only in activities closely related to banking, as permitted by the Federal Reserve.

The current treatment of the securities activities of US banks is discussed in more detail in the next section. In particular, under Section 20 of the 1933 Banking Act, member bank affiliates are permitted to participate in otherwise impermissible securities activities so long as this is not their principal occupation.

Table 10.2 provides a summary of the current policy of regulators, in the different countries of our sample, to major non-bank activities. As can be seen the approaches vary, though recent developments have significantly narrowed the differences. Moreover, even in those countries that allow universal banking (such as the Federal Republic of Germany, and Switzerland), the amount of investment in industrial companies is marginal. For the most part, expansion into non-banking activities has been concentrated in securities and other areas closely related to banking.

10.7 The Current Approach to Securities Activities in the United States

10.7.1 Relevant Regulations

The regulatory treatment of the securities activities of US banks is prescribed by the Glass-Steagall Act (for banks), and the BHC Act (for holding companies).

The Banking Act of 1933 (or more specifically the four sections that are called the Glass-Steagall Act), as amended and interpreted by regulators and the courts, significantly limited the securities activities of banks.

Section 16

Refers to the direct operations of banks. It prohibits banks from issuing, underwriting, selling, or distributing, at the wholesale or retail level or through syndicate participation, securities other than US government bonds (or bonds insured by the federal government), obligations issued by government agencies, and general obligation bonds of states and munici-

Table 10.2 Permissible activities for banking organizations

	Securities	*Insurance*	*Real estate*	*Industrial investment*
1 Switzerland	Unlimited	Subject to separate regulations. Thus do not engage in insurance activities	Generally limited to holding bank premises	No limitations
2 The Federal Republic of Germany	Unlimited	Unlimited, through subsidiaries	Unlimited, through subsidiaries	Permitted, subject to limits based on bank's capital
3 France	Unlimited	Unlimited, usually through subsidiaries	Unlimited	Permitted, subject to regulatory approval of interests in excess of 10%
4 United Kingdom	Unlimited, usually through subsidiaries	Unlimited, through subsidiaries	Unlimited	Permitted subject to consultation with the Bank of England
5 Japan	Limited	Not permitted	Generally limited to holding bank premises	Limited to holding a 5% interest
6 Canada	Unlimited, through subsidiaries	Currently not permitted; unlimited activities through subsidiaries proposed	Generally limited to holding bank premises	Permitted to hold up to 10% interest
7 United States	Limited	Not permitted	Through REITs	Only in permissible activities

Source: The Institute of International Bankers (1988)

palities. It does allow a bank to purchase or sell securities without recourse, solely on the order and for the account of customers.

Section 21

Prohibits any firm engaged in the deposit-taking business from engaging in the business of issuing, underwriting, selling, or distributing securities, except as permitted in Section 16.

Section 20

Refers to commercial bank affiliations. It forbids a member bank from being affiliated with any firm engaged principally in the issue, floatation, underwriting, public sale, or distribution at the wholesale or retail level, or through syndicate participation, of stocks, bonds, debentures, notes, or other securities.

Section 32

Prohibits management and employee interlocks between banks and firms primarily engaged in the issue, floatation, underwriting, public sale, or distribution of securities. Section 32 applies even if there is no common ownership or corporate affiliation between the commercial bank and the investment company.

The BHC Act of 1956 was the first piece of legislation aimed at the group banking movement. Under the 1970 Amendment, the Federal Reserve Board was appointed to administer the law, which required the Board to establish standards for determining the non-banking activities into which BHCs would be permitted to expand. In deciding whether to permit a BHC to engage in a particular activity, the Board determines whether the activity is closely related to banking and whether the performance of the activity by the proposed affiliate is expected to produce benefits to the public that outweigh possible adverse effects (Section 4(c)(8) of the Amendment).

A holding company must, however, comply with the provisions contained in the Glass-Steagall Act. Categories ruled on by the Board are listed in table 10.3.

In 1987, the Board began approving applications submitted by BHCs to allow non-bank subsidiaries to underwrite and deal in certain bank-ineligible securities such as municipal revenue bonds, mortgage-backed securities, commercial paper, consumer asset-based securities (backed by credit card receivables, and consumer auto loans), and corporate bonds. These activities have been permitted for the "Section-20" companies (so-called because they do not breach Section-20 of the Glass-Steagall Act), as long as the revenues of "ineligible" securities activities amount to no more than 10 percent (formerly 5 percent) of the affiliate's total revenues. The Board also required these companies to observe a number of prudential limitations, called firewalls:

1 Capital adequacy conditions
2 Restrictions on financial ties between banks and Section 20 affiliates
3 Prohibitions against banks sharing employees or confidential information with a Section-20 company, or engaging in marketing activities on its behalf.

Table 10.3 Activities permitted as being "closely related to banking"

Activities	*Securities-related*
Making and servicing loans	No
Industrial banking	No
Trust company functions	Yes
Investment or financial advice	Yes
Leasing personal or real property	No
Community development	No
Data processing	No
Insurance agency and brokerage in connection with credit extensions	No
Underwriting insurance related to an extension of credit	No
Providing courier services	No
Management consulting to non-affiliated bank and non-bank deposit institutions	No
Issuing and selling money orders, savings bonds, and travellers checks	No
Real estate and personal property appraising	No
Arranging commercial real estate equity financing	No
Securities brokerage	Yes
Underwriting and dealing in government obligations and money market instruments	Yes
Foreign exchange advisory and transactional services	No
Future commission merchant	Yes
Investment advice on financial futures and options on futures	Yes
Financial counselling for consumers	No
Tax planning and preparation	No
Check-guaranty services	No
Operating a collection agency	No
Operating a credit bureau	No

Source: US General Accounting Office, 1990

As of September 30, 1989, 21 BHCs had Section-20 subsidiaries (see GAO 90–48 Bank Powers). These companies had altogether about $1.8 billion in capital. Section-20 firms represent about 7 percent of the revenue (most of it from eligible activities) of all securities firms registered with the SEC. During the third quarter of 1989, Section-20 firms accounted for 2 percent of the total underwriting volume of the combined market for municipal revenue bonds, mortgage-related securities, and asset-backed securities. It is too early to assess the significance of Section-20 firms' bank-ineligible securities activities. The current regulatory policy of approving Section-20 subsidiaries for BHCs is expected to continue, with securities activities of banks expanding further, mainly by increasing the 10 percent revenue limitation, and allowing banks to underwrite equity issues. This expansion can be justified simply by interpreting more liberally the term "engaged principally" as it appears in the Glass-Steagall Act.

The policy of expanding the permissible securities activities of commercial banks through the BHCs reflects both the need to allow banks more competitive power, and the concern over the effect of such expansion on the riskiness of banks. Moreover, the current approach to securities activities of commercial banks is ambivalent in regard to the BHC form of organization. In the past, the regulatory approach was that the holding company and the affiliated bank should be treated equally. This approach finds expression, for example, in the allowing of the same non-banking activities to the holding company and the affiliated bank, in the imposition of capital adequacy requirements on both organizations, and in the rescuing of the holding company as well as the affiliated bank when circumstances arise (e.g., the Continental Illinois Corp.).

Currently, regulators are attempting to *separate* a bank from its securities activities (through firewalls), while at the same time having the BHC serve as a source of financial and managerial strength to its subsidiary banks.[6] Securities industry officials have also expressed concerns that the firewall requirements are not stringent enough to insulate banks from the activities of Section-20 firms, and to prevent them from having access to funds at lower costs (because they are at least partially insured). It is our belief that following a transition period regulators will be able to impose an enforceable financial separation between bank and non-bank affiliates with a strict message that liabilities of affiliated securities subsidiaries and the holding company are not insured by the FDIC. Thereafter, the regulation of these Section-20 firms will be partially relaxed.

The major firewalls currently used to separate a bank from its affiliates engaging in securities activities are:

1 Revenue restriction – 10 percent limitation on the level of revenue that can be generated from ineligible securities activities is in force.
2 Capital adequacy condition – these companies are subject to a SEC minimum net worth capital ratio, with capital investment from the holding company deducted from the holding company's capital adequacy calculation, to prevent double counting.
3 Restrictions and prohibitions on financial ties between banks *and* Section-20 companies – credit extension from a bank to its affiliates (directly or indirectly)

is prohibited, as is extension of bank credit to the affiliate's customers for purposes related to securities underwriting. Issuing of bank credit enhancement instruments (such as letters of credit) to back a Section-20 firm's issue of ineligible securities is prohibited.

4 Prohibition against banks sharing employees or confidential information or engaging in marketing activities on behalf of a Section-20 affiliate.

The main purpose of these firewalls is to protect the bank's safety and soundness, and to prevent potential conflicts of interest. However, they are costly and reduce the profitability of the activities, while entailing other risks. For example, the 10 percent revenue restriction has created the incentive for the holding company to shift eligible activities to the Section-20 firms, hence increasing risk to the bank. The restriction on joint production and marketing may prevent synergistic profits (due to economies of scope), while the capital adequacy standard imposed on the holding company (by the Federal Reserve) and the Section-20 subsidiary (by the SEC) impose further costs.

10.8 The Significance and Future of Non-banking Activities

In examining the areas of non-banking activities to which banks can expand it can be seen that the most significant is the securities field. In other popular fields such as real estate and industrial firms (even if they are allowed under the system of universal banking), the volume of bank expansion has never been significant. To some extent this is consistent with the synergistic hypothesis, which implies that the rationale for non-bank expansion is to attain economies of scope, for example, by joint production and consumption. The evidence suggests that the expansion of US banks into real estate (through REITs) had a significant negative impact on their performance in the 1970s, and even brought a number of banks to the brink of bankruptcy.

The fields most likely to provide economies of scope are securities activities and insurance.

Saunders (1990), thoroughly examines the potential risk and return inherent in three types of non-banking activities: casualty/property insurance, life and health insurance, and securities. His conclusions are:

> In sum, if banks are allowed to expand into casualty/property insurance they are likely to concentrate on lines such as auto- and home-insurance, that have relatively predictable loss rates and provide natural economies of scope with their lending business. In addition, since this insurance is likely to be

> written in-house (or direct), underwriting risks would be directly monitorable and underwriting commissions and costs more controllable... so that any costs are outweighed by economies of scope and other benefits (p. 19).
>
> ... Most life insurance lines would appear to offer relatively low-risk underwriting opportunities for universal banks as well as potentially important economies of scope especially in the areas of distribution via branches and linking the savings element of banking type products to pure insurance aspects of life products (e.g., variable life plans linked to indices of deposit rates)... the relatively low risk nature of most life lines is enhanced by the presence of conservative reserve policies, mortality assumptions, sizable capital, surplus reserves and availability of reinsurance where required, as well as relatively few moral hazard incentive problems emanating from the current insurance safety net[7] (pp. 23–24).
>
> ... Securities firms like property-casualty firms also appear to enjoy cyclical periods of high and low profitability. This is perhaps surprising in view of the low risk nature of brokerage activities and the relatively low risk nature of most new securities underwriting. However, the problems of Drexel-Burnham may be symptomatic of a major change in the source of securities firms revenues in the 1980's and the types of risk undertaken. Specifically there has been a major shift towards so-called risk-based revenue activities in which the securities firms themselves often take a significant principal position (the SIA defines risk-based revenues as the sum of underwriting and trading revenues plus other securities-related revenues (private placements, M and A fees, and non-margin interest revenues).
>
> For example, the non-syndicated share of US debt underwritings alone has increased from 1 percent in 1980 to 89 percent in 1989 largely as a result of Rule 415 off-the-shelf issues. And the recent passage of Rule 144A by the SEC may mean that high quality low-risk issues will be offered via the private placement market while the high-risk issues will form the remaining pool of public equity and debt offerings. That is, the average quality of public offerings may decline and underwriting risk increase (p. 28).

The potential synergistic gains from securities activities deserve further discussion. The flow of funds in any financial system can be either direct, or indirect using intermediaries.

These methods are described in the diagram opposite.

The relative importance of each method in the financial system varies among countries and changes over time, due to factors such as regulatory rules and intervention, tax policy, level of development, and economic structure. For example, underdeveloped countries, lacking efficient capital markets, usually rely heavily on financial intermediaries, especially banks. Due to the primary role of banks and lack of alternative financial markets, and the high-risk environment, the level of regulation in these countries is usually very high.

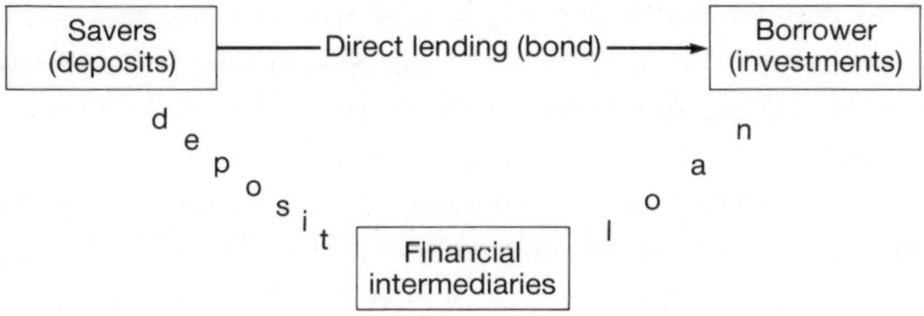

Figure 10.3

In more developed countries, however, technological and economic conditions are more favorable to the development of capital markets, enabling direct financing to compete with intermediaries. Moreover, regulatory restrictions imposed on intermediaries, primarily commercial banks including minimum capital ratios and liquidity requirements (and the monetary tax they imply), can inhibit the ability of intermediaries to compete with direct financing. As such restrictions on intermediaries become broader and more effective, their share of financial activity shrinks, compared to that of direct financing. Thus, in the 1980s commercial banks in many countries lost their comparative advantage as providers of credits to large borrowers. Many large businesses replaced borrowing from the banking system with issuing securities such as bonds, commercial paper or Euronotes. While retail markets have been less affected, wholesale markets have seen a marked impact of such securitization, that is the replacement of intermediated financial flows with direct obligations. In considering these two channels it is clear that in an economy with capital markets in which all agents are price-takers and there is neither friction nor private or costly information, intermediaries need not exist, since they have no advantage over capital markets.

Lending through a bank rather than directly imposes two principal costs on investors. One is the cost of the bank's operations, including a normal return on its capital. The second is the cost of determining whether the bank is limiting and controlling the risks of the loans it makes with (in effect) the investors' funds (deposits). With respect to the first cost, one reason that a bank exists is that it has a competitive advantage over individuals and other organizations in acquiring and analyzing information to reduce risk, such as screening borrowers, collecting and interpreting data, writing the loan contract, recording payments, monitoring performance, checking collateral, and enforcing the terms of the contract.[8] Bank-customer relationships play an important role in this process since they provide both parties with lower-cost information and monitoring.[9] The broad bank-customer business relationships resulting from various services provided by a bank (such as corporate demand deposits, letters of credit, and wage payments to employees) provide it with almost cost-free and continuous sources of information about customers' activities and performance. In addition, a bank might hold shares of firms with which it does business. Such affiliations between the banks and borrowing firms result in lower information and monitoring costs. A bank can often provide these services at a lower cost than can be achieved by investors who lend directly.

But the bank is a borrower with respect to the investor (depositor). Hence, like any borrower, it has an incentive to convince investors that it will repay their funds as promised. To the extent that it does not succeed in convincing investors, the bank bears the cost in the form of higher interest and other payments. Several methods can (and have been) employed to establish the bank's credit worthiness in the eyes of depositors.

Firstly, the bank's owners (residual investors) provide capital that absorbs the cost of defaulted loans and other losses before the investments of depositors and other contractual investors are reduced. In this respect, a bank's situation is no different from that of any other firm. The residual investors (equity holders) have the incentive to avoid the costs of bankruptcy. (Since these costs include the real resource costs of legal fees and other foregone tax write-offs, they cannot be diversified away.) A bank also resembles other firms in that it bears the costs of having less capital relative to debt, *ceteris paribus*, since the greater risk to debt holders is compensated for by a higher cost of debt.[10] Furthermore, should a bank fail, its residual owners stand to lose the valuable asset of depositor trust.[11]

The cost of getting depositors to believe in a bank's safety is usually spread over many years, in such forms as a good investment record and the reputation of its principals for probity and good judgment. Should the bank fail, this trust will be damaged and probably lost, even if the bank is taken over by other investors. Additionally, if entry into commercial banking is restricted by chartering requirements, the owners lose the value of the charter if the bank fails and is purchased by others.

Secondly, a bank will tend to hold a diversified portfolio of assets to reduce the probability that an unexpected event will result in a loss that exceeds its capital. This diversification will be over geographic areas, industries, and maturities such that unexpected changes in economic activity and interest rates will tend to lead to offsetting cash flows, resulting in a lower net variance. As is the case for other decisions, diversification will be carried out to the point where the expected marginal benefits equal expected marginal costs (which include the additional costs of serving various and dispersed customers).

Thirdly, a bank can provide investors (depositors) with information and can bind itself with covenants (such as preferences in the event of bankruptcy and guarantees by respected persons) and collateral (such as funds held in escrow and specie available on demand). A bank might also have persons whose probity is respected as senior officers or directors. Groups of bankers might join groups that monitor each other or that provide guarantees of repayment to depositors. In fact, all these practices have been followed in periods when banks have not been regulated.[12]

The involvement of banks in capital market activities as a substitute and supplement for conventional banking intermediation has resulted in the stabilizing of overall bank income. The cycle of market activities is compensated for by traditional banking. In other words, capital markets serve as a natural substitute to banking over time and among countries. The involvement of banks in securities activities allow them to participate in any form of credit channeling in the economy.

Notes

1 For example, in the United States prior to the 1970 amendment to the Bank Holding Company Act, bank holding companies expanded primarily into other financial service fields, and, albeit to a lesser extent, into various industrial fields such as metal mining and petroleum refining, too. (See *Federal Reserve Bulletin*, December 1972, p A99 for a detailed list.)

2 See Volcker (1986), Corrigan (1982, 1987) and Saunders (1988) for a discussion of the uniqueness of banking services.

3 Benston (1990) in studying the pre-Glass-Steagall period did not find support for abuses and conflicts of interest on the part of banks involved in securities transactions.

4 The analysis presented here draws heavily upon Global Survey of Permissible Activities for Banking Organizations in Major Financial Centers Outside the United States, Institute of International Bankers, April 1988.

5 The Gessler Commission, appointed to examine the non-banking activities of banks, issued its report in May 1979. The report endorsed the continuation of the universal banking system while dismissing the two major concerns of non-bank expansion, i.e., potential conflicts of interest and undue concentration of power.

6 The exact conditions under which a BHC can be required to use non-banking assets to support bank subsidiaries have not been set out.

7 Note that the ability of policyholders to make a run on (i.e., cancel and liquidate) insurance policies is less than in the case of deposits because of

liquidity and penalty features that are invoked when policyholders try to switch or cash-in on their policies. Nevertheless, it is still conceivable that panics or runs on insurers could occur in the absence of any insurance guarantee scheme.

8 See Barro (1976) for a discussion of the role of collateral.

9 Black (1975) (among others) emphasizes this relationship.

10 However, unlike other firms, most of the bank's debts are held as demand (or near demand) deposits. Should these debt holders fear the non-repayment of their claims, they can ask for immediate redemption, thereby imposing considerable costs on the bank. Hence, banks have a greater incentive than do other firms to continuously convince these investors that they face a very small probability of non-repayment as promised.

11 Depositors tend to invest through banks rather than directly in part because they believe that they thereby incur less risk.

12 The founding and management of a bank by well known, respected and usually wealthy individuals is commonplace, particularly in smaller communities. In the United States, for example, the Suffolk Group of Banks and the New York Clearing House operated as self-policing agencies in the early 1800s.

References

Barro, Robert J. (1976) The loan market, collateral, and rates of interest, *Journal of Money, Credit and Banking*, vol 8, 441–56.

Benston, George J. (1990) The Separation of Commercial and Investment Banking: The Glass–Steagall Act Revised and Reconsidered, Oxford University Press, New York.

Black, Fischer (1975) Bank funds management in an efficient market, *Journal of Financial Economics*, vol 7, 323–39.

—— Merton H. Miller and Richard A. Posner (1978) An approach to the regulation of bank holding companies, *Journal of Business*, vol 51, 379–412.

Boyd, John H. and Stanley L. Graham (1986) Risk, regulation and banking holding company extension into non-banking, *Quarterly Review*, The Federal Reserve Bank of Minneapolis, 2–17.

—— The profitability and risk effects of allowing bank holding companies to merge with other financial firms: a simulation study, *Quarterly Review*, The Federal Reserve Bank of Minneapolis, vol 10, 3–20.

Boyd, John H., Gerald A. Hanweck and Pipat Pithyachariyakul (1980) Bank holding company diversification, Proceedings of a Conference on Bank Structure and Competition, The Federal Reserve Bank of Chicago, 102–21.

Brewer, Elijah A note on the relationship between bank holding company risk and nonbank activity, The Federal Reserve Bank of Chicago, *Occasional Paper* 5–88.

——Diana Fortier and Christine Pavel (1988) Bank risk from non-bank activities, *Economic Perspectives*, The Federal Reserve Bank of Chicago, vol 12, 14–26.

Cable, John (1985) Capital market information and industrial performance: The role of West German banks, *Economic Journal*, vol 95, 118–32.

Corrigan, E. Gerald Are banks special?, The Federal Reserve Bank of Minneapolis, *Annual Report 1982*.

—— Coping with globally integrated financial markets, The Federal Reserve Bank of New York, *Quarterly Review*, Winter 1986–87, 1–5.

—— Financial market structure: A longer view, The Federal Reserve Bank of New York, *Annual Report 1986*.

Desai, Anand S. and Roger D. Stover (1985) Bank holding company acquisitions, stockholder returns, and regulatory uncertainty, *Journal of Financial Research*, vol 8, 145–56.

Eisemann, Peter C. (1976) Diversification and congeneric bank holding company, *Journal of Bank Research*, vol 7, 68–77.

Eisenbeis, Robert A. (1983) How should bank holding companies be regulated?, *Economic Review*, The Federal Bank of Atlanta, vol 68, 42–7.

Federal Reserve Bulletin, Board of Governors of the Federal Reserve System, various issues.

Gilligan, Thomas and Michael Smirlock (1984) An empirical study of joint production and scale economies in commercial banking, *Journal of Banking and Finance*, vol 8, 67–77.

Heggestad, Arnold A. (1975) Riskiness of investments in non-bank activities by bank holding companies, *Journal of Economics and Business*, vol 27, 219–23.

Institute of International Bankers, *Global Survey of Permissible Activities for Banking Organizations in Major Financial Centers Outside the US*, New York, April 1988.

Jessee, Michael A. and Steven A. Seelig (1977) *Bank Holding Companies and the Public Interest*, D. C. Heath and Co., Lexington Massachussets, Toronto.

Johnson, Rodney D. and David R. Meinster (1974) Bank holding companies: Diversification opportunities in non-bank activities, *Eastern Economic Journal*, vol 1, 316–23.

Karna, Adi (1979) Bank holding company profitability: Non-banking subsidiaries and financial leverage, *Journal of Bank Research*, vol 10, 28–35.

Liang, Nellie J. and Donald T. Savage (1990) The non-bank activities of bank holding companies, *Federal Reserve Bulletin*, vol 76, 280–92.

Litan, Robert E. Assessing the risk of financial product deregulation, paper presented to the American Economics Association, New York, 1985.

—— *What should banks do?*, Washington, D.C., The Brookings Institution, 1987.

Mayne, Lucille S. (1978) New directions in bank holding company supervision, *Banking Law Journal*, vol 95, 729–49.

—— Bank holding company characteristics and the upstreaming of bank funds, *Journal of Money, Credit and Banking*, 1980, vol 12, 209–14.

Meinster, David R. and Rodney D. Johnson (1979) Bank holding company diversification and the risk of capital impairment, *The Bell Journal of Economics*, vol 10, 683–94.

Orgler, Yair E. and Benjamin Wolkowitz (1976) *Bank Capital*, Van Nostrand Reinhold, New York.

Rose J. I. and Samuel H. Talley (1984) Financial transactions within bank holding companies, *Journal of Financial Research*, 209–17.

Saunders, Anthony (1988) Bank holding companies: Structure, performance and reform, in *Restructuring Banking and Financial Services in America*, W. Haraf and R. M. Kushmeider (eds), AEI, Washington D.C.

—— Universal banking in the US: Implications for bank risk and the Federal safety net, Working Paper, New York University Graduate School of Business, May 1990.

—— and Michael Smirlock (1987) Intra and interindustry effects of bank securities market activities: The case for discount brokerage, *Journal of Financial and Quantitative Analysis*, vol 2, 467–81.

Silverberg, Stanley C. (1975) Bank holding companies and capital adequacy, *Journal of Bank Research*, vol 74, 202–7.

Stover, Roger D. (1980) The single subsidiary bank holding company, *Journal of Bank Research*, vol 11, 43–50.

Swary, Itzhak (1981) Bank acquisition of mortgage firms and stockholders' wealth: An empirical analysis, *Journal of Banking and Finance*, vol 5, 201–15.

Talley, Samuel A. (1975) Bank holding companies financing, Proceedings of a conference on bank structure and competition, The Federal Reserve Bank of Chicago, 124–35.

US General Accounting Office, *Bank Powers: Activities of Securities Subsidiaries of Bank Holding Companies*, GAO/GGD 90-48, Washington D.C., March 1990.

Volcker, Paul A., Statement before the Subcommittee on Commerce, Consumer and Monetary Affairs of the Committee on Government Operations, United States House of Representatives, June 11, 1986.

Wall, Larry D. (1985) Regulation of banks' equity capital, *Economic Review*, The Federal Reserve Bank of Atlanta, vol 70, 4–18.

—— Non-bank activities and risk, *Economic Review*, The Federal Reserve Bank of Atlanta, vol 71, 19–34.

—— and Robert A. Eisenbeis (1984), Risk considerations in regulating bank activities, *Economic Review*, The Federal Reserve Bank of Atlanta, vol 69, 6–19.

Ra/Lp
Neg X

11

The International Convergence of Capital Adequacy Requirements

11.1 Background

The issue of capital adequacy has attracted continuous attention from bank management and regulatory authorities alike. The primary role of bank capital is to provide a cushion against unexpected losses, and to prevent bank failures (defined as the inability of a bank to meet its obligations). The larger a bank's capital to debt ratio, the smaller the probability of it not meeting its obligations. Accordingly, equity capital serves as a source of funds which determines when (*ceteris paribus*) a bank is insolvent.

The rationale behind the supervision of the banking industry has been considered in several studies (Benston, 1973; Black, Miller, and Posner 1978; Buser, Chen, and Kane, 1981; Paroush, 1988). These studies have suggested the following justifications:

- Supervision protects bank customers who lack the ability to assess bank risk.
- The viability of a bank is profoundly dependent upon public confidence. Supervision can prevent external diseconomies generated by the loss of public confidence due to bank failure. A bank that fails to meet its obligations introduces instability into the whole banking system.

The studies mentioned above have found that bank regulators are vitally concerned with maintaining bank "safety and soundness." Consequently, regulators impose solvency standards on banks through capital adequacy requirements which define upper limits on acceptable probabilities of ruin (or bank risk). Such policies effectively impose a risk-of-ruin constraint on a bank's portfolio. As noted by Buser, Chen, and Kane (1981), capital requirements, bank activity or portfolio restrictions, and bank examination may be thought of as regulatory taxes, which create increasing deadweight losses to the value of the banking firm as it adjusts to increased risk levels.

In particular, numerous studies have been devoted to the analysis of different aspects of capital adequacy regulations.

11.1.1 The Contagion Effect of Bank Failures

The "contagion effect" of bank failures states that the bankruptcy of a single bank, especially a large institution, may cause runs on other banks. The contagion effect is like the "domino" effect; regardless of the cause of bank failure, its effect may spread to other banks as well. The losses caused to these banks and their depositors disrupts the monetary system and general economic stability.[1] The significance of the contagion effect, which has in part motivated the behavior of regulators ever since the Depression, has been assumed by government officials with no empirical evidence to support it.

For example, during the Continental Illinois Bank crisis, fears of contagion were frequently expressed by regulators. In 1984, the FDIC chairman warned that "the cost of the domino effect, as other banks failed, would have been incalculable." However, the chairman of the House Banking Committee charged that the FDIC had promulgated a misleading "domino theory" to justify the rescue of Continental Illinois Bank. This controversy resulted in a call for empirical studies, which were in fact difficult to implement.

In any event it is clear that bank failures could potentially affect other banks in two ways. Firstly, a bank failure might cause the public to loose confidence in solvent banks, a phenomenon referred to here as the "bank-run effect." Secondly, information about regulatory policy and asset quality as revealed by a bank failure can lead depositors to revise their valuation of other banks, and this is called the "informational effect" (Aharony and Swary, 1983).

The bank-run effect predicts that any bank failure leads depositors to become less confident in the solvency of their own institutions and, hence, to withdraw their funds. Such withdrawals force these banks to borrow more costly funds or to liquidate assets, thus reducing shareholder profits. The potential losses motivate government authorities to take action or to adopt policies limiting this behavior. The informational effect states only that the response to a bank failure is based on information revealed. Depositor, regulator, and investor reaction may be interpreted simply as a response to a common type of previously unobservable information revealed in the bank failure.

Two empirical studies have used capital market data in an attempt to detect contagion effects on the performance of the banking industry.

Aharony and Swary (1983), examined the three largest bank failures in US history. They concluded that

> ... when the failure of a large bank is caused primarily by problems specific to the bank such as fraud, no contagious effects are observed. When the failure of a large bank is caused by problems whose revelation is correlated across banks, the observed fall of solvent bank stocks may be interpreted as investors' response to a common type of unfavorable signal, rather than a contagious effect.

Swary (1986), examined the stock market reaction to the Continental Illinois Bank crisis and found

> ... while there was a clear market reaction to information revealed in the crisis about banks' asset quality and regulatory policy, depositors apparently did not withdraw funds in the massive way that regulators anticipated. ... Finally, the informational effect might indeed have led to the kind of domino effect that chairman Isaac alluded to, but this is by no means evidence of bank runs.

In other words, empirical findings are not necessarily consistent with the rationale of capital adequacy requirements.

11.1.2 Optimal versus Adequate Capital

Optimal bank capital is determined by the decision-making process of the bank, which is presumably governed by an objective of maximizing some appropriate criterion such as stockholder wealth. Capital adequacy is determined by that probability of bank failure viewed as socially optimal by regulators. The main concern of most analyses of capital adequacy is to determine to what extent optimal and adequate capital differ.

Studies by Robinson and Pettway (1967), Pringle (1974), and Taggart and Greenbaum (1978), are concerned with the role of capital in the financial management of the individual bank. They concluded that the amount of equity capital is an important management-decision variable, and that maximizing behavior with respect to shareholder wealth does not necessarily lead to a low capital position. They reasoned that banks are pressured by profit-maximizing behavior to hold the optimal leverage position dictated by capital market forces. Thus, these studies call for the abandonment of regulatory standards on capital in favor of market discipline.

Specifically, Pringle assumed that the bank is a private wealth-maximizing economic unit that operates in imperfect markets, and concluded that optimal capital policy is determined by relative transaction costs of alternative financing sources and investment opportunities. Taggart and Greenbaum based their analysis on the assumption that transaction services (to depositors) provide the bank with profit opportunities offset by regulatory constraints (e.g., reserve requirements). Provision of such services leads to an optimal amount of deposits, and an optimal financial structure in the absence of constraints. It should be emphasized that the impact of equity capital on the probability of a bank's failure and the expected costs of bankruptcy, which are the main interest of regulators, were entirely ignored in these studies. In contrast to the approaches of the foregoing studies, the explanation advanced by regulatory authorities and some economists to justify supervision of the banking system is the possible difference between each bank's optimal capital structure, reflecting private benefits and costs, and what society considers an adequate amount of capital, reflecting social benefits and costs (Watson, 1974; Santomero and Watson, 1977).

11.1.3 The Impact of Regulation on Bank Capital

Several studies have attempted to evaluate the effectiveness of US regulatory agencies. Mayne (1972), analyzed differences in the amount of capital required by each of the regulatory agencies in order to determine whether different agencies have different impacts on bank capital. Since there are variances in the capital standards required by each agency (as discussed above), effective implementation of the various regulatory standards could lead to significant differences in observed capital positions among banks. In her empirical study, Mayne reported that such differences are statistically insignificant. This empirical evidence is compatible with either of the following hypotheses:

- there are similarities in applied capital standards of the supervisory agencies, or
- regulators are unable to impose their capital standards upon the banks they presumably regulate.

Peltzman (1970), computed estimates of the magnitude of the effect of government regulations on capital investment in commercial banking, and also examined whether deposit insurance is a substitute for capital. His results indicated that, during the period studied, "there was no evidence that bank investment behavior conforms to the standard set forth for it by the regulatory agencies" (p. 20). The basis for this conclusion was the finding of a significantly negative (cross-sectional) relationship, over a three-year period, between the flow of capital into banking and various measures that approximate regulatory-determined capital adequacy. Furthermore, the deposit insurance variable (percentage of insured deposits) was found to be negatively related to capital investment. Peltzman concluded, therefore, that deposit insurance is substituted for capital and that capital requirements of regulators are ineffective, i.e., the capital investment process in banks is not affected significantly by regulation.

Peltzman's study, however, was criticized by Mingo (1975), who followed Peltzman's approach closely and attempted to correct two apparent errors:

- a specification error in the measurement of the impact of the regulatory process. The relationship between capital and regulatory pressure is nonlinear, i.e., the regulator puts much more pressure on banks that are considered to be very deficient in capital;
- an error in the use of data unsuitable for such an inquiry, namely, data aggregated by states.

Mingo found that the lower the ratio of actual capital to capital required by the regulators, the more likely the bank is to increase its capital over the next period, to satisfy the demand of the bank regulator.

Consideration of the effectiveness of capital requirements imposed by regulators leads to fundamental questions regarding capital adequacy. Firstly, is regulatory supervision of capital standards appropriate? Secondly, is the current bank regulation process efficient?

11.1.4 Social Costs and Benefits of Capital Adequacy Regulation

Santomero and Watson (1977), discussed determinants of the social costs and benefits of increased capitalization in a general equilibrium framework. Benefits result from a decrease in the expected costs of bank failure both to society as a whole and to the individual bank.

Social costs are the opportunity costs of overcapitalization, which must be borne both by the banking system and by society at large. Any excess capital in banking generates undesirable effects on output and productivity in the economy through misallocation of resources. However, the social and private impact of the regulatory process on both individual bank market value maximization (in particular, the bank's investment policy), and the volume of intermediation in the economy were ignored in the Santomero and Watson study.

The impact of capital adequacy regulation on the behavior of individual banks has been analyzed, to some extent, by Blair and Heggestad (1978), and Kahane (1977), who found that regulators often use capital requirements or portfolio regulations to maintain a sound banking system (defined as a lower probability of bank failure). These requirements, however, cannot completely ensure a decrease in the probability of ruin, since they may adversely affect other decisions (and their attendant risks) as well. Blair and Heggestad suggested that portfolio regulations are rather inefficient and might also be ineffective, since regulatory attempts to maintain soundness can be achieved without altering the mean-variance efficient frontier faced by the bank, by constraining the feasible set of assets a bank can hold. A serious shortcoming of both studies was their use of improper objective functions (mean-variance utility functions) for individual banks, which makes it unlikely that the authors detected the actual consequences of the regulatory process on an individual bank's behavior, and on the social costs involved.

The social benefits of capital adequacy regulation result from a decrease in the expected costs of bank failure. The theoretical relationship between failure and capital is clear. In practice, however, this link depends on the ability of examiners to identify problem banks before failure, i.e., on the efficiency of the identification process. This issue has been analyzed and tested in several empirical studies. Cotter (1966), tested the usefulness of the capital ratio in predicting bank failures. He found that the mean values of capital ratios for banks that failed, and for those that did not, were not statistically different. Benston (1973), compared the ratio of capital to assets adjusted by the quality (riskiness) of a bank's assets, according to the FDIC evaluation approximately a year before failure. His findings indicated that "a relatively large number of banks that failed were severely under-capitalized" (p. 45). Inadequate capital, however, does not occupy a prominent position on the list of causes of failure provided by Benston, a fact which, in his study at least, implies that capital plays a small role in the prevention of failure.

Sinkey (1978), examined the FDIC-adjusted capital ratio and found that loan classification was an important variable in identifying problem banks. Almost all banks that failed in the late 1970s evidently had a large volume of substandard loans for several years preceding their failure. The FDIC identification process was found to be inefficient however, since almost all banks with low adjusted capital ratios did not fail. Santomero and Vinso (1977), also estimated the cross-section riskiness of the banking structure and its sensitivity to variations in bank capital. Their results indicated that

> the industry is exposed, on average, to a very small risk of suspended operation, and this probability changes very little with variations in the capital account buffer. However, some banks within the sample do exhibit higher risk potential. These can be explained, to a large part, by relatively low capital ratios and/or high variability over the sample period (p. 204).

The Sinkey and Santomero-Vinso studies imply that the existence of inadequate capital or a high probability of bankruptcy is not a common characteristic of the industry as a whole, but rather is specific to a group of problem banks. The implied conclusion, therefore, is that rather than being imposed upon the entire industry, capital adequacy constraints should be limited to these high-risk banks alone.

In summary, findings on the social benefits of capital adequacy regulation raise many questions about regulatory practice. Changes resulting from the set of portfolio constraints may lead to effects that are adverse to other regulatory goals. In other words, attempts to increase capital are frequently offset by portfolio adjustments. Moreover, the major cost of bank regulation is that of opportunities lost, to the extent that bank capital regulation inhibits the efficient allocation of resources.

11.2 Pre-Basle Capital Adequacy Requirements

Although the concept of capital adequacy is easily defined in terms of the primary function of bank capital as a reduction of the probability of bank failure, its translation into practical supervisory terms is difficult and complex. The intended effect of bank regulation can best be analyzed if it is assumed that regulators are able to specify, measure, and enforce a direct constraint on the probability of bank failure. Direct constraints induce change in the shadow price of risk-taking, thereby controlling the bank's overall risk, and influencing various decisions.

In practice, however, regulators in different countries impose a set of portfolio constraints that are intended to restrict the freedom of an individual bank to engage in risky activities or to hold a high-risk portfolio of assets and liabilities. Portfolio constraints deal separately with each type of risk, and do not allow substitution among these different types, within the general constraints of the probability of bankruptcy.

As indicated above, bank regulation is imposed as a means of controlling the risks assumed by banks. Three major types of provisions are identifiable in different countries: portfolio (solvency) constraints, bank examination, and deposit insurance. The primary method complementing these provisions to control bank risk is, of course, the use of capital adequacy standards.

11.2.1 Portfolio (Solvency) Constraints

Portfolio constraints restrict the freedom of an individual bank to engage in risky activities or to hold a high-risk portfolio of assets and liabilities. In banking, attention should be paid to intermediation between sources and uses, which may differ as to terms of maturity and currency of denomination.

In particular, the following major types of provisions are identifiable.

Constraints on financing decisions

Three capital ratios are common: capital/public deposits, capital/total liabilities, and capital/risky assets. The first two ratios are general, and do not refer to the different degrees of risk involved in different operations and assets. The third ratio is aimed more directly at relating capital to those assets likely to require a buffer against unforeseen losses.

Constraints on investment decisions

These include constraints on both the minimum degree of asset diversification and on activities banks can pursue, namely a ceiling on the size of any single asset in a bank's portfolio ("size constraint"), and a limit on the kind of assets banks are allowed to hold ("activity constraint").

Constraints on liquidity management

Two requirements can be distinguished. First, capital must cover fixed assets. Such constraints are imposed, for example, in Belgium, the Netherlands, Luxembourg, and the Federal Republic of Germany. In banking, a fixed asset is used for the production of banking services, and thus will usually not be sold so long as the bank is a going concern. Accordingly, capital available to maintain an adjustment between the maturity of assets and liabilities is reduced by the amount invested in fixed assets.[2]

The second requirement is that of *required reserves*. In most countries reserve requirements are based on a percentage of deposits, applied according to the maturity of the various deposits; the longer the repayment period, the lower the liquidity ratio. However, banks may use only a fraction (the reserve ratio) of required reserves to meet unexpected withdrawals. Therefore, this constraint primarily affects the composition of a bank's asset portfolio rather than its liquidity position. Under these conditions reserves are riskless assets.

In a few countries, including the Netherlands, Switzerland, and the Federal Republic of Germany, relevant laws refer to the mutual relationship that should exist between the maturity dates of assets and liabilities (and, consequently, between capital and liquid assets).

Constraints on foreign exchange operations

Some countries (again, the Netherlands, Switzerland, and the Federal Republic of Germany) impose restrictions on uncovered positions in foreign currency as a percentage of equity capital.

Other regulations

In addition to the provisions reviewed above, the following regulations are imposed by various authorities: restrictions on the distribution of dividends (in most countries); restrictions on a single stockholder's bank shares (designed to prevent self-dealing and fraud); specifications as to the internal composition of capital (the proportion of debentures to total capital in the United States); and a ceiling on the amount of any single deposit.

11.2.2 Bank Examination

The major tasks of bank examination are to detect possible mismanagement and dishonesty; to acquire information regarding the adequacy of a bank's capital, and accordingly to enforce capital requirements; and to ensure that laws regulating bank activities are being followed. Benston (1973, p. 40), found that fraud and other irregularities were the major cause of failure in two-thirds of the 56 banks that failed between 1959 and 1971. In recent years, however, there has been a trend toward progressively larger banks experiencing failure (Aharony and Swary, 1983).[3]

Therefore, bank examination and portfolio constraints are complementary measures of capital adequacy regulation. Bank examination is directed mainly toward small banks, where internal control is generally inadequate and the potential for fraud and defalcation greater. However, in larger banks where internal control is more efficient, any failure would more likely be due to mismanagement, defined as the use of practices that involve high risk.

11.2.3 Deposit Insurance

In some countries, bank risk is limited through mandatory government insurance and portfolio constraints.[4] In the United States, for example, a constant rate insurance premium per dollar of domestic deposit is charged, whether or not the deposit is covered by insurance.

Deposit insurance not only protects depositors (to a limit of $100,000 on an individual account in the United States), but also indemnifies the banking system against destructive runs on deposits. Government guarantees for deposits are provided because of economies of scale in information and monitoring costs, and in the provision of large-scale guarantees to the banking system (Kreps and Wacht, 1971; Gibson, 1972). Holders of deposits in excess of the $100,000 ceiling, however, partially bear the default risk and may tend to withdraw their funds, thereby adding to a bank's problems.

An important factor in determining the consequences of deposit insurance is the FDIC policy at the time of bank failure. The FDIC may, at its discretion, either provide assistance for purchase or merger into another bank, or liquidate the failed bank. The purchase and assumption transaction effectively provides 100 percent insurance to uninsured depositors. In fact, FDIC policy has been such that most deposits during the period 1935–80 were 100 percent insured, despite the official maximum on the amount of deposit insured (Barnett et al, 1977).

The major problem that occurs over time with the current deposit insurance structure is the fixed premium of deposit insurance and the moral hazard of induced incentive to increase bank risk. (Marcus and Shaked, 1984; Flannery, 1989).

Bank capital and its definition

Since the central concern of bank capital regulation is bank failure, anything within the balance sheet that absorbs this risk is viewed as part of capital. There is general agreement on the criteria for inclusion of a potential component of "core" capital: it must be permanently available, it must not impose contractual charges against earnings, and it is not redeemable at holders' request. Nevertheless, the definition for solvency purposes of a bank's core capital varies significantly from country to country, as a result of differences in accounting principles, varying rates and determinations of inflation, and the existence of "semi-equity" instruments.

Other elements possessing some of the characteristics of core capital (Tier 1) can be treated as components of equity capital, including:

- Asset revaluation reserves. Most countries that allow such revaluation include it in the definition of capital. Such countries include France, Norway, Spain, and the United Kingdom.
- Loan loss reserves. Specific provisions are not part of capital. General provisions are held against the risk of losses that are latent but not attributable to a specific asset. As such they have some of the characteristics of capital and are included, in most countries, in the capital base. These countries include Canada, France, the United Kingdom, Switzerland, Japan, and the United States.
- Subordinated debt. The treatment of long-term debt varies substantially among the countries considered here. Faced with regulatory pressure to

increase capital, banks have issued debt rather than equity to prevent dilution of their capital. They have argued that debt, because of its subordination, protects the depositor in the event of failure. Innovations, such as perpetual maturities and automatic convertibility clauses, have contributed to supervisor agreement in some countries that subordinated debt is to be included. This is the case in Canada, France, Switzerland, the United Kingdom, and the United States.

The issue of book value to market value differential is far more complex than the simple revaluation of securities portfolio. While recognizing the ambiguity associated with book valuation, regulators in different countries have nonetheless persisted in this fiction, which causes considerable hardship and inefficiency within the banking community.

Measurement of capital adequacy

Several methods have been devised to relate capital to overall bank risk. Two basic approaches can be used in a complementary fashion – the leverage ratio and the risk asset ratio. The leverage ratio relates capital to banking liabilities or claims. This constraint puts a ceiling on the maximum expansion of a bank for a given amount of capital resources, and has been applied in Canada, the United States, and Japan, among other countries. The major drawbacks of this system are the difficulty in incorporating off-balance-sheet activities, and the fact that the level of required capital is not directly related to the level of risk.

In applying the risk asset ratio, varying weights are attached to the different categories of assets to be related to the capital base. These weights reflect the perceived riskiness of the various types of bank business. Countries adopting this approach differ markedly with respect to the number of categories of risk defined: the Federal Republic of Germany has three or four classes, Switzerland has fifteen, the United Kingdom has eight, and Spain six classes of risk.

Nevertheless, neither measure of capital adequacy is likely to capture the overall quality of a bank's portfolio. It is generally agreed that the measurement of capital adequacy is only one element in evaluating a bank's soundness. Thus some countries, such as Canada and the United Kingdom have refrained from prescribing precise quantitative ratios. In the Federal Republic of Germany and Switzerland, a fixed ratio is set by statute, but the authorities have the power to change the ratio in specific circumstances.

11.3 The International Convergence of Capital Adequacy

Confronted with a perceived deterioration of asset quality, and with increasing risks on and off the balance sheet, supervisors in all developed countries have taken steps to prevent a further erosion of capital ratios. These regulatory efforts have been designed to encourage a significant increase in the level of bank capital, to formalize the assessment of risk in capital ratios, and to adopt measurement techniques for new financial instruments and for off-balance-sheet activities. In highly competitive global banking, market imbalances may place at a disadvantage banks subject to comparatively strict capital adequacy rules, so that international coordination becomes vital.

Recent goals of the BIS (Cooke Committee) have been to strengthen capital adequacy requirements, to arrive at a greater convergence of approaches in different countries, and to improve comparability of the definition and measurement of capital adequacy. Differences in accounting conventions, and in the assessment of the value and risk of assets and liabilities, remain very large. These inconsistencies represent a formidable obstacle to the accurate quantitative comparison of banks in different countries. In the early 1980s a process of harmonization was initiated both within the European Community (EC), and in the broader forum of the Basle Committee on Banking Regulations and Supervisory Practices. After several years of work, the Basle Committee issued in December 1987 an international convergence of capital adequacy standard for commercial banks. The proposed guidelines have recently been accepted by all member countries.

In December 1989, the EC finance ministers signed the Solvency Ratio Directive, which essentially imparts legal force to the BIS standards throughout the EC from January 1991. The agreed framework is designed to establish minimum levels of capital for internationally active banks. In some instances member nations have extended the proposals to apply to domestic banks and bank holding companies. The EC solvency ratio applies to all banks active in the EC, and not only those which are internationally active.

Capital adequacy is one of several factors to be taken into account when assessing the strength of banks. Tax treatment and accounting standards, particularly those for certain loss provisions, may affect the comparability of capital adequacy in banking systems from country to country.

The Basle agreement is applied to banks on a consolidated basis. The position of a given bank within the banking group may affect the quantification of its strength. The current requirements deal exclusively with credit risk. The BIS committee intends to broaden the coverage of capital adequacy requirements to include interest rate risk and foreign exchange risk (basis risk).

The new risk-based capital standard includes four parts: a definition of capital, risk-based requirements, the target standard ratio, and transitional and implementation arrangements.

Definition of capital

An important feature of the standard is that capital is redefined and divided into two types: narrow and broad. The narrow measure is called Tier 1 (or core), and consists essentially of common equity and retained earnings, including minority interests, net of both intangible assets such as goodwill, and investment in banking subsidiaries. The broad measure is called Tier 2, and is equal to the sum of core capital and "supplementary" capital. Supplementary capital includes:

- Subordinated debt and intermediate term preferred stock (original average maturity 5+ years) up to a maximum of 50 percent of the core capital.
- Hybrid capital instruments (perpetual debt, mandatory convertible securities, etc.) and other instruments that can support losses on an ongoing basis, such as long-term preferred shares in Canada, and Genusscheine in the Federal Republic of Germany.
- Undisclosed reserves that have been passed through the profit and loss account, and are accepted by the supervisory authorities.
- Revaluation reserves from a formal revaluation (when allowed), or from hidden values, due to the practice of holding securities in the financial statement at historic cost (below market value). In the latter case a substantial discount (to reflect market volatility) of 55 percent on the revaluation is required.
- General provision or general loan loss reserves, the general provisions of which should be included in capital. (However, in practice it is difficult to distinguish among freely available provisions that have been created against particular assets' identified losses.) This reflects the diversity of accounting, supervisory, and fiscal policies. The committee wishes to ensure a consistent definition of general loan loss provisions eligible for inclusion in the capital base. By 1992, the loan loss reserve should not exceed 1.25 percent of the risk-weighted asset base. The maximum amount of supplementary capital that may be used for regulatory purposes is 100 percent of Tier 1 capital.

Classes of risk

In order to tie a bank's capital requirements to its estimated credit risk, risk classes were created for all assets and off-balance-sheet items. This procedure allocates assets into four risk categories, each with a different weight designed to reflect the degree of credit risk. The lowest category carries a zero weight and consists of items not subject to default risk (Appendix 1). The committee recognizes some market risk in the holding of government securities (10 percent for all securities with a maturity date under one year, and 20 percent for those maturing in one year or more). Claims against the private sector are generally weighted at 100 percent.

Country transfer risk

The committee differentiates countries considered to be of high credit standing. It is the committee's belief that transfer risk varies greatly among countries, and that this risk is significant. Also, the European Community is firmly committed to the principle that all member countries should be treated in the same way. Accordingly, all OECD member countries are treated as one group. However, different treatment of short-term and long-term interbank assets does exist.

Off-balance-sheet commitments

A bank's credit risk from off-balance-sheet activities is treated according to the same approach, after converting notional amounts of each off-balance-sheet instrument into an on-balance sheet "credit equivalent amount" (Appendix 2). Prior to this approach, letters of credit, loan commitments, and other direct credit substitutes were seen by banks as a source of fee income (with no risk).

The conversion factors are as follows:

- 0 percent conversion factor. Short-term commitments with an original maturity of one year or less, or that can be unconditionally cancelled at any time.
- 20 percent conversion factor. Short-term, self-liquidating, trade-related contingencies, including commercial letters of credit.
- 50 percent conversion factor. Transaction-related contingencies (e.g., standby letters of credit), unused contingencies with an original maturity in excess of one year, revolving underwriting facilities, note issuance facilities and similar arrangements.
- 100 percent conversion factor. Direct credit substitutes, acquisitions of risk participation in bankers' acceptances and direct credit, repurchase agreements, and forward agreements to purchase assets.

Credit equivalent amounts for foreign exchange and interest rate swaps are computed (Appendix 2) in one of the following ways:

1 Calculating the present replacement cost by marking to market (capital against the bank's current exposure) and adding a factor to represent potential exposure during the remaining life of the contract.
2 Conversion factors based on the notional principal sum underlying each contract according to its type and maturity.

The majority of member countries have selected the first approach.

A target standard ratio

Finally, a bank's risk-based requirement is computed. Two requirements must be met, corresponding to the two measures of capital: Tier 1 capital must equal 4 percent of risk-adjusted assets, and the ratio of total capital to risk-adjusted assets must ultimately equal 8 percent.

These ratios are common minimum standards, which international banks in member countries will be expected to hold; however, they do not come into effect until the end of 1992.

Transitional arrangements

The new standards will be phased in over a three-year period. By year-end 1990, total capital (core and supplementary) had to equal or exceed 7.25 percent of risk-weighted assets, including off-balance-sheet exposures. The core stockholders' equity ratio, had to reach at least 3.25 percent. The 8 percent requirement must be fully satisfied by all international banks before year-end 1992. Core capital will be at least 4 percent by that time. Additionally, general loan loss reserves will be limited at year-end 1992 to 1.25 percent, or exceptionally and temporarily to 2.0 percent within supplementary elements only. (Transitional arrangements are summarized in Appendix 3.)

11.4 Limitations of the New Standard

The simplicity of the approach used to measure capital and risk in the BIS requirements is a measure of both its strength and weakness. The most favorable effect of the new standard will be to induce risky banks to increase their capital base, shift to less risky activities, and decrease their volume of activities, thereby reducing their overall risk, and the probability of failure. A second potential benefit of the plan is to increase competition and allow for the comparison of banks in different countries, all of whom participate in the international banking market. However, the agreement will increase the costs of bank intermediation, thereby putting banks at a competitive disadvantage vis a vis non-bank intermediaries.

The measurement problem is the major limitation of the new standard. An ideal capital adequacy requirement would include a measure of capital reflecting a bank's true cushion against unexpected losses, and a measure of risk reflecting a bank's true chance of experiencing unexpected losses. The new plan imperfectly measures both components.

11.4.1 Book Value versus Market Value

The new standard measure relies on book value accounting. However, the inclusion of part of the unrealized capital gains on securities holdings in supplementary capital is allowed. To analyze the issue of book vs. market value, a bank's entire balance sheet must be converted to a market value basis. But because it is difficult to obtain reliable estimates for market value, regulators adhere to the book value historical cost basis, with its well known measurement biases. This approach exposes the new standard to the accounting practices used in different countries and to banking policies used by different banks. As a result there are several difficulties that may cause a major bias:

- The impact of inflation on equity is measured mostly as a result of investment in premises. Several countries have used inflation-adjusted accounting practices, such as the United States, the United Kingdom, and Israel, though most recently the UK and the US have abandoned this practice. The impact of inflationary adjustment is to increase measured equity; the significance of this adjustment depends on the level of inflation, the timing of investment in premises, and the magnitude of such investment.
  The difference in inflation across countries may lead to a major measurement bias. For example, inflation-adjusted accounting was implemented in Israel in 1984; and as a result of this change in accounting measure, the capital-to-asset ratio of Israel's banking system increased four times in one year, from about 1 percent in 1983 to 4 percent at year-end 1984.
- Most bank assets and liabilities are long-term contracts whose value is sensitive to changes in interest rates. The sensitivity of a bank's capital is measured by the duration of its assets and liabilities, i.e., their average weighted maturity.
  Banks that liquidate one side (assets or liabilities) during changes in interest rates, can generate additional biases to the book value of equity. For example, the managements of many savings and loans institutions in the US have been accused during the 1980s of liquidating profits on their assets side while retaining liabilities with high interest rates. Their "true" position was revealed in their books only several years later. This event has created a public call for the implementation of market value accounting for banks.
- The practice of revaluating assets and then capitalizing the sum of the revalued fixed assets, and thereby increasing its Tier 1 capital. This results from the

dependence of the new standard on accounting rather than market valuation. An example of this practice is the National Westminster bank (United Kingdom), which increased its Tier 1 capital by £600 million. This practice is not allowed in most other countries.

11.4.2 Definition of Risk Measures

The new standard focuses exclusively on credit risk, and ignores other types of risk which combine sources and uses, such as interest rate and foreign exchange risk. These additional sources of risk have become more significant with the increased volatility of interest rates and foreign exchange. As a result, the committee intends to continue working on the definition of these risks.

The addition of other risks has made necessary the measurement of interactions, defined as covariances among the different types of risk and their combined impact on a bank's overall risk and return. This measure may prove difficult to obtain (Grammatikos, Saunders, and Swary, 1986). The committee will undoubtedly discuss this issue in the future, in order to improve the measure of overall bank risk.

11.4.3 Imperfect Measure of Credit Risk

No distinction is made between highly creditworthy and risky borrowers. In a sense, given the shadow price of extending credit, the BIS standard encourages banks to increase their risk. For banks whose capital requirement is binding (or potentially binding), extending credit to one borrower means reducing credit to others. Moreover, where the borrower is less risky, the small margin may become insufficient to cover the shadow price of the capital requirement. This lacuna may lead to the perverse affect of increased risk.

11.4.4 Portfolio Considerations

The BIS standard ignores the interaction of different assets within a bank's portfolio. In other words, the risk of a given asset should be measured by its marginal contribution to the risk of total assets (Benston and Kaufman, 1988; and Swary, 1980). A highly diversified loan portfolio is treated in the same manner as a portfolio of loans concentrated in one industry or region. Given the significance of substandard loans in the process of bank failure, while ignoring the quality of assets and portfolio considerations, major biases could develop in measuring bank risk. Sinkey (1978) found that almost all failed banks had a large volume of substandard loans for several years preceding their failure.

11.4.5 Earnings Stream

The probability of bank failure is measured in the risk-return domain. However, the new standard (as well as previous capital requirements) concentrates on risk measures and ignores the return impact. Thus banks that invest in risky assets expect higher returns as a cushion against unexpected losses, and in some cases investing in risky assets may actually reduce the probability of bank failure.

Vojta (1973), proposed two capital adequacy measures based on this concept: an earnings test requiring current earnings to amount to at least twice the level of total expected normal annual losses; and a "capital cushion" test requiring a bank to hold capital funds amounting to 20 times the last five years' moving average of actual total loss experience.

11.4.6 Other Capital Adequacy Measures

As mentioned above, the new standard ignores other capital adequacy measures intended to control bank risk. These measures significantly differ from country to country. It is to be hoped that the convergence of capital requirements in general will be followed by the convergence of other capital adequacy standards, which will make possible the accurate comparison of international banks in different countries.

11.4.7 Off-Balance-Sheet Items

The weights assigned to different assets and off-balance-sheet items allow banks to create low-risk weight synthetic securities. This is achieved by combining low risk-weight spot investments with interest rate contracts that provide the same yield and have performance characteristics similar to those of high-risk weight spot securities or loans (Goldman Sachs, 1988). Obviously, creation of this situation was not the intention of the committee; identical assets should of course be assigned the same weight.

Finally, it should be noted that most of the limitations and the shortcomings mentioned here existed in the pre-Basle capital requirements as well.

11.5 Impact on Banks

The new risk-based capital adequacy standard has had profound and immediate implications for all banks. Despite the fact that the new standard becomes effective only at year-end 1992, banks whose risk- weighted capital ratio falls below the target ratio will clearly be under pressure to increase their ratio in the least expensive way possible. Even for banks with sufficient capital, additional capital will still be required to provide stand-by capacity, allowing for the expansion of bank volume. Additional capital helps banks to increase their investment in high-risk-weighted assets, permits their acquisition of other banks when such opportunities arise and are otherwise feasible. Therefore, given competitive pressure, some excess capital is desirable and even essential for banks. Additionally, the level and type of Tier 2 capital will constitute one of the principal determinants of reported return on bank shareholder equity. As a result, banks that are currently or potentially bound by capital requirements can be expected to direct their activities at improving their capital position.

11.5.1 Restructuring Considerations

Risk weights assigned to each asset will affect both the relative attractiveness of such assets and the relative yield relationship. Banks, in an attempt to retain a target level of profitability, will tend to sell off their prime loans (due to their low margin), while retaining higher-risk but equally-weighted loans. In a sense, banks will seek profitability by restructuring their portfolio toward higher risk-return assets, thereby adversely affecting the intended outcome of the new standard.

11.5.2 Off-Balance-Sheet Activities

Because capital requirements for swaps and forward exchange exposure are low, such instruments may become attractive for creating synthetic instruments.

11.5.3 Securitization

Securitization and asset sales will play a key role in shrinking the balance sheet and increasing fee generating business (loan sales).[5]

11.5.4 Mergers and Acquisitions

The acquisition market for institutions or subsidiaries is expected to be reduced under the new measures for two reasons. Firstly, an acquisition is frequently carried in excess of book value (i.e., goodwill), which in return is deducted from the core capital. Secondly, the new risk-based standard is being imposed on a consolidated basis, whereas acquisitions increase the volume of business without affecting the given capital base. Merged banks may prefer the exchange of bank shares as a method of payment; under the pooling of interest method no goodwill is created, and the equity of the merged firm is equal to the sum of equities of the two separated banks (Accounting Principles Board (APB) ruling 18). Since hostile takeovers normally also require compensation packages, the new standard will limit the possibility of aggressive consolidation.

11.5.5 Profitability

The major cost of the new capital and equity requirement is that of forgone opportunities to the public and banks, to the extent that regulation inhibits the efficient allocation of resources. Additionally, banks seeking a target return on equity will have to respond to investor concerns of over-capitalization (defined as the dilution of earnings per share caused by capital infusions induced by the new guidelines).

11.5.6 Asset Prices and Yields

The new capital adequacy standard will, by altering bank behavior with respect to loan mix, portfolio, and off-balance-sheet exposures, affect the relative yield relationships between general classes of securities and loans. The significance of this impact depends on the change in relative risk-weight differentials and the share of the instrument currently or likely to be held by banks. Additionally, the proposed capital adequacy rules will affect the yield relationship among different types of securities within a given class.

11.5.7 Risk-Taking

Raising capital standards increases the proportion of a bank's risk borne by shareholders. It therefore reduces the benefit to a bank's shareholders of high-default risk investment, e.g., the moral hazard problem. However, by increasing the costs of bank intermediation mainly for low-risk assets, banks may be encouraged to invest in more risky assets, and to increase securitization of low-risk assets.

11.6 Comparative Analysis

By 1993, the best watched measurement of a bank's strength will be its capital adequacy ratio, as a result of banks worldwide conforming to the guidelines on capital adequacy produced by the BIS. Since non-BIS regulators have already begun to emulate the new standards, banks in many locales will also be concerned with their capital ratio. It is of interest to attempt a comparison of the relative position of different countries with respect to this requirement, and to analyze the reaction of banks to their starting position. The 1988 figures given below reflect differences in accounting practices and tax policies, making it difficult to compare banks from different countries.

Table 11.1 International comparison of bank capital ratios

	Bank capital ratio end of 1988	
	Tier 1	*Total*
	(%)	
France	3.9	7.5
Japan	4.1	8.2
United Kingdom	5.9	10.2
United States (money center)	6.4	10.3
Canada	5.1	7.6
Switzerland	6.2	n.a.
Federal Republic of Germany	5.0	9.0

Source: Salomon Brothers Inc., various publications

Competitive pressures in international banking suggest that most banks will be obliged to stay well above the required minimum, and that a capital ratio of 10 percent will become the new benchmark. A summary of the current situation in these countries reveals a variegated pattern of responses.

11.6.1 Switzerland

The required capital-to-asset ratio in Switzerland is among the highest in Europe. Actual ratios are higher yet; the banks have built up substantial hidden reserves that have swollen their effective capital ratios.

11.6.2 The Federal Republic of Germany

The supervisory authorities in the Federal Republic of Germany follow a narrow definition of capital. German banks already meet the 1992 target ratio, and have been expanding their balance sheets, using marked increases in share prices to raise new funds. As a result, FRG banks have improved their already conservative ratios to about 6 percent for Tier 1 capital and about 10 percent for total capital.

11.6.3 France

French banks are likely to hover close to the minimum capital requirements. Legislation for securitization may well provide the solution, by shrinking the balance sheet. Nationalized French institutions face restrictions on the issuance of new shares; they may issue only non-voting stock, with a ceiling of 25 percent of all equity. They also issue Credit Enhanced Perpetual Capital (CEPC) votes, a kind of perpetually subordinated and non-cumulative bond. It is unclear as to whether CEPC stock belong to Tier 1 or to Tier 2.

11.6.4 The United Kingdom

In general, the Bank of England has taken a hard line on capital adequacy in determining the weights assigned to different assets. During 1988 and 1989, the four largest British banks raised small amounts of capital for cash and a number of banks capitalized part of their property revaluation reserves. Also during this period, British banks issued about £2.5 billion of perpetual variable rate notes and term debt (mostly in 1988). The continued growth in lending, and the substantial provisions for LDC debt, resulted in a decline in the average capital ratio in 1989 to 9.3 percent. Nevertheless, all the big four British clearing banks comfortably exceeded the 1992 target.

11.6.5 *Japan*

The implementation of the risk-adjusted capital rules based on the BIS proposal was expected to have had a significant impact on Japanese banks. Regulatory authorities in the United States and Europe conceived the capital adequacy standards partly as a way to restrain the international growth of Japanese banks. It was claimed that the Japanese banks' relatively low levels of capital constituted a funding advantage. The substantial shortfall of Tier 1 capital was therefore expected to severely affect the strategic direction of the banks by slowing down the massive growth in Japanese bank assets.

The contribution of unrealized profits to Tier 2 capital, and the increased weight of overseas operations, made Japanese banks' capital ratios extremely sensitive to fluctuations in both asset prices and the exchange rate of the Japanese yen. Thus, although the big five banks raised a huge three trillion yen (21 billion dollars) by issuing equity and convertible bonds by March 1989, and attained an average ratio of 8.2 percent, a few months later that ratio was estimated to have fallen to about 6.7 percent, leaving almost all the major banks under target. Most of the decline was the result of the fall in the Nikkei stock index of approximately 20 percent in that period, which substantially reduced unrealized securities profits. A weaker yen also increased the weight of foreign currency assets, while leaving the size of yen-denominated equity unaffected, further depressing ratios. Assuming a continuation of these trends, or other developments (such as a sell off in Japanese real estate) the shortfall of capital might assume tremendous proportions. The banks will probably respond by acting on both sides of the ratio: raising additional capital, both equity and increasingly subordinated debt; and downsizing assets, including the elimination of high-volume, low margin activities, increased securitization of assets, and the reduction of activities abroad (see Salomon Brothers, 1990).

The agreements will be mandatory only for 35 Japanese banks with overseas subsidiaries or branches. All other banks will have the option of conforming to domestic capital adequacy regulations.

11.6.6 *Canada*

The Superintendent of Financial Institutions in Canada follows a liberal approach in implementing the BIS capital ratios. While Canadian banks meet Tier 1 ratios, they do not yet meet Tier 2 requirements. However, they are in a relatively favorable situation, since their need to raise Tier 2 capital (such as subordinated debt) will have only a marginal effect on their reported profitability.

11.6.7 The United States

Despite sizable off-balance-sheet assets, most US multinational banks should comfortably exceed the 1992 guidelines. A few multinational banks, however, will have difficulty complying with the minimum ratio. At least until year-end 1990, US regulators expect banks and bank holding companies to also satisfy the old 6 percent unweighted standard. The figures for 1989 show an improvement in the capital adequacy ratio for US banks despite the increase in provision for losses from LDC debt. The average qualifying total capital ratio for 12 money center banks reached 10.4 percent (5.9 percent Tier 1 and 4.5 percent Tier 2), and for a sample of 24 regional banks 10.6 percent (8.4 percent Tier 1 and 2.2 percent Tier 2). Only one bank in the entire sample (Security Pacific with a ratio of 7.25 percent) falls short of the 1992 required ratio.

The implementation and dynamic changes in the capital ratio in different countries reveal that, despite the shortcomings and limitations of the BIS proposals, the underlying aim of increasing capital and reducing risk is already being achieved. Only in a few cases will the target ratio be reached through accounting measures. In most instances the target will be attained through an infusion of cash capital, as well as changes in the level of risk.

Table 11.2 Elements of US banks capital

	Elements of Tier 1 capital (US$ billions)	
	Money center group (12 banks)	*Regional banks group (24 banks)*
Common equity	33.0	43.8
Perpetual preferred	5.7	2.5
Minority interest	0.2	0.1
Less: goodwill	(2.8)	(3.7)
Total	36.1	42.7

Table 11.2 *contd.*

	Elements of Tier 2 capital (US$ billions)	
	Money center	*Regional banks*
Hybrid securities	7.2	4.4
Tier 2 debt	20.2	13.5
Loan loss reserve	24.2	12.1
Others	1.0	0.7
Total	52.6	30.7

Source: Salomon Brothers (1990), A Review of Bank Performance

11.7 Improving Risk-based Capital Ratios

The importance of the new capital adequacy measure lies in its dynamic method of controlling the level of bank risk. Banks that are short of the required capital, for example due to rapid expansion or heavy losses, may correct the situation through one of several measures. Most of these measures result in distortions in bank decision-making, such as the composition of assets and liabilities, the leverage position, or the optimal size of the bank. The optimal adjustment (shadow price) of each bank depends on its decision-making at several key points, as follow.

11.7.1 Capitalized Revaluation of Assets

The most painless means of improving the Tier 1 capital ratio is by using accounting techniques with no economic implications. The most important such technique is capital issued against revaluation of assets. Revaluation of assets is allowed by accounting standards in only a few countries, the United Kingdom being most notable. Therefore, the large UK banks made wide use of this technique in 1989. The BIS standard allows for the inclusion of revaluation reserves in Tier 2 capital, if assets are prudently valued and fully reflect the possibility of price fluctuation and forced sale. The issue of capital against such reserves is not prohibited in the BIS standard.

This practice is an extreme example of the use of accounting techniques to improve Tier 1 capital. Other issues such as the treatment of profit and realization on long-term investment in securities, and the policy toward provision of doubtful loans, differ widely across countries.

11.7.2 *Dividend Policy*

Cutting distributed dividends may seem to be an easy adjustment in a bank's policy. However, the importance of dividend policy as a signalling device may significantly affect the market value of banks.

11.7.3 *Issue of Capital*

The issuance of financial claims does not necessarily coincide with the bank decision-making process, since it only affects reported profitability. The straight issue of equity against cash (including rights issues) is widely used in the United Kingdom, the Federal Republic of Germany, the United States, and Japan. (For example, Deutsche Bank has issued DM 12.3 billion, and Barclays Bank £921 million.) A new popular kind of Tier 1 equity, called "perpetual non-cumulative preference shares," is widely used in the United Kingdom and France (i.e., the Bank of Scotland and Crédit Lyonnais). Another type of issue is the variable rate loan, a liquid subordinated term debt (Tier 2 capital), issued for example, by Lloyds and National Westminster in the United Kingdom.

11.7.4 *Asset Restructuring*

The shadow price of undercapitalized banks can increase the cost of holding high-risk weight assets and off-balance-sheet items, and induce banks to change the composition of their assets. However, the profitability of transactions should be considered as well. In this respect low-margin, high-risk weighted loans are not attractive (due to their high shadow price). The reduction of these assets can lead to the adverse effect of increasing bank risk.

11.7.5 *Shrinking Bank Size*

Undercapitalized banks are expected to lose market share to more capitalized banks. The undercapitalized banks may recapture part of the lost business by using securitization (and fee income). Japanese banks, for example, are phasing out the system of compensating balances, and are increasing the use of government guarantee programs.

11.7.6 *Mergers and Acquisitions*

Mergers using exchange of shares falling in the category of "pooling of interest," are neutral in respect to the capital ratio of the merged firm (the sum of the two firms). Furthermore other purchasing methods reduce the capital adequacy ratio of the acquiring bank because of the expansion of assets and the potential creation of goodwill. Consequently, most mergers are expected to be in the form of exchange of shares among institutions having high capital ratios with banks having low capital ratios.

Appendix 1

Risk weights by category of on-balance-sheet asset

0%	(a)	Cash[6]
	(b)	Claims on central governments and central banks denominated in national currency and funded in that currency.
	(c)	Other claims on OECD[7] central governments[8] and central banks.
	(d)	Claims collateralized by cash or OECD central-government securities,[9] or guaranteed by OECD central governments.[10]
0,10,20 or 50% (at national discretion)	(a)	Claims on domestic public-sector entities, excluding central government, and loans guaranteed[11] by such entities.
20%	(a)	Claims on multilateral development banks (IBRD, IADB, AsDB, AfDB, EIB)[12] and claims guaranteed by, or collateralized by, securities issued by such banks[13].
	(b)	Claims on banks incorporated in the OECD and loans guaranteed[14] by OECD incorporated banks.
	(c)	Claims on banks incorporated in countries outside the OECD, with a residual maturity of up to one year and loans with a residual maturity of up to one year, guaranteed by banks incorporated in countries outside the OECD.
	(d)	Claims on non-domestic OECD public-sector entities, excluding central government, and loans guaranteed[15] by such entities.
	(e)	Cash items in process of collection.
50%	(a)	Loans fully secured by mortgages on residential property that is or will be occupied by the borrower or that is rented.
100%	(a)	Claims on the private sector.
	(b)	Claims on banks incorporated outside the OECD with a residual maturity of over one year.

(c) Claims on central governments outside the OECD (unless denominated in national currency – and funded in that currency – see above).
(d) Claims on commercial companies owned by the public sector.
(e) Premises, plant and equipment, and other fixed assets.
(f) Real estate and other investments (including non-consolidated investment participation in other companies).
(g) Capital instruments issued by other banks (unless deducted from capital).
(h) All other assets.

Source: Basle Committee on Banking Regulations and Supervisory Practices, 1988

Appendix 2

Off-Balance-Sheet Assets

Conversion of off-balance-sheet items to on-balance-sheet equivalents

Conversion factor (%)	Off-balance-sheet exposure
100	Direct credit substitutes, e.g., general guarantees of indebtedness (including standby letters of credit serving as financial guarantees for loans and securities) and acceptances (including endorsements with the character of acceptances)
50	Certain transaction-related contingent items (e.g., performance bonds, bid bonds, warranties, and standby letters of credit related to particular transactions)
20	Short-term self-liquidating trade-related contingencies (such as documentary credits collateralized by the underlying shipments)
100	Sale and repurchase agreements[16] and sales with recourse where the credit risk remains with the bank.
100	Forward asset purchases, forward deposits and partly paid shares and securities, which represent commitments with certain drawdown
50	Note issuance facilities and revolving underwriting facilities
50	Other commitments (e.g., formal standby facilities and credit lines) with an original maturity of over one year[17]
0	Similar commitments with an original maturity of up to one year, or which can be unconditionally cancelled at any time

Interest rate and foreign exchange swaps differ from the above, because banks are not exposed to the full face value of the contracts and only to the cost of replacing the cash flows if the counter party defaults. The credit equivalent amount depends on the maturity of the contract as well as the volatility of rates underlying the particular instrument. National authorities have two alternative ways in which to measure the risk:

1. The current exposure method

Current replacement cost is used to measure credit risk, by marking to market all contracts with a positive value. To this is added a factor to represent the remaining exposure during the rest of the contract, calculated on the basis of the total notional principle and the residual maturity as follows:

Table 11.3 The current exposure method

Residual Maturity	*Interest rate contracts*	*Exchange rate contracts*
Less than one year	nil	1.0%
One year and over	0.5%	5.0%

2 Original Exposure Method

A conversion factor, based on notional principle amounts underlying each contract according to its type and original maturity, is used to arrive at the credit equivalent amount.

Table 11.4 The original exposure method

Maturity	*Interest rate contracts*	*Exchange rate contracts*
Less than one year	0.5%	2.0%
One to two years	1.0%	5.0% (ie 2% + 3%)
For each additional year	1.0%	3.0%

(NB All the above conversion factors are subject to change as a result of changes in interest and exchange rate volatilities.)

Since exchange rate contracts involve a transfer of capital at expiry they are generally more risky, consequently they carry a higher conversion factor.[18] Subject to certain constraints,[19] banks may weight the net rather than gross claim arising out of swaps and similar contracts with the same counterparties.

Weights are applied according to the category of the counterparty once the credit equivalent amounts have been calculated, whether according to the current or original exposure method. A 50 percent weight will be applied in respect of counterparties which would normally attract 100 percent weight, though some national authorities reserve the right to apply the 100 percent weight.

Appendix 3

Table 11.5 Transitional arrangements

		Initial	*End – 1990*	*End – 1992*
1	Minimum standard	The Level prevailing at end – 1987	7.25%	8.0%
2	Measurement formula	Core elements plus 100%	Core elements plus 100% (3.625% plus 3.625%)	Core elements plus 100% (4% plus 4%)
3	Supplementary elements included in core	Maximum 25% of total core	Maximum 10% of total core (i.e. 0.36%)	None
4	Limit on general loan loss reserves in supplementary elements[a]	No limit	1.5 percentage points exceptionally up to 2.0 percentage points	1.25 percentage points, or exceptionally and temporarily up to 2.0 percentage points
5	Limit on term subordinated debt in supplementary elements	No limit (at discretion)	No limit (at discretion)	Maximum of 50% of Tier 1
6	Deduction for goodwill	Deducted from Tier 1 (at discretion)	Deducted from Tier 1 (at discretion)	Deducted from Tier 1

[a] This limit would only apply in the event that no agreement was reached on a consistent basis including unencumbered provisions or reserves in capital (see paragraphs 20 and 21).

Source: Committee on Banking Regulations and Supervisory Practices (July 1988, Annex 4)

Notes

1 See e.g., Dean and Giddy, 1981; Diamond and Dybvig 1983; and Bernanke 1983.

2 In England and Ireland, evaluation of bank capital adequacy ratios is based upon the amount of "free capital," defined as equity capital less buildings, equipment, commercial investments and goodwill.

3 Until 1971 the largest US bank to fail had total deposits of $93 million, whereas Franklin National Bank of New York, which failed in 1974, had total deposits of $1.4 billion.

4 Governmental deposit insurance arrangements exist in only a few countries: the United States, Lebanon, India and Canada.

5 Securitization is defined here as the process by which a bank removes assets from its balance sheet by selling them in the form of securities.

6 Included (at national discretion) gold bullion held in own vaults or on an allocated basis to the extent backed by bullion liabilities.

7 The OECD group is considered here to be comprised of countries which are full members of the OECD or which have concluded special lending arrangements with the IMF.

8 Some member countries intend to apply weights to securities issued by OECD central governments to take account of interest rate risk. These weights would, for example, be 10 percent for all securities or 10 percent for those maturing in up to one year and 20 percent for those maturing in over one year.

9 See note 8.

10 Commercial loans partially guaranteed by these bodies will attract equivalent low weights on that part of the loan which is fully covered. Similarly, loans partially collateralized by cash or securities issued by OECD central governments and multilateral development banks will attract low weights on that part of the loan which is fully covered.

11 See note 10.

12 Claims on other multilateral development banks in which G-10 countries are shareholding members may, at national discretion, also attract a 20 percent weight.

13 See note 10.

14 See note 10.

15 See note 10.

16 These items are to be weighted in accordance to the type of asset and not the type of counterparty with whom the transaction has been entered into. Reverse repos are to be treated as collateralized loans and where the asset temporarily acquired is a security which attracts a preferential risk-weight, this would be recognised as collateral and the risk-weighting reduced accordingly.

17 During the transition period up to the end of 1992 but not beyond, supervisory authorities will have the discretion to apply residual maturity as a basis for measuring commitments.

18 Interest rate swaps include single currency interest rate swaps, forwards, interest rate futures and options. Exchange rate instruments are similar to interest rate swaps but also include a cross-currency transaction. Exchange rate contracts with an original maturity of less than fourteen days are excluded, as are instruments traded on exchanges, which are subject to daily margin requirements.

19 Banks may net contracts subject to novation (supervisory authorities can

require a phase-in period before a novation agreement is recognised in the weighting process). Also the contract cannot be subject to close-out clauses.

References

Aharony, Joseph and Itzhak Swary (1981) Effects of the 1970 Bank Holding Company act: Evidence from capital markets, *Journal of Finance*, vol 36, 841–53.

—— Contagion effects of bank failures: Evidence from capital markets, *Journal of Business*, vol 56, 213–30.

Bank for International Settlements *Annual Reports*, various issues.

Barnett, Robert E., Paul M. Horovitz and Stanley C. Silverberg (1977) Deposit insurance: The present system and some alternatives, *Journal of Banking Law*, vol 94, 304–32.

Basle Committee on Banking Regulations and Supervisory Practices, *International Convergence of Capital Measurement and Capital Standards*, July 1988.

Benston, George J. (1983) Bank examination, *The Bulletin* of the Institute of Finance, Graduate School of Business Administration, New York University, no 89–90.

—— and George G. Kaufman, Risk and solvency regulation of depository institutions: Past policies and current options, *Monograph Series in Finance and Economics*, Monograph 1988–1 (Salomon Brothers Center for the Study of Financial Institutions, Graduate School of Business Administration, New York University).

Bernanke Ben (1983) Non-monetary effects of the financial crisis in propagation of the Great Depression, *American Economic Review*, vol 73, 257–76.

Black, Fischer, Merton H. Miller and Richard A. Posner (1978) An approach to the regulation of bank holding companies, *Journal of Business*, vol 51, 379–412.

Blair, Roger D. and Arnold A. Heggestad (1978) Bank portfolio regulation and the probability of bank failure, *Journal of Money, Credit and Banking*, vol 10, 88–93.

Cotter, Richard V. (1966) Capital ratios and capital adequacy, *National Banking Review*, vol 3, 333–46.

Dean, James W. and Ian H. Giddy (1981) Averting international banking crisis, *Monograph Series in Finance and Economics*, Monograph 1981–1 Salomon Brothers Center for the Study of Financial Institutions, New York University, Graduate School of Business Administration, New York University.

Diamond, Douglas W. and Philip H. Dybvig (1983) Bank runs, deposit insurance and liquidity, *Journal of Political Economy*, vol 91, 401–19.

Flannery, Mark J. (1989) Capital regulation and insured banks' choice of individual loan default risks, *Journal of Monetary Economics*, vol 24, 235–8.

Gibson, William E. (1972) Deposit insurance in the United States: Evaluation and reform, *Journal of Financial and Quantitative Analysis*, 1575–94.

Goldman Sachs (1988) Risk-based capital adequacy standard: Impact on bank portfolio and fixed income markets, Special Study, Economic Research.

Grammatikos, TheoHarry, Anthony Saunders and Itzhak Swary, (1986) Returns and risks of U.S. bank foreign currency activities, *Journal of Finance*, vol 41, 671–83.

Kahane, Yehuda (1977) Capital adequacy and the regulation of financial intermediaries, *Journal of Banking and Finance*, vol 1, 207–18.

Kreps, Clifton H. and Richard F. Wacht (1971) A more constructive role for deposit insurance, *Journal of Finance*, vol 26, 605–13.

Marcus, Alan J. and Israel Shaked (1984) The valuation of FDIC deposit insurance using option-pricing estimates, *Journal of Money, Credit and Banking*, vol 16, 446–60.

Mayne, Lucille S. (1972) Supervisory influence on bank capital, *Journal of Finance*, vol 27, 637–51.

Mingo, John J. (1975) Regulatory influence on bank capital investment, *Journal of Finance*, vol 30, 1111–22.

Paroush, Jacob (1988) The domino effect and the supervision of the banking system, *Journal of Finance*, vol 43, 1207–18.

Peltzman, Sam (1970) Capital investment in commercial banking and its relationship to portfolio regulation, *Journal of Political Economy*, vol 78, 1–26.

Pringle, John J. (1974) The capital decision in commercial banks, *Journal of Finance*, vol 29, 779–95.

Robinson, Ronald I. and Richard H. Pettway (1967) *Policies for Optimum Bank Capital*, a study prepared for the Trustees of the Banking Research Fund Association of Reserve Bankers Association.

Santomero, Anthony, M. and Ronald D. Watson (1977) Determining an optimal capital standard for the banking industry, *Journal of Finance*, vol 32, 1267–82.

Santomero, Anthony M. and Joseph D. Vinso (1977) Estimating the probability of failure for commercial banks and the banking system, *Journal of Banking and Finance*, vol 1, 185–205.

Sinkey, Joseph F. (1978) Identifying 'problem' banks. How do the banking authorities measure a bank's risk exposure, *Journal of Money, Credit and Banking*, vol 10, 184–93.

Swary Itzhak (1986) *Capital Adequacy Requirements and Bank Holding Companies*, Ann Arbor Michigan, UMI Research Press.

—— Bank acquisition of non-bank firms: An empirical analysis of administrative decisions, *Journal of Banking and Finance*, vol 7, 213–30.

Taggart, Robert A. and Stuart I. Greenbaum (1978) Bank capital and public regulation, *Journal of Money, Credit and Banking*, vol 10, 158–69.

Vojta, George T. (1973) *Bank Capital Adequacy*, First National City Bank, New York.

Watson, Ronald D. (1974) Insuring some progress in the bank capital hassle, *Business Review*, The Federal Reserve Bank of Philadelphia, 3–18.

12

The 1992 Single European Market in Financial Services

12.1 The EC and the Single European Act

The commitment of the twelve members of the European Community (EC) to achieving a fully unified internal market by 1992, was a major decision with important implications for virtually all aspects of international business, including, of course, banking. In the words of one highly regarded banking analyst:

> In our judgement, the advent of a single European banking market has far-reaching ramifications for the U.S., Japanese and European banking systems and may eventually be regarded in the annals of bank history as the single most important banking event of the twentieth century.[1]

Since the repercussions of 1992 will be quite extensive, a survey of the process itself is in order.

The first step towards a single European economy was the adoption in 1957 of the Treaty of Rome, which led to the creation of the six-member European Community (EC). While its immediate goal was the creation of a customs union to facilitate trade in goods, from its very inception the EC included as its objectives the achievement of free movement of people, capital, and services, as well as the development of common policies regarding agriculture, legislation, social affairs, and foreign affairs.

Implicit in the EC's goals was the laying of the groundwork for eventual European economic and political integration and even union. Nevertheless, until the early 1970s, the EC basically concentrated on completing the internal market for goods by consolidating and perfecting a customs union among its members. To this end it adopted an approach of harmonization, whereby laws, regulations, and standards of member countries were brought in line with each other. As a result, the Community achieved a significant degree of success in removing the most obvious obstacles to free trade in goods, such as tariffs and quantitative restrictions (quotas).

The period from the early 1970s until the mid-1980s was for the EC a time of geographic expansion. By 1986, the original six members had become twelve. It is moreover by no means certain that the EC will not expand still further. Future members could be countries on the "periphery of Europe", including European Free Trade Association (EFTA) members such as Norway, Sweden, and Finland, or others, such as Turkey; countries not in the EC for reasons of political stance, such as Austria and Switzerland, or even former Comecon members such as Czechoslovakia and Hungary.

Despite its physical expansion, a general dissatisfaction with the EC's economic performance had become apparent by the 1980s. The EC's share of world trade in manufactured goods declined from 45 percent in 1973 to 36 percent in 1985.[2] Furthermore, Europe seemed to be lagging in the high-tech and rapid-growth areas that were so vital to further achievement: in the mid-1980s these accounted for 22.4 percent of EC industry, compared to 27 percent for the United States and 28 percent for Japan.[3]

Perhaps the most dramatic effect of the perceived Euro-sclerosis was the virtual inability of the EC to produce new jobs, compared with the United States, Japan, and the newly industrialized countries (NICs) of Asia. At the same time, political and social changes in a number of member countries made them more receptive to seeking market-oriented solutions to the economic stagnation that seemed to be afflicting Europe.

As a result, the EC Commission in a 1985 White Paper, proposed a fully unified and integrated single European market as the best possible framework for ensuring Europe's economic progress. The proposal was subsequently adopted by the EC as the 1986 Single European Act. This definition of a single European market, which was clearly in harmony with the original goals of the EC, was visualized as "an area without internal frontiers in which the free movement of goods, services, persons and capital is ensured in accordance with the provisions of the Treaty (of Rome)."[4]

The present 12–nation single European market is the largest in the world by population – 323 million in 1987, compared to 244 in the United States and 122 million in Japan, while its GNP is approximately the same as that of the United States, and one and one-half times that of Japan. The European Commission proposed 277 specific measures to achieve the internal market. By the end of 1989, 90 percent had been formally tabled, with over 45 percent adopted. These measures comprise a program of three main goals:

1 Eliminating physical barriers (borders).
2 Removal of technical barriers.
3 Removal of fiscal barriers.

The economic benefits that will follow from the formation of the internal market will stem from four sources:

1 Higher productivity due to economies of scale.
2 Greater efficiency and rationalization resulting from increased competitive pressures.
3 Increased exploitation of comparative advantages made possible by an integrated market.
4 Dynamic benefits, such as increased innovation, resulting from the unification process.

12.2 The Single Market for Financial Services

The European Commission's 1985 White Paper, which was spurred by the inability of European business to compete on a global scale, detailed a timetable for the completion of the internal market by the end of 1992. As the internal market for goods was already well advanced by 1985, the White Paper placed its emphasis on progress toward attaining the remaining goal of free movement of people, capital, and services. The Single European Act, subsequently passed in 1986, contained a provision allowing for products that are approved and regulated under the laws of one member state to be sold throughout the Community.

Disagreement and dispute are thus substantially reduced, since each member state remains free to set its own laws, subject to minimum standards.

Financial services, and especially banking, received considerable attention, due to their impact on achieving efficient allocation of capital, and their resultant importance in attaining the overall goals of the internal market.

Moreover, financial services form an especially important sector of EC economic activity: they constituted 6.5 percent of GDP, and provided 3.5 million jobs, or 3 percent of total employment in 1988.[5] A 1985 study[6] of the structure of the three main economic groupings by value added on a sectoral basis, demonstrated the comparative importance of financial services in the EC, which generated value added of 253 billion ECU in that year compared to 163 billion in the United States, and 69 billion in Japan. On a relative basis, these services constituted 8 percent of EC value added, but only 3.1 percent in the United States and 3.8 percent in Japan.

The twelve EC countries are home to some 2,100 commercial banks and 550 branches of foreign banks, in addition to approximately 1,400 savings banks and 4,000 cooperative banks. The United States has over 14,000 commercial banks, 3,000 savings institutions and 14,000 credit unions, while Japan has approximately 1,165 banks.

The EC countries have 160 of the 500 largest banks in the world. Table 12.1 shows the relative share of the major trading blocs' banking systems.

The size of the EC banking system in relation to GDP was 151 percent, compared to 100 percent in the United States and 224 percent in Japan.

Table 12.1 Distribution of the 50 largest commercial banks, 1970 and 1988

Home area	*Number of banks*		*Total assets $US, billions*		*Percent of top 50 banks assets*	
	1970	*1988*	*1970*	*1988*	*1970*	*1988*
EEC (12)	16	17	156	2,258	31	29
US	15	4	188	484	38	6
Canada	4	1	35	82	7	1
Japan	11	24	89	4,662	18	59
Other	4	4	28	422	6	5
Total	50	50	496	7,908	100	100

Source: Hufbauer, Gary Clyde (ed) (1990) *Europe 1992, An American perspective*, The Brookings Institute, Washington D.C., p. 4

The proposal for an internal market in financial services is based on three pillars: the removal of restrictions on the free flow of capital, the removal of barriers to cross-border marketing and the provision of financial services and products, and a "level playing field" in terms of the supervisory and prudential rules governing financial services.

The first pillar, the requirement to liberalize capital movements, entails a number of difficulties, including national control of monetary policy and exchange rates, and problems of tax evasion and fraud that are bound to arise with the removal of capital controls. In response to these problems, a number of safeguards were adopted, so that the EC undertook a phased removal of all capital controls by 1990. Extensions were granted to certain countries up to 1995.

The second pillar, the goal of removing barriers to the cross-border supply of financial services and markets, is based on the general, long-held principles of the EC, and the third is the Commission's advanced approach to the regulation of the banking sector. The following specific concepts regarding financial service regulation have been adopted:

1 *Non-discrimination* between foreign and domestic residents in financial services has resulted in "national treatment," or providing foreign firms with the same opportunities as domestic firms, within a given state.
2 *Harmonization* of key standards concerning prudential supervision of institutions and consumer protection of investors and depositors is being effected. Previous legislation seeking Europe-wide harmonization has met with limited success. Currently, the Commission's approach is one of minimum harmonization.
3 *Mutual recognition* by member states of supervisory processes and authority is being instituted.
4 *Home-country control* will be instituted, the principle being that a financial institution will be ultimately controlled and supervised by the authorities in the country in which it has its head office, even when it has established branches, or is directly supplying services, in another member state.[7]

It should be noted that it is the combination of all these factors, and especially the principle of home-country control, which make possible a unified market. Non-discrimination alone, while providing a "level playing field" in each member state, would not eliminate the fragmentation resulting from having 12 distinct markets, while harmonization of all rules and regulations is too complicated to be feasible.

Although the principle of home-country control is essential to the process, it is not absolute. Host countries retain the right to protect the "public good" and public interest, in such matters as monetary policy or the regulation of branches, which can still be subjected to their controls.

The implications of the adoption of these rules are many and varied. Essentially, a single banking license will be valid throughout the EC. Any bank licensed in a member country will be free to provide, throughout the EC, any services allowed it in its home country, either by establishing branches or providing services directly across borders, without the need to obtain any further authorization in the host country.

In addition to banking, other financial services will also be affected. Investment services will be affected by the EC in two main areas: the provision of services to customers, and the trading of securities in the marketplace. The overall approach is to achieve both unified market efficiencies, as well as consumer protection, and system stability and safety. This will be accomplished by encouraging:

1 a single, accessible market for the trading and issuing of securities;
2 full disclosure of information to enable the proper evaluation of risk.

Prudential regulation is more difficult in the case of investment services than in banking, due to the greater diversity among national standards and regulatory structures, and the lack of harmonization among them. For example, in the area of capital standards there is nothing similar to the Basle Accord pertaining to banks. Nevertheless, the Investment Services Directive proposed by the EC Commission in 1988 will permit branching and supply of services throughout the EC on the basis of home-country control, analogous to the treatment of banks. To ensure competition, access to stock exchanges, futures and options markets will be equalized. Other EC measures and proposals deal with harmonizing listing and information requirements for securities issues, disclosure of major transactions, regulation of insider trading, and capital adequacy requirements for firms in the investment service business.

The insurance sector, though increasingly in competition with banks and investment firms in the supply of financial services, is much further behind on the path to integration. Aside from the reinsurance business, insurance has been highly protected in most countries, the regulations and restrictions inhibiting integration being much more extensive then in other areas.

For this reason, Community proposals have been much more modest and cautious in the case of insurance than for banking and investment services. The Second Nonlife Insurance Directive of 1988, calls for liberalized cross-border provision of insurance but not community-wide branching: host-country authorization and regulation will still be mandatory. In addition, even this liberalization will apply only to wholesale business, explicitly excluding the small-consumer, retail sector.

With the completion of the integrated internal market in financial services the overall impact of the steps in all three areas will be

> ... to bring down the costs of insurance, mortgage credit, consumer credit and brokerage services, which in many member states have remained high because of lack of national and international competition.[8]

12.3 EC Legislation on Banking

EC policy on banking has evolved gradually towards its present goal of allowing Community-wide provision of services based on home-country control with as little need as possible for host-country approval. Actual policy has been formed through specific EC legislation concerning banking, which, due to its importance, is briefly described here.

Abolition of Restrictions 1973 – The direct impact of this first effort to reduce national restrictions on banking services was very limited.

First Banking Directive 1977 – This was the first effort to coordinate bank regulation and to mandate cooperation between the supervisory authorities of the different countries. It defines banks, sets certain standards regarding solvency and liquidity ratios, secrecy, and capital adequacy, and eliminates home-country identity as a basis for refusing authorization.

Consolidated Supervision Directive 1983 – This piece of legislation mandates the supervision of banks on a consolidated basis. It was a first step toward the adoption of home-country control. It requires annual (at the minimum) assessment of the banking group by the responsible supervisor.

The 1985 White Paper on Completing the Internal Market, proposed some 307 directives towards achieving the unified market. Later, in 1986, the Single European Act amended the Treaty of Rome to expand and improve the Community's activities and decision-making powers. In its reform of EC decision-making rules and its setting of European unity as a concrete goal, it marked a significant shift of national sovereignty from members to the Community, and shaped the Community's subsequent powers and role in implementing changes.

Winding-Up Directive – Proposed in 1985, though still not adopted, this directive establishes the principle of home-country control in the treatment of unstable institutions. If a bank in an EC country fails, it will be rescued according to its home rules. Countries with deposit protection must extend that protection to branches in other EC countries, if the host countries do not have protection schemes of their own.

Accounts of Banks – Proposed in 1986, the directive on this issue specifies the format and contents of published accounts; standards should be harmonized by 1991 and publication mandatory by 1993.

Large Exposure – Proposed in 1987, this directive recommends standards for controlling large exposures, defined as 15 percent or more of capital, with single loan exposures limited to 40 percent of capital, and aggregate large exposures limited to 100 percent of capital.

Deposit Guarantee – This 1987 directive, completes the winding-up directive by requiring member states to establish deposit guarantee schemes. Deposit protection schemes were in place in Belgium, the Federal Republic of Germany, Spain, France, the Netherlands, and the United Kingdom. Italy, Ireland, Portugal and Denmark were expected to adopt them by 1990.

Bank Branch Accords – Legislated in 1989, this directive eliminates the need for branches of EC–domiciled banks to publish separate accounts in most cases. Non-EC banks may be made to publish accounts, depending on the level of standards and reciprocity in their home countries.

Own funds (*capital*) – A 1989 directive adopted the Basle Committee definitions for the EC. While the BIS standards refer to international banks and are not legally enforceable, the EC regulations cover all banks and carry the force of law.

Solvency Ratio – A 1989 directive proposed a minimum own-funds (capital) ratio of 8 percent of risk-weighted assets. Similar to, but not exactly the same as, the BIS proposals.

Mortgage Credit – The directive on this issue, which has not yet been adopted, extends the home country control principle to mortgage banks, so that mortgage lenders will be able to operate throughout the EC.

Second Banking Directive – This 1989 directive, which will become effective on January 1, 1993, essentially completes the single European market for banking by expanding the first banking directive of 1977, mandating mutual recognition of rules as the principle behind the Community's approach to the banking industry, and harmonizing supervisory rules.

Permitted activities will be allowed throughout the EC on a single-license basis for EC members, and on the basis of reciprocity for non-EC banks. It defines banking activities, and forbids discrimination against foreign banks. It mandates home-country control rather than business law harmonization, but allows for host country control regarding consumer protection laws and "public good" laws.

Other directives and recommendations cover electronic banking standards, consumer credit, payment systems, and sundry issues, while further legislation will undoubtedly be called for as the single European market develops.

With the exception of the second directive and the directive on mortgage credit, EC directives all concentrate on the harmonization of various aspects of the banking sector. The two above mentioned directives, which are likely to have the greatest impact on the banking sector, both stem from the concept of minimum harmonization.

12.4 The Issue of Reciprocity

A key issue is that of reciprocity between the EC and non-EC countries. Whereas EC legislation determines the nature, structure, and rules of the Single European Market for EC member banks, the application and interpretation of reciprocity will determine the treatment of non-EC member banks within the Single European Market, as well as having important implications for the domestic banking systems of non-member countries. The issue of reciprocity is controversial, highly charged, and very politically sensitive. It is also far from being resolved. Moreover, to a larger extent than other issues it revolves around subtle aspects of organizational behavior and decision-making which can be hard to specify unambiguously. Rather than being a clear-cut matter of legislation, the impact of reciprocity will depend upon many individual rulings of governments, EC bodies and other authorities, foot-dragging, timing and so forth. The main lines of the issue can nevertheless be discerned.

The starting point is the EC position that it will not automatically extend the benefits of the single European market (such as a single banking license) to non-members, unless it is required to do so by an existing international treaty. Since no existing treaty, particularly not the General Agreement on Tariffs and Trade (GATT), currently contains such a requirement, the EC will ask third country non-members who wish to receive the benefits of the single European market to provide reciprocity to EC countries in the given area. It is the definition, measurement, and application of such reciprocal agreements that form the heart of the issue.

While the GATT approach to reciprocity measures the benefits of mutual concessions in terms of the changes in trade, the EC calls for the evaluation of the level of trade. For example, were the EC and Japan reciprocally to grant each other banking concessions which increase each party's share of the other's market by 5 percent, this would be viewed as fair treatment according to GATT, even if the Japanese began with a 20 percent share of the European market, as opposed to Europe's 2 percent share of the Japanese market.

The EC approach would be to compare total market shares after benefits take effect, – in this case 25 percent against 7 percent – and ask if this is the result of truly reciprocal treatment.

The second banking directive caused great concern among non-EC countries when it appeared to require "mirror-image" reciprocity – i.e., in order for banks in countries such as the United States, Japan, and Switzerland to enjoy the benefits of the single European markets, they would have had to allow EC banks to operate in their countries exactly as they operate at home in the EC.

Such a requirement would have caused enormous difficulties, for example, in the United States and Japan, where the Glass-Steagall Act and Article 65 of the Security Law, respectively, still largely prohibit commercial banks from most securities activities. Whereas EC banks are permitted these activities at home, US and Japanese authorities are prohibited from allowing banks to pursue them. As a result, a demand for mirror-image reciprocity would have effectively barred such countries from enjoying the benefits of the single European market.

The Community has responded to this problem by formulating a more flexible definition of reciprocity. The essence of the solution is "national treatment," i.e., EC banks in third countries are to be treated no differently to domestic banks. This is essentially a call for a "level playing field" within the third country, though not necessarily the same field as in the EC. In addition, the European Commission enunciated a policy of "effective access," i.e., "European firms (in foreign countries) will enjoy market access and opportunities comparable to those granted by the Community". Clearly, granted the complexity and ambiguity of the issues, the resolution of the question of reciprocity will be a lengthy and difficult one, calling for a great deal of case-by-case treatment, and specific responses to different situations and circumstances. The EC has already indicated that its approach will be case specific and pragmatic. The current circumstances and atmosphere clearly indicate that Japan will be the most important test of the reciprocity doctrine, even though it is vital to all non-EC countries.

12.5 Impact on the Banking System

The impact on national banking systems of the 1992 process has become the subject of considerable debate. A preliminary assessment would seem to indicate that 1992 will not provide the impetus for drastic or revolutionary change in banks or the banking system, but will be another milestone in the continuing evolution of banking in response to a changing environment. Indeed, it can be assumed that many of the developments that will occur will be responses not to 1992 specifically but to associated and correlated trends, and thus would likely have occurred regardless of the specific EC timetable for the single European market in financial services.

The importance of the free market in financial services is the fact that it affects not only the efficiency of the financial industry itself, but the allocational efficiency of all the other sectors of the economy that rely upon financial services. The macroeconomic goal of improved allocation of savings and investments should result from the financial sector achieving: a higher return to savers; a lower spread between creditory and debitory interest rates; lower cost of capital; and better hedging and diversification techniques.

The theoretical sources of increased efficiency in banking are:

1 Economies of scale
2 Economies of scope
3 New entry into protected markets
4 Exploitation of comparative advantage
5 Convergence of regulatory policy.

These factors do not affect all areas of banking activity equally. In general, it can be assumed that the potential benefits are greatest in the area of retail banking services, though this is exactly where the greatest obstacles and counterweights are found. In the area of wholesale banking, where obstacles are relatively few, the potential benefits have already been almost totally exploited, since wholesale banking services have long been provided in a relatively unrestricted and thus efficient market. Moreover, there are significant countervailing forces acting upon the advantages cited above. Specialization and localization retain certain advantages; differences in national tastes and behavior will presumably remain; and the legislated formal abolition of restrictions will not necessarily carry through in the interpretation, application, and day-to-day policy of authorities in their treatment of foreign banks. Matters of the public good and monetary policy will not be affected by EC legislation, and certain "irregularities" will remain in even the most level of playing fields. Thus, it is quite possible that the actual impact of 1992 will be less than might be expected from a review of the legislation.

The existence of economies of scale and scope in banking are also the subject of considerable debate. What seems clear is that most European banks have probably already achieved a size where most economies of scale have already been realized. In wholesale banking this is undoubtedly true, as any economies of scale are probably fairly minor and easily achieved, while in retail banking which offers greater economies of scale, economies of specialization are also greater. Moreover, if there is still room for greater economies of scale, there is no necessity for a cross-border dimension: they can be achieved at least as effectively by domestic consolidation.

This is probably why up to now, domestic restructuring, as in Spain and Italy (with their low-efficiency banking systems) has been more pronounced than any cross-border expansion. Comparative advantages may allow some improvements in banking efficiency. It should be noted, however, that many apparent cases of comparative advantage (and disadvantage) probably stem from causes such as discriminatory tax or regulatory policies that will themselves be reduced in the post-1992 market, thus negating any impact from this source.

New forms of providing services may allow banks to achieve certain economies of scale, scope, and function without any change in organization, size, structure, or ownership. Salient examples include credit card corporations and automatic teller machine networks, which allow even small banks to compete on a more or less equal basis with much larger banks, even in those areas where large size would seem to be a basic prerequisite for effective competition.

Within the EC, the post-1992 era will probably see increasing convergence among banks in terms of product, cost, and structure. As already mentioned, this will probably be a result of a large number of factors, of which the specific 1992 legislation is only a part.

The European Commission, in its basic findings on "The Cost of Non-Europe", indicated the considerable theoretical price decreases possible in financial services (table 12.2).

Table 12.2 Estimate of potential price decreases in financial services (in percentages)

	Belgium	*Germany*	*Spain*	*France*	*Italy*	*Luxem-bourg*	*The Nether-lands*	*The UK*	*European 8 average*
Consumer credit	−41%	136%	39%	105%	n.a.	−26%	31%	121%	52%
Credit cards	79	60	26	−30	89	−12	43	16	34
Mortgages	31	57	118	78	−4	n.a.	−6	−20	36
Average retail	23	84	61	51	n.m.	n.m.	23	39	41
Letter of credit	22	−10	59	−7	9	27	17	8	16
Foreign exchange	6	31	196	56	23	33	−46	16	36
Traveler's checks	35	−7	30	39	22	−7	33	−7	19
Commercial loans	−5	6	19	−7	9	6	43	46	15
Average non-retail	15	9	76	20	16	17	12	16	22
Total banking	15	33	34	25	18	16	10	18	21
Total insurance	31	10	32	24	51	37	1	4	23
Total securities	52	11	44	23	33	9	10	12	25
Overall total	23	25	34	24	29	17	9	13	22
Indicative price reductions for all services	6–16	5–15	16–26	7–17	9–19	3–14	0–9	2–12	6–16

n.a. – not available.
n.m. – not meaningful.

Source: Adapted from Emerson, Michael, *et al.*, *The Economics of 1992*, p. 105

The average of the four lowest national price levels for a given service was taken to represent a low competitive price, from which theoretical price decreases were computed. Interestingly, indicative (as opposed to theoretical) price-level decreases were computed as being in a ±5 percent range around one-half of the theoretical price decrease (with additional adjustments in specific cases).

Among the interesting results is the fact that the possible price decreases in banking (21 percent) are significantly less than those of insurance (24 percent), and securities (25 percent), indicating that banking is already a relatively competitive industry. Moreover, there are significant differences both between countries and among products within a single country. Retail services show a potential decrease (41 percent), almost twice that of wholesale services (22 percent), confirming the thesis that the market for wholesale banking services is already a fairly competitive one. As one might expect, Belgium, Luxembourg, the United Kingdom, the Netherlands, and somewhat less expectedly, Italy, represent low-price banking centers, while Spain, the Federal Republic of Germany, and France are higher cost areas. While Spain is expensive and the Netherlands and Belgium are inexpensive in all areas, Germany is very competitive in wholesale banking, though it is high-cost in retail banking. The United Kingdom and France also display much greater efficiency in wholesale activities than in retail.

Table 12.3 Interest margins and operating expenses

	Belgium	*Denmark*	*France*	*FRG*	*Italy*	*The Netherlands*	*Spain*	*The UK*
Average margin on[a] demand deposits								
(1980–1985)	11.2%	16.2%	11.7%	6.5%	4.3%	5.6%	14.5%	10.8%
(1986–1989)	7.6%	12.4%	8.8%	5.5%		5.0%	9.3%	11.4%
Average margin on[a] saving deposits								
(1980–1985)	5.6%	8.9%	4.3%	2.8%	3.4%	2.8%	10.7%	2.5%
(1985–1989)	3.4%	8.9%	4.3%	3.2%		3.1%	9.1%	5.8%
No. inhabitants per branch	1807	1495	2176	1532	4187	1976	1185	
Operating expenses[b] per asset in banks	3.65%		3.3%	3.13%	2.95%	2.84%	3.4%	4.4%
Operating expenses in savings banks[b]	2.55%		2.5%	2.2%	2.3%		4.1%	

[a] Current short-term rate minus interest rate paid on deposits.
[b] Excludes interbank assets. Expenses on non-interbank transactions are calculated as follows: Total expenses minus (interbank assets X 1.8%) (end of 1986).

Source: Jean Dermine, (1990) "The Gains from European Banking Integration, A Call for a Pro-Active Competition Policy," Conference on World Banking and Securities Markets after 1992, Geneva

Data regarding interest margins, ratio of operating expenses over assets, and wage costs (tables 12.3 and 12.4), while not conclusive, do indicate the existence of considerable price differences across countries. Nevertheless, this does not indicate the inevitability of price convergence due to the existence of market imperfections, objective differences across countries, or externalities affecting the banking industry. It seems likely that these factors exist and will continue to have an impact on bank competition even after 1992. Hawawini and Rajendra (1990), and Ruthenberg (1990), examined the evolving structure and dynamics of the EC's banking sector. The creation of a single European market is expected to lead to mergers, acquisitions, establishment of de novo branches, and joint ventures between banks within and among countries. These changes will in turn affect the banking systems concerned in two major aspects:

Table 12.4 Salaries in the banking sector, 1984–1986

Country	*Remuneration per employee national average*	*Assets per employee (thousands ecus)*	*Average cost per employee (ecu)*
Belgium	1.856	916.54	37.672
Germany	1.099	1022.16	26.000
France	1.559	787.85	31.716
Italy	2.134	939.63	37.631
The Netherlands	1.193	1034.90	26.792
Luxembourg	1.904	3701.1	36.440
Spain	1.699	821.7	n/a
Denmark	1.259	749.56	n/a
The UK	1.994	1387.3	27.854

n/a: not available
Source: Dermine, Jean, ibid

1. The trade-off between structure (concentration) and performance (profits).
2. Operating efficiency as reflected in economies/diseconomies of scale.

These expected long-run effects are indicated by the fact that at present the European market is comprised of banking systems (EC as well as non-EC) that are overbanked, with intense competition and low price-cost margins, along side systems which are characterized by low to moderate competition and operational inefficiencies. This should attract new, well-run entrants into the less competitive markets. Moreover, convergence of banking regulations between countries, the harmonization of essential supervisory requirements, the standard range of products available to EC banks (the Second Banking Directive defines the core of permitted activities that fall within the definition of banking services), and the adoption of the principle of mutual recognition of national supervisory systems, will further stimulate change in the long-run.

Ruthenberg (1990), examined empirically the hypothesis that the cross-border activities will increase competition and thus reduce and possibly eliminate existing differences in cost inefficiencies, and arbitrage away price-cost margins.

His major findings are that:

- The estimated coefficient of the concentration variable (Herfindahl index) (H) and performance variables are positive and highly significant.
- Banks that have high net operating expenses tend to compensate themselves by increasing interest rate margins on loans relative to the marginal cost of raising deposits.
- Banks that assume higher risks in their operations (credit risk, interest rate risk, basis risk, foreign exchange risk, etc.) tend to support those risks by, ceteris paribus, higher loan rates.
- Banking systems that are characterized by low entry barriers (high ratio of population per branch-PNBR) are vulnerable to increased competition and thus lower margins and a lower Lerner Index (defined as interest rate spread divided by interest rate).
- The inflation rate and central bank discount rates were found to exert a significant effect on the performance of banks in the European Community. As hypothesized, higher rates of inflation tend to lower the Lerner index. The significant positive effect of the discount rate on interest margin suggests that banks adjust their loan rates in line with changes in monetary policy.
- The empirical results suggest that an integrated European market provides the opportunities for cost savings in large banking systems (e.g., the UK) as well as in small, inefficient banking systems (e.g., Ireland and Spain). These opportunities can be exploited through cross-border expansion.

The ownership structure of European banks in the post-1992 era is another area for concern. While initial reactions foresaw a wave of acquisitions and mergers resulting in a small number of mega-banks with Community-wide networks, more recent evaluations have been much more guarded.

As already noted, the economic and business rationale for creating banking behemoths is ambiguous at best. In addition, the present ownership of many large banks in the EC mitigates against their being acquired by a foreign bank: they are either nationalized (as in France), publicly-owned (as in Italy), cooperative institutions, or simply too large and important to allow foreign takeovers.

Outright acquisition of a large bank by a foreign concern has not yet occurred. Indeed, rather than true international mergers, other forms of restructuring are more likely to take place, such as domestic consolidations (as in Spain and the Federal Republic of Germany), acquisition of small to medium-sized banks which maintain their national identity, interlocking of minority interests, or the creation of alliances of financial firms.

In terms of business strategy, the overall impact of 1992 will probably be to reinforce and possibly accelerate existing economic and business trends, rather than to generate any totally new approaches. In the retail market, banks are likely to emphasize and exploit their existing, primarily domestic, markets, and see some expansion of their product line. Some reduction of cross-country price differentials will probably occur. Wholesale markets will probably see continued emphasis on export of products and services rather than factors of production, i.e., direct cross-border marketing of banking services rather than physical expansion of banks across borders. In the corporate area, banks are likely to increase their involvement in investment banking activities. In part, this will result from continued securitization and faster growth in the securities area than in commercial banking, and in part it will be a response to greater demand for these services due to widespread corporate restructuring in Europe, itself a result of the completion of the internal market. Thus, commercial banks will have to show increased expertise in so-called financial engineering, in financial advisory and corporate restructuring services (mergers and acquisition, leveraged buy-outs), investment and liability management roles, and sophisticated derivative products, in order to meet customer needs.

Gardener (1989), considered the impact of 1992 on the development of securitization in Western Europe. The post-1992 scenario for securities markets and related business appears to be one of increased capital market activity. In examining the two major forms of securitization – commercial paper and mortgage securitization – Gardener concludes that (p. 19):

> The impact of 1992 on the future of securitization should be positive but not dramatic if the recent deregulatory experiences of countries like the U.K. are any guide, ... the general prognosis is one of steady progress for asset securitization after 1992 as European capital markets and institutions continue to evolve.

Bank regulation within the EC seems virtually certain to converge on a low level of operative interference, and a concomitantly low regulatory burden. Indeed, the greater mobility of banking services post-1992 will lead to a migration of banking to those areas with low regulatory burdens. This will put pressure on national authorities to equalize the regulatory burden.

Norman (1989), attempted to assess the strategic impact of regulation on the location of banking institutions in member states of the EC. The study examined the current regulatory environments of the twelve member countries, and ranked them in terms of regulation, in order to establish which of them will provide the most appealing regulatory environment to take advantage of the provisions of the single banking license. The results are given in table 12.5 (based on a detailed comparison of the regulations in these countries). The weighting values were chosen arbitrarily, and while the final index figures are in themselves meaningless, they do provide a convenient way of establishing a regulatory ranking for each country. The findings are that the well-established banking centers provide the most appealing regulatory environment (the Federal Republic of Germany, Luxembourg, the Netherlands, and the United Kingdom). These countries, with their tradition of being international financial centers, would appear to offer the most hospitable regulatory environment to banks wishing to establish a presence in Europe.

Table 12.5 Regulatory comparison

	Establishment regulations	*Continuing regulations*	*Total bank regulation*	*Capital controls*	*Total regulation*	*Rank*
Belgium	9	31	40	8	48	5
Denmark	13	31	44	13	57	6
France	16	37	53	17	70	8
Germany	10	25	35	0	35	2
Greece	28	43	71	15	86	11
Ireland	14	34	48	13	61	7
Italy	30	40	70	21	91	12
Luxembourg	8	13	21	8	29	1
The Netherlands	13	29	42	0	42	4
Portugal	21	43	64	13	77	9
Spain	25	40	65	15	80	10
The UK	11	28	39	0	39	3
Average	16.5	32.8	49.3	10.3	59.6	

Source: Norman, 1989

Nevertheless, national differences, political risk, and perceived credit differentials will maintain a certain level of regulatory differences. Institutional segmentation seems virtually certain to decline as well, as savings institutions (such as building societies in the United Kingdom), cooperatives, and regional institutions come to resemble core commercial banks more closely.

Indeed, not only will regulatory convergence be felt within the EC; it will be felt between the EC and third countries as well. The greater weight of the united European market, as well as the specific applications of the reciprocity doctrine, are sure to put substantial pressure on the United States, Japan, Canada, Switzerland, and other countries to evolve toward the EC model of banking with few geographic or product limitations.

In addition to the immediate effects on the banking system of the internal market in financial services, a number of developments concerning the EC will have an important impact. The future of the political process of European integration will have a decisive impact on economic activity. The future of the European monetary system, the adoption of a common European currency, and the proposal for a single European central bank will have immediate consequences for the banking system, as will the achievement of free capital movements, already planned. In addition, a number of key issues, crucial to the future of the banking system, remain unresolved, such as tax harmonization, capital adequacy, and control of monetary policy.

12.6 The Response of National Banking Systems

It is likely that the process leading up to 1992's integrated European market will affect banks in a variety of fashions, although it is by no means clear that national identity will be an important factor in determining the banks' responses. In fact, the key effect of the process might be to induce regulatory convergence among countries, thus actually attenuating the importance of the national home.

If this is indeed the case, then the performance of banks will be determined by fundamental factors such as basic economic trends, performance in specific products markets, productivity, home-market success, and overall competitive health, rather than specific responses to 1992. Nevertheless, certain general comments can usefully be made regarding national groupings.

12.6.1 The Federal Republic of Germany

The preparation of most German banks for 1992 can be described as cautious. Indeed, German banks probably had a preference for exploiting new products in the domestic market, rather than international or pan-European activity, even before German unification became a reality.

There can be little doubt that recent events will decisively shift the focus of the strategic expansion of German banks to new domestic territory, geographically as well as product-wise.

German banks, with their relatively long tradition of free capital movements and openness to foreign banks, should be well prepared for the post-1992 environment; though their conservative managerial style and somewhat protected domestic market may have hampered the development of their competitive skills. They are thought to be particularly susceptible to foreign (especially American and Japanese) competition in the aggressive and dynamic investment banking type of activities, such as securities trading, fund management, and mergers and acquisitions work. On the other hand, they are exploiting their existing strong ties with industrial and commercial firms, and attempting to attain similar depth of penetration into the strong growth sector of middle-sized and newer firms. Insurance activities are another prime area for German bank expansion.

The Bundesbank and its regulatory policies will have to adapt to the post-1992 reality as well. Capital regulations will need to be expanded to deal with the definition of Tier 2 capital. The Bundesbank's traditional reliance on gentlemen's agreements in establishing codes of conducts for banks will also have to be brought in line with more formal pan-European policies.

12.6.2 France

The extensive reform of the French financial system in recent years has resulted in a banking system much better equipped to deal with international integration than would have been the case in the absence of the reforms. The traditional openness of France to foreign ventures has also helped prepare the country for European integration, while two other characteristics of the French financial tradition have probably had a negative impact – the extensive reliance on capital controls, and the strong role of government intervention.

Overall, the French banking system will bring a number of strengths into the 1992 market, including commercial banks of sufficient size and well-respected investment banks (banques d'affaires); considerable international experience; advances in application of financial technology, including ATMs and EPOS, and experience gained from adapting to a rapidly changing financial market within the country during the recent period of accelerated reform. Relative weaknesses include a generally low level of productivity; heavy dependence on interest margin income rather than fee income; a high-cost structure of intermediation; and still heavy state intervention.

The extensive branch network and evident surplus of banking capacity domestically will undoubtedly help to protect the French bank's domestic base, though this will be at the not inconsiderable cost of heavy overheads and expenses. Even though French banks have usually been considered weakly capitalized, they will evidently have little trouble meeting the Cooke Committee ratio of 8 percent by 1992, though there is a great deal of variation among them regarding this target. The 4 percent target of core capital will probably be more difficult to reach, due to the traditional reliance of the banks on subordinated and participating debt. Due to size and ownership characteristics, French banks do not appear to be especially attractive targets for mergers and acquisitions. While the large variety of banking institutions in France will likely pursue an equally wide range of strategies, it appears that they will have to emphasize fee-generating activity and universal banking activities to compensate for the high-cost, low-profit traditional intermediation they have relied upon in the past. They have already begun to make serious efforts in the areas of insurance and securities activities.

12.6.3 The United Kingdom

Due to their open, relatively deregulated environment and strong international presence, the London financial markets are probably already closer to the post-1992 European model than those of any other EC member. For the same reason, of course, projected changes are probably fewer, since the UK banking system has long experience in an environment similar to that projected for post-1992.

Since there are already few barriers to entry into the London market, 1992 should mean very little in terms of increased foreign competition in domestic markets. As surveys indicate, the costs of UK banking services are already among the lowest of all the countries in the EC, and only slight reductions in banking costs can be expected. Despite their substantial presence in London, foreign banks have remained overwhelmingly concentrated in wholesale and interbank markets, and have met with little success in capturing shares of the retail banking market. There is little reason to expect that 1992 will change this.

The foreign operations of UK banks may see a continuation of the existing tendency to shift attention to EC countries rather than the South American and Commonwealth markets, though this will be less because of the incentives to operate in post-1992 Europe and more out of a desire to avoid negative conditions in the non-industrialized countries. In so far as the cross-border provision of services is made easier after 1992, London's role as an international financial center might be enhanced even further.

British banks, due to their depressed share prices (with the lowest price/earnings ratios in the EC) and lack of either direct or indirect government ownership, appear to be relatively attractive acquisition targets for foreign banks. For many of the same reasons it appears unlikely that they will engage in large-scale acquisitions overseas themselves. Instead, they will probably try to expand into new product lines, both domestically and on the continent, utilizing, where feasible, strategic alliances and joint marketing ventures, rather than outright control of foreign ventures.

The issue of reciprocity between EC countries and non-members is of considerable interest to the members of the London financial community, as they have no wish to endanger London's unique international standing by subjecting it to EC policy constraints. Nevertheless, the overall impact of 1992 on British banks and banking is likely to be extremely limited.

Table 12.6 Stock market capitalization (outstanding) market value at 31 December, 1988

	Equity of domestic companies	*Bonds and debentures ($, billions)*	*Commercial paper*
US (NYSE)	2,366	1,561	420
Japan	3,789	1,135	29.7
Luxembourg	46	677	n.m.
France	223	365	10.5
Italy	135	n/a	5.2
The UK	711	559	5.0
Spain	91	67	3.3
Norway	16	32	3.1
Switzerland[a]	402	144(Zurich)	n.m.
Germany	251	n/a	n.m.
The Netherlands	104	131	0.9
Belgium	59	99	n/a
Denmark	27	159	n/a
Portugal	84	64	n/a

[a] Includes Basle, Zurich and Geneva.
n/a – not available
n.m. – not meaningful.

Source: Gardener (1989), tables 1 and 5

12.6.4 Non-EC Countries

Non-EC countries share a number of common concerns, many of which center around how third countries will be able to operate within the internal European market after 1992. The Community's application of the reciprocity doctrine is of overriding concern. As already noted, any insistence by the EC for mirror-image reciprocity on the part of third countries will cause great difficulties, especially for the United States and Japan. Even if national treatment is adopted rather than mirror-image reciprocity, there will still be pressure upon third countries to expand permissible activities and bring their regulatory policy into line with that of the EC. The size and importance of the European market will ensure that it is a powerful force in promoting convergence of structure and regulation among the relevant countries, and between them and the EC. Capital adequacy will likewise be increasingly mandated through international standards, with countries adopting similar policies and definitions as a result.

It should be noted that the impact of 1992 should not be over-emphasized. Many of the changes projected for the various banking systems will be the result of long-term general trends affecting all banks, and are likely to occur even without the completion of the internal market, though the latter event might accelerate the process to some extent.

12.6.5 Switzerland

Swiss banks are in many ways well positioned for competing in post-1992 Europe. They are accustomed to operating in a free and largely deregulated environment, have considerable experience in securities (either organic or acquired), and certainly have vast experience in international issues. The increased ease of post-1992 cross-border marketing of services, along with the increased freedom of capital movements, should provide Swiss banks with many new opportunities. In fact, adjusting to post-1992 conditions is likely to be easier for Swiss banks than for many EC-domiciled banks.

On the other hand, Switzerland is not likely to be a high priority target for EC bank expansion, as profitable areas of endeavor would appear to be few and far between, and the domestic market would appear to be of little interest.

In areas where some cartelization on the part of the domestic banks still remains, foreign competition might put some pressure on fees and income.

Switzerland will have some difficulty in adapting to EC expectations in a number of areas, including securities trading, bank secrecy, and tax policy, which might cause some friction in terms of reciprocity agreements.

12.6.6 Japan

The reciprocity issue is paramount in any discussion of the EC and the Japanese banking system. Japanese banks are the most susceptible to EC sanctions, and clearly have the farthest to go in meeting even minimal EC demands for reciprocity. The resolution of the issues involved is likely to be difficult and acrimonious.

EC-based banks, like all other foreign banks, have had a difficult time penetrating the Japanese market. Potentially lucrative as it is, few of the obstacles, formal or otherwise, appear likely to disappear quickly or easily. The increased leverage of the EC representing twelve nations in its dealings with the Japanese, might increase the pace at which the Japanese markets will open up.

The Japanese banks have been assiduously laying the foundations for their post-1992 activities in Europe. Due to fear of reciprocity-based limitations on their activities, both the "grandfathering" of institutions and the use of subsidiaries to attain domestic status have been used. On account of previous experience, Japanese banks are increasingly preferring organic growth rather than acquisition, necessitating a rather slow and measured pace for their expansion. It is unlikely that they will duplicate the large-scale and retail-oriented expansion strategy they used, for example, in the California market.

12.6.7 Canada

Canadian banks, which are already de-emphasizing the international aspects of their businesses, are unlikely to be greatly affected by EC moves. The deregulation of the Canadian financial system, along with the implications of the US-Canada free trade area, are likely to occupy them more than European developments. They are likely to pursue opportunities opened up domestically and in the United States, and only compete in those relatively narrow product areas in Europe where they have a specific advantage.

12.6.8 The United States

The impact of 1992 on US banks is difficult to predict. Direct effects will be limited to a tiny percentage, 20 or so in number, for which international activity is important (though they constitute only a small percentage of US banks by number, they do account for close to half of the banking system in terms of assets). Even for them, however, the immediate impact will be limited, as they have, with only one or two exceptions, concentrated on wholesale banking business, which will be little affected by 1992. They are, therefore, adopting a relatively low profile toward the European markets. They are likely to continue to forgo (or spin-off) retail operations, while emphasizing cross-border product-based and "niche" specialties, such as foreign exchange and interest rate risk management, rather than trying to provide a supermarket of services. Due to the expected growth of corporate structuring in post-1992 Europe, American banks may encounter a strong demand for their services in mergers and acquisitions advice and financing, because of their experience, perceived skills in the area, and relative objectivity – a result of their detachment and distance from the corporate entities involved. Insofar as the internal European market draws increased attention from US non-financial firms, American banks of all types might "follow their customers" into greater involvement with the European market, though this process would develop slowly, and certainly not in the short term. Its key impact might be on the regional and super-regional banks with little international exposure, who will have to provide such services to middle-market domestic customers attracted to the European market.

Approximately 80 EC-based banks currently operate over 200 offices in the United States, engaging primarily in wholcsale business. The possibility exists that with larger retail bases in Europe, and declining product and geographic segmentation in the United States, EC banks might find the United States an attractive area in which to pursue retail banking, as Japanese banks in California and various other foreign banks (usually targeting ethnic markets) already have. The EC as an entity uniting twelve nations might be able to exert its increased influence to accelerate the development of the necessary conditions.

In fact, the greatest impact of 1992 is likely to be its acceleration of structural change in the United States. Both geographic restrictions and product restrictions (based on the McFadden and Glass-Steagall Acts, respectively) are likely to come under increasing pressure. Thus, the convergence of the US and the EC banking structures might, sooner or later, lead to US banks developing more along the lines of European universal banks, with multi-state branch networks and investment banking and securities capabilities. Such restructuring will entail considerable consolidation in the banking system, along with functional and operational changes and increased and varied competitive pressures.

Regulation in the United States is likely to undergo structural changes as well. As regulatory policy and structure become more uniform and coordinated internationally, the segmented structure of US bank regulation, divided as it is between the states and the federal government, and even between different bodies at the same level, will become less and less tenable. Calls (and legislative proposals) for a single regulatory body to represent the United States in international forums have already been heard.

Assuming that the changes envisaged are brought about by pressure generated on the United States by a united European market, the net, long-run effect might be a strengthening of the competitive position of US banks vis a vis EC banks, resulting from the greater powers and firmer foundations of their US activities.

Notes

1 Hanley, Thomas H., et al (1989) *European banking integration in 1992*, Salomon Brothers, New York, p. 1.
2 Price, Victoria Curzon (1989) *1992: Europe's last chance?* in Dahrendorf, p. 11.
3 Emerson, Michael et al. (1988) *The Economies of 1992*, Oxford, p. 13.
4 The Single European Act, quoted in Overview: European financial markets – the Commissions proposals," in Jean Dermine, 1990 (ed), *European Banking in the 1990s*, p. 8.
5 Emerson, Michael et al. (1988) *The Economics of 1992*, Oxford, p. 98.
6 Emerson, Michael et al. (1988) *The Economics of 1992*, Oxford, p. 12.
7 This approach is similar to the regulation of foreign banks' activities in different states in the United States (International Banking Act of 1978).
8 Fitcher Geoffrey Overview: European Financial Markets – the Commission's proposals," in Jean Dermine (ed), *European Banking in the 1990s*.

References

Dahrendorf, Ralf, *et al.* (1989) Whose Europe? Competing visions for 1992, *Institute of Economic Affairs*, London.

Dermine, Jean (ed) (1990) The gains from European banking integration, a call for a pro-active competition, Policy paper prepared for conference on World Banking and Securities Markets after 1992, Geneva, February 1990.

—— European Banking in the (1990s) 1990, Basil Blackwell, Oxford.

Emerson, Michael *et al.* (1988) The economics of 1991 The EC Commission's assessment of the economic effect of completing the internal market, OUP, Oxford.

Gardener, Edward P. M. (1989) Regulation and convergence of capital adequacy, *Institute of European Finance Research Papers in Banking and Finance* 89/1, University College of North Wales, Bangor.

—— 1992 and the future of securitization in Western Europe (1989) *Institute of European Finance Research Papers in Banking and Finance* 89/2, University College of North Wales, Bangor.

Hanley, Thomas H. *et al* (1988) European banking integration in 1992 the competitive challenges facing US multinational bonds, Salomon Brothers, New York.

Hawawini, Gabriel and Eric Rajendra (1990) The transformation of the European financial services industry: From fragmentation to integration, *Monograph Series in Finance and Economics* 1984–9, Salomon Brothers Center for the Study of Financial Institutions, Graduate School of Business Administration, New York University.

Hufbauer, Gary Clyde (ed) (1990) Europe 1992 An American Perspective, The Brookings Institute, Washington D.C.

Norman Richard (1989) Regulation of Banking in the Member States – The EEC and its Impact on the Location of Banking Institutions in Europe post 1992, Price Waterhouse.

Ruthenberg, David (1990) Structure-performance and economies of scale in banking, in an emerging unified European market by 1992, unpublished manuscript, the Bank of Israel.

13

Trends and Developments

13.1 Bank Regulation: The Banking Industry Perspective

The underlying justification for bank regulation is usually presented from the point of view of society's overall welfare. Due to external diseconomies, bank failures carry a high social cost which is usually attributed to the so-called contagion effect, or the possibility that a single bank failure can cause a domino effect, leading eventually to widespread failures throughout the banking system.[1] At the same time, the social costs of bank regulation are usually seen as allocation inefficiencies caused by intervention in bank operations.

The rationale for bank supervision can be clarified by examining the regulatory process from the point of view of the management of the banking firm and the decision-making process of the banking industry. From this point of view, most regulatory structures represent a *quid pro quo* between interference in the bank's operation (which is costly to the bank), on the one hand, and protection of the bank's market, on the other hand. Examples of the most widespread constraints upon bank decision-making include capital adequacy standards, reserve requirements, solvency ratios, single-borrower limitations, and restrictions on permissible activities.

Table 13.1 summarizes the regulatory constraints placed on banks in our sample countries. These are intended to control the risks borne by banks, even though they may distort the decision process and result in the foregoing of profit opportunities.

At the same time, the regulatory regimes in most countries provide the banking systems with various benefits, usually involving the protection of market share. The nature of this protection is such as to complement and offset, to a degree, the inefficiency caused by regulatory interference. Notable examples of protective regulation include:

Table 13.1 Regulations governing continuing banking operations

Country	*Solvency*	*Large exposures*	*Reserve requirements*	*Investment restrictions*	*Other*
Switzerland	Adequate capital very conservatively defined include off-balance-sheet activities.	Unsecured loan Obligations may not exceed 20% and secured loans may not exceed 40% of a capital.	Primary liquidity – 2.5% from certain short-term liabilities. Secondary liquidity – 33% of excess short-term liabilities.	None	Banks must establish as a legal reserve 5% of net profit.
FRG	Loans and investments max. of 18x issued share capital + retained earnings. BIS capital requirements.	Max. 50% equity to 1 customer. Total loans > 15% equity limited to 800% of equity.	Must hold interest free deposits on ratio determined by maturity of liabilities.	None	Daily foreign exchange exposure max. 30% of all equity capital.
France	Fixed assets to fund 60% of equity + long resources. Liquid assets min. 100% of short term liabilities. BIS capital requirements.	Max. 40% equity to 1 customer. Total loans > 15% of equity is limited to 800% of banks equity.	Varies, 1–5% of some short term-items.	Max. 20% holding in a company that is not a financial institution.	Only authorised banks (French or foreign) are foreign transfer intermediaries.
United Kingdom	Capital to weighted risk assets of 8%, core capital element 4% (BIS requirements).	Max. 25% equity to 1 customer without prior notification. Over 10% must notify after the event.	If liability > 10m must hold 0.45% at central bank in non-interest bearing account.	None	FSA of 1986 introduced self-regulation and "polarization".

Country	*Solvency*	*Large exposures*	*Reserve requirements*	*Investment restrictions*	*Other*
Japan	Capital to asset – 4%, banks with foreign branches – 6% foreign risky assets 3.5 net worth. In 1988 BIS requirement implemented.	Max. 20% of the bank's capital.	Time deposit and CDs – 0.25%-2% (according to size of bank, and maturity).	Only banking activities primarily deposit taking and lending of money.	Individual ceiling on foreign currency position at the end of any working day.
Canada	Primary and secondary capital based on each bank's risk. In 1988 the BIS requirements were implemented.	Schedule I banks Max. 25% to single borrower. Foreign banks Max. 50%, and aggregate large exposure 400% of equity.	10% of demand deposit 2–3% of other deposits.	Banks are prohibited from making investments greater than 10% of equity and are not allowed to engage in most non-bank activities.	
The US	5.5%-6% primary and total capital according to bank size. BIS capital requirement since 1989.	Max. 15% of unimpaired capital additional 10% of additional loans if fully secured.	Transaction accounts 3% up to $41.1 million 12% above.	The Glass-Stegall Act and the Bank Holding Company Act, separate commercial and investment banking.	

Source: See the corresponding chapters in this book

1 Entry (and branching) barriers, shielding banks from competitors in different geographic areas, abroad, or in different industries.
2 Segmentation and specialization of the banking market between, for example, commercial and mortgage banks.
3 Interest rate controls to reduce competition amongst commercial banks.
4 Deposit insurance and other aspects of the "safety net."

Tables 13.2 and 13.3 summarize the major ways in which bank markets are protected in our sample countries.

Overall, countries can be grouped into three categories, according to the degree of regulatory intervention in bank decision making:

- Loose – the United Kingdom, West Germany, Switzerland
- Mild – France, Canada
- Heavy – the United States, Japan.

Observation reveals that there is a close positive correlation between the level of interference in banking operations and the level of protection provided by regulators. For example, in the United States and Japan regulators intervene heavily in bank decision-making, while providing the banks with a high level of protection as compensation.

Within this framework it can be seen that the cost of bank regulation includes the inefficiency caused by intervention in bank operations. This cost consists of foregone potential economies of scale, economies of scope, and lending opportunities. Empirical evidence suggests that larger banking organizations do not have a cost advantage over smaller banks, indicating that mergers between financial firms which increase the scale of operations will not yield cost savings. It should be noted however, that these findings were obtained under a regulatory framework within which the existence and profitability of small banks was protected not merely by efficiency but also by regulation. The result of this type of regulation is a low level of bank failures in countries with heavy regulatory intervention. This may be seen as evidence supporting the contention that the main aim of bank regulation is the prevention of bank failures and bank runs. Thus, current regulations represent a fragile balance between protection and intervention. The process of bank deregulation should create a new balance between protection and intervention: deregulation reduces supervisory protection (geographic barriers, interest rate control, segmentation, etc.) while also reducing intervention (expanding the bank's powers, reducing reserve requirements, etc.).

Without doubt, the newly less-regulated banks operating in an environment of increased competition and efficiency will be more vulnerable to risk. The effect of deregulation in banking is expected to be similar to that

Table 13.2 Regulations governing competition in banking

Country	*Licencing*	*Foreign purchase of an indigenous bank*	*Foreign establishment*	*Segmentation among banks*	*Branching*	*Bank merger*	*Interest rate control*
Switzerland	SFr 2 million. Most management must reside in Switzerland.	Permitted.	Branching of foreign banks is regulated reciprocity required.	Geographical segmentation between Grossbanken Cantonal and regional banks.	Authorization required only for branches of foreign banks.	Only the acquisition of major participation in foreign-owned banks requires authorization.	None.
Germany	Min. required Capital DM 6 million. In practice DM 10 million.	Permitted.	No specific restrictions.	No regulatory segmentation. banks differ in legal form and regional orientation.	Notification to the FBSO and the Bundesbank.	Notification to FBSO and the Bundesbank.	Interest rate decree March 1965–April 1967.
France	Authorization of French Treasury. Min. Capital FFr 30m if assets > FFr 1.2 billion, FFr 15m if assets < FFr 1.2 bil.	Purchase above 20% of equity requires authorization by ministry of Economy and of the central bank.	No specific restrictions.	Essentially eliminated although specialization remains.	Notification to the banking commission.	Authorisation by the committee on credit Institutions.	Direct control on bank lending and deposit rate since 1967 still in force with changes in maturity.
United Kingdom	5 million U.K. bank. No minimum capital for branches.	Permitted-central bank approval if above 15% (foreign and domestic bidders).	No specific restrictions.	Declining, although retail, building societies, other restrictions remain.	Notification to the Bank of England.	Subject to Fair Trading legislation. Prior approval if above 15%.	Recommended interest rate system of building societies. Clearing banks cartel on bank lending and deposit rate 1960–71.

Country	*Licencing*	*Foreign purchase of an indigenous bank*	*Foreign establishment*	*Segmentation among banks*	*Branching*	*Bank merger*	*Interest rate control*
Japan	Ministry of Finance approval Min. capital Yen 1 billion.	Purchase above 5% of equity required approval of MOF.	Restrictions on entry, branching, and activities, i.e., bond issuance.	Highly segmented: commercial, long term, trust, sectoral banks.	Authorization of the Ministry of Finance.	Approval of the Ministry of Finance. Above 5% subject to Anti-monopoly law.	Direct control on interest rates on all bank deposits and loans (end 1960) Currently no control on large deposits and negotiable instruments.
Canada	Schedule I bank no one shareholder more than 10% of equity. Minimum capital 2C$ million. Schedule II min. capital 5 C$ million.	The share of all schedule II banks should not exceed 16% of total assets in the banking system.	Restricted entry, branching, controls on aggregate market shares.	Chartered banks, trust companies, mortgage loan companies still distinct.	Prior approval for schedule II banks.	Mergers and acquisitions are subject to licencing as de novo establishments.	Interest rate (maximum) on banks loans of 6% per annum during the period 1961–86.
United States	Approval by comptroller of currency or state bank charter based on capital adequacy.	Purchase above 25% of equity subject to BHC Act and prior approval according to Bank Holding Company Act.	International Banking Act of 1978 generally ensures "national treatment" for foreign banks, but some special regulation (federal and state) remains; reciprocity is a factor.	Commercial, Thrift and Investment banking are distinct.	Under the McFadden Act, 1927, subject to state control including: – unit banking – state wide branching – limited state branching.	Bank Merger Act of 1960. Prior approval based in effect on efficiency and competition more liberal recently.	Reg. Q 1933–80 prohibition of interest payment on demand deposit and ceiling on interest on time deposits.

Source: See the corresponding chapters of this book

Table 13.3 Deposit insurance

Country	*Established*	*Condition of membership*	*Administration*	*How funded*	*Bank's annual contribution*	*Deposits covered*	*Accumulated interest covered*	*Level of protection for depositors*
Switzerland	1984	voluntary	private	no funds collected	–	Savings accounts and wage accounts. Swiss fr. deposits.	Yes	SFr 30,000 ($22,800)
FRG	1966	voluntary	private	contributions from participating institutions.	0.03% deposits	all	yes	maximum of 30% of bank's liable capital per depositor.
France	1980	compulsory	private	calls on participating institutions in event of loss.	depends on losses, annual maximum for small banks 1% of deposits.	FFr only	yes	FFr 0.4 million per depositor. ($76,170)
The UK	1982	compulsory	official	contributions from participating institutions. Fund ceiling is 6m.	minimum initial contribution of 10,000 further calls when necessary up to 300,000 ceiling of 0.3% of bank's deposit base.	£ only	yes	75% of deposits up to £20,000 per depositor. (£37,300)

Table 13.3 Deposit insurance—*contd.*

Country	*Established*	*Condition of membership*	*Administration*	*How funded*	*Bank's annual contribution*	*Deposits covered*	*Accumulated interest covered*	*Level of protection for depositors*
Japan	1971	compulsory	semi-official	contributions from participating institutions and government.	0.012% of savings deposits at year end annually.	Yen only	yes	Up to Y 10 mil. per depositor. ($74,000)
Canada	1967	compulsory	official	contributions from participating institutions.		Since 1983 private sector domestic Canadian dollars deposits.	yes	C$ 60,000. ($50,720)
The US	1936	voluntary	official	contributions from participating institutions.	0.083% of insured deposits (0.23% from 1991).	all	yes	$100,000

Dollar equivalent at exchange rates prevalent at the end of 1990.

Source: *The Economist*, March 10, 1990, and various other sources

in other industries, such as the airline and trucking industries in the United States. It can be expected to lead in the first stage to a major restructuring that will be accompanied by bank failures and bank mergers. In an unregulated banking environment the uniqueness of the banks is greatly reduced and competition is enhanced. In other words, in a less regulated, and thus less protected, banking industry, an inefficient bank is more likely to disappear, and any potential economies of scale and scope are more likely to be exploited.

The US experience of regulation-deregulation and their effect on banks represents a radical change in the structure of the banking system. As the change appears to be essentially the same in other countries, even though it may be of a different order of magnitude and involve considerably more leads and lags (as in Japan), the US experience deserves further examination.

13.2 The Regulation–deregulation Process in the United States

Concern for safety and soundness prompted much of the restrictive bank legislation of the 1933–4 period. The package of regulation which followed the banking system crisis of 1933 is based on the two basic components mentioned earlier.

The Risk Control Component:

1 Separation of commercial and investment banking.
2 Capital adequacy regulation.

Protection:

1 Regulation Q (interest rate control).
2 The McFadden Act (prohibition on interstate branching).
3 Deposit insurance and the federal safety net.
4 Separation of depository and non-depository institutions.

13.2.1 The Risk Control Component

1 The Banking Act of 1933 (The Glass-Steagall Act) mandates the separation of commercial and investment banking. Moreover, it prohibits banks and bank holding companies from underwriting or dealing in corporate debt or equity securities, from owning stock and from managing mutual funds. Banks are also prohibited from underwriting insurance or directly investing in real estate. They are limited to investing in, dealing in, and distributing US government securities. Two concerns underlie the Glass-Steagall Act: potential conflicts of

interest, and the safety and soundness of the banking system. In other words, the motivating force was the fear that involvement in securities activities would increase bank risk.

2 The capital adequacy requirements imposed since 1933 by US regulators are intended to protect depositors and to prevent bank failures (thus protecting FDIC funds). In 1978, the three regulatory agencies issued a uniform rating system called CAMEL, which included a capital adequacy test. In 1982, the Federal Reserve and the comptroller of currency adopted a capital standard (5.5 percent primary and 6.0 percent total equity), and, finally, the BIS capital adequacy requirements were adopted in 1989. The purpose of capital adequacy requirements is to control bank risk, albeit at the expense of foregone opportunities.

13.2.2 Protection

The major regulations that protect commercial banks include the following:

1 Regulation Q prohibits banks from paying interest on demand deposits and sets a ceiling on interest payments on time and saving deposits. On the other hand, the interest rate banks can charge non-business borrowers is usually limited by state usury laws.

2 The McFadden Act of 1927 and the Banking Act of 1933, prohibit interstate branching by making all branching subject to state authority. The Douglas Amendment to the Bank Holding Company Act of 1956 prohibits bank holding companies from acquiring banks in more than one state.

3 The Federal Deposit Insurance Corporation was established in 1933 to provide protection for deposits held at commercial banks. Deposit insurance generally extends to checking, time, and savings accounts, or any combination of such accounts held by individuals or businesses up to $100,000 in aggregate in domestic branches of an insured bank. The bank pays a constant rate premium per dollar of deposits.

In addition, competition between banks and other financial institutions is limited by restrictions on the kind of services each can offer (such as deposit insurance). The federal safety net as developed and practised by regulators includes (in addition to deposit insurance) federal intervention to prevent crisis or failure in the banking system.

The structure of the regulation instituted following the banking crisis of the 1930s emphasized the dual need of controlling bank risk-taking, while also providing protection to the banks. In this setting, competition among banks, and between banks and other financial institutions, was suppressed. Interstate branching was prohibited by federal law, and the ability of banks to compete for demand deposits was limited by Regulation Q. The major purpose of these anti-competitive laws was to ensure the "safety and soundness" of banks by preventing destructive competition, which regulators believed had caused the collapse of the banking system in the 1930s. The FDIC intended to prevent bank runs caused by bank failures. The outcome of the effort to maintain the fragile balance between safety requirements, which control bank risk, and protection, which limits competition, was a banking system comprising a large number of small banks that relied heavily on their immediate local area as a source of deposits and loan demand. Against this background, it is not surprising that no economies of scale or economies of scope are to be found in empirical studies covering the period from the beginning of the 1940s to the beginning of the 1970s, or that the number of bank failures remained low.

By 1970, banks were facing a much more competitive environment, due to the decreasing effectiveness of protective regulation. The developments which exposed banks to competition included: rising interest rates, inflation, non-bank competition (from commercial firms exploiting loopholes in banking laws), exposure to international banking (partly to avoid domestic regulation), and the development of the capital market as a substitute for banking (securitization).

These factors contributed to the process of liberalization which began in the 1970s with the removal by the Federal Reserve of the Regulation Q ceiling from negotiable CDs and other instruments. The major steps in this process included the following.

Deregulation

The Depository Institutions and Deregulation and Monetary Control Act of March 1980 (DIDMCA) and the Depository Institution Act of 1982 (DIA), are widely considered to be the most significant pieces of bank legislation passed since the Banking Act of 1933 (see Aharony, Saunders, and Swary, 1988). A key component of these acts was the removal of interest rate ceilings and entry barriers with respect to thrift institutions wishing to provide financial services previously preserved for commercial banks. Thus, the acts increased competition and risk in banking.

Relaxation of geographic expansion restrictions

The relaxation of geographic restrictions on bank operations has encouraged greater merger activity. The limitation on geographic expansion, made official in the McFadden Act and the Douglas Amendment to the Bank Holding Act, prohibits multi-bank holding companies from acquiring a bank in another state unless that state allows for such entry. However, from 1982, when New York became the first state to endorse legislation providing for cross-border affiliations, to mid-1989 44 states had sanctioned some type of interstate expansion provision.

To date, 11 states – Alaska, Arizona, Idaho, Maine, New Mexico, Nevada, Oklahoma, Oregon, Texas, Utah and Wyoming – have enacted legislation permitting unrestricted interstate banking.

Capital adequacy requirements

The Federal Reserve Board implemented a risk-based capital requirement in January 1989. This has established a systematic analytical framework which is more sensitive to differences in risk profiles among banking organizations, and takes off-balance-sheet exposures explicitly into account in assessing capital adequacy. These capital requirements are expected to be binding and to substantially affect banking policies.

Bank powers

In 1987, the Federal Reserve Board began approving applications submitted by bank holding companies to allow wholly-owned, non-bank subsidiaries to underwrite and deal in certain bank-ineligible securities. It is believed that bank powers will be further expanded in the future.

As a result of this dynamic process of deregulation and decreased protection, commercial banks found themselves competing with investment banks, finance companies, and other financial institutions. The increased competition and reduced protection had the immediate effect of causing a widespread restructuring of the banking industry, as can be seen in table 13.4. There has been a dramatic increase in bank failures since the beginning of the 1980s, a sharp rise in the number of problem banks, and an acceleration of bank merger activity. The forces behind this restructuring include both the sharp decline in asset quality, and the effect of increased competition and reduced protection. This process has put the federal safety net in general, and deposit insurance in particular, under heavy criticism in recent years, since they contradict the basic philosophy behind deregulation. Specifically, the advance of deregulation requires a basic change in regulatory protection as well.

In sum, the non-competitive banking market which developed in the United States as a result of regulatory interference, was shielded by the protective facets of that same regulatory regime. The deregulatory process tempered both these features, increasing competition and leading to a rise in problem banks, mergers, and failures. The intensity of the process, which is basically similar in all countries, is a function of the prior level of both regulation and protection. Thus, the process in Japan, with its heavily regulated environment similar to that of the United States, will probably

Table 13.4 Restructuring of the US banking system

	Bank failures			*Bank mergers and acquisitions*	
Year (period)	*Number of banks*	*Total deposits ($ millions)*	*Number of problem banks*	*Number*	*Assets acquired ($ millions)*
1941–1950	7.3[a]	9.9[a]		n.a.	n.a.
1950–1960	4.3[a]	10.5[a]		n.a.	n.a.
1960–1964	5.1[a]	14.0[a]		152.4[a]	1,780.2[a]
1965–1969	7.2[a]	45.0[a]		148.8[a]	2,800.2[a]
1970	8	55.2		247	6,663
1971	6	132.1		195	5,647
1972	6	99.8		280	9,000
1973	6	971.3		321	10,864
1974	4	1,575.8		262	9,118
1975	14	340.6		137	6,819
1976	17	865.7		135	5,348
1977	6	205.2		138	7,873
1978	7	854.2		144	5,520
1979	10	110.7		179	7,491
1980	10	216.3		188	9,330
1981	10	3,826.0	196	359	19,546
1982	42	9,908.4	326	422	37,129
1983	48	5,441.6	603	432	42,952
1984	79	2,883.2	800	553	82,900
1985	118	8,059.4	1,098	553	64,725
1986	138	6,471.1	1,457	625	89,100
1987	184	6,281.5	1,559	910	131,410
1988	200	24,931.3	1,334	n.a.	n.a.
1989	206	24,090.0	1,093	n.a.	n.a.

n.a.: not available.

[a] Annual average for the period.

Sources: 1 Federal Deposit Insurance Corporation, Annual Report, various issues

2 Burns, Arthur F. (1988) The Ongoing revolution in American banking, American Enterprise Institute for Public Policy Research, Washington D.C.

3 Rhoades, Stephen A. (1985) Mergers and acquisitions by commercial banks; 1960–1983, Staff Studies, Board of Governors of the Federal Reserve System, no. 142.

4 The FDIC, *Quarterly Banking Profile*, various issues

display a pattern close to the American one, including increased bank mergers and even failures. However, the large-scale restructuring of the banking industry is probably transitory, representing a process of adjustment to the new environment of financial services.

13.3 Performance – A Comparative Analysis

The analysis in this section relates to the profit and loss statements of the 49 large banks in our seven sample countries, (table 13.5) and is based on the IBCA data. It should be noted, however, that the comparison is limited in nature and can only serve to illustrate general trends. Among the factors responsible for this constraint are the following:

Table 13.5 Indicators of operation of the major banks in sample countries

Country	*Number of banks*[a]	*Total assets*	*Average bank size (assets)*
Switzerland	5	319	64
FRG	3	394	131
France	4	705	176
UK	4	563	141
Japan[b]	13	2,929	225
Canada[c]	5	315	63
US	15	1,027	68
Total	49	6,252	128

[a] The names of the banks included in each country are given in the corresponding chapter.
[b] Data for March 31, 1989.
[c] Data for October 31, 1988.

Source: See corresponding chapters in this book

- Because of differences in the accounting system from one country to another, and inconsistency in accounting treatment among countries, biases may exist. The most important parameter in this context is undoubtedly the loan loss provision.
- Due to regulatory intervention, competition, capital market status, etc., the function of the banking system may differ from one country to the next.
- Different countries may be at different stages in the deregulation process. Whereas deregulation has been having a major impact in the United States

since the beginning of the 1980s, it reached Japan only at the end of that decade.

- Developments in the big banks do not necessarily represent the performance of the entire banking system.

Table 13.6 Indicators of operations – the major banks in seven countries (All figures are in percentages)

Year	*Swiss*	*FRG*	*France*	*UK*	*Japan*	*Canada*	*US*
a The annual increase in loans (real terms)							
1988	14.5	4.4	15.9	15.9	10.2	2.4	-2.6
1987	9.3	6.4	6.5	-0.7	14.5	1.3	-4.10
1986	7.4	7.6	1.3	1.9	6.9	-0.3	3.77
1985	4.5	0.0	-7.8	-7.4	12.7	4.4	1.25
1984–8	40.4	19.5	15.2	8.7	52.1	8.0	-1.9
b Annual nominal growth of earning assets							
1988	8.4	6.1	15.4	15.8	15.1	2.1	0.2
1987	6.0	13.2	9.4	2.1	14.6	4.1	1.3
1986	12.0	6.9	1.8	8.1	16.5	3.4	8.2
1985–8	28.7	28.4	28.2	28.0	51.6	10.0	10.7
c Net spread							
1988	0.75	1.87	1.97	3.16	0.99	3.08	3.32
1987	0.69	1.95	2.07	3.15	1.06	2.78	3.10
1986	0.76	2.29	2.09	3.05	1.13	2.76	3.05
1985	0.78	2.15	2.07	3.05	0.97	2.59	2.96
1984	0.71	2.16	1.98	2.95	1.10	2.36	2.70
d Annual growth of net interest income							
1988	14.3	4.9	8.8	12.1	11.3	14.1	12.1
1987	0.2	-5.7	6.3	5.3	10.0	3.8	2.6
1986	4.1	13.2	3.2	6.6	19.2	8.4	6.4
1985–8	19.3	12.0	19.3	25.1	46.0	28.4	22.3
e Non-interest income/net interest							
1988	162	49	35	60	24	38	68
1987	185	44	30	58	26	37	73
1986	177	37	33	53	25	31	65
1985	161	38	27	50	17	29	53
1984	161	33	28	55	17	27	47

Table 13.6—*contd.*

Year	*Swiss*	*FRG*	*France*	*UK*	*Japan*	*Canada*	*US*
f Personnel expenses/operating income							
1988	40	44	40	39	28	32	33
1987	39	44	42	40	30	32	35
1986	37	41	41	40	33	32	34
1985	37	41	43	40	42	33	32
1984	39	41	41	41	38	35	–
g Deposits/loans							
1988	98	67	82	132	128	96	103
1987	107	67	85	139	125	97	104
1986	114	66	91	140	125	98	99
1985	117	62	86	139	124	97	98
1984	126	61	81	147	131	97	–
h Equity/total assets							
1988	6.2	3.6	2.7	7.1	2.7	5.7	5.1
1987	6.2	3.6	2.6	6.6	2.4	5.3	4.4
1986	6.1	3.7	2.5	6.7	2.0	5.6	5.1
1985	6.0	3.5	1.8	5.8	2.1	4.8	4.9
1984	5.4	3.1	1.5	3.8	2.3	4.2	4.7

13.3.1 Net Interest Income

Net interest is still the major source of income in our sample, prior expectations of a decline in this source notwithstanding. Changes in the magnitude of net interest income have been caused primarily by four factors:

1 The growth of the loan portfolio.
2 The spread between the interest paid on sources and interest charged on uses.
3 Changes in the composition of the loan portfolio, due to different spreads on international, and domestic retail and wholesale lending.
4 Competition among financial institutions.

In terms of size, as can be seen in table 13.6, during the period examined the real growth of the loan portfolio in Japanese and Swiss banks was the most impressive (52.1 and 40.4 percent, respectively). The net spread in almost all the countries remained quite stable during this period. However, in all our sample countries, the stability of the net spread resulted from the combination of a decline in interest rate margins and an offsetting change in the composition of the loan portfolio, for example, by increasing the proportion of loans with high interest margins (mostly retail) and decreasing the proportion of wholesale loans (often international). This produced a significant increase in net interest income in Japan. In addition, the continual elimination of low margin loans extended during the period of rapid bank expansion, either by maturation or write off, contributes to a higher reported net spread.

13.3.2 Provision for Doubtful Loans

The provision for doubtful loans was a major factor in determining the performance of banks during the period examined. However, the level of disclosure with respect to this item is insufficient and its treatment is inconsistent among countries and over time, not to speak of the special treatment of South American debt, which made the analysis of this item almost impossible. These contingencies notwithstanding, our effort to determine the overall "regular" provisions for doubtful loans as a percentage of net interest income, yielded the following figures for the period examined:

Canada	– 26.2 percent
France	– 23.8 percent
FRG	– 14.7 percent
Japan	– 4.2 percent
UK	– 23.2 percent
US	– 23.1 percent

13.3.3 Non-interest Income

The proportion of non-interest income to net interest income increased significantly in all countries, except for the special case of Switzerland. Swiss banks have always enjoyed a large share of non-interest income, produced by the special nature of Swiss banking, including fiduciary accounts. In addition, the rapid growth in their loan portfolios produced correspondingly rapid growth in net interest income, keeping the non-interest/net interest ratio approximately stable.

However, the general picture of an increased share of non-interest income clearly demonstrates an important trend in these banks – a de-emphasis of traditional intermediation, which produces interest income, and a turn toward fee income generating activities.

13.3.4 *Personnel Expenses/Operating Income*

This ratio represents the cost of personnel expenses to operating income. Figures for employees of different levels are included, the assumption being that on average, employees in non-banking activities are of higher quality and therefore more costly. The figures in table 13.6 indicate that countries with a higher proportion of non-interest income do in fact have a slightly higher personnel expense to operating income ratio (see figures for Switzerland and the Federal Republic of Germany). However, the differences are not significant. The special rigidities of wages and labor markets make the interpretation of this ratio very difficult.

The end result of comparing the performance of banking systems in different countries seems to indicate that, in the short run, performance is mostly affected by macroeconomic factors such as the level of interest rates, the level of economic activity (recession), the deregulation process, and specific factors such as the South American debt crisis or stock exchange performance.

Unexpected changes in the interest rate

Conventional wisdom has long viewed financial intermediaries, such as banks, as being susceptible to interest rate risk. This is so because of their propensity to undertake a maturity transformation, or intermediation function, by lending long (often at fixed rates) and borrowing short (often at variable rates). Although there is no generally accepted view as to why banks have an advantage in undertaking this asset transformation function compared to other firms,[2] banks typically keep title to the relatively long-term loan portfolios they originate while selling deposit contracts of short maturity. A priori, such mismatched asset-liability structures make the earnings of banks (stock values) more susceptible to interest rate surprises than those of firms who choose not to specialize in providing maturity transformation services.

The empirical evidence on the sensitivity of bank earnings (stock values) to interest rate surprises is less than clear cut. Specifically, Flannery (1981, 1983), in examining the sensitivity of large and small bank net current operating earnings to interest rate movements, found a significant long-run impact for only two of the 15 large banks sampled, while for small banks only seven out of 60 were significantly affected (all in a positive direction). Elsewhere, Maisel and Jacobson (1978), arrived at basically the same conclusions. By comparison, Flannery and James (1984), and Aharony, Saunders and Swary (1986), using a variant of the capital asset pricing model to analyze the separate effects of market returns and unexpected interest rate changes on bank stock returns, found that (1) on average there was a statistically significant negative relationship between bank stock returns and (unexpected) interest rate changes (over the January 1976 to November 1981 period), and (2) this effect varied cross-sectionally according to the maturity of a bank's net nominal assets. This result suggests that the monetary policy environment may have an important effect on the relationship between interest rates and stock returns. However, Chance and Lane (1980), using a similar methodology over an earlier, more stable interest rate period (1972–6), found that unexpected interest rate changes had no effect on bank stock returns (beyond their impact on market returns in general).

In general, the empirical evidence has tended to support a negative association between the banks' market value and interest rate shocks, especially in periods of relatively high monetary policy/interest rate uncertainty.

The increased level of interest rates in West Germany and Japan in 1989 negatively affected bank performance in both countries. The, as yet only partially reported, losses include the decline in the market value of bond portfolios and the implicit value of loan portfolios, which will be fully reflected in financial statements with a delay.

Bank losses on loans due to recession in certain industries

The losses on real estate and property loans in the United States and the United Kingdom led to the poor performance of banks in 1989 and 1990.

Deregulation

As discussed earlier, the deregulation process entails a transition period for banks in which restructuring occurs, and increased risk and reduced profits are observed. This process, especially in the United States and Japan, has resulted in a large number of bank mergers and bank failures.

Exposure to South American debt

This, and the LDC debt crisis in general, caused heavy losses to large banks in all our sample countries. However, these losses were reported in the financial statements in an inconsistent and unsystematic fashion.

Capital market involvement

Exposure of banks to stock market volatility resulted from both the value of their investment portfolios and from capital market activity as a source of income. The stock market decline of 1987 had a negative effect on Swiss banks' performance, although fixed income portfolio gains partially compensated for equity market losses. Rising interest rates caused losses for German banks in their bond portfolios in 1989 and 1990, while the combination of the Tokyo Stock Exchange decline and rising interest rates in Japan in 1990, had a pronounced negative effect on Japanese bank performance.

13.4 The Future of International Banking

13.4.1 Historical Overview

Virtually all the data for the aggregate size of international banking yield very high rates of growth over the last 25 years. In studying international banking, it is essential to distinguish between:

- Cross-currency transactions: foreign currency denominated claims on, or liabilities to, domestic and foreign residents.
- Cross-border transactions: claims on, or liabilities to, foreign residents denominated in domestic or foreign currency.

It is also important to distinguish among types of customer (interbank, private, public sector).

Unfortunately, such data are not readily available for most countries. Bryant (1987), provides an excellent breakdown (see table 13.7) for a specific single date (December 31, 1982). He estimated that all accounts with cross-currency or cross-border characteristics came to nearly \$3.5 trillion on December 31, 1986 (about 32 percent of the total bank system balance sheet).

In analyzing the data, Bryant reached the conclusion that less than 30 percent of international banking represents lending to non-banks, with the remainder consisting of lending to other banking offices. It seems that foreign-owned institutions are especially likely to initiate cross-border and cross-currency transactions. Thus, international banking is much more a means of channelling funds among financial institutions in different countries than of providing direct and maturity intermediation between investors and borrowers.

Table 13.8 provides a comparison of international involvement in banking in our sample countries, including the foreign bank share of the domestic market, the activity of domestic banks abroad, and cross-border transactions.

The Euro-currency market is a major component of what is considered to be international banking. Levich (1990), provided data on the growth of the Euro-currency deposit market, from essentially zero in 1960 to over

Table 13.7 Assets (including interbank claims) reported by banking offices in seven countries, December 31, 1982 (US$ billions at end-1982 exchange rates unless otherwise indicated)

	Assets with one or more international characteristics			*Traditional domestic assets*	*Total assets*	*Subtotal of assets with international characteristics*	
	Claims on Foreign residents denominated in foreign currencies	*Claims on Foreign residents denominated in home currency*	*Claims on home residents denominated in foreign currencies*	*Claims on home residents denominated in home currency*	*(Gross size of banks' balance sheets) (1+2+3+4)*	*Amount (1+2+3)*	*Percent of total balance sheet [(6÷5)×100]*
Country	*(1)*	*(2)*	*(3)*	*(4)*	*(5)*	*(6)*	*(7)*
Switzerland	33	38	5	184	260	76	29
FRG	19	64	2	1,054	1,140	86	8
France	124	24	40	466	654	188	29
UK	437	26	183	248	893	646	72
Japan	66	25	87	1,437	1,615	178	11
Canada	37	2	26	171	236	65	27
US	8	356	a	1,745	2,109	363	17
Swiss trustee accounts	93				93	93	100
Grand total	817	535	343	5,305	7,000	1,695	24.2

[a] Data not reported with this breakdown, but the amount is believed to be small (less than $0.5 billion).

Source: Bryant, Ralph C. (1987) International financial intermediation, The Brookings Institute, table 3–2

$4.5 trillion on a gross base ($2.2 trillion on a net of interbank deposits basis) in March 1988 (with 65 percent denominated in US dollars). This represents a compound annual growth rate of about 20 percent.

13.4.2 The Rationale for Internationalization

The rapid growth in cross-border financial intermediation can be explained by several factors:

- Real sector demand
- Capital flows
- Minimizing of the regulatory burden
- Response to taxes and foreign exchange controls.

Table 13.8 Indicators of international banking activity

Country	Year	Foreign banks share of market	Foreign branches of domestic banks	Assets and liabilities held against foreigners: Assets	Liabilities
		(percentage)[a]			
Switzerland	1984	12.2	16.4	40.0	31.9
	1989	12.1[a]	15.2	36.9	29.8
Germany	1984	6.7	12.6	7.8	5.9
	1989	6.2	13.1	12.1	6.4
France	1984	18.2	n.a.	19.8	21.0
	1988	n.a.	n.a.	17.0	17.8
UK	1984	56.1	n.a.	56.1	61.0
	1988	50.8	n.a.	64.2	71.5
Japan	1984	2.2	18.9	5.7	
	1989	1.4	18.3	12.1	
Canada	1984	4.2	n.a.	16.2	17.0
	1988	7.3	n.a.	10.7	11.2
US	1984	7.9	13.2	11.8	
	1987	12.0	11.3	12.1	

n.a. – not available.

[a] Percent of total assets of the domestic banking system.

Source: Swary and Topf (1990), own calculations

Real sector demand

As indicated by Bryant (1987), the postwar expansion of international trade was faster than that of income and output, because of reduced barriers to trade and the fall in the relative cost of transportation. The greater volume of trade has induced a significant increase in international assets and liabilities (bankers' acceptances and short-term bank loans). Thus, just as international trade has grown faster than domestic activity, international banking activity has grown faster than world trade in goods.

Capital flows

Capital flows between countries are the result of both the financing counterpart of real sector transactions and portfolio adjustments. Technological progress in communications and data processing has facilitated the large-scale movement of funds across national markets; the movement itself having grown in importance due to the development of significant imbalances in the international flow of funds (such as the petrodollar recycling of the 1970s and the Japanese capital surplus of the 1980s). Meanwhile, capital movements have come to vastly outweigh trade transactions – it was estimated in 1988 that 95 percent of global foreign exchange represented portfolio activity. Although a great deal of the cross-border intermediation was electronic in nature, many financial institutions saw fit to establish a physical presence overseas.

However, by the mid-1980s most industrialized countries had removed all capital controls, and those countries which were not advocates of totally free capital movements (such as France and Japan) were experiencing great difficulties in maintaining controls.

Minimizing the regulatory burden

Bank regulation that interferes in bank decision-making (reserve requirements, interest rate controls, and restrictions on non-bank activities) encourages international banking. A complex set of regulations has evolved to monitor the risk-taking of financial institutions. As discussed earlier, this intervention has been accompanied by compensating protection. The difference between these costs and benefits constitutes the regulatory burden placed on banks and private firms. In an open world economy, banks may attempt to operate in a regulatory framework outside their home country if the regulatory burden is thereby reduced. The Euro-currency market (and its offspring – Euro-deposits and Euro-commercial paper) is a natural outcome of differential national regulations.

An important variant of behavior for minimizing the regulatory burden occurred as national regulatory authorities permitted banks to establish offshore facilities for conducting transactions with foreign customers, or transactions in foreign currencies (while limiting transactions with domestic residents). Examples of such arrangements are the International Banking Facilities (IBFs) in the United States, and the Japanese Offshore Market (JOM).

In evaluating the internationalism of the US and Japanese banks and the activities of German banks in Luxembourg, there is no doubt that factors such as interest rate controls and restrictions on permitted activities played a crucial role in inducing them to expand their international activities.

Tax and foreign currency considerations

Tax considerations and foreign currency controls have also been incentives for banks to escape domestic regulation.

It is likely that all these factors have contributed to the growth of international banks. However, given the fact that about 70 percent of the market is interbank activity, it seems that the capital flow incentive has been the most dominant.

13.4.3 The Future of International Banking

In considering the future of international banking it seems that the growth of this market will slow, and that the slowdown will be accompanied by a basic change in its nature. This expectation is based on several factors:

- The Basle Capital Adequacy requirements have imposed equivalent standards on all international banks. Even though the rules have shortcomings in defining capital and in treating interest rate and exchange risk, they will have a far-reaching impact on bank operations. The growth of banking intermediation is expected to be severely impaired even in those countries that are currently above the required ratio. Banks will attempt to manage lending capacity so as to gain a comparative advantage over competitors. In other words, with the constraint on size imposed by capital requirements, each loan has a shadow price in terms of the overall constraint. Within this framework, international banking, with its low profitability, is a prime candidate for contraction.
- The widespread process of deregulation in all developed countries, and the eventual removal of the Glass-Steagall Act in the United States, and Article 65 in Japan, will reduce or eliminate one of the prime incentives for international banking. The introduction of consistent regulation across the major countries (the BIS and the EC) is further improving the degree of substitutability among currencies and across national markets. Reductions in tax rates in most countries further decrease the potential benefits from reducing the regulatory burden via international banking.
- Developments in communications technology have been especially important. Innovations in electronic equipment – computers, switching devices, telecommunications, satellites – have permitted the processing and transmission of information, and completion of transactions, in a much less costly manner. Therefore, it is becoming increasingly difficult for a state or nation to impose regulatory burdens that deviate from world norms. Moreover, interbank and international banking do not require a physical presence.
- Some international lending that would formerly have taken the form of assets on banks' balance sheets has become "securitized" (i.e., flows are transmitted through international capital markets rather than through bank intermediation). At the same time, however, banks have begun holding larger amounts of marketable securities, as part of their involvement in the securitization process.
- Innovative financial instruments such as Note Issuance Facilities (NIFs), Forward Rate Agreements (FRAs) and interest-rate and currencies swaps have developed. These instruments allow unbundling of different risks (exchange risk, interest rate risk, and credit risk) that were combined in traditional cross-

border and cross-currency bank lending, thus further encouraging securitization.

- The institutionalization of savings and investments has meant that many bank customers have acquired the scale and expertise to dispense with bank services in the field of diversification and asset transformation. This has affected international banking as well: combining technological advances and easier access to capital markets, many former bank customers are essentially replicating bank functions in-house at lower cost.

Impeding further internationalization of banking are a number of additional factors. Due to the personal nature of the bank-customer relationship, banking services differ from other goods. Moreover, most countries maintain some sort of special treatment of cross-border financial transactions. Additional limits on foreign presence in banking are justified by the argument that banking is a strategic industry, and that foreign institutions may cause interference with central banks' conduct of monetary policy.

Moreover, as a result of deregulation and increased competition, almost all banking systems are in a situation of overbanking, resulting in restructuring in the form of bank failures and bank mergers. Thus, opportunities for cross-border activity would appear to be limited.

The conclusion of this analysis is that banks have no comparative advantage in traditional intermediation as a source of diversification and growth. They are expected, therefore, to participate in the process of capital flows among countries without a physical foreign presence; a process which improves capital allocation globally without changing the local nature of banking institutions.

13.5 The Outlook for Commercial Banking

Commercial banking has come under great pressure in the past decade, and will likely undergo extensive and even painful change as a result. However, to view the restructuring of commercial banking as a straightforward process of industry "rationalization" squeezing inefficiency out of the banking system, might be overly simplistic. An examination of the unprecedented changes which have occurred in the financial system in the recent past indicate that changes in commercial banking represent a real transformation in their economic role. Although the restructuring is costly, the process may involve the recognition as real of costs which were always present, but hidden by the regulatory and protective system.

13.5.1 *The Macroeconomic Environment*

Developments in the banking industry must of necessity be viewed against the broader economic background. Firstly, the real volume of financial activity, including both banking and capital market activity, has increased greatly during the recent past. Secondly, relatively large financial imbalances have developed and undergone rapid change, both domestically (central government deficits, sectoral crises) and internationally (petrodollar recycling, the LDC debt burden, the Japanese capital surplus). Thirdly, the volatility of financial variables (inflation, exchange rates, interest rates, asset prices) has increased by a large order of magnitude. Fourthly, the current period seems to be characterized not only by rapid change, but also by a steady acceleration of the rate of change, necessitating extensive adaptation of economic behavior.

13.5.2 *Structural Changes*

Such changes include the following:

- Technological change has led to a quantum leap in all aspects of information processing, including communications and data processing.
- Institutionalization of financial management has extensively transformed the nature, quality, and capabilities of financial decision-makers.
- Globalization of real and financial markets, both geographically and functionally, regional organizations (such as the EC, the US-Canada free trade agreement), international cooperation (on, for example, capital adequacy requirements), and economic pressures, are producing a convergence of operating conditions around the world.
- The growth of capital markets, a natural byproduct of increased levels of development, reinforced by the other trends described here, has changed the basic supply and demand conditions of financial markets. The growth of securitization, as well as the development of derivative financial products, have been of special significance.

13.5.3 *Regulatory Policy*

The regulatory framework, in many ways the primary determinant of the institutional structure of financial markets, is continuing to evolve at a rapid pace. Some of the changes have been independent initiatives, leading to changes in the regulated institutions; others are themselves a response to industry initiatives and other trends described here. The result is a dynamic process which will continue to play a major role in determining the future of commercial banking i.e.,

- Liberalization of financial markets has been the result of the turn to market mechanisms in economic decision-making. Government involvement in economic and allocative decisions has declined, and the role of the market in determining price and quantity has increased.
- Operative interference in banking systems has declined, as has the regulatory protection accorded to the supervised institutions. However, the timing and extent of both these changes were not necessarily synchronized, which was in itself of considerable importance.
- Prudential supervision of financial markets, as well as consumer protection, have retained their high priorities.

The cumulative impact of these developments has been an extensive erosion in the uniqueness of the commercial banks. Once a very special firm in the financial structure, banks are becoming increasingly similar to other economic agents. Functionally, bank products are becoming increasingly indistinguishable from the products of other financial and even non-financial firms, including transaction accounts (Money Market Mutual Funds, credit and debit cards) and short-term credit (bridge loans, finance company loans, commercial paper). Institutionally, market segmentation has been reduced to the extent that banks now face competition in previously protected markets from other financial and non-financial firms, including other depository institutions, investment banks, securities houses, insurance firms, and large retail and industrial corporations.

Geographically, technological change and regulatory reform have largely reduced much of the protection or advantage based on locale. As a result, banks will increasingly have to depend upon their own economic usefulness to justify their existence in a more purely competitive environment. Rents and public stipends, which they previously received by virtue of their unique and privileged position in the financial structure, will disappear, so that their performance will be a function of their own efficiency and competitiveness.

This being the case, the outlook for commercial banks depends upon the economic function they serve. Most analyses identify two roles for commercial banks: asset transformation and information processing. The asset transformation role involves changing the maturity, denomination, liquidity, and risk characteristics of financial assets so as to better meet the needs of final savers and borrowers. As information processors, banks exploit relative advantages in the gathering, analysis, and management of data, to produce economically valuable services. In the first role, banks act as direct intermediaries, holding assets on their balance sheets; in the second role of indirect intermediation, they help determine the distribution of financial assets without themselves holding any such assets.

Virtually all of the developments described here have decreased any relative advantage enjoyed by commercial banks in the asset transformation role. Increasingly, institutional investors, with access to large and liquid securities markets, using deviative products and advanced financial techniques, are having less and less need for commercial banks to provide for their needs in terms of denomination, liquidity, or risk characteristics of financial assets. Large borrowers with access to extensive capital markets can dispense with the intermediary role of commercial banks, and have indeed done so. In fact, the regulatory burden still borne by most commercial banks probably constitutes a competitive disadvantage in many cases.

The trend, therefore, is for banks to abandon their traditional role as direct intermediaries and increase their role as indirect intermediaries, to the point where they become, essentially, pure information processors. In this role, by contributing to the efficiency of the financial system, they will earn a return on services rendered. It can be seen that the existence of direct financial intermediaries is, to a certain degree, predicated on the existence of market imperfections. As markets become more efficient, perfect, and complete, the direct intermediary is eliminated. However, as information is the sine qua non for maintaining efficient markets, the demand for information processing is assured.

The clearest example of this process is the case of securitization. In the market for asset-based securities, banks favor the roles of origінization, evaluation, packaging, and servicing, while removing themselves from the borrower or lender roles. The process of securitization is essentially the conversion of commercial banks from asset transformers into information processors. Fiduciary accounts at Swiss bank are an interesting transitional example combining elements of the two roles. One of the most successful US banks, the Boston-based State Street Bank, has already nearly completed the transformation. It

> ... has closed 90 percent of its branches. Two thirds of its assets are in cash or investments. It has no third world debt and makes no loans ... State Street's customers are large investing institutions ... [who] use State Street to do the complex reporting [they] are required to make. ... The bank has become a data processing company with a portfolio of trust and custodial businesses. In effect, it is now a computerized bookkeeper cum accountant, not a banker in a traditional sense.[3]

One of the clearest indicators of this trend is the increasing share of non-interest income, or fees produced by information processing, as opposed to interest income, i.e., the creditory-debitory interest spread earned on traditional intermediation (table 13.6).

Banks will probably continue to play a key role in payment systems, since these are, essentially, large-scale data management operations. John Reed, Chairman of Citicorp, has described money as "information on the move."[4] In fact, as supervisory authorities deal with the issue of the increasingly problematic nature of today's large-scale payment and safe-keeping services, they will probably reduce the riskiness of the systems to the extent that these services become pure information management tasks for the banks involved. The Fedwire payments system and Federal Reserve Book Entry System for eligible securities in the United States are examples of such a development.

Against the background of an apparent surplus of banking capacity in most industrialized countries, as well as continued expected growth of capital markets, the developments described above have the following implications:

- Economies of scale, not present under conditions of regulatory interference and protection, will become more important. In a competitive environment, cost efficiencies will lead to greater concentration in the banking industry, i.e., there will be fewer but larger, banks acting as information handlers.
- Economies of scope involving information will also take on a greater role. It can be expected that banks will expand activities whenever they can take advantage of joint production of information services, that is, in credit card systems, trust activities, and insurance.
- In so far as information services do not require the physical presence of large branch and office systems, banks will be able to reduce their overheads. As already mentioned, this will be especially true on the international level.
- The move from direct to indirect intermediation will increase the involvement of banks in capital markets. They will benefit from both economies of scope in handling information, and the "smoothing" effect capital market activities have on overall income when combined with income from traditional banking activities.

Notes

1 See, for example, Volcker (1986), Corrigan (1982) and (1987), Baltensperger and Dermine (1987), Saunders (1988), Aharony and Swary (1983), and Swary (1986).

2 For a review of the theory of the banking firm, see Santomero (1984). It should be noted that most modern theories have concentrated on the advantages of banks in information processing.

3 *The Economist*, April 7, 1990, p. 31.
4 *The Economist*, April 7, 1990, p. 21.

References

Aharony, Joseph and Itzhak Swary (1983) Contagion effects of bank failures: Evidence from capital markets, *Journal of Business*, vol 56, 213–30.

Aharony, Joseph, Anthony Saunders and Itzhak Swary (1986) The effects of a shift in monetary policy regime on the profitability and risk of commercial bank, *Journal of Monetary Economics*, vol 17, 363–77.

—— The effects of DIDMCA on bank stockholders' return and risk, *Journal of Banking and Finance*, vol 12, 317–31.

Baltensperger, Ernst and Jean Dermine (1987) Banking Deregulation, *Economic Policy*, vol 2, 63–109.

Bryant, Ralph C. (1987) International Financial Intermediation, Washington: The Brookings Institute.

Burns, Arthur F. (1988) The Ongoing revolution in American banking, American Enterprise Institute for Public Policy Research, Washington, D.C.

Chance, Don M. and William R. Lane (1980) A re-examination of interest rate sensitivity in the common stocks of financial institutions, *Journal of Financial Research*, vol 3, 49–55.

Corrigan E. Gerald (1982) Are banks special?, The Federal Reserve Bank of Minneapolis, *Annual Report*.

—— Coping with globally integrated financial markets, The Federal Reserve Bank of New York, *Quarterly Review*, vol 11, 1–5.

[The] Economist Bank Deposit Insurance – Protecting Auntie, March 10, 1990, 98–100.

—— A Survey of International Banking, April, 7, 1990.

Flannery, Mark J. (1981) Market interest rates and commercial bank profitability: An empirical investigation, *Journal of Finance*, vol 36, 1085–1101.

—— Interest rates and bank profitability: Additional evidence, (1983) *Journal of Money, Credit and Banking*, vol 15, 355–62.

—— and Christopher M. James (1984) Market evidence on the effective maturity of bank assets and liabilities, *Journal of Money, Credit and Banking*, vol 16, 435–45.

FDIC, *Quarterly Banking Profile*, various issues.

—— *Annual Reports*, various issues.

Levich, Richard M. (1990) The Euromarkets After 1992, in *European Banking in the 1990s*, Jean Dermine (ed.), Basil Blackwell, Oxford.

Maisel, Sherman J. and Robert Jacobson (1978) Interest rate changes and commercial bank revenue and costs, *Journal of Financial and Quantitative Analysis*, vol 13, 687–700.

Rhoades, Stephen A. (1985) Mergers and acquisitions by commercial banks 1960–1983, Federal reserve system, *Staff Studies* no 142.

Saunders, Anthony (1988) Bank holding companies: Structure, performance and reform, in *Restructuring Banking and Financial Services in America*, W. Haraf and R.M. Kushmeider (eds), AEI, Washington D.C.
Swary Itzhak (1986) Stock market reaction to regulatory action in the Continental Illinois crisis, *Journal of Business*, vol 59, 451–73.
Volcker, Paul A., Statement before the Subcommittee on Commerce, Consumer and Monetary Affairs of the Committee on Government Operations, United States House of Representatives, June 11, 1986.

14

Conclusion

At the time of this writing, the world banking system is in a period of considerable turmoil. Stresses and strains affecting individual banks and even entire banking systems seem to be on the increase, as banks appear to be lurching from one crisis to the next. While continued change is the one certainty facing commercial banks in the future, we believe that the aggregate effect of the process now occurring will be a comprehensive transformation of the banking industry. Although the future character and nature of commercial banking obviously cannot be predicted, we believe that a review of the major developments of the recent past can serve to indicate the general direction banking is likely to take.

The nature of commercial banks up to now has been based on two factors: their function has been a product of the uniqueness of their role in the financial system, and their structure has been a specific institutional response shaped by the regulation which was so dominant in the banking industry. As their uniqueness wanes and the regulated environment changes radically, the banks must make concomitant adjustments if they are to survive in the new circumstances.

Basic economic forces are prompting banks to replace intermediation with capital marked activity, so that they become information processors rather than asset transformers. Utilizing joint production efficiencies in the gathering and analysis of information, banks will exploit newly achievable economies of scope and scale. The former will lead banks to expand into other financial services, including investment banking, capital markets, and insurance services. The latter will lead to increased concentration in the banking system, with many smaller units leaving the industry. There is little reason to expect banks to expand into other commercial or industrial areas.

Clearly, the future shape of banking systems is the universal banking model prevailing in Europe, rather than the highly segmented American/Japanese model. Interestingly, the universal banking systems, such as those of Germany and Switzerland, have exhibited much greater stability and resilience to shocks than the narrowly-based, segmented banking systems.

The convergence of financial systems globally, will reduce the role of international banking in the flow of funds. International intermediation will become just another type of intermediation, increasingly accomplished through cross-border provision of services rather than the export of factors of production (that is the establishing of bank offices). As borders diminish in importance, even this activity will decline. In a truly united Europe, with a single currency, all banking, transnational or otherwise, will be essentially domestic banking.

The transformation of banking does not mean that all banks will be alike. As in any activity, relative advantages will yield a variety of business strategies: even where fully universal banking is already permitted, banks have developed functional specialization based on economic activity. Competition will focus on products and services, rather than organizational identity, so that many of the banks' competitors will include other financial or non-financial firms as well as other banks.

The largest banking organizations will be the "supermarkets", attempting to provide a broad range of retail as well as wholesale services in many countries, or even globally. Citibank, Deutsche Bank, and Barclays Bank are examples of such organizations that already exist. Wholesale banks will focus on corporate and capital market activities, like the Industrial Bank of Japan, and some may even abandon traditional intermediation entirely, as Bankers Trust might. Since there will still be a need for intermediation to serve the non-institutional market, efficient retail banks such as First Wachovia and other successful super-regional banks in the United States will prosper.

Finally, pure agents, such as the State Street Bank, will provide portfolio, processing, and advisory services on a fee basis. The regulation of banks will need to keep pace with the evolution of the banking industry. If banks decrease their role as principals in financial transactions, and if payment system risk can be eliminated through technological progress and supervisory innovations, the traditional arguments for regulatory interference will become irrelevant.

Since non-bank competitors will be undertaking "banking" activities, regulation will need to be applied on a functional and product basis, rather than by institutional identity. This will equalize the regulatory burden and reduce distortions in the financial system. While capital adequacy standards will be expanded and improved, they will not be a complete answer to the regulatory problem, and assessment of asset quality and financial risk will need to be improved.

Finally, the widespread changes in the banking industry will also have wider implications. Monetary policy will need to adapt both its tools and its strategies to deal with a changed financial system. In so far as the financial system is made more efficient, allocational efficiency of financial flows should improve, providing benefits to the entire economy. As financial institutions become more efficient, they should be able to reduce their consumption of real resources, especially labor, and the real cost of banking systems in the economy should decline. And for the immediate future, as in the ancient Chinese curse, everyone involved in banking, or concerned with its development, will probably be fated to live in interesting times.

Further Reading

Aber, Jack W. (1988) Securitization in the retail banking world, *Journal of Retail Banking*, vol 10, 5–12

Aliber, Robert Z. (1984) International banking: A survey, *Journal of Money, Credit and Banking*, vol 16, 661–78

Amel, Dean F. and Michael J. Jacowski (1989) Trends in banking structure since the mid 1970s, *Federal Reserve Bulletin*, vol 75, 120–33

Bailey, John, M. and Charlene G. Valenza (1990) Regulating capital adequacy, *Bank Management*, vol 66, 30–3

Bank for International Settlements, *Recent Innovations in International Banking*, Basle, April 1986

Bank of England (1983), The nature and implications of financial innovation, *Quarterly Bulletin*, vol 23, 358–62

—— The Single European Market: Survey of UK financial services industry, *Quarterly Bulletin*, August 1989, vol 29, 407–12

—— *Loan transfers and securitization*, Banking Supervision Division Consultative Paper 8/87, December 1987

Beaty, Randolph P., Antony M. Santomero and Michael L. Smirlock, Bank mergers premiums: Analysis and evidence, *Monograph series in finance and economics*, 1987–3, Salomon Brothers Center for the Study of Financial Institutions, Graduate School of Business Administration, New York University

Benston, George J. (1989) The Federal safety net and the repeal of the Glass–Steagall Act's separation of commercial and investment banking, *Journal of Financial Services Research*, vol 2, 287–305

Berger, Allen N., and Lawrence M. Benveniste (1987) Securitization with recourse, Board of Governors of the Federal Reserve System, *Research Paper* No. 97

Berlin, Mitchell (1988) Banking reform: An overview of the restructuring debate, *Business Review*, The Federal Reserve Bank of Philadelphia, July–August, 3–14

Bishop, Graham (1990) Asset-backed securities and the changing European market, paper presented at the BRI International Conference on Securitization in Europe, Paris

Bishop, Graham and O'Kelly, Ann (1989) *1992 and Beyond*, Salomon Brothers Inc., New York

Boyd, John H., Stanley L. Graham and Hewitt (1990) Bank holding company mergers with non-bank financial firms: Effects on the risk of failure, The Federal Reserve Bank of Minneapolis, *Working Paper*

Broaddus, Alfred (1985) Financial innovation in the US-Background, current status and prospects, *Economic Review*, The Federal Reserve Bank of Richmond, vol 71

Burda, Michael C. (1990) The consequences of German economic and monetary union, Center for Economic Policy Research Discussion Paper 449

Callen, T. S. and J. W. Lomax (1990) The development of the building societies sector in the 1980s, *Bank of England Quarterly Bulletin*, vol 30, 503–10

Chandler, Clark J. and Christopher Jenkins (1989) Merger and acquisitions: accounting and regulatory considerations, *Bank Accounting and Finance*, vol 3, 3–8

Clarke, Stephen, V., American banks in the international interbank market, Monograph 1983–4, *The monograph series in finance and economics*, Salomon Brothers Center for the Study of Financial Institutions, Graduate School of Business Administration, New York University

Comité de la Réglementation Bancaire, *Rapport Annuel 1989*

Commission of the European Communities, The cost of non-Europe in financial services, Research on the cost of non-Europe, basic findings, 1988, 9

—— *Europe without frontiers – Completing the internal market*, 2nd ed, Luxembourg: Office for Official Publication of the Communities, February 1988

Comptroller of the Currency, *Quarterly Journal*, various issues

Corrigan, E. Gerald (1987) A perspective on the globalization of financial markets and institutions, The Federal Reserve Bank of New York, *Quarterly Review*, vol 12, 1–9

Crouhy, Michel and Dan Galai (1986) An economic assessment of capital requirements in the banking industry, *Journal of Banking and Finance*, vol 16, 231–41

Cumming, Christine (1987) The economics of securitization, The Federal Reserve Bank of New York, *Quarterly Review*, vol 12, 11–23

Deutsche Bundesbank (1982) The Deutsche Bundesbank: Its monetary policy instruments and functions, *Deutsche Bundesbank Special Series* No. 7

Dohner, Robert S. and Henry S. Terrell (1988) The determinants of the growth for multinational banking organizations 1972–86, Board of Governors of the Federal Reserve System, *International Finance Discussion Paper* No. 326

Donahoo, Kathleen and Sherrill Shaffer (1988) The impact of capital requirements on the securitization decision, The Federal Reserve Bank of New York, *Research Paper*, No. 8820

Donaldson, T. H. (1989) *Credit Risk and Exposure in Securitization and Transactions*, Macmillan, London

Federal Reserve Bank of Kansas City, *Restructuring the financial system*, a symposium sponsored by The Federal Reserve Bank of Kansas City, August, 1987

Ford, Theresa (1987) Global banking, financial integration, major conference themes, *Economic Perspectives*, The Federal Reserve Bank of Chicago, vol 11, 23–7

Frankel, Allen B. and Catherine L. Mann (1986) A Framework for analyzing the process of financial innovation, Board of Governors of the Federal Reserve System, *International Finance Discussion Paper* No. 283

Freedman, Charles (1983) Financial innovation in Canada: Causes and consequences, *American Economic Review*, vol 73, 101–6

Friesen, Connie M. (1986) *International Bank Supervision*, Euromoney Publications, London

Gardener, Edward P. M. (1989) The capital adequacy problem in modern banking, *Institute of European Finance Research Papers in Banking and Finance* 89/2, University College of North Wales, Bangor

—— (ed), *The Future of Financial Systems and Services*, St. Martin's Press, New York, 1990

Germany, J. David and John G. Morton (1985) Financial innovation and deregulation in foreign industrial countries, *Federal Reserve Bulletin*, Board of Governors of the Federal Reserve System, Washington D.C., vol 71, 743–53

Giddy, Ian H. (1985) Is equity underwriting risky for commercial bank affiliates?, in *Deregulating Wall Street*, Walter Ingo (ed), John Wiley, New York 145–69

Gorton, Gary and Anthony M. Santomero (1990) Market discipline and bank subordinated debt, *Journal of Money, Credit and Banking*, vol 22, 119–28

Greenbaum, Stuart, I. and Anjan V. Thakor (1987) Bank funding modes: securitization versus deposits, *Journal of Banking and Finance*, vol 11, 379–401

Greenspan, Alan (1988) Innovation and Regulation of Banks in the 1990's, *Federal Reserve Bulletin*, vol 74, 783–7

Havrilesky, Thomas M. and Robert Schweitzer (1987) *Contemporary developments in financial institutions and markets*, Harlan Davidson Inc., Arlington Heights, Ill.

Hawawini, Gabriel and Itzhak Swary (1990) *Mergers and Acquisitions in the US Banking Industry*, Elsevier Science Publishers

Hayes, Samuel L. III (1984) Investment banking: Commercial banks' inroads, *Economic Review*, The Federal Reserve Bank of Atlanta, vol 69

Heaton, Gary C. and Constance R. Dunham (1985) The growing competitiveness of credit unions, *New England Economic Review*, The Federal Reserve Bank of Boston, May–June

Heimann, John (1984) Market-driven deregulation of financial services, *Economic Review*, The Federal Reserve Bank of Atlanta, vol 69, 36–41

IMF (1988) *International Capital Markets Developments and Prospects*, IMF, Washington D.C.

Institute of International Bankers (1989) Economic benefits to the United States from the activities of the international banking community, Institute of International Bankers, New York

Jacklin, Charles J. and Sudipto Battacharya (1988) Distinguishing panics and information – Based banks runs; welfare and policy implications, *Journal of Political Economy*, vol 96, 568–92

James, Christopher (1987) Off-balance-sheet-banking, *Economic Review*, The Federal Reserve Bank of San Francisco, Fall

Japan Center for International Finance (1988) Tokyo as a center of world finance, *Policy Study Series* No. 1, Washington D.C.

Journal of International Banking Law, various issues, ESC Publishing Ltd, Oxford

Kane, Edward J. (1981) Accelerating inflation, technological innovation and the decreasing effectiveness of banking regulation, *Journal of Finance*, vol 36, 355–67

Key, Sydney J. and Henry S. Terrell (1988) International banking facilities, Board of Governors, Federal Reserve System, *Washington Staff Studies* No. 333

Key, Sydney J (1989) Mutual recognition: Integration of the financial sector in the European Community, *Federal Reserve Bulletin*, vol 75, 591–609

Kim, Deasik and Antony M. Santomero (1988) Risk in banking and capital regulation, *Journal of Finance*, vol 43, 1219–1233

Koehn, Michael and Anthony M. Santomero (1980) Regulation of bank capital and portfolio risk, *Journal of Finance*, vol 35, 1235–44

Kwast, Myron (1987) The impact of underwriting and dealing on bank returns and risk, Board of Governors of the Federal Reserve System, *Research Papers in Banking and Financial Economics*, 95

Levich, Richard M. (1987) Economic consequences of innovations in international financial markets, Paper presented at the 7th International Symposium National Bureau of Economic Research of Ministry of Finance Tokyo

Lomax, David E. (1987) *London Markets after the Financial Services Act*, Butterworths, London

Love, Brian and Jonathan Todd (1989) The EC's single market in banking services, *European Report* No. 1507

Mcleay, Stuart and Philip Molyneux (1989) Bank profitability and structure in France, the United Kingdom, West Germany and Japan: Some preliminary findings, *Institute of European Finance Research Papers in Banking and Finance* 89/12, University College of North Wales, Bangor

Metais, Joel (1987) Financial innovations and new patterns of financing in France, *Institute of European Finance Research Papers in Banking and Finance* 87/14, IEF, University College of North Wales, Bangor

—— Toward a restructuring of the international financial services industry: Some preliminary empirical and theoretical insights, in *The Future of Financial Systems and Services*, Edward P. Gardener (ed) (1990) St Martin's Press, 170–92

Molyneux, Philip (1989) The Single European Market and the implications for large scale bank acquisitions, *Institute of European Finance Research Papers in Banking and Finance* 89/8, University College of North Wales, Bangor

Moulton, Janice (1985) Non-bank banks: Catalyst for interstate banking, *Business Review*, The Federal Reserve Banks of Philadelphia, December, 3–18

Mullineux, Andrew (1987) *International Banking and Financial Systems: A Comparison*, Graham & Trotman, London

OECD (1984) *Electronic Funds Transfer, Plastic Cards and the Consumer*, OECD, Paris

Pardee, Scott E. (1987) Internationalization of financial markets, *Economic Review*, The Federal Reserve Bank of Kansas City, vol 72, 3–7

Parry, Robert T. (1987) Major trends in the US financial system: Implications and issues, *Economic Review*, the Federal Reserve Bank of San Francisco, Spring

Pavel, Christine (1986) Securitization, *Economic Perspective*, The Federal Reserve Bank of Chicago, vol 10, 16–31

Pavel, Christine and Harvey Rosenblum (1985) Banks and non-banks: The horse race continues, *Economic Perspectives*, The Federal Reserve Banks of Chicago, vol 9, 3–17

Pavel, Christine and John M. McElravey, Globalization in the financial services industry, *Economic Perspectives*, The Federal Reserve Bank of Chicago, vol 14, 3–18

Peat, Marwick (1986) *Banking in Germany*, Peat Marwick Mitchell and Co., Frankfurt

Pecchioli, R. M. (1987) *Prudential Supervision in Banking*, OECD, Paris

Poulsen Annette B (1986) Japanese Bank Regulation and the Activities of US Offices of Japanese Banks, *Journal of Money, Credit and Banking*, vol 18, 366–73

Rosenblum, Harvey (1985) On banks, non-banks and overlapping markets, *Staff Memoranda 85–1*, The Federal Reserve Bank of Chicago

Santomero, Anthony M. (1984) Modelling the banking firm, a survey, *Journal of Money, Credit and Banking*, vol 16, 576–602

—— The changing structure of financial institutions: A review essay, *Journal of Monetary Economics*, 1989, vol 24, 321–8

Silber, William L. (ed) (1983) The process of financial innovation, *American Economic Review*, vol 73, 89–95

Simpson, Thomas D. (1988) Developments in the US financial system since the mid 1970s, *Federal Reserve Bulletin*, vol 74, 1–13

Swoboda, Alexander (1990) Swiss banking after 1992, in *European Banking in the 1990s*, Jean Dermine (ed), Basil Blackwell, Oxford 335–53

Van Den Bempt, Paul and Marc Quintyn (eds) (1989) *European financial integration and monetary cooperation*, European Policy Study Group, IFR Publishing, London

Wall Larry D. (1987), Has bank holding companies' diversification affected their risk of failure?, *Journal of Economics and Business*, vol 39, 313–6

Walter, Ingo (1988) Global *Competition in Financial Services*, Ballinger Publishing company, Cambridge, Massachusetts

—— Smith, Roy C. (1989) *Investment Banking in Europe; Restructuring for the 1990s*, Basil Blackwell, Oxford

Weatherstone, Dennis (1988) An American perspective on Europe 1992, *The World of Banking*, vol 7, 3–16

Whinney, Ernest, (1987) International Bank Accounting, 2nd ed Euromoney Publications, London

Whitehead, David (1988) Moving toward 1992: A common financial market for Europe?, *Economic Review*, the Federal Reserve Bank of Atlanta, November–December

Wilson, John Stuart Gladstone (1986) *Banking Policy and Structure, a Comparative Analysis*, New York University Press, New York

Wolfbrandt, Marianne (1989) Economic effects of EC financial integration, *Sveringes Riksbank Quarterly Review I*

Wright, Richard W. and Gunter A. Pauli (1987) *The Second Wave: Japan's Global Assault on Financial Services*, Waterlow, London

Young, Arthur (1988) *Managing International Bank Taxation*, Euromoney Publications, London

Zimmerman, Gary C. (1989) The growing presence of Japanese banks, *Economic Review*, the Federal Reserve Bank of San Francisco, Summer, 3–17

INDEX